Common Law

The International Library of Essays in Law and Legal Theory
Series Editor: Tom D. Campbell

Schools

Natural Law, Vols I & II *John Finnis*
Justice *Thomas Morawetz*
Law and Economics, Vols I & II *Jules Coleman and Jeffrey Lange*
Critical Legal Studies *James Boyle*
Marxian Legal Theory *Csaba Varga*
Legal Reasoning, Vols I & II *Aulis Aarnio and D. Neil MacCormick*
Legal Positivism *Mario Jori*
American Legal Theory *Robert Samuel Summers*
Postmodernism and Law *Dennis Patterson*
Law and History *David Sugarman*
Law and Language *Fred Schauer*
Sociological Theories of Law *Kahei Rokumoto*
Rights *Carlos Nino*
Law and Psychology *Martin Lyon Levine*
Feminist Legal Theory, Vols I & II *Frances Olsen*
Law and Society *Roger Cotterrell*
Contemporary Criminological Theory *Francis T. Cullen and Velmer S. Burton Jr.*

Areas

Criminal Law *Thomas Morawetz*
Tort Law *Ernest J. Weinrib*
Contract Law, Vols I & II *Larry Alexander*
Anti-Discrimination Law *Christopher McCrudden*
Consumer Law *Iain Ramsay*
International Law *Martti Koskenniemi*
Property Law, Vols I & II *Elizabeth Mensch and Alan Freeman*
Constitutional Law *Mark V. Tushnet*
Procedure *D.J. Galligan*
Evidence and Proof *William Twining and Alex Stein*
Company Law *Sally Wheeler*
Privacy, Vols I & II *Raymond Wacks*
Lawyers' Ethics *David J. Luban*
Administrative Law *D.J. Galligan*
Child Law *Harry D. Krause*
Family Law, Vols I & II *Harry D. Krause*
Welfare Law *Peter Robson*
Medicine and the Law *Bernard M. Dickens*
Commercial Law *Ross Cranston*
Environmental Law *Michael C. Blumm*
Conflict of Laws *Richard Fentiman*
Law and Religion *Wojciech Sadurski*
Human Rights Law *Philip Alston*
European Community Law, Vols I & II *Francis Snyder*
Tax Law, Vols I & II *Patricia D. White*
Media Law *Eric Barendt*
Labour Law *David L. Gregory*
Alternative Dispute Resolution *Michael D.A. Freeman*

Legal Cultures

Comparative Legal Cultures *Csaba Varga*
Law and Anthropology *Peter Sack*
Hindu Law and Legal Theory *Ved Nanda*
Islamic Law and Legal Theory *Ian Edge*
Chinese Law and Legal Theory *Michael Palmer*
Russian Legal Theory *W. Butler*
Common Law *Michael Arnheim*
Japanese Law and Legal Theory *Koichiro Fujikura*
Law and Development *Anthony Carty*
Jewish Law and Legal Theory *Martin P. Golding*
Legal Education *Martin Lyon Levine*
Civil Law *Ralf Rogowski*
African Law and Legal Theory *Gordon Woodman and Akintunde Obilade*

Future Volume
Cumulative index

Common Law

Edited by

Michael Arnheim

Barrister at Law, Lincoln's Inn
Sometime Fellow of St John's College, Cambridge

NEW YORK UNIVERSITY PRESS
REFERENCE COLLECTION

First published in the U.S.A. in 1994 by
NEW YORK UNIVERSITY PRESS
Washington Square
New York NY 10003

Library of Congress Cataloging-in-Publication Data
Common law / edited by Michael Arnheim.
p. cm. — (International library of essays in law and legal theory. Legal cultures ; 6)
"New York University Press reference collection."
Includes index.
ISBN 0-8147-0625-8
1. Common law. 2. Jurisprudence. I. Arnheim, M. T .W. (Michael T. W.) II. Series.
K588.C66 1994
340.5'7—dc20 94-18805
CIP

Contents

Acknowledgements

The editor and publishers wish to thank the following for permission to use copyright material.

Blackwell Publishers for the essays: P.S. Atiyah (1985), 'Common Law and Statute Law', *The Modern Law Review*, **48**, pp. 1–28; A.W.B. Simpson (1957), 'The *Ratio Decidendi* of a Case', *The Modern Law Review*, **20**, pp. 413–15; A.W.B. Simpson (1958), 'The *Ratio Decidendi* of a Case', *The Modern Law Review*, **21**, pp. 155–60.

Cambridge Law Journal for the essay: Philip Allott (1979), 'The Courts and Parliament: Who Whom?', *The Cambridge Law Journal*, **38**, pp. 79–117.

The Journal of Legal Studies for the essays: George L. Priest (1977), 'The Common Law Process and the Selection of Efficient Rules', *The Journal of Legal Studies*, **6**, pp. 65–82; Paul H. Rubin (1977), 'Why is the Common Law Efficient?', *The Journal of Legal Studies*, **6**, pp. 51–63.

Oxford University Press for the essays: J.W. Harris (1990), 'Towards Principles of Overruling – When Should a Final Court of Appeal Second Guess?', *Oxford Journal of Legal Studies*, **10**, pp. 135–99; Stephen R. Perry (1987), 'Judicial Obligation, Precedent and the Common Law', *Oxford Journal of Legal Studies*, **7**, pp. 215–57; T.R.S. Allan (1983), 'Parliamentary Sovereignty: Lord Denning's Dexterous Revolution', *Oxford Journal of Legal Studies*, **3**, pp. 22–33; S.L. Hurley (1990), 'Coherence, Hypothetical Cases, and Precedent', *Oxford Journal of Legal Studies*, **10**, pp. 221–51; R.B. Ferguson (1983), 'The Horwitz Thesis and Common Law Discourse in England', *Oxford Journal of Legal Studies*, **3**, pp. 34–58.

Southern California Law Review for the essay: Larry Alexander (1989), 'Constrained by Precedent', *Southern California Law Review*, **63**, pp. 3–64. Reprinted with the permission of the Southern California Law Review.

Stanford Law Review and Fred B. Rothman & Co. for the essay: Frederick Schauer (1987), 'Precedent', *Stanford Law Review*, **39**, pp. 571–605. © 1987 by the Board of Trustees of the Leland Stanford Junior University. Reprinted by permission of Stanford Law Review and Fred B. Rothman & Company from the Stanford Law Review, Vol. **39**, pp. 571–605.

Sweet & Maxwell Limited for the essays: George Winterton (1976), 'The British Grundnorm: Parliamentary Supremacy Re-examined', *The Law Quarterly Review*, **92**, pp. 591–617; Rupert Cross (1976), 'Blackstone v. Bentham', *The Law Quarterly Review*, **92**, pp. 516–27; S.F.C. Milsom (1965), 'Reason in the Development of the Common Law', *The Law Quarterly Review*, **81**, pp. 496–517.

The University of California Press for the article: Frederick Schauer (1989), 'Is the Common Law Law?', *California Law Review*, **77**, pp. 455–71.

The Yale Law School and Fred B. Rothman & Co. for the essays: George P. Fletcher (1981), 'Two Modes of Legal Thought', *The Yale Law Journal*, **90**, pp. 970–1003; Joseph Raz (1972), 'Legal Principles and the Limits of Law', *The Yale Law Journal*, **81**, pp. 823–54. Reprinted by permission of The Yale Law Journal and Fred B. Rothman & Co.

Every effort has been made to trace all the copyright holders, but if any have been inadvertently overlooked the publishers will be pleased to make the necessary arrangement at the first opportunity.

Series Preface

The International Library of Law and Legal Theory is designed to provide important research materials in an accessible form. Each volume contains essays of central theoretical importance in its subject area. The series as a whole makes available an extensive range of valuable material which will be of considerable interest to those involved in the research, teaching and study of law.

The series has been divided into three sections. The Schools section is intended to represent the main distinctive approaches and topics of special concern to groups of scholars. The Areas section takes in the main branches of law with an emphasis on essays which present analytical and theoretical insights of broad application. The section on Legal Cultures makes available the distinctive legal theories of different legal traditions and takes up topics of general comparative and developmental concern.

I have been delighted and impressed by the way in which the editors of the individual volumes have set about the difficult task of selecting, ordering and presenting essays from the immense quantity of academic legal writing published in journals throughout the world. Editors were asked to pick out those essays from law, philosophy and social science journals which they consider to be fundamental for the understanding of law, as seen from the perspective of a particular approach or sphere of legal interest. This is not an easy task and many difficult decisions have had to be made in order to ensure that a representative sample of the best journal essays available takes account of the scope of each topic or school.

I should like to express my thanks to all the volume editors for their willing participation and scholarly judgement. The interest and enthusiasm which the project has generated is well illustrated by the fact that an original projection of 12 volumes drawn up in 1989 has now become a list of some 60 volumes. I must also acknowledge the vision, persistence and constant cheerfulness of John Irwin and the marvellous work done by Mrs Margaret O'Reilly and Sonia Hubbard.

TOM D. CAMPBELL
Series Editor
The Faculty of Law
The Australian National University

Introduction

'The life of the law has not been logic: it has been experience.' This famous remark made by Oliver Wendell Holmes Jr comes from the beginning of his book on *The Common Law* (Boston: Little, Brown & Co., 1881, p. 1). What is meant by this is that the common law is not a set of fixed and immutable axioms, but instead is made up of rules which are the product of history, some of which may owe their existence to circumstances which have long passed away. As Holmes put it elsewhere, 'the whole outline of the law is the resultant of a conflict at every point between logic and good sense – the one striving to work fiction out to consistent results, the other restraining and at last overcoming that effort when the results become too manifestly unjust' (*Collected Legal Papers*, p. 50). By 'logic' Holmes means a consistent, rigorous set of rules. Yet a third of Holmes's aphorisms perhaps explains his attitude to the common law best of all: 'The prophecies of what the courts will do in fact, and nothing more pretentious, are what I mean by the law' ((1897) *Harvard Law Review*, **10**, 457–78).

This concept of 'prophecy', or prediction, provides a useful bridge between jurisprudential theory and the practice of law in the real world. The legal practitioner is concerned to advise his client on a particular practical problem and to suggest a course of action. This can only be done effectively on the basis of a prediction as to what the outcome of the case is likely to be. But how is such a prediction to be reached? If we adopt Holmes's analysis, the answer must lie in balancing 'logic' with 'good sense' – or tempering the strict rules of the law with the requirements of justice.

This of course presupposes that such predictions *can* indeed be made. The chief problem of English common law today is that such predictions are increasingly difficult to determine. More and more cases are what may be termed 'yo-yo cases', with one decision at first instance, which is reversed on appeal to the Court of Appeal and then reversed back again by the House of Lords – usually with the result that the loser in the House of Lords has to pay the costs of the winner at all levels.

The problem is best illustrated by an example. One of the many recent cases which underline the difficulty of predicting the outcome with any certainty even on pretty straightforward facts is *Ogwo v Taylor* [1987] 1 All ER 668; [1987] 3 All ER 961. This is not in fact a yo-yo case, but rather one where the first instance decision was reversed by the Court of Appeal and that decision then affirmed by the House of Lords.

The facts were simple enough. Robert Taylor was preparing to paint his small terraced house, 91 Laburnum Avenue, Hornchurch, Essex, England. He used a blowlamp to burn off the paint on the fascia boards beneath the eaves, which set the house on fire. He called the fire brigade. Two firemen duly arrived, one being Michael Ogwo, the plaintiff. The fire was in the roof space and was eventually brought under control by playing water on it. The heat in the enclosed space was intense. This was relieved to some extent by the firemen kicking out some of the roof tiles. But even so, Michael Ogwo was badly burnt by scalding steam which had penetrated under his fireman's tunic, and he proceeded to sue Robert Taylor for negligence.

The judge at first instance found that Taylor had been negligent in starting the fire but nevertheless dismissed the fireman's claim on the ground that his injuries were not a reasonably foreseeable consequence of Taylor's negligence. The Court of Appeal unanimously reversed this finding and awarded Ogwo damages of £14,402. The basis of this decision was that, though Michael Ogwo had been injured by steam rather than by the flames themselves, his injuries were nevertheless essentially of the same kind and were therefore reasonably foreseeable within the requisite rule. The House of Lords affirmed this decision, also unanimously.

Neill LJ in the Court of Appeal enumerated the following as 'matters which can be treated as not being in dispute in this appeal' (p. 673e):

> (a) The fire was started by the negligence of the defendant.
> (b) The contents of the attic were not unusually combustible and there was nothing unusual about the fire. Indeed attendance at fires in terraced houses is a regular part of the work of firemen in this part of Essex.
> (c) The plaintiff was wearing the standard protective clothing, but such clothing did not provide complete protection to the plaintiff against the steam generated by the water which he and his colleague were pouring on the fire.
> (d) The plaintiff was not guilty of any contributory negligence.

Lord Bridge, who gave the leading speech in the House of Lords, with which all his fellow law lords agreed, summed up the issues in the case (p. 963a):

> The finding of negligence is not challenged. Counsel for the defendant expressly disclaimed any intention to rely on the defence of *volenti* and accepted that the appeal turned solely on the issues of foreseeability, proximity and causation.

Far from justifying the decision, these points raised by Neill LJ and Lord Bridge are, if anything, likely to increase one's disquiet about it:

1. *Why* was the doctrine of *volenti non fit injuria* not relied upon by the defendant? The facts that, as Neill LJ pointed out, 'there was nothing unusual about the fire' and that fires in terraced houses formed a regular part of firemen's duties in the area concerned, should surely have led the firemen in question to expect the sort of problem that they in fact encountered at 91 Laburnum Avenue. And, considering their choice of career, is it really so difficult to conclude that they must have accepted the risks involved?
2. In view of the routine nature of the fire, *why* were the firemen not adequately protected against steam burns? Surely, that could well have formed the basis of a claim of contributory negligence against the fireman – and then possibly of a third party action by him against his employers.
3. It is strange to read that in neither appeal was the negligence of the defendant challenged. Thus Dillon LJ in the Court of Appeal (p. 670b): 'The plaintiff put his case against the defendant on the ground that the defendant had been negligent at common law in starting the fire and allowing it to get out of the defendant's control. ... The judge had no hesitation in finding that the defendant had been negligent, and that finding has not been, and could not be, challenged in this court.' And yet, the selfsame judge who had found the defendant 'negligent' gave judgment in favour of the defendant on the ground that the injury was not reasonably foreseeable! Foreseeability, proximity and

causation were also identified by Lord Bridge, as we have seen, as the issues on which the appeal turned.

But what is negligence at common law if it does not include the elements of foreseeability, proximity and causation? The answer is that the concept of negligence under English common law is a composite one made up of the following ingredients:

1. duty of care,
2. breach of duty,
3. foreseeability/proximity/causation, and
4. injury, loss or damage.

If any one of these ingredients is missing, there is no negligence at all. So, by holding that the fireman's injury was not reasonably foreseeable, what the judge was really saying was that the damage was too remote; in other words, that the degree of proximity between Mr Taylor's breach of duty and Mr Ogwo's injury was not close enough to establish liability. In short, Mr Taylor's breach did not *cause* Mr Ogwo's injury.

The judge was evidently using the term 'negligence' in a rather loose and colloquial sense when he said that Mr Taylor had been 'negligent' in starting the fire and allowing it to get out of control. Certainly, in terms of the law, it is not possible to say, as the judge did, *both* that Mr Taylor was negligent *and* that the fireman's injuries were not reasonably foreseeable – because, to put it very simply, the absence of foreseeability means that there can be no negligence. The point is that the term 'negligence' *means* liability. So, strictly speaking, the judge was actually saying that Mr Taylor both was and was not liable at the same time! But since the judge did not find Mr Taylor liable, he must have been using the word 'negligent' in a broad colloquial sense, meaning merely that Mr Taylor was in breach of his duty to Mr Ogwo.

However, if the first instance judge was confusingly broad in his use of the term 'negligent', the Court of Appeal and House of Lords seem to have taken an unduly narrow approach to the case as a whole. After all, if Mr Taylor was liable to a fireman for injuries arising out of an unremarkable fire in a regular type of setting, then surely any fireman ever injured in a fire could sue the owners of the premises? But would that not be contrary to public policy? For who is going to call out the fire brigade if he suspects that it is likely to cost him his life savings?

One of the most remarkable features about the case is the disdainful way in which both the Court of Appeal and the House of Lords waved aside the American precedents pointing in the opposite direction. The case of *Krauth v Geller* (1960) 157 A 2d 129, decided by the Supreme Court of New Jersey, was cited to both courts. This extract from the judgment of Weintraub CJ was quoted in the judgments of both Neill LJ and Lord Bridge, only to be rejected:

> That the misfortune here experienced by a fireman was well within the range of foreseeability cannot be disputed. But liability is not always co-extensive with foreseeability of harm. The question is ultimately one of public policy, and the answer must be distilled from the relevant factors involved upon an inquiry into what is fair and just. ... [I]t is the fireman's business to deal with that very hazard [the fire] and hence, perhaps, by analogy to the contractor engaged as an expert to remedy dangerous situations, he cannot complain of negligence in the creation of the very occasion of his

> engagement. In terms of duty, it may be said there is none owed the fireman to exercise care so as not to require the special services for which he is trained and paid. Probably most fires are attributable to negligence, and in the final analysis the policy decision is that it would be too burdensome to charge all who carelessly cause or fail to prevent fires with the injuries suffered by the expert retained by public funds to deal with those inevitable, although negligently created, occurrences' (at pp. 130–31).

Why could the English courts not bring themselves to accept this eminently sensible approach? One might at least have expected some argument, some reasons, why this widespread American approach should not be followed. Neill LJ admitted that the rule espoused here by Weintraub CJ 'has been widely applied', but rejected it simply on the basis that '[t]here is ... no "firemen's rule" to be found in the cases decided in this country' (p. 675d). Lord Bridge in the House of Lords gave the rule even shorter shrift. After quoting the passage from Weintraub CJ's judgment, he commented: 'In oral argument, however, counsel for the defendant did not feel able to derive any assistance from this source and, as I think prudently, did not pursue the matter' (p. 966g). It appears from this that even the defendant's counsel, who presumably first drew the court's attention to the American rule, abandoned it during the appeal hearing, though quite why he was so positively congratulated for doing so is not explained.

Unsettling and disquieting though the decisions of the Court of Appeal and House of Lords are in *Ogwo v Taylor*, this is only one of many cases that could have been selected to illustrate the way the English courts have tended to treat the common law in recent years. As we have seen, there is an alarming shortage of legal analysis and reasoning in the judgments. The judge at first instance did not apply the correct test of 'reasonable foreseeability', as both the Court of Appeal and House of Lords held. He also used the term 'negligence' loosely and confusingly, so that he was able to find the defendant 'negligent' and yet enter judgment for him. If the judge was concerned to find for the defendant, why did he not do so on the basis of absence of duty, as Weintraub CJ did in *Krauth v Geller*? As for the Court of Appeal and House of Lords, after correcting the judge on the test of foreseeability, they seemed to treat the matter as settled in favour of the plaintiff. There was no systematic examination to see whether all the ingredients required by law were really present.

Some of the legal problems raised by this case can be summarized as follows:

1. The existence of a duty of care, as we have seen, is something that could by no means be taken for granted in these circumstances. Does a householder really owe a duty to a fireman essentially to put that fireman out of work? That problem, identified by Weintraub CJ, is not even mentioned in any of the judgments in *Ogwo v Taylor*.
2. One problem here is the confusing terminology adopted by the English courts in recent years. 'Reasonable foreseeability' is now the basis of not one, but two, of the legal ingredients of the tort of negligence. Unless it was 'reasonably foreseeable' that the defendant's breach of duty would lead to injury of the kind suffered by the plaintiff, the third ingredient – namely *proximity* or *causation* – is absent, so that liability cannot be found. It is this aspect of foreseeability that exercised all the courts in *Ogwo v Taylor*. But 'reasonable foreseeability' is of course also a necessary element of the first legal ingredient of the tort of negligence – *duty of care* – as was established in *Donoghue v Stevenson* [1932] AC 562. Despite the use of the same term ('reasonable foreseeability') for both, the two concepts are really very different. It may be reasonably foreseeable

that the defendant's acts will affect the plaintiff in a general way, without it being reasonably foreseeable that the plaintiff's actual injury (or some similar injury) will result from the relevant act of the defendant concerned. In the *Ogwo* case, it is thus quite possible to say that it was reasonably foreseeable that Mr Taylor's setting fire to his house might have some effect on Mr Ogwo, but that it was not reasonably foreseeable that Mr Taylor's act would cause Mr Ogwo the type of injury he suffered. In such circumstances there would be a finding of the existence of a duty of care, but not of sufficient proximity or causation. Mr Taylor would then win the case. No discussion of these points is to be found in any of the judgments in either the Court of Appeal or the House of Lords.

3. A proper legal analysis of the question of whether or not a duty of care existed in the first place would have to be concluded one way or the other. But even if Taylor did owe Ogwo a duty of care (which was essentially taken for granted at all three levels), this surely raises a public policy question, of which again there is no mention at all in any of the judgments. The public policy question is quite stark: if a householder is to risk his life savings by calling the fire brigade, is this likely to make householders more careful in the way they remove paint from their fascias – or is it more likely to result in householders being afraid to call out the fire brigade? If the latter, then do not public policy considerations effectively cancel out a duty of care in these circumstances?
4. Another problem area is of course causation, which was also not specifically discussed in any of the judgments in *Ogwo v Taylor*. Although closely connected with the concept of foreseeability, it is not exactly the same thing. Did Robert Taylor's attempt to burn off the paint from his fascia board really *cause* the fireman's injuries? Or was there a *novus actus interveniens*, such as in the way in which the firemen handled the blaze or in the design of their protective clothing which allowed steam in under the tunic? Was it really advisable to use water against a fire in an enclosed space to begin with? That fundamental question does not even appear to have been raised – and yet it was the water from the firemen's hoses which of course gave rise to the steam in the first place.
5. Nor does the decision conform to any other recognizable rational principle. Could it be said, for instance, that the interests of justice were served by this decision? Nor was the question of insurance ever raised. This is in keeping with the traditional view of English law that it is irrelevant whether a case is being fought by the party named in the writ or by an insurer by subrogation. Yet such questions do of course have important practical effects and *have* been taken into account by some judges, notably Lord Denning. In the *Ogwo* case, it would obviously have made a huge difference in practice if Mr Taylor had been covered by some form of liability insurance. There is no indication from the record whether he was insured or not.
6. Moreover, a victory for Mr Taylor would not necessarily have meant a defeat for Mr Ogwo. If a fireman attending a non-extraordinary fire such as this was injured because his protective clothing was not able to prevent steam entering and burning his skin, that must surely be the fault of the fireman's own employers for not providing him with *adequate* protective clothing. Yet the fire authority does not appear to have been involved at any stage of this case. This can hardly be the fault of the unfortunate householder, who should surely be able to rely on a fireman's ability to do the job for which he is being paid without getting injured in the process.

7. What is perhaps strangest of all is that, if anything, this decision actually flies in the face of the general trend of negligence cases under English law, thus underlining the problem of unpredictability mentioned above. Even cases quite closely comparable to *Ogwo v Taylor* have largely gone the other way, in favour of the defendant; indeed, if there is a discernible trend in English law, it is towards a shrinking of liability in tort generally. See for example *D & F Estates Ltd v Church Commissioners* [1989] AC 177 and the cases following on from it.

A number of recent cases reveal an approach to the common law by the English courts increasingly characterized by:

A. A literal-minded approach to the law.
B. A lack of concern for the consequences of a decision for the parties involved (see further under C, below).
C. A lack of concern for justice. 'Justice' is a word which judges are increasingly shy of using in court. A good example of this occurred in *Harlingdon Ltd v Hull Fine Art Ltd* [1990] 1 All ER 737, where Stuart-Smith LJ, in dissenting from his fellow judges in the Court of Appeal, was at pains to point out that the reason for his disagreement had nothing to do with the justice of the case, although he clearly felt that justice had not been served by the majority decision. The case involved the sale of a painting supposedly by Gabrielle Münter which in fact was a fake. Both buyers and sellers were art dealers. The buyers sold the painting on, but refunded their customers when the truth about the painting emerged. The buyers then claimed the purchase price back from the sellers but lost, largely on the ground that, because the buyers knew more about Gabrielle Münter than the sellers, there was no *reliance* placed by the buyers on the sellers. Stuart-Smith LJ put in a minority judgment in favour of the buyers, arguing that reliance was irrelevant to a case of sale of goods and concluding:

> For these reasons I consider that the judge reached the wrong conclusion on this issue and I would allow the appeal. In reaching this conclusion I am in no way influenced by the fact that the judge's decision appears to produce an unjust result. It is trite that hard cases make bad law. But it is undoubtedly a hardship on the plaintiffs, who have refunded the price to their purchaser, that they are left holding the loss, when the defendants or their client would appear to have a claim over against those who sold the painting to them (at p. 749).

D. A tendency to ignore basic principles. This is perhaps the most alarming trend of all. Many English lawyers, including some judges, pride themselves on the supposed fact that English common law is based on precedent rather than on principle – differing in this respect from the Roman-based civil law systems in use in most countries in Europe and elsewhere. But in the absence of principle, how can one decide which cases should be treated as precedents and which not? This can surely only be done on the basis of a set of guiding principles. What is more, it is quite wrong to believe that English law lacks a basic underpinning of principle. A number of very ancient principles underlie the leading cases of the past, but there are alarming signs that these principles are now being lost sight of. Moreover, they are hardly ever taught to law students or trainees. There are all too many recent decisions which can be used to illustrate this, but few which disregard so many basic principles as *Wood v Smith* [1991] 3 WLR 514; [1991] 2 All ER 939. The facts of the case were as follows:

> Two days before he died the testator wrote out a document by hand headed 'My Will by Percy Winterbone'. He did not sign it at the foot of the document, but it was signed at the foot by two attesting witnesses. One of these pointed out to him that he had not signed, but he said: 'Yes I have. I've signed it at the top', referring to the heading, adding that he could sign it anywhere.

The first question before the court was whether the heading constituted a signature. The plaintiff executors did not seek to dispute this, but they argued that the position of the words 'Percy Winterbone' invalidated them as a signature. The judge agreed with the contention. The Wills Act 1837 s 9 had originally required that a will be signed 'at its foot', but this requirement was abolished by s 17 of the Administration of Justice Act 1982. On what basis, therefore, was the signature held to be invalid? The argument was that at the time the testator put his name to the paper in question, there was no disposition of property on it, so *at that moment of time* the piece of paper was not a will. The argument is a clever-clever schoolboy's debating point, which ought to have been laughed out of court in the circumstances of the case. For there was never any doubt of the following:

1. that the *whole* instrument was in Percy Winterbone's handwriting,
2. that it *did* contain dispositions of property,
3. that the dispositions were penned immediately after the heading containing the signature,
4. that the signature was attested by two subscribing witnesses who signed at the foot of the holograph will and only after the dispositions of property had been made, and
5. that the phrase 'My Will by Percy Winterbone' is itself evidence of a clear intention on Mr Winterbone's part that the document he was executing *should* constitute a will.

Despite all these points, the first instance judge held that the will had not been duly executed and could not be admitted to probate. The Court of Appeal reversed this part of the decision, holding that the will had been duly executed; however, it still refused to allow it to be admitted to probate on the ground of insufficient testamentary capacity: [1992] 3 All ER 556.

But why did it take a trip to the Court of Appeal in order to obtain the right decision on the validity of the will in these circumstances? The first instance decision in my view offends against no fewer than three fundamental principles of the common law:

A. *Omnia praesumuntur rite et solemniter esse acta* ('Everything is presumed to have been done rightly and properly'). This principle was cited by Coke on Littleton (*6b*, *323b*) but goes much further back. It is applicable to public and private law alike, and to a huge variety of circumstances. It is essentially a presumption of fact requiring strong counter evidence in order to rebut it. Thus, in *Re Sandilands* LR 6 CP 411 there was an attestation clause to a purported deed stating that the deed had been signed, sealed and delivered. The presumption that the deed had been properly sealed was held to operate, even though there was no sign of any seal on the face of the document. This is not irrelevant to the case of *Wood v Smith*, yet the presumption was apparently never cited in this case either to or by the court, either at first instance or on appeal.

B. *Benigne faciendae sunt interpretationes ... ut res magis valeat quam pereat* (Coke on Littleton 36a); *et verba intentioni, non e contra, debent inservire* (Fox's Case, Coke's Reports VIII 93b). ('A document should be construed in a liberal spirit, so that it is held valid rather than that it should be destroyed; and the words of a document ought to serve the intention of the parties and not the contrary.') These two closely related maxims of the common law are fundamental to the interpretation of any kind of document, enjoining a broad purposive approach. The first maxim requires a court to treat a purported contract as a contract, a purported will as a will, a purported deed as a deed – subject to negative evidence rebutting this presumption. Despite its obvious relevance to *Wood v Smith*, this maxim was also not cited in that case. Applying it to Percy Winterbone's will would obviously have resulted in holding it valid, while an application of the second maxim would have resulted in an interpretation of the will in the way intended by the testator.

But these two maxims are doubly relevant. They apply not only to the will, but also to the statute governing the execution of wills, the Wills Act 1837. The relevant section is s 9, which now reads as follows (as amended by s 17 of the Administration of Justice Act 1982):

> No will shall be valid unless – (a) it is in writing and signed by the testator, or by some other person in his presence and by his direction; and (b) it appears that the testator intended by his signature to give effect to the will; and (c) the signature is made or acknowledged by the testator in the presence of two or more witnesses present at the same time; and (d) each witness either – (i) attests and signs the will; or (ii) acknowledges his signature, in the presence of the testator (but not necessarily in the presence of any other witness), but no form of attestation shall be necessary.

The first instance judge interpreted s 9(b) as meaning that the testator 'must have made his will before signing it'. It is hard to see how this extremely restrictive interpretation could be derived from the wording; indeed, this interpretation was rejected on appeal. But not only does this narrow interpretation serve no practical purpose; it also flies in the face of a fundamental principle of construction of the law.

C. *Precedent*. Precedent is of course the very life-blood of the common law, and there is no shortage of authority on the validity of wills. In *Smith and Smith v Smith* (1866) LR 1 P&D 143, for example, the attesting witnesses to a will saw the testatrix write something, but did not see what she was writing. Indeed, they did not even know it was a will: when they signed at the bottom, they did not see the attestation clause containing the testatrix's signature nor any of the actual text of the will itself. This was surely a far weaker case for validity than *Wood v Smith*, yet the disputed will was upheld in the earlier case, which was not cited to or by the court in *Wood v Smith*. The relevant passage in the judgment of Sir J.P. Wilde reads as follows:

> The presumption *omnia rite esse acta* is strong in a case like the present, and the Court ought to be very careful not to defeat the intention of the testatrix by setting aside the will, unless the evidence clearly rebuts that presumption. It is proved that the testatrix intended to execute

> some paper, and to have it attested by the witnesses, and that she wrote out a holograph will with a full attestation clause at the end of it, part of which was probably written in the presence of one of the witnesses, and there was nothing in the evidence tending to show that she copied it from anything before her. ... The conclusion of fact which I draw is, that what she then wrote was her name. The next question is, what did the witnesses see and attest? They both saw her write that which I am now satisfied was her name, but they did not see the name and did not know that it was her name. The question is whether that is a sufficient attestation. If the Court were to hold that it is not, it would invalidate a great many wills, because it must often happen that when a testator calls witnesses into a room to attest his will, they stand at some distance from him, perhaps at the opposite end of a large table, and see his pen going but do not see what he is writing, and that they then write their names without seeing his signature in consequence of a piece of blotting paper being placed over it, of their not being asked to look at it, and nothing occurring to direct their attention to it. I am therefore unwilling to hold that it is not sufficient for the attesting witnesses to have seen the fact of writing, which I am satisfied was the signature, take place, unless they also saw what that writing was; nor does the statute, in my opinion, require such a decision. For the signature was 'made in the presence of' the two witnesses; they saw the act of writing, and they were, I consider, aware that they had been called in for the express purpose that it should be made in their presence. I therefore hold that here was a good execution, and pronounce for the will.

The real problem, therefore, is not that the common law is lacking in clear principles, but that these principles are no longer taught at university or law school and also are no longer applied by the courts. As far as English common law specifically is concerned, no recent attempt has been made to codify it, even informally. Perhaps most worrying of all is the tendency mentioned above for English lawyers and judges to deny that the common law of England is based on principle at all.

Academic writers unfortunately do not usually appreciate the practical problems. Thus, Melvin Eisenberg in his much-praised book on *The Nature of the Common Law* (Harvard University Press, 1988, pp. 2ff.) identifies what he refers to as three leading 'lines of analysis', all of which he rejects in favour of his own classification. The three 'lines of analysis' identified by Eisenberg are:

1. The view to be found in such works as Joseph Raz's *The Authority of the Law* (1979) and J. Bell's *Policy Arguments in Judicial Decisions* (1983) that a distinction must be drawn between 'cases that can be decided solely on the basis of binding doctrinal propositions and cases whose decision requires the employment of social propositions'. The law, under this line of analysis, consists of the doctrinal propositions found in its binding official texts. Cases that can be decided solely on the basis of such propositions, without the employment of social propositions (except insofar as the terms of a doctrine require the latter), are put into one category, sometimes called 'easy', 'clear' or 'regulated' cases. Here the judge is said to act as a law-finder. Cases in which the employment of social propositions figures in establishing (rather than merely applying) the deciding rule are put into another category, sometimes called 'hard', 'indeterminate' or 'unregulated' cases. Here the judge is said to act with the power of a legislator, making new law by employing those social propositions he thinks best and adopting the rule he thinks best.
2. The view expressed by R. Sartorius in *Individual Conduct and Social Norms*, pp. 181–210 (1975), which has often been attributed to Ronald Dworkin (as in his *Taking Rights Seriously*, pp. 81–130 (1978). According to Eisenberg, however: 'While Dworkin

did once hold this view, he later abandoned it'.) Those espousing this position maintain 'that the judge always acts as a law-finder'. This analysis also distinguishes between hard and easy cases, but on different grounds. Easy cases are those controlled by relatively specific doctrinal rules. Hard cases are those that can be decided only by the application of relatively general doctrinal rules. The judge is said to decide hard cases by 'determining what general rule best fits prior institutional decisions and applying that rule to the case before him'.

3. The view expressed in Ronald Dworkin's *Law's Empire* (*passim*, 1986) 'that the judge decides hard cases by determining what rules would satisfy some threshold test of fit with prior institutional decisions and then selecting, from among these, the rule he thinks best on the basis of his own moral and political convictions. In so deciding, the judge determines rather than makes law'.

Eisenberg responds to these three lines of analysis as follows (*op. cit.*, p. 2):

> I will show that none of these analyses properly accounts for common law adjudication. Under the institutional principles that govern the common law, social propositions are relevant in all cases. To put this differently, all common law cases are decided under a unified methodology, and under this methodology social propositions always figure in determining the rules the courts establish and the way in which those rules are extended, restricted, and applied.

By 'social propositions' Eisenberg means 'all propositions concerning the world other than doctrinal propositions, such as propositions of morality, policy, and experience' (*ibid*, pp. 1f.). 'Doctrinal propositions', by contrast, are defined as 'propositions that purport to state legal rules and are found in or easily derived from textual sources that are generally taken to express legal doctrine. The most obvious group of doctrinal sources consists of official texts that are generally regarded as binding on a deciding court – principally, the so-called primary legal sources, such as statutes and precedents of the deciding court's jurisdiction. A second group of doctrinal sources consists of official texts that are not regarded as binding on a deciding court, such as precedents of other jurisdictions. A third group consists of texts that are the product of analyses by members and students of the profession who replicate the process of judicial reasoning and publish their analyses in forums that are conventionally regarded as secondary legal sources, such as treatises and law reviews' (*ibid*, p. 1).

'Most modern analyses of law and adjudication', Eisenberg roundly states (including his own brand of analysis), 'can be largely defined in terms of their treatment of the interplay between doctrinal and social propositions' (*ibid*, p. 2).

The question that all these modern analysts are asking is essentially the same: do judges merely 'find' the appropriate law and apply it to the case in hand or do they 'make' the law? This is not a new question. Indeed, it is the same question posed by Jeremy Bentham in his furious attack on Blackstone's *Comment on the Commentaries* written about 200 years ago. Blackstone saw the common law of England as derived from immemorial custom, natural or divine law, and reason. Judges merely declared and interpreted it. Blackstone conferred on the common law an august status which elevated it above any human agency, including that of the legislature:

> Those rights then which God and nature have established and are therefore called natural rights, such as life and liberty, need not the aid of human laws to be more effectually invested in every man than they are; neither do they receive any additional strength when declared by the municipal laws to be inviolable. On the contrary, no human legislature has power to abridge or destroy them, unless the owner shall himself commit some act that amounts to forfeiture (I *Commentaries on the Laws of England*, 49).

It was this belief in the sanctity and immutability of the common law and of the rights of the individual that law was seen to enshrine that turned Blackstone into the hero of American jurisprudence that he remains to this day – even though his writings are largely ignored in the land of his birth. Bentham, by contrast, laughed to scorn the whole concept of natural rights, as in his oft-quoted comment on the French Revolutionary Declaration of the Rights of Man: '*Natural rights* is simple nonsense: natural and imprescriptable rights, rhetorical nonsense – nonsense upon stilts'. It may seem paradoxical that Blackstone – the conservative judge – upheld the concept of natural rights whereas Bentham – the radical reformer – roughly rejected it. But it is not really a paradox at all since, for Bentham, all law was a human creation and he looked to the legislature to implement reform.

Because of the centrality of the clash between Blackstone and Bentham to an understanding of the nature of the common law, I have included an illuminating essay on the subject by Rupert Cross as Chapter 16 in this volume.

The four modern analyses of law identified by Eisenberg do not really take us any further than this 18th-century debate between Blackstone and Bentham. All four presuppose that there are 'doctrinal propositions' as well as 'social propositions', the only question being which of the two is dominant in any set of circumstances. The rigidity of Eisenberg's own formulation is particularly unhelpful, stating as he does (see above) that '*all* common law cases are decided under a unified methodology, and under this methodology social propositions *always* figure in determining the rules the courts establish and the way in which those rules are extended, restricted, and applied' (emphasis added). What this presumably means is that *all* cases are decided by a combination of legal and non-legal 'propositions' – a sweeping generalization which will not stand up to scrutiny. For example, what 'social propositions' can be identified in the first instance decision in *Wood v Smith* (discussed above)?

None of the four modern analyses helps us to answer the real problems that confront the lawyer in practice or, for that matter, the layman seeking legal advice. Indeed, what has struck me as a practising barrister acting here as editor of a collection of essays is the tremendous chasm that divides practitioners of law from legal academics – something which bodes ill for the future of the law as a whole.

The chief reason for this chasm is that the questions posed by legal academics tend to be irrelevant from the practitioner's point of view. This is not because of any shortage of really serious problems and fundamental questions that would be of relevance to practitioners but which neither they nor legal academics have addressed.

One of the most important aspects of common law is precedent – important from a practical as well as from a theoretical point of view. I therefore made a point of seeking out several essays on various aspects of this subject for inclusion in this volume, notably Chapters 3, 8, 9 and 12.

Stephen Perry (Chapter 3) sets out to answer the question, 'What is the nature of judicial obligation?', which he characterizes as 'perhaps the most prominent question of legal theory over the past 20 years'. He concludes that 'the most fundamental obligation of a common law court is to settle disputes in accordance with the applicable principles of morality, so that even though judges systematically weight their assessment of the balance of reasons in favour of continuity with the past, they never lose touch with those substantive principles in doing so'.

This, unfortunately, is not a description of the common law that many practitioners – including judges – would recognize. It also does not help to use the categorical word 'never'. In fact, the place of morality in a common law court is far from clear-cut, but it can be said quite confidently that deciding cases 'in accordance with the applicable principles of morality' (whatever that may mean) is *not* the most fundamental obligation of a common law court. There are some judges who would like to think that their decisions combine law with justice and morality, the most notable modern judge of this type being Lord Denning who expressed his own attitude to the doctrine of precedent in the following terms:

> Whilst ready to applaud the doctrine of precedent when it leads to a just and fair result, they [*viz* most judges] become restless under it when they are compelled by it to do what is unjust or unfair (*Discipline of Law*, 285).

This succinct comment goes to the true heart of the problem. It recognizes that, far from being obliged to decide cases on the basis of moral principles, judges may indeed find themselves obliged by precedent to do the opposite: to decide cases in a manner which not only others but even they themselves consider to be unfair or unjust. Sometimes judges who feel so constrained actually have the courage to say so from the bench. Thus, in *Pirelli v Faber* [1983] 1 All ER 65, Lord Scarman's speech (i.e. judgment) in the House of Lords was particularly frank in this regard (at 72):

> My Lords, I agree that the law is now as set out in the speech of my noble and learned friend Lord Fraser. But it is no matter for pride. It must be ... unjustifiable in principle that a cause of action should be held to accrue before it is possible to discover any injury (or damage). A law which produces such a result ... is harsh and absurd.

'No matter for pride', 'unjustifiable in principle', 'harsh and absurd'? Lord Scarman, it may be supposed, was delivering a dissenting judgment? Not at all. He was concurring with the decision of Lord Fraser, who gave the leading speech – and who was also far from happy with the decision that he felt constrained by precedent to reach. Indeed, the decision of the House of Lords was a unanimous 5–0. Both Lord Fraser and Lord Scarman called upon Parliament, in Lord Fraser's words, 'to remedy the unsatisfactory state of the law on this subject', though that could have been but cold comfort to the losing party in the House of Lords!

It is perhaps worth noting that by the time that *Pirelli v Faber* was decided, the House of Lords was entitled to overrule its own previous decisions as well as those of any lower court. Why then did the House of Lords not choose simply to act upon what its own members regarded as fair and sensible rather than uphold a view of the law which they found repugnant to justice and reason alike? Indeed, in following the latter course in the *Pirelli* case, they actually reversed the decision of the Court of Appeal!

Pirelli v Faber underlines the subordinate role the judiciary plays in England in comparison with the US, a fact which has important ramifications for the common law. According to

Morton J. Horwitz's *Transformation of American Law, 1780–1860* and other writers on American legal history, the approach of American judges to the common law underwent a number of discernible changes over time, one of the most important aspects of which concerned the judicial treatment of precedent. The first period, prior to the American Revolution, was characterized as one in which judges saw their role as 'declaratory' only and in which a strict doctrine of precedent prevailed. This was succeeded, from about 1780 to 1840, 1850 or possibly even 1860, by a period in which the character of judicial discourse was identified as 'grand' or 'instrumentalist', marked by an independent attitude to precedent on the part of American judges. In the words of R.B. Ferguson (Chapter 9 in this collection): 'Judges adopted a critical approach to precedents: precedents were regarded as more or less persuasive depending on the reputation of the judge who set the precedent, but were to be followed only if in conformity with "principle" and embodying "sound policy".' This attitude was replaced in the latter half of the 19th century by a 'formalistic' approach, paying much more respect to precedent and suppressing policy considerations as 'extraneous and irrelevant'.

This shift from 'instrumentalism' to 'formalism' is rejected by Ferguson on the basis of an analysis of the reasoning adopted by English judges in sale of goods cases in four distinct periods: 1801–1805, 1881–90, 1896–1905 and 1971–75. Ferguson's conclusions are however open to a number of objections, as follows:

1. He seeks to disprove 'the Horwitz thesis', as he calls it, by means of English cases alone, insisting that: 'It is beyond question that this account [*viz* that of the Horwitz school] is meant to apply to England as much as to America' (p. 314). It is clear, however, that there are important differences between the two. According to Horwitz, there was a period of strict precedent before the American Revolution and again from the mid-19th century onwards, with a more freewheeling attitude to precedent sandwiched in between. One obvious explanation for this shift is the fact that the precedents available in the first decades of the new Republic were largely English decisions; at least one of the reasons for the rejection of the doctrine of binding precedent at that time must have been hostility to England and to the British establishment.
2. Ferguson also concentrates exclusively on sale of goods cases. He recognizes the possibility of criticism on this score only to dismiss it out of hand: 'More plausibly the point might be pressed that it is impossible to extrapolate from findings based on sale of goods cases to other branches of the law. This point is well made. Nevertheless sale of goods transactions are at the heart of trade and commerce; surely, therefore, sale of goods law is a suitable arena in which to examine the impact of capitalist development upon judicial discourse? In any case, sales law is not obviously unrepresentative of commercial law and contract law.' What Ferguson does not seem to realize is that sale of goods law does not really belong to the common law tradition at all, being essentially an adaptation of the *law merchant*, with its roots going back to Roman law. That is why some of the fundamental principles of sale of goods law are at loggerheads with those of the common law, notably the common law doctrine that *nemo dat quod non habet* as compared with the law merchant maxim: *en fait de meubles possession vaut titre*. (See Factors Act 1889 and Sale of Goods Act 1979, sections 21 and 25, under which it is possible in certain circumstances for someone to pass on a better title to goods than he himself possesses.) The fundamental difference between the two concepts is that the common law doctrine

is concerned to prevent fraud, while the law merchant doctrine is designed to prevent the risk of insolvency and to facilitate trade. (See *Sanders v Maclean* (1883) 11 QBD 327 at 343 (CA), *per* Bowen LJ.)

3. Unlike any other branch of English contract law, sale of goods law has been codified in the form of the Sale of Goods Act 1979 (a slightly amended version of the original 1983 Act). 'This is not to say that the Act made no difference', admits Ferguson (p. 333n), who then attempts to discount this fact. But the point is not that sale of goods law is in statute form, but that it represents one (of only two or three examples in the totality of English law) attempt to *codify* a whole area of the law.

A related, if broader, question is posed by Atiyah in Chapter 1 of this collection: 'Does our law constitute, in some sense, a single coherent, integral body of law, or does it consist of two separate entities, two streams running on parallel lines one of which occasionally feeds into the other, but which are destined for ever to retain their separate identities?' The two entities referred to here are common law and statute law; Atiyah concludes that, despite some caveats, there is evidence that the courts have sometimes applied doctrines identified in statutes analogously to common law rules. Atiyah, correctly in my view, remarks on the difference between England and America in this regard, notably: 'American legislatures are accustomed to being told what they can and cannot do by the courts. Our legislature is not, nor would it take kindly to being criticised by the courts' (p. 27).

Conclusion

One of the biggest problems besetting the common law is the fact that the issues emphasized by those teaching and writing about it are to a large extent extremely remote from the concerns of those practising and applying it in the law courts. The difficulties that I would single out as being of the greatest importance to practitioners are not often discussed in academic journals or, if they are, tend to be treated from a theoretical standpoint. Here are a few such issues.

1. *Are there any legal principles to be found in the common law?*
I am not here concerned to distinguish between 'principles' and 'rules', a question which has exercised some academic writers. The practical question is whether the common law consists of identifiable and recognizable principles at all – as distinct from being based purely on individual precedents (as a surprising number of English lawyers believe). My own view is that this pragmatic approach is dangerous, as it may tend to obscure or even prevent the recognition and understanding of the fundamental principles that I, for one, believe most certainly are present at the very heart of the common law.
2. *If so, what are these principles and where are they to be found?*
There is no shortage of student textbooks entitled 'The Principles of Hog Law' or the like, but the word 'principles' in such contexts has come to mean no more than 'introduction to'. Most such books do *not* in fact set out the principles of the branch of law in question – nor (with a few notable exceptions) do most 'advanced' law texts. Most lawyers would probably be very hard pressed to enunciate any basic principles of common law. Indeed, the last time any attempt was made to publish such principles was

in Francis Bacon's unfinished (and largely unknown) collection of ***Maxims of Law*** written about four centuries ago. Some of the most fundamental principles (as cited in the discussion of *Wood v Smith*, above) remain unknown to the mass of practitioners – including many judges – and academic lawyers alike.

3. *How predictable is a decision of the court in any given case?*
This is one of the most important practical questions confronting a lawyer in just about any case. The figure of Justice is traditionally portrayed as blind (i.e. impartial), but all too often it is the lawyers on either side – and, worst of all, their clients – who enter the hallowed portals of justice blindfold. Especially in England, where the loser normally has to pay the winner's costs as well as his own, this can amount to a travesty of justice. If the result of a case could be predicted with at least some degree of certainty beforehand, a lot of misery would be saved. For the outcome of a case to be predictable, however, there has to exist a strong body of clearly enunciated and well understood legal principles. It is precisely the lack of this sure foundation – or rather its erosion – that has resulted in the spate of yo-yo cases in England in recent years (see above), cases decided one way at first instance, reversed on appeal and then reversed back again on final appeal – with whoever finally loses paying everybody's costs all the way up!

This Introduction has dealt chiefly with the law of England, where my own experience has been largely concentrated. As the 20th century draws to a close, the health of English common law gives genuine cause for concern. One of the great strengths of the common law in the past has been its adaptability and capacity for growth. English law has rather lost these characteristics. Thus, for example, not only has it failed to develop a law of privacy, as US common law has successfully done, but has set its face against the possibility of any such development. If a law of privacy comes to England, it will have to be introduced by statute.

Also, as we have already seen, there is a tendency on the part of the English courts to construe statute law – and even procedural rules enacted by statutory instrument – in a literal-minded spirit. This is contrary to another traditional strength of the common law, namely its flexibility. English common law has become very rigid again. It is an ailment first diagnosed over a century ago and supposedly successfully treated then, but there has been a serious relapse.

English law has long served as a model for other Commonwealth jurisdictions with common law systems, so the loss of its adaptability and flexibility bodes ill, not only for English law, but also for that of a number of other countries. Common law in the 52 US jurisdictions, by contrast, appears alive and well, partly because of a constitution interpreted to place the judiciary on a par with the executive and legislature, and also probably because of the survival of the jury system in civil as well as in criminal trials.

Bibliography

Bell, John (1983), *Policy Arguments in Judicial Decisions*, Oxford: Oxford University Press.

Blackstone, William (1765–69), *Commentaries on the Laws of England* (reprint 1979) Chicago & London: University of Chicago Press.

Denning, Lord (1979), *The Discipline of Law*, London: Butterworth.
Dworkin, Ronald (1978), *Taking Rights Seriously*, London: Duckworth.
Dworkin, Ronald (1986), *Law's Empire*, London: Fontana.
Holmes, Oliver Wendell Jr (1920), *Collected Legal Papers*, Boston: Little, Brown & Co.
Horwitz, Morton J. (1977), *The Transformation of American Law, 1780–1860*, Cambridge, Massachusetts: Harvard University Press.
Raz, Joseph (1979), *The Authority of the Law*, Oxford: Oxford University Press.
Sartorius, R. (1975), *Individual Conduct and Social Norms*, New York.

[1]

THE

MODERN LAW REVIEW

Volume 48 January 1985 No. 1

COMMON LAW AND STATUTE LAW*

I PROPOSE in this lecture to address a question which has attracted very little attention in our legal literature[1] although it is, I believe, of considerable theoretical, and potentially also some practical importance. The question concerns the relationship between the common law and statute law. Does our law constitute, in some sense, a single coherent, integral body of law, or does it consist of two separate entities, two streams running on parallel lines one of which occasionally feeds into the other, but which are destined for ever to retain their separate identities? In posing this question, I must make it clear that I am not concerned with the question how *well* common law and statute law fit together, but with the logically prior question, of *how* they fit together. All lawyers, of course, know that large areas of both the common law and the statute law are a shambles, but is it one shambles or are there two? This may seem a very theoretical, or even metaphysical question, but there are a number of important practical issues involved here, particularly when it has once become accepted that the common law is a dynamic, developing body of law just as much as statute law. It may well be that the reason these issues have attracted so little attention hitherto is that until very recently the prevailing orthodoxy of English law was that the judges had no power to change the law. But now that this fairy tale has been abandoned, the relationship between common law and statute law must be seen as the relationship between two developing and moving bodies of law; and the way in which they interact on each other becomes a matter of no little importance.

I

Now there is one respect in which, when a statute is passed, it becomes part of a large ongoing enterprise, just as a new piece of case law does. Obviously, it may reverse or modify existing law; but less obviously it takes a great deal of existing law for granted.

* The Chorley Lecture, 1984.

[1] Virtually the only discussion of which I am aware is in Cross, *Precedent in English Law*, 3rd ed., Oxford, 1977.

Very few statutes are self-contained instruments even when they deal with a remote or esoteric branch of the law. At the very least they are subject to the rules of interpretation, and hence to the provisions of the Interpretation Act. But in addition, most statutes attract huge bodies of existing law—both statute and common law—in a wide variety of ways. For example, there is the relationship of the statute to the courts: a statute is law, and prima facie matters of law fall within the jurisdiction of the courts. If it is a matter of public law, judicial review may be available, and the whole body of law governing judicial review may thus be attracted by the Act. Alternatively, if the Act creates private rights, huge bodies of civil law may be attracted. Rules of general application drawn from the substantive law of contract or tort or restitution or trusts may become relevant. Other statutes, where appropriate, such as, for instance, the Contributory Negligence Act or the Frustrated Contracts Act, may become applicable, via the common law rules which they amend, and which may themselves be drawn within the orbit of an Act creating civil liabilities. Or again, the Act may create offences. At once, the whole body of general principles of criminal law becomes relevant: rules concerning the criminal capacity of minors, rules concerning the criminal responsibility of secondary parties, rules concerning sentencing, all these will become part of the machinery for the enforcement of the new Act without one word being said about them. Beyond and behind all these rules of substantive law, there lie still further bodies of rules about enforcement of the law: apart from rules of jurisdiction, procedure and evidence, there are the powers of the police, the powers of prison governors and sheriffs, and in the case of civil liabilities a whole battery of enforcement mechanisms such as garnishee orders, attachment of earnings orders and bankruptcy laws—which of course bring in their train yet further rules about the powers and procedure of the courts with bankruptcy jurisdiction.

So in all these ways, a new statute becomes part of a very large body of law even though not one word is said about these things in the Act itself. Furthermore, the Act itself may now become part of this ongoing, all pervasive body of laws which will attach itself to later Acts as and when they come to be passed. What is more, it is not just the *ipsissima verba* of the Act which thus becomes part of this mass of laws, apparently floating in the sky and ready to fasten on any new passing statute. It is the Act as interpreted by the proper organs entrusted with the job. As we all know, many statutes, as living pieces of law, are in substance an amalgam of the legislative wording and judicial exegesis, and it is this amalgam which attaches itself to new statutes in the manner I have just sketched. Furthermore, judicial exegesis is itself the subject of yet further rules which necessarily get attached to the Act, and therefore to other statutes to which this one may become attracted: rules about the authority of the expounder, about the status of the court in which he was sitting, about how the exegesis was made and so on.

Much of what I have so far said is just as true of case law even in areas which may seem to be matters of pure common law. A new decision, like a new statute, must be fitted into the existing body of the law. The very courts which pronounce the decision are today, creatures of statute; the substantive rules being applied may remain pure and unsullied rules of common law, but statute obtrudes in the most unlikely corners when we look carefully. If either of the parties is a company, or some public body, or even a married woman, the capacity of that party to sue or be sued, and indeed, in the case of corporations, its very existence, may be a matter of statute law; the rules of procedure of the court in question will probably be an amalgam of enacted and traditional or common law; the enforcement mechanisms for the courts' ultimate decrees may well be statutory.

In all these ways, the law does indeed seem to be a seamless web, a huge network of interrelated rules of common law or case law, and of statute law. Let me now single out for more detailed attention three particular types of situation where the work of Parliament and the work of the courts is still more closely interwoven. There are, first, statutes which have deliberately adopted a very open-textured type of language, and thereby delegated to the courts the responsibility for creative development of case law. One thinks, for example, of the old Workmen's Compensation Acts with their famous formula about accidents "arising out of and in the course of employment." The case law which developed around these words was, in a sense, a mixed legislative and judicial creation. The courts had been in effect delegated the task of finding principles to solve the many marginal cases which arose under the Act; and they performed this task as they perform most common law tasks—that is by gradually building up a body of cases along principled lines. This case law has long had a bad name among lawyers, but it seems unlikely that the results would have been better if some minister had been given the power to make regulations when the first Workmen's Compensation Act was passed, and had had to anticipate the many different types of case which in fact arose. But my main point is that the working of the Acts illustrates a legislative–judicial partnership which is not untypical in modern law. The statute was the starting point; and statutory amendments were, of course, introduced from time to time. But within the framework of the statute, the common law methodology prevailed: that is to say, case by case, *ex post facto* decision making, but decision making with reasoned explanations and attempts at finding principles to govern future cases. Although the system may have worked badly in the end, it is a grave mistake to suppose that the volume of case law to which it gave rise itself demonstrates that fact. After all, even under the old system, thousands of cases were dealt with every year without litigation.

A second type of situation which also illustrates the legislative–judicial partnership, and which is perhaps more typical of modern law than the Workmen's Compensation Acts, is to be found in statutes openly conferring discretion on the courts to resolve conflicts or disputes as they think just and equitable, or in some such formula. One has, for instance, the extremely wide discretion exercised by the courts in matrimonial property cases, or in claims under the Inheritance (Family Provision) Legislation. Once again, one finds the case law method being used: reasoned explanations, the search for principles, classification of differing factual situations, and so on. True it is that this is a more obviously discretionary field than the old Workmen's Compensation law, and true it is that the courts have been unwilling to tie themselves down to rigid application of principles. But the difference may lie as much in a general loosening up of the strict doctrine of precedent, as in the difference between an overt discretion and an apparent rule of law. Perhaps if the doctrine of precedent had been operated more loosely under the Workmen's Compensation Acts, there would have been less dissatisfaction with their results.

On the other hand, if all principle is to be abandoned, and everything left to the discretion of a single trial judge, the whole value of the case by case methodology of the common law will be lost. For that reason I confess to feeling great anxieties at the signs in a number of recent cases that discretionary power to do what seems just and equitable are to be exercised solely by a trial judge, with virtually no appellate supervision unless manifest errors of principle are made. In the *George Mitchell* seeds case,[2] for instance, the House of Lords stressed that the "reasonableness" requirement of the Unfair Contract Terms Act was a matter for the decision of the trial judge alone; in the *B.P. Exploration*[3] case under the Frustrated Contracts Act, the Court of Appeal likewise insisted that it was for the trial judge to assess what was a "just sum" to award under section 1(3) of that Act and the Court of Appeal would not interfere with his decision merely because they thought that there were better ways of assessing the just sum: in the *Hadmor Productions* case,[4] likewise, the House of Lords stressed that the decision to grant an interlocutory injunction is discretionary, and that the discretion is that of the trial judge not subject to appellate control unless he errs in principle. One understands, of course, why the courts are reluctant to multiply appeals where discretion rather than strict rule is in question: if the matter is one of discretion, there are no ultimate standards by which to determine whether the decision is "right" or "wrong," so the decision of one

[2] [1983] 2 A.C. 803.
[3] [1981] 1 W.L.R. 232. The appeal to the H.L. did not involve this question.
[4] [1983] 1 A.C. 191.

judge may be thought as acceptable as the decision of another. Yet this line of reasoning seems to me essentially fallacious. Once it is agreed, as it now seems to be, that even in matters of strict law, appellate courts are rarely driven to one inexorable result, but have in reality to choose between alternative ways of developing the law, and it should be apparent that decisions on matters of strict law do not differ in the relevant respect from discretionary decisions. Furthermore, as I suggested in my inaugural lecture at Oxford in 1978,[5] we are apparently moving to an era when a great deal of strict law is being replaced by discretions of one kind or another. The proliferation of these discretions appears to me to arise at least in part from the realisation that legislation, even when fleshed out by detailed subordinate legislation, simply cannot anticipate and provide for the great variety of cases which are likely to arise; and that Parliament therefore prefers to proceed in partnership with the judiciary. Prima facie rules of law which are displaceable by discretions in exceptional cases are now almost the norm in many forms of legislation: this kind of legislation seems to me to open the door to a possible new type of law making in which the traditional common law method of *ex post facto,* case by case analysis is integrated into a general statutory framework. But if the courts insist that all these discretions are not to be subject to the advantage of reasoned discussion in appellate courts, with the interchange of opinion available in multi-judge courts, the possibility of fruitful development along these lines will be stifled.

My third example of a type of law in which common law and statute law develop together relates to areas of law in which statutes have been passed amending a very active living part of the common law. When this happens, the Act may be interpreted and applied, often in parallel with analogous areas of the common law, and the legislation almost takes on the characteristics of a living graft which develops a life of its own. The example which comes to my mind—doubtless there are others—is the law governing claims for damages by the dependants of those killed in accidents. In this area, first the Fatal Accidents Act of 1846, and later the Law Reform Act of 1934 became closely interwoven with the general common law rules about the assessment of damages, as well as the substantive principles of liability governing such claims. The result is that the law is today an amalgam of common law and statute law of such an interdependent kind that it is often difficult to say whether a particular result is determined by the statute or by ordinary case law. Except for the recent disastrous situation caused by *Pickett* v. *British Rail,*[6] from which we may or may not have been rescued by the Administration of Justice Act 1982, it is my impression that this amalgam worked tolerably well—setting aside, of course, the very wide issues raised about the suitability in

[5] *From Principles to Pragmatism*, Oxford, 1978.
[6] [1980] A.C. 136.

modern times of the whole nature of the action for damages for personal injury and fatal accidents. Yet it will be noticed that the original Fatal Accidents Act was not drafted with a myriad of detail in the way of most modern legislation. It was a bare skeletal framework which the courts fleshed out in a manner which, if it did not give universal satisfaction, will, I believe, prove in retrospect to have been more successful than the amending legislation of 1982. Nevertheless, neither Parliament nor the courts can take much comfort from their performance in this area of the law. If the 1846 Act enabled Parliament and the courts to work out a reasonable amalgam, the 1934 Act was an unmitigated disaster. Like many Acts emanating from the Law Revision Committee, it was ill-conceived, and its relationship with the Fatal Accidents Act, simply not properly thought through. But if the Act was bad, the judicial handling of it was even worse. I need not rehearse the whole lamentable story which is well enough known. The only point I want to make is that where legislation impinges on daily law in action, some modicum of co-operative partnership between courts and legislature is absolutely necessary. This partnership can be achieved by the legislature dealing only with general principles, and leaving the courts to flesh out the details, or it can be achieved by a greater willingness on the part of the courts to iron out defects in an ill-considered statutory scheme. Unfortunately, in this instance, neither of these was done.

II

I have so far said nothing very controversial, nor, perhaps, anything very original though I have possibly offered a new side-light on the relationship between common law and statute law. But I now want to move on to a more difficult and controversial subject. If, as I have suggested, statute law and common law do, at least in many areas, work together in some kind of legal partnership, creating sometimes amalgams of law of various kinds, it is possible for the courts to take account of statute law, in the very development of the common law itself? Can the courts, for instance, use statutes as analogies for the purpose of developing the common law? Can they justify jettisoning obsolete cases, not because they have been actually reversed by some statutory provision, but because a statute suggests that they are based on outdated values? Could the courts legitimately draw some general principle from a limited statutory provision, and apply that principle as a matter of common law? It must be clear that using statutes in this way is fundamentally different from any process of construction, however benevolent or liberal that might be. Construction, as a matter of theory at least, requires the court to give effect to what it thinks the legislation actually enacts. Using statutes by way of analogy quite clearly involves using them to produce results which the legislation does *not* enact. The questions I now wish to address are whether the courts already do this, and if so whether any principles can be discerned by which they do so, and whether there is scope for further development along these lines.

I must disclaim any pretence to being the first person to ask these questions. In 1907 Roscoe Pound raised the basic issue in an article in the *Harvard Law Review.*[7] He suggested there that there were four different ways in which the common law could respond to legislation. First, judges might give statutes a strict and narrow interpretation, and refuse to reason from them by analogy. Secondly, they might interpret legislation in a more liberal way, while still refusing to receive the statute into the general body of the law, and therefore using it as a source of values and analogies for the development of the common law. Thirdly, the judges might receive statutes fully into the body of the law, to be reasoned from by analogy in the same way as cases themselves, but without necessarily giving superior status to analogies drawn from legislation. Fourthly, he suggested, judges might go to the extreme extent of treating statutes as a higher source of analogy than cases or other sources of law. Pound suggested that the general tendency of common lawyers seemed to be to treat statutes in the first of these four ways—to refuse to receive them fully into the body of the law, to treat them as interlopers, and interpret them narrowly, giving them no further effect than a direct application requires.

In his book on *Precedent in English Law*[8] Sir Rupert Cross suggested that English law had already reached the third if not the fourth stage referred to by Pound, and he gave a number of examples, though mostly of some antiquity, in which common law rules had apparently been developed by analogy to statutes. He referred for instance, to the presumption of death after seven years' absence as having originated in the early nineteenth century from some early statutes of limited application; and also to the well-known development of limitation periods both at common law and in equity, by analogy to some very early legislation.[9] I shall refer to this view as the Cross thesis.

The problem seems to me a good deal more complex than Sir Rupert Cross suggested, however, and his discussion of the topic is somewhat flawed by his failure to refer to the historical variations in the way statutes have been treated by the courts. For it is well enough known that in the sixteenth century Plowden enunciated his theory of the "equity of a statute"[10] which seems to closely resemble the idea that courts can develop the law by analogy to a statute. Undoubtedly many remarkable instances of what would today be called extremely liberal statutory interpretation occurred

---

[7] "Common Law and Legislation" (1907) 21 Harv. Law Rev. 383.

[8] *Op. cit.*

[9] *Ibid.*, at pp.167–168.

[10] *Eystone* v. *Studd* (1574) 2 Plow. 459, 465–469. See generally, Allen, *Law in the Making* (7th ed., Oxford, 1964), pp.451–455.

in the medieval period; perhaps the most extreme is the case in which it was held that a statute forbidding interference with the Bishop of Norwich in his spiritual jurisdiction extended to all the Bishops.[11] But the idea that it was permissible to develop the law in this way fell into disfavour in the eighteenth century[12] and was effectively discarded altogether in the nineteenth.[13] The editors of *Maxwell*[14] and *Craies*[15] treat the whole doctrine of the equity of a statute as obsolete today. Now I have said that using legislation to justify changes and developments in the common law is conceptually a different exercise from construction, however liberal; but it remains a serious question how far it is possible to reconcile the idea that no effect can be given to the statute, *as a statute,* beyond what it actually enacts, and the idea that the statute can nevertheless be applied as a source of analogy or principle to justify changing the common law. Let me consider a number of problem areas which have traditionally been thought to be purely questions of statutory construction or application.

Consider, first, the straightforward *casus omissus*: an Act simply fails to deal with a case within the general purview of the legislation. Until very recently, the strict orthodoxy of English law was that a court could not fill in the gaps left by Parliament.[16] If Parliament had blundered, the remedy lay with Parliament. The gap in the Act could only be filled if, on the true construction of the Act, there was in truth no gap. If, after all endeavours had been made, the gap was still obstinately there, then the law remained as though there was no statutory provision. As Craies on *Statute Law* uncompromisingly puts it "*a statute may not be extended to meet a case for which provision has clearly and undoubtedly not been made.*"[17] Now it may be that the decision of the House of Lords in *Wills* v. *Bowley*[18] marks some retreat from this extreme position. Faced with a statutory power of arrest for an offence for which the accused was subsequently acquitted the House here extended the statute to authorise the arrest of a suspected offender and not just an actual offender. Counsel for the police frankly conceded that he was inviting their Lordships to read some words into the Act which were not there, and it is striking that in a case where the liberty of the subject was at stake, the House should have acceded to this invitation not for any

[11] *Platt* v. *Sheriffs of London* (1550) 1 Plow. 35, 36.

[12] Thus Lord Mansfield treated the equity of the statute as synonymous with the intent of the legislature. *R.* v. *Williams* (1758) 1 W.Bl. 93, 95.

[13] See, *e.g.* Lord Tenterden in *Brandling* v. *Barrington* (1827) 6 B. & C. 467, 475; Lord Brougham in *Gwynne* v. *Burnell* (1840) 7 Cl. & F. 572, 696; Pollock C.B. in *Miller* v. *Solomons* (1853) 7 Ex. 475, 558.

[14] See Maxwell, *Interpretation of Statutes* (12th ed., 1969), p.237: "This kind of construction would not be tolerated today."

[15] Craies on *Statute Law*, p.102.

[16] See, *e.g. Magor & St. Mellons R.D.S.* v. *Newport Corpn.* [1952] A.C. 189; *R.* v. *Wimbledon JJ.* [1953] 1 Q.B. 380; *Fisher* v. *Bell* [1961] 1 Q.B. 394.

[17] p.17: the italics are in the original.

[18] [1983] 1 A.C. 57. See Bennion on *Statute Law* (2nd. ed., 1983), pp.131–141.

compelling reasons of construction, but because they thought it desirable to introduce some clarity and uniformity into a confused area of statute law.

Of course lip service was paid to the traditional dogma that the court was merely construing the Act, though we need not pay too much attention to that. But it remains difficult to see this as a case in which the court has in any sense developed the common law with the aid of statutory material; the truth may be that it extended the operation of the Act to give effect to its views on sound policy, but that—within limits which vary and are difficult to define—is a well-established function of the courts and does not seem to illustrate the kind of legal development I am addressing.

Consider now another clear example of a *casus omissus* where it never seems to have occurred to anybody that the problem could be dealt with by altering the common law by analogy with the statute. The Law Reform (Miscellaneous Provisions) Act 1971[19] enacted that in assessing damages payable to a widow under the Fatal Accidents Act, no account should be taken of the remarriage or prospect of remarriage of the widow. But the Act made no provision for the like problem which arises when damages have to be assessed for a child under the Fatal Accidents Act. Before the passing of the Act it was settled law that account had to be taken of the fact or possibility of a widow's remarriage, when assessing damages payable to her or to her children.[20] This "settled law" was, of course, a part of that common law-statutory amalgam governing fatal accident claims to which I have already referred: it is hard to say whether it was a rule of the common law, or a statutory rule. It was, at any rate, quite clearly a judge-made rule. Now when the interpretation of the 1971 amendment came before the courts, in *Thompson* v. *Price,*[21] it was treated in the traditional way as a *casus omissus*. Counsel for the child argued, quite correctly, that the whole purpose of the amendment was to free the court and the widow of the requirement that her prospects of remarriage should be assessed by the judge; and it was therefore obvious that this policy would be defeated if the old law remained in force as regards the assessment of the damages awardable to the child. If Sir Rupert Cross was right in his assessment of the courts' ability to use statutes by analogy, this would seem to have been a very strong case for the application of such methodology. The court could have said: the Act clearly does not apply to this case, but it does show quite plainly that the old law laid down by the courts does not commend itself to Parliament, and therefore we are free to depart from the old law. But the argument only has to be stated to show how contrary it is to traditional methods and it

[19] s.4(1), now re-enacted as s.3(2) of the Fatal Accidents Act 1976.
[20] *Goodburn* v. *Thomas Cotton Ltd.* [1968] 1 Q.B. 845.
[21] [1973] Q.B. 338.

does not even seem to have been considered as a possibility by the judge, or by counsel.

The same statutory provision illustrates my next point. If the courts are free to change or develop the common law by analogy to legislation, what should they do with statutes which are not yet in force? In *Wilson* v. *Dagnall*[22] the trial of a widow's action under the Fatal Accidents Acts took place five days before the coming into force of the 1971 Act. The trial judge rather courageously decided to apply the Act; but the majority of the Court of Appeal condemned this decision as "wrong and contrary to law."[23] Lord Denning dissented, but only on the ground that the trial judge should have post-dated his judgment. The question that arises in the present context is whether the court could, or should have declared that the Act not yet being in force, the matter was to be resolved according to the law apart from the Act, but that that law was judge-made law, and Parliament having shown its dislike for the law, it was now open to the judges to alter the pre-Act law. In the majority judgment Megaw L.J. said that because the Act expressly stated that it was only to come into force on August 1, 1971, this meant "that Parliament has ordained that up to that date, August 1, 1971, the law is to remain as before." With respect, this is clearly wrong. A commencement provision ordains nothing as to the state of the law before the commencement date. It neither approves, modifies nor reverses the law before the commencement date: it is simply silent.[23a] It would, for instance, have been open to the House of Lords to overrule the earlier authorities requiring account to be taken of the prospects of remarriage of the widow. If that question had indeed arisen, then the House might have had to consider what weight, if any, to place on the fact that Parliament had altered the law for future cases. But if the House of Lords could do it, why could not the Court of Appeal? The earlier authorities were it is true, Court of Appeal decisions binding on that court in the ordinary way. But if statute can be resorted to by way of analogy, for development and change in the law, surely the analogy—at least if pressing enough as this one clearly was—ought to be given greater weight than a mere judicial decision. Nevertheless, nobody thought to make this argument.

But if no English court has ever applied an Act not yet in force, there is one remarkable decision of the House of Lords which seems to have applied an Act after it was repealed. Lord Cairns' Act of 1858 was repealed by the Statute Law Revision Act 1883, though with a savings provision which is not easy to understand,

[22] [1972] 1 Q.B. 509.

[23] At p.519.

[23a] However, interesting questions could arise as to the duty of a Minister to make a commencement order, where he fails or refuses to do so. Could a new government, for instance, evade the need for repealing an Act by simply refusing to make a commencement order?

and which was itself repealed by the Statute Law Revision Act 1898 with yet further savings. In *Leeds Industrial Co-operative Society* v. *Slack*[24] the House of Lords applied Lord Cairns' Act as though it were still in force. Lord Finlay, delivering the leading judgment, attempted to penetrate the jungle of savings provisions but ended up by saying, that there had been since 1883 a general consensus of opinion that Lord Cairns' Act "or something equivalent to it" was still in force. It seems almost as though the House accepted that the principle of the Act remained in force although it had been repealed; but it is not wholly clear whether this holding was in reliance on the savings' provisions or by some other alchemy. The case is so extraordinary that it cannot be treated as serious support for the Cross thesis.

My next problem with the Cross thesis arises from the large number of cases concerning attempts to escape the provisions of an Act by casting a transaction in a form which the Act does not seem to strike. One thinks particularly of taxing statutes, of course, but there are many other examples; for instance, there is a line of cases in which refinancing transactions have been held not to fall within the Bills of Sale Acts on the ground that the owner of the goods is not granting a charge but selling the goods and then re-acquiring them on hire purchase terms.[25] There are many cases recognising that workers may contract out their labour as independent contractors in such a way as to escape the provisions—both benefits and burdens—of the law of employment, even though in reality and in substance, they are employees.[26] There are the well-known cases holding that many protections accorded to tenants can be evaded by adopting the form of a licence rather than a lease.[27] The record of the courts in dealing with these problems has been patchy and sometimes unpredictable. Where a transaction can be characterised as a complete "sham" it may be possible for the courts to treat the case as falling within the relevant statutory provisions,[28] but it will be seen that this is in complete accord with the traditional approach to the relationship of common law and statute law. If the form of the transaction is a sham, as defined by the court, then the "real," *i.e.* the legal nature of the transaction is one which falls within the direct control of the legislation. Nobody has suggested that it is possible to extend the legislation, by analogy or in any other way, to cover cases which actually succeed in escaping the direct effect of the statute, merely because they are designed to achieve the same purpose, or fall within the mischief of

---

[24] [1924] A.C. 851.

[25] See, *e.g. Snook* v. *London & West Riding Investments Ltd.* [1967] 2 Q.B. 786; *Stoneleigh Finance* v. *Phillips* [1965] 2 Q.B. 537; *Kingsley* v. *Sterling Industrial Securities* [1967] 2 Q.B. 747.

[26] See Chitty, *Contracts* (25th ed., 1983), § 3404.

[27] *Somma* v. *Hazelhurst* [1978] 1 W.L.R. 1014.

[28] See Andrew Nicol, "Outflanking Protective Legislation—Shams and Beyond" (1981) 44 M.L.R. 21.

the Act, or because policy suggests that they should be treated in the identical way. Even the recent House of Lords decisions in the *Ramsay*[28a] and *Dawson*[28b] cases do not seem to go this far, or to reason in this way.

One further difficulty with the Cross thesis concerns the way in which the courts usually treat cases which have been reversed by statute. As a general rule, the courts tend to regard the statutory reversal of judicial decisions as not affecting the underlying principles of those decisions. Indeed, a very large number of the cases cited by standard textbooks on the law of contract, to take one example, are annotated with footnotes indicating that the actual decision in the case has been reversed by legislation, but that the case is still authority for some general principle. One thinks, for instance of *Derry* v. *Peek*[29] and *Dunlop* v. *Selfridge*[30] in contract law, but examples can be found in nearly all branches of the law.[30a] Furthermore, attempts to argue that statutory reversal of common law rules is evidence of a parliamentary policy hostile to those rules, is often met with the counter argument that if the statute has only reversed part of the common law rules, it must have impliedly confirmed the remainder. For example in *Admiralty Commissioners* v. *S.S. America*[31] Lord Sumner argued that the rule in *Baker* v. *Bolton*[32]—that death gave no cause of action in tort—was impliedly recognised by Parliament's enactment of the Fatal Accidents Act 1846; because that Act, though largely rendering nugatory the effect of *Baker* v. *Bolton,* did not in terms completely reverse the principle that death could not give rise to a cause of action in tort. However, I don't want to make too much of this objection to the Cross thesis, because there are in fact a number of instances of treatment by the courts of statutory reversals of judicial decisions which support his general view of the relationship of common law and statute law. I shall deal with these presently.

III

I come now to deal with a number of legal areas in which it seems that the courts do develop the common law, either by analogy to statutes, or at least in a way which is somehow influenced by statute law, and in which the law appears to develop as a coherent integral whole.

I will take first the action for breach of statutory duty. As all lawyers know, the theory of the civil action for breach of statutory

[28a] *W. T. Ramsay Ltd.* v. *I.R.C.* [1982] A.C. 300.
[28b] *Furniss* v. *Dawson* [1984] 1 All E.R. 530.
[29] (1889) 14 App.Cas. 337.
[30] [1915] A.C. 847.
[30a] See, *e.g.*, as to the effect of the Criminal Attempts Act 1981 on the common law offence of incitement, to which the Act does not apply, Smith & Hogan, *Criminal Law* (5th ed., 1983), p.226 and *R.* v. *Fitzmaurice* [1983] 1 All E.R. 189.
[31] [1917] A.C. 38.
[32] (1808) 1 Camp. 493.

duty is that the courts find in some legislative prohibition an implied intention on the part of Parliament to create civil liability for its breach; equally, as all lawyers know, this legislative intention is nearly always a complete fiction. But the search for this intent is more than just a fiction. It plainly runs counter to the accepted contemporary methods of statutory interpretation. Were it not that the action for breach of statutory duty is now a well established part of the law, it seems to me almost unthinkable that a court could today justify the creation of civil liability out of some exiguous statutory provision creating an offence. To do this plainly involves reading in words wholesale into the Act without any grammatical or literal justification. There are cases without number in which far less dramatic extensions or adaptations of statutory language have been rejected by the courts as exceeding the permissible bounds of statutory interpretation. So we must, I think, accept that in most cases the recognition that a penal statutory provision creates civil liability is a creative act on the part of the courts. But that does not wholly answer our question because there are two distinct ways in which this creative act could be characterised. First, it could be said that this is an illustration of the Cross thesis, that it does truly involve recognition that common law and statute law should be treated as one body of law, that an action for breach of statutory duty is created by way of analogy to, or extension of, the statute, in order to integrate the law of negligence as closely as possible with the penal provisions of statutes. A reasonable man, it might be said, must always comply with statutory duties, so any breach of statutory duty should *per se* be treated as negligence. Some American courts do adopt this theory,[33] and the House of Lords came close to endorsing it in *Lochgelly Iron & Coal Co. Ltd.* v. *M'Mullan*[34] in 1933. But there is an alternative way of explaining the creative act of the court in these cases: it could be said that there is a general rule of the common law that, subject to various conditions, breaches of duty give rise to civil liability, and that these breaches of duty may arise at common law or by statute. On this theory, there is no extension or adaptation of the statute when a court recognises a penal provision as creating civil liability; all that happens is that the court uses the statute to fill in the blanks, as it were, in the pre-existing common law rule that various types of breach of duty create civil liability. As I shall suggest below, there are in fact quite a large number of points of contact between the common law and statute law which can be explained in this sort of way, and for my part I find this theory fits the practice of the courts better than the Cross thesis.

I say this for two reasons. First, the practice today is to treat the cause of action for breach of statutory duty as quite separate from

[33] See Prosser, *Torts* (4th ed., 1971), pp.190–192.
[34] [1934] A.C. 1.

the cause of action for negligence, even though they are often pleaded together and arise out of one set of facts. A particularly striking example is to be found in *Chipchase* v. *British Titan Products Co. Ltd.*[35] in 1956. The plaintiff was a workman who fell off a plank on which he was standing to do some work. The plank was only nine inches wide, and was six feet off the ground. Statutory regulations provided that if the plank had been six feet six inches off the ground, the plank should have been at least 34 inches wide, and the plaintiff's counsel tried to persuade the court to look at the regulations as a guide to what would have been a reasonable size plank. Clearly if you need 34 inches when you are six feet and six inches off the ground, it might reasonably be thought that you need more than nine inches of plank when you are six feet high. But the Court of Appeal would have none of it. The statutory regulations and the common law duty were different things, they insisted, and must be considered independently. There was no lack of reasonable care on the facts of the case. This case seems plainly inconsistent with the Cross thesis unless it is possible to argue that delegated legislation stands on a different footing from statutes. There may well be a case for drawing such a distinction, but it is not recognised in current legal doctrine except of course for the *ultra vires* rule.

My second reason for thinking that the present law and practice relating to breach of statutory duty does not proceed on the basis of any analogical or other extension or adaptation of the statute, is that once a claim of this kind is before the courts, they will construe the statutory provision according to their normal strict, somewhat literal, methods of interpretation to see if there has indeed been a breach. So far as I am aware, nobody has ever suggested that because the whole action is the creation of the courts, it therefore falls to be treated as though it were a common law claim, in which case it might be suggested that the spirit of the legislation is more important than the precise words.

So although matters might have developed otherwise, it seems to me that as matters now stand, the action for breach of statutory duty does not truly reflect any serious fusion or integration of common law and statute law in the way argued for by Sir Rupert Cross. Many other areas of contact between common law and legislation can, I think, be explained in the same way. There is, for instance, the law of illegality in contract. Here again, the courts go through the pantomime of looking for a parliamentary intention to prohibit the making of the relevant class of contracts.[36] And here again, this exercise is plainly a creative one, and can be explained by the same two distinct theories as I suggested in the case of breach of statutory duty. It is possible to argue that the courts are extending the operation of the statutes by treating breach as

[35] [1956] 1 Q.B. 545.

[36] See, *e.g. St. John Shipping Corpn.* v. *Joseph Rank* [1957] 1 Q.B. 267, 285.

depriving a party of the right to enforce a contract; or alternatively, it can be argued that there is a pre-existing rule of the common law that certain types of unlawful conduct may render a contract unenforceable. One then only has to recognise that what is unlawful conduct for this purpose can be prescribed by Parliament as much as by the courts themselves, and it becomes unnecessary to regard the rules governing illegal contracts as an instance of analogical extension of the statutory provisions. I am less sure that there is any real difference between these two theories in this instance, but I incline to think that the second explanation again fits the practice of the courts more closely than the first, mainly on the ground that here also the courts do not look to the spirit of the legislation but to its precise wording to see whether there has been any violation. Exactly the same explanation can be offered of a number of other similar areas of the law in which the concept of an illegal or unlawful act constitutes a part of a common law rule, as for instance, in the law relating to intimidation or duress.

I will mention two other cases of a similar character which appear to me rather more interesting, though again it is far from clear whether they really did involve any analogical extension of statutory provisions—certainly it is plain that in neither case did the judges think they were engaged on any such exercise. The first is the decision of the House of Lords in *The Towerfield*[37] in 1951. The case arose out of the Pilotage Act 1915 which made a shipowner vicariously liable for the negligence of a compulsory pilot—as opposed to a pilot voluntarily engaged. Nineteenth-century judges with their individualist value systems, and their belief in freedom of choice, had recoiled from the idea that a shipowner could be liable for the negligence of a pilot foisted on him without his choice, but the Act of 1915 reversed this common law rule. But the draftsman of the Act had overlooked a point (which is indeed very commonly overlooked in statutory extensions of vicarious liability); he had failed to make it clear whether the negligence of the compulsory pilot was to be imputed to the shipowner in a case where the shipowner was the plaintiff, suing for damage to the ship, and the defence of contributory negligence was set up. What the Act provided was that the shipowner was to be "answerable for any loss or damage caused by" his vessel when under the control of the pilot. The House of Lords treated the case as solely depending on the true construction of these words, and with much difficulty and some hesitation, they persuaded themselves that the words were capable of extending to the case where the shipowner was plaintiff and the question was one of contributory negligence. Two alternative ways of arriving at the same conclusion do not appear to have been canvassed at all. The first was, of course, to apply the Cross thesis and simply extend the common

[37] [1951] A.C. 112.

law rule by analogy to the statute; and the second was to declare that there was a common law rule to the effect that whenever one person is vicariously liable for the acts of another (whether at common law or by statute) he must also be vicariously responsible for the acts of that other when contributory negligence is in issue.

My second illustration of this same theme is the decision of the Court of Appeal in *Travers* v. *Holley*.[38] Until 1937 English courts had uniformly held that domicile was the sole basis on which English courts would assume jurisdiction to grant decrees of divorce and likewise, it was only a decree granted by a foreign court where the parties were domiciled which would be recognised by English courts.[39] In 1937 the Matrimonial Causes Act gave English courts jurisdiction to grant divorces in certain limited circumstances to a wife who was not domiciled in England, but nothing was said in the Act about the circumstances in which foreign divorces would be recognised in English law. In *Travers* v. *Holley* the Court of Appeal was faced with a divorce decree granted in New South Wales to a wife not domiciled there, but under legislation closely comparable to that of the English Act of 1937. Almost without argument, the court held that the New South Wales decree ought to be recognised in England. The judgments are so brief that it is difficult to find any principle or theory underlying the decision, but again I would suggest that there are two alternative explanations: either the decision can be seen as an extension of the common law rules regarding the recognition of foreign decrees by analogy to the 1937 Act—and certainly there is one cryptic phrase in the judgment of Hodson L.J. which seems to support this; or alternatively it can be said that what the court did here was to restate or reformulate the common law rule. Originally the rule appeared to be that only divorces granted by the courts of the domicile would be recognised, but *Travers* v. *Holley* could be understood as saying that this was an incorrect statement of the common law rule: the true rule was that foreign divorces would be recognised in England if they were granted by courts claiming substantially the same jurisdiction as English courts. If that is the theory of the case, then there is no need to invoke the idea that the statute was in any sense extended or applied beyond what it actually enacted.

I turn now to another point of contact between statute law and common law, namely the declaratory Act—a matter of less practical importance perhaps, but of considerable theoretical interest. If an Act is truly declaratory of the common law, then extension of the Act by analogy becomes more permissible. Strictly speaking, perhaps, at least according to traditional orthodoxy, the court does not actually extend the statute itself; it simply develops and extends the common law rules which are partly embodied in the statute. Certainly this seems to have occurred with the Sale of Goods Act

[38] [1953] P. 246.

[39] *Le Mesurier* v. *Le Mesurier* [1895] A.C. 517.

where, it is well known, various provisions have been applied, more or less by analogy, to contracts not strictly falling within the definition of a contract of sale of goods.[40] It also seems to be true that the courts have felt more free to interpret the statutory provisions of the Sale of Goods Act as though that Act remained largely a matter of common law. So, for instance, in the *Ashington Piggeries* case,[41] Lord Diplock insisted that the Act was to be construed against the general common law background of freedom of contract, and the implied conditions set out in the Act

> "ought not to be construed so narrowly as to force on parties to contracts for the sale of goods promises and consequences different from what they must reasonably have intended. They should be treated rather as illustrations of the application to simple types of contract of general principles for ascertaining the common intention of the parties as to their mutual promises and their consequences, which ought to be applied by analogy in cases arising out of contracts which do not appear to have been within the immediate contemplation of the draftsman of the Act in 1893."[42]

So also the treatment by the courts of the enigmatic section 13 (which requires the goods to correspond with their description) seems, after taking a weary and tortuous path through a labyrinthine maze, to have emerged as a pure piece of common law. As I understand the effect of section 13 as now interpreted, it means something like this:

> "Where any words of description are used by the seller which apart from the provisions of this section would be treated as a condition of the contract, then those words are a condition of the contract."[43]

Similarly, the recent case law[44] on intermediate terms, and the rejection of the condition/warranty dichotomy as applicable to contracts not governed by the Act shows that—at least in the case of a declaratory Act—the courts feel quite free to reject the analogy of the statutory provisions and to continue to develop the common law along different lines. Whether this would be appropriate if the courts were to use non-declaratory Acts to develop the law by analogy is clearly a more difficult question. With a declaratory Act like the 1893 Sale of Goods Act, the courts have felt free to criticise the condition/warranty dichotomy and to refuse to extend it because it was, after all, their own creation. True, Parliament enacted it, but in doing so, it only gave a new and simpler form to the law created by the courts. We reach here

[40] See, *e.g.* *Stewart* v. *Reavell's Garage* [1952] 2 Q.B. 545 where Sellers J. stated the common law rule in almost the exact words of s.14(1) of the Sale of Goods Act 1893.
[41] [1972] A.C. 441.
[42] At p.501.
[43] See the (forthcoming) 7th ed. of my *The Sale of Goods* for a full explanation.
[44] See, *e.g.* the *Reardon Smith Lines* case [1976] 1 W.L.R. 989.

the distinction between Roscoe Pound's third and fourth possible methods of receiving statutes into the full body of the law: the third, it will be recalled, involves using statutes as analogies, and the fourth involves using them as analogies of superior status to common law decisions. It will, by now, be evident, I think, that even if the very concept of using statutes by analogy is acceptable, the choice between the third and fourth possibilities cannot take the form of a general across-the-board solution.

Another interesting question concerning declaratory Acts arises out of Fox's Libel Act of 1792, and here we do seem to have a clear example of a relatively modern extension of statute by analogy. The Act was designed to give the jury the power to return a general verdict in libel cases, and to prevent the judge from requiring the jury to render a verdict only on the issue of publishing, while reserving to himself the question of libel or no as a matter of law. It is indisputable that the Act by its terms extends only to criminal cases, but it seems at a very early date to have become the practice of judges trying civil cases to apply the Act, and when the issue was squarely raised before the common law courts in two cases in 1840–41, they unanimously upheld this practice and rested it on the analogy of the statute.[45] But the judges justified their decision in part at least by the fact that Fox's Act was stated to be a declaratory Act. There was, said the judges, no distinction on this matter between civil and criminal libel cases, so if the law in criminal cases was as it had now been declared by Fox's Act, then the same law must apply in civil cases. The problem with this bland explanation is that although Fox's Act *claimed* to be a declaratory Act, it is perfectly well known that this was a political gesture. In the *Dean of St. Asaph's* case[46] the Court of King's Bench under Lord Mansfield had most emphatically ruled, despite the passionate eloquence of Erskine, that the judge was entitled to decide the issue of libel as a matter of law, and to leave to the jury only the responsibility of deciding whether the defendant was guilty of publication. It is true that Erskine maintained to his dying day that this decision was wrong, and that the common law was not as laid down by the King's Bench; and it is true that Erskine had the support of the parliamentary Whigs in this, and that it was for this very reason that the Act took the form of a declaratory Act. The Act was indeed designed as a rebuke to the judges. But this hardly overcomes the point that the common law, as declared by the judges, was different from the common law as declared by Fox's Act. In modern times the practice would, I think, be to amend the law but to make the amendment retrospective. This double-barrelled process is Parliament's way of acknowledging the supremacy of the judges in the matter of

[45] *Parmiter* v. *Coupland* (1840) 6 M. & W. 105; *Baylis* v. *Lawrence* (1841) 11 Ad. & E. 920.

[46] (1784) 4 Doug. 73.

declaring what the law is, but reserving to itself the power of altering it, and of altering it even for past cases if this is deemed desirable.

This more modern technique appears to me to run counter to the Cross thesis, while the technique used in Fox's Act would tend to support the Cross thesis. If statute law and common law really constitute one integral body of law, there seems no reason why our sovereign Parliament should not be able to declare the common law to be something different from what the judges say it is. But I incline to think that most lawyers and even most parliamentarians would today think this improper, if not indeed in some sense conceptually impossible.[46a] I think a lawyer today would say that the common law is by definition what the judges say it is; Parliament may command the judges to change the rules they apply, even retrospectively, but Parliament cannot make the common law different from what the judges say it is any more than it can alter a historical fact. But these are rather deep waters of constitutional theory, and I propose to leave them to discuss a number of other areas of law where it seems to me clear that there is some real support for the Cross thesis.

IV

I will pause to mention, but not to discuss at any length, that there are in the books a number of illustrations of very dramatic statutory construction, which are difficult to reconcile with the traditional canons of interpretation, but which could easily be justified if the courts had the power to extend statutes by analogy. Consider, for instance, the case of the *Edison Telephone Co.*[47] in 1880 where it was held that a telephone conversation was a telegram transmitted by telegraph within the meaning of the Telegraph Act 1869, or the Privy Council ruling in 1932 that broadcasting falls within the definition of "telegraphs,"[48] or in very recent times, the decision that a microfilm record is a bankers' book within the meaning of the Bankers Books Evidence Act 1879.[49] There must be scores, perhaps hundreds of courageous decisions of this character; but almost certainly there are just as many on the opposite side where such decisions could possibly have been made, but were not. If it were permissible for the courts—subject no doubt to appropriate limitations—to apply statutes by analogy, it is possible that cases of this nature could be dealt with in a more principled and hence more predictable way.

[46a] One other example of a declaratory Act which changed the law laid down by the courts is the Territorial Waters Jurisdiction Act 1868, but it is interesting to note that while the preamble claimed the Act to be declaratory, the sidenote to s.2 recognises that the law was being changed.

[47] (1880) 6 Q.B.D. 244.

[48] *Re Regulation and Control of Radio Communication in Canada* [1932] A.C. 304.

[49] *Barker* v. *Wilson* [1980] 2 All E.R. 81.

I turn now to one or two illustrations of a different kind. Where an important new common law question is raised for decision the courts may sometimes look at statutory provisions by way of direct analogy, or sometimes as simply part of the general background against which the common law decision must be made. It is surprisingly hard to find clear illustrations of true analogical reasoning in modern times—the cases may exist, but they cannot easily be traced through Digests or Indexes—but one such case is the House of Lords decision in *Parry* v. *Cleaver*.[50] The question here was whether in a common law action for damages for personal injuries, the receipt by the plaintiff of a disability pension should be taken into account by way of reduction of the damages. Lord Reid invoked the analogy of the Fatal Accidents Acts which clearly exclude from consideration any pension or life insurance; the decision, he said, was largely a matter of policy, and it was desirable to have regard to the policy adopted by Parliament in a closely analogous field. But the speeches of the other Law Lords show the difficulties involved in this kind of reasoning by analogy from statute. Lord Morris, for instance, thought there was a manifest difference between claims under the Fatal Accidents Acts and claims by living plaintiffs; indeed, he suggested, it might be inferred that because Parliament had *not* legislated for living plaintiffs in the same way that they had legislated for fatal claims, a contrary inference could be drawn as to how the case should be decided. Lord Wilberforce pointed to a still greater difficulty. The Law Reform (Personal Injuries) Act 1948 dealt with the deduction from damages of social security benefits, and it could well be suggested that this was a closer analogy than that of the Fatal Accidents Act. But "this type of solution" added Lord Wilberforce, "is not open to the courts." He did not explain why not, but it is not difficult to guess. The 1948 Act provides for the deduction from common law damages of half the value of the benefits receivable over a five-year period. It is thus evidently not a principled piece of legislation but a political compromise of some kind, and one can see that there are great difficulties about using legislative analogies from which no clear principles can be drawn. But then, what is to be done where, as in the instant case, there is one good statutory analogy which cannot be applied because no principle can be deduced from it, and a much less good statutory analogy which can be applied because a principle can be drawn from it?

Another case which perhaps deserves a passing mention here is *Jobling* v. *Associated Dairies*[51] where the House of Lords wrestled with the almost insoluble problems arising from multiple sufficient causation, first brought into prominence by *Baker* v. *Willoughby*.[52] One of the arguments made in support of the decision in *Baker* v.

[50] [1970] A.C. 1.
[51] [1982] A.C. 794.

Willoughby, to the effect that a tortfeasor should not lightly be relieved of liability as a result of a subsequent concurrent cause, was that those responsible for the subsequent injuries might be men of straw, unable to meet any awards of damages.[53] In the *Jobling* case this argument was rejected by Lord Wilberforce and Lord Edmund-Davies on the ground that the injured plaintiff might still be entitled to compensation from some other source such as the Criminal Injuries Compensation scheme, or statutory social security benefits. It is not yet clear whether this means that arguments about fairness and justice in possible extensions of the law of personal injuries must now be conducted against the statutory background of the social security schemes. This is not, of course, a case of extending or developing the common law by analogy to a statute; but it is very close to the converse case of restricting or confining developments of the common law because of the existence of statutes which are to some degree in *pari materia.* It should be added that the whole House of Lords in *Jobling* rejected one of the main planks of Lord Reid's argument in *Baker* v. *Willoughby* on the ground that it was a mistaken application of a statutory analogy. Lord Reid had relied heavily on a decision[54] under the Workmen's Compensation Acts which is another clear instance of the use of a statutory analogy in a common law case; but the utility of the illustration as a precedent is somewhat weakened by the fact that the analogy was so manifestly defective.

I return now to a series of cases concerning the effect of statutes which overturn common law decisions. I suggested earlier that the general tendency of the courts seems to be to treat such statutory reversals as not affecting the principles of the case in question; but there are a number of clear exceptions to this general tendency. In particular it is possible to identify two types of case where the courts are apt to treat such legislative reversals of common law cases as wiping the slate clean and enabling the common law to be reformulated and developed along new lines. The first type of case concerns common law rules which have become totally out of line with the general judicial approach to the subject, so that if it were not for the restrictions which the judges place on their own powers they would clearly overrule the older cases themselves. One thinks, for instance, of the doctrine of common employment which the courts would certainly have abrogated before it was abolished by Parliament in 1948, if they had not thought that this was too drastic an exercise of legislative power. So when in *Broom* v. *Morgan*[55] counsel sought to argue by analogy from the now-abolished doctrine of common employment, Lord Denning declared that the doctrine "should be disregarded in the same way as if it

---

[52] [1970] A.C. 467.
[53] See, *e.g.* McGregor, *Damages* (14th ed.), §1146.
[54] *Harwood* v. *Wyken Colliery Co.* [1913] 2 K.B. 158.

had never been enunciated. Statute law and common law should," he went on, in full support of the Cross thesis, "be integrated as one law."[56] If the authority of Lord Denning is thought too suspect to support such a dramatic result, it is possible to point to a Privy Council decision of 1885 where the judges refused to apply as a part of the common law of Canada, a series of decisions "which have been swept away by the legislature [that is, in England] as fraught with inconvenience and mischief."[57]

There is a second kind of case, where the courts have shown willingness to regard legislative reversal of common law doctrines as justifying further re-adjustment of the common law, beyond the scope of the enactment itself. In both the examples I have in mind the common law led to results which the judges themselves came to find unsatisfactory, and they were led to use shifts and devices to evade these results. Subsequent legislation freed the judges from the need to resort to these devices. The first example is the Law Reform (Contributory Negligence) Act 1945. It is well known that before this Act the judges had often used strained causation arguments to hold that a defendant was solely responsible for an accident even though on any normal use of causal principles the plaintiff would have been regarded as partly to blame. The Act itself said nothing about the rules of causation, and in *Davies* v. *Swan Motor Co.*[58] Bucknill L.J. insisted that these rules had not been altered by the Act.[59] Of course if that were true the absurd result would have followed that the defendant would still have been held solely to blame in cases where this result, in defiance of all common sense, had been arrived at before the Act was passed. In the same case, however, Denning L.J. said that a distinction must be drawn between the legal effect of the Act and its practical effect. The legal effect might be the narrow one referred to by Bucknill L.J., but the practical effect was to lead to a broader view of questions of causation. There is no doubt that in the result Denning L.J.'s view has been entirely vindicated, but his statement of the position is open to one criticism. What Denning L.J. refers to as the practical effect of the Act is in fact also a legal effect. It is not possible to say that what judges rule on issues of causation is not part of the law. So it must be recognised that the effect of the Act was indeed to enable the judges to alter the law beyond the scope of the direct enactment that the Act achieved.

If this conclusion is once again to be regarded as a trifle suspect because it rests upon the sole authority of Lord Denning, the same cannot be said of the second illustration. I refer to the doctrine of

---

[55] [1953] 1 Q.B. 597. For some more extreme (and manifestly erroneous) dicta by Lord Denning in this general area, see *Beverley Acceptances* v. *Oakley* [1982] R.T.R. 417.

[56] At p.609.

[57] *McGibbon* v. *Abbott* (1885) 10 App.Cas. 653.

[58] [1949] 2 K.B. 291.

[59] At p.310.

fundamental breach and the rules of construction of exclusion clauses. The story is too well known and too recent to need rehearsing here. What is quite clear, as it seems to me, is that the House of Lords has now accepted the legitimacy of altering the rules of construction of exclusion clauses and perhaps even, though more arguably, the doctrine of fundamental breach, as a result of the passing of legislation which did not itself make these changes in the law.

To take the rules of construction first. As we all know, there was a long history of severe and restrictive construction of exclusion clauses until the passing of the Supply of Goods Act in 1973, and its replacement by the Unfair Contract Terms Act 1977. In the *George Mitchell*[60] case substantially the same conflict of opinion occurred that had taken place in *Davies* v. *Swan Motor Co.* On the one side Lord Denning was still there—34 years later—to argue that with the passing of this legislation the need for the special rules of construction of exclusion clauses had disappeared, and that the exclusion clause in the instant case ought to be given its natural and ordinary meaning, and then struck down under the statute. On the other side, the majority of the Court of Appeal insisted with traditional orthodoxy, like Bucknill L.J. in *Davies* v. *Swan Motor Co.*, that the Act had no effect on the law outside its immediate area of application, and that the old rules of construction had to be applied. Fortunately, on this occasion the House of Lords was at hand to uphold Lord Denning's judgment and his whole approach, with one or two minor exceptions concerning the difference between limitation clauses and exclusion clauses. There is no escaping the fact that this judgment of the House of Lords has recognised that, at least in this type of situation, statutory alterations in the law can be used as a justification for reformulation or redevelopment of the common law, quite apart from the changes directly made by the Act. This is not a matter of developing the common law by analogy, because the change is more in the nature of a consequential amendment, as a parliamentary draftsman might call it. But it certainly is supporting evidence for the Cross thesis of the integrity of common law and statute law.

Of course, to recognise what actually happened in the *George Mitchell* case at once raises questions about the possible use of this technique. How far does it go? Getting rid of artificial rules of construction is one thing, but what about other shifts and devices adopted by the courts as ways round unreasonable exclusion clauses in recent years? What about *Adler* v. *Dickson*,[61] for instance, and similar cases holding that an employee can be sued in tort when his employer is protected by a contractual exclusion clause? If the exclusion clause is held to be reasonable and valid under the 1977

60 [1983] Q.B. 284 (C.A.); [1983] 2 A.C. 803 (H.L.).
61 [1955] 1 Q.B. 158.

Act, is this result still to be permitted?[62] Then there are questions about the binding effect of appellate court decisions. In the *George Mitchell* case no suggestion was made in the House of Lords that the result at which they arrived could not appropriately and properly have been arrived at by the Court of Appeal, despite many earlier cases in the House of Lords supporting the restrictive rules of construction of exclusion clauses. Does that mean that in this sort of case, a judge of first instance can use a statute to declare a decision of the House of Lords obsolete even where the Act clearly does not actually reverse that decision?[63]

I will leave these questions for the future to deal with, and pass on to say a few words about the very similar process by which the doctrine of fundamental breach was eventually disposed of. Again the story is well enough known. First, the series of Court of Appeal decisions enunciating the doctrine of fundamental breach as a rule of substantive law, then the *Suisse Atlantique* case,[64] apparently rejecting this doctrine, only to be followed by further Court of Appeal and first instance decisions finessing their way round the speeches in the House of Lords; and finally, the *Photo Productions* case,[65] in which the House made no mistake about giving the final quietus to the doctrine. But what I want to draw attention to are some remarks of Lord Wilberforce in this latter case:

> "The doctrine of 'fundamental breach'" he said, "in spite of its imperfections and doubtful parentage has served a useful purpose. There were a large number of problems, productive of injustice, in which it was worse than unsatisfactory to leave exclusion clauses to operate."[66]

He then referred to the Unfair Contract Terms Act, even though the Act did not actually govern the facts in *Photo Productions* and went on to say that "after this Act" it was better to allow freedom of contract to operate, at least in commercial matters generally, when the parties are not of unequal bargaining power. Jurisprudentially speaking, these remarks are of enormous interest, and it is not surprising to see them emanating from Lord Wilberforce to whom I would like in passing to pay my tribute as one of the greatest Law Lords of the twentieth century. For it will be seen that Lord Wilberforce refused to pronounce the old fundamental breach cases as right or wrong: they served a useful purpose, he insists,

[62] I may be permitted to say that in my submissions to the Law Commission over 10 years ago I recommended that, once some method of controlling unreasonable exclusion clauses was enacted, the rule in *Adler* v. *Dickson* ought to be reversed. My recommendation was never commented on.

[63] In the *Photo Productions* case [1980] A.C. 827 where the same question was also discussed, Lord Scarman approved the refusal of McKenna J. at first instance to follow the "sophisticated refinements" into which the courts had previously been led.

[64] [1967] 1 A.C. 361.

[65] [1980] A.C. 827.

[66] At p.843.

which implies that they were a proper exercise of the judicial function. But after the new Acts were passed, they were no longer needed and ought to be overruled. It may be objected that this fails to explain the *Suisse Atlantique* decision, and Lord Wilberforce's own concurrence in that decision. But the answer to this objection, I think, is that it was already manifest at the time of the *Suisse Atlantique* decision that some consumer protection legislation dealing with unfair contracts was imminent. Indeed, Lord Reid specifically said that as a result of the decision in that case "there [would] certainly be a need for urgent legislative action but [he added] that is not beyond reasonable expectation."[67]

Had this expectation not been fulfilled, and had it continued to seem that Parliament did not propose to do anything about unfair contract terms, then it is highly probable that by the present time the courts would already be busy retreating from the *Suisse Atlantique* decision, or at least looking for alternative ways of meeting the problem. The importance of this is that it involves recognising the reality that the development of the law always must involve some degree of mutual co-operation between Parliament and courts. It is no longer possible to say of legal decisions or legal doctrines that they are in some immutable or absolute sense right or wrong: they may be right and appropriate when the Statute Book is in one condition, and wrong and unnecessary when the Statute Book is in a different condition.

V

Any attempt to draw conclusions of general application from the above scattered and fragmented illustrations of odd happenings in the relationship of common law and statute law seems to me premature. So far as English law was concerned, the whole subject was only put on the agenda by Sir Rupert Cross and he dealt with it briefly. I have indicated that it is a great deal more complex than he suggested, and I have drawn on my own, and some of my colleagues' memories for useful illustrations of the subject. But illustrations are difficult to come by using traditional research methods, and other memories may be better than my own. We need more research and more examples before we can even begin to think very coherently about the subject, though I think I have shown that the approach of the courts to the subject has hitherto lacked consistency. But some warnings are in order.

The first is a warning about a blind alley down which there are signs that the courts have sometimes been tempted to venture. If the courts are to be free to use an Act as an analogy, or to extend its area of operation indirectly by reformulating the common law, there may be a temptation to speculate about the reasons for Parliament's failure to make the alterations itself. In *Herrington* v.

[67] [1967] 1 A.C. at p.406.

British Rail[68] the House of Lords indulged in such speculations on a considerable scale. Parliament, in enacting the Occupiers' Liability Act had omitted to do anything about the law relating to trespassers. What was the significance of this omission? Lord Reid's initial reaction was to say that Parliament's "pointed" omission to alter the law must be taken as affirmation of the existing common law rule laid down in *Addie's* case[69]; but he then retreated from the position, saying that it was "just possible" that Parliament's omission was due to its inability to make up its mind what to do about the law relating to trespassers. Lord Morris was inclined to think that Parliament's deliberate abstention from legislation as to trespassers made it "not fitting" for the courts to make fundamental changes in the law. Lord Wilberforce thought that Parliament must have intended the courts to be free to continue to develop the common law in their traditional way. In my view it was a serious blunder for the House of Lords to indulge in these speculations, both on practical and on constitutional grounds. As to practical grounds, it must be perfectly plain that, given the limited material available to the courts for the discovery of Parliament's intentions, it is quite hopeless for the judges to ask why Parliament has failed to legislate on a given topic. There are all sorts of possible reasons—lack of time, lack of ministerial energy, lack of agreement as to the alternatives, satisfaction with the existing law, and so on. Even if the courts could consult *Hansard* they would often find no answer to the question; without such consultation the quest is futile. As we all know, it is often difficult enough to know what Parliament intended even on those subjects that it *has* legislated upon; how is it to be supposed that Parliament's intentions can be divined on those subjects on which it has *not* legislated? But it is anyhow a constitutional mistake to ask the question at all. There is one, and only one, way in which Parliament is entitled to make its intentions known to the judges, and that is by passing an Act. The intentions of Parliament, when not enshrined in a statute, have no legal or constitutional validity. Resolutions of the House of Commons, statements of Ministers, have no legal validity; how can it be suggested that some mysterious parliamentary intention not enshrined in a text can even be relevant to the decisions of the courts? In my view the courts should completely eschew the attempt to ascertain the intentions of Parliament as to a piece of non-existent legislation.

Unfortunately, the House of Lords has recently repeated these heresies, and even acted upon them. In *La Pintada*[69a] the House refused to depart from the common law rule that interest is not in general payable on an overdue debt on a number of grounds, one of which was that Parliament had failed to give statutory effect to

[68] [1972] A.C. 877.
[69] [1929] A.C. 358.
[69a] [1984] 3 W.L.R. 10.

the Law Commission's proposed amendments to the law relating to interest.[69b] but had merely included one minor provision in the Administration of Justice Act 1982, dealing with this subject.[69c] I remain unpersuaded that this is a constitutionally permissible ground of decision. I accept, of course, that within the narrow confines of a single provision (a single section, or subsection, for instance) what is omitted may be a proper aid to the construction of what is included. And I can see that it might be appropriate in some cases for the courts to take account of the mere failure of Parliament to pass legislation in deciding how the common law ought to be developed. But what seems to me quite wrong is to treat the failure of Parliament to pass a Bill as though it were an actual enactment to the opposite effect. In fact, as is perfectly well known, the reason why Parliament did not enact the Law Commission's proposed Bill on interest, was not because Parliament rejected the proposals, but because the government decided not to introduce the Bill. Now the government has no legislative powers, and their decision not to introduce a Bill into Parliament cannot be treated as though it were a decision by Parliament itself.

My second warning is of a more general nature. The idea of using statutes as analogies or as a source of principles in the development of the common law has an initial attraction, and it has been widely,[70] though still cautiously[71] used in America during the past few decades. The Uniform Commercial Code specifically recommends application of its provisions by analogy, and a considerable case law has grown up demonstrating the practicability of this methodology. But there are very real differences between the American political and constitutional system and our own which make this methodology much more difficult to operate in England. For one thing, our legislature is much more active than American legislatures, especially state legislatures. The need for judicial creativity is much greater there, and there is a corresponding need for methods by which the courts can jettison obsolete laws based on out-dated values.

For another thing, American legislatures are accustomed to being told what they can and cannot do by the courts. Our legislature is not, nor would it take kindly to being criticised by the courts. Yet consider how difficult it would be for a judge empowered to act on the analogy of a statute to reject the analogy because he thought a better analogy was to be found in the common law cases. Could a judge, for example, refuse to apply a statute by analogy before it has come into force on the ground that he thinks the common law rule being reversed by the statute was

[69b] Law Commission, *Report on Interest,* Cmnd. 7229.

[69c] s.15.

[70] See especially Traynor, "Statutes Revolving in Common Law Orbits" (1968) 17 Cath Un.L.R. 401; and see U.C.C., Art. 1-102.

[71] See Note, (1965) 65 Col.L.Rev. 880. But things have moved quite significantly since 1965.

actually a better rule?[72] And yet the power to apply by analogy could not be a compulsion: the judges would have to be able to pick and choose. Would this not tend to force the judges into embarrassing and invidious comparisons between those statutes they prefer to apply by analogy and those they do not? Are there political problems here? As was once said by Lord Shaw of Dunfermline in a case where the House of Lords refused to interpret an Act by analogy to a common law rule, "analogies are dangerous."[73] Other problems arise from the fact that some legislation is party political in its nature and the courts could hardly be expected to reason by analogy from Acts of that kind. Yet how are judges officially to distinguish party political Acts from other Acts?[74]

Yet despite all the dangers there does seem to me to be some scope for a cautious and coherent development here, and there is adequate support for such a development in the case law I have discussed. If I may conclude with an example of a recent statute which seems to me eminently suitable for extension by the courts in the ways I have discussed, one need look no further than the Forfeiture Act 1982. Here is an Act which clearly shows that a famous and age old common law principle—that no person shall benefit from his wrong—is, at least in many cases, based on outdated values. Yet the 1982 Act only nibbles away at one corner of the principle. Surely the judges would be justified in using the Act to narrow the application of this common law principle?[75]

P. S. Atiyah*

[72] In California, statutes have been applied by analogy before they are in force, see Traynor, *op. cit.*

[73] *Gray* v. *Ashburton* [1917] A.C. 26, 37.

[74] Another problem about reasoning from the analogy of statutes is that the common law in different parts of the Commonwealth would then gradually diverge, though the importance of maintaining the unity of the common law in the Commonwealth may have been exaggerated.

[75] Another example of a principle which could be extracted from statute law and developed in the common law itself is the principle against racial (or perhaps also sexual) discrimination. As to this, see the remarks of Lord Morris in *Charter* v. *Race Relations Board* [1973] A.C. 868, 889, where it is suggested that the Race Relations Acts had introduced a new guiding principle of fundamental and far-reaching importance into the law.

* Professor of English Law, Oxford University. I am greatly indebted to Mr. F. A. R. Bennion for some helpful suggestions and interesting discussion about the theme of this article.

[2]

Towards Principles of Overruling—When Should a Final Court of Appeal Second Guess?[†]

J. W. HARRIS*

Their Lordships regard the use of precedent as an indispensable foundation upon which to decide what is the law and its application to individual cases. It provides at least some degree of certainty upon which individuals can rely in the conduct of their affairs, as well as a basis for orderly development of legal rules.

Their Lordships nevertheless recognise that too rigid adherence to precedent may lead to injustice in a particular case and also unduly restrict the proper development of the law. They propose, therefore, to modify their present practice and, while treating former decisions of this House as normally binding, to depart from a previous decision when it appears right to do so.

In this connection they will bear in mind the danger of disturbing retrospectively the basis on which contracts, settlements of property and fiscal arrangements have been entered into and also the especial need for certainty as to the criminal law. This announcement is not intended to affect the use of precedent elsewhere than in this House.[1]

1. A 'Jurisprudence of Overruling'?

In the third edition of his *Precedent in English Law*, published in 1977, the late Sir Rupert Cross wrote '. . . it does seem that a jurisprudence of overruling is developing at the highest level and, for this reason alone, the 1966 Statement must be regarded as a legal event of considerable significance'.[2]

At the time when these words were written, there were only three cases in which the House of Lords had unambiguously employed the power it assumed in 1966 to overrule its own decisions, and not many more in which reasons had been advanced by the House for declining an invitation to use it. Other commentators took a far more sceptical view than did Cross of the significance of the Practice Statement.[3] It

* Keble College, Oxford.

† Earlier versions of this paper were delivered in 1987 when I was the visiting Allen, Allen and Hemsley Professor at the University of Sydney. I am indebted to helpful comments made on those occasions. I wish to express my thanks to the Law Faculty of Sydney University and to the partners of Allen, Allen and Hemsley and their associated firms for their hospitality throughout my visit.

1 Practice Statement (Judicial Precedent) [1966] 1 WLR 1234.

2 R. Cross, *Precedent in English Law*, 3rd ed, Clarendon Press, 1977, 135.

3 See, for example, Lyndel V. Prott, 'When Will a Superior Court Overrule Its Own Decision?' (1978) 52 *ALJ* 304. Robert Stevens, *Law and Politics: the House of Lords as a Judicial Body 1800–1976*, Weidenfeld and Nicolson, 1979,

  continued on page 136

was pointed out that there were already, before 1966, ample techniques wherewith the House could escape the fetters of decisions it disliked. The availability of the new power might have had a psychological effect impelling members of the House to make greater use of these traditional techniques, but it had not resulted in anything so grandiose as a 'new jurisprudence'. Given the paucity of occasions on which the question of exercising the power played a central role in their Lordships' speeches, such a sceptical attitude may well have been appropriate in 1977. It should not go unchallenged today.

As late as 1985, we read in the 5th edition of *Lloyd's Introduction to Jurisprudence*: 'Not until 1974 did the House of Lords refuse to follow an earlier decision of its own, and only once since has the new power been invoked. Dogma has changed: little else'.[4] In fact, there were in 1985 already five instances in which the House had unambiguously exercised its power to overrule its own decisions and, as we shall see, there are now seven. There is no flood, but there is quite enough to suggest that the change goes beyond the rhetorical surface.

Of course, the older distinguishing techniques continue to flourish. But that very fact should cause us to ask why, in any particular case, the House does or ought to resort to its overruling power rather than employ one of these techniques. Conversely, on what grounds does (or should) the House refrain from exercising the power even if convinced that an earlier decision was erroneous? Such questions raise the possibility that there could be principles justifying and delimiting the exercise of the power. I shall suggest that there are indeed such principles of overruling implicit in the decisions. It must, however, be stressed that this suggestion has, at present, no more than a tentative status. There is, as yet, no *settled* jurisprudence of overruling.

A settled jurisprudence would require two things: first, that it is possible to articulate principles which would support the exercise of the power in those cases in which it has been used and also the refusal to exercise it in other cases; and secondly, evidence that such putative principles had the support of the bulk of judicial dicta on the subject. A settled jurisprudence, exhibiting these two features, does exist in relation to other areas of the English doctrine of precedent. The rule in *Young* v *Bristol Aeroplane Co Ltd*,[5] for example, is settled in this way. It announces principles by reference to which the Court of Appeal may or may not overrule its own past decisions, and it has the authority of the majority of judicial dicta behind it. There is room for debate in the interpretation of its terms; but, for the most part, such uncertainty as exists about the rule concerns, not its terms, but where the power resides to change it.[6]

continued from page 135
617–21; Julius Stone, *Precedent and Law: Dynamics of Common Law Growth*, Butterworths, 1985, chs 10 and 11. For a more favourable view of the Practice Statement's significance, see Alan Paterson, *The Law Lords*, Macmillan, 1982, ch 7.

[4] Lord Lloyd of Hampstead and M. D. A. Freeman, *Lloyd's Introduction to Jurisprudence*, 5th ed, Stevens, 1985, 1104.

[5] [1944] KB 728.

[6] In *Davis* v *Johnson* [1979] AC 264, one member of the Court of Appeal (Cumming-Bruce LJ at 311), and at least three members of the House of Lords (Lord Diplock at 323–8, Lord Dilhorne at 336, and Lord Scarman at 349)

continued on page 137

It will be my contention that, in the context of the House of Lords Practice Statement power, the first feature of a settled jurisprudence does exist—that there are principles supporting the decisions. The second feature—explicit judicial affirmation of these putative principles—is largely absent. True, we have the terms of the Practice Statement itself (set out at the beginning of this article). Sometimes, as we shall see, these are appealed to in cases in which the House accepts or rejects a submission that it should invoke its freedom under the Practice Statement. There is usually, however, no question of subjecting the phraseology of the Statement to analysis or exegesis,[7] as might be done with announced guidelines governing the exercise of some other judicial discretion. Occasionally, opinions delivered in one Practice Statement case cite dicta pronounced in others, but nothing like as often as where the House is developing a body of case law.

Having regard to the peculiar status of judicial observations on precedent, it is not to be expected that they should be regarded as laying down 'rules' with the same obligatory force as are possessed by substantive rules of case law. As Cross has argued, the doctrinal distinction between ratio decidendi and obiter dicta, which is applicable to substantive rules, has no application in the context of rules of precedent.[8] Furthermore, what we are seeking in the present context are principles governing the *exercise* of a power, as compared with those principles delimiting the *existence* of a power which are contained in the *Young* v *Bristol Aeroplane* rule. Nevertheless, more might have been expected in the way of judicial attempts to explain why it is right to exercise, or not to exercise, the power to overrule in the case at bar, whilst the contrary was true in other reported cases. A rare instance occurred in *Fitzleet*,[9] where the House 'distinguished' *Miliangos*[10] by pointing out that there had been an important change of circumstance justifying departure from an earlier decision in that case whereas nothing similar could be appealed to in the instant case. Such explicit distinguishing in relation to Practice Statement cases is, however, rare. There is, rather, a judicial shyness about the whole topic. In the last of the seven cases in which the power has been exercised (*Howe*),[11] for example, of the five members of the House only Lord Hailsham LC explicitly mentioned the

continued from page 136
assumed that, constitutionally, this power must reside with the House of Lords. Three members of the Court of Appeal (Lord Denning MR at 27–83, Baker P at 288–90, and Shaw LJ at 307–9) contended that a five-man Court of Appeal could modify the *Young* v *Bristol Aeroplane* rule. One member of the Court of Appeal (Goff LJ at 295) and one member of the House of Lords (Lord Salmon at 344) said this could be done by a unanimous full Court of Appeal. In delivering the opinion of the Privy Council in *A-G of St Christopher Nevis and Anguilla* v *Reynolds* [1980] AC 637, at 659, Lord Salmon noted that the Court of Appeal of the West Indies Associated States had been correct to hold itself bound by prior decisions just as was the English Court of Appeal under the Young rule; but went on to say that the opinion of the Privy Council or of the House of Lords on this question could only be of persuasive authority because the point could never come before them for decision.

[7] Lord Simon in *Knuller* (case ix, below, p 146) said that, since the Practice Statement was a constitutional convention of the sort analysed by Dicey, 'the actual terms of the declaration must provide essential guidance to your Lordships in making use of the new freedom vouchsafed by it' ([1973] AC 435, 485). For criticism of this view of the status of the Practice Statement, see Anthony Blackshield, 'Practical Reason and Conventional Wisdom: the House of Lords and Precedent', in Lawrence Goldstein ed, *Precedent in Law*, Clarendon Press, 1987.

[8] R. Cross, 'The House of Lords and the Rules of Precedent', in P. M. S. Hacker and J. Raz eds, *Law, Morality, and Society*, Clarendon Press, 1977.

[9] Case x, below, p 146.

[10] Case ii, below, p 143.

[11] Case vii, below, p 145.

Practice Statement at all, even though the submissions for the Crown and the outcome make it clear, beyond peradventure, that the House was exercising its power and did overrule its decision in *Lynch*.[12] Despite the protests of Lord Simon in *Miliangos*,[13] opinions continue to employ the mild term 'depart' rather than the more robust 'overrule'.[14]

The question arises in widely divergent legal contexts and, typically, their Lordships concentrate on giving reasons for or against exercising the power in the instant case, focusing on the substantive issue of law at stake. It may be that there is a widespread assumption, both among the judges and within the profession, that nothing much of a general nature can be said, outside the context of a particular substantive issue, about the propriety of overruling. Even law reporters seem to share this assumption. It is not uncommon for the summary contained in case headnotes to omit any reference to the fact that the Practice Statement power was exercised or declined.

In *Vestey*,[15] Lord Wilberforce stated that the House should try to keep the discretion conferred by the Practice Statement 'governed by stated principles'. He immediately added, however, 'but the fact that the circumstances of one particular case cannot be brought precisely within the formulae used in others of a different character should not be fatal to its exercise'.[16]

In *Blumenthal*,[17] Lord Roskill expressed the view that no useful purpose would be served by reviewing other decisions where the House has or has not departed from earlier decisions, since cases where the 1966 Practice Statement should or should not apply 'cannot be categorized'.[18]

Before we surrender to such principle-nihilism, it is at least worth asking whether there might be criteria underlying the ad hoc reasoning to be found in the cases. If there are none, what are we to make of the oft-repeated assertion that a case should not be departed from merely because it is now thought to have been wrongly decided? Why should it not? If a reason can be given, it is implausible to suppose that it is one which could never bear on some other case in which the House is asked to invoke its power. In other words, statements by their Lordships to the effect that wrongness is not enough are either isolated whistlings in the wind, or else the overruling power is being exercised subject to some (relatively inarticulated) principles of constraint. If there are indeed no such principles, invitations to counsel to make submissions on the question of the exercise of the Practice Statement power, as distinct from submissions addressed to the substantive question of law in dispute, are a time-wasting ritual.

[12] *Lynch* v *DPP for Northern Ireland* [1975] AC 653.

[13] 'I say "overrule" expressly. It is better to avoid euphemisms like "depart from". A wise decision is more likely to be achieved if the reality is faced' ([1976] AC 443, 470).

[14] In *Dick* (case iii, p 144, below) and in *Vestey* (case iv, p 144, below), most of the opinions do employ the word 'overrule'. In subsequent cases, 'depart' has returned as the standard term. Judges in the High Court of Australia usually employ 'overrule'.

[15] Case iv, p 144, below.

[16] [1980] AC 1148, 1178.

[17] Case xi, p 147, below.

[18] [1983] 1 AC 845, 922.

Scepticism about the existence of overruling principles might take this form. When judges say that a decision ought not to be departed from whether or not it was wrong, in reality they are simply not convinced that it was after all mistaken. If they have formed a definite opinion that the impugned decision was erroneous, they overrule it. If they think it was probably right, they throw in the bromide—about wrongness not being enough to warrant overruling—as a rhetorical device to lend weight to their approving opinions.

It is true that, during almost two decades of the Practice Statement's operation, there were only two notable opinions in which members of the House of Lords had stated of an earlier ruling of the House that (1) it was clearly mistaken, but that (2) it would be wrong to overrule it, so that (3) it should continue to represent the law. These were the speeches of Lord Simon in *Hudson*[19] and of Lord Reid in *Knuller*.[20] However, in two recent cases—*La Pintada*[21] and *Antclizo*[22]—the House of Lords, as a body, has reached just this conclusion.

Thus, recent developments include both a greater tendency to use the Practice Statement power, and a tendency to decline to do so even when an impugned decision is openly disapproved. Consequently, although there is all too little straw for the making of bricks, the question whether there may be real justificatory principles underlying the exercise of the overruling power ought to be raised.

If there are principles which not merely explain, but also actually justify the exercise of (or refusal to exercise) the Practice Statement power, one would expect them to have counterparts in comparable common law jurisdictions whose ultimate courts of appeal have assumed a similar power to second-guess earlier decisions—allowing for any difference which the presence of a written constitution might make. I shall therefore compare the principles which (I shall suggest) have emerged in the case of the House of Lords with the much older overruling jurisdiction of the High Court of Australia.[23] In that jurisdiction also, whilst overrulings have been taking place throughout most of this century, it has frequently been repeated that it is not enough that a decision is thought to be merely 'wrong'.[24] In what follows I shall seek to unearth, both for the United Kingdom and for Australia, what it means for a final appellate court to conclude that an earlier decision of its own should no longer represent the law, and why wrongness is not enough. The enquiry

[19] Case viii, p 146, below.
[20] Case ix, p 146, below.
[21] Case xii, p 147, below.
[22] Case xiii, p 147, below.
[23] The power of the High Court of Australia to overrule its own decisions was first assumed in *Australian Agriculture Co v Federated Engine Drivers and Firemens Association of Australasia* (1913) 17 CLR 261. Justification for such a step was sought in the comparable practice of the Privy Council and of the Supreme Court of the United States. The power was assumed at a time when appeals lay from the High Court to the Privy Council. Such appeals were abolished in relation to constitutional matters by the Privy Council (Limitation of Appeals) Act 1968, and in relation to all other matters by the Privy Council (Appeals from the High Court) Act 1975. It was suggested by Aickin J in *Queensland v The Commonwealth* (1978) 139 CLR 585, 630, that such abolition must change the approach of the High Court to overruling its own decisions 'at least to some extent'. It appears, however, from the Australian overruling cases considered below that the approach has not differed as a result of this change in the status of the High Court as a final appellate court.
[24] For a survey of the cases in which this has been said, see the judgment of Aickin J in *Queensland v The Commonwealth* (1978) 139 CLR 585, 620–30.

has to encompass, among other things, a jurisprudential reflection on what it means to say of a decision about a proposition of law that it was 'wrong'.

2. Copper-bottomed Overruling Cases

The focus of our enquiry is not the freedom which the House of Lords has, in light of all available judicial techniques, for escaping the shackles of unpalatable precedents. We are concerned with cases in which a proposition of law which the House recognized to be part of the ratio decidendi of an earlier case is challenged, and in which either the proposition is rejected by virtue of the Practice Statement overruling power, or it is left to stand because the House considers that, whether that proposition should or should not form part of the law, it would be inappropriate to remove it by exercise of that power. These are the copper-bottomed overruling cases. The exercise of the overruling power has, as a necessary premise, the assumption that some proposition (x) has until this present judgment formed part of the law by virtue of the authority of the now-impugned earlier decision. In *Miliangos*,[25] for example, the members of the House of Lords were at pains to stress that the decision which they now proposed to overrule had, prior to the present judgment, been binding on all inferior courts.[26] If the House concludes, by whatever strained process of reasoning, that (x) is not a proposition for which the earlier decision is conclusive authority, or if it finds that (x) is in any event not part of the present law—because, for example, it is inconsistent with a statute enacted after the earlier decision—the case is not an overruling one.

On that basis, there have been only seven instances in which the Practice Statement power has been unambiguously exercised.[27] It is more difficult to draw a line around negative overruling cases—instances in which the House has concluded that it would not be right to exercise the power in relation to an earlier decision, whether they approved of it or not. Clearly, not all cases in which a decision is followed are included. The House may take the view that the decision is so obviously right that no question of exercising the power arises.[28] A negative

[25] Case ii, p 143, below.

[26] [1976] AC 443, 459 Lord Wilberforce, 470–7 Lord Simon, 496 Lord Cross, 501 Lord Edmund-Davies, 503 Lord Fraser. The same point was made in *Dick* (case iii, p 144, below) by Lord Wilberforce: 1976 SLT, 22, and by Lord Kilbrandon, ibid 25. In contrast, in *The Despina R* [1979] AC 685, where the House of Lords substituted the rule that damages for torts committed abroad should be awarded in the currency in which the loss was sustained for the rule (for which its earlier decision in *The Volturno* [1921] 2 AC 544 was authority) that such damages should be the sterling equivalent of the loss at the date of breach, no criticism was voiced of the lower courts which had not followed *The Volturno*. The change in the law effected by *Miliangos*, allowing judgments in England to be rendered in currencies other than sterling, had so undermined the reasoning in *The Volturno* that the rule established by that case was no longer law at the time of *The Despina* litigation. In consequence 'departure' from *The Volturno* did not require an exercise of the Practice Statement power.

[27] Alan Paterson has argued that the number of overruling cases is greater than this—*The Law Lords*, Macmillan, 1982, pp 163–5. He includes cases in which, although in their opinions Law Lords did not indicate that they were overruling, they have, after the event, told him in personal interviews that they consider that that was what they were doing. Such anecdotal information is of value to the role-analysis in which Paterson is engaged, since it throws light on the psychological significance of the Practice Statement. It cannot be used in the present enquiry, since we are concerned with principles which underlie the reasons actually given in announced instances of the exercise of the power.

[28] For example, in *DPP* v *Nock* [1978] AC 979, the House of Lords accepted the principle laid down in its decision in *Haughton* v *Smith* [1975] AC 476—that steps on the way to the doing of something which is thereafter done and which is no crime cannot be regarded as attempts to commit a crime, and they extended the principle from attempts to

continued on page 141

overruling case requires that the House be pressed to overrule, and that opinions are delivered to the effect that, on the assumption (arguendo) that the earlier decision was mistaken, it would nonetheless be inappropriate to overrule it. I shall list the more important instances of such copper-bottomed negative overrulings of the House of Lords, and a selection from those cases in which the High Court of Australia has had to consider whether or not to overrule its own decisions.

Of course, any judicial comments on the overruling power, whether contained in the copper-bottomed cases or not, may be prayed in aid for or against putative overruling principles—above all, the terms of the Practice Statement itself. The copper-bottomed cases must, however, be our primary focus, since if there are no principles which might justify the outcomes in those cases, then there is no jurisprudence of overruling.

Consequently, I leave largely to one side those cases in which the House of Lords departed from propositions which appeared to have the imprimatur of previous decisions of the House, but did so without relying on its Practice Statement power.

In *Conway* v *Rimmer*,[29] the House rejected the wide statement of principle for which its decision in *Duncan* v *Cammell Laird Ltd*[30] had been regarded as authority, to the effect that the court would not question an executive decision that a document must remain secret in the public interest. It did so by confining the principle to the special facts of that case rather than by overruling the case.[31]

In *British Railways Board* v *Herrington*,[32] the House departed from the principle stated in *Addie* v *Dumbreck*[33] that occupiers of land owe no duty of care to trespassers beyond the duty not to injure them intentionally or recklessly. They did so by 'developing the law' as laid down in *Addie*, that is, by expressing their perception of its rationale in novel terms. Whereas *Addie* had allowed for the possibility that there could be a relationship between an occupier and a potential trespasser which should be interpreted as an implied licence to enter, the majority of their Lordships in *Herrington* preferred to express that relationship as one of a duty of care owed to a potential trespasser, thus avoiding the unnecessary terminology of a fictitious licence.[34]

continued from page 140
do the impossible to conspiracies to do the impossible. It was suggested in argument that relevant passages in the speeches in *Smith*'s case could be regarded as dicta or, if they were not, that the House might overrule them ([1978] AC 979, 990). Lord Scarman, delivering the leading speech in *Nock*, said: 'It was—somewhat half-heartedly—suggested by the Crown that the House might reconsider the decision, which we were told is causing difficulties in some respects. It is, however, a very recent decision; and a unanimous one reached after full argument which brought to the attention of this House the relevant case law and exposed the difficulties. More importantly, the decision is, in my respectful opinion, correct in principle' ([1978] AC 979, 997). Both *Haughton* v *Smith* and *Nock* have been overtaken by the Criminal Attempts Act 1981, whose interpretation was the issue in *Shivpuri* (case vi, p 145, below). Similarly, in *Bird* v *IRC*, the House declined an invitation on the part of the taxpayer to overrule its decision in *IRC* v *Cleary* ([1968] AC 766) without requiring argument for the Crown in its support, on the ground that there could be no doubt about the correctness of the decision: [1989] AC 300, 304, 310, 317.

[29] [1968] AC 910.

[30] [1942] AC 924.

[31] Only Lord Morris unequivocally favoured overruling *Duncan* ([1968] AC 910, 958). Lord Hodson's position is unclear since, on the one hand, he held that *Duncan* had been binding on the Court of Appeal (ibid 976), yet, on the other hand, he appears to have regarded it as distinguishable from the instant case on its facts (ibid 979). The other members of the House were clear that it was distinguishable.

[32] [1972] AC 877.

[33] *Addie and Sons (Collieries) Ltd* v *Dumbreck* [1929] AC 358.

[34] [1972] AC 877, 900–11 Lord Morris, 911–22 Lord Wilberforce, 931–4 Lord Diplock. None of their Lordships stated, in so many words, that the *Addie* rule should be departed from by virtue of the Practice Statement power. However, whether or not this was the proper course had been the subject of submissions in argument (ibid 883, 884,

continued on page 142

In *Hyam* v *DPP*,[35] the House repudiated the view, for which its earlier decision in *DPP* v *Smith*[36] had been thought by many commentators to be authority, that the mental element in murder was to be assessed objectively rather than subjectively. However, they found it unnecessary to overrule this aspect of *Smith*, since it was far from clear that such an objective test was a necessary part of the ratio decidendi of that case, and in any event an objective test could not be part of the present law in view of the intervening enactment of section 8 of the Criminal Justice Act 1967.[37] When the ratio decidendi of a House of Lords decision has, on the true interpretation of a subsequent Act of Parliament, been derogated from (even if it has not been expressly abrogated), no question of exercising the Practice Statement power need arise. In such a situation, even a first instance judge (or anyone else) is bound to regard that ratio as no longer forming part of the law.[38]

In *R* v *Moloney*[39] the House of Lords in turn departed from the proposition, which appeared to have the support of the majority in *Hyam*, that an intention to kill or to do some grievous bodily harm was either not an essential requisite for malice aforethought or else was a mental element which must necessarily be found to be present where such an outcome was foreseen as highly probable. But again, given the inconclusiveness of the ratio decidendi in *Hyam*, the House in *Moloney* did not find it necessary formally to overrule it.

continued from page 141
890); and the speeches of Lord Reid and Lord Pearson may be read as invoking the power, in view of Lord Reid's conclusion that any acceptable 'development' of *Addie*'s case must mean that if it arose today it would be decided the other way (ibid 898), and Lord Pearson's assertion that the *Addie* rule was an obsolete anomaly which should be discarded because it impeded 'the proper development of the law' (ibid 929–30). Lord Diplock also, having demonstrated how *Addie* could be developed without being overruled, added that, since the Practice Statement, it did not matter which course was adopted (ibid 934–5). In this, it is submitted, Lord Diplock was mistaken. The principal obstacle to outright overruling, as revealed in argument and the speeches, was the contention that Parliament had implicitly endorsed *Addie* when it enacted the Occupiers' Liability Act 1957. The fact that their Lordships in effect interred *Addie* but without unequivocally invoking the Practice Statement left unclear the significance of such an alleged constraint on the overruling power. See p 179, below.

[35] [1975] AC 55.

[36] [1961] AC 290.

[37] See especially Lord Hailsham LC [1975] AC 55, 69, 71–2. Two members of the House were, however, willing to overrule another aspect of the ratio decidendi of *Smith*, namely, the proposition that an intention to cause grievous bodily harm is sufficient malice aforethought for murder—[1975] AC 55, 93–5 Lord Diplock, 98–9 Lord Kilbrandon. That this aspect of *Smith* should be overruled had not been argued on behalf of the appellant, and the majority of their Lordships expressed no view as to what course they would have taken had they considered this proposition to be erroneous. In *R* v *Cunningham* [1982] AC 566, the House of Lords unanimously affirmed the proposition. Lord Hailsham LC (with whose speech Lord Wilberforce, Lord Simon and Lord Bridge expressed complete agreement) said that to reverse the proposition would entail overruling both *Smith* and *Hyam*, but that that was a course he was spared from having to consider since the proposition had his full approval—[1982] AC 566, 574, 580–1. Lord Edmund-Davies, although he thought the law ought to be otherwise, agreed that the Practice Statement power should not be invoked in this context (ibid 582–3).

[38] Alan Paterson contends that the decision of the House of Lords in *DPP* v *Camplin* [1978] AC 705 was an example of overruling under the Practice Statement—*The Law Lords*, Macmillan, 1982, 165. There the House concluded that, on a true reading of section 3 of the Homicide Act 1957 (which redefines the defence of provocation), its decision in *DPP* v *Bedder* [1954] 2 All ER 801 had ceased to have any authority. *Bedder* had held that the 'reasonable man', by reference to whom the reaction of the accused must be tested, was not to be regarded as sharing any physical characteristics peculiar to the accused. The Court of Appeal in *Camplin* had distinguished *Bedder*, holding that its ruling did not apply to the age of the accused. The House of Lords whilst acknowledging that such a distinction was possible, also found that it was unnecessary because the definition contained in the act permitted the accused's physical characteristics, as well as his age, to be taken into account. If that is a correct interpretation of section 3, it follows that it is one which the Court of Appeal, or any judge, could and should have adopted. *Bedder* was not law when *Camplin* was decided and consequently the Practice Statement power was not needed.

[39] [1985] AC 905.

The holdings in these cases—as opposed to any relevant dicta contained in the opinions—provide no guidance as to principles governing the exercise of the Practice Statement power. On the contrary, they illustrate the continuing ability of the House of Lords to 'develop' the law of which its past decisions are thought to be authoritative statements without using that power.[39a]

(a) Overruling cases—Affirmative

The seven cases in which the House of Lords has unequivocally exercised its Practice Statement power are as follows:

(i) *Oldendorff*: In *The Johanna Oldendorff*,[40] four out of five members of the House of Lords concurred in overruling the House's decision in *The Aello*.[41] The issue concerned the point at which a ship sailing under a port charterparty could be said to be arrived at its port of destination, so as to make the charterers liable to the owners for lay-time pending her loading or unloading. The rule laid down in *Aello* was that this point is not reached until the ship is in that part of the port where a ship can be loaded or unloaded when a berth is available. In *Oldendorff*, the House substituted the rule that the point is reached so soon as the ship is in a position where she is at the immediate and effective disposition of the charterers, and that she will be presumptively in such a position if she is at a place within the port where ships usually lay while awaiting a berth. The 'usual place' rule was thought preferable to the 'available to load' rule since it was easier to apply for shippers and arbitrators and so introduced more certainty into the law. All the members of the House in *Oldendorff*, save Lord Morris, who had been one of the majority in *Aello*, held that *Aello* was not distinguishable and had been wrongly decided.

(ii) *Miliangos*: In *Miliangos* v *George Frank (Textiles) Ltd*,[42] the House, by a majority of four to one, overruled its decision in the *Havana Railways* case.[43] The rule accepted in *Havana* was that an English court can render judgments only in sterling even in suits for breach of contractual obligations to make payment in a foreign currency, and that the amount ordered to be paid should be the sterling equivalent of the sum due under the contract at the date of breach. In *Miliangos*, the House substituted the rule that, in such circumstances, the plaintiff was entitled to recover judgment in the foreign currency and, if necessary, to enforce payment in the sterling equivalent at the time payment was made. All five members of the House agreed that the earlier case was indistinguishable. The majority took the view that the *Havana* rule worked an injustice on creditors. Lord Wilberforce, Lord Edmund-Davies and Lord Fraser found it unnecessary to determine whether the *Havana* decision was erroneous at the time when it was laid down. It was sufficient to conclude that it should not represent the law today, in view of intervening changes in rates of exchange and developments in procedural rules governing the form in which court judgments can be rendered.

[39a] The same must be said of cases in which the House has departed from its earlier pronouncements in the area of recoverable economic loss in tort, culminating in *D. and F. Estates Ltd* v *Church Commissioners for England* [1989] AC 177.

[40] *E. L. Oldendorff and Co GmbH* v *Tradax Export SA, The Johanna Oldendorff* [1974] AC 479.

[41] *Societad Financiera de Bienes Raices SA* v *Agrimpex Hungarian Trading Co for Agricultural Products, The Aello* [1961] AC 135.

[42] [1976] AC 443.

[43] *Re United Railways of Havana and Regla Warehouses Ltd* [1961] AC 1007.

(iii) *Dick*: In *Dick* v *Burgh of Falkirk*,[44] the House of Lords unanimously overruled an 80-year-old decision of the House in *Darling* v *Gray and Sons*.[45] What was at stake was whether, according to the common law of Scotland, where a victim of a negligently-caused injury first institutes proceedings and then dies, a dependant may bring a separate action for solatium and loss of support. In *Darling* the House ruled that no action lies. In *Dick* they decided that it did. The *Darling* rule was held to lack doctrinal cogency and to produce unjust consequences for persons in the position of the appellant (the widow of an employee whose death had been cause by the negligence of a fellow employee of the respondents). *Darling* had stated Scottish common law erroneously (although the rule it had laid down had been binding on all inferior courts). The rule should now be replaced by one allowing the action to be brought since, according to contemporary standards, it was clearly unjust that a person like the appellant should be refused relief simply because her husband had commenced proceedings before he died.

(iv) *Vestey*: In *Vestey* v *Inland Revenue Commissioners*,[46] the House of Lords unanimously overruled its decision in *Congreve*.[47] At stake was the interpretation of section 412 of the Income Tax Act 1952, which provided that 'for the purpose of preventing the avoiding by individuals ordinarily resident in the United Kingdom' of liability to tax by the transfer of assets to persons resident abroad, the resulting income should be deemed for tax purposes to be that of 'any such individual' who has rights of enjoyment over the income or receives any payment of capital. In *Congreve* it was ruled that 'any such individual' included any resident of the United Kingdom who obtained rights as a result of the transfer. The House in *Vestey* substituted the proposition that 'any such individual' referred only to the person who made the transfer of assets. All members of the House held *Congreve* was not distinguishable and that, if applied to facts such as those in *Vestey*, it would have had arbitrary and unjust consequences which were not foreseen by the Lords who decided *Congreve*. In *Vestey*, settlements had been made under which property was transferred to trustees resident abroad to hold on discretionary trusts for descendants of the settlors. On the *Congreve* interpretation of section 412, each and every beneficiary resident in the United Kingdom would be liable to income tax and surtax on the whole of the income of the trustees. This result could only be obviated by the Revenue voluntarily choosing not to exact tax on the whole income over and over again from each beneficiary, but instead (as it proposed) by making what it considered to be an equitable apportionment of liability amongst them. Such an exercise of executive discretion in relation to the levying of tax was stated, in *Vestey*, to be 'unconstitutional'. The *Vestey* ruling, in contrast, had the consequence that, on the facts, no tax was payable at all.

(v) *Khawaja*: In *Khawaja*,[48] at least four members of the House of Lords

[44] 1976 SLT 21.

[45] (1892) RHL 31 (reported more fully sub nom, *Wood* v *Gray and Sons* [1892] AC 576).

[46] [1980] AC 1148.

[47] *Congreve* v *Inland Revenue Commissioners* [1948] 1 All ER 948.

[48] *R* v *Secretary of State for the Home Department, ex parte Khawaja* [1984] AC 74.

concurred in overruling the decision of the House in *Zamir*.[49] The issue concerned the interpretation of section 33 (1) of the Immigration Act 1971, and the scope of judicial review in respect of an immigration officer's power to order the detention and deportation of an immigrant on the ground that, having obtained entry to the United Kingdom by practising a deception, he was an illegal entrant. The relevant ruling in *Zamir* was that the function of the court was limited to determining whether the immigration officer had reasonable grounds for his decision. In *Khawaja*, the House substituted the rule that the court had itself to be satisfied on the civil standard of proof (to a high degree of probability) that the person in respect of whom the power was exercised was in fact an illegal entrant. The new ruling was based on the constitutional principle that, where an executive officer's power to restrict or take away a subject's liberty was dependent on the existence of precedent facts, it was for the court itself to determine whether those facts existed. Lord Wilberforce's speech is equivocal on the question whether *Zamir* could be distinguished. The other members of the House were clear that it could not, and must be overruled.

(vi) *Shivpuri*: In *R* v *Shivpuri*,[50] the House unanimously overruled its one-year-old decision in *Anderton* v *Ryan*.[51] The issue was the proper construction of section 1 of the Criminal Attempts Act 1981. The section provides that if, with intent to commit an offence, a person does an act which is more than merely preparatory to the commission of the offence, he is guilty of attempting to commit the offence; that a person may be so guilty 'even though the facts are such that the commission of the offence is impossible'; and that a person shall be regarded as having had an intent to commit an offence if his intention would have been so regarded 'if the facts of the case had been as he believed them to be'. In *Ryan* the majority ruled that a person who erroneously believed that he was committing an offence was not guilty under the section if his acts were throughout innocent. Mrs Ryan, who bought a video cassette recorder believing it to be stolen when it was not, could not, therefore, be convicted of attempting to handle stolen goods. In *Shivpuri* the House substituted the ruling that the section covered any person who intended to commit an offence and did acts which would be more than merely preparatory to its commission were the facts as he supposed. Shivpuri, who took custody of a suitcase which he believed to contain heroin or cannabis, could, therefore, be convicted of attempting to deal in or harbour prohibited drugs even though the suitcase in fact contained only snuff. Their Lordships all concurred in overruling *Ryan*, even though at least two of them believed that it was distinguishable. They accepted that *Ryan* failed to achieve the reform in the law of attempts which Parliament had wished to bring about.

(vii) *Howe*: In *R* v *Howe*,[52] the House of Lords unanimously overruled its decision in *Lynch*.[53] The issue was the availability at common law of the defence of

[49] *R* v *Secretary of State for the Home Department, ex parte Zamir* [1980] AC 930.
[50] [1987] AC 1.
[51] [1985] AC 560.
[52] [1987] AC 417.
[53] *Lynch* v *DPP for Northern Ireland* [1975] AC 653.

duress to a person charged with murder. In *Lynch* the majority ruled that the defence could be pleaded by a person charged as principal in the second degree, but left open the question whether it was also available to the actual killer. In *Howe* the House laid down the rule that duress is no defence to any class of murderer. They took the opposite view to the *Lynch* majority on the question of moral principle, whether one who kills an innocent person out of fear for his own life should be exempted from criminal sanction as a concession to human frailty. They concluded that *Lynch* had been an inappropriate exercise of judicial power, since it had purported to change the historic common law on a matter of fundamental principle. The question of whether duress should be available to accomplices to murder did not have to be answered in order to dispose of the appeals. Nevertheless, their Lordships took the opportunity to overrule *Lynch* as a distinction, in relation to the defence, between actual killers and aiders and abettors was a blemish on the law.

(b) Overruling Cases—Negative

(viii) *Hudson*: In *Hudson*,[54] a specially empanelled seven-judge sitting of the House of Lords refused, by a majority of four to three, to overrule *Dowling*.[55] Section 36 (1) of the National Insurance (Industrial Injuries) Act 1946 provided that a decision by a statutory tribunal (determining a claim for industrial injury benefit) that the claimant's injury arose out of an accident suffered in the course of his employment was 'final'. The House ruled in *Dowling* that a medical board (in assessing a subsequent claim for disability benefit) was precluded by the subsection from finding that the injury was not so caused. The majority in *Hudson* took the view that this interpretation was a matter of impression about which different minds might draw opposite conclusions, and that therefore the House should not second guess its earlier ruling.

(ix) *Knuller*: In *Knuller*,[56] four out of five members of the House of Lords declined to overrule *Shaw*,[57] which had established the existence of the crime of conspiracy to corrupt public morals. They stressed the need for certainty in the criminal law, and pointed out that some thirty convictions had already been obtained on the assumption that *Shaw* correctly stated the law without unlooked-for unjust results. For some of the *Knuller* majority, the fact that Parliament had passed legislation in the relevant area without abrogating *Shaw* was also material.

(x) *Fitzleet*: In *Fitzleet*,[58] the House unanimously refused to overrule its decision in the *Chancery Lane* case.[59] At stake was the liability of a taxpayer to account to the revenue for tax deducted from interest on a loan when the taxpayer already had taxed profits equal to the interest in question. It had been held in the earlier case,

[54] *R* v *National Insurance Commissioner, ex parte Hudson* [1972] AC 944.
[55] *R* v *Deputy Industrial Injuries Commissioner, ex parte Amalgamated Engineering Union, re Dowling* [1967] AC 725.
[56] *Knuller (Publishing, Printing and Promotions) Ltd* v *DPP* [1973] AC 435.
[57] *Shaw* v *DPP* [1962] AC 220.
[58] *Fitzleet Estates Ltd* v *Cherry (Inspector of Taxes)* [1977] 3 All ER 996.
[59] *Chancery Lane Safe Deposits and Offices Co Ltd* v *IRC* [1966] AC 85.

by a majority of three to two, that such liability to account existed where the interest had been capitalized by being debited to the cost of land in a taxpayer company's balance sheet. The House in *Fitzleet* took the view that, since no contention was being put forward which was not present in the *Chancery Lane* case, it was inappropriate to allow the question to be re-opened.

(xi) *Blumenthal*: In *The Hannah Blumenthal*,[60] the House unanimously refused to overrule its two-year-old decision in *The Bremer Vulkan*.[61] In *Bremer Vulkan*, a majority of three to two of the House had ruled that, where a claimant under an arbitration agreement had been guilty of inordinate and inexcusable delay, the respondent was not entitled to treat the agreement to refer the dispute to arbitration as repudiated, since, in contrast to the position in an action at law, the obligation to proceed with dispatch was mutual. The House in *Blumenthal* held that they ought not to depart from this decision (whether it was right or wrong) because nothing had occurred in the meantime to warrant re-consideration of the issue and to take such a course would detract from that certainty in the law which was of especial importance in relation to commerce.

(xii) *La Pintada*: In *La Pintada*,[62] the House unanimously refused to overrule its decision in the *London, Chatham and Dover Railway* case,[63] which had established, as a rule of common law, that a creditor who receives late payment cannot recover interest on his debt by way of general damages. The House considered the rule unjust, but declined to change it on the ground that Parliament had enacted a statutory code partially dealing with the whole question of interest on damages, and that a reversal of the common law rule would not cohere with this code.

(xiii) *Antclizo*: In *The Antclizo*,[64] the House again unanimously declined to overrule *Bremer Vulkan*. They disapproved of that decision and of the supporting reasoning, and were prepared to find that it had given rise to deleterious consequences where claimants had allowed arbitrations to 'go to sleep' for many years. They nevertheless declined to review it as, on the facts of the instant appeal, overruling *Bremer Vulkan* could not affect the outcome.

(c) Australian Overruling Cases

(xiv) *Thomas*: In *Thomas*'s case,[65] the High Court of Australia unanimously refused to overrule its earlier decision in *Milne*'s case.[66] The issue was whether, for the purpose of estate duty law, a deceased partner had a beneficial interest in the good will of a business which devolved on surviving partners, notwithstanding an option to purchase the share of the deceased on terms which excluded payment for good will. *Thomas* followed *Milne* in holding that a beneficial interest did devolve in

60 *Paal Wilson and Co AS* v *Partenreederei Hannah Blumenthal, The Hannah Blumenthal* [1983] 1 AC 854.
61 *Bremer Vulkan Schiffbau und Maschinenfabrik* v *South India Shipping Corp, The Bremer Vulkan* [1981] AC 909.
62 *President of India* v *La Pintada Compania Navigacion SA* [1985] AC 104.
63 *London, Chatham and Dover Railway Co* v *South Eastern Railway Co* [1893] AC 429.
64 *Food Corporation of India* v *Antclizo Shipping Corporation, The Antclizo* [1988] 2 All ER 513.
65 *Perpetual Executors and Trustees Association of Australasia Ltd* v *The Federal Commissioner of Taxation (Thomas's case)* (1949) 77 CLR 493.
66 *Trustees Executors and Agency Co Ltd* v *The Federal Commissioner of Taxation (Milne's case)* (1944) 69 CLR 270.

such circumstances. The High Court declined to overrule *Milne* because the only basis of the contention that it should do so was the fact that *Milne* was a majority decision and the composition of the court had changed.

(xv) *AG* v *Perpetual Trustee*: In *Attorney-General for New South Wales* v *Perpetual Trustee Co Ltd*,[67] five out of six members of the High Court followed the decision of the court in *Quince*,[68] in holding that the action *per quod servitium amisit* does not lie at the suit of the Crown in respect of the loss of the services of a member of the police force against a party whose negligence had caused injury to the officer. Dixon J concurred in the decision even though he considered *Quince* to have been wrongly decided, on the ground that the question was highly disputable and had been thoroughly considered in *Quince*.

(xvi) *Geelong*: In the *Geelong Harbour Trust* case,[69] a majority of three out of five of the High Court followed its decision in the *Townsville Harbour Board* case.[70] The issue was whether legislation should be interpreted as imposing strict liability on the agents of a vessel for damage done by the vessel to harbour installations. In *Townsville* it had been held that earlier similar legislation should be interpreted as incorporating a requirement of fault. The majority in *Geelong* took the view that whether or not the reasoning in *Townsville* had been correct, the decision should not be overruled since it may have been the basis on which commercial transactions had been entered into. The decision of the High Court in *Geelong* was approved on appeal to the Privy Council.[71]

(xvii) *Queensland*: In *Queensland* v *The Commonwealth*,[72] the issue raised was one of the highest importance for Australian constitutional law. Was legislation of the Commonwealth Parliament which granted direct representation in the Senate to Australian territories (not being states of the Commonwealth) valid within the constitution? Two years earlier, in *Western Australia* v *The Commonwealth*,[73] it had been held that the legislation was valid. The decision had been reached by a majority of four to three of the full court. Since then there had been one change in the composition of the court. In *Queensland*, four members of the seven-judge full court were of the view that the *Western Australia* decision was erroneous. Of these, two (Barwick CJ and Aickin J) considered that, on such a question, the court ought to overrule a wrong decision. Two (Gibbs and Stephen JJ) disagreed. They considered that, as nothing had changed since *Western Australia* except that one judge had retired and another had replaced him, and further that expectations as to senatorial representation had been raised by the earlier decision, it should now be followed (even though it was wrongly decided). In the result, the full court in *Queensland*, by a majority of five to two, followed *Western Australia* in upholding the validity of the legislation.

[67] (1952) 85 CLR 237.
[68] *The Commonwealth* v *Quince* (1944) 48 CLR 227.
[69] *Geelong Harbour Trust Commissioners* v *Gibbs, Bright and Co* (1970) 122 CLR 504.
[70] *Townsville Harbour Board* v *Scottish Shire Line Ltd* (1914) 18 CLR 306.
[71] *Geelong Harbour Trust Commissioners* v *Gibbs, Bright and Co* [1974] AC 810.
[72] (1978) 139 CLR 585.
[73] (1975) 134 CLR 201.

(xviii) *Jones*: In *Jones* v *The Commonwealth*,[74] a majority of six to one of the High Court held that it would be inappropriate to overrule its decision in *Hilton* v *Wells*.[75] In the earlier case, by a majority of three to two, the court had upheld the constitutional validity of legislation which conferred on judges the power to issue warrants for the interception of telephonic communications. The majority in *Jones* took the view that the issue turned solely on the true meaning of the legislative provisions, and since that was a question of pure statutory interpretation they should not reconsider it.

(xix) *Zecevic*: In *Zecevic* v *Director of Public Prosecutions for Victoria*,[76] a majority of five to two of the High Court overruled its decisions in *R* v *Howe*[77] and *Viro* v *R*[78] and held that where an accused had used excessive force in self-defence and in consequence killed his assailant his offence should not be reduced from murder to manslaughter. The principal ground which, in the view of the majority, justified this alteration in Australian criminal law was that the *Howe/Viro* rule (which dictated a manslaughter conviction in such circumstances) had proved unworkable in practice since it necessitated over-complex directions to juries.

3. When, Prima-Facie, Should a Decision be Overruled?

It emerges from the overruling cases that, subject to the constraining principles discussed in the succeeding sections of this article, the following must be shown before the overruling power may rightly be invoked. The present law, all things considered, would be improved were some proposition, forming part of the ratio decidendi of the earlier decision, entirely discarded and replaced by a new proposition to be formulated in the overruling decision. As appears from our earlier discussion of cases like *Conway* v *Rimmer*, *Herrington*, *Hyam* and *Moloney*,[79] resort to the overruling power is not strictly needed unless the rejected proposition, in the view of the present court, did indeed form part of the ratio decidendi of the earlier case and is still current law.

The prima-facie requirement (that the present law, as a whole, be improved) does not vary with the type or field of law in question, although, as we shall see, the operation of the constraining principles may do so. The power may be exercised in relation to issues turning on statutory interpretation (*Vestey*,[80] *Khawaja*,[81] *Shivpuri*[82]), as well as matters of common law (*Oldendorff*,[83] *Miliangos*,[84] *Dick*,[85]

[74] (1987) 61 ALJR 348.
[75] (1985) 157 CLR 257.
[76] (1987) 162 CLR 645.
[77] (1958) 100 CLR 448.
[78] (1978) 141 CLR 88.
[79] Above, pp 141–142.
[80] Case iv, p 144, above.
[81] Case v, p 144, above.
[82] Case vi, p 145, above.
[83] Case i, p 143, above.
[84] Case ii, p 143, above.
[85] Case iii, p 144, above.

Howe[86]). The Practice Statement[87] suggests caution where contracts, settlements and fiscal arrangements are concerned. Yet *Vestey* overruled a tax case; and, although in *Blumenthal*[88] the House of Lords stressed the need for certainty as to commercial law, they indicated in *Antclizo*[89] that such considerations alone would not have deterred them from overruling a commercial law case. *Oldendorff* and *Miliangos* were both commercial law overrulings. *Khawaja* related to public law. Nor is criminal law an area peculiarly to be exempted from the exercise of the power, despite the Practice Statement's reference to 'the especial need for certainty as to the criminal law'. In *Shivpuri* and *Howe*, House of Lords' decisions on issues of criminal law were overruled with the effect, in both cases, that the scope of the criminal law was extended.

The prima-facie proper exercise of the power does not turn on the age of the decision under review. It has been applied to decisions whose antiquity varied from eighty years (*Dick*) to one year (*Shivpuri*). Lord Bridge in *Khawaja* described the age of a decision as a 'neutral factor'.[90]

(a) Present Law Improved

The focus of inquiry for the all-things-considered improvement is the present law. It is consequently not required to establish that the earlier decision was 'wrong' at the time when it was pronounced. In *Miliangos*, most of the Law Lords who now concurred in overruling *Havana* found it unnecessary to decide whether that decision was mistaken at the time when it was handed down. It was sufficient to establish that, in the light of developments since 1961, the law ought not now to embody a rule limiting creditors to damages assessed according to the sterling equivalent of contractual debts at the time of breach. In the words of Lord Wilberforce:

> My Lords, even if I were inclined to question some of the arguments used in the speeches, I should find it inappropriate and unnecessary to say that, in the circumstances of the time and on the arguments and authorities presented, the decision was wrong or is open to distinction or explanation.
>
> What we can do, and what is our responsibility, is to consider whether this decision, clear and comparatively recent, should be regarded as a binding precedent in today's circumstances. For that purpose it is permissible to examine the speeches in order to understand the considerations upon which the opinions there reached were based, for the ultimate purpose of seeing whether there have emerged fresh considerations which might

[86] Case vii, p 145, above.
[87] Set out at the beginning of this article.
[88] Case xi, p 147, above.
[89] Case xiii, p 147, above.
[90] [1984] AC 74, 125. Aickin J expressed a similar view in the *Queensland* case: 'Neither do I find it persuasive to say that a case is either so recent or of such long standing that it should not be overruled. It cannot be the proper approach to say that only cases which have stood for a moderate, but not excessive, length of time may be overruled. Neither common sense nor precedent supports such a view'—(1978) 139 CLR 585, 630.

have appealed to those who gave those opinions and so may appeal to their successors.[91]

It is not sufficient for the House to conclude that the law laid down in the earlier decision ought to be changed. It must itself be able to formulate a proposition which, if substituted for that contained in the ratio decidendi of the earlier case, would improve the present law.[92] The Practice Statement, having noted that rigid adherence to precedent may lead to injustice and unduly restrict the proper development of the law, goes on to state that, while former decisions will be treated as 'normally binding', they will be departed from 'when it appears right to do so'. In *Khawaja*, Lord Scarman commented on these words as follows:

> This formula indicates that the House must be satisfied not only that adherence to the precedent would involve the risk of injustice and obstruct the proper development of the law, but also that a judicial departure by the House from the precedent is the safe and appropriate way of remedying the injustice and developing the law. The possibility that legislation may be the better course is one which, though not mentioned in the Statement, the House will not overlook (a recent illustration is its decision in *Pirelli General Cable Works Ltd* v *Oscar Faber and Partners*).[93]

In *Pirelli*[94] the House followed and applied its decision in *Cartledge* v *E. Jopling and Sons Ltd.*[95] That decision had laid down that, for the purposes of statutes of limitation, an action in tort accrues when damage is done and not at some later date when the damage is discovered or could with reasonable diligence have been discovered. Lord Fraser, delivering the leading speech in *Pirelli*, accepted that such a result appeared to be unreasonable and contrary to principle and called for legislation to remedy the matter; but he took the view that only legislation, and not the courts, could produce a better rule for it might require introducing some long-stop data on accrual of actions which only Parliament could devise.[96] The House was not asked to overrule *Cartledge* in *Pirelli*,[97] and only Lord Scarman's speech contains any reference to the Practice Statement. He said:

> It is tempting to suggest that in accordance with the Practice Statement . . . the House might consider it right to depart from the decision in *Cartledge*. But the reform needed is not the substitution of a new principle or rule of law for an existing one but a detailed set

[91] [1975] AC 443, 460. Lord Edmund-Davies (ibid 498) and Lord Fraser (ibid 501) agreed with Lord Wilberforce. Lord Cross alone (ibid 494–7) gave reasons for holding that *Havana* had been wrongly decided. In *R* v *Cunningham* ([1982] AC 566, 582) Lord Edmund-Davies said: 'The cases are probably rare where your Lordships' House would think it right to invoke the Practice Statement notwithstanding the conclusion that a relevant earlier decision had been *correctly* arrived at. But that such a power exists is recognised in the Practice Statement itself, and *Miliangos* . . . is an instance . . .' (italics in original).

[92] See, for example, *Oldendorff* [1974] AC 479, 535–6 Lord Reid, 552 Viscount Dilhorne; *Miliangos* [1976] AC 443, 467–70 Lord Wilberforce.

[93] [1984] AC 74, 106.

[94] [1983] 2 AC 1.

[95] [1963] AC 758.

[96] [1983] 2 AC 1, 19. Lord Fraser's call for legislation was implemented by the Latent Damage Act 1986.

[97] The question argued before the House was whether the Court of Appeal in *Sparham-Souter* v *Town and Country Developments Ltd* [1976] QB 858 had correctly applied the *Cartledge* decision when it had ruled that, in the case of damage to property, damage does not occur (and hence action does not accrue) until a defect causes the plaintiff some economic loss. It held that it had not and overruled the *Sparham-Souter* decision.

> of provisions to replace existing statute law. The true way forward is not by departure from precedent but by amending legislation.[98]

'Waiting for legislation' is not a distinct constraining principle (although, as we shall see,[99] comity with the legislature is). The House reserves an issue for Parliament when, although convinced that the existing law is unsatisfactory, it is not in a position itself to improve it (as in *Pirelli*). If a rule of common law for which the earlier decision is authority can be isolated and simply reversed—and assuming that there are no sufficient grounds for supposing that Parliament has given its affirmative sanction to the rule—then the House in the present case may be satisfied that the law would be improved by such a reversal, notwithstanding that legislation in the area in question is already on the horizon. In *Dick* the House was confronted with a rule of Scots common law which denied recovery of damages to a dependant in one strictly confined situation, namely, where the deceased had commenced proceedings which were still pending at his death. As the House was aware, the whole topic of dependants' rights of recovery was one of which the Scottish Law Commission was seised, and legislative reform had from time to time been enacted. These were not sufficient reasons for delaying in bringing about an improvement in the law through overruling its previous decision. As Lord Wilberforce said: '. . . this particular issue stands by itself, can be dealt with by judicial decision and needs to be so dealt with if justice is to be done to the present appellant'.[100]

(b) Measuring Improvement—Justice, Certainty and Coherence

What considerations are to be taken into account in order to determine whether the law would be improved by an overruling? The Practice Statement speaks of adherence to precedent being undesirable when it 'may lead to injustice in a particular case and also unduly restrict the proper development of the law'. These two conditions are in form distinct and cumulatively necessary. So to understand them would, however, be pedantic and misleading. 'Injustice in a particular case' cannot refer to a situation in which although a rule is generally satisfactory it happens to entail injustice on the particular facts of a single case. It must point to a legal proposition which, in view of the consequence of its universalized application,

[98] [1983] 2 AC 1, 19.

[99] Section 6 below.

[100] 1976 SLT 21, 24. Lord Kilbrandon, who delivered the only other leading speech, expressed the same view (ibid 28–9). In contrast, in *Hesperides Hotels Ltd* v *Muftizade* [1979] AC 508, where the House of Lords refused to overrule its decision in *British South Africa Co* v *Companhia de Moçambique* [1893] AC 602, their Lordships took the view that the rule established in that case—that English courts have no jurisdiction to award damages for trespass to foreign land—could not be altered without consequential changes in other parts of the law, and that such innovations involved sensitive political questions with which only the legislature should deal—[1979] AC 508, 536–7 Lord Wilberforce, 541 Viscount Dilhorne, 542 Lord Salmon, 543–45 Lord Fraser, 545 Lord Keith. Similarly, in *Lim Poh Choo* v *Camden and Islington Health Authority* [1980] AC 174, the House of Lords refused to overrule its decision in *H West and Son Ltd* v *Shephard* [1964] AC 326, which had established that substantial damages for negligently-caused injury are recoverable in respect of loss of amenities notwithstanding that the plaintiff's mental condition is such that he is unaware of the loss. Lord Scarman, delivering the leading speech, said that any reversal of this rule should be done, not judicially, but legislatively within the context of a comprehensive enactment dealing with all aspects of damages for personal injury—[1980] AC 174, 188–9.

would fail to do justice to a class of those affected by it. If that is so, adherence to the proposition would inevitably 'unduly restrict the proper development of the law'.

The perceived injustice may consist of over-harsh or over-lenient treatment of the class in question. Thus, the injustice to creditors of the judgment-in-sterling rule was a crucial factor swaying the majority in *Miliangos*, as was the injustice to dependants of the rule unanimously overturned in *Dick*; and in *Vestey*, the members of the House were appalled by the injustice entailed by the *Congreve* rule, whereby a taxpayer might become liable to pay income tax and surtax on income which he had never received. Conversely, in *Howe* it was held that justice required an overruling of *Lynch*, because the *Lynch* rule would allow those who ought to be convicted of murder to escape criminal liability altogether.

A rule which results in 'injustice in a particular case' is, then, merely an instance of a legal proposition which 'unduly restricts the proper development of the law'. The converse is not true. There may be grounds for holding that a rule ought to be changed which are not based on the injustice its implementation perpetrates on an assignable class. Or, even when a rule is thought unjust in this sense, other factors may militate against a proposed new (just) ruling. The rule (or the proposed new rule) may, owing to its inherent imprecision, be difficult of predictable application and thus infect the law with uncertainty. Or it may be that, whatever the merits of the rule taken in isolation, its implementation in conjunction with other rules forming part of the present law would lead to a degree of incoherence. Two propositions lack mutual coherence when it is implausible to attribute to the law any abstract purpose which fully justifies them both. Certainty and coherence are factors which have been taken into account in the overruling cases, in addition to justice. They all contribute to the determination of the question whether the law as laid down in an earlier decision ought, all things considered, to be changed.

'Certainty', as both the cases and the terms of the Practice Statement, reveal, is an ambiguous aspiration. Certainty as to what? Certainty that the law will not be changed, or certainty as to the content of the law's demands? In the former sense, 'certainty' points as we shall see[101] to one of the constraining principles, that of 'justified reliance'. The Practice Statement recognizes that the use of precedent 'provides at least some degree of certainty upon which individuals can rely in the conduct of their affairs'. Lord Simon of Glaisdale, in *Knuller*, insisted that this was the only kind of certainty envisaged by the Practice Statement:

> The declaration was, in other words, concerned with that certainty which comes from following rules of law already judicially determined, not with any such certainty as may come from the abrogation of those judicially determined rules of law which involve issues of fact and degree.[102]

On that view, 'certainty' always tells one way, against overruling. Lord Simon was there disagreeing with the view of Lord Diplock (who dissented in *Knuller*).

[101] Section 5 below.
[102] [1973] AC 435, 488–9.

Lord Diplock argued that overruling *Shaw* would increase the certainty of the law because 'conspiracy to corrupt public morals' denoted an inherently uncertain range of conduct.[103] On his view, if overruling would replace some hazy rule with a clearer one, then 'certainty' favours overruling. Support for this latter view of certainty is to be found in *Oldendorff* and *Miliangos*. In *Oldendorff*, it was not established that the *Aello* rule was unjust to ship-owners, but rather that, by referring to availability-to-load-or-unload as the test for when lay-time should start to run, it provided a standard which it would be difficult for commercial men and arbitrators to apply. In *Miliangos*, although injustice was a primary factor in determining that the law should be changed, the majority still required to be satisfied that the new rule would be no less unambiguous than the old.[104]

The judgment of the High Court of Australia in *Zecevic*[105] provides a particularly striking example, in the context of a final court overruling its decisions, of considerations of 'certainty' (in the sense of clarity of content) prevailing over considerations of justice. The majority took the view that the rule which had previously prevailed, allowing excessive force in self-defence to reduce murder to manslaughter, had necessitated the formulation of directions to be given by trial judges which were far too complex for the average jury to apply. The law already required the judge to make it plain to the jury that, for a charge of murder to be made out, the prosecution must prove that there was an intention either to kill or to do some grievous bodily harm and must further negative any plea of provocation or reasonable self-defence. A further refinement separating out situations in which force was used in self-defence but to an excessive degree was more than the trial process could bear. Wilson, Dawson and Toohey JJ reached this conclusion although they recognized some force in the view that 'this may result in the conviction for murder of a person lacking the moral culpability associated with that crime'.[106] Mason CJ, who had been a party to the majority ruling in *Viro*,[107] concurred in the view that that decision should now be overruled even though the earlier doctrine 'expresses a concept of self-defence which best accords with acceptable standards of culpability'.[108]

In determining whether the law would, all things considered, be improved by an overruling, considerations of justice may also be outweighed by the requirements of coherence. In *La Pintada*,[109] the question was whether ship-owners, who had received late payment of freight from charterers and subsequently instituted proceedings, were entitled to interest by way of general damages. The House of Lords held that they were not. They unanimously took the view that the rule of common law which the House had laid down in the *London-Chatham* case, denying interest on late payment of debts, constituted an injustice to creditors. Lord

[103] [1973] AC 435, 480.
[104] [1976] AC 443, 467–9 Lord Wilberforce, 497 Lord Cross, 500–1 Lord Edmund-Davies, 501 Lord Fraser.
[105] Case xix, p 149, above.
[106] (1987) 162 CLR 645, 664. Brennan J concurred with their judgment (ibid 666).
[107] (1978) 141 CLR 88.
[108] (1987) 162 CLR 645, 653.
[109] Case xii, p 147, above.

Scarman and Lord Roskill called for prompt legislation to provide for interest in cases where payment had been delayed, since the present state of the law put small creditors at a grave disadvantage against influential debtors (whom they might fear to offend by instituting proceedings).[110] Nevertheless, all members of the House agreed that it would not be right to exercise the Practice Statement power, for the reasons given by Lord Brandon.

Lord Brandon distinguished three cases in which the absence of any common law remedy for late payment of a debt may be important: (1) where a debt is paid late but before any proceedings have been begun; (2) where a debt is paid after the commencement of proceedings but before their conclusion; (3) where a debt remains unpaid until, as a result of proceedings being prosecuted to conclusion, a money judgment is given in which the original debt becomes merged. Reversal of the *London-Chatham* rule would entail that interest was recoverable at common law in all three cases. He rejected the invitation to exercise the Practice Statement power for three reasons. First, although ideally there ought to be a remedy in all three cases, the greater part of the injustice to creditors had been removed since Parliament had provided (in the Administration of Justice Act 1982) a discretionary remedy in cases 2 and 3, and because *London-Chatham* had been properly distinguished so as to allow recovery of special (as distinct from general) damages in appropriate situations. Secondly, Parliament had declined to enact a Law Commission recommendation in so far as it related to case 1. This is a consideration to which we shall return in discussing that constraint on the overruling power which arises from comity with the legislature.[111] Lord Brandon's third reason invokes what is here called 'coherence'.[112]

> My third reason is this. Suppose that your Lordships were to depart from *London-Chatham* in such a way as to give all creditors, whose debts either remained unpaid or were paid late, whether before or after action brought, a cause of action for interest by way of general damages for breach of contract, what would be the result?. The result, as it seems to me, would be that such cause of action would be available to a creditor not only in case 1, in respect of which he still has no remedy except where he can prove special damages, but also in cases 2 and 3, in respect of both of which, since the coming into force of the Act of 1982, he already has a statutory remedy. What is more, the new cause of action so applicable to cases 2 and 3 would constitute a remedy as of right for a creditor, whereas the statutory remedy would remain discretionary only. There would, accordingly, exist, in relation to cases 2 and 3, two parallel remedies, one as of right and the other discretionary; and the likelihood would be that creditors would, because of this difference, come to rely mainly on the former, rather than the latter, right.[113]

There would be no logical conflict between the proposition that interest *must* be paid, and the proposition that interest *may* be paid, in the same circumstances; but

[110] [1985] AC 104, 111–2.

[111] Below, pp 178–179.

[112] For a fuller discussion of the requirements of coherence in law, see Neil MacCormick, *Legal Reasoning and Legal Theory*, Clarendon Press, 1978, ch 7.

[113] [1985] AC 104, 131.

no possible ground could be found to support their separate and simultaneous validity within a normative field of meaning.[114]

When 'certainty' is appealed to as a ground for overruling, it is often conjoined with coherence considerations. This occurs when the fact that a decision has been subjected to subtle distinguishing is put forward as a reason why the decision should be discarded. Distinguishing is 'subtle' when an initial and a subsequent ruling, taken together, leave the law in an unsatisfactory state. If it would be implausible to imagine any contemporary legislator wishing to enact both rules, they are incoherent. Where such incoherence exists, there will be uncertainty in the law because, since no underlying principle or policy justifies both rulings, there can be no basis upon which further decisions can be allocated within the reach of either the initial or the subtly distinguished ruling. To that extent, prediction of future decisions becomes haphazard. Thus in *Oldendorff* and *Howe*, it was accepted that the cases under review (*Aello* and *Lynch*) had been distinguished on inadequate grounds in subsequent cases, with a consequent increase in the disharmony of the law. In *Shivpuri*, too, those members of the House who considered that a distinction was possible between the present case and *Ryan*[115] were nevertheless willing to concur in overruling *Ryan*. They accepted, in effect, that it was implausible to attribute to Parliament any workable distinction between different classes of impossible attempts, some of which should be criminal and others not.

In Lord Reid's view, expressed in *Hudson*,[116] the unfortunate consequences of subtle distinguishing was one of the primary grounds for the adoption of the Practice Statement power:

> It is notorious that where an existing decision is disapproved but cannot be overruled courts tend to distinguish it on inadequate grounds. I do not think that they act wrongly in so doing: they are adopting the less bad of the only alternatives open to them. But this is bound to lead to uncertainty for no one can say in advance whether in a particular case the court will or will not feel bound to follow the old unsatisfactory decision. On balance it seems to me that overruling such a decision will promote and not impair the certainty of the law.[117]

If it is established, in the light of considerations of justice, certainty and coherence, that the present law would be improved, all things considered, were a case to be overruled, that merely determines the prima-facie propriety of the exercise of the Practice Statement power. We must now turn to those principles of constraint which have emerged in the overruling cases.

4. *The First Constraining Principle—No New Reasons (Finality)*

It has been frequently pointed out in the overruling cases that it is not sufficient warrant for the House of Lords to exercise its Practice Statement overruling power

[114] Cf J. W. Harris, *Law and Legal Science*, Clarendon Press, 1979, 10–14, 41–3, 65–73, 97–103, 111–22.
[115] Below, pp 181–182.
[116] Case viii, p 146, above.
[117] [1972] AC 944, 966.

that, in the view of the members of the present appellate committee, the earlier decision was simply 'wrong'.[118] Why should this be so? Once it is concluded that the ruling in the earlier case ought not to have been laid down as it was and consequently, a fortiori, it ought not to form part of the law today, and that some alternative proposition rejected in that case ought then and ought now to represent the law, why should the decision not be overruled? 'Wrongness' is not, as we have seen, necessary for a decision to be overruled, but why is it not sufficient?

It will be my contention that four distinct constraining principles underlie the terms of the Practice Statement and the overruling cases. They invoke, respectively, considerations of finality, reliance, comity with the legislature, and mootness. The first of these is the one with the widest theoretical scope. It will be considered in this section, and the others in the three succeeding sections.

(a) The No-New-Reasons Principle

Some issues of law are so inherently poised between counter-weighted reasons that a court which second-guesses an earlier court cannot, in principle, deny the possibility of third-guessing. As Lord Pearson put it in *Hudson*:[119]

> If a tenable view taken by a majority in the first appeal could be overruled by a majority preferring another tenable view in a second appeal, then the original tenable view could be restored by a majority preferring it in a third appeal. Finality of decision would be utterly lost.[120]

Lord Morris spoke to the same effect in *Cassell and Co Ltd* v *Broome*:

> I do not think that the power that was referred to in the statement of July 26th 1966 was intended to encourage a tendency periodically to chop and change the law. In branches of the law where clarification becomes necessary there may well be decisions which as a matter of policy are not universally welcomed or where some may think that some variant of the decision one way or the other would have been more acceptable. But this does not mean that decisions of this House should readily be reviewed whenever a case presents itself which is covered by a decision. There must be something much more.[121]

The finality consideration played a decisive role in *Blumenthal*.[122] There the buyers of a ship invoked the arbitration provisions of the contract of sale but, as all the members of the House of Lords recognized, they had been guilty of such delay that no arbitration could now be 'satisfactory'. The House nevertheless held, following *Bremer Vulkan*, that such delay did not constitute repudiation. They rejected the sellers' submission that that case should be departed from. Lord Roskill said:

[118] See especially Lord Reid in *Hudson* [1972] AC 944, 996, and in *Knuller* [1973] AC 435, 445; Lord Wilberforce in *Fitzleet* (1977) 3 All ER 996, 999; Lord Edmund-Davies, ibid 1001–3; Lord Brandon in *Blumenthal* [1983] 1 AC 854, 911–3.

[119] Case viii, p 146, above.

[120] [1972] AC 944, 996–7.

[121] [1972] AC 1027, 1098.

[122] Case xi, p 147, above.

> Were your Lordships to yield to the respondents' submissions a few years have only to elapse and other litigants might hope to persuade a differently constituted appellate committee once again to reconsider the position and to restore the *Bremer Vulkan* decision to its present role.[123]

The fact that the House of Lords can now overrule its decisions inevitably adds something to the unpredictability of legal outcomes. No doubt such 'uncertainty' would be exacerbated if there were any serious likelihood of reconsideration—that is, if the House, having in case B departed from case A, were subsequently to overrule B and reinstate A. This has not yet happened, but the following somewhat cryptic observation of Lord Bridge in *Shivpuri*[124] appears to recognize it as a possibility. He said that if, contrary to his present view, there was a valid distinction between *Ryan* and *Shivpuri*, 'my present opinion on that point would not foreclose the option of making such a distinction in some future case'.[125] This comment is particularly unsettling as at least two of his colleagues, although they concurred in overruling *Ryan*, were of opinion that it could have been distinguished.[126]

If the argument from lack of finality is a cogent ground for not overruling a decision merely because it is perceived to have been wrongly decided, why does it not apply in every such case? The problem has been approached, in some cases, in an *ad hominem*, rather than a principled, fashion. If Law Lords who decided an impugned case are actually sitting in the instant case and indicate that they have changed their minds, as did Lord Fraser and (less explicitly) Lord Wilberforce in *Khawaja*,[127] and Lord Bridge in *Shivpuri*, their colleagues have, for that reason, been the more willing to overrule.[128] Similar pragmatic *ad hominem* considerations played a large part in the reasoning of the House of Lords in *Davis* v *Johnson*,[129] when they rejected the view that the Court of Appeal should be generally free to overrule decisions of its own. Given that the Court of Appeal consisted of seventeen judges and usually sat in divisions of only three, there would be a real danger of reconsideration. This danger did not exist, so it was assumed, to anything like the same degree where the House of Lords overrules one of its decisions, because of its smaller size and the fact that it normally sits in panels of five. The risk of lack of finality may be thought to be even less where members who participated in the impugned decision are present wearing the white sheet of repentance.

[123] [1983] 1 AC 854, 922–3.

[124] Case vi, p 145, above.

[125] [1984] AC 1, 23. In *Anclizo*, Lord Goff recognized the possibility of reconsideration in the converse situation, that is, where the House of Lords has in case B declined to overrule case A but accepts the invitation to do so in case C—[1988] 2 All ER 513, 516.

[126] Below, pp 181–182.

[127] Case v, p 144, above.

[128] In *Khawaja*, Lord Bridge said that the fact that Lord Wilberforce and Lord Fraser had, on the hearing of the present appeals, changed their minds about the view they had expressed in *Zamir* was what weighed most heavily with him in reaching the conclusion that the House should depart from *Zamir*—[1984] AC 74, 125. In *Shivpuri*, Lord Hailsham LC said, of the consideration that the sooner a serious error was corrected the better, that it had all the greater force when the error was to be corrected by a panel comprising one of the original authors of the *Ryan* majority judgment—[1987] AC 1, 11. Similarly, in *Miliangos* the fact that Lord Denning, who was a party to the decision in *Havana*, had demonstrated a change of view in the Court of Appeal was a consideration of which account was taken—[1976] AC 443, 462 Lord Wilberforce.

[129] [1979] AC 264.

This pragmatic approach to distinguishing instances in which finality tells against overruling 'wrong' decisions from those in which it does not is unsatisfactory. The phenomenon of announced change of mind can occur, of course, only when the decision under review is a comparatively recent one. More importantly, members of the House are in no position to predict, on an *ad hominem* basis, what the minds of their successors will be on a particular question when they and their current colleagues have retired.

If there is a class of case where the House should not, for fear of lack of finality, overrule a 'wrong' decision, is it identifiable in terms of principle? Such a category can be identified, it is submitted, by reference to the idea of 'no new reasons'. When all the reasons canvassed for or against a proposition of law in the instant case were also canvassed in the decision under review, then what remains for the judge is a subjective weighing of them one against the other. He may, for his part, be convinced that his brethren in the earlier case read the scales wrong. But since, ex hypothesi, he cannot give a distinct reason in support of this impression, he cannot, in principle, describe as 'demonstrably mistaken' any third guess on the issue which a future judge, faced with the same catalogue of reasons, might make.[130]

There are, in Lord Pearson's words,[131] two 'tenable' views in just this class of case. If judge X reflects on judge Y's opinion and concludes that he disagrees with it, it may be that X can point to a reason, *r*, which played no part in Y's reasoning. X can then give as the ground for his disagreement with Y the fact that *r* was overlooked or not foreseen. There would not be, in such a case, two tenable views, as X sees it. If, however, X can point to no such overlooked or unforeseen reason, how does he explain his disagreement with Y? In a milieu subject to different institutional or social constraints, he might say: 'On the reasons we both have, that old fool should have realized that the question was to be settled the other way, since no other outcome could follow from those reasons'. Within the constraints of an adjudicative institution, he says (and probably genuinely believes) that the weighting to be given to the competing reasons on either side of the question is a matter of subjective impression—that he is sure, for his part, which way the scales should come down, but that the other view is 'tenable'.

The need for finality on disputed questions of law thus justifies the constraint that the House of Lords should not overrule a decision of its own if no new reasons are in play. The connection between finality and no-new-reasons appears explicitly in the speech of Lord Wilberforce in *Fitzleet*,[132] when he was justifying the refusal of the House to depart from its 1966 decision in the *Chancery Lane* case:

> My Lords, two points are clear. (1) Although Counsel for the taxpayer developed his argument with freshness and vigour, it became clear that there was no contention advanced or which could be advanced by him which was not before this House in 1966

[130] Cf J. W. Harris, *Legal Philosophies*, Butterworths, 1980, 186–8.
[131] Cited at, p 157, above.
[132] Case x, p 146, above.

. . . (2) There has been no change of circumstance such as some of their Lordships found to exist in *Miliangos* v *George Frank (Textiles) Ltd*, such as would call for or justify a review of the 1966 decision . . .

There is therefore nothing left to the taxpayer but to contend, as it frankly does, that the 1966 decision is wrong. This contention means, when interpreted, that three or more of your Lordships ought to take the view which appealed then to the minority.

My Lords, in my firm opinion, the 1966 Practice Statement was never intended to allow and should not be considered to allow such a course. Nothing could be more undesirable, in fact, than to permit litigants, after a decision has been given by this House with all appearance of finality, to return to this House in the hope that a differently constituted committee might be persuaded to take the view which its predecessors rejected. True that the earlier decision was by a majority: I say nothing as to its correctness or as to the validity of the reasoning by which it was supported. That there were two eminently possible views is shown by the support for each by at any rate two members of the House. But doubtful issues have to be resolved and the law knows no better way of resolving them than by the considered majority opinion of the ultimate tribunal. It requires much more than doubts as to the correctness of such opinion to justify departing from it.[133]

Lord Brandon, delivering the leading speech in *Blumenthal*, cited the above passage from Lord Wilberforce's speech in *Fitzleet* and concluded that it constituted guidance which should be followed in the present case.[134] He said that:

. . . where two eminently possible views of a question may be taken; where a decision between them has to be made by the best method known to the law; and where, once such decision has been made, it must for the future be followed and acted upon without the risk of its later being held to have been wrong and departed from on that account. In this connection I would lay stress on what is generally accepted to be the special need for certainty, consistency and continuity in the field of commercial law.[135]

In both *Fitzleet* and *Blumenthal*, the decision which (right or wrong) the House declined to overrule had been by a bare majority. Consistently with the no-new-reasons principle and its finality rationale, the fact that, in an earlier case, the House was divided gives no warrant for overruling. On the contrary, where dissenting speeches have been delivered, it is more likely that all pertinent reasons were considered than where unanimity prevailed. The finality rationale presupposes that the House of Lords, when asked to exercise its Practice Statement power, is seised of an issue in a way quite different from that which arises in the case of an ordinary appeal from a lower court. In the latter context, even where 'two eminently possible views of a question may be taken', it would be inconsistent with the role of an appellate court to declare that, although in its view the lower court had got the law wrong, nonetheless that incorrect holding should not be disturbed.[136] When the Practice Statement is invoked, the House is not in the

[133] [1977] 3 All ER 996, 999.

[134] [1983] 1 AC 854, 911–12.

[135] [1983] 1 AC 854, 913.

[136] The assumption is that the final court takes the view, however impressionistically, that the correct conclusion as to the present state of the law is different from that reached by the lower court in the instant case. The situation would be different if the final court simply regretted that the ruling contained in the lower court's judgment was part of the law, yet was unable itself, for reasons considered in the last section, to substitute a ruling which would have the

continued on page 161

notional position of a court yet higher in the judicial hierarchy than was the House which rendered the impugned decision. It is therefore consistent with its role, as a final court of appeal one of whose functions is to keep the law under review, to hold that, though the earlier decision may have been a mistake, it should not now be altered. That is so unless new reasons—matters which were not or could not have been considered in the earlier case—can be advanced for holding that the law ought now to be changed.

The no-new-reasons principle has a long pedigree in the Australian overruling cases, although it has been most commonly expressed in the negative form: that a mere change in the constitution of the bench is not a sufficient ground for the High Court to overrule a decision. Soon after the High Court assumed its overruling jurisdiction, Barton J said:

> I have never thought that it was not open to this court to review its previous decisions upon good cause. The question is not whether the court can do so but whether it will, having due regard to the need for continuity and consistency in judicial decision. . . . Changes in the number of appointed justices can I take it never of themselves furnish a reason for review.[137]

The above statement has been frequently cited with approval in subsequent cases, for example by Latham CJ in *Thomas*[138] (who added that it applied equally to changes in the personnel of the court as to changes in numbers)[139] and by Gibbs J in *Queensland*.[140] It is clear that this negative form has the same import as the no-new-reasons principle. Manifestly no counsel would ever submit that the *fact* that the bench has changed is a reason for overruling. The point is that if the High Court is pressed to reach a different conclusion from its predecessor and nothing is put by way of argument which was not advanced on the earlier occasion, the court should not allow itself to be persuaded to a different view even if, had the matter been *de novo*, the present majority might have seen the outcome in the way contended for.

The matter was put more positively in terms of no-new-reasons by Dixon J in *A-G* v *Perpetual Trustee*:[141]

> But there appears to me to be no ground for reconsidering the decision in *Quince*'s case unless it be a sufficient ground simply that the opposite conclusion is to be preferred. It is evident that the decision was reached only after a very full examination of the question. It cannot be said that any compelling consideration or important authority was overlooked or that the decision conflicts with well-established principle or fails to go with a definite stream of authority.[142]

continued from page 160
consequence that the totality of the present law would, all things considered, be improved. In the latter situation, it could properly take the view that 'reform' must await legislative initiative.

137 *The Tramways Case* (1914) 18 CLR 54

138 Case xiv, p 147, above.

139 (1949) 77 CLR 493, 496.

140 (1978) 139 CLR 585, 599. Whether the no-new-reasons principle should have been applied as it was to the sort of issue raised in *Queensland* (case xvii, p 148, above) is discussed below, pp 190–191.

141 Case xv, p 148, above.

142 (1952) 85 CLR 237, 244.

(b) Implementing the Principle

What, after all, does it mean to say that a decision on a question of law was 'wrong'? I have elsewhere suggested that the kinds of reason which may be advanced in support of legal propositions fall into four models of legal rationality: the will model, which appeals to historical information about the motives or intentions of those who created a legal rule; the natural-meaning model, which invokes the linguistic-conventional import of the words employed in the canonical formulation of a rule; the doctrine model, which prays in aid of a proposition some maxim belonging to an official tradition; and the utility model, which supports one legal proposition against another by reference to their respective consequences.[143] A decision may be considered 'wrong' in two quite different ways: first, if reasons belonging to one or more of these models, which were relevant to the case, were not invoked and should have led to a contrary holding if they had been; and secondly when, although all pertinent reasons were in play, the view is taken that they were not correctly weighted. These two species of wrongness may be distinguished, respectively, as 'structural wrongness', and 'ultimate wrongness'.

When a judge concludes that his predecessor's decision was infected with ultimate wrongness, he is faced with a situation of stark disagreement. Finality and the no-new-reasons principle favour restraint in the institutional implementation of that disagreement (unless, as we shall see in section 8, he is convinced that the issue at stake is so fundamental that it is his duty to enforce his own view). When, on the other hand, he concludes that his predecessor's decision suffered from structural wrongness, he may suggest that there is at bottom no irresolvable disagreement—that, if only omitted reasons had been drawn to the attention of his predecessor, he might have taken a different view.

As we have seen, new reasons may emerge without any finding that the earlier decision was wrong at all. In *Miliangos*, the majority of their Lordships did not find it necessary to conclude the *Havana* decision was wrong at the time when it was rendered. Subsequent events had provided reasons, consonant with the utility model of rationality, for changing the legal proposition it laid down.[144] Where consequences unforeseen in the earlier decision constitute the new reasons which justify overruling it, it makes little difference whether one interprets the overruling as premised on the assumption that the decision, though correct in its day, had been overtaken by events, or as entailing a conclusion that these overlooked consequences give rise to structural wrongness in the decision. Either way, ultimate disagreement has not been joined with the view that a particular conclusion follows from particular reasons.

When in *Vestey*[145] the House of Lords overruled *Congreve*, it was recognized that, viewed purely as a matter of linguistic interpretation, the construction of the income tax legislation which had been adopted in *Congreve* was a 'tenable view'. However, that interpretation had led to disastrous consequences which could not

[143] J. W. Harris, *Law and Legal Science*, Clarendon Press, 1979, ch 5.
[144] Above, pp150–151.
[145] Case iv, p 144, above.

have been intended by Parliament. It had entailed that every potential object of a foreign discretionary settlement was liable to pay tax on the entire income of the fund, and to the unconstitutional assumption by the Revenue of the power itself to decide which beneficiaries should pay tax and how much each should pay. The utility model of rationality was substituted for the natural-meaning model, so that new reasons could be found in these unlooked-for consequences. Lord Wilberforce said:

> . . . it can now be seen, as it certainly was not seen in 1949, that the consequences of the interpretation then accepted must lead, in relation to a large class of settlements . . . to a situation involving results which are arbitrary, potentially unjust, and fundamentally unconstitutional. If these had been seen in 1949—within the ambit of proper argument they could not reasonably have been seen—I cannot believe that the eminent Lords who decided the case would have been willing to ascribe to Parliament an intention to produce such results.[146]

Structural wrongness may take other forms. Consonant with the will model of rationality, a judge may take the view that admissible historical evidence of the goal aimed at by the legislature was overlooked in the earlier case. In *Shivpuri*, Lord Bridge gave as a principal ground for his change of mind the fact that those relatively innocuous examples of attempts which, in *Ryan*, he had supposed Parliament could not have intended to penalize were in fact expressly instanced in the Law Commission's report which led to the passing of the Criminal Attempts Act 1981. It is well established that such a report may be consulted as evidence of the mischief at which a statute is directed. He had overlooked this information in his *Ryan* opinion.[147]

Again, important historical principles, relevant within the doctrine model of rationality, may, in the view of a later court, not have been properly ventilated in an earlier decision. In *Vestey*, the House of Lords recognized that extra-statutory concessions of a universalized kind by the Revenue were legitimate, but they concluded that the power to decide which beneficiaries should pay tax and how much they should pay (which the Revenue had to assume if the *Congreve* rule was to work) was 'unconstitutional'. Lord Edmund-Davies drew attention to the provisions of the Bill of Rights of 1688, which declared: '(1) that the pretended power of suspending of laws, or the execution of laws, by regal authority, without consent of Parliament, is illegal. (2) That the pretended power of dispensing with laws, or the execution of laws, by regal authority, as it has been assumed and exercised of late, is illegal'.[148]

Similarly in *Khawaja*, Lord Scarman and Lord Bridge, who delivered the leading speeches in favour of overruling *Zamir*, concluded that the reasoning in that case had neglected what has now become a principle of constitutional law,

[146] [1980] AC 1148, 1176. Similar views were expressed by Viscount Dilhorne, ibid. 1186, by Lord Edmund-Davies, 1196 and by Lord Keith, 1198. Lord Salmon expressed complete agreement with Lord Wilberforce, 1190.
[147] [1987] AC 1, 21.
[148] [1980] AC 1148, 1195.

namely, Lord Atkin's statement in *Liversidge* v *Anderson*:[149] 'That in English law every imprisonment is prima-facie unlawful and that it is for a person directing imprisonment to justify his act'. The *Zamir* interpretation of the immigration legislation was wrong because, in disregard of this principle, it held that it was enough for an immigration officer exercising power to refuse entry to have reasonable grounds for believing that a person was an illegal entrant.[150]

Where what has here been called 'ultimate wrongness' is perceived in an earlier decision, one judge considers that another reached the wrong conclusion, not because reasons were overlooked, but because the pros and cons were not properly measured one against the other. This will almost inevitably be the case where the issue is thought to turn exclusively on the natural reading of the words of a statute. To such a case the no-new-reasons constraint on overruling paradigmatically applies. The kinds of reason which can be given for asserting that one reading rather than another is the more natural will, in the nature of the case, be of a limited kind—relating to such matters as ordinary usage revealed by dictionaries, special usage indicated from the immediate context, or technical usage deriving from a broader legal context. It will be implausible to suggest that, if judge X believes judge Y misunderstood the most natural reading, it was because he ignored a reason of this kind. The suggestion will usually be one of counter-impression. Such cases are, presumptively, no-new-reasons cases, because semantic questions are prima-facie, inherently independent of special reasons which forensic research may unearth. The presumption could, however, be displaced by showing that there are facets of the text, or of other texts in pari materia, which had been overlooked.

In *Hudson*, Lord Pearson made his oft-cited reference to finality telling against overruling where there were two 'tenable' views[151] in the context of a decision which, in the view of the majority, turned precisely on the natural reading of statutory language—the meaning of a tribunal's decision being 'final'. What the case vividly illustrates is that prior classification of an issue within one or other of the models of rationality will itself often determine whether there are relevant reasons not considered in the earlier case and hence whether the no-new-reasons constraint applies. The minority, who favoured overruling *Dowling*, approached the issue by a familiar mix of the will and utility models of rationality. They contended that there were good grounds, not canvassed in *Dowling*, for holding that Parliament's aim, in setting up the system of tribunals and medical boards, would not be furthered if the question of whether an injury was caused by a particular accident was foreclosed by the decision of the first authority before whom it happened to arise; and they buttressed this historical speculation about the policy goal which those who promoted the legislation had in mind by reference to what they considered to be the arbitrary and unjust consequences of accepting the *Dowling* ruling. The majority classified the issue within the natural-meaning

149 [1942] AC 206, 245.
150 [1984] AC 74, 109–10, 122.
151 Cited above, p 157.

model and hence concluded that different views about the rightness of *Dowling* must necessarily relate, not to the introduction of new reasons, but to different subjective weighings of a closed category of (linguistic-constructional) reasons. Lord Reid said:

> No broad issue of justice or public policy is involved nor is any question of legal principle. The issue is simply the proper construction of complicated provisions in a statute.[152]

Lord Simon, after giving linguistic arguments for holding that *Dowling* was wrong, concluded that it should nonetheless not be overruled. He said:

> A variation of a view on a matter of statutory construction—so much a matter of impression—would, I should have thought, rarely provide a suitable occasion, by itself, that is to say, for it would be different if it were convincingly shown that a previous construction, clearly demonstrated to be wrong, is causing administrative difficulties or individual injustice.[153]

The above dicta were at one time understood by commentators to mean that issues of statutory construction, as such, are peculiarly exempt from the Practice Statement power. In *Vestey*, they were held not to carry this implication.[154] *Vestey*, *Khawaja* and *Shivpuri* all involved questions of statutory construction. But in those cases the issue was not seen as one of the meaning of words. Consequentialist considerations, constitutional principles or historical evidence of Parliament's intentions dictated the interpretations.

The crucial significance of the subsumption of an issue within one of the models of legal rationality may also be illustrated from the decision of the High Court of Australia in *Jones*.[155] Six out of the seven justices refused to overrule an earlier decision of the court interpreting the Telecommunications Interception Act 1979. They took the view that the issue was one of linguistic construction: 'The answer to the question depended on finely balanced considerations, there being room for a difference of opinion, so that it cannot be said that the decision on this point was plainly or manifestly wrong . . .'.[156] Gaudron J, in her dissenting judgment, classified the issue within what I have called 'the doctrine model' of rationality. She contended that what was at stake was a matter of constitutional principle: whether the power purportedly conferred on judges by the legislation to issue warrants for the interception of telephone calls was compatible with the judicial function. This question, she claimed, was not put in *Hilton* v *Wells* and accordingly it was proper for the present court to review that case.[157]

Questions considered by the deciding judge to fall squarely within the natural-meaning model of rationality invariably come within that category of cases where it is considered that all relevant reasons were ventilated in the earlier case, so that the need for finality calls for a refusal to exercise the overruling power. The earlier

152 [1972] AC 944, 966.
153 [1972] AC 944, 1024.
154 [1980] AC 1148, 1186 Viscount Dilhorne, 1196 Lord Edmund-Davies.
155 Case xviii, p 149, above.
156 (1987) 61 ALJR 348, 349, judgment of Mason CJ, Wilson, Brennan, Dean, Dawson and Toohey JJ.
157 (1987) 61 ALJR 348, 349–50.

decision may have been ultimately wrong—'so much a matter of impression'—but it was not structurally wrong—'plainly' or 'manifestly' wrong. Issues thought to turn on historical intention (within the will model of rationality) are also likely to be of this kind, since it will be unusual to find, as was found in *Shivpuri*,[158] that some admissible evidence of what the legislature intended to achieve was overlooked in the earlier case. Where the issue is subsumed within the utility model, so that the comparative consequences of alternative legal propositions are thought decisive, the age of the impugned ruling will be important. If it is an old one, it is highly likely that consequences not adverted to in the earlier decision will be advanced in the present case. In *Dick*,[159] for example, attitudes towards the propriety of claims by dependants arising out of a negligently-caused death had greatly changed during the eighty years since the decision in *Darling*, as evidenced both from legislative and common law developments. In consequence, the House felt free to conclude that the injustice of the *Darling* rule was obvious.[160]

Where the earlier decision is a recent one, the discovery of new reasons in unforeseen consequences is less likely.[161] In *Blumenthal*, for example, it was urged for the sellers that the *Bremer Vulkan* ruling had produced dismay in commercial circles, entailing as it did that respondents to arbitration claims must themselves take the initiative to forward proceedings and could not assume, as defendants to ordinary civil actions may, that inordinate delay by plaintiffs will lead to stale claims being struck out for want of prosecution. That dismay had been recognized and sympathized with in the lower courts. The House rejected the view that these alleged deleterious consequences of *Bremer Vulkan* constituted any new ground for reviewing that decision.[162] Lord Roskill denied that there were in the present case unlooked-for 'practical difficulties' resulting from the earlier decision, such as those which had justified the House in *Oldendorff* in reviewing its decision in *Aello*.[163] As Lord Brightman put it: 'Nothing has occurred since January 1981 in the field of arbitration to warrant such an in-road into the principle of stare decisis . . .'.[164]

Counsel for the sellers had submitted that, if the decision in *Bremer Vulkan* was wrong, the sooner it was departed from the better.[165] Just that contention was

[158] Above, p 163.

[159] Case iii, p 144, above.

[160] 1976 SLT 21, 23 Lord Wilberforce, 25–6, 28–9 Lord Kilbrandon. Lord Diplock agreed with the speech of Lord Kilbrandon (ibid, p 24). Viscount Dilhorne and Lord Edmund-Davies agreed with the speeches of both Lord Wilberforce and Lord Kilbrandon (ibid, pp 24, 29). The House in *Dick* also concluded that *Darling* was doctrinally erroneous. There it had been said that the personal action, which availed only a limited class of relatives, was anomalous and so ought not to be extended; and that there was no precedent for allowing an action in these circumstances. Their Lordships in *Dick* rejected these reasons. Whether or not the action could be characterized as an anomaly, allowing it to proceed where the deceased had himself instituted proceedings did not amount to an 'extension'; and, in the absence of direct precedent either way, the House in *Darling* should have regarded itself as free to settle the matter on principle.

[161] Cf the citation from Lord Scarman in *DPP* v *Nock* quoted at n 28 above.

[162] [1983] 1 AC 854, 911–13 Lord Brandon, 920–3 Lord Roskill, 923 Lord Brightman. Lord Keith (ibid, 920) signified agreement with Lord Brandon's speech. Lord Diplock (ibid, 917) expressed agreement with Lord Roskill, Lord Brandon and Lord Brightman.

[163] [1983] 1 AC 854, 922.

[164] [1983] 1 AC 854, 923.

[165] [1983] 1 AC 854, 899.

accepted in *Shivpuri* in relation to a decision only one year old. However, as we have seen, in *Shivpuri* it was found that crucial evidence as to Parliament's intention had been overlooked in *Ryan*—that is, that the decision involved what has here been termed 'structural wrongness'. Whereas in *Blumenthal*, although counsel for the sellers contended that the majority in *Bremer Vulkan* gave insufficient regard to practical realities, he conceded that there had been no 'change of circumstances' since that decision.[166] In other words, the claim was that *Bremer Vulkan* suffered from 'ultimate wrongness', in that, although all relevant factors had been taken into account, they had been wrongly weighed. The unanimous response of the House of Lords was that, supposing that might be true, finality required that the decision (which was only two years old) should not be reviewed.

However, when, in *Antclizo*,[167] the House was again asked to depart from *Bremer Vulkan*—now a seven-year-old decision—it seems that their Lordships were prepared to consider the consequences for commerce of the decision sufficiently bad to warrant overruling it. Lord Goff delivered the single speech in *Antclizo*. Of the four members of the House who expressed unqualified agreement with him, two (Lord Brandon and Lord Brightman) had been members of the appellate committee in *Blumenthal*. Lord Goff referred to the 'serious disquiet among the whole commercial community' which *Bremer Vulkan* had provoked.[168] Evidently, the accumulated experience of the consequences of the decision would have provided new reasons within the no-new-reasons principle, for Lord Goff expressed a strong inclination to accept the invitation to review *Bremer Vulkan* if the circumstances were appropriate.[169] He concluded that circumstances were not appropriate in the present case because, as we shall see in section 7, the mootness constraint lay in the way.

Where reasoning relates to matters of doctrine, much will depend on the exhaustiveness of the discussion of relevant authorities in the earlier case.[170] If all that is being urged by way of argument in the present appeal was also urged in the earlier case, finality warrants restraint in exercising the overruling power even if the present court would have assessed the strength of the arguments differently. That was the view taken by the House of Lords as to an issue of criminal law in *Knuller*,[171] and by the High Court of Australia as to an issue of tort law in *A-G* v *Perpetual Trustee*.[172]

[166] [1983] 1 AC 854, 899.
[167] Case xiii, p 147, above.
[168] [1988] 2 All ER 513, 515.
[169] [1988] 2 All ER 513, 516.
[170] In *Conway* v *Rimmer*, Lord Morris—the only member of the House to take the view that the disposal of the present appeal required overruling, rather than merely distinguishing, *Duncan* v *Cammell Laird Ltd.* (n 31 above)—stressed the point that Scots authorities had been overlooked in argument in *Duncan*'s case—[1968] AC 910, 958–61.
[171] Case ix, p 146, above.
[172] Case xv, p 148, above. Similarly in *Lim Poh Choo* v *Camden and Islington Health Authority* [1980] AC 174 the House of Lords declined the invitation to overrule its decision in *H West and Son Ltd* v *Shephard* [1964] AC 326 (which had ruled that damages for loss of amenities suffered by an unconscious plaintiff should be substantial, in contrast to

continued on page 168

Knuller arguably represents a high-water-mark of the no-new-reasons constraint and its finality rationale. The House of Lords in *Shaw* had laid down that there was known to the common law an offence of conspiring to corrupt public morals. As is often the case with an issue of common law, reasons advanced for and against this ruling were derived from both the doctrine and utility models of rationality. Could the authorities be read as affirming the existence of such a crime? The majority in *Shaw* held that they could. Would the recognition of such a crime entail undesirable consequences in that it would subject accused persons to the subjective whims of juries and unduly widen the scope of the criminal law? The majority held that it would not. In *Knuller*, no new reasons, under either category, were in play, and hence the majority took the view that 'certainty', in the sense of finality, required that *Shaw* should be followed whether or not it was wrong.

Lord Morris believed that *Shaw* had been correctly decided, but stated that, even if he had been of a different opinion, he would have considered it wholly inappropriate for the House now to review the decision:

> It is accepted that all relevant authorities were examined before this House came to its decision. There comes a stage when further disputation should cease.[173]

Lord Reid had participated in *Shaw* as a dissenting voice. In *Knuller*, he adhered to the view that the decision of the majority in *Shaw* was erroneous but emphatically rejected the suggestion that it should be overruled. No new reasons had emerged. Nothing had occurred since *Shaw* which demonstrated that the decision had had unlooked-for deleterious consequences:

> We were informed that there had been at least thirty and probably many more convictions of this new crime in the ten years which have elapsed since *Shaw*'s case was decided, and it does not appear that there has been manifest injustice or that any attempt has been made to widen the scope of the new crime.[174]

The no-new-reasons principle is deeply embedded in the practice of the final appellate courts of the United Kingdom and Australia. Two caveats should, however, be entered. First, where a court decides, in case B, that case A (even if wrongly decided) should not be overruled since no new reasons have emerged, that decision itself falls outside the reach of the finality rationale. The court may always conclude, in case C, that things have changed since case B was decided, that new reasons have emerged, and that it ought now to respond favourably to an invitation to overrule case A. This was recognized in *Antclizo*, where Lord Goff stated that, in such a situation: 'I cannot for myself think that an earlier refusal to respond to the

continued from page 167
the token damages awarded in fatal accident cases for loss of expectation of life). Lord Scarman, delivering the leading speech, said that the opinions delivered on either side in earlier authorities had displayed equally formidable logic and good sense and that, 'The question upon which opinions differed was, in truth, as old and as obstinate as the philosopher's stone itself'. (ibid, 189).

[173] [1973] AC 345, 463.

[174] [1973] AC 435, 455.

invitation should stand in your Lordships' way if they were now minded to accept it'.[175] He considered that such a situation should be analysed as a repeated invitation to depart from case A, not as an invitation to depart from case B as well as case A.[176] Secondly, as we shall see in section 8, the no-new-reasons constraint is not absolute. There are issues of fundamental principle to which it does not apply.

5. The Second Constraining Principle—Justified Reliance

The Practice Statement announces that their Lordships 'will bear in mind the danger of disturbing retrospectively the basis on which contracts, settlements of property and fiscal arrangements have been entered into and also the especial need for certainty as to the criminal law'.

This formulation might suggest that there is a special need for caution in regard to some areas of law which does not obtain elsewhere. It has indeed sometimes been interpreted in this way. For example, in *Khawaja*[177] Lord Fraser and Lord Bridge alluded to the fact that the case did not concern any of the matters specifically marked out for caution in the Practice Statement among their justifications for overruling *Zamir*.[178] It is submitted, however, that the bulk of the reasoning in the overruling cases supports a more principled distinction. If it seems likely that a class of the citizenry, as distinct from the executive, have acted on the basis of the law laid down in an earlier decision, they have a reliance interest which tells against exercising the overruling power; and such justified reliance may, in principle, be shown to exist in relation to any department of the law. The potentiality of this constraint will be considered first in relation to civil law and then in relation to criminal law.

(a) Civil Law

In practice, no doubt, commercial men, conveyancers and tax-planners are classes of citizens who are more likely than others to enter into transactions in conscious reliance on the law. In *Geelong*,[179] for example, the majority of the Australian High Court refused to overrule a 50-year-old decision which had interpreted legislation as not imposing strict liability on those who damage harbour installations. The decision had been severely criticized, but 'commerce has no doubt been conducted on the footing of the correctness of what this court decided'.[180]

In principle, however, there is no reason to mark out the reliance interests of entrepreneurs for special protection. Decisions in other areas of private and public law might give rise to equally legitimate expectations. *Khawaja* concerned immigration law, and the overruling was in the immigrant's favour. Had it been a

175 [1988] 2 All ER 513, 516.
176 Ibid.
177 Case v, p 144, above.
178 [1984] AC 74, 98, 125.
179 Case xvi, p 148, above.
180 (1970) 122 CLR 504, 517, Mactiernan and Minges JJ.

question of overruling unfavourable to immigrants, surely just as important reliance interests might have been at stake as in the case of commerce, property and fiscal arrangements. In *Queensland*,[181] justified reliance was one of the reasons advanced by those members of the Australian High Court who declined to overrule *Western Australia*, even though they adhered to the view that the majority in that case had been mistaken in their interpretation of the constitution. The earlier case had ruled that federal legislation providing for representation of the Australian territories in the Senate was valid. Although that decision was less than two years old, it had been acted on. Senators had been elected. Consequently, in the words of Gibbs J: 'To reverse the decision now would be to defeat the expectations of the people of the Territories that they would be represented . . . by senators entitled to vote—expectations and beliefs that were no less understandable because in my view they were constitutionally erroneous, and that were encouraged by the decision of this court'.[182]

The significance of the reliance factor should not be exaggerated. In the first place, developments in case law not involving the exercise of a final appellate court's power to overrule its own decisions may, in practice, be just as likely to disappoint expectations. Further, the degree of potentially unfair surprise varies enormously, depending on the age of the impugned decision and the extent to which parties have been put on guard against relying on it by previous adverse comments. In *Oldendorff*,[183] it was strongly urged on behalf of the charterers that to overrule *Aello* would be to upset expectations of parties to hundreds of charterparties which had been entered into on the basis of that test case.[184] This argument was not specifically addressed in the speeches in the House; but it was presumably held to have little force in view of Lord Reid's conclusion that, in the light of the subtle distinguishing to which the *Aello* decision had been subjected, 'there must be numerous cases where parties' advisers can only guess what line the court will take'.[185]

If overruling is otherwise right, there should be some clear demonstration of likelihood that a section of the public who have taken the earlier ruling into account in making their plans will be unfairly surprised, before overruling should be refused on this ground of constraint. In *Dick*,[186] Lord Kilbrandon dismissed as obviously untenable any argument that, by overruling *Darling* and so allowing a relative's action to proceed notwithstanding that the deceased had already commenced proceedings, the House might be upsetting justified reliance:

> But it cannot be said that this is the class of case in which persons may have acted in reliance on old established law; no prospective liability could possibly have been calculated, either by an employer or his underwriters, according to the contingency of

[181] Case xvii, p 148, above.
[182] (1978) 139 CLR 585, 600. Stephen J expressed a similar view (ibid 603–4). Aickin J, however, denied that the previous decision had been 'acted upon' in the sense of cases such as the *Geelong Harbour* case (ibid 630).
[183] Case i, p 143, above.
[184] [1974] AC 479, 523, 527.
[185] [1974] AC 479, 535.
[186] Case iii, p 144, above.

whether a hypothetical injured man would or would not have instituted proceedings before his death.[187]

In *Geelong*, the judges merely appealed to the way in which commerce had 'no doubt been conducted'. When the decision was upheld on appeal to the Privy Council, the Board took the view that the members of the High Court were much better qualified than their Lordships to assess the implications for commerce of such rulings because the High Court sat regularly in the capitals of the various states which are also the main ports and commercial centres of Australia.[188] Judicial notice of facts amounting to justified reliance may indeed be most appropriate in an area of lawyer's law.[189] Nevertheless, whatever the branch of law involved, the question should be one on which argument and even actual evidence should be invited.

In fact no case has so far been reported in which the House of Lords has indicated that the grounds for overruling might otherwise have been sufficient, save that 'the basis on which contracts, settlements of property and fiscal arrangements have been entered into' would be retrospectively disturbed. *Fitzleet*[190] (a revenue case),[191] and *Blumenthal*[192] (a commercial law case) were, as we have seen,[193] decided primarily with reference to the no-new-reasons principle and its finality rationale. On the other hand, the overruling in *Vestey*[194] of a 30-year-old decision, entailing as it did that income tax had been collected for years on an understanding of the law now retrospectively falsified, did far more than merely disturb fiscal arrangements. By its seeming generosity to the rich taxpayers involved, it produced a temporary political storm. The then Chancellor of the Exchequer, Sir Geoffrey Howe, appeared on the media to defend the Revenue: how could they be blamed if the Law Lords suddenly changed the basis on which taxation of the wealthy had proceeded?[195]

187 (1976) SLT 21, 28–9. In contrast, in *Lim Poh Choo* v *Camden and Islington Health Authority* [1980] AC 174, 189, Lord Scarman gave as one ground for the impropriety of overturning the rule that an unconscious plaintiff is entitled to recover substantial damages in respect of loss of amenities, the fact that claims had been settled on the basis of that rule so that judges would be perpetrating an injustice if they changed it. No reliance interest was at stake here since no such settlements would have been invalidated by an overruling. Rather, Lord Scarman appears to have been invoking the maxim 'treat like cases alike'. The applicability of this maxim in the overruling context is criticized below, pp 175–176.

188 [1974] AC 810, 819.

189 In *O'Brien* v *Robinson* [1973] AC 912, the House of Lords rejected an invitation to overrule *McCarrick* v *Liverpool Corporation* [1947] AC 219, which had construed landlords' implied covenants in housing legislation to keep a structure in repair as not imposing liability in respect of defects of which the landlord had neither knowledge nor notice. Lord Morris stated, at 925, that the decision 'must have guided landlords and tenants in their business transactions in the years since 1946'. (cf Lord Diplock, ibid 930.) In any event, the House approved the ruling in *McCarrick*.

190 Case x, p 146, above.

191 Lord Edmund-Davies recited that part of the Practice Statement which includes the cautionary admonition about such cases, but went on to point out that the fiscal arrangements at issue in the case had not been made in reliance on the decision which the House was asked to overrule—[1977] 3 All ER 996, 1001–1002.

192 Case xi, p 147, above.

193 Above, pp 159–160.

194 Case iv, p 144, above.

195 No mention is made in the *Vestey* opinions of the Practice Statement's reference to the 'danger of disturbing retrospectively the basis on which . . . fiscal arrangements have been entered into', Lord Wilberforce merely observing of the *Congreve* ruling that 'No doubt many persons have been taxed on the basis of it without resistance'—[1980] AC 1148, 1175.

Both *Vestey* and *Khawaja* constitute strong support for the view that justified reliance, as a constraint on the overruling power, does not operate at all in favour of the executive. In principle this seems correct. If private citizens have entered into transactions in conscious reliance on the law as laid down by a decision of the House of Lords, the transactions create legal rights of which, prima-facie, it is unfair that they should be retrospectively divested. Yet, so long as the House of Lords does not adopt the device of prospective overruling, such retrospective divesting is, in a clear case of reliance, the inevitable consequence of overruling. In the case of executive reliance, what are at issue are public powers not private rights. If it is concluded that an impugned decision gives the executive more power than by law it ought to have, it cannot be right to refuse to correct the situation for the future simply because that illegitimate power has been exercised in the past.

(b) Criminal Law

Shivpuri[196] and *Howe*[197] proceeded on the basis that if (but only if) it is plausible to suppose that subjects have acted in the faith that certain conduct is not criminal, then it should not be retrospectively made criminal by an overruling decision. These cases thus interpret the reference in the Practice Statement to 'the especial need for certainty as to the criminal law' as doing no more than extending reliance-interest considerations to that field of law. In *Knuller*,[198] however, the reference was given a wider significance, justifying a refusal to overrule a decision where such overruling would have been favourable to the accused. What their Lordships in *Knuller* supposed to be special about criminal law is, as we shall see, not easy to grasp.

In *Shivpuri*, the House unanimously reversed the interpretation of the Criminal Attempts Act 1981 which it had laid down a year before in *Ryan*. It was stressed that no-one could, in the nature of the case, have acted on the faith of the earlier decision.[199] The conduct which *Ryan* held does not, but *Shivpuri* establishes does, amount to a criminal attempt must be perpetrated by someone who believes he is committing an offence. He could hardly be induced to embark upon a course of conduct which he (for his part) is sure is criminal by the thought that, should it turn out that it is not, he will incur no criminal sanction. In *Howe*, the House unanimously reversed the rule laid down twelve years before in *Lynch*—that duress is a defence available to one who aids and abets murder. The question of reliance is not expressly mentioned in the opinions in *Howe*; but Lord Mackay may have had it in mind when he stated: 'The reasoning which persuaded this House in *R* v *Shivpuri* that it was appropriate to reconsider its earlier decision in *Anderton* v *Ryan* applies equally to the present case'.[200] Indeed, it does seem implausible that a man who is threatened with immediate death unless he participates in a murder would

196 Case vi, p 145, above.
197 Case vii, p 145, above.
198 Case ix, p 146, above.
199 [1987] AC 1, 23 Lord Bridge.
200 [1987] AC 417, 456.

be swayed in his decision by the knowledge that duress would (or would not) be available at his subsequent trial. He will either make the heroic choice to sacrifice his own life rather than that of the victim (which the members of the House in *Howe* considered that the common law requires of him), or he will take the path of what Lord Hailsham described as 'the coward' or 'the poltroon'.[201]

The question of justified reliance, in a criminal law context, was raised in the recent decision of the High Court of Australia in *Zecevic*.[202] At first sight, it appears bizarre to suggest that anyone acting in self-defence would use excessive force in reliance on those decisions (overruled in *Zecevic*) which had laid down that killing in such circumstances amounts to manslaughter rather than murder. There was, however, a different context in which the reliance factor could be considered. Might it not be that in trials now pending, defence lawyers had given advice as to appropriate pleadings in reliance on the older decisions and procedural steps been taken which would not have been but for those decisions? The majority thought this unlikely.[203] Deane J, however, in his dissenting opinion, considered that the 'possible consequences' of overruling the earlier decisions would include that some accused awaiting trial were faced by confessional statements which were made on the basis of correct professional advice about the then state of the law 'and which would not have been made if it had been known that the law was not as this court had authoritatively stated it to be'.[204]

Speculation about reliance of this kind seems a weak ground for constraining the overruling power. Does it not prove too much? When a final appellate court is minded to overrule a decision of an intermediate appellate court, it might always be the case that defence lawyers in pending trials have advised their clients on the basis of the law as laid down in the impugned decision. If the court is convinced that the decision is mistaken, should this possibility be considered a sufficient ground for leaving the law in its 'unsatisfactory' state? Much is expected of professional advisers including, one would have thought, taking the possibility of overruling into account.

Shivpuri, *Howe* and *Zecevic* all extended the reach of the criminal law, *Shivpuri* by interpreting an offence more broadly, *Howe* and *Zecevic* by reducing the scope of a defence. No serious issue of reliance may have arisen in these cases, but clearly it could in other situations. If, for example, some previous decision had narrowly construed the elements of the *actus reus* of a technical offence, it would be possible that, in reliance on that ruling, citizens had deliberately engaged in conduct held to fall outside the offence. In such circumstances, even if a final appellate court in a later case took the view that the narrow construction was mistaken, it would be prima-facie wrong to overrule the earlier decision. To do so would be retrospec-

201 [1987] AC 417, 432. It follows, presumably, that arguments from deterrence can play no part in the justification for withdrawing duress from murder. Where the absence of sanction cannot plausibly have given rise to reliance, its presence cannot plausibly deter.

202 Case xix, p 149, above.

203 (1987) 162 CLR 645, 664. Wilson, Dawson and Toohey JJ.

204 (1987) 162 CLR 645, 678.

tively to penalize conduct reasonably thought to be non-criminal at the time of its commission.

Two seemingly weighty arguments might be advanced for the view that the Practice Statement's reference to 'the especial need for certainty as to the criminal law' ought not to be understood, narrowly, as a mere extension to the criminal law of the reliance-interest considerations implicit in 'the danger of disturbing retrospectively the basis on which contracts, settlements of property and fiscal arrangements have been entered into'. The first appeals to the principle of prospectivity, the second to the maxim of formal justice—'treat like cases alike'. Deane J, in his dissenting judgment in *Zecevic*, invokes both these arguments (as well as the refined reliance considerations already discussed).

> The vice of such retrospective abolition of defence to a charge of murder lies not in the prospect of injustice to some imaginary killer who has killed on the basis that his crime will be reduced from murder to manslaughter in the event that he is found to have been acting excessively in self-defence. It lies in the fundamental injustice of inequality under the law which is unavoidable when the administration of the criminal law is reduced to a macabre lottery by what the late Professor Stone described as flagrant violation of the 'well established judicial policies of the criminal law in favorem libertatis, and against ex post facto punishment': *Precedent and Law* 1985 at p 190. It is simply wrong that an accused may be adjudged not guilty or guilty of murder according to the chance of whether his trial is completed before or after this court has abolished a defence which, under the law which the court itself had definitively settled . . . at the time the offence was committed, reduced the offence from murder to manslaughter.[205]

If the prospectivity principle is correctly invoked in this context, it entails that a final appellate court should never overrule a decision of its own if doing so extends the scope of the criminal law (assuming the absence of any practice of prospective overruling). *Shivpuri* and *Howe* would be unsupportable.[206] If the maxim 'treat like cases alike' is correctly invoked, it rules out retrospective overruling of a decision whether it extends or restricts the law's scope. It would condemn *Shivpuri* and *Howe*, but support *Knuller*.

Liberal opinion in western democracies gives an unqualified thumbs-down to retrospective criminal legislation. It is, for example, banned by the fourth protocol to the European Convention on Human Rights and Fundamental Freedoms. Does it follow that the House of Lords ought not to have overruled *Ryan* in *Shivpuri* or *Lynch* in *Howe*, nor the Australian High Court *Viro* in *Zecevic*, even if it was true that the overruled decisions were wholly erroneous? Before accepting such an implication, one should ask why the principle against retrospective criminal legislation enjoys such universal approval.

One explanation is that, from the point of view of deterrence theory, there is simply no point in a legislature enacting retrospective criminal laws. The problem with common law overruling is that, to achieve whatever deterrence or retributive

[205] (1987) 162 CLR 645, 677–8.

[206] Deane J does concede that there might be circumstances in which an overruling which extends the law would be justified, citing *Shivpuri* ((1987) 162 CLR 645, 677). He does not explain how any such case could escape the principled arguments to which he appeals.

value the new ruling is thought prospectively to promote, the ruling has to be retroactive as well—in the absence of adopting the device of prospective overruling. A more important assumption underlying the objection to retrospectivity is that it is unjust to punish someone who had good reason to believe that his conduct was not contrary to law when he engaged in it. This justification for the ban on retrospectivity goes no further than the consideration of justified reliance. It does not extend to cases where no-one could have acted on the faith of his conduct being exempt from criminal liability. It is accordingly suggested that, in so far as no-one has actually been prejudiced by relying on the old decision, the retrospective element in an overruling decision should not, merely because it exists, disqualify it as an improper exercise of judicial power.

The maxim—'treat like cases alike'—might be thought to point to a different objectionable feature in an overruling decision. As Deane J put it in *Zecevic*: 'It is simply wrong' that an accused may be adjudged not guilty or guilty according to whether his trial is completed before or after the overruling decision. The objection would apply whether the overruling has the effect of widening or narrowing the reach of the law. In *Knuller*, the fact that convictions had been obtained on the basis of the ruling in *Shaw* was appealed to as one of the grounds for not departing from that decision,[207] and this appeal may be interpreted as an invocation of the equality maxim.

The significance of the maxim for the doctrine of precedent is obscure.[208] Why should we think that, if some people who engaged in certain conduct have in the past been convicted or acquitted of crime, it is 'simply wrong' that others who engage in it should now be acquitted or convicted (as the case may be)? Wherein does the wrongness lie? Is it that X will feel aggrieved if he was convicted and Y is not (in the case of a decision restricting the scope of the criminal law), and Y will feel aggrieved if he is now convicted when X was not (in the case of a decision extending the law)? Clearly this cannot be the basis of the objection, since such grievances could arise as the result of wholly prospective legislation penalizing or de-penalizing conduct. The injustice of failing to treat like cases alike is a function of the action of the penalizing authority, not of resentment of those who perceive themselves to be differently treated. The legislature which enacts a new criminal statute treats like cases alike if the scope of the statute is universal. There would only be infringement of the formal maxim if we personified, as one entity, both the legislature which is now making the conduct criminal and the former legislature which did not, and concluded that this collective 'they' had allowed some people to engage in conduct without sanction whilst punishing others. Such cross-temporal unitary personification of different legislatures would be absurd. Yet it was just this kind of unitary personification of different benches of the Australian High Court which Deane J made in *Zecevic* when he spoke of a defence not being available,

[207] [1971] AC 435, 455 Lord Reid, 463, 466 Lord Morris, 489 Lord Simon. Lord Kilbrandon (ibid 495) expressed agreement with Lord Simon's reasoning.

[208] Cf Theodore Benditt, 'The Rule of Precedent', in Laurence Goldstein ed, *Precedent in Law*, Clarendon Press, 1987.

after 'this court' had changed the law which 'the court itself' had laid down. The same would be presupposed by a claim that: 'It would be unfair for the House of Lords in *Knuller* to have overruled *Shaw*, since that would mean that some conspirers to corrupt public morals would have been punished and others not so that *the House* would not be treating like cases alike?

The maxim—'treat like cases alike'—is relevant to the doctrine of precedent only where a court cannot, or has decided not to, overrule a prior decision and the question then arises whether the instant case has features making it, in some important respects, unlike the binding (or un-overruled) authority. When a court concedes the continuing validity, as part of the present law, of some proposition for which an earlier case stands as authority, it is its duty to assess the combined effect of that proposition and any proposition it now proposes to lay down, in terms of consistency and coherence, including any considerations of fairness to which the maxim may point. In that sense, it personifies 'the present law'. Where it proposes to overrule a decision, thus announcing that it no longer forms part of the law, no such duty exists. There is no need that the law of the past and the law of the present should speak with a consistent voice.

It might perhaps be argued that, in the context of the power to overrule a decision which would restrict the scope of the criminal law (as in *Knuller*), the maxim embodies, not so much a principle of fairness, but a special kind of policy argument connected with respect for legal processes. Faith in judicial infallibility is always under-mined when earlier decisions are announced to have been in error; but the result is poignantly subversive, it might be said, if it is made public that people have been imprisoned—or, worse still, executed[209]—on a wrong view of the law.[210] The argument has only to be spelled out to lose any credibility. We are dealing with a situation where, ex hypothesi, the court has reasons for holding that a decision was mistaken, but now has to consider whether to decline to overrule it because people have been convicted in reliance on it. How could respect for the judicial process be increased by an open announcement of the form: 'Those imprisoned persons ought not to have been held guilty of crime, but we will not say that the basis of their convictions, or of the convictions of others like them to be prosecuted hereafter, was legally erroneous?' To imagine the policy working, the finding that the earlier decision was mistaken would have to be kept secret. No pragmatic recommendation for suppressing reasons can, logically, constitute an explicit legal principle. A judge cannot say: 'I now give weight to the principle that the fact I have reasons to the contrary should not appear in my judgment'.

It is submitted that, as was assumed in *Shivpuri* and *Howe*, justified reliance by citizens, where it can be proved or reasonably inferred, should be regarded as the

[209] Lord Hailsham stated in *R* v *Cunningham* that if he had entertained any doubt about the merits of the proposition that an intention to cause grievous bodily harm was a sufficient *mens rea* for the crime of murder, one of the considerations which would have deterred him from overruling *DPP* v *Smith* and *Hyam* v *DPP* (see n 37 above), was that it would have amounted to saying that a number of persons executed before the abolition of the death penalty ought only to have been convicted of manslaughter ([1982] AC 567, 581).

[210] J. R. Spencer assumes that this was the operative argument in *Knuller*, and, not surprisingly, condemns such reasoning as 'monstrous' 'because it amounts to saying that where a person has been unjustly locked up in the past it is better to lock another person up unjustly than to admit that a mistake was made'—(1986) 45 *CLJ* 361.

only significance of the Practice Statement's reference to 'the especial need for certainty as to the criminal law' (so far as this reference concerns restraint on the overruling power).[211] Reliance by the executive does not count. On one further understanding of *Knuller*, this latter submission would be inconsistent with that case. When their Lordships indicated that it would be wrong to overrule *Shaw* because thirty convictions had been recorded on the basis of the law there laid down, could they be understood to be appealing, not to some principle of fairness nor to the manifestly unsound policy argument discussed in the last paragraph, but to the simple fact that the prosecution in the present case had relied on *Shaw* and such justified reliance should not be disappointed. If that were so, their approach would be in conflict with that taken in *Vestey* and *Khawaja*. In those cases it was never even suggested that the fact that the Revenue and the immigration authorities had relied on the impugned decisions was a reason for not overruling them.

The most plausible view of the puzzling references in *Knuller* to past convictions is, it is suggested, none of those discussed in this section, but the point made at the end of the last section about the no-new-reasons constraint. Their Lordships took note of the fact that experience of the application of the *Shaw* ruling did not suggest that the decision had produced 'unjust' consequences not taken into account when it was laid down.[212] If that is right, *Knuller* is not inconsistent with the submission that justified reliance, so far as it operates as a constraint on overruling, is limited to reliance by the citizen.

6. *The Third Constraining Principle—Comity with the Legislature*

Some of the overruling cases indicate support for the view that the House of Lords ought not to overrule a prior decision of its own where, subsequent to the decision, Parliament has acted on the assumption that the ruling in the earlier case represents the law. Thus in *Knuller*,[213] one of the grounds which appealed to some members of the House as support for their decision not to overrule *Shaw* was the fact that Parliament had enacted legislation in the area of public morals and had not chosen to abrogate the crime of conspiracy to corrupt public morals.[214] Similarly, in *La Pintada*[215] one reason given for not changing the common law rule which debars a plaintiff who is paid his contractual debt before proceedings are commenced from

[211] It is, however, arguable, as we shall see in section 7, that the reference may be taken to support more rather than less overruling of criminal cases, in that it justifies giving a limited scope to the mootness constraint.

[212] See the citation from Lord Reid at p 168, above. Lord Simon similarly states: 'A number of persons have been prosecuted and convicted on this basis. It was not contended that the rule has led to any injustice'—[1973] AC 435, 489.

[213] Case ix, p 146, above.

[214] [1973] AC 435, 465, 466 Lord Morris, 489 Lord Simon, 496 Lord Kilbrandon. Special significance was attached in these speeches to section 2 (4) of the Theatres Act 1968, as showing that Parliament recognized *Shaw* to be part of the law. The subsection provides that 'no person shall be proceeded against for an offence at common law of conspiring to corrupt public morals' in respect of performance of plays. This argument was rejected by Lord Diplock (ibid 480–1), who was for overruling *Shaw*, and by Lord Reid (455–6) who nevertheless opposed overruling because of the no-new-reasons constraint (p 168, above).

[215] Case xii, p 147, above.

recovering interest by way of general damages, was that Parliament had legislated in this area without changing this rule; and, consequently, to change it by judicial evolution of the law would be to usurp the role of the legislature.[216]

These decisions do not make clear what is the normative basis of the constraint. Presumably, it is something like comity with the legislature. If legislation subsequent to the impugned decision constitutes convincing evidence of a Parliamentary intention that the ruling it laid down should continue to be law, it would constitute lack of proper judicial co-operation if the House were nonetheless to ordain that the ruling shall not be law.

Comity of this kind is an extension of the constitutional deference due from the judiciary to a sovereign legislature. Of course, if Parliament expressly re-enacts the ruling in the earlier decision, there could be no question of its now being overruled; the House of Lords would simply be bound by the re-enacting statute. In our present context Parliament has, ex hypothesi, taken the view that the old ruling should constitute the law but has chosen not to incorporate it explicitly in legislation. For the House now to force Parliament into express enactment by an overruling decision would, so it is assumed, be an unfriendly and unco-operative step.

If this is the correct explanation of the comity principle, it should obviously be applied only with considerable circumspection. The drawing of an inference from the fact that Parliament has enacted legislation in the general area of the impugned decision of the existence of a legislative intention to confirm that decision must always be problematic. It is noteworthy that no such inference was even suggested in *Vestey*,[217] although many statutes had been passed in the field of income tax law since the overruled decision in *Congreve*.

Perhaps the best evidence from which it may be inferred that Parliament has decided that some ruling should continue to form part of the law is the fact that a law reform body has recommended its abrogation and Parliament has subsequently implemented other recommendations but not this one. In *La Pintada*, as we have seen,[218] Lord Brandon (whose reasoning was approved by all his colleagues) gave three distinct grounds for rejecting the invitation to overrule the *London-Chatham* case, notwithstanding that it unjustly denied interest on debts. The second reason concerned what is here called 'comity'. A Law Commission report dealing with the general question of interest on damages[219] had recommended that interest should be recoverable, *inter alia*, where late payment was made before proceedings were commenced. The Administration of Justice Act 1982 implemented other recommendations contained in the report, but not this one. Lord Brandon said:

[216] In *O'Brien* v *Robinson* (above, n 189) Lord Diplock was also apparently prepared to give some weight to this argument ([1973] AC 912, 930) although he had rejected its applicability in *Knuller* (n 214, above). Support for the argument can also be found in the speech of Lord Simon in *Taylor* v *Provan* [1975] AC 194, 220–21 and in the speech of Lord Fraser in *Hesperides Hotels Ltd* v *Muftizade* (n 100, above)—[1979] AC 508, 545.

[217] Case iv, p 144, above.

[218] Above, p 155.

[219] Law Com No 88, 1978.

My second main reason is that, when Parliament has given effect by legislation to some recommendations of the Law Commission in a particular field, but has taken what appears to be a policy decision not to give effect to a further such recommendation, any decision of your Lordships' House which would have the result of giving effect, by another route, to the very recommendation which Parliament appears to have taken that policy decision to reject, could well be regarded as an unjustifiable usurpation by your Lordships' House of the functions which belong properly to Parliament, rather than as a judicial exercise in departing from an earlier decision on the ground that it has become obsolete and could still, in a limited class of cases, continue to cause some degree of injustice.[220]

Lord Brandon went on to reject an argument, advanced on behalf of the ship-owners, which appealed to the course taken by the House in *British Railways Board* v *Herrington*.[221] Parliament had passed the Occupiers' Liability Act 1957 implementing some of the recommendations contained in the third report of the Law Reform Committee of 1954, but not those concerning liability to child trespassers; and it was argued in *Herrington* that that was a reason for not overruling *Addie*. As Lord Brandon put it in *La Pintada*: 'Your Lordships' House, however, rejected that contention and did make a decision which involved *at least some degree of departure* from *Addie*'s case'.[222] He rejected the *Herrington* analogy: unlike the issue in *La Pintada*, the law relating to child trespassers had been 'a matter of serious importance which needed to be dealt with without further delay'; and Lord Reid in *Herrington* had suggested that Parliament's silence might be attributable, not to a rejection of the recommendations of the Law Reform Committee, but rather to Parliament's being unable to make up its mind what to put in the place of the existing law and leaving it to the courts to work out a solution, whereas, it was very doubtful whether that explanation could account for Parliament's decision in the 1982 Act not to give effect to the Law Commission's recommendation.[223]

Since what was in question was whether the House of Lords should exercise its Practice Statement power, the argument based on *Herrington* could have been rejected on a much simpler ground. The comity principle—that the House should not overrule what Parliament has elected not to repeal—appears to have been a major consideration influencing the majority in *Herrington* not to make unequivocal use of its Practice Statement power.[224]

Nevertheless, Lord Brandon's reasons for distinguishing *Herrington* are significant. They suggest, firstly, that the comity constraint should not be understood as an absolute bar on the overruling power, in that there might be urgent situations where the House should act notwithstanding Parliament's seeming acceptance of an old rule. Secondly, they indicate that the existence of a law reform recommendation which has not been implemented in subsequent legislation should not be

[220] [1985] AC 104, 130. If Lord Brandon had been free to consult Hansard, he would have found evidence to support the inference which he drew as to the policy decision taken by Parliament; see North [1984] *LMCLQ* 365.

[221] [1972] AC 877.

[222] [1985] AC 104, 130 (italics supplied).

[223] Ibid.

[224] The argument, which had been strongly advanced on behalf of the appellants ([1972] AC 877, 884), was accepted by Lord Morris (ibid 904) and by Lord Wilberforce (921), and rejected, with hesitation, by Lord Reid (897).

taken as conclusive evidence that Parliament has decided that the law should not be changed. In *Herrington* it would have been preferable, it is submitted, if the House of Lords had frankly exercised the Practice Statement power to overrule *Addie* in spite of the comity constraint rather than, as it did, finding tortuous grounds on which the law as there laid down could be developed without such overruling.[225]

7. *The Fourth Constraining Principle—Mootness*

In the United States, where the Supreme Court plays a much more central role in legal development than does the final appellate court in any other common law jurisdiction, one of the important constitutional techniques developed for adjusting the sphere of the judiciary with that of the legislature, is the doctrine of mootness. According to the doctrine, courts should not undertake review and development of the law where to do so would have no bearing on any litigated dispute. Something comparable exists in the United Kingdom, although less technical terminology is used. Courts will sometimes refrain from undertaking a review of the authorities even though pressed to do so by the parties if nothing in the case at bar will turn on a question, on the ground that such an undertaking would be 'only of academic interest'. (The terminology reflects an interesting assumption about the contrast between the practically important and the merely academic.)

In *Antclizo*,[226] this self-imposed limitation on the courts' proper role in legal review was invoked by the House of Lords in the context of the 1966 Practice Statement power. In *Bremer Vulkan* it had laid down that a party to an arbitration agreement who perpetrated protracted delay in bringing his arbitration claim could not thereby be taken to have repudiated the agreement. The reason was that a mutual obligation rests on both parties to co-operate with the reference. The House in *Antclizo* was asked to depart from this decision.

Lord Goff, delivering the only leading speech, noted that the alleged mutual obligation to proceed with the reference to arbitration had been generally considered to bear no relation to commercial reality.

> Indeed, it is plain that (if it exists) it is honoured more in the breach than in the observance, because in arbitration, as in litigation, where the claimant does not actively pursue his claim, it is the usual practice of the other party, founded on sheer common sense, to do nothing in the hope that the claim will simply die a natural death. In such a case, to expect the respondent to stir up an apparently moribund claim in arbitration proceedings against him is most unreal: . . .[227]

Lord Goff went on to point out that all the members of the Court of Appeal in the present case had expressed anxiety about the present state of the law on this topic 'in terms which have become depressingly familiar'. He said that there was little doubt that the Court of Appeal had given leave to appeal in the hope that the House might undertake a full-scale review of the matter and even that they might exercise

225 Above, p 141.
226 Case xiii, p 147, above.
227 [1988] 2 All ER 513, 515.

their Practice Statement power to depart from *Bremer Vulkan*.[228]

What stood in the way of overruling it? None of the three principles of constraint so far discussed were apparently in point. The adverse reception of the case in commercial circles provided unforeseen consequences, and attempts to distinguish it in subsequent litigation had shown that it had brought about unforeseen uncertainty in the law. There were consequently 'new reasons' within the first constraining principle.[229] No argument was advanced that claimants to arbitration had deliberately delayed in bringing forward references in reliance on *Bremer Vulkan* (within the second constraining principle); and there was no question of legislation in the general area subsequent to the decision so as to give rise to comity considerations (within the third).

However, on the facts of the dispute before the House in *Antclizo*, it was found that the charterers' appeal must fail whether or not *Bremer Vulkan* was overruled. In dismissing claims by the charterers based on mutual agreement to abandon and estoppel, the lower courts had made findings of fact which would entail that, even if protracted delay could amount to repudiation, there had been no repudiation by the owners. Lord Goff stated that, before the power to depart from an earlier decision could be exercised, the House of Lords must be satisfied, not only that the decision and its reasoning were erroneous, but also that it would be of relevance to the resolution of the dispute in the instant case.

> Your Lordships' House has repeatedly stressed that they will not embark on an inquiry into an issue which is only of academic interest: . . . A fortiori they should not do so where the inquiry involves a review of a previous decision of your Lordships' House, because it cannot be right to hold, obiter, that such a previous decision was wrong.[230]

It has earlier been suggested[231] that what makes it difficult to find a settled jurisprudence of overruling is the common failure of the House of Lords, when overruling or declining to overrule an earlier decision to explain why the course adopted is or is not distinguishable from that taken in other overruling decisions. *Antclizo* is a classic instance of this failure. Lord Goff asserts that obiter overrulings 'cannot be right'. Yet in two previous decisions (*Shivpuri*[232] and *Howe*[233]) that is precisely what was done.

In *Shivpuri*, all the members of the House concurred in departing from *Ryan* under the Practice Statement power, yet at least two of their Lordships took the view that *Ryan* was distinguishable and that Shivpuri's appeal would have been dismissed even if *Ryan* had not been overruled. Mrs Ryan thought she was buying a stolen video cassette recorder whereas (as was assumed) the recorder had not actually been stolen. Shivpuri believed he was assisting in the import of prohibited drugs, whereas the suitcase he went to collect contained only snuff. As the result of

228 Ibid.
229 Above, p 167.
230 [1988] 2 All ER 513, 516.
231 Above, pp 137–138.
232 Case vi, p 145, above.
233 Case vii, p 145, above.

the overruling of *Ryan*, both kinds of conduct are now criminal attempts in English law. Lord Hailsham LC, whilst concurring in the overruling, contended that, whereas Shivpuri's sole intent from start to finish was to defeat a customs prohibition, the intention of Mrs Ryan was merely to buy a particular item at a knock-down price. Consequently, whether or not Mrs Ryan was guilty of an offence, Shivpuri certainly was.[234] Lord Mackay agreed with this view,[235] and Lord Elwyn-Jones may also have done so.[236]

In *Howe*, overruling *Lynch* was not technically required in order to dismiss the appeals. *Lynch* had laid down that duress was an available defence to those charged with aiding and abetting murder. In *Howe*, the defence had been allowed at the trial of those defendants charged with such secondary participation. The only issue before the House which strictly had to be decided in order to dispose of the appeals was whether the defence should be extended to the actual killer. That question could have been answered in the negative without overruling *Lynch*. Yet, in Lord Hailsham's words, the case afforded 'an ideal and never to be repeated opportunity' to review the whole matter and, by overruling *Lynch* under the Practice Statement power, to deny a duress defence to all kinds of murderers.[237]

It might be thought that a distinction between *Shivpuri* and *Howe*, on the one hand, and *Antclizo*, on the other, is to be found by reference to the law's need to be free from over-subtle distinctions. We have seen that the elimination of incoherence is one of the goals of 'certainty' in the law.[238] The suggestion would be that, whilst the House should not overrule a decision where doing so cannot affect the outcome of the present appeal, yet there is an exception where such an overruling is the only way to eliminate incoherent rulings. Certainly, in *Shivpuri* those members of the House who believed *Ryan* was distinguishable also evidently concluded that the law would be improved if it did not incorporate esoteric distinctions between different kinds of impossible attempts. So too in *Howe*, the majority were convinced that it was indefensible to have different duress rules for different classes of murderers.[239] The suggestion must, however, be rejected. In *Antclizo* Lord Goff recited a whole string of distinctions which had been canvassed in cases after *Bremer Vulkan* in an attempt to circumvent it, some of which remained open for argument.[240] Overruling *Bremer Vulkan* would have enabled the jungle to be cleared, but the mootness constraint (so it was held) prevented this being done.

In other contexts, mootness is a matter of degree. Very often, where a point of law has been strenuously argued on either side, a court will not take the view that, because a resolution of the issue is not crucial to the outcome, it should be regarded

[234] [1987] AC 1, 12.
[235] [1987] AC 1, 23–4.
[236] The report of *Shivpuri* appearing in the All England Law Reports contains a sentence in which Lord Elwyn-Jones agreed with Lord Hailsham's view on this point ([1986] 2 All ER 334, 337). The sentence is omitted from the report of the case appearing in the Law Reports Appeal Cases ([1987] AC 1, 13).
[237] [1987] AC 417, 427.
[238] Above, p 156.
[239] Below, pp 184–185.
[240] [1988] 2 All ER 513, 515.

as of 'only academic interest'. One example is the decision of the House of Lords in *Hedley Byrne*,[241] where the House recast the law on liability for negligent mistatements even though, on the facts, there had been an effective disclaimer of responsibility. Another is the recent decision of the Court of Appeal in *Ashburn Anstalt* v *Arnold*,[242] where the court, after exhaustively reviewing the authorities, ruled that a contractual licence does not constitute an interest in land, even though it had found that the present case concerned a lease. On the other hand, courts will not stray far beyond the issues arising from the facts of cases and engage in a review of the law simply because that is what the parties would like them to do. The primary function of a common law court is seen to be the resolution of disputed claims. It has an inescapable secondary function as declarer of the law with precedential authority; and where a superior court engages in the review or overruling of earlier authorities, this second function is, at least in substance, quasi-legislative. The point about mootness of issues is the keeping of the secondary function from becoming primary. Courts may inevitably 'make law' in doing what they must do (settling disputes); but they should not go out of their way to make law, for that is the province of the legislature.

The approach taken in *Anteliza* presupposes that the mootness constraint is particularly compelling when the House of Lords is asked to exercise its Practice Statement power. However erroneous an earlier decision is thought to be, it should not be overruled where such overruling could, on the facts, make no difference to the outcome of the appeal. The justification for taking this stance—such as it is—must lie in the assumption that an overruling by the House is a particularly flagrant instance of its secondary, quasi-legislative function.

There remains the problem of reconciling this approach with that taken in *Shivpuri* and *Howe*. This can only be done by assuming that the mootness constraint is compelling only in relation to civil, not to criminal, law overrulings.[243] The Practice Statement speaks of the 'especial need for certainty as to the criminal law'. As we saw in section 5, this was intended as a counsel of restraint in overruling. In the present context, it may be appealed to as a consideration favouring more overruling, as a modification to the mootness constraint. In the modern English legal system, it is recognized that the superior courts have a special responsibility to keep the criminal law under review and, in particular, to iron out uncertainties which may be bedevilling the framing of indictments and directions to juries. It would be a sanguine commentator who claimed that they had achieved uniform success in the discharge of this function; but that the responsibility exists is recognized, *inter alia*, by the practice of the Court of Appeal in certifying whether appeals raise issues of general public importance and in framing questions for consideration by the House of Lords, and by the practice of the Attorney-General in referring acquittals to the Court of Appeal for rulings on points of law.

241 *Hedley Byrne and Co Ltd* v *Heller and Partners Ltd* [1964] AC 465.

242 [1989] Ch 1.

243 It has some force even in regard to criminal cases, in that the House will not, by an obiter pronouncement, overrule a decision where the issue has not been fully argued—see *R* v *Sakhuja* [1973] AC 152, 196 Lord Cross, 200 Lord Salmon.

It is therefore not surprising that the House of Lords has, in the context of criminal appeals, not taken the *Antclizo* line—that it should never overrule a decision of its own by a strictly obiter pronouncement. In *Shivpuri* and *Howe*, it took the opportunity to clarify the law, irrespective of any mootness considerations.

8. Fundamental Principles

It has been argued in section 4 of this article that the overruling cases have adopted, as the primary constraint on the exercise of the overruling power, the no-new-reasons principle. According to this principle, if all the reasons bearing on a contested proposition of law which are advanced in the present case were considered in the earlier decision, that decision ought not to be overruled merely on the ground that the members of the present court take a different view of the conclusion entailed by those reasons. The rationale of this principle is the importance attached to finality.

The decision of the House of Lords in *Howe*,[244] and the views of two of the members of the Australian High Court in *Queensland*,[245] suggest that there may be fundamental principles which escape this constraint. With many disputed questions of law, those who take one view may properly concede to their opponents that—once all reasons on either side have been canvassed—all that divides them is a subjective weighing of those reasons. There are two 'tenable' views,[246] two 'eminently possible' views,[247] 'room for a difference of opinion' where the question depends on 'finely balanced considerations',[248] or the answer is 'so much a matter of impression'.[249] With other disputed questions, both sides share a perception that there is an objectively correct answer and each takes the view—no doubt, with respect—that the other side is objectively mistaken. Where questions of the latter sort relate to issues of fundamental importance, the present court should overrule an earlier decision thought to be wrong even if nothing is argued now which was not argued in the earlier case.

(a) When There Need Be No New Reasons

In *Howe* the House of Lords were asked to extend the ruling in *Lynch*[250] (to the effect that duress may be pleaded as a defence by those charged with aiding and abetting murder) and to hold that it could be pleaded by the actual killer. They declined to do this and, instead, took the opportunity to overrule *Lynch* and to lay down that duress could never be a defence to any kind of murder. All but Lord

[244] Case vii, p 145, above.
[245] Case xvii, p 148, above.
[246] Lord Pearson in *Hudson* [1972] AC 944, 996, cited above, p 157.
[247] Lord Wilberforce in *Fitzleet* [1977] 3 All ER 966, 999, cited above, pp 159–160; and Lord Brandon in *Blumenthal* [1981] 1 AC 854, 913, cited above, p 160.
[248] Majority judgment in *Jones* v *The Commonwealth* (1987) 61 ALJR 348, 349, cited above, p 165.
[249] Lord Simon in *Hudson* [1972] AC 944, 1024, cited above, p 165.
[250] *Lynch* v *DPP for Northern Ireland* [1975] AC 653.

Hailsham LC[251] held that, in the context of this defence, no rational distinction could be drawn between principles in the first and second degree.[252] They were unanimously of the view that the right answer to the question: 'does the common law permit those charged with murder to avail themselves of the defence of duress?' was 'no'.

Did anything bear on the question which had not been considered in *Lynch*? Were there any new reasons? So far as doctrine is concerned, it was not suggested in *Howe* that some authoritative statement of the common law had not been drawn to the attention of their Lordships in *Lynch*. In both cases, consideration was given to important analogous rules whose continuing validity might affect the coherence of the law should duress be admitted as a defence—such as the rule in *Dudley and Stephens*[253] which denies necessity as a defence to murder, the exclusion of murder from the defence of marital coercion,[254] and the rule that superior orders generally constitute no defence as accepted in the Nuremburg war trials. As to utility model reasoning, account was taken in both cases of the argument that, should duress not be available, there might nevertheless be sufficient flexibility built into the criminal justice system in virtue of executive action—such as prosecutorial discretion, the Crown's prerogative of mercy and the parole system. The possible consequential dangers of terrorists, gang-leaders and kidnappers making use of the defence as a shield for their terrified underlings was an important consideration in *Howe*, as it was in the reasoning of the majority in the intervening Privy Council decision in *Abbott*[255] (where it had been held that *Lynch* could not be taken to have altered the common law rule that duress was no defence to the actual killer). This policy consideration was, however, fully canvassed in *Lynch*, where it was among the factors persuading the minority that duress should be no defence to any species of murder,[256] whilst the majority held that it carried little force since juries could be trusted to reject specious defences. In *Howe*, Lord Mackay suggested that the unworkability of the distinction between different degrees of murder (in the context of the duress defence) had become more evident since *Lynch*,[257] citing the decision of the Court of Appeal in *R* v *Graham*.[258] But the question whether such a distinction was appropriate had been fully considered in *Lynch*.[259]

There was one new development since *Lynch* on which two of their Lordships in *Howe* placed some reliance. The Law Commission, in its report on general defences,[260] had recommended that duress should be available in all classes of murder, and Parliament had not acted on this recommendation. The significance of this development is obscure.

251 [1987] AC 417, 429.
252 [1987] AC 417, 437 Lord Bridge, 438 Lord Brandon, 445 Lord Griffiths, 452–3 Lord Mackay.
253 *R* v *Dudley and Stephens* (1884) 14 QBD 273.
254 Criminal Justice Act 1925, s 47; Criminal Justice Act (Northern Ireland) 1945, s 37.
255 [1977] AC 755.
256 Lord Simon coined the phrase: 'A charter for terrorists, gang-leaders and kidnappers'—[1975] AC 653, 688.
257 [1987] AC 417, 457.
258 [1982] 1 WLR 294.
259 The distinction was rejected by the minority—[1975] AC 653, 691–3 Lord Simon, 702 Lord Kilbrandon—and by one member of the majority—[1975] AC 653, 714–15 Lord Edmund-Davies.
260 Law Com No 83, 1977.

Lord Bridge stated that his conviction as to the impropriety of the House of Lords in *Lynch* introducing duress as a defence to murder 'is now immensely strengthened by the knowledge that Parliament, even against the background of the plainly unsatisfactory present state of the law, has in ten years taken no action on the report of the Law Commission'.[261] We have seen, in the context of the comity constraint on overruling, that the House of Lords is sometimes prepared to draw inferences as to Parliament's will from its enactment of legislation in a general area of law. That may be a questionable procedure, but it is surely far more questionable to draw any such inference from its failure to enact anything at all. There may have been any number of reasons why Parliament refrained from giving legislative effect to the Law Commission's proposals on general defences other than a considered disapproval of the particular suggestion about extending duress to all classes of murder—of which pressure of other Parliamentary business is only the most obvious. Parliamentary inaction was no firmer a basis for inferring disapproval of the Law Commission's recommendation than it was for inferring approval of the *Lynch* ruling.

Lord Griffiths said of Parliament's ten-year inertia: 'This must at least be some indication that the community at large are not pressing for a change in the law to remedy a perceived injustice'.[262] Community perceptions of what is just are certainly taken into account by courts among the consequentialist considerations applicable within what I have called 'the utility model of rationality'. The majority in *Lynch* had supposed that contemporary opinion would consider it unjust if someone who acted solely to save his life was afterwards convicted as a murderer. They may have been mistaken in their guess about public opinion, but it seems implausible in the extreme to derive evidence that they were so mistaken from what Parliament has not done.

In substance, then, there were no new reasons since *Lynch*, and *Howe* must be regarded as exemplifying a qualification on the first constraining principle. Although, usually, a final appellate court ought not to overrule an earlier decision of its own if nothing is urged by way of argument now which was not urged then, there are fundamental matters as to which it is enough that the present court is sure that the earlier decision was simply wrong. The House of Lords in *Howe* stressed that the *Lynch* ruling had illegitimately purported to alter a fundamental principle of the historic common law.[263]

Such a conclusion raises complex philosophical and jurisprudential issues. In particular, two questions must be distinguished. First, is it, as a matter of critical morality, just that a person who commits murder under the immediate threat of death or serious injury should be convicted of that crime? Secondly, does the common law embody its own distinctive answer to this first question?

The majority in *Lynch* took the view that it is not just for one acting under sufficient duress to be convicted of murder, on the grounds that the criminal law

261 [1987] AC 417, 437.

262 [1987] AC 417, 443.

263 [1987] AC 417, 430 Lord Hailsham LC, 437 Lord Bridge, 438 Lord Brandon, 439 Lord Griffiths, 448–9 Lord Mackay.

should not demand more in the way of self-sacrifice than can be expected of the ordinary citizen, and that the ordinary citizen cannot be asked to exhibit that degree of heroism which would be required for a man to sacrifice his own life rather than to kill another.[264] From this view Lord Hailsham LC vigorously dissented in *Howe*:

> I have known in my own lifetime of too many acts of heroism by ordinary human beings of no more than ordinary fortitude to regard a law as either 'just' or 'humane' which withdraws the protection of the criminal law from the innocent victim and casts the cloak of its protection upon the coward and the poltroon in the name of a 'concession to human frailty'.[265]

The second question raised by the fundamental issue of principle in these cases revolves about competing conceptions of the common law. On one view, the common law consists of that body of case law which the courts in any particular jurisdiction have evolved at any particular time, so that there may be, in theory, as many common laws as there are common law jurisdictions. Lord Diplock appealed to this conception in *Cassell and Co Ltd* v *Broome*, in support of the view that different rules about punitive damages might properly have emerged in different jurisdictions.

> It has survived because the common law subsumes a power in judges to adapt its rules to the changing needs of contemporary society . . . Your Lordships have the duty, when occasion offers, to supervise the exercise of this power by English courts. Other supreme appellate tribunals exercise a similar function in other countries which have inherited the English common law at various times in the past.[266]

On another view, the common law is a supra-jurisdictional system consisting, in part, of fundamental rules and principles contained in those sources which constitute a common historical heritage. Thus, for example, in *Parker* v *R*,[267] the High Court of Australia refused to follow the decision of the House of Lords in *DPP* v *Smith*,[268] in so far as that decision accepted, as a proposition of the common law relating to malice aforethought in murder, that a man is presumed to intend the natural consequences of his act. The High Court took this course, not because the different circumstances of Australia justified a different rule, but because, in its view, the House of Lords had misstated a fundamental principle of the common 'common law'. Dixon CJ, speaking on this matter with the authority of all his

[264] [1975] AC 653, 670 Lord Morris, 684 Lord Wilberforce, 715 Lord Edmund-Davies.
[265] [1987] AC 417, 432.
[266] [1972] AC 1027, 1127. On this basis, Lord Diplock denied that the decision of the House of Lords in *Rookes* v *Barnard* [1964] AC 129 was out of line with other common law jurisdictions providing any good reason for departing from it. On the other hand, in *Hesperides Hotels* v *Muftizade* (n 100, above) one reason given for the House of Lords not departing from its decision in the *Moçambique* case was the fact that the rule prohibiting actions for trespass in respect of foreign land was followed in almost all common law jurisdictions [1979] AC 508, 536 Lord Wilberforce, 545 Lord Fraser. Lord Salmon and Lord Keith concurred with Lord Wilberforce's speech (ibid 542, 545).
[267] (1963) 111 CLR 610.
[268] [1961] AC 290.

colleagues, stated that there were 'fundamental propositions' laid down in *Smith*'s case which were 'misconceived and wrong'.[269]

The common law is a notoriously elusive concept. For present purposes it is enough to suggest that it embodies elements from both these competing conceptions. It comprises rules and principles emanating from certain English historical texts relating to fundamental rights against the executive and fundamental mutual responsibilities of citizens, together with a mass of particular rulings based on judicial assessments of public policy. The former are basic to the individualistic conception of human society which underlies the common law and are both relatively timeless in quality and also part of the common stock of political aspirations wherever the common law has taken root. The latter change with new social developments and may be thought to require different answers in different jurisdictions because of local circumstances.

Into which category should the duress-murder rule be fitted? The *Lynch* majority held that, even though the bulk of authority was against the admission of duress as a defence, they could develop the common law so as to take account of what they saw as changed community opinion about the just solution to the question. In the view of the majority of the Privy Council in *Abbott*, the House of Lords' decision in *Lynch* could not have had the effect of altering the common law applicable in Trinidad and Tobago. In the view of all the Lords in *Howe*, the rule that duress is no defence to murder is a fundamental principle of the common law which only the legislature should change. The *Lynch* decision had laid down English law for the time being, but it could not change the common law on such a question and should not have tried to do so. Lord Hailsham, as we have seen, was quite certain that the right answer to the moral question was that those who killed under duress were justly convicted as murderers. The other members of the House of Lords were not so emphatic as to that. They were, however, convinced that, whatever the objectively morally correct answer, the common law's answer—given the supreme importance it attached to the value of human life—was Hale's answer: 'He ought rather to die himself than kill an innocent'.[270]

It was suggested in section 4 of this article that perceived 'wrongness' in an earlier decision may be either 'structural' or 'ultimate'. It is structural when pertinent reasons were not taken into account. It is ultimate when a mistaken conclusion was derived from certain reasons. It is now necessary to emphasize an important sub-division within perceptions of ultimate wrongness. In the ordinary run of controverted legal questions, what separates those on either side is a matter of subjective impression added to a set of reasons. There are, in Lord Pearson's words in *Hudson*,[271] two 'tenable' views; or in the words of Lord Wilberforce in *Fitzleet*[272]

[269] (1963) 111 CLR 610, 632. Similarly the Privy Council, in hearing an appeal from the Isle of Man, has asserted that the true common law on the question of malice aforethought had not been affected by *Smith*'s case—*Frankland* v *R* [1987] AC 576.

[270] [1987] AC 417, 439, 443–4 Lord Griffiths; 448–9, 455–6 Lord Mackay. Lord Bridge expressed agreement with Lord Griffiths and Lord Mackay (ibid 438). Lord Brandon agreed with Lord Mackay (ibid).

[271] Cited above, p 157.

[272] Cited above, pp 159–160.

and Lord Brandon in *Blumenthal*,[273] 'two eminently possible views'; or, in the words of the majority judgment of the High Court of Australia in *Jones*,[274] 'room for a difference of opinion'. We may call these instances of 'ultimate impressionistic wrongness'. They may relate to questions of statutory construction (*Hudson*, *Fitzleet*, *Jones*), or of common law (*Blumenthal*). Ultimate impressionistic wrongness is the primary domain of the no-new-reasons constraint. With other examples of ultimate wrongness, the perception may be that the question has an objectively right answer. Reasonable lawyers may, of course, differ as to what the answer is; but it is not supposed on either side that there are two views each of which, in the light of the authorities, is equally plausible. We may call these instances of 'ultimate objective wrongness'.

Within this category of ultimate objective wrongness, a yet further sub-division must be made if we are to reconcile the approach taken to overruling its own decisions by the House of Lords, on the one hand, in *Howe*, and, on the other hand, in *Knuller*.[275] If what is at stake is a fundamental rule or principle, then an earlier decision which is perceived to be ultimately and objectively wrong should be overruled. That should be done even though—the wrongness being ultimate and not structural—nothing is argued on the hearing of the present appeal which was not also put forward in the earlier case. Fidelity to objective legal truth on fundamental matters prevails over the finality rationale which underlies the no-new-reasons constraint (*Howe*). If, on the other hand, the rule or principle is not fundamental, the House should not overrule its earlier decision even on the assumption that it was ultimately and objectively mistaken. The finality rationale holds sway (*Knuller*). In the case of rules and principles of the common law, whether they are fundamental or not will turn on judgments about the importance of the rights against the executive or mutual responsibilities of citizens which they embody.

As we have seen, there were no new reasons in *Knuller*.[276] Nor was it suggested in any of the speeches that the issue was one as to which there were two equally plausible views. The decision in *Shaw*'s case, which the House was asked to overrule, was uniformly assumed to be both ultimately and objectively either right or wrong. A crucial topic on which their Lordships were divided concerned the proposition for which *Shaw* was authority. It had been argued for the appellants that *Shaw* raised a basic issue of constitutional liberty involving the respective functions of the legislature and the courts, since it was part of the ratio decidendi of the case that there was a residual power in the judiciary to create new offences in the area of public morals.[277] Lord Diplock, who favoured overruling *Shaw*, accepted that argument.[278] All the other members of the House decisively rejected it. They held that *Shaw* was authority merely for the proposition that the common

[273] Cited above, p 160.
[274] Cited above, p 165.
[275] Case ix, p 147, above.
[276] Above, p 168.
[277] [1973] AC 435, 441–2.
[278] [1973] AC 435, 469, 479.

law recognized the existence of one particular offence, a conspiracy to corrupt public morals.[279] That narrow proposition might have been objectively wrong—Lord Reid was quite sure that it was[280]—but it was evidently not an issue of such fundamental importance as to escape the finality constraint.

In *Howe*, the crucial question was whether the refusal of the historic common law to admit duress as a defence to murder was something which could properly be modified by judicial decision. The House of Lords had given an affirmative answer to that question in *Lynch*. In *Howe*, their Lordships took the view that that decision had been objectively wrong, and also that the principle involved was of such fundamental importance that *Lynch* must be overruled.

Fundamental questions of this sort comprise only a portion of the common law. Need they be limited to the common law? Obviously, in jurisdictions where there is in force a written constitution, those aspects of the common law which concern rights against the state may be supplemented by or—as in the case of the United States—largely superseded by constitutional principles. What divided the High Court of Australia in *Queensland* was precisely whether the issue before the court was of the fundamental kind which is not subject to the no-new-reasons constraint.

It is arguable that, in a jurisdiction where there is a power of judicial review over ordinary legislation, the final appellate court ought always to regard itself as free to overrule its own decisions on constitutional matters. In *Thomas*,[281] Latham CJ, having accepted the general principle that the court should not overrule a decision where nothing has changed but the composition of the court, added: 'It may be that considerations are present in constitutional cases which do not arise in other cases'.[282]

The *Queensland* case involved the interpretation of constitutional provisions, but it also raised a basic question about the nature of Australian federalism. Australia is a democracy, which suggests that all its citizens, including those resident in the territories, should be entitled to elect representatives in both houses of the Australian Parliament. On the other hand, Australia is a federation of states, which suggests that only representatives of the states should be included in the Commonwealth Parliament. In the *Western Australia* case,[283] four out of seven members of the High Court took the view that the democratic principle should prevail over the federal principle. Two years later in the *Queensland* case, because of one change in the composition of the court, the situation was that four members considered that the federal principle prevailed. Of those four, Gibbs and Stephen JJ were of the view that they should not depart from the *Western Australia* case—although they considered it to have been wrongly decided—because no new

[279] [1973] AC 435, 459 Lord Reid, 465 Lord Morris, 490 Lord Simon, 496 Lord Kilbrandon.

[280] [1973] AC 435, 455. Lord Morris considered that *Shaw*'s case was correctly decided, but stated that he would not have favoured reviewing it even if he had been of a different opinion—ibid 463. Lord Simon thought that *Shaw* should not be overruled, whether wrong or right, so that it was unnecessary to express any opinion whether that decision was 'in an abstract juridical sense' correct in law—ibid 484. Lord Kilbrandon agreed with Lord Simon's speech—ibid 495.

[281] Case xiv, p 147, above.

[282] (1949) 77 CLR 493, 496.

[283] (1975) 134 CLR 201.

reasons were in play. Barwick CJ and Aickin J, however, regarded it as their judicial duty to rule on the question according to their view about the right answer, fidelity to legal truth (as they conceived it) being more important than finality.

Stephen J, though adhering to the opinion that *Western Australia* was mistaken, classified that decision as an instance of what I have termed 'ultimate impressionistic wrongness'. He said that the case 'was very much one upon which different minds might reach different conclusions, no one view being inherently entitled to any pre-eminence as conforming better than others to principle or to precedent'.[284] We have seen that the no-new-reasons constraint holds sway in the context of decisions so classified.

Gibbs J, in contrast, based his adherence to the view that the *Western Australia* decision was erroneous on what he took to be the right answer to a difficult question of constitutional principle. In other words, for him that case was an example of what I have called 'ultimate objective wrongness'. Nevertheless, he was for abiding by the decision. His principal ground[285] was a direct appeal to the no-new-reasons constraint:

> It cannot be suggested that the majority in *Western Australia* v *The Commonwealth* failed to advert to any relevant consideration, or overlooked any aposite decision or principle. The arguments presented in the present case were in essence the same as those presented in the earlier case.[286]

For Aickin J, considerations of this kind should not stand in the way of overruling an earlier decision which concerned a 'fundamental question' of constitutional principle.[287] For Barwick CJ: 'In the case of the constitution, it is the duty, in my opinion, of each justice paying due regard to the opinions of other justices past and present, to decide what in truth the constitution provides'.[288]

(b) Objective Rightness

What these opinions reveal is that the framework of distinctions to which attention has been drawn earlier in this section is no more than that—a framework. Once it is accepted that there are no reasons before the present court which were not put in argument in the impugned decision—so that, if it was wrong, it was ultimately, not structurally, wrong—there is, of course, no mechanical means by which the decision may be slotted into the category of ultimate impressionistic wrongness or that of ultimate objective wrongness, nor by which, supposing it comes within the latter category, the question can be seen as relating to a principle of such

[284] (1978) 139 CLR 585, 603.

[285] As we have seen, both Gibbs J and Stephen J also invoked the justified-reliance constraint—above, p 170.

[286] (1978) 139 CLR 585, 600 Gibbs J went on to say that if Parliament were further to distort the federal balance of the constitution by legislating to provide for the election of more senators for the territories 'that would be a circumstance that might be regarded as sufficient to justify a re-consideration of the question whether *Western Australia* v *The Commonwealth* should continue to be followed' (ibid 600–1). Stephen J, for whom the question turned on an impressionistic interpretation of constitutional provisions, dissociated himself from this qualification of the refusal to overrule (ibid 604).

[287] (1978) 139 CLR 585, 630

[288] (1978) 139 CLR 585, 593

fundamental importance that legal truth should be preferred to finality. For what an English commentator's opinion is worth on so sensitive a question of Australian constitutional jurisprudence, the issue in the *Queensland* case does appear to be one falling outside the 'mere impression' category and also to be one of fundamental importance, so that the approach to overruling taken by Barwick CJ and Aickin J is to be preferred to that of Gibbs and Stephen JJ.[289] As we have seen,[290] attention was drawn in the House of Lords in *Vestey* to the provisions of the Bill of Rights of 1688 which declared suspension of or dispensation with laws illegal, and in *Khawaja* to Lord Atkin's principle that the onus lies on the executive to justify imprisonment. The significance of these constitutional principles had not been taken into account in the cases which the House overruled. If, however, they had been fully considered and held inapplicable or overridden, it may well be that the overrulings would still have taken place on the ground that these are fundamental questions as to which each appellate committee must enforce its view as to the 'correct' answer.

No more is claimed for the framework of distinctions than that it makes explicit the phenomenology of adjudication in the overruling cases in which wrongness is usually, but not always, taken to be an insufficient ground for departing from earlier decisions. That claim, however, flies in the face of a widely held opinion amongst modern jurists, that arguments about disputed questions of law are *always* premised on the assumption that there is an objectively right answer. The most influential exponent of this view is Professor Ronald Dworkin.

As we saw, one of the questions raised by the cases of *Lynch*, *Abbott* and *Howe* was whether it is just that a person who kills under the immediate threat of death or serious injury should be convicted of murder. One who is consistently sceptical and relativistic about moral questions will deny that it can be answered, and indeed will protest that it should not be asked. For such a sceptic, critical morality, as a matter of reasoned conclusions about right and wrong, is no proper endeavour for the human intellect: we can do no more than give tongue to our own (and others') subjective likes and dislikes, and should not suppose that our ethical opinions may be founded on reason. Such sceptics have to be left to one side by those, like judges or debating legislators, who engage in institutional decision-making. Such decision-makers have sometimes to give answers to moral questions and are required to come up with reasons for their answers. The sceptics must also be left aside by anyone who seeks to take issue with what the decision-makers have done and thus takes up a position on institutional ground. If we think that we have reasons which are sufficient to support a moral conclusion—reasons which are stronger than any canvassed for the opposite view—then we presuppose that there is a right answer. Whether or not morality is in some sense 'really' objective, we argue as though it were; and, on a question such as that under consideration, moral philosophers themselves can and do join in.[291]

[289] Nothing is said here about the correct answer to the substantive question of Australian constitutional law, as to which all these four justices were agreed, whilst the opposite view, in the event, received the imprimatur of the court.

[290] Above, p 144.

[291] For example, Anthony Kenny, writing in 1979, recommended the overruling of *Lynch*—Anthony Kenny, *The Ivory Tower: Essays in Philosophy and Public Law*, Basil Blackwell, ch 3. He wrote (at 37): 'It is true that to resist

continued on page 193

Dworkin adopts arguments similar to the above against the moral sceptic.[292] However, he goes much further. He claims that the institutional practices of the law presuppose a right answer to every legal question.[293]

In the overruling context, judicial statements can be found which appear to support this claim. In *Queensland*, Barwick CJ cited with approval[294] the following famous dictum of Isaacs J in the *Engine Drivers* case:

> The oath of a justice of this court is 'to do right to all manner of people according to law'. Our sworn loyalty is to the law itself and to the organic law of the constitution first of all. If then we find the law to be plainly in conflict with what we or any of our predecessors erroneously thought it to be we have as I conceive no right to choose between giving effect to the law and maintaining an incorrect interpretation. It is not in my opinion better that the court should be persistently wrong than that it should be ultimately right. In my opinion where the prior decision is manifestly wrong it is the paramount and sworn duty of this court to declare the law truly.[295]

Taken literally, this dictum obviously proves too much for, as was pointed out in the opinion of the Privy Council in *Reynolds'* case, it could entail that any first instance judge, if he thought that the decision of a superior court was wrong in law, would be bound by his oath to disregard it.[296] In its context, the dictum may be understood as limited to the situation of a judge sitting in a final appellate court which has power to overrule its earlier decisions. It suggests that, so long as the judge is sure that the earlier decision was wrong, it is always his duty to overrule it and to declare what the law 'truly' is. There is no room for a distinction between impressionistic and objective wrongness.

It appears that Dworkin's imaginary super-judge, Hercules,[297] would recognize no such distinction either. Hercules supposes that there is always a right answer to any question of law. He will find it by taking into account the entire body of authoritative legal materials (the dimension of 'fit'), on the one hand, and, on the other hand, considerations of justice, fairness and procedural due process (the 'substantive' dimension).[298] He will never conclude that, in the light of all reasons available on both dimensions, the issue is still one as to which there are equally tenable views so that he must make a decision which is one of mere impression.

Could Hercules ever decline to overrule a wrong decision? It would be question-begging to assume that the wrong decision itself constitutes an element of the legal materials with which Hercules' present opinion must fit. Dworkin tells us

continued from page 192
duress or to refrain from taking life under necessity may call for heroism. It does not follow that it is morally permissible to do anything else.'

292 Ronald Dworkin, *A Matter of Principle*, Harvard UP, 1985, 137–45, 171–7.

293 Op cit, ch 5.

294 (1978) 139 CLR 585, 593.

295 *Australian Agricultural Co* v *Federated Engine Drivers and Firemen's Association of Australasia* (1913) 17 CLR 261, 278–9.

296 *A-G for St Christopher Nevis and Anguilla* v *Reynolds* [1980] AC 637, 660.

297 Hercules emerged in Dworkin's essay on 'Hard Cases' (1975) 88 *Harv LR* 1057 (reprinted in R. M. Dworkin, *Taking Rights Seriously*, Duckworth, 1978, ch 4). I have discussed developments in Hercules' portrait in 'Unger's Critique of Formalism in Legal Reasoning: Hero, Hercules and Humdrum' (1989) 52 *MLR* 42.

298 Ronald Dworkin, *Law's Empire*, Fontana Press, 1986, chs 7–10.

that Hercules must seek to elaborate principles which will justify decisions which have 'not been recanted or in some other way taken as a matter of institutional regret';[299] 'decisions that his court also proposes to uphold'.[300] 'If the courts propose to overrule the decision, no substantive argument of fairness, fixing on the actual decision in the case, survives . . .'[301]

Thus, only if Hercules decides not to overrule it is a decision one which must be taken into account in reaching his conclusions about what the law requires.[302]

Of the constraints on overruling considered in this article, the second, third and fourth could properly play some part in Hercules' reasoning, because they have a bearing on features of the substantive dimension. If it were true that citizens had justifiably relied on the earlier decision, then, as Dworkin makes plain, considerations of procedural due process might tell against overruling because of the unfair surprise that would ensue.[303] If the legislature had enacted statutes in the general area of law without repealing the impugned decision, that might be some evidence that it conformed to community morality so that what Dworkin calls 'fairness'[304] might weigh against overruling. That might account for the third constraint, although its supposed rationale would be subservience to popular moral opinion rather than comity with the legislature. The mootness constraint may be favoured by considerations of procedural due process, since if nothing crucial to the instant appeal turns on whether the earlier decision should stand or not, it may not be apparent that all arguments in its support have been given proper attention. The no-new-reasons principle, however, could play no part in Hercules' deliberations. For him, every instance of ultimate wrongness is also one of objective wrongness and—assuming the absence of the other constraints—should he not always correct error (whether in matters great or small)? Finality, as such, must be nothing to him. Given his definitional super-human capacities, he will always know the true law and would not be deterred from declaring it merely by the possibility that some lesser judge might hereafter again get the law wrong.

Dworkin contends that, in law as in morals or aesthetics, however much reasonable people disagree as to what the answer is, they argue as if there is an objectively right answer and therefore there is an objectively right answer.[305] No quarrel is here taken with Dworkin's rejection of what he calls 'external scepticism'.[306] As earlier stated in connection with the duress-murder rule, in an institutional context at least we have to assume objectivity about difficult legal and moral questions. Scepticism about morals is a private matter. Objectivity, how-

299 Ronald Dworkin, *Taking Rights Seriously*, Duckworth, 1978, 115.

300 Op cit 116.

301 Op cit 118.

302 The citizen, on the other hand, must take the decision of any court into account in making his judgment as to what the law requires, even though the doctrine of precedent, given the possibility of overruling, 'does not make the decisions of any court conclusive' (op cit 211).

303 Ronald Dworkin, *Law's Empire*, Fontana Press, 1986, 403.

304 Op cit 249–50, 340–2.

305 Ronald Dworkin, *A Matter of Principle*, Harvard UP, 1985, 137–45, 171–5; 'A Reply', in Marshall Cohen ed, *Ronald Dworkin and Contemporary Jurisprudence*, Duckworth, 1984, 275–8.

306 Ronald Dworkin, *A Matter of Principle*, Harvard UP, 1985, 175–7; '"Natural" Law Revisited' (1982) 34 *U Flo LR* 165, 173–8.

ever, is not the same thing as determinacy. It may be that a person accepts certain abstract moral principles as objectively true, yet, in a particular concrete dilemma about what ought to be done, finds that he has to make a decision as to which these moral 'facts' give no definitive guidance so that he must make an impressionistic judgment.

Whether or not that is so in moral life, the overruling cases show that it is often true as to questions of concrete legal decision-making. Dworkin's conceptions of law in general and of adjudication in particular are advanced as interpretative concepts, ones which make the best sense of the practices we have.[307] He tells us that 'in the end all my arguments are hostage to each reader's sense of what does and what can happen in court'.[308] By that yardstick his theory ought to have acknowledged, as it does not, that courts frequently recognize instances of impressionistic rightness or wrongness—that, when all reasons on any dimension have been taken into account, there remains to be added a subjective weighing of those reasons.

When a court finds that the issue before it and before the court in an earlier decision was of this kind, the need for finality of decision favours constraint on overruling even if the present court believes that the earlier decision was, impressionistically, erroneous. Furthermore, real judges are not Herculeses. Hence, even where the court is sure that the earlier decision was objectively mistaken, its acknowledged lack of super-human wisdom may suggest that, in the interests of finality, it should not depart from it unless what is at stake is a fundamental principle.

9. *Conclusion*

It is submitted that the following propositions emerge from the overruling cases:

(a) Prior Decision Authoritative and Unacceptable

A prior decision of the House of Lords need not be overruled, in exercise of the Practice Statement power, unless the House in the present case concludes that the prior decision cannot but be understood as a currently binding authority for some unacceptable proposition of law (*Conway* v *Rimmer*, *Herrington*, *Hyam*, *Moloney*).

(b) 'Proper Development of the Law'

A final appellate court should not overrule a prior decision of its own unless it concludes that the present law, all things considered, would be improved were some proposition forming part of the ratio decidendi of the prior decision entirely discarded and replaced by a new proposition (*Pirelli*, *La Pintada*). It is not

[307] Ronald Dworkin, *Law's Empire*, Fontana Press, 1986, 49–54, 65–8, 87–96; *A Matter of Principle*, Harvard UP, 1985, ch 6.

[308] Ronald Dworkin, *Law's Empire*, Fontana Press, 1986, 15.

necessary to conclude that the earlier decision was mistaken at the time when it was made (*Miliangos*).

(c) '*Justice in a Particular Case*'

It counts in favour of holding that the present law would be improved if it can be shown that the impugned ruling results in injustice to an assignable class of persons (*Miliangos*, *Dick*, *Vestey*).

(d) *Certainty*

It counts in favour of holding that the present law would be improved if it can be shown that the impugned ruling is couched in such terms as to make its application to particular instances uncertain (*Oldendorff*, *Zecevic*). Where an impugned ruling is not uncertain of application but is objectionable on some other grounds, it should not, prima-facie, be rejected unless it can be substituted for by some legal proposition which is no less certain (*Miliangos*).

(e) *Coherence*

In deciding whether the law would be improved, the coherence of the impugned ruling and of any proposed new ruling with the rest of the present law is to be taken into account. Coherence is not a problem if the rule in question can be isolated from the rest of the law (*Dick*). If the decision under review has been distinguished on imprecise grounds in subsequent cases, coherence may favour overruling (*Oldendorff*, *Howe*). Parliament is to be presumed to intend coherence (*Shivpuri*). If a new ruling, though more just than the old, would not cohere with a body of legislated rules, coherence may favour not overruling but, instead, awaiting further legislative initiative (*La Pintada*).

(f) *First Constraining Principle—No New Reasons (Finality)*

Even if the present law would be improved, the power to overrule should not (subject to proposition (n) below) be exercised where the contentions for or against the question of law in issue fail to introduce new reasons—that is, reasons not taken into account in the earlier case. The justification for this principle is finality. If the present court differs from the earlier one only in its assessment of the relative strength of the same reasons, the court cannot point to a distinct reason why a third court should not make the same assessment as the first court. The present court is therefore not justified in overruling the earlier decision even if, for its part, it thinks that it was 'wrong' (*Hudson*, *Knuller*, *Fitzleet*, *Blumenthal*, *Thomas*, *A-G* v *Perpetual Trustee*, *Queensland* per Gibbs and Stephen JJ, *Jones*). Wrongness, in such a case, entails ultimate, as distinct from structural, wrongness. It may also be an instance of impressionistic, as opposed to objective, ultimate wrongness, there being two 'tenable' views (*Hudson*, *Fitzleet*, *Blumenthal*, *Queensland* per Stephen J, *Jones*).

(g) Semantic Questions

Where the issue is thought to turn on the most natural reading of a text, the case is presumptively one in which no new reasons are involved (*Hudson*, *Jones*).

(h) Legislative Purpose

Where the issue is thought to turn on historical evidence of legislative purpose, new reasons may be found in evidence of legislative intention properly available, but not adverted to, in the earlier case (*Shivpuri*).

(i) Doctrine

Where the issue is thought to raise doctrinal questions, new reasons may include general principles overlooked in the earlier decision (*Vestey*, *Khawaja*, *Jones* per Gaudron J).

(j) Consequences

Where the issue is thought to turn on the comparative consequences of alternative rulings, new reasons may be advanced by reference to consequences which were not, or could not have been, foreseen at the time of the earlier decision (*Oldendorff*, *Miliangos*, *Dick*, *Vestey*, *Zecevic*).

(k) Second Constraining Principle—Justified Reliance

Even if overruling is prima-facie warranted, it may be right to refrain from exercising the power to overrule if it can be shown that citizens who have relied upon the old ruling would thereby be prejudiced (Practice Statement, *Geelong*, *Queensland* per Gibbs and Stephen JJ, *Zecevic* per Deane J). It must be plausible that such prejudicial reliance has occurred (*Dick*). It need not be assumed merely because an overruling extends the scope of the criminal law (*Shivpuri*, *Howe*, *Zecevic*). Reliance by the executive does not count (*Vestey*, *Khawaja*).

(l) Third Constraining Principle—Comity with the Legislature

Even if the present law would be improved were a decision overruled, the exercise of the overruling power may not be appropriate if the court is satisfied that, subsequent to the impugned decision, the legislature has acted on the assumption that a proposition approved in that decision is part of the law. The inference may then be drawn that the legislature has, for the time being, given its assent to the proposition so that it would break comity between the court and the legislature were the court now to discard it (*Herrington*, *Knuller*, *La Pintada*).

(m) Fourth Constraining Principle—Mootness

In the context of civil litigation, the overruling power should not be exercised where, on the facts of the case at bar, it would make no difference to the outcome whether the impugned ruling were part of the law or not (*Anticlizo*). However, in the context of the criminal law (where the public interest in certainty is paramount), it is not necessary that a departure from the earlier decision is required in order to dispose of the present appeal (*Shivpuri*, *Howe*).

(n) Qualification on First Constraining Principle—Fundamentals

Notwithstanding that the contentions in the present case introduce no reasons which were not considered in the earlier case, a decision may be overruled if the court now takes the view that it introduced a development which is not warranted having regard to fundamental principles underlying the common law (*Howe*, *Knuller* per Lord Diplock). The same may be true where what is at stake are fundamental principles of the constitution (*Queensland* per Barwick CJ and Aickin J, Gibbs and Stephen JJ, contra).

These propositions embody a relatively coherent conception of the proper role of final appellate jurisdiction in the overruling context. Once revealed, this conception can be challenged and will, no doubt, undergo modifications. The mootness constraint (proposition m) appears unduly rigid in its application to civil law jurisdiction. If a court is convinced that the law would be improved were it to overrule an earlier decision, should it stay its hand merely because a question, though fully argued before it, is not one which literally has to be answered in order to dispose of the present appeal? A future appellate committee of the House of Lords might not take the absolutist stance which the House adopted in *Anticlizo*. The rationale of the third constraining principle (proposition l) has never been fully ventilated. Short of specific re-enactment, a final appellate court should surely be slow to draw the inference that Parliament has chosen to retain an impugned ruling as part of the law. As the cases discussed in section 6 make clear, the possibility that Parliament has simply not made up its mind and has left the matter for judicial resolution must always be borne in mind and, in any case, the constraint is not regarded as unqualified. The justified-reliance constraint (proposition k) is normatively cogent provided its proper limits are understood. Its practical significance, as appears from the cases discussed in section 5, has not been great in the United Kingdom context.

Propositions b–j and n reflect unavoidable complexities embedded in the notions of a decision's being 'wrong' and of mere 'wrongness' not being a sufficient ground for overruling. They also reflect a balancing between the demands of finality and those of fidelity to legal truth. Needless to say, these propositions supply no straightforward or 'mechanical' means by which the items in the balance can be identified or the weighing process itself resolved. In the end, the proper reconciliation of finality and truth must turn on one's view of what members of the community can and should expect of their judges. If citizens are entitled to demand the judge's best judgment every time, without reference to what his predecessors have decided or to what his successors may decide, we could eliminate propositions f–j and n. On matters great and small, a final appellate court (on this view) should overrule, overrule and overrule again, always enforcing the present court's opinion of the right answer. It has been my contention that this is not how members of the House of Lords or of the High Court of Australia do or should perceive their roles. Where wrongness in an earlier decision is a matter of impression, or where it relates to issues which are not of fundamental importance, finality properly prevails over the present court's perception of legal truth.

[3]

JUDICIAL OBLIGATION, PRECEDENT AND THE COMMON LAW

STEPHEN R. PERRY*

I. JUDICIAL OBLIGATION AND LEGAL THEORY

What is the nature of judicial obligation? This has become perhaps the most prominent question of legal theory over the past 20 years, and most recent attempts to answer it can be seen to take one or the other of two fundamentally different approaches. According to the first approach, the obligation of a judge coincides with a duty to apply whatever source-based positive rules are recognized within the relevant legal system to be laws, where the most important potential sources of law would generally be legislative enactment, precedent, and custom (either among the population at large, or among a special group such as the judiciary). Where a court is not bound by such a rule its decision always involves an exercise of discretion rather than compliance with any kind of obligation imposed by law. The view of legal theory which is associated with this approach takes the function of law to be the authoritative guidance of conduct by means of positive, publicly ascertainable rules, where the correlative function of courts is to evaluate the conduct of individuals by means of those same rules. The approach is characteristic of modern positivism, and it is best exemplified in the work of H. L. A. Hart[1] and Joseph Raz.[2]

The second approach to law and judicial obligation supposes the function of law to be, at least in part, the institutionalized adjudication and resolution of disputes in accordance with principles of justice or fairness, where the requisite principles need not be source-based in the positivist sense. The obligation of the judge is to apply such principles—which may include some that require him to give special consideration to what legislatures and courts have done in the past—to the facts of particular cases brought before him. He is not generally to be regarded as having the freedom to make discretionary decisions, even when the reach of statute law and precedent has been exhausted. An approach to legal theory along

*Assistant Professor of Law, McGill University, Montreal. I would like to thank the following persons for discussion and comments on earlier drafts: Peter Benson, Paul Craig, Ronald Dworkin, Joseph Raz, Ernest Weinrib and the former editor of this journal. Much of the work on this paper, which is based on material from my DPhil thesis at Oxford, was done while I was a Junior Boulton Fellow at the Faculty of Law, McGill University in 1984–85. I gratefully acknowledge this support.

1 H. L. A. Hart, *The Concept of Law* (Oxford, 1961); *Essays on Bentham* (Oxford, 1982), chs 6, 10.

2 See especially Joseph Raz, *Practical Reason and Norms* (London, 1975), chs 4–5 (hereafter *PRN*); *The Authority of Law* (Oxford, 1979) (hereafter *AL*).

these lines is, of course, a dominant theme in the work of Ronald Dworkin,[3] but it can also be discerned, to a greater or lesser degree and in differing forms, in the work of George Fletcher,[4] Charles Fried[5] and Lon Fuller;[6] a particularly interesting version of the approach, interpreting the form of private law adjudication as Aristotelian corrective justice, has recently been developed by Ernest Weinrib.[7]

Theories which view law from this second perspective are, in essence, natural law theories that are grounded in a certain conception of adjudication and the judicial process; in this they differ from more traditional natural law theories, which attempt to establish a systematic connection of some sort between valid positive law and moral value.[8] One might say that the non-traditional theories are not so much concerned with the relationship between positive law and justice as they are with the *pursuit* of justice within a formal context of adjudication.[9] Law is to be regarded as a certain kind of institutionalized procedure for attempting to settle particular disputes justly or fairly, and this requires, as I shall argue below, an interpretation of the theoretical nature of at least certain manifestations of positive law which differs from the interpretations of either positivism or traditional natural law theories; the process of adjudication itself, rather than the phenomenon of positive law, is taken to be the essence of law, and I shall accordingly speak of such theories as exemplifying the *adjudicative* approach to legal theory.

Both the positivist and the adjudicative conceptions of law can perhaps be thought of as singling out a particular aspect of the legal process as theoretically fundamental, and then as somehow trying to accommodate all remaining legal phenomena within the theory of law that results. Positivism takes the essence of law to be the authoritative guidance of conduct by means of source-based, duty-imposing rules, so that the primary obligation of a judge is to be regarded as the interpretation, application and enforcement of those previously-existing rules. There is, however, no reason to suppose that such a model will fit all areas of law equally well, and although I shall not try to argue the point in detail here I believe

3 See especially Ronald Dworkin, *Taking Rights Seriously* (2nd ed, Cambridge, Mass, 1978), chs 2–4 (hereafter *TRS*).

4 George Fletcher, 'Two Modes of Legal Thought', 90 *Yale LJ* 970 (1981); 'Punishment and Compensation', 14 *Creighton L Rev* 691 (1981).

5 Charles Fried, 'The Laws of Change: The Cunning of Reason in Moral and Legal History', 9 *J of Legal Stud* 335 (1980).

6 Lon Fuller, 'Reason and Fiat in Case Law', 59 *Harv L Rev* 376 (1946); 'The Forms and Limits of Adjudication', 92 *Harv L Rev* 353 (1978).

7 Ernest Weinrib, 'Toward a Moral Theory of Negligence Law', 2 *Law and Philosophy* 37 (1983); 'The Insurance Justification and Private Law', 14 *J of Legal Stud* 681 (1985); 'The Intelligibility of the Rule of Law', forthcoming in Monahan and Hutchinson, (eds), *The Rule of Law: Ideal or Ideology?*; 'The Natural Law of Torts' (unpublished manuscript); 'Liberty and Community in the Theory of Private Law' (unpublished manuscript).

8 The most recent attempt to develop a systematic traditional natural law theory is to be found in John Finnis, *Natural Law and Natural Rights* (Oxford, 1980).

9 Cf Fletcher, 'Two Modes of Legal Thought', *supra* n 4, 981.

that this sort of model offers a much more successful explanation of criminal law than it does of, say, private civil law.

The essence of the positivist model is the forward-looking guidance of conduct by means of pre-established standards of behaviour, with the theoretical emphasis being placed upon the duty to conform to the standards, rather than upon any rights of other persons to be free from whatever harmful effects that the regulated conduct might generate; at least at first glance this seems to be a much more accurate picture of the criminal law than it is of private law, the usual concern of which is with the determination, generally on a retrospective basis, of the rights and liabilities of two parties *inter se*.[10] Unlike the criminal law, where the conduct of a single person comes under the scrutiny of the state, private law does not so much look to the conduct of individuals as such, as it does to the balance of equities between two (or occasionally more than two) persons (whence, for example, the much greater prevalence of objective standards in civil than in criminal law). It thus comes as no surprise that the usual focus of adjudicative theories is on civil law, and particularly private law, rather than on criminal law.[11] This sort of theory places theoretical emphasis upon such civil remedies as restitution and compensatory damages, claiming that liability to make restitution or reparation is mainly determined by historically-oriented, backward-looking principles of justice, not necessarily source-based, that provide redress for unjust enrichment or wrongful injury; the judge's duty is then to ascertain, on an *ex post facto* basis, whether such liability exists.

If it is true that the two sorts of theories can be looked upon in this way as founding themselves on quite different areas of law and the legal process, then it is by no means obvious that they cannot be reconciled under the umbrella of a single unifying theory. I take Lon Fuller, for one, to have been advocating a position of this sort when he maintained, somewhat aphoristically, that both fiat and reason were necessary elements of law.[12] Positivism, however, at least as it has been developed by Hart and Raz, claims to be an all-encompassing theory that sets out the foundations of law in their entirety. The aim of this paper is to challenge that claim of exclusivity by showing that the interpretation which positivism must

10 Cf H. L. A. Hart and Tony Honoré, *Causation in the Law* (2nd ed, Oxford, 1985), 250: 'In criminal law the wrong is not primarily the infringement of someone else's right to life, bodily safety or goods but rather the interference with some state of affairs (the life of another, his possession of goods) contrary to the public interest. . . . But in civil law the position is different. Compensation is there given for the infringement of some right. . . .' One of Hart's criticisms of Austin was that the latter's theory could not be extended very far beyond the criminal law: see Hart, *The Concept of Law*, *supra* n 1, 27–33. Although I shall not try to establish the point here, I believe that modern versions of positivism are, in the end, not very much more successful in this regard than was Austin's.

11 Dworkin's rights thesis, for example, applies to 'ordinary civil cases at law': *TRS* 94, n 1; cf 84, 100.

12 'Reason and Fiat in Case Law', *supra* n 6. Fletcher, in 'Two Modes of Legal Thought', *supra* n 4, 979 ff, also seems to have in mind what might be called a 'mixed' theory of law.

place on a phenomenon that is to be found in a number of different legal systems, namely judicial law-making of the sort associated with the common law, is, in comparison with the rival interpretation of the adjudicative approach to legal theory, an inadequate one.

The central focus of adjudicative theories is, as I have said, on private law, which is the heart of the common law. I shall be speaking, however, of common law reasoning as it manifests itself in civil cases generally. I should emphasize that I do not assume that judges of all legal systems make law, that all judicial law-making is like that of the common law, or that civil law must necessarily be judge-made. I do not argue that positivism is in every respect a wrong-headed theory, nor do I attempt to set out a full-blown alternative conception of law. My aim is the more modest one of showing that there exist certain kinds of legal institutions of which positivism presents a deficient account, and that any adequate general theory of law must consequently incorporate certain of the insights of the adjudicative approach. Since an argument by counter-example is sufficient for this purpose, I do not attempt to make any unnecessary claims of universality or exclusivity on behalf of the adjudicative theory.

Since much of the discussion of this paper will concern the proper interpretation of the common law doctrine of *stare decisis*, I begin the argument with an examination of the logic of practical reason and its possible applications to the interpretation of a practice of following precedent. I then outline Raz's development and defence of what seems to me to be the most powerful version of positivism that has yet been advanced. I discuss and criticize the positivist interpretation, based upon Raz's notion of an exclusionary reason, of both the general concept of judicial obligation and the specific judicial practice of following precedent. Drawing upon certain aspects of the adjudicative approach to legal theory I then offer what I think is a more satisfactory account of both phenomena, at least so far as their manifestation in the common law is concerned.

An important point which should be mentioned before proceeding with the main argument concerns the fact that a conception of the 'function' of law has figured in the preliminary characterizations of both the positivist and the adjudicative approaches to legal theory. Proponents of both approaches routinely make the assumption that law can sensibly be said to have a function, and both rely on that assumption in developing particular theories of law.[13] The attribution of a function to a social institution which is both purposive and yet shaped by the purposes not of one but of many individuals is problematic, however, and unfortunately there are few discussions in the jurisprudential literature that address the question of whether such attribution is meaningful, let alone the

13 See e.g. Raz, *AL*, 50–52; Dworkin, *TRS*, 347–48. In 'Does Law Have a Function? A Comment on the Two-Level Theory of Decision', 74 *Yale LJ* 640 (1965), Dworkin argued against the proposition that law could be said to have a goal or function, but it is clear that he had in mind only those goals or functions that are forward-looking in character (e.g. the maximization of utility).

question of what it means. A notable exception is the work of John Finnis, who argues both that a theory of law cannot help but take some position on what the point or function of law is, and that in taking such a position the theory will necessarily be adopting an evaluative viewpoint.[14] I take Dworkin to have been making an essentially similar point when he says in *Taking Rights Seriously* that positivism is, like his own theory, 'a political theory about the point or function of law';[15] he has since elaborated on what this sort of claim involves in his discussion in a number of different works of the general nature of interpretation and of its place in law and legal philosophy.[16] If Dworkin and Finnis are, at least in a general sense, correct in this regard, as it seems to me that they are, then, contrary to what has sometimes been claimed, a neutral, value-free description of legal phenomena cannot be given. It is not possible to explore this issue here, important though it obviously is. For present purposes I will simply assume that the attribution of a function either to law generally or to particular legal institutions, whether by positivist or by adjudicative theorists, is a notion which can, one way or another, be put on a sound theoretical footing.

2. THE LOGIC OF PRACTICAL REASON AND THE DOCTRINE OF PRECEDENT

2.1 *Raz on practical reason*

In his valuable discussion of the logic of practical reason Joseph Raz draws a formal distinction between two modes of reasoning about what ought to be done.[17] The first, which involves consideration of and action upon what he calls the balance of reasons, presupposes both that all the relevant reasons which might bear on whether or not one ought to perform a given action have a certain weight or strength, and that all such reasons are commensurable. A rational agent who is acting in accordance with this conception of practical reason first determines the total weight of the various reasons that favour each alternative course of action, and then acts upon that alternative which has the greatest overall support. He

14 *Supra* n 8, ch 1. Raz would seem to be in agreement with Finnis on this point: see Raz, 'The Problem about the Nature of Law', 21 *Univ West Ont L Rev* 203, 217–18 (1983); 'Authority, Law and Morality', 68 *The Monist* 295, 320–22 (1985). This does not, of course, commit him to the position that the identification of particular laws within a particular legal system depends on evaluative considerations: see the discussion of what he calls the sources thesis in section 3 of this paper, *infra*.

15 *TRS*, 347. Cf 'A Reply by Ronald Dworkin', in Marshall Cohen, (ed), *Ronald Dworkin and Contemporary Jurisprudence* (Totowa, NJ, 1984), 254: 'In my view any theory of law, including positivism, is based in the end on some particular normative political theory.' Finnis, unlike Dworkin, does not expressly characterize the relevant evaluative considerations as being political in nature.

16 See Dworkin, '"Natural" Law Revisited', 34 *Univ Flor L Rev* 165, 165–69 (1982); *A Matter of Principle* (Cambridge, Mass, 1985), chs 5–7; *Law's Empire* (Cambridge, Mass, 1986).

17 *PRN*, 35–48.

acts, that is to say, on the balance of reasons, taking into account the weight of each relevant reason in doing so. Since this account is a formal one, no distinctions are drawn among substantive types of reasons; the reasons that figure in the balance of reasons could be, for example, moral, prudential or desire-based.

The second mode of practical reason which Raz distinguishes involves what he calls an exclusionary reason, which is a second-order reason to refrain from acting on a reason or on some category of reasons. Such reasons are, in effect, reasons to refrain from acting on the balance of reasons. The idea of acting in accordance with an exclusionary reason is, again, a formal one, and so does not depend on whether there ever could in fact be a justification for refusing to act on the balance of reasons. Raz nonetheless claims both that acting on the basis of an exclusionary reason is a common phenomenon, and that in at least some sorts of situations it can be defended as the rational thing to do. He supports this claim by pointing to the different sorts of rules that persons often do in fact follow, and to the sorts of reasons that might be given for their doing so. Consider, for example, a rule not to take a major investment decision when one is tired or drunk.[18] Adherence to such a rule will sometimes entail forgoing an investment possibility entirely, and so amount to a decision on the substantive question of whether or not to invest. That decision has not been taken on the balance of reasons, but it may nonetheless be justifiable if one will be better off in the long run by always following a predetermined course of action whenever it is necessary to make certain sorts of decisions under conditions of impaired rationality or incomplete information.[19] Rules of thumb of this sort can also be justified on efficiency grounds; calculating the balance of reasons involves costs, in the form of time and effort consumed, and one may well be better off in the long run if one avoids incurring these costs by adhering, within a certain range of circumstances, to a preconceived plan of action.

Raz further illustrates the concept of an exclusionary reason by pointing to rules issued by authority.[20] Such rules are exclusionary reasons because they are, in effect, directions to comply with the authority's judgment of what is right on the balance of reasons, rather than with one's own judgment. Compliance with authoritative rules can, says Raz, be justified in a number of ways. One might have reasonable grounds to believe, for example, that the authority is wiser or more knowledgeable than oneself. Alternatively, it might require authoritative direction to coordinate in an effective way the activities of the various members of a group.[21] This is not to say, of course, that one necessarily has a moral obligation to comply with authoritative rulings simply because the coordination to which they give rise has social value (although, as Raz points out, the claim that coordination does have value figures in many of the classical justifications of

18 Ibid, 37–38.
19 Ibid, 59–62.
20 Ibid, 62–65.
21 But see Leslie Green, 'Authority and Convention', 35 *Phil Quart* 329 (1985).

political authority).[22] Raz's claim here is simply that, given certain reasonable background assumptions, it can be *rational* to comply with authority.

Raz recognizes that exclusionary reasons have a dimension of what he calls scope,[23] which is simply to say that the range of first-order reasons that are pre-empted by an exclusionary reason can vary. Thus an exclusionary reason need not be absolutely exclusionary. Even the standards of conduct imposed by the criminal law, which are archetypal instances of exclusionary rules, are not unlimited in scope while Raz does not discuss these particular examples, the defences of necessity and duress can plausibly be interpreted as involving a recognition that action which is taken on the basis of a certain very limited range of reasons falls beyond the proscriptive reach of the criminal law. It should be emphasized that the concept of scope is, like that of an exclusionary reason, a formal one; it does not tell us, in and of itself, how the particular range of excluded reasons which is defined by these defences is to be justified.

2.2 *Practical reason and precedent*

Raz's distinction between acting on the balance of reasons and acting on the basis of an exclusionary reason is a powerful conceptual tool in the analysis of practical reason. It yields a precise and illuminating characterization of what a rule is, for example—viz an exclusionary reason of general application which is also itself a first-order reason to perform (or refrain from performing) some action[24]—and this characterization can be employed, in turn, to clarify the foundations of positivism. It is important to note, however, that Raz's distinction is not exhaustive of the possible modes of practical reason. To see why this is so, it will be helpful to concentrate on the particular practical phenomenon that is of interest here, namely the common law doctrine of *stare decisis*. In what ways could a previous judicial decision figure in a later decision in such a way that a court could be said to be 'following precedent'? One obvious possibility is that the prior case is regarded as constituting, or as somehow giving rise to, an exclusionary rule in the sense just discussed. This, as we shall see, is Raz's own positivistic interpretation of precedent. An alternative conception would regard a court as being bound by a previous decision, itself decided on the basis of a balance of reasons, only until such time as it was convinced both that the balance of reasons had been wrongly assessed on the prior occasion, and that the correct assessment in fact led to the opposite result. A court could not depart from a previous decision, in other words, unless it had a positive reason for doing so. On this conception of precedent, which I will call the weak Burkean conception,[25] it obviously takes very little to

22 Raz discusses this and related issues in *AL*, ch 12. He outlines his own (limited) justification of political authority in 'Authority and Justification', 14 *Phil and Pub Aff* 3 (1985).

23 *PRN*, 40.

24 Raz calls exclusionary reasons that are also first-order reasons *protected* reasons: *AL*, 18.

25 I use the term 'Burkean' not in order to invoke the political philosophy of Burke, but simply to convey the idea of a presumption of some sort in favour of previously-accepted practices.

overcome the binding force of an earlier case. Despite this evident lack of strength, however, the weak Burkean conception *is* a form of following precedent. It is distinguishable from an adjudicative system based on absolute discretion insofar as its application would be non-trivial in the following two sorts of situations: first, where the previously-accepted balance of reasons had been cast in doubt but no new assessment had won recognition, and second, where the previous assessment had been rejected and the reasons on each side of the issue in question were now regarded as being evenly weighted.

The two conceptions of precedent just described correspond, in a fairly obvious way, to the two modes of practical reason distinguished by Raz. The first conception regards precedents as giving rise to exclusionary rules, and the second regards them as giving rise to a certain kind of weak constraint on departing from past decisions that is at the same time consistent with a case-by-case consideration of the balance of reasons. There is a third conception of precedent, however, which corresponds to a mode of practical reason that Raz does not discuss. Consider a court which does not look upon a previous decision as precluding it from taking account of any particular reason or set of reasons, as happens on the model of exclusionary rules, but which nonetheless will not depart from a prior holding unless it is first satisfied that the collective weight of the reasons supporting the opposite result is of greater strength, to some specified degree, than the weight which would otherwise be required to reach that result on the ordinary balance of reasons. The intuitive idea is that a court is bound by a previous decision unless it is convinced that there is a *strong* reason for holding otherwise. This conception of precedent, which I will call the strong Burkean conception, differs from the weak Burkean model in that one needs more than just *a* reason to overcome the binding force of a precedent, but at the same time it differs from the exclusionary model in that no relevant first-order reasons are excluded from consideration as a matter of course.

The mode of practical reason underlying the strong Burkean conception of precedent might be characterized as action in accordance with a *weighted* balance of reasons. One would be acting on this basis if one were to accept a second-order reason to give some first-order reason a greater or lesser weight than it would otherwise receive in an assessment of the ordinary balance of reasons. (By directing that a particular set of reasons, which would now be regarded as tipping the ordinary balance of reasons in favour of a given result, nonetheless has to attain a somewhat higher threshold of strength before being allowed to prevail, the strong Burkean conception of precedent is, in effect, attaching to that set of reasons a lower collective weight than the one which it would ordinarily receive.) It is important to notice that reliance on this kind of second-order weighting principle does not entail that the first-order reason (or set of such reasons) which is being 'given' a new weight actually *has* that new weight; the idea is, rather, that at least under certain specified circumstances one is being directed to act *as if* the first-order reason in question had a different weight than in fact one thinks it has.

The mode of acting on a weighted balance of reasons does not, therefore, simply collapse into the mode of acting on the ordinary balance of reasons.

Raz characterizes second-order reasons as reasons to act on or refrain from acting on first-order reasons,[26] but this is clearly too narrow. A second-order reason is a reason for treating a first-order reason as having a greater or lesser weight than it would ordinarily receive, so that an exclusionary reason is simply the special case where one or more first-order reasons are treated as having zero weight. The two modes of practical reason which Raz distinguishes can thus be regarded, in effect, as the two extremes of a continuum; at one end action is to be assessed on the basis of a balance of reasons in which no reason has been assigned anything other than its ordinary weight, while at the other end action is to be assessed by a balance of reasons some of which have been assigned, on the basis of second-order reasons, a non-ordinary weight of zero. Between these two extremes lies an indefinitely large number of further possibilities, all of which are variations on the idea of a weighted balance of reasons.[27]

2.3 *Dworkin's conception of precedent in 'the model of rules I'*

The conception of precedent which is suggested by Ronald Dworkin in his article 'The Model of Rules I'[28] must be interpreted, I would argue, as a strong Burkean conception. In that paper Dworkin drew a logical distinction between rules and principles. A rule, which was said to operate in an all-or-nothing fashion, gives rise to an obligation to perform (or refrain from performing) a specified action whenever the rule's conditions of application have been met, a characterization of rules which is obviously compatible with Raz's exclusionary account. A principle, on the other hand, favours one course of action over others but does not, by itself, require that that course of action be followed; it possesses, rather, a dimension of weight or importance, which is to be factored into the determination of what ought to be done whenever the relevant principles do not at all point to the same result. Dworkin argued that in law not only are there rules which are legally binding on judges but certain sorts of principles as well, and that among these are included a number which 'reflect . . . the equities and efficiencies of consistency . . [and which] incline toward the *status quo* . . .';[29] this cluster of principles, taken together, constitutes the doctrine of precedent.

26 *PRN*, 39; *AL*, 17.

27 The distinction between the exclusionary conception of precedent and the weak Burkean conception is, I think, a homologue of Rawls' distinction between what he called the practice and the summary conceptions of rules: see Rawls, 'Two Concepts of Rules', 64 *Phil Rev* 3 (1955), reprinted in P. Foot, (ed), *Theories of Ethics* (Oxford, 1967) 144. It seems to me that Rawls erred in characterizing the difference between the two conceptions at least partly in terms of the description of actions, rather than, as here, in terms of reasons for action alone. It is only when one utilizes the properly generalized notion of a second-order reason for action that it becomes clear that the practice and summary conceptions of rules are, correctly understood, just the two extremes of a continuum.

28 *TRS*, ch 2.

29 Ibid, 37.

Dworkin's conception of acting in accordance with principles, where the appropriate course of action is to be determined by a comparison of the overall weight of the various sets of principles that support each possible outcome, clearly corresponds to Raz's conception of acting on the balance of reasons, where the reasons that a judge may legitimately take into account are restricted to certain kinds of moral and political considerations.[30] The doctrine of precedent is not a rule, in Dworkin's view, but rather a set of principles which judges must somehow weigh into the general balance of principles when deciding cases at law. Precedential principles cannot be ordinary first-order reasons, however, as most of the principles envisaged by Dworkin presumably are, since they have no independent content at the first-order level; the result to which they point in any given case will vary with the prior course of institutional history. Precedential principles do not, in other words, enter into the balance of reasons by invariably pulling towards a particular result regardless of context, but rather they affect the assessment of the balance of reasons in a way that varies with what has been decided by the courts in the past.

Thus it is perfectly conceivable that what observers would agree is essentially the same doctrine of precedent could point to quite different results in two jurisdictions where the courts had previously come to opposite conclusions concerning the proper disposition of a certain type of case. One can also speak of the different result that the same doctrine of precedent could hypothetically have required in a single jurisdiction, if the courts had decided an earlier case or line of cases other than as they did. The principles which make up Dworkin's doctrine of precedent are therefore best interpreted as second-order reasons for judicial action, directing that a set of first-order principles must be regarded as possessing a somewhat stronger threshold weight than that which would be required on the ordinary balance of reasons before it may permissibly be substituted for the set of principles which was relied upon in a previous similar case. This is, of course, precisely the strong Burkean conception of precedent.

It is worth remarking here that Dworkin's explanation of judicial obligation by reference to a process of reasoning that must be interpreted as involving a weighted balance of reasons is not limited, in the 'The Model of Rules I', to his interpretation of the doctrine of precedent. Dworkin seems at times in that paper

30 In 'The Model of Rules I' Dworkin used the term 'principle' to refer to standards that have the logical property of weight, as described in the text. He also drew a substantive distinction between principles and policies, where a principle 'is a requirement of justice or fairness or some other dimension of morality' and a policy 'sets out a goal to be reached, generally an improvement in some economic, political or social feature of the community': ibid, 22. A similar distinction was later relied upon by Dworkin in 'Hard Cases', ibid, ch 4, in the formulation and defence of the 'rights thesis'. In 'The Model of Rules I' he did not put the distinction which he had drawn there to work, however, and 'principle' in the logical sense was used generically to refer to standards which could be either policies or principles in the substantive sense. Although I believe that a version of the rights thesis can be defended, I will not try to show that here. Throughout this paper I will therefore use 'principle' in Dworkin's generic sense only.

to maintain that the balancing of principles is a source of judicial obligation *in addition to* that which is imposed by rules, but his theory of adjudication can be seen, when properly interpreted, to be a much more radical one than this would suggest. Dworkin argues, for example, that the bindingness of a legal rule is nothing more than the collective normative force of the principles which, taken together, can be regarded as justifying the particular course of action that the rule demands; when that support is considered to have evaporated, or never to have existed at all, then the rule is no longer to be treated by a judge as binding.[31] What this means, of course, is that all-or-nothing exclusionary rules have no place whatever in the theory of adjudication which Dworkin advances in this paper, appearances to the contrary notwithstanding; it would seem that if there is any place at all within this theory for a conception of rules, it is one in which a rule is regarded as nothing more than a device of convenience, a kind of *aide-mémoire* for recording the perceived aggregate consequences of the various principles that bear on the resolution of a specific kind of dispute.[32] The nature of judicial obligation is completely determined by a duty to act on the balance of first-order principles, as modified by certain second-order weighting principles of the sort represented by the doctrine of precedent. Even statute law is not considered to be obligatory in itself; whatever binding force that a legislative enactment possesses which is not simply attributable to its content derives from certain principles of 'legislative supremacy', which require no more than that the courts 'pay a qualified deference to the acts of the legislature'.[33]

This general conception of judicial obligation, which Dworkin does not appear to have carried forward in quite such a strong form from 'The Model of Rules I' into his later work, is an interesting and provocative one. It suggests, for example, that the Diceyan doctrine of parliamentary sovereignty is neither an inevitable constitutional arrangement nor one that has somehow just come to be accepted in British courts; it is to be regarded, rather, as the upshot of principles of political morality that have won judicial recognition because they are taken to state the proper relationship that should obtain between courts and democratically-elected legislatures. This suggests in turn that the courts of Britain and of other countries with similar constitutions could perhaps legitimately reach the conclusion that some alternative, less deferential conception of that relationship is the correct one; an example would be the doctrine of an implied bill of rights that has surfaced from

31 *TRS*, 37–38.

32 Cf Rawls' summary conception of rules, *supra* n 27.

33 *TRS*, 37. It is worth remarking here that the case of *Riggs* v *Palmer* (1889) 22 NE 188, which is one of Dworkin's main examples in 'The Model of Rules I', involved, as a result of judicial reliance on a principle, the modification or qualification of a statutory rule. On this point see Colin Tapper, 'A Note on Principles', 34 *Mod L Rev* 628, 629–31 (1971).

time to time in Canadian constitutional law.[34] These are not matters that can be considered here, and I raise them simply to show how an adjudicative theory of the sort described at the beginning of this paper has potential application not simply to the analysis of a judge's duty where no statute law is applicable, but also to the characterization of judicial obligation generally.[35] It is with judge-made law that the present paper is chiefly concerned, however, and I will be turning to consider its proper theoretical analysis once I have outlined, in the following section, Raz's discussion of the foundations of positivism and of the interpretation of precedent to which positivism gives rise.

3. POSITIVISM, JUDICIAL OBLIGATION AND PRECEDENT

3.1 *The foundations of positivism*

Law, according to Raz, is an institutionalized system of norms.[36] More particularly, it is a system of norms which is directed primarily towards guiding the conduct of the population at large, and which a particular kind of state-backed social institution, loosely identifiable for present purposes as a court, is bound to apply in evaluating that conduct. A norm belongs to the system—i.e. it counts as a law—either if it is a customary rule or principle that the courts accept as binding, or if it is a rule or principle that a norm belonging to the system identifies as valid. Following Hart, Raz calls customary norms which set out the system's ultimate criteria of validity rules of recognition. Particular laws which belong to the system can impose duties, confer powers, or take any of a number of other logical forms, but it is duty-imposing rules, which are simply one type of exclusionary rule, that constitute 'the ultimate basis of the law';[37] the significance of all other kinds of laws resides in their logical relation to duty-imposing laws, so that the point of such legal regimes as contract and trust, for example, is that they confer a power

34 See especially *Switzman* v *Elbling* [1957] SCR 285, 326–28 per Abbott J. See generally Peter Hogg, *Constitutional Law of Canada* (2nd ed, Toronto, 1985), 636–38. The doctrine of an implied bill of rights was rejected by Beetz J in *A G Canada* v *Dupond* [1978] 2 SCR 770, 796, and has in any case been overtaken by the coming into force in 1982 of the *Canadian Charter of Rights and Freedoms*. The possibility of a less deferential conception of the relationship between the British courts and Parliament was rejected by Lord Simon of Glaisdale in *Miliangos* v *George Frank (Textiles) Ltd* [1976] AC 443, 472–73.

35 A somewhat different theoretical conception of statute law and of the judicial practice of statutory construction, which I think is closer to Dworkin's own view in this work after 'The Model of Rules I', is sketched below in section 4.6. This theory allows that legislatures enact exclusionary rules, but maintains that interpretive principles grounded in considerations of political morality must be brought to bear to determine just what rule they have enacted. Depending, of course, on one's understanding of what the appropriate interpretive principles entail, this approach still allows for the possibility of something like a doctrine of an implied bill of rights.

36 See generally *PRN*, ch 4; *AL*, chs 3, 5, 6.

37 *AL*, 176.

upon individuals to create new duties for themselves and others which are of a legally binding character.

On Raz's view, then, a legal system must contain laws which are capable of guiding the behaviour of individuals, and it must also make provision for courts which evaluate the conduct of individuals by means of those very same laws.[38] Raz also maintains that there is an overarching theoretical constraint on the means by which a law can be identified within the system as valid, which is that its existence must be established, and its content determined, on the basis of social facts alone. Raz calls this constraint the *sources thesis*, and he elaborates it in the following way: 'A jurisprudential theory is acceptable only if its tests for identifying the content of the law and determining its existence depend exclusively on facts of human behaviour capable of being described in value-neutral terms, and applied without resort to moral argument.'[39] Whenever a court relies on standards that do not meet this test it is, in Raz's view, not applying law but exercising discretion.[40]

The sources thesis draws attention to the fact that law is in some sense a human creation, a perception which lies at the heart of the positivist tradition in legal philosophy, and Raz further emphasizes that law is a social phenomenon; a legal system arises out of, and helps to order, the interactions and relations among persons which are characteristic of community life. But the sources thesis goes well beyond the recognition of what Raz calls the primacy of the social,[41] insisting that law cannot incorporate moral rules or principles even by reference;[42] law is not simply a normative system which is located within a social framework, but one in which each individual norm is necessarily identifiable by reference to social facts alone.[43]

In *The Authority of Law* Raz advances two arguments in support of this strong claim.[44] The first is that the sources thesis orders and systematizes the intuitive

38 See *AL*, 112: '[L]aw contains both norms guiding behaviour and institutions for evaluating and judging behaviour. The evaluation is based on the very same norms which guide behaviour.' See also *PRN*, 142: 'The official evaluation of behaviour by the primary organs [i.e. courts] must of course coincide with the guidance given by the system to ordinary individuals.'

39 *AL*, 39–40; see also 47.

40 Ibid, 59.

41 Ibid, 103.

42 Ibid, 46.

43 A weaker version of positivism, in which the rule of recognition might identify at least some legal standards by reference to moral considerations rather than social facts, has been argued for by a number of theorists: see Philip Soper, 'Legal Theory and the Obligation of a Judge: The Hart/Dworkin Dispute', 75 *Mich L Rev* 473, 511–12 (1977); David Lyons, 'Principles, Positivism and Legal Theory', 87 *Yale LJ* 415, 425–26 (1977); Jules Coleman, 'Negative and Positive Positivism', 11 *J of Legal Stud* 139, 148 (1982). In *TRS*, 345–50, Dworkin has, however, offered persuasive reasons for thinking that this approach cannot be reconciled with positivism. Raz agrees, although his argument is different: see *AL*, 47, n 8; 'Authority, Law and Morality', *supra* n 14, 311–15. A recent attempt to revive the Lyons-Soper-Coleman line of argument can be found in W. J. Waluchow, 'Herculean Positivism', 5 *Oxford J Legal Stud* 187 (1985).

44 *AL*, 48–52.

distinctions which, he maintains, we draw between settled and unsettled law, and between applying the law and developing it; it is the 'normal', or 'common' view, says Raz, that when judges interpret and apply the settled law they are using purely legal skills which involve no recourse to moral considerations, so that they only have occasion to use moral skills when they are called upon to decide cases where the law is unsettled or otherwise in need of development. These distinctions to which Raz adverts, however, are not so much systematized by the sources thesis as they are implied by it, in the sense that they do not constitute incontrovertible social facts, hard empirical data which a theory of law must acknowledge and explain or else be accounted unacceptable; they are, rather, claims about the theoretical character of the legal process which presuppose the acceptance, explicit or implicit, of a certain philosophical interpretation of that process. Distinctions of this sort have no place in Dworkin's rights thesis, for example, which, as Dworkin says, 'presents not some novel information about what judges do, but a new way of describing what we all know they do; and the virtues of this new description are not empirical but political and philosophical'.[45] Our pretheoretical conception of law does not, in other words, draw Raz's distinctions in such a sharp and unequivocal way that we have no choice but to accord them theoretical recognition.

The second of Raz's two justifications for the sources thesis, however, takes the form of an argument for, rather than from, the positivist interpretation of what it is that judges do, and for that reason is the more fundamental of the two. Raz remarks that this argument 'captures and highlights a fundamental insight into the function of law', where that function is taken to be '[the provision of] publicly ascertainable standards by which members of the society are held to be bound so that they cannot excuse non-conformity by challenging the justification of the standard'.[46] The reason for regarding the function of law in this way has to do with the fact that law 'helps to secure social cooperation not only through its sanctions providing motivation for conformity but also through designating in an accessible way the patterns of behaviour required for such cooperation'.[47] (This does not, of course, commit Raz to the position that actual laws are such that general compliance with them will necessarily lead to social cooperation, or even that it would be a good thing if that were to happen.)[48] The designation of the required patterns of behaviour is achieved by means of rulings which are issued by political authority. The actual argument for the sources thesis is then presented in the following terms: 'Since it is of the very essence of [an] alleged authority that it issues rulings which are binding regardless of any other justification, it follows that it must be possible to identify those rulings without engaging in a justificatory argument, i.e. as issuing from certain activities and interpreted in the

45 *TRS*, 90; cf 352.
46 *AL*, 50, 52.
47 Ibid, 51.
48 See 'Authority, Law and Morality', *supra* n 14, 321.

light of publicly ascertainable standards not involving moral argument.'[49] As this justification for the sources thesis makes clear, Raz regards rulings issued by political authority, and therefore laws, as being, at least in the eyes of the authority itself, exclusionary reasons which pre-empt any other reasons (perhaps within a certain range) that citizens could have for performing or refraining from performing a given type of action.

In a recent article Raz has advanced a different version of this second argument for the sources thesis. He there defends what he calls the 'service conception' of authority, according to which authorities are to be regarded as 'mediating between people and the right reasons which apply to them, so that the authority judges and pronounces what they ought to do according to right reason'.[50] A de facto authority will only be justified if it is likely to assess the requirements of right reason better than its alleged subjects. But it can only carry out this mediating role if its subjects actually do guide their actions by its instructions and not by what *they* think right reason demands. Authoritative directives must therefore pre-empt the subjects' own assessment of what action is required by right reason, i.e. the directives must be regarded by the subjects as exclusionary reasons (although Raz does not use that term here). The sources thesis is then justified because the subjects of the authority can benefit from its decisions 'only if they can establish their existence and content in ways which do not depend on raising the very same issues which the authority is there to settle'.[51] This version of the second argument for the sources thesis, like the version presented in *The Authority of Law*, clearly presupposes that the central function of law is the authoritative guidance of conduct. The main difference between the two is that the newer version is based on a more sophisticated conception of what 'the authoritative guidance of conduct' involves.

In addition to its role in justifying the sources thesis, this idea that the function of law is to provide authoritative guidance for conduct by means that transcend individual judgment is also the foundation, in Raz's theory, of the related positivist thesis concerning the nature of judicial obligation. Raz envisages the social regulation of conduct in terms of a distinction between what he calls the deliberative and executive stages of public decision-making.[52] At the deliberative stage, the paradigm instance of which is the law-making process of a legislature, various possible social choices are evaluated, on whatever basis is considered appropriate, and one of them is selected as the preferred alternative. At the executive stage, where the necessary course of action is carried out or enforced, there can be no further assessment of the wisdom of the initial choice, and, in

49 *AL*, 52.

50 'Authority, Law and Morality', *supra* n 14, 299 (emphasis deleted from original). On the service conception see also 'Authority and Justification', *supra* n 22.

51 'Authority, Law and Morality', ibid, 304.

52 *The Concept of a Legal System* (2nd ed, Oxford, 1980), 213–14. See also 'The Problem about the Nature of Law', *supra* n 14, 214–16.

particular, no further assessment of its moral merit. The deliberative stage, in other words, issues in—and sometimes amends or repeals—authoritatively declared and publicly ascertainable standards of conduct which then belong to the executive stage and which constitute exclusionary rules for both ordinary citizens and courts: citizens are legally obligated to comply with the declared standards of conduct, and courts, which are the primary institutional reflection of the executive stage of the process, are legally obligated to employ those same standards when they evaluate citizens' behaviour.

If a court happens to be called upon to resolve a dispute that is not regulated by the settled law, or if it is authorized to change the settled law in some respect in the course of deciding a case, then it will have itself assumed the role of acting at the deliberative stage of decision-making, and the constraining obligations that are associated with its usual executive function no longer apply.[53] It is in this sense that the nature of judicial obligation is not only initially determined but ultimately limited by the duty to apply pre-existing positive laws: where a court makes a decision that is not governed by such laws, basing itself instead on standards which are drawn from morality, for example, then it is exercising a discretion in exactly the same sense that a legislature is when it enacts one statute rather than another; within the limits of any general constraints that might be imposed by a particular constitutional arrangement, the one kind of deliberative decision-making body is no more bound by a *legal* obligation than is the other.[54] This assertion is subject to the possible qualification discussed by Raz that the scope of judicial discretion might sometimes be limited by general principles which, so long as they are source-based, themselves have the status of law. But the existence of such principles, and their applicability to any given case, are contingent matters on the positivist model, and in any event they do not impose a solution on the judge; rather they simply provide guidance for him in the exercise of his discretion.[55]

3.2 *Positivism and precedent*

It can thus be seen that on the positivist view the primary obligation of courts, and therefore their most basic function, is to apply pre-existing source-based laws,

53 *AL*, 113.

54 Raz recognizes in *AL* at 195–201 that courts are, owing to their institutional character, more restricted than legislatures in their ability to introduce far-reaching reforms; this is, however, a practical rather than a theoretical matter. It should also be noted that in *AL*, 197, after first saying that in making law 'courts . . . should act just as legislatures do, namely, they should adopt those rules which they judge best . . .', Raz characterizes this duty as a *legal* duty because it 'follows directly from the fact that by law the courts are not allowed to act arbitrarily. . . .' It would appear that Raz regards the duty not to act arbitrarily as applying to all judges and not just to those of, say, the English legal system: see e.g. Raz, 'Legal Principles and the Limits of Law', 81 *Yale LJ* 823, 847–48 (1972), where a similar point is made without reference to any particular legal system. But the existence of a valid law or, more likely, of a general judicial custom, that unregulated cases not be decided arbitrarily, can be, on the positivist model, a contingent matter only; there is nothing in the model itself to exclude arbitrary exercises of discretion in a given legal system.

55 *AL*, 113.

but, as has just been made clear, positivism is not committed to regarding this as their only function. Where a dispute arises which is not regulated by pre-existing law, it will generally be the case that a court will not simply decline jurisdiction but will assume the role of a deliberative decision-maker, settling the dispute through an exercise of discretion. In legal systems where this is true the courts will thus have a secondary function of dispute-settlement that extends beyond the application of pre-existing laws.[56] In some legal systems, moreover, such acts of discretion may themselves be accepted by the judiciary as sources of law, in which case the court will effectively be acting, as it is sometimes put, as though it were a deputy legislature or a body exercising delegated rule-making power. This law-making role may be limited to the interpretation and supplementation of an independently-legislated regime of rules, since any such regime will inevitably give rise to indeterminacies and gaps, or, as with the common law, it may be that the regulation of certain areas of activity has been left over to the courts more or less entirely. In either of these two situations a judicial decision in an unregulated case will become a binding precedent, offering authoritative guidance both to the population at large and to the courts themselves in their disposition of subsequent similar cases.

Thus while it is not a necessary fact about courts that they make law as well as apply it, it is nonetheless true, on the positivist model, that if judges do have a law-making function then they make law in very much the same way that legislatures do: precedents are to be regarded as, or as giving rise to, exclusionary rules that are binding for both citizens and courts alike.[57] It follows that a court can only overrule such a binding precedent when its justification for doing so lies outside a certain range of reasons; it is not free to depart from a previous decision simply because it thinks that, all things considered, that would be the best thing to do on the overall balance of reasons.[58] Raz's formal analysis of a rule as an exclusionary reason whose scope may be less than absolute thus plays a crucial role at this point in his theory, since it is only by relying on this idea that he is able

56 At times Raz seems to suggest that a normative system is not a legal system unless it fulfils the function of settling unregulated disputes: see *AL*, 172–75. While he maintains there that the settlement of unregulated disputes is in fact a primary function of law, he does not try to relate this claim to his most central and fundamental thesis that '[i]t is of the essence of law to guide behaviour through rules and courts in charge of their application' (*AL*, 225). But even if one were to grant that Raz's theory can legitimately categorize the settlement of unregulated disputes as a primary function of law, he still could not maintain, at least not without moving from a purely positivist theory to one which incorporated elements of the adjudicative approach, that such a function necessarily involves attempting to settle disputes in a just or a rational or even a non-arbitrary way: see n 54, *supra* n 65, *infra*, and accompanying text.

57 *AL*, 114, 195, 197. See also *PRN*, 144: 'The courts are in effect bound to regard individuals as acting in accordance with legal standards to the exclusion of all other reasons. Since . . . the rules of the system which apply to ordinary individuals are identical with the rules by which the primary organs [i.e. courts] ought to judge individuals it follows that *all* the legal rules are both first-order and exclusionary reasons' (emphasis added).

58 *PRN*, 140–41; *AL*, 114–15, 189–90.

plausibly to maintain both that courts can be bound by a given precedent, and that they may nonetheless have a discretion under certain circumstances to depart from it.[59] It is probably fair to say that the apparent paradox concerning how this could be so, which had been an obstacle to previous attempts by Richard Wasserstrom[60] and others to characterize the bindingness of judge-made law, has received in Raz's analysis its first satisfactory resolution, in a formal sense at least, from a positivist perspective.[61]

The idea that the essential (i.e. theoretically-determinative) function of law is the authoritative guidance of individual conduct[62] thus constitutes the focal point of an elegant and powerful interpretation of our unrefined, pretheoretical perceptions of law and the legal process. The aspects of this theory that are of the greatest interest for our present purposes, however, are the following two theses: first, that the theoretical contours of judicial obligation are shaped almost entirely by the duty to apply positive laws, where the central case of such a law is an authoritatively-enacted exclusionary rule which is intended to guide the conduct of ordinary citizens and which judges are obligated to apply in evaluating that conduct; and second, that the common law doctrine of *stare decisis* is, like the legislative process of enactment, to be interpreted as giving rise to positive laws in precisely this sense.

The importance of these two theses in Raz's model is given emphasis by what he has to say about so-called systems of absolute discretion.[63] Raz asks us to imagine a certain kind of adjudicative institution which has authority in a community to settle all disputes referred to it, but which in doing so need not apply a particular set of legislated or customary standards, whether these are of its own or anyone else's creation. These 'courts', while they are not bound even by their own precedents, are nonetheless not free to settle disputes in an arbitrary way: they must always 'make that decision which seems to them the best in the

59 Although nothing turns on the point for present purposes, there would in fact seem to be two levels of exclusion. The first level is that of individual rules which have been created by precedent; since each such rule can have its own exclusionary scope, 'departure' from the rule would be possible whenever there are sufficiently weighty reasons which fall outside the range of excluded reasons. The second level is that of the doctrine of precedent itself; here, reasons falling outside the scope of the doctrine could warrant the modification or complete abrogation of rules at the first level. In practice the distinction between the two levels would be likely to be quite blurred.

60 Richard Wasserstrom, *The Judicial Decision* (Stanford, 1961), 160 ff.

61 In 'The Model of Rules I', *supra* n 28, Dworkin argued at 37–38 that a positivist could only account for the bindingness of a legal rule by supposing that it coincides with the collective, aggregate bindingness of a set of principles. (This conception of judicial obligation is discussed in the text accompanying n 31, *supra*.) Raz's alternative explanation in terms of exclusionary rules shows Dworkin to have been mistaken on this point, at least in a formal sense.

62 By a function which is 'theoretically-determinative' I mean one which is attributed by a theory to law, or to some particular aspect of the legal process, and which affects in a direct and significant way the theory's interpretation of the pre-theoretical data.

63 *PRN*, 137–41; *AL*, 111–14, 173–75.

circumstances, taking account of all the considerations which seem to them relevant'.[64] This requirement that decisions must be justified by reasons could be expected to lead, says Raz, to some measure of regularity in rulings, but because cases will be heard by different judges holding divergent opinions, each of whom might in any event change his mind on any given issue, the degree of consistency over time is not likely to be high. An adjudicative system of this sort would therefore not provide any standards which individuals could use to guide their conduct, and so, according to Raz, could not be characterized as a legal system. This conclusion underscores the importance of the first positivist thesis that I singled out above, relating to the nature of judicial obligation, because it makes clear that any duty which a judge might have to decide an unregulated case in the way that he thinks is independently (morally) correct is not, on the positivist view, a *legal* obligation.[65]

What Raz has to say about systems of absolute discretion also bears on the second positivist thesis to which I have drawn attention, namely the contention that precedents give rise to legal rules in the sense of exclusionary reasons for action, since he apparently does not envisage any possible interpretation of a practice of *stare decisis* other than the exclusionary approach: either adjudicative institutions follow their own precedents on an exclusionary basis, or else they cannot be said to be bound by their previous decisions at all (except possibly in the very attenuated sense that is represented by a weak Burkean conception of precedent); if the latter alternative holds, then, as in a system of absolute discretion, each case is decided through individual consideration of the balance of reasons. (Even if the system contained customary, discretion-guiding principles of the sort which Raz discusses elsewhere,[66] this would not give rise to a different interpretation of precedent, since these principles would just be another kind of first-order reason to be taken into account in the ordinary balance of reasons.) Raz simply does not allow, in other words, for the possibility that judges might be bound by their own decisions in the manner suggested by a strong Burkean conception of precedent.

64 *AL*, 111–12.

65 This is so, at least, unless the particular legal system under consideration contains a law which directs judges to decide cases in that way, where the requisite law might either be embodied in a judicial custom or recognized by the rule of recognition as valid. However, as was indicated in n 54, *supra*, Raz has occasionally seemed to contend that judges always have a legal obligation to decide cases in a non-arbitrary way. As I there pointed out, on the positivist model there could only be such an obligation if it was imposed by an appropriate law, and the existence of such a law is always a contingent matter. One is nonetheless led to ask whether the obligation not to decide cases arbitrarily which Raz attributes to the judges of a system of absolute discretion is considered by him to be a *legal* obligation. If it is not, then in what respect is this obligation different from the apparently similar one which he attributes to other judges? On the other hand, if it is a legal obligation, then why is the system not a legal system, even if only in some peripheral sense?

66 See generally Raz, 'Legal Principles and the Limits of Law', *supra* n 54.

In section 4 of this paper I will argue that the common law doctrine of *stare decisis* is best interpreted as a strong Burkean conception of precedent rather than as an instance of the exclusionary approach. This will show that common law precedents should not be regarded as giving rise to rules which are exclusionarily binding on judges (one aspect of the second positivist thesis),[67] and at the same time will point the way towards a more complex picture of judicial obligation than is drawn by the first positivist thesis. Although it will not be possible to complete that picture in this paper, I at least hope to be able to show that it can only be properly filled in by utilizing elements of the adjudicative approach to legal theory. Unlike the positivist view of law which underlies the sources thesis, the adjudicative approach does not take the function of law which is theoretically determinative in this context to be the authoritative guidance of conduct. One conclusion towards which the arguments of section 4 will accordingly point is that the sources thesis is not applicable, in any theoretically significant sense, to the common law.

4. LEGAL THEORY AND THE COMMON LAW

4.1 *Rules, principles and justification*

Bentham maintained that the common law was 'fictitious' and 'a mere non-entity',[68] or, at best, a manifestation of 'sham',[69] 'mock', or 'impostrous'[70] law which in reality amounted to little more than the exercise of arbitrary power.[71] This scepticism was the consequence of his belief that the common law could not in any plausible way be characterized as a system of authoritatively-enacted rules, which, in the positivist tradition, he took to be the only tenable model for law of any sort. I will argue that while Bentham was correct to deny that the common law consists of rules—at least where rules are understood in Raz's exclusionary sense—common law precedents are nonetheless meaningfully binding on judges in a way which still makes it sensible to assert that the common law exists as a

67 I will not be able to deal in this paper with another aspect of the second thesis, which is that precedents give rise to rules which are exclusionarily binding for *citizens* as well as for courts. I would want to argue, however, that this aspect of the second claim is false as well.

68 Jeremy Bentham, 'Papers Relative to Codification and Public Instruction', in John Bowring, (ed), *The Works of Jeremy Bentham* (Edinburgh, 1843), 483. Bentham's claim that the common law did not exist is discussed by A. W. B. Simpson in 'The Common Law and Legal Theory', in Simpson, (ed), *Oxford Essays in Jurisprudence*, second series (Oxford, 1973) 77, 88–89.

69 Bentham, ibid, 485.

70 Ibid, 460.

71 Ibid, 460: 'Of unwritten [i.e. common] law (for such is the term in use), but much more properly of uncomposed and unenacted law (for of writing there is, beyond comparison, more belonging to this spurious than to the genuine sort) . . . the perpetual fruits . . . are . . ., in the breast and hands of the judge, power everywhere arbitrary, with the semblance of a set of rules to serve as a screen to it.' 'Genuine' law is 'written or statute law' (ibid, 460), which is 'the only real sort of law' (ibid, 484).

rational and non-arbitrary regime of practical reason. There is a coherent mode of practical reason underlying the doctrine of ***stare decisis***, but it consists of a weighted balance of reasons and not, despite Raz's contention to the contrary, of a system of exclusionary rules.

In order to preserve a measure of neutrality in terminology I will use the term 'proposition' of the common law rather than the expression 'rule'. That liability for unintentional injury to the person or property of another is to be determined in accordance with the negligence standard of fault is, for example, a proposition of the law of torts. The most obvious characteristic of such propositions, and one that has frequently been remarked upon, is that they are not expressed in a canonical form of language, or, as Pollock put it, they 'have never been committed to any authentic form of words'.[72] This feature of the common law was in fact one of the reasons for Bentham's belief that it did not constitute a system of genuine rules,[73] and the connection which he perceived between a rule and a definitive linguistic formulation of the rule is perhaps plausible in the following way. The very nature of a rule is, as Raz correctly observes, both to exclude a certain range of first-order reasons from consideration in deciding what to do, and at the same time to serve as a first-order reason itself for performing (or refraining from performing) some specified action. A rule can do neither of these things very efficiently, however, unless the nature of the appropriate action, and the circumstances under which it becomes mandatory, are specified with some degree of exactitude, and this is more likely to be the case where a fixed form of words is employed. I of course do not mean to suggest that there cannot be rules which have not been given a canonical formulation, and the difference between rules which have been so formulated and those which have not is in any event a matter of degree; every rule, no matter how precisely worded, will always have a measure of open texture. But there is perhaps something to be said for the claim that the central case of a rule is one that has been 'committed to [an] authentic form of words', especially since conventions of construction can then be brought to bear which will have the effect of further restricting the initial range of potential indeterminacy.

If common law propositions were simply exclusionary rules that were defective because they had not received a definitive linguistic formulation, then there is no reason to suppose that such a defect could not and would not have been remedied by the judiciary. In fact, however, a reform of this sort would be pointless. A proposition of the common law is not generally regarded as important in itself, but only as a kind of convenient but informal statement of the outcome that is perceived as flowing from a particular set of justifying principles in a particular type of case. A judge who is considering a precedent is generally more interested in the principles which were taken to justify the decision reached, and, in particular, in whether they apply to the facts of the present case, than he is in any

72 Frederick Pollock, *A First Book of Jurisprudence* (6th ed, London, 1929), 253.

73 *Supra* n 71.

baldly-stated proposition or 'rule' that the earlier decision could be said to stand for. It is true that the appeal to such principles may not always be explicit; this happens, for example, whenever a judge relies upon a determination that the facts of the case before him are 'relevantly' similar (or dissimilar) to those of the previous case, without attempting to give a (complete) justification for drawing the distinction in the way that he does.[74] The utilization of such a concept of relevant similarity can only be understood as an implicit claim that the principles that must be taken as justifying the decision in the earlier case require that a similar result be reached in the case at hand.

The pervasiveness of this tendency on the part of common law judges to appeal both explicitly and implicitly to justifying principles is significant, since it demonstrates that propositions of the common law do not possess 'the relative independence . . . from . . . their justifying reasons' which Raz says is typical of rules, and which explains why we hypostatize rules and treat them as 'complete reasons in their own right':[75]

> Thus norms [i.e. exclusionary rules] have a relative independence from the reasons which justify them. In order to know that the norm is valid we must know that there are reasons which justify it. But we need not know what these reasons are in order to apply the norm correctly to the majority of cases. . . . It prevails in virtue of being an exclusionary reason.

This relative independence of rules from their justifying reasons is an important element in Raz's defence of positivism, since the basis of the argument for the sources thesis is that legal standards must be identifiable without recourse to justificatory argument, and, in particular, without recourse to moral argument. This does not, however, appear to be true of propositions of the common law (at least so far as judges are concerned), since it is a direct appeal to the principles underlying those propositions which ultimately seems to lie at the foundations of common law reasoning. This would seem to be the point, for example, of the common law maxim 'cessante ratione legis, cessat ipsa lex'.[76]

It might seem that there is a fairly straightforward reply which the positivist could make to this line of argument. The reply would grant that common law judges do look to the reasoning behind previous decisions and not simply to propositions which summarize the upshot of that reasoning. But, the reply would run, this state of affairs is not inconsistent with the model of exclusionary reasoning, since the rationale of a previous decision must itself be regarded as exclusionarily binding on a common law judge. The judicial task which is associated with the doctrine of *stare decisis* is to determine which principles were

74 Perhaps an even more common formulation to the same effect is that there is 'no distinction in principle' between the way that the two sets of facts should be regarded by the court: see e.g. *Bannister* v *Bannister* [1948] 2 All ER 133, 136.

75 *PRN*, 79.

76 This is not to deny Lord Simon of Glaisdale's conclusion, in *Miliangos* v *George Frank (Textiles) Ltd*, *supra* n 34, 476, that the maxim 'is not a licence to courts to change the law . . .'. In section 4.2 I offer an analysis of the constraints on judicial freedom.

taken to be relevant in previous similar cases, assess what relative weights were thought to attach to each, and then ascertain whether and how that received understanding of the normative situation applies to the case in hand. According to this view, the entire *ratio decidendi* of a common law precedent is to be regarded as constituting an exclusionary reason for judicial action in any subsequent cases in which the facts fall within the *ratio*'s scope. Principles are important in the common law, but it is only the previous judicial understanding of which principles apply when that actually binds judges; in cases that are covered by a precedent there is no room for a fresh reassessment. The reply would no doubt concede that this variety of exclusionary reasoning differs from the central case of a rule which is expressed independently of its justification, especially since a large measure of judgment is called for in determining what the *ratio decidendi* of a judicial decision is. But the point that would be insisted upon is that this interpretation of common law reasoning *is* exclusionary, and so is capable of being accommodated within the positivist model.

This reply will not do as it stands, since it is clearly not true that the process of common law reasoning categorically rules out fresh reassessments of which principles apply in which types of case, and of what specific results they point to; not only do judges frequently refine, qualify or revise the reasoning that was relied upon in earlier cases, they sometimes reject the rationale of a previous decision entirely. It is conceivable, however, that a more sophisticated version of the simple model of exclusionary reasoning that was sketched in the last paragraph could be developed which would be able to take account of these facts. Raz's attempt in chapter 10 of *The Authority of Law* to reconcile the doctrine of precedent with the revisability of the common law suggests the form that such a theory might take.[77] Raz distinguishes between two categories of judicial revision in the common law, namely those where the change involves overruling a previous decision and those where it does not, and for purposes of exposition it will be convenient to follow him in this regard. The latter category will be considered in the remainder of this section, but the former will not be considered until section 4.3.

Raz suggests that revisions of the common law which do not amount to instances of overruling must be explained by reference to the judicial practice of distinguishing.[78] Sometimes judges distinguish a previous case by means of a straightforward determination that the reasoning which was given in support of the earlier result does not apply to the facts of the case at hand. If the practice of distinguishing were limited to such determinations then it would obviously not be capable of remedying the inadequacies of the simple 'exclusionarily binding *ratio*'

77 Note that Raz accepts the distinction which I earlier rejected between a common law rule and its rationale, and that he frames his proposed reconciliation in these terms. This is not important in the present context, however, since almost everything that Raz says in his discussion of precedent can be translated into a terminology that does not employ this distinction: see e.g. n 79, *infra*.

78 *AL*, 184–85, 189, 195.

model discussed above. Raz describes a stronger form of distinguishing, however, which permits a judge to add a further restricting condition to a common law rule, but only if the newly-stipulated condition was present in the reported facts of the earlier case; the new version of the rule must still support the old result.[79] Having characterized the 'special revisability' of judge-made law in this way, Raz concludes that such law has 'a different status from legislated law'.[80] It can, he says, be said to be 'metaphorically' less binding than statutory law, but, even so, '[s]trictly speaking judge-made law is binding and valid, just as much as enacted law;'[81] common law rules are, according to Raz, 'binding in their essential rationale.'[82] (I will assume for present purposes that statutory law can properly be characterized as giving rise to exclusionary rules.)

The problem with this attempt to reconcile the revisability of the common law with an exclusionary interpretation of the doctrine of precedent is that it depends on too narrow a characterization of the ways in which, even short of overruling, the common law can be revised. Judges do not limit themselves, in reassessing the justificatory principles which were employed in a previous case, to restricting the reach of those principles; very commonly a court will recognize that the true scope of the relevant principles requires that their range of potential application be extended beyond what had been contemplated by the court which made the original decision. Raz explains such cases as instances of analogical reasoning, in which an entirely new rule is created through reliance on the rationale that justified an old one: '. . . if a certain reason is good enough to justify one rule then it is equally good to justify another which similarly follows from it'.[83]

The first point to be noted about this explanation which Raz offers for common law cases in which the range of previously-accepted principles is extended is that it utilizes the distinction between a rule of the common law and the rationale for the rule which I argued earlier to be unimportant. It also depends (as does the entire positivist model of the common law) on a much sharper theoretical distinction between making and applying law than any which is drawn by the judges themselves.[84] But more significant than either of these points is the fact that this explanation does not even seem to give Raz a way to avoid saying that on at least some occasions analogical reasoning leads judges 'to extend [an old] rule . . . by dropping a condition [of applicability] . . .' (as opposed simply to leading them in all such situations merely 'to create another rule').[85] Thus, even

79 Ibid, 185–86. Essentially the same idea could be captured, but without reference to rules, by saying that judges are permitted to reformulate the principles which were used to justify a previous decision if the effect is to restrict those principles' range of applicability while still supporting the result of the previous decision itself.

80 Ibid, 195.

81 Ibid.

82 Ibid, 189.

83 Ibid, 204.

84 Raz acknowledges this in *AL*, 206–9.

85 Ibid, 204.

within the terms of Raz's own model, the strong form of distinguishing is not the only means by which a common law rule can be modified; so long as the results of previous cases are still upheld, a judge may, if he thinks that the extant version of a rule can be improved upon, *either* add new conditions of applicability *or* drop old ones. It is therefore no longer clear how, on Raz's view, a common law rule can be said to possess an exclusionarily binding 'essential rationale'. This conclusion is reinforced by the observation that the process of reassessing the reasoning in previous cases sometimes takes a more radical form than mere restriction or extension, amounting to what is, in effect, the articulation of a new justificatory basis for a whole line of prior decisions. This kind of modification of the common law, which is not discussed by Raz, is particularly characteristic of landmark cases: *Donoghue* v *Stevenson*[3] and *MacPherson* v *Buick Motor Co*[4] are, perhaps, the most celebrated examples in modern times of such general restatements of the law, but they are by no means the only ones.

4.2 *The strong Burkean interpretation of precedent*

Let me try to summarize what has emerged from the discussion in section 4.1. Propositions of the common law must be characterized as informal statements of the upshot of a particular balance of justifying principles, as these principles are thought to apply to a particular kind of case. This is evidenced by the fact that such propositions lack a canonical formulation, so that their content and scope must be primarily determined by direct reference to the underlying principles rather than by reliance upon techniques resembling those of statutory construction. Common law propositions therefore cannot be regarded as being instances of Raz's central case of exclusionary rules, which are rules that possess a relatively large measure of independence from their justifying reasons. But neither can such propositions be construed as exclusionary rules in some secondary sense, according to which the formulation of underlying principles that was arrived at in the relevant precedents is itself exclusionarily binding. This is because the possibility of reconsidering and modifying the underlying balance of justifying principles, far from being excluded, seems to be left open in some way in almost every case. Moreover the extent to which the common law can thus be restated and revised is, even without any previous cases being overruled, sufficiently great that it does not appear to be capable of being accommodated within a more sophisticated version of this 'exclusionarily binding *ratio*' approach. It is nonetheless obvious that the doctrine of precedent places *some* constraints on the revisability of the common law, but the nature of these constraints seems to elude the exclusionary model completely.

There is an alternative interpretation of the doctrine of *stare decisis* which, while it is capable of accounting for the extensive revisability of the common law, makes clear at the same time that the process of revision is not an unconstrained

86 [1932] AC 562.
87 (1916) 111 NE 1050.

one. This interpretation is based upon the strong Burkean conception of precedent, and it is accompanied by an account of judicial obligation which, being drawn from the adjudicative approach to legal theory, differs markedly from the positivist account. The most basic obligation of the common law judge is not, on this view, to evaluate the conduct of individuals in accordance with exclusionary rules which were created, as the positivist interpretation of *stare decisis* would have it, by a judicial procedure that closely resembles statutory enactment. Instead the judge is taken to be obligated to decide the cases that come before him on the basis of whatever principles of justice and other relevant dimensions of morality properly apply in the resolution of disputes of that kind, where the nature of these principles is very much as described by Dworkin in 'The Model of Rules I'.[88]

On this view the judge is nonetheless not free, as he would be in the system of absolute discretion described by Raz, for example, simply to ignore what has been done in the past and to decide the case presently before him in the way that he now happens to think is correct. If the present case falls within the scope of the reasoning that was enunciated in an earlier similar case, then he can only rely on a modified (or completely different) formulation of principles if the collective weight of the latter appears to him to be, in the manner of the strong Burkean conception, above a threshold of strength which is higher than what would be required on the ordinary balance of reasons. (The factors which determine this threshold will be considered shortly.) Otherwise he is bound to make the decision that is indicated by the precedent, which can therefore be loosely thought of as having itself been assigned a certain weight (i.e. beyond whatever intrinsic weight is perceived as attaching to the reasoning which supported the result). The intuitive idea is that a legal system can change its mind, so to speak, about which principles apply to a given type of case, about what relative weight each possesses, and about what concrete results they collectively point to, but it cannot do so too hastily.

Propositions which summarize the upshot of the train of judicial reasoning in one or more precedents can no doubt be spoken of in a loose and derivative way as being binding upon judges. Within the bounds of this locution, however, judge-made law can be seen to be not merely metaphorically less binding than enacted law, as Raz suggests, but *really* less binding. The reason for this has to do with the nature of the strong Burkean conception of precedent: previous judicial reliance upon the set of principles for which a given proposition stands does not exclude action upon a subsequently reconsidered balance of reasons, but is simply deemed, in effect, to confer a somewhat greater weight upon those principles than they would otherwise have received when reconsideration occurs. The process of common law adjudication, the central function of which is taken on this view to be the resolution of individual disputes in accordance with the appropriate principles of morality, thus gives rise, as a kind of by-product, to a body of dispute-settling standards which possess a certain degree of stability. But the propositions which

88 See n 30, *supra*. As I there explained, in this paper I am using 'principle' in the generic sense of 'The Model of Rules I' and not in the substantive, rights-oriented sense of 'Hard Cases'.

set out these standards have a very different status from statutory enactments. Besides lacking a canonical formulation and being, in the sense just explained, less binding, even the degree to which they do bind need not be fixed; as we shall see in a moment, the threshold which is established by the strong Burkean conception of precedent can vary among propositions, and for any given proposition it can change with context and over time.

It would therefore be very misleading to speak of a proposition of the common law as having been brought into full-blown existence, through a process analogous to the enactment of legislation, simply because the principles underlying it had served as the basis of decision in one or more cases. Such propositions are, rather, established as a part of the law to a greater or lesser degree, in the sense that they can vary in the extent to which they resist reformulation, qualification, revision and replacement. This is a convenient but, again, a somewhat loose way of speaking, since it is really the underlying set of justifying principles, and not the proposition itself, which constitutes the locus of resistance to change; the extent to which a particular proposition can be said to be established as a part of the law is determined by the extra threshold weight that a proposed new formulation of the balance of justifying principles must be thought to attain before it can replace the formulation of principles for which the proposition presently stands.[89] (For the sake of convenience I will sometimes refer to the proposition itself as carrying a certain relative weight.) That liability for unintentional injury to the person or physical property of another is to be determined in accordance with the negligence standard is, in this sense, a well-established proposition of the law of torts. That recovery may be had for negligently-caused economic loss is, by contrast, a proposition that is less well established.

The relative weight that is to be assigned to any given proposition of law will generally be a complex function of many different factors, including the position in the judicial hierarchy of the courts that have relied upon the proposition in the past, the number of times that it has been so relied upon, and the age[90] of the relevant precedents. Where the threshold is set will also vary with the extent to which a particular area of the law should be regarded as appropriately inducing

89 The idea of a principle (or proposition) of the common law being settled or established to a greater or lesser degree has been given expression in a number of different metaphors in judicial opinions. See, for example, *Hedley Byrne & Co Ltd* v *Heller & Partners Ltd* [1984] AC 465, 519 per Lord Devlin: 'I cannot feel, therefore, that there is any principle enunciated in *Le Lievre* v *Gould* which is now so deeply embedded in the law that your Lordships ought not to disturb it.'

90 The effect of this factor is complex and possibly confused: see the discussion in Alan Paterson, *The Law Lords* (London, 1982), 161. Generally speaking, however, a proposition of law that has been enunciated in a very recent case seems to carry less weight than one enunciated in a case which has stood for a longer time: see e.g. *Jones* v *Secretary of State for Social Services* [1972] AC 944, 993 per Viscount Dilhorne. On the other hand, a proposition that was stated in a very old precedent may, if it has not been reaffirmed for some time, carry less weight than it would have if it had been associated with a more recent case.

reliance; being able to predict and rely upon what a court is likely to decide is undoubtedly more important in contract law than in negligence law, for example.[91] It is also possible that a certain weight may sometimes be accorded to a given proposition by reason of its having been recognized and relied upon by the higher courts of certain other jurisdictions. The nature of the factors which have just been canvassed should not, however, lead one to conclude that the weight of a proposition is a determinate property which is fixed, at any given moment in time, independently of the context in which the proposition is being considered: its weight is also relative to the position in the judicial hierarchy of whatever court is contemplating modifying it, as well as to the extent of the modification which is proposed. A suggested reformulation of the balance of justifying principles underlying a given proposition can range from, on the one hand, a relatively minor reassessment (which might take the form, for example, of a slight variation in the relative weight attributed to each relevant principle) to, on the other, a proposal which entails that the principles properly applicable in the resolution of a given kind of dispute are radically different from those which have been applied heretofore.[92] A very minor change will generally involve little perceptible alteration in the threshold of strength above the ordinary balance of reasons, and it will probably be capable of implementation by most of the courts in the system; a major restatement of the law, on the other hand, along the lines of *Donoghue* v *Stevenson,* will involve a much higher threshold, and implementing the change will in general be the prerogative of the higher courts of appeal.

The relative weight that is to be assigned on any given occasion to a particular proposition of the common law—and hence its degree of bindingness on that occasion—thus varies with the precise configuration of the different factors just enumerated (and no doubt others as well); contrary to Raz's claim, such propositions are not binding or not-binding, valid or invalid, in the all-or-nothing fashion that is usually associated with statute law.[93] Strictly speaking, of course, they are not even variably binding except in a derivative sense, since the basic process of practical reason which underlies the common law is to be found at the more fundamental level of a weighted balance of principles; propositions of the common law are, to repeat, essentially devices of convenience, undoubtedly useful

91 The fact of justified reliance, as opposed to an assessment of the relative importance of predictability, is a consideration which can directly affect the balance of substantive reasons. See the discussion in section 4.4 below.

92 Note that a proposed reformulation could entail that one or more previous cases should have been decided differently. This will be discussed in section 4.3, where overruling is considered.

93 I thus disagree as well with the following claim made by Finnis, *supra* n 8, 312, at least so far as it applies to the common law: 'The black-and-white quality of legal obligation (like the all-or-nothing quality of legal validity) is part of the data, which an explanation of law must take into account and explain (and not explain away).' The idea that propositions of the common law are valid in an all-or-nothing sense is, for both positivism and for the traditional natural law theory defended by Finnis, not part of the data but the consequence of an interpretation of the data.

but ultimately dispensable. Moreover, as has already been pointed out, judges, at least, frequently do dispense with them; it is often remarked that common law judges do not generally write their judgments in a way that shows direct reliance upon, or permits the ready extraction of, proposition-like statements of the law (or rule-like statements, as it is usually put).[94] Casting the law into the form of concise propositions is, to a certain extent at least, a task that has been undertaken by treatise-writers rather than by judges.

In connection with the observation that propositions of the common law are only derivatively binding, it is also worth noting that judges characteristically speak of being bound by cases rather than by propositions (or by 'rules'); this is consistent with the idea that second-order weighting principles ultimately apply not to propositions as such but to sets of first-order principles, where the actual degree of weighting is determined by what has been done in previous cases. Cases are usually said, moreover, to possess not validity but authority,[95] which is a variable rather than an all-or-nothing concept, and one which can be fitted quite easily into the account of common law reasoning being presented here: the authority of a case is a function of, first, the perceived strength of the actual arguments that were given in support of the result reached, and, second, of the various characteristics of the case—its age, the hierarchical status of the deciding court, etc—that might affect the threshold of weight that would have to be met by a proposed revised set of justifying principles in a subsequent similar case. It is thus quite conceivable that a well-reasoned lower court decision can have greater authority than a poorly-reasoned decision by a higher court, and the history of the common law in fact offers many such examples.

4.3 *Overruling*

In the discussion in the preceding section of the way in which propositions of the common law can be said to be established to a greater or lesser degree, I was assuming that all potential revisions of the law could only take place within the limits of a more fundamental constraint that is imposed by previous cases, namely the limitation on overruling. Overruling is simply the necessary implication of a sufficiently drastic restatement of the law that an earlier case would now be decided differently. It is to a consideration of this constraint, which is the one that judges probably most often have in mind when they speak of being bound by an earlier decision, that I now wish to turn. The question that will be of particular interest is whether the common law practices relating to overruling can be accommodated within the theoretical interpretation of the doctrine of precedent that I have been developing up to this point.

94 See e.g. A. W. B. Simpson, 'The *Ratio Decidendi* of a Case and the Doctrine of Binding Precedent', in A. G. Guest, (ed), *Oxford Essays in Jurisprudence* (Oxford, 1961) 148, 166; Dworkin, *TRS*, 111.

95 See e.g. Simpson, *supra* n 68, 86. Weinrib also discusses this point in 'The Natural Law of Torts', *supra* n 7.

According to Raz, the constraint on overruling is always exclusionary in character: judges cannot, he says, modify the law to such an extent that a previous decision would now be reversed except on the basis of certain sorts of reasons, i.e. reasons that fall outside the scope of an exclusionary reason.[96] Now it is certainly generally true that a lower court in a common law jurisdiction cannot, on the basis of however cogent a reason, overrule a decision by a court that is higher than itself in the judicial hierarchy, and often it cannot overrule a decision by a court at the same level. It is also true that between its decision in the *London Street Tramways*[97] case in 1898 and its Practice Statement of 1966,[98] the House of Lords regarded itself as being completely precluded from overruling its own decisions. These are examples of situations in which the constraint on overruling has taken on (absolutely) exclusionary status. As has already been explained, however, an exclusionary reason is simply a special case of a more general conception of a second-order reason, which is a reason for assigning a first-order reason a greater or lesser weight than that which it would ordinarily carry. It does not follow from the fact that the constraint on overruling sometimes assumes this special form that it must always do so.[99]

That lower courts are bound by the decisions of higher courts in a strong exclusionary sense can easily be explained by a general requirement of institutional consistency: the state cannot justifiably permit the parties in one of its courtrooms to be treated in a manner that is at variance with how they (or any other set of litigants) would be treated in the courtroom next door.[100] It is a requirement of consistency such as this which justifies the generally greater degree of constraint alluded to earlier on the ability of lower courts to modify the common law; in the case of the drastic sort of modification of the law which is represented by overruling, this limitation takes the strong form of an exclusionary prohibition (at least where the prior decisions of higher courts are concerned). The picture of the judicial process which is associated with such a requirement is one in which the responsibility for major revisions of judge-made law is vested mainly in the highest courts of appeal, whose decisions are then to be taken as imposing systemic constraints of consistency throughout the entire judicial hierarchy.

What then can be said of the highest courts of appeal themselves? Are they necessarily constrained by an exclusionary prohibition from overruling their own previous decisions, except, possibly, where they do so on the basis of reasons that

96 *PRN*, 140–41; *AL*, 114–15, 189–90.

97 *London Street Tramways Co Ltd* v *London County Council* [1898] AC 375.

98 [1966] 3 All ER 77.

99 Note, however, that in terms of the distinction drawn in n 59, *supra*, Raz's discussion of overruling would seem mainly to be concerned with second-level exclusion. For the strong Burkean conception of precedent, which does not give rise to a distinct category of hypostatized standards corresponding to Raz's exclusionary rules, such a distinction between levels of exclusion is without significance.

100 The ultimate justification for such a requirement is presumably related to Dworkin's doctrine of political responsibility: see *TRS*, 87, 162.

fall outside a certain scope? The House of Lords, as I have already mentioned, certainly adhered (or at least claimed to adhere) to such a practice from 1898 until 1966, the year in which Lord Gardiner stated that the House would in future continue to treat its former decisions as 'normally binding', but would 'depart from a former decision when it appears right to do so'.[101] Was this a shift from an absolute exclusionary doctrine to one with a more limited exclusionary scope? Or was it, rather, a shift from a strong Burkean conception of precedent in which the threshold that had to be achieved by a new perception of the balance of justifying principles was, if an overruling were involved, unobtainably high, to one in which this was no longer so?

Raz is clearly committed to the first of these two alternative interpretations of the 1966 change. He says of overruling generally that there is a 'permissible list' of reasons for overruling a previous decision which includes, but is apparently not exhausted by, injustice, iniquitous discrimination, and being out of step with the court's conception of the relevant area of law.[102] Now quite apart from the fact that this list is stated at such a general level that it seems to capture most of the reasons that a court would ever be likely to have for overruling a previous decision, so that an exclusionary prohibition would be left with very little work to do and one would be led to expect overruling to occur much more frequently than it does, common law courts do not appear to have even an implicitly limited list of possible reasons in mind when they consider overruling an earlier case. Judges in the House of Lords, for example, emphasize that the decision being reconsidered must be 'clearly wrong',[103] and they tend to speak of the necessity for 'a very good reason'[104] to overrule rather than for a reason of one or another sort. This is language which argues for a strong Burkean over an exclusionary interpretation of overruling, since it emphasizes the degree of strength of the balance of justifying reasons as presently

101 *Supra* n 98.

102 *PRN*, 140; *AL*, 114.

103 *Fitzleet Estates Ltd* v *Cherry* [1977] 3 All ER 996, 1000 per Viscount Dilhorne: 'If the decision in the *Chancery Lane* case was wrong, it certainly was not so clearly wrong and productive of injustice as to make it right for the House to depart from it.' See also *O'Brien* v *Robinson* [1973] AC 912, 930 per Lord Diplock; *Jones* v *Secretary of State for Social Services*, *supra* n 90, 993 per Viscount Dilhorne.

104 *Knuller Publishing Promotions* v *DPP* [1973] AC 435, 455 per Lord Reid: '[O]ur change of practice in no longer regarding previous decisions of this House as absolutely binding does not mean that whenever we think that a previous decision was wrong we should reverse it. In the general interest of certainty in the law we must be sure that there is some very good reason before we so act.'

perceived, rather than categories of excluded and non-excluded reasons.[105]

When I say that common law courts, and the House of Lords in particular, do not have a limited list of possible reasons in mind when they consider overruling a previous decision, the emphasis should be placed on the word 'limited'. I do not, of course, mean to imply that the House of Lords has not worked out standards for the overruling of its own prior decisions, but only that these standards can best be understood in terms of the strong Burkean conception of precedent. Alan Paterson has recently attempted to distil from the relevant cases a number of criteria which he says that the House of Lords has developed to help determine when one of its own previous decisions should be overruled.[106] There are several positive criteria (by which I mean ones that would favour departure from a previous decision), these being that the holding in the earlier case is outmoded, unjust, or itself the cause of great uncertainty. Like Raz's list of reasons for overruling these criteria are very broadly-stated, almost to the point of being all-encompassing. Even so, there does not seem to be any implication, either on Paterson's part or in the cases, that the categories of overruling are closed. Moreover these positive criteria must be considered in conjunction with what I would regard as the most important of Paterson's negative criteria, which is that 'a decision ought not to be overruled merely because the Law Lords consider that it was wrongly decided'[107] (the 'precedent merely wrong' criterion). When one examines the language in which the Law Lords themselves have formulated this criterion, examples of which were given in the previous paragraph and accompanying footnotes, I think it becomes clear that it is best understood simply as a statement of the strong Burkean conception of precedent.[108]

As for Paterson's other negative criteria, one involves a current inability to assess the balance of principles (the 'unforeseeable consequences' criterion), and so is consistent not only with the strong but with the weak Burkean conception. The rest are either compatible with the strong Burkean conception (the 'use sparingly'

105 Canadian common law judges have not explicitly addressed the question of when previous decisions should be overruled to the same extent that English judges have, but what they have said seems to be best understood in terms of the strong Burkean conception of precedent. See, for example, former Chief Justice Bora Laskin's article 'The Role and Function of Appellate Courts: The Supreme Court of Canada', 53 *Can Bar Rev* 469, 478 (1975): 'We are now able [in Canada] to view [*stare decisis*] as simply an important element of the judicial process, a necessary consideration which should give pause to any but the most sober conclusion that a previous decision or line of authority is wrong and ought to be changed.'

106 *Supra* n 90, 156–57.

107 Ibid, 157.

108 Sometimes judges in the House of Lords have spoken of the 1966 Practice Statement in terms that are more reminiscent of the *weak* Burkean conception of precedent than they are of the strong version, let alone the exclusionary model; see e.g. *Saif Ali* v *Sydney Mitchell & Co* [1980] AC 198, 217 per Lord Diplock: 'In this House, . . . since the Practice Direction of 1966, all propositions of law laid down in the speeches in previous appeals are persuasive only. . . .' Such a characterization does not, however, seem to accord very well with actual English practice.

criterion), involve statutory interpretation rather than the common law (the 'construction' criterion),[109] or are concerned with a possible *change* in the balance of principles since the previous decision was rendered (the 'legitimate expectations' and 'need for comprehensive reform' criteria). Changes in the balance of principles will be discussed in the following section.

The House of Lords' exclusionary approach to overruling its own decisions between 1898 and 1966 is probably best regarded as an extreme and somewhat aberrant application, to the specific constraint on overruling, of a more general conception of change in the common law that even during that period could be seen to take a strong Burkean form;[110] it was an approach, moreover, that the House of Lords itself obviously came to think was mistaken.[111] Even so, since 1966 English judicial practice seems generally to be interpretable as requiring that a reason to overrule be of a threshold strength well beyond what would otherwise be decisive on the ordinary balance of reasons. Both the earlier and the later English practice can thus be contrasted with the approach of the higher American courts, which have traditionally appeared to take the view that, at least in certain areas of the law, a reason for overruling must meet a threshold of strength that is only slightly (if at all) above what would be sufficient on the ordinary balance of reasons. At times the American practice seems more consistent with a weak than with a strong Burkean conception of precedent.[112] Judicial decisions in the United States are nonetheless generally regarded as giving rise to law in much the same way as they are in England, and a theory that can explain how and why this could be so is clearly preferable to one that cannot. The general account of precedent that I have presented in this paper is capable of providing such an explanation,

109 There is a brief discussion of statutory construction in section 4.6 below.

110 I am referring here to changes in the common law which fall short of overruling, of the sort discussed in sections 4.1 and 4.2, and also to the overruling of lower court decisions by the House of Lords. That judicial reasoning in the latter sort of situation took a strong Burkean form even during the *London Tramways* period is evidenced by, for example, *Admiralty Commissioners* v *Valverda* [1938] AC 173, 194, where Lord Wright said that the House of Lords would overrule a long-established course of decisions 'only in plain cases where serious inconvenience or injustice would follow from perpetuating an erroneous construction or ruling in law'.

111 See Paterson, *supra* n 90, ch 6.

112 This has been especially true in the case of constitutional law. See e.g. *Smith* v *Turner* (1849) 48 US 282, 470 per Taney CJ: 'I . . . am quite willing that it be regarded hereafter as the law of this court, that its opinion upon the construction of the Constitution is always open to discussion when it is supposed to have been founded in error, and that its judicial authority should hereafter depend altogether on the force of the reasoning by which it is supported.' Cf *Burnett* v *Coronado Oil & Gas Co* (1932) 285 US 393, 406–10 per Brandeis J (dissenting); *Smith* v *Allwright* (1944) 321 US 649, 665 per Reed J. However, in '"Overruling" Opinions in the Supreme Court', 57 *Mich L Rev* 151 (1958), Albert Blaustein and Andrew Field have argued that the United States Supreme Court has generally observed certain constraints in overruling its own previous decisions (including, it would seem, those in the constitutional area). These constraints can, I believe, be best understood in terms of a strong Burkean conception of precedent.

since the differences between various versions of the strong Burkean conception of precedent are merely differences of degree, and even the weak Burkean conception is, as was explained in section 2.2, just one extreme of the same continuum.

Raz himself speaks at times in his discussion of overruling in terms that are more reminiscent of the strong Burkean conception of precedent than they are of the exclusionary model. He says at one point, for example, that 'a court should not overrule unless it is certain that the new rule is an improvement compared with the old'.[113] This kind of 'restraint of caution', as Raz calls it, is very much in the spirit of the strong Burkean approach, which builds a kind of conservative inertia into the adjudicative process but without in general completely excluding any particular reason or type of reason from further consideration. Generally speaking, there does not appear to be any distinction between the types of reasons that could be (and are) given by the courts for modifications to the common law that fall short of overruling, and those that could be (and are) given for modifications which imply that a previous case should have been decided the other way. Rather there seems to be a requirement that the more drastic change which is involved in the latter kind of situation be justified by the reasons for it being seen to carry a greater weight than would otherwise be necessary; this suggests, in turn, that the constraint on overruling is simply one more factor—albeit an important one—to be taken into account in determining the threshold of perceived strength which must be met before a different conception of the proper balance of justifying principles in a given area of the law can be substituted for the presently-accepted conception.

4.4 *Changes in the balance of principles*

There may well be a number of grounds why a court would adhere to a strong Burkean conception of precedent. One of the most important of these would seem to be that by doing so it could take into account, in the dispute-settling process itself, the fact that it is always of value to the parties to a potential dispute to know in advance how the dispute would be likely to be settled; this is a consideration which is relevant to the resolution of those disputes which do in fact subsequently arise. The only way that a court could otherwise take account of this sort of consideration (apart from adopting a weak Burkean or exclusionary approach to precedent, either of which would just be a variation on the same theme), would be to try to factor it directly into the ordinary balance of reasons. The only apparent way that it could do this, in turn, would be to look to the actual expectations either of the litigants presently before it or of the general population. While it is true that even if the court did not adhere to any sort of doctrine of precedent there would still always be an expectation that it would settle disputes on the basis of the applicable substantive considerations, these are often controversial; there would, therefore, often be no *concrete* expectations concerning

113 *AL*, 190.

what the court was likely to do which could be of any assistance to potential litigants in arranging their affairs.

A court might therefore want to ensure a degree of predictability in an indirect way by adhering, with respect to the balance of substantive reasons, to a strong Burkean conception of precedent.[114] In doing so it would presumably try to assess and take into account, with respect to the various sorts of disputes that might arise, the relative importance of maintaining a measure of predictability as against that of deciding each case on the basis of the applicable substantive considerations. This, I would argue, is the reason why common law courts vary the determining threshold of the strong Burkean conception in accordance with certain of the factors which were discussed in section 4.2. The relative importance of predictability is obviously higher, for example, with respect to voluntary transactions such as contracts than it is with respect to involuntary transactions of the sort dealt with by the law of torts.[115]

In adhering to a strong Burkean conception of precedent a court would, of course, be generating new concrete expectations, of a greater or lesser strength, in favour of the status quo. Potential litigants would often be justified in relying on these expectations, so that in some sorts of situations, particularly those where voluntary transactions were concerned, it might become appropriate for the court to take account of such reliance directly, i.e. in the ordinary balance of principles.[116] There would be, in other words, a kind of feedback effect from the strong Burkean conception of precedent to the balance of substantive reasons, and very often it might become difficult—perhaps impossible—to distinguish the two different sources of conservative pull. In this way certain kinds of dispute-settling procedures might become so entrenched that even where a court felt that the original case giving rise to the procedure had obviously been wrongly decided, it would nevertheless not feel justified in overruling it because the balance of reasons *now* required that the same result be reached again. Raz recognizes that the balance of reasons can be affected by the judicial process in this way.[117] It is interesting to remark that where this has happened the resulting dispute-settling procedures might resemble exclusionary rules, even though this is not what they would be, either in origin or in present form. Rather such procedures would be directly justified on the basis of the present state of the ordinary balance of principles.

The foregoing discussion serves to clarify the nature of the 'legitimate expectations' criterion which Alan Paterson includes in his enumeration, discussed

114 Cf the 1966 Practice Statement, *supra* n 98: '[The use of precedent] provides at least *some degree* of certainty upon which individuals can rely in the conduct of their affairs . . .' (emphasis added).

115 See e.g. *BTC* v *Gourley* [1956] AC 185, 211–12 per Lord Reid.

116 Cf the 1966 Practice Statement, *supra* n 98: '[Their Lordships] will bear in mind the danger of disturbing retrospectively the basis on which contracts, settlements of property and fiscal arrangements have been entered into. . . .'

117 *AL*, 191.

in the previous section, of the criteria which he thinks that the House of Lords has developed for overruling its own decisions.[118] Another of Paterson's criteria which is relevant here is the following: 'A decision ought not to be overruled if to do so would involve a change that ought to be part of a comprehensive reform of the law' (the 'need for comprehensive reform' criterion).[119] This criterion is also concerned with a change in the balance of principles, but of a different sort from that which has just been discussed. Where the justification for a previous decision has become an integral part of an interlocking network of dispute-settling procedures, the fact that the judicial process of decision-making is necessarily limited in its capacity to make an immediate, sweeping change in the settled law can undoubtedly count as a reason against overruling that decision and thereby introducing inconsistency into the larger network. We have here an instance of an *institutional* consideration, of the same general sort that is invoked by the *de minimis* principle and perhaps also by the infamous floodgates argument, which is being taken into account in the ordinary balance of reasons. If (and to the extent that) such considerations affect the general capacity of the courts to settle disputes in a just and consistent manner, then judges should clearly weigh them into the balance of principles in deciding particular cases.

4.5 *The nature of the common law*

The idealized picture of common law reasoning that has been presented in previous sections is for the most part quite sharply and precisely drawn, whereas in practice, of course, the way in which precedents figure in judicial argument tends to be much more impressionistic and elusive, with the whole process often giving rise to much unclarity and controversy. A. W. B. Simpson has said in this regard that the common law is 'more like a muddle than a system', that its character is 'essentially shadowy', and that it operates 'as if [it] placed particular value upon dissension, obscurity, and the tentative character of judicial utterances'.[120] The value of the idealized picture which is associated with the strong Burkean conception of precedent is that, by seeming accurately to reflect an underlying logic in the common law process of reasoning, it demonstrates that that process need not be interpreted as a muddle in anything other than a superficial sense: if the strong Burkean account is correct then we are not forced, for example, to regard the common law as an attempt by the judiciary to create a system of exclusionary rules that has somehow spectacularly misfired.

That the common law nonetheless sometimes appears to be a muddle is the consequence of at least three factors. The first is that some degree of indeterminacy in the characterization of judicial reasoning results from the

118 *Supra* n 90, 156: 'A decision ought not to be overruled if to do so would upset the legitimate expectations of people who have entered into contracts or settlements or otherwise regulated their affairs in reliance on the validity of that decision. . . .'

119 Ibid, 156–57.

120 Simpson, *supra* n 68, 87, 90, 99.

feedback, described in the previous section, from the strong Burkean conception of precedent to the balance of substantive reasons. The second is that reasoning on the basis of a (weighted) balance of reasons can never be a matter of precise mechanical calculation: the determination of the weight that should properly be attributed to different reasons for action, and their subsequent aggregation and balancing, is a process that we constantly and necessarily rely upon but which is inevitably impressionistic in its actual manner of operation.

The third factor underlying the appearance of muddle, which is related to the second, might be called the element of moral uncertainty. We have available to us no formal decision procedure which will make clear, in a reliable and certain way, which principles are applicable to which sorts of cases, what weight they carry, and what concrete results they support. The answers we give to these questions depend on a constant search for overall coherence among our various moral judgments at all levels of generality, along the lines suggested by Rawls' conception of reflective equilibrium,[121] and so in general can never be, at any one time, anything other than presumptive and provisional in character. We necessarily operate, in other words, with a moral picture which, because it is at best only an approximation of the truth, is always open to revision. It is this possibility of conflict between what was previously and what is presently thought to be morally correct that underlies whatever need there might be for second-order weighting principles that try to regulate the transition from one judicial approximation of moral truth to another. And it is this same possibility, together with the further layers of inexactitude and uncertainty which are introduced by the second-order principles themselves—they are, of course, as subject to revision and qualification as are first-order principles[122]—that gives rise to the 'dissension, obscurity and . . . tentative character of judicial utterances' to which Simpson draws our attention.

Despite the occasional appearance of muddle and obscurity the common law can, I have argued, be shown to be ultimately grounded in a consistent and rational process of practical reason which is nonetheless not rule-based in character. The strong Burkean interpretation of common law reasoning thus affords, for example, a coherent explanation of how it is both that the authority of precedents appears to be variable rather than all-or-nothing in nature, and that particular propositions of the common law seem in a related way to be established as a part of the law to a greater or lesser degree. It offers a plausible answer to the persistent puzzle concerning 'how [the] process of perpetual change [in the

121 See John Rawls, *A Theory of Justice* (Cambridge, Mass, 1972), 20–21, 48–51. Rawls assumes that the search for coherence will eventually result in a point of equilibrium being reached, although it may not be a stable equilibrium. This assumption is not, however, a necessary one.

122 Note, however, that in order to avoid upsetting legitimate expectations concerning the operation of the doctrine of precedent itself, second-order weighting principles should ideally be reassessed in a way that does not take anyone by surprise. Thus when the House of Lords decided to depart from its practice of not overruling its own previous decisions, it made that decision known not by actually overruling a case but by issuing a Practice Statement.

common law] can be reconciled with the principle of authority and the rule of *stare decisis*'.[123] At the same time it provides a non-metaphorical rendering of Lord Mansfield's aphorism that 'the common law . . . works itself pure by rules drawn from the fountain of justice. . . .'[124]

The understanding of judicial obligation which is associated with the adjudicative approach to legal theory serves, moreover, both to explain and to underscore the significance of the systematically ambiguous way in which lawyers speak of 'the common law'. While use of that expression often carries with it a reference to the settled law as it exists at present, the more dominant and fundamental reference, as illustrated by the quote from Lord Mansfield, is to the dynamic, institutionalized process of rational dispute-settlement itself; in addition, there are usually overtones concerning what the courts *should* do in order to settle a given sort of dispute justly or fairly.[125] The adjudicative interpretation of the common law process offers an explanation of why the last two of these three different senses which attach to the expression 'the common law' figure as prominently in our linguistic usage as they do, since the function of the common law is, on this view, precisely to settle disputes in accordance with justice and whatever other moral principles may be relevant.

The body of settled common law is, therefore, not to be regarded as the productive machinery of the common law process, which is essentially how it is conceived on the positivist model, but as a by-product; it is never more than a weighted but nonetheless provisional approximation to those requirements of morality the determination and application of which constitute the ultimate obligation of the common law judge. This, I think, is the true basis for Dworkin's repeated rejection of any picture of 'existing law' which takes it to consist of 'a distinct collection of rules and principles . . . such that it is a sensible question to ask whether, at any given moment, a particular rule or principle belongs to that collection'.[126] It also provides a reason for questioning the significance of the sources thesis for the common law, even though the existence and content of the various propositions of the settled law may be determinable at any particular moment by reference to social facts alone, since in any given case the solution indicated by the currently-accepted settled law is always liable to be retrospectively displaced, within the constraints of the strong Burkean conception

123 Lord Wright, *Legal Essays and Addresses* (Cambridge, 1939), xvi.

124 *Omychund* v *Barker* (1744) 1 Atk 21, 33, (argument of Solicitor-General Murray, later to become Lord Mansfield). The aphorism presupposes that successive approximations of what morality requires form an asymptotic progression towards the truth. I make no comment here on whether this optimistic presupposition is plausible.

125 Cf Simpson, *supra* n 68, 79: 'In the common law system no very clear distinction exists between saying that a particular solution to a problem is in accordance with the law, and saying that it is the rational, or fair, or just solution.' (This point does not, however, seem to sit very well with Simpson's own account of the common law in terms of custom; this sort of theory is discussed and criticized below.)

126 *TRS*, 343; cf 76, 292.

of precedent, by the requirements of justice as they come to be perceived by the court.

This is perhaps an appropriate place to point out that a strong Burkean interpretation of the doctrine of *stare decisis* differs not only from Raz's exclusionary model of valid, source-based rules, where the criteria of validity are set out in a rule of recognition, but also from any account of the common law in which it is treated as a form of custom among the judiciary (or possibly among the judiciary and bar together).[127] Such an account, which in any event could only offer a plausible explanation of the common law as it is found in a jurisdiction with a highly homogeneous judiciary or legal profession, must suppose that a judge applies a given proposition of law because—and only because—that proposition is generally accepted among a certain group of persons (judges and perhaps other lawyers). The strong Burkean conception of precedent, on the other hand, supposes that a judge applies a given proposition of the law because of the reasons that can be given in support of it, and while general acceptance of a practice among a group of persons can sometimes count as a reason for doing the same thing, such as when the practice provides the solution to a coordination problem, it would be most implausible to think that the doctrine of *stare decisis* could be given a general justification along these lines.[128]

It is true that the strong Burkean theory looks upon a proposition of the common law as in effect carrying a certain weight simply by reason of having figured in previous judicial decisions, and so in that respect appears to be at least

127 See e.g. Simpson, *supra* n 68, 9:–99.

128 On the view being considered in the text, each individual proposition of the common law (putting aside any problems of individuation that might arise) would be regarded as an instance of judicial custom. *Stare decisis* is, on this view, a kind of emergent phenomenon; judges do not so much comply with a rule that they should follow precedent as simply decide cases in the generally accepted way. This differs from the position of Hart and Raz, who regard the doctrine of *stare decisis* as part of the rule of recognition; that rule, but not the particular propositions of the common law which it identifies as valid, is regarded as customary in character. One might therefore be tempted to argue, as Gerald Postema has done in 'Coordination and Convention at the Foundations of Law', 11 *J of Legal Stud* 165 (1982), that the rule of recognition itself can be 'reconstructed' so as to show it to be a solution to a coordination problem. The coordination problem he envisages is the identification and interpretation of valid laws, and while it is true that the Hartian rule of recognition sets out criteria for this purpose, it also imposes a duty upon officials to apply those laws. (See Raz, *AL* 92–93.) No doubt some conventional solutions to coordination problems can give rise to duties, but the only such duty which Postema can arguably demonstrate to exist is the duty to identify and interpret valid laws correctly. He in effect simply builds the anterior duty to *apply* valid laws into the defining conditions of the coordination problem, and so does not ever provide an answer to the question of why there is such a duty in the first place. This question is, however, just another way of asking why the rule of recognition possesses normative force, which is the very question Postema purports to be answering. John Finnis attempts a more ambitious application of coordination theory to the foundations of law: see *supra* n 8, ch 9. The resulting theory is effectively criticized by Leslie Green in 'Law, Coordination and the Common Good', 3 *Oxford J of Legal Stud* 299 (1983).

superficially similar to an explanation in terms of custom, but it must be remembered that the strong Burkean approach also permits—indeed requires—a sufficiently strong reformulation of the principles underlying the proposition to prevail over the formulation that had previously been accepted; the approach can thus account for a fact that seems to lie beyond the explanatory reach of a purely custom-based theory, which is that changes in the common law do not simply happen but are typically the by-product of a reasoned judicial argument. The strong Burkean approach also differs from a custom-based theory insofar as it recognizes that judges do not simply identify particular propositions as belonging to the common law through reliance on a crude and undifferentiated conception of general acceptance, but rather assign different relative weights to different propositions as a function of a number of more or less independent factors concerning, *inter alia,* how and how often the proposition has been employed in previous judicial decisions.

It is worth pointing out that the differences between a strong Burkean conception of precedent and an explanation of the common law in terms of custom also serve to deflect certain criticisms that have been made of Dworkin's account of how principles figure in legal argument, as that account was developed in 'The Model of Rules I'. Dworkin maintained that we would go about backing up a claim that a given principle was a legal principle by pointing to certain kinds of 'institutional support' that it enjoyed,[129] the most notable instance of which would be the fact that it had been relied upon in earlier judicial decisions. Raz replied that such institutional support was really just a sign of general customary acceptance among the judiciary, which indicated that principles of which this was true possessed a social source that was compatible with positivism after all. (Raz further allowed for the possibility that a legal system might also contain non-ultimate principles that could be identified as valid by a sufficiently sophisticated rule of recognition.)[130] Dworkin subsequently pointed out in 'The Model of Rules II' that courts frequently treat principles as binding even in cases where they are given judicial expression for the first time,[131] which shows that institutional support cannot be a *necessary* condition for a principle to be a legal principle. But such support is not a *sufficient* condition either, since, as Dworkin had already made clear in 'The Model of Rules I', it is just one of the factors to be taken into account in determining the status and strength of a principle in legal argument;[132] sometimes a sufficiently strong change in the way that a court perceives the balance of reasons will lead it to conclude that a given principle should not be taken into account in a particular legal context at all, even though the courts had themselves previously regarded it as being applicable.

129 *TRS*, 40.
130 Raz, 'Legal Principles and the Limits of Law', *supra* n 54, 851–54.
131 *TRS*, 65; cf 344.
132 *TRS*, 41.

In a legal system based on a strong Burkean conception of precedent it would in fact be misleading to speak of *any* kind of general test for establishing whether or not a given principle is a 'legal' principle; institutional support in particular is simply a reason for attributing what amounts to an additional increment of weight to the (moral) weight that a principle is perceived as independently possessing. (More accurately, extra weight is effectively attributed to a *set* of principles, and only to the extent that they are collectively taken to justify a particular limited range of earlier decisions.) It is true that Dworkin does sometimes speak in this misleading way in 'The Model of Rules I', but it seems to me that that is a superficial and inessential feature of the theory of adjudication which he presents there.[133] The notion of institutional support clearly coincides at a more fundamental level with the effect of second-order weighting principles in a strong Burkean model of judicial reasoning; for the reasons already given, it therefore cannot plausibly be construed as an indication of general judicial acceptance amounting to an instance of custom.

4.6 *The construction of statutes*

Courts in common law jurisdictions follow their own previous decisions concerning the construction of statutory and constitutional provisions in much the same way that they do when common law precedents are in play, and in fact some of the cases that I cited earlier in describing the doctrine of precedent fell into the first rather than the second category. No theoretical distinction is drawn between the two types of situation (although judges in England, at least, clearly give more weight to a decision if it involves the construction of a statute).[134] One might therefore want to ask whether this univocal character of *stare decisis* is in any way at odds with the theoretical distinction argued for in section 4.2 between the status of legislative enactments and the status of propositions of the common law.

This is not the place to try to develop a full-blown theory of statutory construction, but the answer that I would want to give to the question just raised can be briefly sketched out in the following way. The consideration of moral principles in common law reasoning leads to the tentative judicial formulation of

133 Dworkin's own elaboration of the idea of institutional support in 'The Model of Rules II' involved the idea that 'a principle is a principle of law if it figures in the soundest theory of law that can be provided as a justification for the explicit substantive and institutional rules of the jurisdiction in question': *TRS*, 66. This way of explaining institutional support, which Dworkin developed at much greater length in 'Hard Cases', amounts in my view to a departure from the insights of 'The Model of Rules I' for the reason that it seems to require acceptance of an exclusionary model of the common law.

134 The result is, where overruling is concerned, Paterson's 'construction criterion' (*supra* n 90, 156). See e.g. *Jones* v *Secretary of State for Social Services*, *supra* n 90, 966 per Lord Reid, 995 per Lord Wilberforce, and 1024 per Lord Simon; *Vestey* v *IRC* [1980] AC 1148, 1187 per Viscount Dilhorne, and 1196 per Lord Edmund-Davies. As Lord Edmund-Davies noted in the latter case, however, 'there can be no absolute veto against overruling decisions turning on the construction of statutes or other documents—or, indeed, any other type of decision'.

specific dispute-settling standards, as enunciated in propositions of the common law. Such standards can be thought of as attempts to articulate the moral rule which properly applies to the sort of dispute in question. Instances of statutory construction, on the other hand, can be thought of as attempts to articulate, not an independent moral rule, but rather a rule which is taken to have been created by an act of legislation. The enacted rule cannot, of course, simply be equated with the particular (canonical) text which the legislature adopted; the rule must in effect be constructed from that text by means of interpretive principles which are, as Dworkin has rightly insisted, principles of political morality.[135] The strong Burkean conception of precedent can then be thought of as applying to previous attempts to state, in accordance with these principles, the rule which the legislature 'really' enacted,[136] and so can be seen to be operating in this context in very much the same way that it does with respect to prior attempts in common law cases to state an independent moral rule.

The univocal nature of *stare decisis* is thus accounted for, but without collapsing the theoretical distinction between statutory enactments and propositions of the common law: the former represent rules that have been created by particular legislative acts, whereas the latter represent direct judicial approximations of the requirements of justice and other relevant dimensions of morality. Furthermore, while the need for interpreting legislative enactments is unavoidable, this does not preclude treating the provisions of, say, the criminal law (including, incidentally, those derived from the common law as well as those from statute) as exclusionary guides to conduct of very much the sort which are described in Raz's version of positivism. Judicial attention to the basically exclusionary and action-guiding character of criminal law accounts for the concern evinced, for example, in the 1966 Practice Statement for 'the especial need for certainty' in this area of the law. It is also consistent with the fact that one of the most important principles of political morality which is applicable to the interpretation of criminal statutes is that they are to be construed strictly, in favour of the subject. Adherence to this principle means that much potential uncertainty is eliminated concerning what conduct on the part of an individual is being statutorily required or proscribed, thereby making it easier for him to guide his actions in accordance with what the legislature has enacted. Considerations of this sort also serve to explain the asymmetry which can be seen to operate in the doctrine of precedent in criminal cases.[137] Finally, a judicial concern with the action-guiding character of legislative provisions generally, and not just those which can be characterized as criminal law, seems to underlie the greater weight

135 See e.g. Dworkin, *A Matter of Principle*, *supra* n 16, chs 1, 2; *Law's Empire*, *supra* n 16, ch 9.

136 Cf Dworkin, *Law's Empire*, *supra* n 16, 16–17.

137 See e.g. *Merriman* v *DPP* [1973] AC 584, 605 per Lord Diplock: '[A]lthough the Criminal Division of the Court of Appeal is not so strictly bound by its own decisions as is the Civil Division, its liberty to depart from a precedent which it is convinced was erroneous is restricted to cases where the departure is in favour of the accused.'

which the House of Lords, at least, attributes to previous decisions involving statutory construction.

5. CONCLUSION

I have argued in this paper that Raz's model of exclusionary rules does not provide a satisfactory account of the common law process of reasoning, and, in particular, that it gives rise to a misleading characterization of the doctrine of *stare decisis*. A more accurate interpretation of what goes on in common law courts is provided by the strong Burkean conception of precedent, together with the understanding of judicial obligation which is generated by the adjudicative approach to legal theory: the most fundamental obligation of a common law court is to settle disputes in accordance with the applicable principles of morality, so that even though judges systematically weight their assessment of the balance of reasons in favour of continuity with the past, they never lose touch with those substantive principles in doing so. On this view 'the common law' is best regarded as the institutionalized process of adjudication itself, rather than as the body of relatively stable (but nonetheless constantly changing) dispute-settling standards which emerge from that process. This characterization of the common law, which calls into question the universality of the sources thesis, is not an arbitrary one.[138] Rather it begins with a different evaluative understanding from positivism of what the essential function of certain aspects of the legal process is.

What I have not argued, however, is that the function which Raz sees as fundamental to the theoretical characterization of legal phenomena generally, namely the guidance of conduct by means of authoritative, exclusionary reasons for action, has no part to play in legal theory. That would not be a defensible claim to make. Even within the context of common law adjudication it is clear that not only are lower courts exclusionarily bound not to overrule the decisions of higher courts, but the final ruling in a given case is, as between the litigants themselves, exclusionary in nature. I have also suggested at various points, although it has not been possible in this paper to elaborate, that other aspects of law and the legal process are also best understood in terms of Raz's analysis. Law is a complex social phenomenon, and it can no more be forced into a purely adjudicative mould than it can into a purely positivist one. An adequate and comprehensive legal theory must take account of the fact that law has more than one theoretically determinative function.

138 In 'The Problem about the Nature of Law', *supra* n 14, 212, Raz says that what he calls the lawyer's perspective, which is similar in important respects to what I have called the adjudicative approach, 'is arbitrary as an ultimate starting point'.

[4]

THE BRITISH GRUNDNORM: PARLIAMENTARY SUPREMACY RE-EXAMINED

I. Introduction

The recent referendum strongly endorsing British membership of the European Economic Community (EEC) makes it inevitable that Britain, like her co-members, must squarely face the prospect of Community law prevailing over inconsistent domestic legislation. This makes timely a reconsideration of the nature of the British constitution. Because Britain lacks a written constitution [1] and her courts, unlike those of the United States, decline to review the validity of parliamentary legislation, British lawyers have seldom examined the nature of the constitution in depth; in fact, such examinations have usually been spurred by a "constitutional crisis" in the Dominions. However, in the century since Dicey, Bryce, Anson, Hearn and Bagehot there has been a profusion of disparate views on the nature of the British constitution.

The "grundnorm" [2] (if one is a Kelsenian) or the "ultimate rule of recognition" [3] (if one is Hartian) of the British constitution is that the supreme legislative power rests in the Queen in Parliament, comprised—at least at present and for most purposes—of the House of Commons, House of Lords and the Queen, theoretically sitting

---

1 Viscount Radcliffe has described the British Constitution as "partly unwritten": *Adegbenro* v. *Akintola* [1963] A.C. 614, 628.

2 See D. Lloyd, *The Idea of Law* (1964), 195, 198. Mr. Fazal (quoting Salmond and Sir Rupert Cross in support) argues that "the rule that judicial decisions have the force of law" is a second "basic norm" of the English legal system: M. A. Fazal, "Entrenched Rights and Parliamentary Sovereignty" [1974] Pub.L. 295, 305. We disagree; although Mr. Fazal may be correct in asserting that the norm does not (expressly) derive its validity from the rule of parliamentary supremacy, it is impliedly derived therefrom because it exists at the mercy of Parliament. Hence, a result of the validity of the "first basic norm" is that the "second" is not "basic," whereas the "first" is. With respect, Mr. Fazal and Sir Rupert Cross miss the mark in asserting that "the fact that a statute can reverse the effect of a judicial decision" is irrelevant here (Fazal, *ibid.*, quoting Cross). Of course it is; what is relevant is that the so-called "second basic norm" can be altered by Parliament. If so, how can it be "basic"? See generally J. Stone, *Legal System and Lawyers' Reasonings* (1964), 81, 113. Those who, relying on Hughes C.J.'s. famous aphorism that "the Constitution is what the judges say it is," would assert that the above reasoning could be applied conversely—*i.e.* that the courts could refuse to recognise the rule of parliamentary supremacy—may be reminded that Parliament can dismiss judges, and controls the purse: see, *e.g.* the Abolition of Ship Money Act 1640 (16 Car. 1, c. 14) and the impeachment of six judges involved in the *Ship Money Case* (1641) 3 St.Tr. 1260. More cynically, it is ultimately Parliament, not the judiciary, which controls the army. *Cf. Ex p Merryman*, 17 Fed.Cas. 144 (No. 9487) (C.C.D. Md., 1861).

3 H. L. A. Hart, *The Concept of Law* (1961), 145.

together[4] but in fact sitting separately.[5] This rule was established during the eighteenth century when the political theories of Hobbes and Bodin were in vogue, with the result that over the years the "ultimate rule of recognition" has more frequently been stated by such slogans as "Parliament is sovereign"[6] or "Parliament is omnipotent."[7] In fact, in large measure slogans were employed to cover the fact that the real nature of the limits of Parliament's legislative power was not understood; fortunately, Britain's history since the "Glorious Revolution" of 1688 has been both peaceful (internally) and prosperous, with the result that questions as to the limits of the constitution could be virtually ignored.

The law relating to the powers of Parliament derives from *obiter dicta* of judges[8] and the writings of jurists and, hence, the relevant rules are usually classified as rules of "common law."[9] In reality, they are *sui generis*; it is by no means conceded that Parliament can alter these rules as it can other rules of the common law and it would only exacerbate the confusion about the nature of parliamentary supremacy if any importance is attached to the fact that these rules are classified as part of the "common law."

There are essentially two problems concerning the nature of the British constitution. First, does Parliament's power to legislate on any subject include the power to limit the area of competence or jurisdiction of future parliaments?: to adopt the phraseology of Professor Hart, is the supremacy of Parliament "continuing" or is it "self-embracing"?[10] If the former, each Parliament will have exactly the same powers as its predecessor; it will be able to legislate on every subject bar one—it will not be able effectually to restrict the area of

4 W. I. Jennings, *The Law and the Constitution* (5th ed., 1959), 137–138.

5 Sir Ivor Jennings was uncertain whether the two Houses must sit separately (*ibid.*, 140), but R. T. E. Latham asserted that "The King, Lords and Commons meeting in a single joint assembly, and voting by majority, or even unanimously, could not enact a statute": *The Law and the Commonwealth* (1949), 523 note 3. But *cf. Ndlwana* v. *Hofmeyr N.O.* [1937] A.D. 229, 238 (disapproved in *Harris* v. *Minister of the Interior* 1952 (2) S.A. 428, 471–472, A.D.).

6 Use of "sovereign" in this context has, inevitably, led to confusion between "parliamentary sovereignty" and "national sovereignty." Much ink has been spilt to remove this confusion: see *e.g.*, D. V. Cowen, "Legislature and Judiciary"—Part 1 (1952) 15 M.L.R. 282, 292 *et seq.*; G. Marshall, *Constitutional Theory* (1971), 35–53.

7 See 313 H.L.Deb. (5th ser.) 259 (1970) (Lord Hailsham L.C.); 1 J. Bryce, *The American Commonwealth* (3rd ed., 1907), 36. *Cf. McCawley* v. *R.* (1918) 26 C.L.R. 9, 82–83. "Omnipotent" has also caused confusion, such as analogising to the theological debate whether an omnipotent God is capable of terminating his omnipotence. See J. Latham (1957) 31 A.L.J. 253.

8 For a collection of these *dicta*, see O. Hood Phillips, *Constitutional and Administrative Law* (5th ed., 1973), 47–48.

9 O. Dixon, *Jesting Pilate* (1965), 40, 43, 198, 199 and "The Common Law as an Ultimate Constitutional Foundation" (1957) 31 A.L.J. 240, 242, 245; Jennings, *supra* note 4 at 156.

10 Hart, *supra* note 3 at 146. See also R. Latham, *supra* note 5 at 523; J. Latham, *supra* note 7; P. FitzGerald, "The 'Paradox' of Parliamentary Sovereignty" (1972) 7 Irish Jurist (n.s.) 28.

legislative competence of future Parliaments. There are two aspects to "self-embracing" supremacy, and we shall consider both: while Parliament may be unable to restrict the substantive power of future Parliaments, it may be able to impose procedural restrictions on them. Alternatively, it may be able to impose any restrictions whatever—substantive or procedural—on future Parliaments. If substantive restrictions are imposed, it would no longer be realistic to speak of such restricted Parliament as "omnipotent"—although it may still be "supreme" in the sense that no body is superior to it in legislative competence. But such terminological questions are, ultimately, irrelevant. Secondly, if Parliament is able to impose limitations on itself do the courts have jurisdiction to review the validity of subsequent legislation?

Like other doctrines of the common law, the English constitutional rules have, at all stages of their development, reflected the practical political realities in the Kingdom.[11] It is, therefore, appropriate that our analysis should begin with a brief treatment of the history of the evolution of the rule of parliamentary supremacy, which, in fact, is the history of the doctrine of the Rule of Law in England.

II. PARLIAMENTARY SUPREMACY: AN HISTORICAL PERSPECTIVE

The mediaeval conception of the Rule of Law was that the governmental institutions were created by the common law and, therefore, their powers were defined by it.[12] To quote Bracton's classic *dictum*: "The King must not be under man but under God and under the law, because law makes the King." [13] The growth of royal power under the Tudors and Stuarts challenged this doctrine but the courts generally reasserted it,[14] most significantly against Parliament in the famous case of *Dr. Bonham*.[15]

Although debate still rages as to whether Coke purported, in *Dr. Bonham's* case, to lay down a general rule that Acts of Parliament

11 See J. D. B. Mitchell, *Constitutional Law* (2nd ed., 1968), 70 note 32, 89; Jennings, *supra* note 4 at 159, 167.

12 This idea subsists: see Hood Phillips, *supra* note 8 at 76. *Cf.* the argument that a legislature must be bound by the instrument which created it: *The Bribery Commissioner* v. *Ranasinghe* [1965] A.C. 172, 198, P.C.; *Minister of the Interior* v. *Harris* 1952 (4) S.A. 769, 791, A.D.; *Harris* v. *Minister of the Interior* 1952 (2) S.A. 428, 464, A.D.; *Victoria* v. *Commonwealth* (1975) 7 A.L.R. 1 *esp.* at 46–47.

13 2 *De Legibus et Consuetudinibus Angliae* (Thorne transl., 1968), 33.

14 See *e.g.*, *Case of Proclamations* (1611) 12 Co. Rep. 74, 76, 77 E.R. 1352, 1354. Lord President Bradshawe quoted Bracton to King Charles I at his trial in 1649: see 4 St.Tr. 1009.

15 *Dr. Bonham's* Case (1610) 8 Co. Rep. 113b, 118a, 77 E.R. 638, 652.

contrary to the common law were void[16] or merely enunciated a rule of statutory interpretation,[17] it is clear that even by 1610 the Rule of Law had generally come to mean rule of the law as enacted by Parliament,[18] at least where the Act was not contrary to Scripture[19] or some very basic conception of the constitution, such as Magna Carta.[20] The authority of *Dr. Bonham's* case is shaky if Coke intended to assert that statutes could be declared invalid by the courts, for the precedents he cited were "obsolescent"[21] and he himself made contrary statements elsewhere.[22]

Nevertheless, in the turbulent political atmosphere of the early seventeenth century legal doctrine was frequently used to bolster a political argument. The conception of "fundamental law"[23] embodying the common law[24] or "natural equity"[25] or the ancient liberties of Anglo-Saxon England, as embodied in Magna Carta,[26] was employed by all sides of political controversies until the end of the eighteenth century.[27] The idea that Parliament could not change

16 As Raoul Berger maintains: *Congress* v. *The Supreme Court* (1969), 349–368. Although later judges supported, in *dicta*, Coke's argument that an Act of Parliament making a man judge in his own cause was invalid (*Day* v. *Savadge* (1614) Hob. 85; 80 E.R. 235; *City of London* v. *Wood* (1701) 12 Mod. 669, 687–688, 88 E.R. 1592, 1602 *per* Holt C.J.), the argument that an Act might be invalid for being contrary to the common law does not appear to have extended much beyond this particular common law conception: G. Marshall, *Parliamentary Sovereignty and the Commonwealth* (1957), 70. But see *infra* note 28. *Cf. The Mersey Docks & Harbour Board Trustees* v. *Gibbs* (1866) L.R. 1 H.L. 93, 110, 123, 126.

17 As asserted by Professor Thorne: "Dr. Bonham's Case" (1938) 54 L.Q.R. 543.

18 4 W. S. Holdsworth, *A History of English Law* (hereinafter "*Holdsworth*") (3rd ed., 1945), 187.

19 See 2 *Holdsworth* (4th ed., 1936), 444; 10 *Holdsworth* (1938) 527; *R.* v. *Love* (1653) 5 St.Tr. 43, 172.

20 See Berger, *supra* note 16 at 358, 365. Sir Francis Bacon who, like Coke, was inconsistent in his views regarding the possible invalidity of parliamentary legislation, once asserted that an Act contrary to Magna Carta would be void: see 4 *Holdsworth*, 186 note 4. See also E. S. Corwin, "The 'Higher Law' Background of American Constitutional Law" (1928) 42 Harv.L.Rev. 149, 178. As late as 1793 FitzGibbon asserted that Magna Carta could not be repealed (13 *Holdsworth* (1952), 169 note 7), though provisions of it have been (see 6 *Halsbury's Statutes of England* (3rd ed., 1969), 402–407), and such repeal has been judicially recognised: *Murphy* v. *Gardiner* [1951] N.Z.L.R. 549, 553.

21 T. F. T. Plucknett, "Bonham's Case and Judicial Review" (1926) 40 Harv.L. Rev. 30, 45. *Accord* 2 *Holdsworth*, 442–443; Jennings, *supra* note 4 at 320. Keir and Lawson somewhat overstate the position in asserting that, even in the seventeenth century, it was "a commonplace" for Acts to be declared invalid: see D. L. Keir and F. H. Lawson, *Cases in Constitutional Law* (5th ed., 1967), 1–2.

22 See *e.g.* 4 *Institutes of the Laws of England*, 36. See also Hood Phillips, *supra* note 8 at 44 note 30; Plucknett, *supra* note 21 at 54.

23 For an excellent analysis of the history of "fundamental law" in England, see J. W. Gough, *Fundamental Law in English History* (rev. ed., 1971).

24 *Dr. Bonham's* case *supra* note 15. See also *infra* note 28; P. G. Kauper, "The Higher Law and the Rights of Man in a Revolutionary Society" (1974) 18 Law Quadrangle Notes (Univ. of Michigan) No. 2, pp. 9, 10.

25 *Day* v. *Savadge*, *supra* note 16; 2 *Holdsworth*, 444.

26 *Supra* note 20: Corwin, *supra* note 20 at 170 note 66, 177–178, 179 note 95.

27 See 10 *Holdsworth*, 530; 13 *Holdsworth*, 169. For views favouring "fundamental law," see Gough, *supra* note 23 at 140, 166, 179–186, 192 (Otis), 193–194 (Lord Camden), 194–195 (Earl of Chatham), 198 (Sharpe), 201 (Burke), and for rejection of the doctrine see *ibid.* 119, 138 (Milton), 152, 171, 202 (Lord Kenyon L.C.).

certain principles of the common law was, however, soon seen to favour the Royalists, for the Royal Prerogative was clearly a major doctrine of the common law.[28] Accordingly, the parliamentarians gained the support of the common lawyers who realised that if Royal claims were to be rejected by the law, the Rule of Law must come to mean rule of the law as enacted by Parliament, and not the rule of the ancient common law.[29] This alliance and mutual respect between Parliament and the common lawyers has had a profound effect on the development of English law, particularly in judicial recognition of parliamentary supremacy [30] and parliamentary acceptance of judicial independence.[31] Thus, by the eighteenth century [32] and, for all practical purposes, by the time of the "Glorious Revolution" of 1688, the supremacy of Parliament was clearly established.

Two important themes must be noticed. First, Parliament can trace its origins to the Norman *Curia Regis*, and probably beyond that to the Anglo-Saxon *Witenagemot*, which functioned long before the concept of the separation of powers was conceived. These bodies exercised judicial as well as legislative functions and, as a result, the mediaeval Parliament was conceived of as a court, the highest in the realm, and was usually called the "High Court of Parliament." [33] The rule that the ordinary courts lacked jurisdiction to review the validity of statutes was a natural consequence of this conception for surely, the argument went, a lower court cannot review the "judgments" of the highest court.[34] The conception of Parliament as a court was, in fact, perfectly sensible in view of both the origin of Parliament and the mediaeval jurists' failure to treat parliamentary legislation as different—other than by being written—from common law and custom.[35] It was only after 1688 that the role of Parliament in creating new law was understood but, even so, not until the nineteenth century was Parliament clearly seen as a body which not only could, but also *should*, reform the common law. Nevertheless, the influence of the notion of Parliament as the

[28] See *R.* v. *Hampden* (The Ship Money case) (1637) 3 St.Tr. 825, 1235; *Godden* v. *Hales* (1686) 11 St.Tr. 1165. See also Plucknett, *supra* note 21 at 53.

[29] 2 *Holdsworth*, 441–442; 4 *Holdsworth*, 187–189.

[30] For a discussion of the reconciliation of the Rule of Law with the supremacy of Parliament, see Dixon, *Jesting Pilate* (1965), 39 *et seq.*; A. V. Dicey, *The Law of the Constitution* (10th ed., 1959), 406–414.

[31] Act of Settlement 1700, s. 3.

[32] 10 *Holdsworth*, 527. See also F. Pollock. "A Plea for Historical Interpretation" (1923) 39 L.Q.R. 163, 165.

[33] C. H. McIlwain, *The High Court of Parliament and its Supremacy* (1910). In the Crown and Parliament Recognition Act 1689 the phrases "High Court of Parlyament," "Parlyament" and "Parliament" are all used. As recently as 1974 Lord Morris of Borth-y-Gest spoke of the "High Court of Parliament": *British Railways Board* v. *Pickin* [1974] A.C. 765, 790.

[34] See 4 *Holdsworth*, 182–186.

[35] See T. F. T. Plucknett, *Legislation of Edward I* (1949), 13–15.

highest court long persisted, adding greatly to the arguments against judicial review of legislation.[36]

Secondly, motivations for rebelling against royal authority were multifarious but many political thinkers were not delighted at the prospect of substituting the tyranny of Parliament for that of the King; the behaviour of the Long Parliament certainly did not allay their fears. Accordingly, they saw the 1688 " revolution settlement " as the occasion for the assertion of individual liberty, indeed the restoration of ancient rights and liberties.[37] This concern was manifested in the passage of the Bill of Rights in 1688 and the Act of Settlement in 1700, as well as a number of earlier measures.[38] Fears of parliamentary tyranny were allayed by the passage of these statutes and the return to " normalcy." The supremacy of Parliament was justified by the theory that because " the people " elected Parliament, its supremacy meant, in effect, the " sovereignty of the people." [39] Of course, Parliament was not even remotely representative of " the people " until the Reform Act of 1832 [40] the passage of which, accordingly, lent great support to the doctrine of parliamentary supremacy.[41]

Nowhere is the development of this doctrine demonstrated more clearly than in the writings of Blackstone and Dicey. Blackstone, writing in the mid-eighteenth century, clearly asserted the doctrine of parliamentary supremacy, but he could not resist expressing his ethical compunction,[42] at times in the language of a much earlier era.[43] By the time we reach Dicey, more than a century later, parliamentary supremacy, bolstered by the Reform Acts, wide-ranging social reforms inspired by Bentham and others, and a long history of legislation governing a quarter of the globe, is seen in absolute, unquestioned, positivist terms, plagued by neither ethical nor religious compunctions.[44] There has been no important development of the doctrine in Britain since Dicey's formulation.

III. PARLIAMENTARY SUPREMACY: THREE INTERPRETATIONS

The dichotomy between " continuing " and " self-embracing " parliamentary supremacy has led to three interpretations:

[36] But this influence has, occasionally, been overstated: *e.g.* H. Pope, " The Fundamental Law and the Power of the Courts " (1913) 27 Harv.L.Rev. 45 esp. at 46, 51, 57, 59.

[37] See 10 *Holdsworth*, 528–530.

[38] The Petition of Right 1627 and the Habeas Corpus Acts of 1640 and 1679.

[39] See Marshall, *supra* note 16 at 68. This conception persists: see *e.g.*, 840 H.C. Deb. (5th ser.) 623, 629 (1972).

[40] Representation of the People Act 1832.

[41] 10 *Holdsworth*, 22; Mitchell, *supra* note 11 at 70.

[42] 1 *Commentaries on the Laws of England* (11th ed., 1791), 42–43.

[43] *Ibid.*, 41. At first, he rather reluctantly accepted the political reality of parliamentary supremacy (*ibid.*, 91) but later he employed virtually Diceyian absolutism to express the " sovereign and uncontrollable authority " of Parliament: *ibid.*, 160–161.

[44] See Dicey, *supra* note 30 at 39–40.

(*a*) The composition of Parliament, the manner and form in which it exercises its power and the limitless ambit of its power are the subject of a " fundamental," unalterable rule.

(*b*) Parliament can change its procedure and the manner and form in which it legislates, but cannot impose limits on the content of legislation.

(*c*) The rule of parliamentary supremacy is totally " self-embracing " *i.e.* it can be amended by Parliament in any respect whatever.

'A. Substantively and Procedurally " Continuing " Supremacy.'

1. The Doctrine

This view, which has commended itself to some of Britain's leading constitutional lawyers, is, supposedly, a realistic assessment of the actual political situation. Parliament, it is asserted, is politically unable to bind itself in any way and, therefore, as the ultimate rule of law or *grundnorm* is a reflection of political reality, the supremacy of Parliament must be " continuing." This is clearly the perspective of Professor H. L. A. Hart.[45]

Although Professor Dicey never explicitly stated that the supremacy of Parliament was, in all respects, " continuing," his writings leave a clear impression to that effect [46]; this opinion is certainly adopted by his disciples, led by Professor H. W. R. Wade. Professor Wade's conclusion [47] that Parliament cannot alter the rule of parliamentary supremacy in any way is derived, as it must be, from an assumption that the rule must be one of " continuing " supremacy; in other words, the argument is circular. Wade begins his analysis by noting that " the rule enjoining judicial obedience to statutes is one of the fundamental rules upon which the legal system depends." [48] He then quotes Sir John Salmond's well-known pre-Kelsen recognition that there must be an ultimate rule of law the origin of which is " historical only, not legal." [49] From this observation—which is neutral so far as the " continuing " or " self-embracing " dilemma is concerned—Wade immediately draws his conclusion that *in law* the " sovereignty " of Parliament must be " continuing "

[45] *Supra* note 3 at 146. It is, however, far from " clear " what the " presently accepted " rule is.

[46] See Dicey, *supra* note 30 at 68 note 1.

[47] H. W. R. Wade, " The Basis of Legal Sovereignty " [1955] C.L.J. 172.

[48] *Ibid.*, 187.

[49] J. Salmond, *Jurisprudence* (12th ed., 1966), 111. It is ironic that Wade should quote Salmond at the crux of his exposition, for Salmond wondered whether the rule of parliamentary supremacy might not be alterable by Parliament: " The exercise of legislative power is admittedly subject to legal *conditions*: why not, then, to legal *limitations*? If the law can regulate the *manner* of the exercise of legislative power, why not also its *matter*? " *ibid.* (11th ed., 1957), 522. Emphasis Salmond's. Professor Wade, of course, denies that Parliament can alter even the *manner* of exercise of legislative power: *supra* note 47 at 190.

as to both substance and procedure: "Once this truth is grasped, the dilemma is solved. For if no statute can establish the rule that the courts obey Acts of Parliament, similarly no statute can alter or abolish that rule. The rule is above and beyond the reach of statute, as Salmond so well explains...."[50] In essence, Wade's analysis amounts to an assertion that *in actual fact*[51] parliamentary supremacy is "continuing." Unfortunately, he seeks to suggest that the opposing view is anything more than an alternative (and, in his view, wrong) mode of looking at the same political facts.[52]

Is Parliament able to impose procedural or "manner and form"[53] limitations upon itself? "Parliament," said Dicey, "means . . . the Queen, the House of Lords, and the House of Commons . . ."[54] but he did not state whether it must always mean these three.[55] It seems clear, however, that the neo-Diceyians, especially Wade,[56] do believe the present composition of Parliament and the manner and form of the exercise of its legislative power to be unalterable by Parliament.[57] Moreover, there are some judicial dicta to the same effect.[58]

Although the second formulation of the rule of parliamentary supremacy offers Parliament greater flexibility so far as its procedure and the manner and form of legislating are concerned, both interpretations of parliamentary supremacy ensure that there is no

---

[50] *Ibid.*, 187. This, with respect, does not follow. Here Wade makes his assumption that "sovereignty" must be "continuing."

[51] See *ibid.*, 188. Mr. Fazal rejects Professor Wade's analysis, substantially (though not solely: see Fazal, *supra* note 2 at 307) on the ground that Wade's argument is based on the proposition that "parliamentary sovereignty . . . cannot be altered . . . short of revolution" (*ibid.*, at 296). This does Professor Wade rather less than justice; all he asserted was that "the relationship between the courts of law and Parliament is first and foremost a political reality": *supra* note 47 at 188.

[52] See *ibid.*, 189. See also S. A. de Smith, *Constitutional and Administrative Law* (2nd ed., 1973), 79 note 67. R. F. V. Heuston criticises Wade for "miss[ing] the point that the argument turns upon whether the measure which the courts are called upon to enforce is a *statute*. The issue . . . is one of manner and form, and not of area of power": "Sovereignty" in *Oxford Essays in Jurisprudence* (Guest ed., 1961), 217. Emphasis Heuston's. In fact, for Wade the rules as to both the area of power and the manner and form of legislation are unalterable by Parliament, so the ultimate "fundamental" rule enables a court to determine whether the measure is a statute. Professor Heuston seems to recognise this: *ibid.*

[53] This phrase is derived from the Colonial Laws Validity Act 1865, s. 5.

[54] *Supra* note 30 at 39.

[55] Dicey did suggest that Parliament could abolish the Monarchy, but this conclusion was derived from his view that Parliament could transfer its powers to another body (*ibid.* 79). *Cf. Clayton* v. *Heffron* (1960) 105 C.L.R. 214, 251.

[56] *Supra* note 47 at 190.

[57] W. A. Wynes, *Legislative, Executive and Judicial Powers in Australia* (5th ed., 1976), 546. Hood Phillips, *supra*, note 8 at 69; E. C. S. Wade, "Opinion to South African Government" (1952) in Marshall, *supra* note 16 at 252, 255, 258.

[58] See *South-Eastern Drainage Board (S. Aust.)* v. *The Savings Bank of S. Aust.* (1939) 62 C.L.R. 603, 633 (Evatt J.); *Ellen Street Estates Ltd.* v. *Minister of Health* [1934] 1 K.B. 590, 597 (Maugham L.J., *obiter*); *McCawley* v. *R.* [1920] A.C. 691, 705–706 (Lord Birkenhead L.C., *obiter*).

legislative vacuum.[59] From the point of view of national policy, it is important that Parliament be unable to create an area over which it may not legislate; even in countries with "controlled"[60] constitutions, such as the United States, Canada and Australia, the constitution can be amended—at least in most respects—so that there is virtually no area which is a permanent legislative vacuum.

Conversely, however, the calcification of rules of law into "fundamental," unchangeable rules has its own danger, for the process, once begun, may spread, resulting in areas of legislative vacuum. It can be argued that the supremacy of Parliament is only one of a number of very basic conceptions of British constitutional law. For centuries, and certainly at the time of the 1688 revolution, the concept of practically "inalienable" personal liberties has been a very strong feature of the British constitution[61]: it is implicit in the British concept of the Rule of Law,[62] and has led to the doctrine of natural justice in administrative law, as well as the rules for interpreting statutes so as not to threaten individual liberty. Moreover, in the United States, belief in ancient Anglo-Saxon liberties, recognised by Magna Carta, embodied in the common law, and allegedly shown to be inalienable by John Locke, played a vital role in both the argument for a Bill of Rights and the actual framing of the document.[63] In fact, the Ninth Amendment to the United States Constitution has been regarded by some as a recognition that the rights guaranteed by the Bill of Rights predate that document and do not owe their existence to it.[64]

There is, therefore, a strong argument that if one basic concept of the British constitution is "fundamental," why should others

[59] However, Parliament could, possibly, impose on itself a "manner and form" limitation (*e.g.* that a Bill on a specific subject must be approved by 80 per cent. of the electors at a referendum before being submitted for the Royal Assent) which amounts to a substantive limitation: this problem is discussed *infra.*

[60] See *McCawley* v. *R.* [1920] A.C. 691, 703–705.

[61] "In England the right to individual liberty is part of the constitution . . .": Dicey, *supra* note 30 at 197. But Dicey was probably using "constitution" loosely. *Cf. Liversidge* v. *Anderson* [1942] A.C. 206, 261. A British jurist has written of the *grundnorm* that "it is insufficiently appreciated that not only effectiveness but also conformity to morality and justice is among the very springs of its being and continued life": R. W. M. Dias, "Legal Politics: Norms Behind the Grundnorm" [1968] C.L.J. 233, 255.

[62] *Cf.* the doctrine of the "implied Bill of Rights" which some Canadian judges have derived from the preamble to the British North America Act 1867 (providing that Canada should have "a Constitution similar in principle to that of the United Kingdom"): see *Switzman* v. *Elbling* (1957) 7 D.L.R. (2d) 337, 371 S.C.; *Saumur* v. *City of Quebec* [1953] 4 D.L.R. 641, 671 (see *contra* Cartwright and Fauteux JJ. at 724), S.C.; *R.* v. *Hess (No.* 2) [1949] 4 D.L.R. 199, 208–209, B.C.C.A.

[63] E. S. Corwin, "The 'Higher Law' Background of American Constitutional Law" (1928–29) 42 Harv.L.Rev. 149, 365. See also B. Bailyn, *The Ideological Origins of the American Revolution* (1967), 175 *et seq.*

[64] Kauper, *supra* note 24 at 11, 13–14; *Griswold* v. *Connecticut* (1965) 381 U.S. 479, 488–493 (but see *contra* at 520). *Cf. Lassalle* v. *Att.-Gen.* (1971) 18 W.I.R. 379, 395 (T. & T. C.A.); *Chabot* v. *School Commissioners of Lamorandiere* (1957) 12 D.L.R. (2d) 796, 807.

not likewise be "fundamental" and unalterable? Nevertheless, there is no reason why an all-or-nothing approach should be adopted for, to adopt Justice Holmes' aphorism, the life of the law has been experience, not logic.[65] If, as appears to be the case, it is still uncertain which of the three formulations of the rule of parliamentary supremacy should be adopted, the policy considerations mentioned here must be taken into account.

2. Abdication of Sovereignty

Dicey saw his theory of "parliamentary sovereignty" as an explanation of the political reality of Great Britain; hence, his theory had to take into account those occasions on which, contrary to his maxim that Parliament cannot bind its successors, Parliament had sought to do just that—for instance by giving independence to Ireland[66] and America.[67] Dicey, accordingly, sacrificed consistency and logic and declared, merely in a footnote, that, while Parliament could not bind its successors, it could abdicate "sovereignty" altogether.[68] This abdication could be effected either without a transfer of "sovereignty" to another body or with transfer.

Mere Abdication. Dicey argued, giving no reason other than a comparison between Parliament and the Russian Czar, who could abdicate his throne, that "Parliament could extinguish itself by legally dissolving itself and leaving no means whereby a subsequent Parliament could be legally summoned."[69] The principal objection to this argument is, of course, that a legislative vacuum would be created and it is obvious that if the British Parliament decided to disband, the British people would simply substitute some other legislature in its place. There seems to be no precedent for Parliament simply "abdicating," for in all cases where independence has been given to a British territory and Parliament has declared that the United Kingdom's sovereignty is terminated the territory has had its own legislature, thereby avoiding any legislative vacuum. In fact, it is difficult to understand why Dicey made his assertion: it was probably merely a point of legal purity, declaring the truism that one occasion when Parliament's "sovereignty" ends is when Parliament itself disappears.

Transfer of Sovereignty. It appears that Dicey envisaged the transfer of sovereignty over the whole area of legislative power.[70]

[65] O. W. Holmes, *The Common Law* (1881), 1.
[66] 23 Geo. 3, c. 28 (1783).
[67] See 22 Geo. 3, c. 46 (1782); Statute Law Revision Act 1964, repealing the American Colonies Act 1766.
[68] Dicey, *supra* note 30 at 69.
[69] *Ibid.*
[70] *Ibid.*

for he gave the Act of Union 1706 as an example.[71] The policy argument against total abdication of sovereignty does not apply here, for no legislative vacuum is created. Moreover, if the United Kingdom Parliament transferred all its legislative power to another person or body and then dissolved itself, as a practical matter it could not repeal the Act as it would no longer exist.[72] Accordingly, most writers agree with Dicey that Parliament could effectually transfer the totality of its powers to another body.[73]

Parliament could transfer part of its legislative authority in two respects: it could, and has purported to, transfer its authority over British territory to another legislature [74] or it could transfer to another body power to legislate for the United Kingdom with respect to certain matters.[75] The difficulty with both these transfers of authority is that Parliament, as usually constituted, remains in existence and could pass repealing legislation. If a court adopted the Dicey/Wade interpretation of parliamentary supremacy, namely that the supremacy is " continuing " both substantively and procedurally, the later

[71] *Ibid.* But see K. W. B. Middleton, " New Thoughts on the Union Between England and Scotland " (1954) 66 Jur.Rev. 37, 53.

[72] Whether the old Parliament could impose limitations on the new has been much debated. The argument, typically, has usually proceeded by interpretation of the maxim " Parliament cannot bind itself or its successors." The issue resolves itself, it is said, into the question whether the new body's position is sufficiently analogous to that of the old Parliament to be called its " successor." (English writers generally regard the Parliament of Great Britain, created by the Union with Scotland Act 1706, as the " successor " of the English Parliament and, therefore, not bound by the Act and the Treaty of Union: Scottish lawyers are less certain.) The clearest exposition of this interpretation of the maxim was the debate on the Government of Ireland Bill in 1886. Mr. McIver said: " [Bryce] says ' We cannot divest ourselves of the supremacy,' and ' We cannot bind our successors.' All that is true; but it is beside the point; for it is true of this Parliament, which will cease to exist if this Bill becomes law. . . . Sir, we shall have no successors. . . . This Parliament will have no legitimate successors, but only the bastard ' Imperial Parliament,' which does not succeed to the title.": 305 Parl.Deb. (3rd ser.) 1720, 1721 (1886). Sir William Anson also wrote: " But if the Irish Government Bill had become law the Parliament of 1885 would have had no successors. . . . A repudiation of the Acts of the Parliament of 1885 by [the new legislature] would not have been a repeal by one Parliament of the Acts of another Parliament *similarly constituted* . . .": W. R. Anson, " The Government of Ireland Bill and the Sovereignty of Parliament " (1886) 2 L.Q.R. 427, 436. Our emphasis. Dicey seems to have had a similar view, for he wrote, after defining Parliament as the Queen, Lords and Commons, that the principle of " parliamentary sovereignty " means " that Parliament *thus defined* has . . . the right to make or unmake any law whatever . . .": *supra* note 30 at 39–40. Our emphasis. On the other hand, Ferguson J. explained the maxim to mean that " the sovereign legislature of today, however constituted, cannot pass a law which the equally sovereign legislature of tomorrow *however it may be constituted* cannot repeal ": *Trethowan* v. *Peden* (1930) 31 S.R.(N.S.W.) 183, 207. Our emphasis. See also Wade, *supra* note 47 at 197.

[73] See *e.g.* de Smith, *supra* note 52 at 76: D. V. Cowen, *The Foundations of Freedom* (1961), 180: W. A. Wynes (1957) 31 A.L.J. 251.

[74] See *e.g.* the numerous Acts granting independence to members of the Commonwealth since 1947 (*e.g.* the Indian Independence Act 1947, s. 6 (4)) and the Statute of Westminster 1931, s. 4, discussed *infra.*

[75] Arguably, the European Communities Act 1972, s. 2 (1) and (4), does this: this Act is discussed *infra.* The Parliament Acts 1911 and 1949 do not purport to transfer " sovereignty " irrevocably.

Act would effectually repeal the earlier transfer of authority. Accordingly, the present position regarding transfer of partial authority is unclear.[76]

Professor Wade has, in fact, recognised the inconsistency in Dicey's assertion that Parliament can irrevocably transfer its "sovereignty" over a portion of territory,[77] though the inconsistency has not worried a number of leading constitutional lawyers.[78] The various arguments have most frequently been formulated in response to the perennial academic question whether the British Parliament could validly repeal section 4 of the Statute of Westminster 1931: "No Act of Parliament of the United Kingdom passed after the commencement of this Act shall extend, or be deemed to extend, to a Dominion as part of the law of that Dominion, unless it is expressly declared in that Act that that Dominion has requested, and consented to, the enactment thereof." While, admittedly, on its face section 4 requires only a declaration that the Dominion has requested and consented,[79] it is conceded by most writers that, when interpreted in light of paragraph 3 of the statute's preamble, section 4 requires the Dominion to have actually requested and consented.[80]

The opinions expressed regarding section 4 reflect, as one would expect, the various formulations of the rule of parliamentary supremacy: some followers of Dicey, not worried by the inconsistency of their position, assert that section 4 is an abdication of sovereignty [81]; the purists who believe in "continuing" parliamentary supremacy in all respects claim that the British Parliament could validly repeal

[76] See D. V. Cowen, "Legislature and Judiciary"—Part II (1953) 16 M.L.R. 273, 297. *Cf.* his greater certainty eight years later: *supra* note 73 at 183–184. Most of the evidence on which Professor Cowen's opinion was based related to the territorial abdication of sovereignty, which some writers feel must be viewed differently from the abdication of jurisdiction over a subject-matter within the United Kingdom: see the distinction between "horizontal" and "vertical" sovereignty in N. M. Hunnings, "Constitutional Implications of Joining the Common Market" (1968) 6 C.M.L.Rev. 50, 57–58. But see Professor Mitchell's doubts about the validity of this distinction: "British Law and British Membership" (1971) 6 Europarecht 97, 105 note 36.

[77] *Supra* note 47 at 196. Accord Bryce, 305 Parl.Deb. (3rd ser.) 1218, 1219 (1886). See also *infra* note 82.

[78] See Anson, "The Government of Ireland Bill and the Sovereignty of Parliament" (1886) 2 L.Q.R. 427; Cowen, *supra* note 73 at 182–183.

[79] This is emphasised by Dr. Wynes: *supra* note 57 at 546.

[80] See *e.g.* H. V. Evatt, *The King and His Dominion Governors* (2nd ed., 1967), 274, 309.

[81] H. ver Loren van Themaat, "The equality of Status of the Dominions and the Sovereignty of the British Parliament" (1933) 15 J.C.L. (3rd ser.) 47. See also S. A. de Smith, "The Constitution and the Common Market: A Tentative Appraisal" (1971) 34 M.L.R. 597, 612–613; *Blackburn* v. *Att.-Gen.* [1971] 1 W.L.R. 1037, 1040, *per* Lord Denning M.R. Contrary to the view of some writers (Mitchell, *supra* note 11 at 79 and *supra* note 76 at 105: F. M. Auburn, "Trends in Comparative Constitutional Law" (1972) 35 M.L.R. 129, 133), a dictum of Viscount Radcliffe in *Ibralebbe* v. *R.* [1964] A.C. 900, 924 does not support the abdication theory. Viscount Radcliffe was not referring to the power of the British Parliament; he was concerned solely with legislation by means of Orders in Council.

section 4 [82]; and the supporters of the second formulation argue that section 4 redefines " Parliament " to include the relevant authority in the Dominion as well as the Queen, Lords and Commons.[83]

On this issue at least, the plethora of opinions is practically reconcilable: section 4 is not an express abdication of power to legislate for the Dominions, but redefines the legislature which can enact a statute extending to a Dominion (which would include an Act repealing section 4 itself, if that Act purported to apply to a Dominion) to include the relevant organ of the Dominion as well as the three parts of the British Parliament. However, it is sensible to distinguish between the law applying in a Dominion and the law applying in the United Kingdom [84]: it is compatible with most of the views expressed on section 4 to say that it is merely a rule of statutory construction as far as British law is concerned,[85] but constitutes a new quadripartite legislature as far as the Dominion's law is concerned.[86] Judicial opinion in Eire (in the days of the Irish Free State [87]) and South Africa [88] supports this interpretation.

It is submitted that, as Professor Wade recognised,[89] it is essentially inconsistent with the theory of the " continuing " substantive and procedural supremacy of the British Parliament to admit that, at least as far as British law is concerned, Parliament can legally abdicate its powers or irrevocably transfer them to another body. If there is one area in which Parliament *can* bind itself and its successors, why should it not be able to do so in others? [90] Once the adherents of the first formulation of the rule of parliamentary supremacy admit that it

---

[82] See *British Coal Corp.* v. *R.* [1935] A.C. 500, 520; E. C. S. Wade in Introduction to Dicey, *supra* note 30 at lxiv, lxxxviii.

[83] H. R. Gray, " The Sovereignty of Parliament Today " (1953) 10 U.Tor.L.J. 54, 70. See *contra* Wynes, *supra* note 57 at 545, 546.

[84] The phrase " as part of the law of that Dominion " in s. 4 itself lends support to this dichotomy.

[85] See K. C. Wheare, *The Constitutional Structure of the Commonwealth* (1960), 27–28. *Cf. Copyright Owners Reproduction Society Ltd.* v. *E.M.I. (Aust.) Pty. Ltd.* (1958) 100 C.L.R. 597, 612–613, 615.

[86] Arguably, s. 2 (2) of the Statute of Westminster enables a Dominion to declare inapplicable, as far as its law is concerned, any attempted British repeal of s. 4 (see Marshall, *supra* note 6 at 62–63), unless s. 2 (2) were also repealed. But the Dominion's case may be stronger if its exercise of the power recognised by s. 2 (2) had preceded the British repeal of that section.

[87] Latham, *supra* note 5 at 534–540. Irish opinion was more consistent with the abdication of " sovereignty " theory.

[88] *Harris* v. *Minister of the Interior*, 1952 (2) S.A. 428, 467. There is also some support for this view in Canada and Australia: see I. C. Rand, " Some Aspects of Canadian Constitutionalism " (1960) 38 Can. Bar Rev. 135, 149; P. J. Hanks, " Redefining the Sovereign: Current Attitudes to Section 4 of the Statute of Westminster " (1968) 42 A.L.J. 286, esp. discussion of *Ex parte Bennett* [1967] 2 N.S.W.R. 597, 602.

[89] *Supra* note 47 at 196.

[90] See J. D. B. Mitchell, " What Do you Want to be Inscrutable *For*, Marcia? " (1967) 5 C.M.L.Rev. 112, 119–120. See *contra* F. A. Trindade, " Parliamentary Sovereignty and the Primacy of European Community Law " (1972) 35 M.L.R. 375, 388.

can be " self-embracing " they have denied the fundamental proposition on which their theory is built.

B. *Substantively " Continuing " and Procedurally " Self-Embracing " Supremacy*

1. *The Doctrine*

Although Dicey's formulation of the rule of parliamentary supremacy, largely unchallenged until the early 1930s, ensured the avoidance of legislative vacuums, it was inflexible regarding the manner and form of legislating. True, by 1930 Parliament had enacted the Parliament Act 1911 but, as we shall see, it was possible to regard that statute as merely an example of delegated legislation and not as redefining " Parliament " for certain purposes.

It was the *Trethowan* case [91] (based on the interpretation of section 5 of the Colonial Laws Validity Act 1865 [92]) in Australia and the *Harris* case [93] in South Africa (based on the interpretation of section 2 (2) of the Statute of Westminster 1931 [94]) which first alerted English lawyers to the possibility of differentiating between Parliament's powers on the one hand and the manner and form of their exercise on the other. Put shortly, they began to see that, even though the powers of Parliament may be illimitable, it might be possible to redefine, at least for some purposes, the " Parliament " which exercised these unlimited powers.[95] Two objections to this formulation, one philosophical and the other practical, must be noted.

First, both the first and the third interpretations of the rule of parliamentary supremacy are internally consistent; depending on one's initial premise, it is perfectly consistent to believe either in totally " continuing " supremacy or totally " self-embracing " supremacy, but there is no consistency in asserting that the doctrine is half of each. Does it make sense to claim that the common law, by a fundamental, unchangeable rule, declares that " Parliament " is the supreme legislative body in the realm, and can efficaciously enact any measure it wishes except one which purports to bind itself and its successors, but does not define the body called " Parliament " in which the powers inhere? It does not, for the reason so well stated by R. T. E. Latham: " Where the purported sovereign is any one but a single actual person, the designation of him must include the

---

91 *Att.-Gen. (N.S.W.)* v. *Trethowan* (1931) 44 C.L.R. 394, aff'd. [1932] A.C. 526.

92 *Ibid.*, 44 C.L.R. at 418, 421, 423–424, 425, 426, 427, 434, 435; [1932] A.C. at 539; *Clayton* v. *Heffron* (1960) 105 C.L.R. 214, 240, 249, 255.

93 *Harris* v. *Minister of the Interior* 1952 (2) S.A. 428, A.D. For a detailed discussion of the whole episode, see Marshall, *supra* note 16 at 139–248.

94 *Harris*, 1952 (2) S.A. at 463.

95 Hart, *supra* note 3 at 147. *Cf. Trethowan*, 44 C.L.R. at 419, 420 (*contra* at 412, 448–449); *Harris*, 1952 (2) S.A. at 463.

statement of rules for the ascertainment of his will, and these rules, since their observance is a condition of the validity of his legislation, are rules of law *logically prior to* him." [96]

Secondly, because the second formulation of the rule of parliamentary supremacy gives greater flexibility than the first, lawyers, and maybe judges also, may be prepared to overlook its logical difficulties; it certainly would not be the first time English law took the pragmatic, rather than the logical, course.[97] However, this formulation of the rule presents in addition a practical difficulty: the line between the manner and form of legislating and the power of Parliament is one of degree only. By imposing stringent "manner and form" requirements, such as approval by 90 per cent. of the electorate at a referendum, Parliament could effectively limit the power of future Parliaments. This was first recognised by McTiernan J. in his dissenting judgment in *Trethowan*: "It was argued . . . that if the Legislature said that an Act should not be repealed except in the 'manner' required by an Act of the Legislature, the first Act could be repealed only in that 'manner.' The label 'manner' does not conclude the matter: the true nature of the law may be disguised." [98] Whether a "manner and form" provision which practically limits the power of future Parliaments would be effective depends upon the courts' approach to the question of judicial review. A court would probably hold that a later Act of "Parliament," as ordinarily constituted, could expressly or impliedly repeal an earlier one which, under the guise of a "manner and form" provision, had sought to deny Parliament the power to pass the later Act [99]; in support of this view is the old maxim that "what cannot be done directly cannot be done indirectly." [1]

Although both *Trethowan* and *Harris* turned on the interpretation of British statutes, jurists have argued that their reasoning is more general; that is, that the common law (the Rule of Law) obliges Parliament to legislate in the manner and form provided by the presently existing law (which Parliament can alter by legislating in the stipulated manner and form), just as did section 5 of the Colonial Laws Validity Act 1865 with respect to the colonies,[2] and that

[96] *Supra* note 5 at 523. Our emphasis.

[97] Heuston appropriately calls the second formulation "so Anglican a solution": *supra* note 52 at 202.

[98] 44 C.L.R. at 442. See also Gavan Duffy C.J. at 413.

[99] *Cf.* W. Friedmann, "Trethowan's Case, Parliamentary Sovereignty, and the Limits of Legal Change" (1950) 24 A.L.J. 103, 106, 107; *South-Eastern Drainage Board (S. Aust.)* v. *The Savings Bank of S. Aust.* (1939) 62 C.L.R. 603, 618, 623, 625, 633–634, 636; *Ellen Street Estates Ltd.* v. *Minister of Health* [1934] 1 K.B. 590, 597; *Vauxhall Estates Ltd.* v. *Liverpool Corp.* [1932] 1 K.B. 733, 743.

[1] See D. K. Singh, "What Cannot be Done Directly Cannot be Done Indirectly: Its Meaning and Logical Status in Constitutionalism" (1966) 29 M.L.R. 273.

[2] See Heuston, *supra* note 52 at 218–219.

Harris demonstrated that a "sovereign" legislature can be constituted in more than one way.[3] Opponents find it fallacious to apply *Trethowan* to the British Parliament because the latter is "sovereign" but the New South Wales legislature is not[4] and argue that, even though the South African Parliament was admittedly "sovereign" in 1952, it was constituted by a document which defined its composition, whereas the British Parliament can look only to the common law which is not specific on the question of its composition. All these arguments have some merit but, of course, they neither prove nor disprove the validity of the second formulation of the rule; they merely debate the validity of an analogy between the British Parliament and the legislatures of South Africa and New South Wales. It cannot be asserted that the *ratio decidendi* of either *Trethowan* or *Harris* itself applies to the British Parliament. This was clearly realised by Dixon J. in the *obiter dictum* giving birth to the second formulation of the rule of parliamentary supremacy.[5]

Although weak judicial *dicta*[6] and some leading constitutionalists[7] oppose the second formulation of the rule, the great majority of modern constitutional lawyers favour it[8]; in fact, in *The Bribery Commissioner* v. *Ranasinghe*[9] the Privy Council, comprised of English judges, observed that the fact that a legislature is "sovereign" does not mean that it must always be constituted in the same way.[10] There is now, accordingly, the authority of senior English judges supporting the argument that the "sovereignty" of the British Parliament is not, *per se*, an obstacle to acceptance of the second formulation of the rule of parliamentary supremacy.[11]

---

[3] See Gray, *supra* note 83 at 56, 57, 61–62, 65.

[4] See E. C. S. Wade, *supra* note 82 at lxxiv–lxxv; H. W. R. Wade, *supra* note 47 at 182–183.

[5] *Trethowan*, 44 C.L.R. at 426.

[6] See *Ellen Street Estates Ltd*. v. *Minister of Health* [1934] 1 K.B. 590, 597 *per* Maugham L.J.; *McCawley* v. *R*. [1920] A.C. 691, 705–706 *per* Lord Birkenhead L.C. Neither judge really addressed the present issue.

[7] Hood Phillips, *supra* note 8 at 68–69; H. W. R. Wade, *supra* note 47 at 190; E. C. S. Wade, *supra* note 57 at 252, 255; Wynes (1957) 31 A.L.J. 251–252.

[8] See *e.g.* de Smith, *supra* note 52 at 88–92; Marshall, *supra* note 6 at 53; Gough, *supra* note 23 at 212; Heuston, *supra* note 52 at 204; Dixon, *supra* note 9, 31 A.L.J. at 244. Professor B. Beinart offers solace to those determined to view the position through the maxim "Parliament cannot bind itself or its successors": a "manner and form" law does not bind "Parliament," he observes, but only its component parts: "Sovereignty and the Law" (1952) 15 Tydskrif vir Hedendaagse Romeinhollandse Reg 101, 126, 129.

[9] [1965] A.C. 172.

[10] *Ibid*., at 200. See also *Akar* v. *Att.-Gen. (Sierra Leone)* [1970] A.C. 853, 867; *Victoria* v. *Commonwealth* (1975) 7 A.L.R. 1, 47.

[11] Moreover, the Supreme Court of Canada appears to have held (albeit *obiter*) that the "sovereign" Canadian Parliament has, in s. 2 of the Canadian Bill of Rights 1960, imposed upon itself a binding form for the enactment of certain legislation: see *R*. v. *Drybones* [1970] S.C.R. 282; 9 D.L.R. (3d) 473; *Att.-Gen. (Canada)* v. *Lavell* [1974] S.C.R. 1349, 1382, 1388; 38 D.L.R. (3d) 481, 507, 511. This also appears to be the meaning of an enigmatic *dictum* of Abbott J. (dissenting): [1974] S.C.R. at 1374; 38 D.L.R. at 484. But see W. E. Conklin, "Pickin and its Applicability to Canada" (1975) 25 U.Tor.L.J. 193, 205–206.

The discussion of this formulation is not purely academic; Parliament has specified the manner in which the Royal Assent shall be given to legislation [12] and, on at least three occasions, has enacted legislation which may be regarded as having redefined " Parliament " for certain purposes. Though there are contrary interpretations,[13] the Parliament Acts of 1911 and 1949 may be regarded as having provided an alternative legislature (comprising the House of Commons and the Monarch) for the enactment of most subjects of legislation.[14] The European Communities Act 1972, when read with article 189 of the Treaty of Rome, may be regarded as having established, for some purposes, a new legislature comprising the Monarch, Lords, Commons and the legislative organs of the European Economic Community; and the Northern Ireland Constitution Act 1973—if it is not regarded as a merely political declaration of intention—could have established a new legislature, comprising the British Parliament and a majority of the people of Northern Ireland, for the enactment of legislation to terminate British jurisdiction over Northern Ireland or any part thereof. Nevertheless, the fact that Parliament has enacted legislation does not establish that the legislation is valid or will be effective; although none of the Acts mentioned has been challenged in court,[15] it has been alleged that one of them is invalid.[16]

Although it is possible that " manner and form " legislation which merely binds Parliament—or its component parts—but is not enforceable in the courts would be effectual in practice,[17] the efficacy

[12] Royal Assent Act 1967.

[13] Some commentators characterise the Acts as a delegation of legislative power, possibly because Parliament has not precluded itself from continuing to enact legislation on any subject in the usual way. See Hood Phillips, *supra* note 8 at 73; Wade, *supra* note 47 at 193–194; Beinart, *supra* note 8 at 113 note 44. However, the British Parliament, in enacting the Parliament Act 1949 pursuant to the 1911 Act's procedure, seems to have treated the latter Act as more than a mere delegation of power, for it expanded the ambit of the powers of the legislature acting pursuant to the Parliament Acts, something a mere " delegate " could not ordinarily do without an express conferral of power.

[14] A Bill to extend the maximum duration of Parliament beyond five years is expressly excluded: Parliament Act 1911 s. 2 (1).

[15] In a general sense, the European Communities Act 1972 was challenged, unsuccessfully, in *Blackburn* v. *Att.-Gen.* [1971] 1 W.L.R. 1037.

[16] Professor Hood Phillips, who regards the Parliament Act 1911 as a mere delegation of legislative power, has questioned the validity of the Parliament Act 1949 (*i.e.* whether it is an " Act of Parliament "): *supra* note 8 at 74. Were his premise correct, it is probably true that the 1949 Act is *ultra vires* the powers of the delegate, especially in view of the preamble to the 1911 Act which shows that it was intended as a temporary measure. However, it is more realistic to view the 1911 Act as a redefinition of " Parliament," for most purposes, as two alternative legislatures. The phrase " Any Public Bill " in s. 2 (1) of the 1911 Act is certainly, on its face, wide enough to include the 1949 Act.

[17] Constitutional " manner and form " provisions are not always judicially enforceable in British countries: *e.g.* Australian Constitution ss. 53, 54 and 56 (*Osborne* v. *Commonwealth* (1911) 12 C.L.R. 321). *Cf.* s. 57: *Cormack* v. *Cope* (1974) 131 C.L.R. 432, 461 (McTiernan J.) (*contra* at 460 (Barwick C.J.), 466–467) (Gibbs J.), 473–474 (Mason J.)); *Victoria* v. *Commonwealth* (1975) 7 A.L.R. 1; *Western Australia* v. *Commonwealth* (1975) 7 A.L.R. 159.

of the legislation would depend on parliamentary good faith, which might not always be forthcoming. Accordingly, the second formulation of the rule of parliamentary supremacy raises the question of judicial review of legislation in the United Kingdom.

2. Judicial Review

Review of " Enacted Legislation." The conception that Parliament could alter its composition or the " manner and form " of its legislation led inevitably to re-examination of the question of judicial review of legislation, and it is appropriate that the first tentative steps in this direction were taken by Dixon J. in *Trethowan.* " [T]he Courts *might be called upon* to consider [whether the body which purported to enact the measure had authority to do so]," he declared,[18] but he left the question unresolved, merely observing enigmatically that " the answer . . . would be deduced from the principle of parliamentary supremacy over the law." [19]

The common law, as an aspect of the Rule of Law, always recognised that the courts, in applying the law to cases before them, must ensure that what purport to be Acts of Parliament have in fact been approved by all three parts thereof.[20] But, as we have seen, until the 1930s it was not thought that Parliament could alter either its composition (including the " manner and form " of legislating) or its powers; hence judicial *dicta* to the effect that the courts cannot question the validity of an Act passed by all three parts of Parliament [21] are irrelevant to the question whether " manner and form " provisions can be judicially enforced; that question had not been conceived of when most of the *dicta* were uttered.

When considering whether to apply to a dispute what purports to be an Act of Parliament, a court which does not accept the first formulation of the rule of parliamentary supremacy must inquire

18 44 C.L.R. at 426. Our emphasis.

19 *Ibid.*

20 *The Prince's* case (1606) 8 Co.Rep. 1a, 20b; 77 E.R. 481, 505. The courts will not enforce a resolution of only one House: *Stockdale* v. *Hansard* (1839) 9 A. & E. 1, 108, 112 E.R. 1112, 1153–1154; *Bowles* v. *Bank of England* [1913] 1 Ch. 57, *Edinburgh & Dalkeith Railway Co.* v. *Wauchope* (1842) 8 Cl. & F. 710, 725, 8 E.R. 279, 285 suggests that the court is concerned only with what appears on the Parliament Roll, not with what actually happened. This is an application of the " enrolled Bill rule," namely that the court will not look behind the Parliament Roll except where an irregularity appears on the face of the Roll. The rule stems from the notion that Parliament is a court of record, not from parliamentary supremacy: see Jennings, *supra* note 4 at 139, 155. See also B. Beinart " Parliament and the Courts " [1954] Butterworth's S.A.L.Rev. 134, 165–176; D. V. Cowen, *supra* note 76 at 275 *et seq.*

21 See the general comments of Willes J. in *Lee* v. *Bude & Torrington Junction Ry. Co.* (1871) L.R. 6 C.P. 576, 582. Other *dicta* denying judicial review refer to substantive limitations on Parliament's power: *e.g. British Railways Board* v. *Pickin* [1974] A.C. 765, 782, 798: *Cheney* v. *Conn* [1968] 1 W.L.R. 242, 247: *R.* v. *Jordan* [1967] Crim.L.Rev. 483; *MacCormick* v. *Lord Advocate* 1953 S.C. 396, 413, 416–417; *Ex parte Selwyn* (1872) 36 J.P. 54, 55.

whether the measure has in fact been enacted by a body which is authorised, under the existing law, to pass it, and whether it was enacted in the correct manner and form; this is merely an application of the Rule of Law,[22] expressed so well 173 years ago in *Marbury* v. *Madison*.[23] Accordingly, British constitutional lawyers favouring the second formulation argue for judicial review,[24] but there is at present neither parliamentary[25] nor judicial support for it. We must, therefore, be wary of assuming that the courts will necessarily do what the Rule of Law suggests they should.[26]

It is vital to remember that before a court will consider the validity of what purports to be an Act of Parliament it must go through two stages. First it must decide which of the three formulations of the rule of parliamentary supremacy it will adopt[27] and, secondly, if it adopts the second or third formulation, it must consider whether it *should* exercise jurisdiction; this depends on the " separation of powers " and " political questions "[28] doctrines. Especially in view of legal developments in the Commonwealth, recognised by the Privy Council,[29] it is becoming increasing likely that British courts will adopt the second formulation of the rule. Moreover, it is likely that their present willingness to examine constitutional arguments innovatively[30] will lead to acceptance of judicial review of the validity of legislation; or, in other words, consideration of whether a measure really has been enacted by *Parliament*.

Judicial Intervention Prior to Enactment. If Parliament has provided a new " manner and form " for the enactment of legislation, say approval by the electors at a referendum held after passage of a Bill by the two Houses but before submission for the Royal Assent, the

[22] Heuston, *supra* note 52 at 211. See also W. S. Tarnopolsky, *The Canadian Bill of Rights* (2nd rev. ed., 1975), 112.

[23] (1803) 5 U.S. (1 Cranch) 137, 177–178.

[24] *e.g.* Mitchell, *supra* note 11 at 82–89, 91 (a masterly analysis) and *supra* note 90 at 108–109.

[25] Some scant and inferential parliamentary support can be found in s. 3 of the Parliament Act 1911, providing that the Speaker's certificate under the Act " shall be conclusive for all purposes, and shall not be *questioned in any court* of law "; by so providing, Parliament seems to admit the possibility of questioning an Act in court. Of course, Parliament can authorise judicial review, as it did in s. 116 (2) of the National Insurance Act 1965. But that was a special situation in which regulations, enacted as delegated legislation, were incorporated into a new statute.

[26] Although the prospects for judicial review appear brighter now than they seemed to Professor Friedmann in 1950: *supra* note 99 at 107.

[27] This is probably what Dixon J. meant when he wrote that the answer " would be deduced from the principle of parliamentary supremacy over the law ": *Trethowan*, 44 C.L.R. at 426.

[28] See G. Sawer, " Political Questions " (1963) 15 U.Tor.L.J. 49, 55–56.

[29] *Esp. The Bribery Commissioner* v. *Ranasinghe* [1965] A.C. 172.

[30] See *e.g. Blackburn* v. *Att.-Gen.* [1971] 1 W.L.R. 1037, 1040; *MacCormick* v. *Lord Advocate* 1953 S.C. 396, 411; *Pickin* v. *British Railways Board* [1973] Q.B. 219. However, the innovative spirit of Lord Denning M.R. and his Court of Appeal colleagues has yet to seize the House of Lords: see *British Railways Board* v. *Pickin* [1974] A.C. 765 (reversing C.A.).

question naturally arises whether the courts may intervene before the Bill is enacted to ensure that the new " manner and form " requirements are not ignored. It may be thought that the discretion which, by law, the Crown still has to withhold assent to legislation would make litigation prior to the Royal Assent moot; however, unlike American Presidents who have a constitutional power to withhold assent, often do, and have sometimes claimed the right when considering veto to follow their own view of the law,[31] the British Monarch, by a convention established since the reign of Queen Anne, does not refuse Assent to Bills passed by both Houses. Hence, in Britain, for all practical purposes a Bill is certain to become " law " once it is submitted for the Royal Assent, with the result that litigation to prevent the submission of a Bill for the Royal Assent is not hypothetical or moot.

As with so many ideas in this area of constitutional law, the notion of judicial intervention prior to the Royal Assent owes its origin to *Trethowan*, in which the Supreme Court of New South Wales issued an injunction against submission of the Bills for the Royal Assent.[32] Debate has raged ever since both as to whether the courts could [33]

[31] See the view of President Jackson, quoted in W. H. Taft, *The President and His Powers* (1916), 137.

[32] *Trethowan* v. *Peden* (1930) 31 S.R.(N.S.W.) 183, 205, 221. Long Innes J. reluctantly concluded that " on the balance of . . . inconvenience " an injunction would be appropriate: at 235. The High Court and Privy Council did not consider whether an injunction should issue. With respect, Lord Diplock was incorrect in suggesting (*Rediffusion (Hong Kong) Ltd.* v. *Att.-Gen. (Hong Kong)* [1970] A.C. 1136, 1156) that the High Court and Privy Council can be taken to have agreed that the courts had jurisdiction to issue an injunction. Certainly, Dixon C.J. felt that *Trethowan* v. *Peden* may have been wrong on this issue: *Hughes & Vale Pty. Ltd.* v. *Gair* (1954) 90 C.L.R. 203, 204–205; (1957) 31 A.L.J. 254. A weak precedent for the issue of the injunction in *Trethowan* was *Taylor* v. *Att.-Gen.* [1917] S.R.Qd. 208, 219 (reversed on another ground (1917) 23 C.L.R. 457). Although in both *Taylor* and *Trethowan* injunctions were issued to prevent the commission of unlawful acts, the position in *Trethowan* was the converse of that in *Taylor*. In the latter the injunction was granted to prevent implementation of an (allegedly) invalid " manner and form " requirement (a referendum), not to secure compliance with a valid " manner and form " provision (requiring a referendum), as in *Trethowan*. Moreover, in *Taylor* the question whether an injunction should be issued was neither given detailed consideration nor treated as one involving " interference " in the parliamentary process. See [1917] S.R.Qd. 208, 223.

[33] Support for the issue of an injunction can be found in *Tonkin* v. *Brand* [1962] W.A.R. 2, 15; *Cormack* v. *Cope* (1974) 131 C.L.R. 432, 453, 466. Barwick C.J. observed that " it is not the case in Australia, as it is in the United Kingdom, that the judiciary will restrain itself from interference in any part of the law-making process of the Parliament ": *ibid.*, at 454. This observation as to the position in Britain seems, with respect, to be based on a confusion between the powers of a legislature and the manner and form of their exercise, for Barwick C.J. began his analysis by observing that " [w]e are not here dealing with a Parliament whose laws and activities have the paramountcy of the Houses of Parliament in the United Kingdom " (at 452). Ironically, Barwick C.J. then quoted a passage from *Ranasinghe* in which Lord Pearce acknowledged the difference between limitations of power and procedural limitations. For views against the issue of an injunction see *Masai* v. *Jansen, N.O.* [1936] C.P.D. 361, 364 (*obiter*); *Hughes & Vale Pty. Ltd.* v. *Gair* (1954) 90 C.L.R. 203, 204; *Clayton* v. *Heffron* (1960) 105 C.L.R. 214, 264; *Cormack* v. *Cope*, 131 C.L.R. at 464–465, 572.

or should [34] grant such relief. A strong argument can be made that, at least in cases where the Bill, when assented to by the Crown, could be held invalid by the courts [35] litigation should await its attempted enforcement, for, until then, the whole proceedings of Parliament can be regarded as merely a wasteful exertion, but not unlawful.[36] Consequently, it is important to remember that in *Trethowan*—still the only occasion on which such an injunction was issued—the existing legislation [37] expressly forbade the submission to the Governor of a Bill not approved at a referendum,[38] so that submission of the Bill to him was unlawful.

In view of the courts' traditional reluctance to " interfere " in the " legislative process " [39] or to issue any injunction when a declaration will probably suffice,[40] it is highly unlikely that the British courts would issue an injunction, even in circumstances similar to those in *Trethowan.*[41] However, the courts show far less reluctance to make a declaration,[42] leaving it to the appropriate officers to decide whether or not to comply with their legal obligations.

C. *Substantively and Procedurally " Self-Embracing " Supremacy*

Although it has no judicial support, a third interpretation of the rule of parliamentary supremacy is logically indicated: that Parliament's supreme power enables it to redefine itself, impose " manner and form " requirements for the enactment of future legislation, *and*

---

34 See *ibid.*, 131 C.L.R. at 460, 467.

35 For the view that courts may be more inclined to intervene prior to the Royal Assent if intervention thereafter were impossible, see *Rediffusion (Hong Kong) Ltd* v. *Att.-Gen. (Hong Kong)* [1970] A.C. 1136, 1156–1157; *Cormack* v. *Cope*, 131 C.L.R. at 472.

36 *Rediffusion* [1970] A.C. at 1161, 1169.

37 Constitution Act 1902–1929 (N.S.W.) s. 7A (2).

38 *Clayton* v. *Heffron* (1960) 105 C.L.R. 214, 234. For discussion of the relevance of such a provision, see *Rediffusion* [1970] A.C. at 1169.

39 *Cf. Bilston Corp.* v. *Wolverhampton Corp.* [1942] Ch. 391, 393. Professor Derham has argued that " [i]n a case such as *Trethowan* . . . the interference by the court . . . would not in any sense be an interference with the legislative process but a protection of it ": (1957) 31 A.L.J. 248. (*Cf.* Lord Denning M.R. in *Pickin* [1973] Q.B. at 231. But see *contra* [1974] A.C. 765 *esp.* at 790, 799). Regarding *Trethowan*, it must be remembered that courts show less reluctance to intervene in the legislative process of a colonial legislature than in that of the United Kingdom: see *Rediffusion* [1970] A.C. at 1157.

40 *McDonald* v. *Cain* [1953] V.L.R. 411, 438; *Mayland* v. *Lymburn* [1931] 2 D.L.R. 698, 704 (Alta. A.D.).

41 *Hughes & Vale Pty. Ltd.* v. *Gair* (1954) 90 C.L.R. 203, 204; Dixon (1957) 31 A.L.J. 254. But see E. Campbell, *Parliamentary Privilege in Australia* (1966), 88–89.

42 *Trethowan* 44 C.L.R. at 426 *per* Dixon J.; *Tonkin* v. *Brand* [1962] W.A.R. 2, 22 (approved by Windeyer J. in *Marks* v. *Commonwealth* (1964) 111 C.L.R. 549, 565); *McDonald* v. *Cain* [1953] V.L.R. 411, 438 *per* O'Bryan J. (Gavan Duffy J. doubtful at 420). In *Clayton* v. *Heffron* (1960) 105 C.L.R. 214 the High Court did not question (nor did it affirm) the appropriateness of the declaratory suit there.

impose substantive limitations on the future exercise of its powers.[43] We have seen that only the first and third interpretations of the rule of parliamentary supremacy are internally consistent; consequently, it may be argued that the inconsistency inherent in the second formulation supports the third, for the second, if it is to be consistent, must admit that the rule of parliamentary supremacy is alterable by Parliament.[44] However, despite the logical attraction of the third formulation, its adoption by the courts seems very remote for two reasons.

First, although it gives Parliament the procedural flexibility given by the second formulation, unlike the first two interpretations it would enable Parliament to deny future Parliaments the power to legislate on certain subjects, thereby enabling the creation of permanent legislative vacuums which could be eliminated only by resort to extra-constitutional devices. It is unlikely that the courts would adopt an interpretation which could lead to such practical difficulty that a "revolution" and replacement of the *grundnorm* may follow.

Secondly, there is simply no judicial support whatever for a rule which would enable Parliament to impose limitations on the content or ambit of future legislation.[45] While legislation seeking to limit the power of future Parliaments may not be void *ab initio*,[46] it would, under the present view of the law, clearly be ineffective,[47] exerting only a moral pressure, at most, on future Parliaments. This conclusion is borne out by the history of those statutes by which Parliament has sought to entrench legislation by providing that it was to last "for ever after" or "in all times to come": the Bill of Rights 1688, the Union with Scotland Act 1706 and the Union with Ireland Act 1800. Each of these statutes has been amended,[48] the Union with Ireland Act has been effectually repealed,[49] and most commentators

[43] See Jennings, *supra* note 4 at 152–153. *Cf.* Beinart, *supra* p. 606, note 8, at 109. Jennings repeats his assertion (*supra* at 160–161) but the illustration he gives (at 161) is one imposing a "manner and form" requirement. Hence, it is possible that Jennings is asserting only the second formulation of the rule, though his comments are wide enough to embrace the third.

[44] See Salmond, quoted *supra* note 49.

[45] *Godden* v. *Hales* (1686) 11 St.Tr. 1165, 1197 (Herbert C.J.); *Blackburn* v. *Att.-Gen.* [1971] 1 W.L.R. 1037, 1041 (Salmon L.J.); Dixon, *Jesting Pilate* (1965), 48.

[46] See *contra* Sir Francis Bacon, quoted in Cowen, *supra* note 73 at 181.

[47] Wade, *supra* note 47 at 186.

[48] Accession Declaration Act 1910 s. 1, Universities (Scotland) Act 1932 s. 5 but see Mitchell, *supra* note 11 at 73) and Irish Church Act 1869, s. 2. It has been suggested that Britain's entry into the EEC is a "breach" of Art. XVIII of the Treaty of Union (Trindade, *supra* note 90 at 389), but the argument is unconvincing and seems a misapplication of the maxim *expressio unius est exclusio alterius*. Interestingly, a different clause of Art. XVIII was relied upon in *Gibson* v. *Lord Advocate* [1975] 1 C.M.L.R. 563 (Outer House).

[49] Government of Ireland Act 1920 s. 1 (1).

acknowledge that they impose no legal limitation whatever on the powers of Parliament.[50]

It is submitted that the second formulation of the rule of parliamentary supremacy will be endorsed by British courts. The only circumstance in which the courts might accept the third formulation is one in which the traditional political setting is radically altered, enabling the courts to say that in effect a new *grundnorm*, or a new customary constitutional rule has emerged. The only presently foreseeable occasion for such a change of attitude by the courts is the complete integration of Britain into the political, economic, constitutional and social structure of the European Economic Community. Accordingly, an assessment of the future of the ultimate rule of her constitution must take the European Economic Community into consideration.

IV. The Future: Parliamentary Supremacy and the EEC

Since the impact of membership in the EEC on the rule of parliamentary supremacy has been subjected to detailed, although, of necessity, speculative analysis elsewhere,[51] our discussion is confined to examining the implications of British membership on the relative claims of the various formulations of the rule of parliamentary supremacy.

The Treaty of Rome, in article 189,[52] provides for the direct application in each member-State of Community regulations. To fulfil its obligations under that article, Parliament enacted section 2 (1) of the European Communities Act 1972 which provides:

> All such rights, powers liabilities, obligations and restrictions from time to time created or arising by or under the Treaties . . . as in accordance with the Treaties are *without further enactment* to be given legal effect . . . in the United Kingdom shall be recognised and available in law. . . .[53]

---

[50] This is the view of most English constitutional lawyers; *e.g.* Dicey, *supra* note 30 at 65. Scottish lawyers have tended to see the Treaty of Union as a "fundamental" law which cannot be amended, except where expressly authorised: see T. B. Smith, "The Union of 1707 as Fundamental Law" [1957] Pub.L. 99, 109–113. See generally Mitchell, *supra* note 11 at 70–73. The most significant expression of the Scottish viewpoint is that of Lord President Cooper in *MacCormick* v. *Lord Advocate* 1953 S.C. 396, 411–412 (Lord Carmont in accord, at 414). But is it important to note that the Lord Advocate had conceded that some "fundamental" articles of the Treaty could not be abrogated: *ibid.*, at 409. The more traditional view is that of Lord Guthrie, in the lower court: *ibid.*, at 403. See also *Gibson* v. *Lord Advocate* [1975] 1 C.M.L.R. 563, 569 (Outer House).

[51] Most of the authorities are reviewed in Trindade, *supra* note 90.

[52] (1958) 298 U.N.T.S. 11, 79.

[53] Our emphasis. Mr. Michael Foot observed of s. 2 (1): "[I]f in a single subsection we are to deal a blow to the cause for which Hampden died on the field and Sidney died on the scaffold, we might at least get the punctuation right" (831 H.C.Deb. (5th ser.) 738 (1972)). For discussion of the effect of s. 2 (1), see *Application des Gaz S.A.* v. *Falks Veritas Ltd.* [1974] Ch. 381: *Gibson* v. *Lord Advocate*

The possibility exists of conflict between Community regulations and subsequent British statutes, so Parliament sought to establish the priorities in section 2 (4) " [A]ny enactment passed *or to be passed*, other than one contained in this Part of this Act, shall be construed and have effect subject to the foregoing provisions of this section. . . .[54] Moreover, the final decision as to the meaning of a Community treaty or instrument is to be made by the European Court in Luxembourg.[55]

So far as parliamentary supremacy is concerned, two possible infringements of the rule arise: conflict between a statute and a later inconsistent EEC regulation, and the converse position. The former situation presents no insuperable problem, for, as we saw earlier, if the second formulation of the rule or parliamentary supremacy is adopted, section 2 (1) may be regarded as creating a new legislature comprising the three elements of the British Parliament, which have, by section 2 (1), given their permanent consent to EEC regulations, and the legislative organs of the Community.[56] Moreover, in this situation the British Parliament could be seen as an alternative legislature and need not be entirely replaced in this area of power by the new legislature. In the event of a conflict between a statute and subsequent EEC regulations the normal rule that the later enactment repeals the earlier would apply; there need be no break with traditional ideas of parliamentary supremacy.

The second area of conflict presents greater difficulty. The European Court, whose interpretation of the Treaties binds British courts,[57] has held that, where Community regulations and subsequent national legislation are irreconcilable, the Community law prevails.[58] Here, again, the second interpretation of the rule of parliamentary supremacy (but not the first) enables Britian to satisfy both her Community obligations and the ultimate rule of her constitution: section

[1975] 1 C.M.L.R. 563, 568; J. W. Bridge, " Community Law and English Courts and Tribunals. General Principles and Preliminary Rulings " (1975) 1 European L.Rev. 13, 14–16.

[54] Our emphasis. Section s. 2 (6), likewise, seeks to bind future Parliaments. *Cf.* the comments of Pigeon J. (dissenting) on the words " construed and applied " in s. 2 of the Canadian Bill of Rights 1960: *R.* v. *Drybones* (1969) 9 D.L.R. (3d) 473, 490.

[55] European Communities Act 1972, s. 3 (1).

[56] Lord Diplock would probably characterise s. 2 (1) as a delegation of legislative power to the Community's leglislative organs: " The Common Market and the Common Law " (1972) 6 *The Law Teacher* 3, 7.

[57] European Communities Act 1972, s. 3 (1).

[58] *Costa* v. *E.N.E.L.* [1964] C.M.L.R. 425, 456; *Re Export Tax on Art Treasures (No. 2)* [1972] C.M.L.R. 699, 708. *Cf. Minister for Economic Affairs* v. *S.A. Fromagerie Franco-Suisse " Le Ski "* [1972] C.M.L.R. 330, 373 (Belg. Cour de Cass.); *Frontini* v. *Ministero delle Finanze* [1974] 2 C.M.L.R. 372, 386–387 (Ital. Const.Ct.). E.E.C. law prevails even when in conflict with the constitution of a member-State: *Internationale Handelsgesellschaft mbH* v. *Einfuhr & Vorratsstelle für Getreide & Futtermittel* (Case 11/70) [1972] C.M.L.R. 255, 283 (Eur.Ct.). (For the interesting sequel in the German Federal Constitutional Court, see [1974] 2 C.M.L.R. 540 *esp.* at 550–551, 562–565 (dissenting opinion)).

2 (1) of the European Communities Act 1972 should be regarded as creating a new legislature, as we saw above, but section 2 (4) must be interpreted as making the new legislature the *only* legislature in the subject areas governed by Community law. In Diceyian terms, section 2 (4) must be regarded as a transfer of " sovereignty " over matters regulated by the EEC to the new legislature. Faced with a conflict between a Community regulation and a subsequent statute, British courts would have to rule that Parliament as usually constituted did not, under the present law, have power to enact the measure, so that the purported statute was not, in fact, an Act of Parliament.[59] With the possible exception of section 4 of the Statute of Westminster, Britain has never sought either to exclude Parliament as usually constituted from an area of legislative power or include a foreign body in its legislative process; nevertheless, the fact that it has not been done before is a weak argument against recognising that it has been done now. A stronger argument against the above analysis is that section 2 (4) is far too unclear to have such far-reaching consequences.[60]

A third matter, which was much discussed in Parliament when the European Communities Bill 1972 was debated, and was raised by the recent reconsideration of membership, is whether section 2 (4) prevents a future Parliament from repealing the European Communities Act and withdrawing Britian from the Community. Although it is true that a statute to effect Britain's withdrawal would, in a general sense, conflict with the continued direct applicability of Community regulations under section 2 (1) and, therefore possibly be subject to section 2 (4), a British court is unlikely to so conclude, because it would interpret section 2 (1) literally, bearing in mind its break with usual constitutional practice. Britian's obligation to remain within the Community arises under international law and not under section 2 (1), for it is not one " created or arising by, or under the Treaties . . . as in accordance with the Treaties [is] without further enactment to be given legal effect . . . in the United Kingdom. . . ." Accordingly, there is nothing in the European Communities Act 1972 to prevent Parliament passing an Act to withdraw Britain from the Community.[61]

Although our conclusions are consistent with those of the Conservative Government, it must be conceded that our argument leading

[59] See *contra* Diplock, *supra* note 56 at 5, 8; 838 H.C.Deb. (5th ser.) 1320 (Sir Geoffrey Howe S.G., 1972).

[60] See Sir Elwyn Jones (Now Lord Chancellor): 839 H.C.Deb. (5th ser.) 251 and 840 *ibid.* 559 (1972). The possibility of adopting the second formulation of the rule of parliamentary supremacy as a way of reconciling the rule with Britain's EEC obligations was not discussed in Parliament: but see Lord Gardiner L.C., 282 H.L.Deb. (5th ser.) 1203 (1967). See also Lord Hailsham L.C., 333 H.L.(Deb. (5th ser.) 1230 (1972).

[61] *Cf.* de Smith, *supra* note 52 at 673 note 14.

to reconciliation of parliamentary supremacy and Britian's Community obligations was not articulated in Parliament during the long debates on the European Communities Bill 1972. Opponents of the Bill argued that section 2 would end the rule of parliamentary supremacy,[62] but the leading lawyers on the Government side asserted that the rule was not affected as it *could not* be[63]; the debate demonstrated, in fact, how deep the British legal world's commitment still is to the Dicey/Wade formulation of the rule of parliamentary supremacy. Nevertheless, the attempt to reconcile the strict Dicey/Wade theory with Britian's Community obligations and the political reality once Britian joined the Common Market resulted in some rather confusing explanations, such as that of Mr. Geoffrey Rippon, the Minister responsible for the Bill:

> By accepting the directly applicable law in [s. 2 (1)] and accepting the jurisprudence of the European Court in [s. 3 (1)] the Bill provides the necessary precedence. In relation to statute law, this means that the directly applicable provisions *ought to prevail over future Acts of Parliament* in so far as they might be inconsistent with them. In practice, this means that . . . quoting the Leader of the Opposition [Harold Wilson]: "It would be implicit in our acceptance of the Treaties that the United Kingdom would, in future, refrain from enacting legislation inconsistent with community law." [Section 2 (4)] accordingly provides that present and future enactments shall be construed and have effect subject to [s. 2]. . . . Of course, nothing in this Bill abridges the *ultimate sovereignty* of Parliament.[64]

At present it appears that it is in relation to Britain's position in the European Economic Community that developments will be seen in the rule of parliamentary supremacy. We have argued that, despite arguments of logical inconsistency, it is the second formulation of the rule which British courts are most likely to adopt in future, especially as it will help to reconcile the rule with Britain's Community obligations. Even if the courts are not, at first, prepared to accommodate political reality to that extent, it is inevitable that they will

[62] See *e.g.* 831 H.C.Deb 699: 832 *ibid.* 1307; 333 H.L.Deb. 1236, 1240, 1400.

[63] 840 H.C.Deb. 627–629; 334 H.L.Deb. 764, 812-813, 911; 335 *ibid.* 292–293. Principally for this reason, the Government opposed, successfully, an amendment, proposed in both Houses, to preserve expressly the rule of parliamentary supremacy: see 840 H.C.Deb. 556–647; 334 H.L.Deb. 893–915; 335 *ibid.* 287–301 (1972).

[64] 831 H.C.Deb. 278 (1972). Our emphasis. Likewise, Sir Geoffrey Howe, S.G.: "But at the end of the day if repeal, lock, stock and barrel was proposed, the ultimate sovereignty of Parliament must remain intact" (838 H.C.Deb. 1319 (1972)).

eventually change their view of the rule of parliamentary supremacy [65]; for, as Mr. Middleton observed some years ago, albeit in a different context, " when the facts cannot be made to fit the law, then the law must be made to fit the facts." [66]

GEORGE WINTERTON.*

[65] The same view has been expressed by Mr. Denzil Davies (832 H.C.Deb. 1302 (1972)) and Professors de Smith (*supra* note 81 at 614) and Lloyd (*supra* note 2 at 192, 198). However, if the experience of the national courts of the original " six " is any guide, the adaptation is likely to take quite a while: see G. Bebr, " How Supreme is Community Law in the National Courts? " (1974) 11 C.M.L.Rev. 3; *Internationale Handelsgesellschaft* [1974] 2 C.M.L.R. 540, 550–551 (but see also the dissenting opinion of three judges at 562–565).

[66] *Supra*, note 71 at 57 note 53. *Cf.* Murphy J.'s reference to " the silent operation of constitutional principles ": *Commonwealth* v. *Queensland* (1975) 7 A.L.R. 351, 378–379; *Att.-Gen. for Australia* v. *Commonwealth* (1975) 7 A.L.R. 593, 642.

* Senior Lecturer in Law, University of New South Wales, Sydney, Australia.

[5]

Cambridge Law Journal, 38 (1), *April* 1979, pp. 79–117.
Printed in Great Britain

THE COURTS AND PARLIAMENT: WHO WHOM?

PHILIP ALLOTT

ALL government is a conspiracy. Each governmental conspiracy has a constitution as its alibi. The constitution describes the way in which the political power of the society is concentrated and places the source of that concentration somewhere other than in the mere fact of power. Because of that dislocation, the constitution is the source not only of political power but also of political duty. The subjection of the organs of government to the constitution runs parallel to the subjection of the people governed to the constitutional power of the organs of government. The constitution justifies constitutional power and constitutional duty by making both of them derivatives from one and the same source.

The prior question of whence the constitution itself derives its authority is, for all everyday practical purposes, answered by the mere fact of the constitution. The constitution is self-proving in practice because it is used as the source of maxims affecting the behaviour of those who exercise physical force with actual impunity, or who control its exercise. To preach or to act against the constitution may or may not be permitted by the legal rules of the given society (themselves derived ultimately from the constitution), but it will in any event be ineffective whenever it comes into collision with power exercised, to the point of physical force, under authority derived from the constitution. A revolution occurs when the exercise of constitutional power, to the point of physical force, ceases or is overridden by the exercise of unconstitutional power, if necessary by the application of greater physical force. A functioning political system is a suspension of revolution. It is civil war by other means.

A constitution thus presents itself as higher law in relation to everyday adjective and substantive law. It is *higher* in the sense that its existence and validity are a pre-condition of the validity of the adjective and substantive law. It is *law* in one or other of two senses, either because it is seen to belong to the same systematic structure as the adjective and substantive law and is, directly or indirectly, applicable and enforceable by the same methods, or else because it is seen to be derived from a source outside the substantive legal system but is felt as a constraint on the operation of the legal system, of a kind which may be labelled, directly or by analogy, as law. In this latter sense, it is derived in modern constitutions, especially and typically, from the so-called sovereignty of the people or of the nation, whose decisive, and perhaps only, exercise of power is in willing the constitution. In the case of newly formed States, the constitution may have a validating source, in addition to or in place of the will of the popular sovereign, in its being an integral part of the coming into existence of the State. The State and the constitution are assimilated and reciprocally validate each other. In such circumstances, the character of the constitution as higher law most plainly speaks for itself.[1]

Such considerations seem to apply in a special way to the British constitution, if they apply at all. The absence of a basic constitutional document has made the source of constitutional authority seem to be a matter of fact or a matter of speculation, rather than a matter of law. The particular form which speculation took in the work of Dicey, the most influential of modern constitutional theorists, has led to the widespread acceptance of an endogenous validation of the constitutional system. Brilliantly in his articulation of the concept of the Rule of Law, less comfortably in his articulation of the concept of the Sovereignty of Parliament, Dicey sought to demonstrate the validity of the system in terms of its own coherence. Dicey's is a coherence theory of a constitutional system. It invited us to understand why it works by understanding how it works. The purpose of the present study is to recall that it is possible to take another view of our constitutional system, in particular a "higher law" view, and to suggest that there are grounds for thinking that such a view is now not only possible but also necessary. The particular form of "higher law" view which will be proposed would not include a principle of "the sovereignty of Parliament", at least in its familiar Diceyan form.

In *British Railways Board* v. *Pickin*,[2] decided as recently as 1974, the House of Lords dealt unanimously, unequivocally and apparently conclusively with a particular kind of challenge to the validity of a provision in an Act of Parliament:

> The idea ... that an Act of Parliament, public or private, or a provision in an Act of Parliament, could be declared invalid or ineffective in the courts on account of some irregularity in Parliamentary procedure, or on the ground that Parliament in passing it was misled, or on the ground that it was obtained by deception or fraud, has been decisively repudiated by authorities of the highest standing from 1842 onwards. The remedy for a Parliamentary wrong, if one has been committed, must be

[1] Particular problems of the location of sovereignty arise in Commonwealth countries. See Marshall, *Parliamentary Sovereignty & the Commonwealth* (1957); de Smith, *The New Commonwealth & its Constitutions* (1964), 109 *et seq.*

[2] [1974] A.C. 765; [1974] 1 All E.R. 609.

sought from Parliament, and cannot be gained from the courts. The law in my opinion is correctly summed up in *Halsbury's Laws of England* [3] in these words:

> If a Bill has been agreed by both Houses of Parliament, and has received the Royal Assent, it cannot be impeached in the courts on the ground that its introduction or passage through Parliament, was attended by any irregularity, or even on the ground that it was obtained by fraud.
>
> (*per* Lord Wilberforce).[4]

It is interesting to note how closely Lord Wilberforce's opinion was related to the kind of challenge in issue in the *Pickin* case. Lord Reid, on the other hand, went wider in setting out the considerations underlying his opinion. Those considerations may be analysed as falling into three categories. They are considerations on three different levels.

(1) The first level is the level of positive law:

> In my judgment the law is correctly stated by Lord Campbell in *Edinburgh & Dalkeith Railway Co.* v. *Wauchope* [5]... He said [6]:
>
> > ...all that a court of justice can look to is the parliamentary roll; they see that an Act has passed both Houses of Parliament, and that it has received the royal assent, and no court of justice can inquire into the manner in which it was introduced into Parliament, what was done previously to its being introduced, or what passed in Parliament during the various stages of its progress through both Houses of Parliament... (*per* Lord Reid).[7]

(2) The second level is the level of constitutional fact:

> For a century or more both Parliament and the courts have been careful not to act so as to cause conflict between them. Any such investigations as the respondent seeks could easily lead to such a conflict, and I would only support it if compelled to do so by clear authority.[8]

(3) The third level is the level of constitutional theory:

> The idea that a court is entitled to disregard a provision in an Act of Parliament on any ground must seem strange and startling to anyone with any knowledge of the history and law of our constitution, but a detailed argument has been submitted to your Lordships and I must deal with it.
>
> I must make it plain that there has been no attempt to question the general supremacy of Parliament. In earlier times many learned lawyers seem to have believed that an Act of Parliament could be disregarded in so far as it was contrary to the law of God or the law of nature or natural justice but

[3] 3rd ed., Vol. 36, p. 376, para. 560.

[4] At pp. 792, 622.

[5] (1842) 1 Bell 252.

[6] At p. 279.

[7] At pp. 786, 617.

[8] At pp. 788, 618.

> since the supremacy of Parliament was finally demonstrated by the Revolution of 1688 any such idea has become obsolete.[9]

Of the remaining members of the House of Lords, Lord Simon also took the matter up to the level of the constitutional theory of " the sovereignty of Parliament," whereas Lord Morris adopted the narrower, more positive-law approach which Lord Wilberforce had favoured, and Lord Cross associated himself with everything which Lord Wilberforce had said on this aspect of the case.

Lord Reid's approach, put in the form of a single proposition, was that his conclusion accorded with constitutional theory, with the policy and practice of the organs of the constitution, and with the law to be found in decided cases. It is a strong conclusion which can claim such a degree of coherence, and the decision in *Pickin* seems, in consequence, to be exceptionally definitive. Indeed, it is possible to see the three levels of considerations used by Lord Reid as characteristic of much of British constitutional discourse. It is worth considering the hypothesis that British constitutional development has precisely consisted of a prolonged effort to maintain the coherence of those three levels. Current concern about the state of the constitution would then be seen as caused by a deep sense that such coherence is not being maintained.

Positive Law

Bonham's Case (1609)[10] is a notorious episode in the long history of the relationship between the judicial and the legislative powers. Itself purporting to be an extrapolation from medieval precedents, it became, in this country, a symbol of something which would have to be resisted or at least clarified in the course of prolonged constitutional change and, in the United States, an element in the ideological substructure of the constitution. Sharing in the constitutional ambiguity of its begetter, Coke, its significance remains uncertain 370 years later. The uncertainty relates to the validity of the decided-case precedents used by Coke, to the meaning of the principle actually stated by Coke, and to the role of the decision in subsequent constitutional development.

About Coke's use of the precedent cases in *Bonham* it may be said, in the first place, that he over-used the cases which he cited, even if there were other cases, of not much weight, which he might have cited had he known them.[11] Secondly, it seems that there had

9 At pp. 782, 614.

10 8 Co.Rep. 107a; 77 E.R. 638.

11 Plucknett, " Dr. Bonham's Case & Judicial Review," 40 Harv.L.Rev. 30 (1926); McIlwain, *High Court of Parliament* (1910), p. 286; Gough, *Fundamental Law in English History* (1955), p. 33: Vinogradoff, " The Yearbooks & Constitutional Law " (1917) 29 L.Q.R. 283; Holdsworth, *H.E.L.*, II, 442 *et seq. Cf.* Wormuth, *The Royal Prerogative 1603–49* (1939), p. 63: there was " abundant authority " for Coke's general proposition.

been a stage of constitutional development, in the fourteenth century, when the relationship between statute and common law was inchoate and when there was some room for a controlling role for the common law.[12] Thirdly, law-making and law-enforcement had not, even in Coke's own day, come to be perceived as intrinsically separate functions, so that his statement must be read against the background of a much more fluid relationship between them.[13] These considerations suggest a cautious approach in determining what exactly Coke meant by the most notorious passage in his lengthy report of the case:

> . . . And it appears in our books, that in many cases the common law will controul Acts of Parliament, and sometimes adjudge them to be utterly void: for when an Act of Parliament is against common right and reason, or repugnant, or impossible to be performed, the common law will controul it, and adjudge such Act to be void . . .[14]

The maximalist view of this statement is that it asserts the supremacy of fundamental law over statute law:

> "Common right and reason" is, in short, something fundamental, something permanent; it is higher law. One thing seems to be assured at the outset—Coke was not asserting simply a rule of statutory construction . . . Coke was enforcing a rule of higher law deemed by him to be binding on Parliament and the ordinary courts alike.[15]

The minimalist view is that the statement is, indeed, a statement about statutory interpretation:

> . . . the argument is derived from the ordinary common law rules of statutory interpretation . . . [Coke was referring to cases] on statutes repugnant and statutes impossible to be performed. . . . There can be no doubt, we think, that it was from these precedents, rather than from any natural law theories, that Coke's argument stems.[16]

(Thorne suggests that repugnancy in this context approximately equals contradictoriness) An intermediate view regards the state-

[12] Plucknett, "Statutes & their Interpretation in the First Half of the 14th Century," *Cambridge Studies in Legal History* (1922); Chrimes, *English Constitutional Ideas in the 15th Century* (1936), p. 289; Corwin, "The 'Higher law' Background of American Constitutional Law," I and II, 42 Harv.L.Rev., 149, 365 (1928).

[13] McIlwain, *op. cit.*, 163 *et seq.*; Pollard, *The Evolution of Parliament* (1926), 246 *et seq.*; Smith, *De Republica Anglorum*, ed. Alston (1906), ed.'s Intro. xxxiii.

[14] 8 Co.Rep. 118a; 77 E.R. 652.

[15] Corwin, *op. cit.*, pp. 370, 372. *Cf.* Jennings, *The Law & the Constitution*, 5th ed. (1959), App. III; Pollock, *Expansion of the Common Law* (1904), p. 22.

[16] Thorne, "Dr. Bonham's Case" (1938) 54 L.Q.R. 543; Holdsworth, *H.E.L.*, *loc. cit.* (note 11); *cf. ibid.*, IV, 186; Gough, *op. cit.*, p. 31; Knafla, *Law & Politics in Jacobean England* (1977), p. 149n.

ment as essentially a statement about statutory interpretation but emphasises that contemporary ideas about the role of Parliament and legislation would have led to some rather substantive presumptions, for example about the principle of *nemo iudex.*[17] Finally, there is what may be called the Ellesmere view, that Coke's statement was simply an instance of judicial over-reaching, and that it was properly for the King and Parliament to judge what was common right and reason and to revise statutes when necessary.[18]

In favour of a reductionist view are two particularly striking considerations. The first is the actual content of Coke's report of the case. At least if modern standards of case-analysis are applied, the case looks like a case of laborious statutory interpretation. It is not easy to know how much to discount of the verbiage and Latinisms of the report, but it does not include any categorical invalidation of the statutory provision, even if, it must be admitted, the outcome of the case is a bold piece of statutory interpretation, even judged by the standards of the most reconstructive of modern judicial techniques. By "adjudging void" Coke may well have meant something considerably less than what we mean by formal invalidation. On the basis of the report itself, it is as much a leading case on the *nemo iudex* principle as on any great constitutional question.[19] The second consideration is that Coke himself in the *Institutes* did not include the supposed *Bonham* principle as a fundamental constitutional principle. Indeed, he was, in his own way, a Parliament man and, as noted further below, spoke of the power of Parliament in seemingly absolutist terms in the *Institutes.* Coke's reply to the King's request in 1616 for an explanation of the *Bonham* decision was equivocal, merely repeating the terms of the report and stressing that it was supported by precedents.[20]

In favour of a more dramatic view of the decision is the interest which it has aroused, from the day it was given to the present day. It is the phrase "common right and reason" which is difficult to explain away in statutory interpretation terms and whose potential scope was as broad as a Lord Chief Justice's foot.[21] However, the echoes of the decision in subsequent decided cases are few and un-

[17] Judson, *The Crisis of the Constitution* (1949), p. 101; McIlwain, *op. cit.*, p. 286; Gough, *op. cit.*, p. 31.

[18] 77 E.R. 652; Knafla, *op. cit.*, pp. 306–307; McIlwain, *op. cit.*, p. 294. On Coke's relationship with Ellesmere, see Knafla, *op. cit.*, *passim*; Holdsworth, *H.E.L.*, V, 236 *et seq.*

[19] *Cf.* Yale, "*Iudex in Propria Causa*: an Historical Excursus" [1974] C.L.J. 80, 83.

[20] Bacon, *Works*, ed. Spedding, XIII, 89.

[21] Coke may have taken the phrase from a petition against a statute said to be "contre Ley et contre reson": R.R.ii.41 (4 Ed. III no. 52). See Vinogradoff, *op. cit.* (note 11).

impressive.[22] It has not been used as authority for holding statutory provisions invalid or for reforming or supplementing them. If it had been Coke's intention to re-establish the common law's precedence over statute law, then, as a matter of fact, he did not achieve his purpose by means of the *Bonham* decision. On the contrary, what has happened is that the courts have declined, time and time again, to apply extrinsic controls to the substantive validity of statutory provisions. Litigants have pleaded one or other of the four limits to constitutionality known to other constitutional systems—fundamental rights and freedoms,[23] fundamental principles of justice and of the constitutional structure,[24] treaties and general international law,[25] and improper legislative procedure.[26] The courts have listened with courtesy but have resisted the interesting temptation. Instead, they have found their views epitomised in the words of Willes J. in *Lee* v. *Bude & Torrington Railway Co.*[27]:

> I would observe, as to these Acts of Parliament, that they are the law of the land; and we do not sit here as a court of appeal from Parliament. It was once said—I think in Hobart—that, if an Act of Parliament were to create a man judge in his own case, the Court might disregard it. That dictum, however, stands as a warning, rather than an authority to be followed. We sit here as servants of the Queen and the legislature. Are we to act as regents over what is done by Parliament with the consent of the Queen, lords and commons? I deny that any such authority exists. If an Act of Parliament has been obtained improperly, it is for the legislature to correct it by repealing it; but, so long as it exists as law, the Courts are bound to obey it. The proceedings here are judicial, not autocratic, which they would be if we could make laws instead of administering them.

Ellesmere would have applauded and Mr. Justice Willes's words have been recalled with approval in many subsequent cases. In compensation for such self-denial, the courts have retained and refined two substantial powers in relation to statutes: the power to interpret and apply to individual cases,[28] and the power to create a

22 Corwin, *op. cit.*, 375 *et seq.*; Gough, *op. cit.*, 49; McIlwain, *op. cit.*, 271, 281–3, 329.

23 *R.* v. *Jordan* [1967] Crim.L.Rev. 483; *Thakrar* v. *Home Sec.* [1974] 2 All E.R. 261, C.A.; *R.* v. *Home Sec., ex p. Bhajan Singh* [1975] 2 All E.R. 1081.

24 *British Coal Corp.* v. *King* [1935] A.C. 500, P.C.; *MacCormick* v. *Lord Advocate*, 1953 S.C. 396; *Blackburn* v. *Att.-Gen.* [1971] 1 W.L.R. 1037.

25 *Mortensen* v. *Peters*, 1906 14 S.L.T. 227; *Chung Chi Cheung* v. *R.* [1939] A.C. 160, P.C.; *Cheney* v. *Conn* [1968] 1 W.L.R. 242; *Trendtex Trading Corp.* v. *Central Bank of Nigeria* [1977] 1 Q.B. 529 and cases there considered.

26 *Ellen St. Estates* v. *Min. of Health* [1934] 1 K.B. 590, C.A.; *Hall* v. *Hall* (1944) 88 S.J. 383; *Pickin* v. *B.R.B.* [1974] A.C. 765.

27 (1871) L.R. 6 C.P. 576.

28 "The law is what the judges say it is": Devlin, *Samples of Lawmaking* (1962), p. 2.

common law of statute law in the form of principles and presumptions of interpretation.[29] They are formidable powers resting on the simple facts that a statutory provision has merely potential content until it is made actual through application in practice and that a statutory provision is not autonomous but takes its place within a vast structure of existing law.

Constitutional Fact

If it is, accordingly, correct to attach such small significance to *Bonham's Case* at the level of positive law, what significance, let alone authority, can it be said to have in any other context? To answer that question it is necessary to move to the second level of constitutional discourse—the level of constitutional fact. What was significant about *Bonham* was its timing. It was decided at the very moment when it was becoming possible to distinguish three aspects of the governmental system: the activity of the King in Parliament, the activity of the King outside Parliament, the activity of the King's courts. The prolonged constitutional struggle of the seventeenth century would throw into relief three corresponding institutions—Parliament, the King and the courts—and the problem of the constitutional relationship between them. We live with the uncomfortable legacy of this double separation of functions and organs of government which, with equal force, illuminates and distorts our everyday experience of the British system.

Bonham's Case may be seen as a catalytic event in a fundamental process of constitutional change. As with the other notorious constitutional cases of the seventeenth century, it should be regarded as an event rather than as a source of law. Cases decided in the courts were one of the material forms which political forces took. The debates and decisions of the House of Commons, the words and deeds of the King, and the application of constitutional and unconstitutional force were the other forms. If *Bonham* were given its most dramatic interpretation, if it had been treated as authoritative in subsequent cases, if it had been left unchallenged in political terms, it could have substantially altered the course of constitutional development, reflecting a different hierarchical structure from that which is generally said to have been created by the events of the seventeenth century.

Demarcation disputes among political authorities were not a seventeenth-century novelty. They had been characteristic of the establishment and development of the kingdoms of western Europe

[29] On presumptions, see Maxwell, *Interpretation of Statutes*, 12th ed. (1969), Chaps. 7 and 8; Cross, *Statutory Interpretation* (1976), Chap. VII.

from their earliest days. Three kinds of such disputes had dominated political life in England until at least the high-Tudor period—the relationship with Rome, the relationship with France, and the relationships of authority within a quasi-feudal system. It is difficult now to capture the inner perspective, how it must have felt to live in a world in which the individual was a subject not only of his local lord, his local king and, in much of continental Europe, the Holy Roman Emperor, but also of the immaterial empire of the Church of Rome.[30] For the time being, it is enough to call to mind the degree to which participation in the supra-national organisation of the Church involved participation in what was virtually a parallel system of government, with its own legal system, courts, taxation, and administrative authorities. It may be illustrated, paradoxically but conveniently, by one of the legislative acts which sought to terminate it:

> ...And to the intent that all usurped and foreign power and authority, spiritual and temporal, may forever be clearly extinguished and never to be used nor obeyed within this realm or any other your Majesty's dominions or countries: May it please your Highness that it may be further enacted by the authority aforesaid that no foreign prince, person, prelate, state or potentate, spiritual or temporal, shall at any time after the last day of this session of Parliament use, enjoy or exercise any manner of power, jurisdiction, superiority, authority, pre-eminence or privilege spiritual or ecclesiastical, within this realm or within any other your Majesty's dominions or countries that now be or hereafter shall be, but from thenceforth the same shall be clearly abolished out of this realm and all other your Highness' dominions for ever; any statute, ordinance, custom, constitutions or any other matter or cause whatsoever to the contrary in any wise notwithstanding (*Act of Supremacy* of 1559).[31]

An important part of the process of establishing the modern nation-state was the domestication of political authority. In post-Reformation England, the perennial problem of the distribution of political authority among the actual centres of power at last presented itself as the problem of organising an independent self-contained political system.

In the same period, the nation at last acquired relative territorial specificity. The political unification of England and the political unification of France followed separate courses leading to different destinations in the modern forms of the two states. But, in the period

[30] Gierke, *Political Theories of the Middle Age*, trans. Maitland (1900), III; Wilks, *Problem of Sovereignty in the Later Middle Ages* (1963), Pt. I; Ullmann, *Short History of the Papacy in the Middle Ages* (1972), Chap. 10.

[31] *Statutes of the Realm*, IV, 350; Stephenson & Marcham, *Sources of English Constitutional History* (1937), p. 344.

from 1066 to the middle of the sixteenth century, the two emerging nations were entangled in complex ties of dynasty and jurisdiction based on conquest, inheritance, marriage, feudal landholding, treaty and gift. The confusion was such that there is difficulty in saying whether the Kings of England had been Kings of France or the Kings of France had been Kings of England.[32] The prolonged interaction of England with France had an important effect on English political development, especially on the position of the King in relation to his principal subjects. In the long run, as would Tudor resistance to the Papacy, it assisted in establishing the internal structure of power and, by way of cultural contrast, the external identity of the nation.

Within the English system, the jurisdictional relationships between the king and the magnates and the other levels of a quasi-feudal structure had been too fluid and too intricate, in the period before, say, 1550, to allow of simple ideas about the distribution of power. However ingeniously we use the remaining documentary evidence, we shall never be able to reconstruct a finally convincing picture of the political structure, to put alongside the schemes which the simplifying modern mind has imposed on political development since 1600. And yet the constitutional historian has had to struggle with the period before 1600 for reasons which go beyond its intrinsic intellectual interest. The participants in the constitutional events of the seventeenth century extrapolated from the events of the medieval period as they saw them, partly in obedience to polemical conventions, partly because of the antiquarianism which dominated the law and the minds of lawyers, but primarily because they believed in institutional continuity. There is a mystical capability of the English mind which co-exists with its notorious pragmatism. It is a capability which has been exercised primarily, but not exclusively, in relation to institutions of all kinds and which is applied, to this day, in relation to the Constitution. The Constitution, because it does not exist in material form, has been given a hypostatic existence and, because of its very immateriality, it must be protected with especial care. That Constitution, we have believed and still believe, is organically linked with all that has gone before, down to its Anglo-Saxon roots.

In the late Tudor period, therefore, the necessary conditions were emerging for a new kind of distribution of political authority; but the forms and substance of political authority already had a long and complex lineage which would radically affect their subsequent development. Their past was big with their future.

[32] William & Mary were invited to the thrones of England, France and Ireland.

In the turbulent political history of medieval England, such events as the baronial resistance to John in the years up to 1215 and the coups of 1399 and 1485 were not structural discontinuities in the manner of modern revolutions. Unconstitutional events they may have been, in some narrow sense of the term, but, like so many of the other leading events of our constitutional history, they are better described as reconstitutional. The participants, seeking to further their own interest within new circumstances, believed that they were re-adjusting the balance of an established system. Such events seem to be the working-out of a limited number of perennial problems about the distribution of political authority, problems which each king and each political generation has had to resolve in its own way, offensively or defensively, or by *laisser-aller*. The statement of the "crimes and defaults" of Richard II, the justification of his deposition, may be used to illustrate the point:

> *Item*, in the parliament recently held at Shrewsbury, the same king, proposing to oppress his people, subtly procured and caused it to be granted that, by the counsel of all the estates of his realm, the power of parliament to decide certain petitions ... should devolve upon certain persons. By colour of which concession the persons thus deputed proceeded with other matters of common concern to that parliament—and this at the will of the king and in derogation of the estate of parliament, to the great damage of the entire kingdom, and [thereby setting] a pernicious example ...
>
> *Item*, when the king of England was able, without oppressing his people, to live honourably from the issues of his kingdom, and from the patrimony belonging to his crown, since the kingdom was not burdened with the expense of wars, the same king ... not only gave the greater part of the said patrimony to unworthy persons, but also, on that account, threw such burdens of taxation on his subjects in nearly every year of his reign that he widely and outrageously oppressed his people, to the impoverishment of his kingdom ...
>
> *Item*, the same king refusing to keep and defend the just laws and customs of his kingdom, but [wishing] at his own arbitrary will to do whatever appealed to his desires, sometimes—and very often when the laws of the kingdom had been declared and explained to him by his justices and others of his council, and when, according to those laws, he was to administer justice to those seeking it—expressly said, with an austere and determined countenance, that his laws were in his own mouth or occasionally, in his own breast; and that he alone could establish and change the laws of the realm. And he, seduced by that opinion, would not permit justice to be done to many of his lieges, but by threats and intimidation compelled many to abstain from the pursuit of common justice ...
>
> And since it seemed to all these estates ... that these statements of his crimes and defaults were notoriously sufficient for

> deposing the same king, . . . all the estates aforesaid unanimously agreed that the deposition of the said king was abundantly justified . . .[33]

Very much of subsequent constitutional history is prefigured in those allegations, and not only British constitutional history. Not only Richard II but also Charles I, James II, George III, Louis XVI and, we might add, President Nixon would have recognised the polemical tone. It is a tone which, in our own day and substituting " the Executive " for " the king," can be heard in the extra-judicial polemics of the successors of Coke (Hewart, Denning, Scarman and Hailsham).[34]

The perennial distribution-of-power issues reflected in such allegations are: who or what makes the King? who judges the King? what is the King's power in Parliament? what is the King's prerogative? to whom are the King's servants answerable? We owe it to the exceptionally vigorous personalities of the Tudor monarchs that the day-to-day business of answering those questions took on a new, aggressively realistic character, more or less free from the mysteries of decayed feudalism, allegiance, jurisdiction, tenure, and service. Instead, the old problems presented themselves in a more schematic form. The King, echoing a distant Trinitarian analogy, was three powerful persons in one—in his person, in Parliament, and in his courts. By enhancing all three, he ensured a balance of sorts in the constitution, but securing for himself a potential position of unique power, since he alone was really present in all three of his manifestations.

Like the Hanoverian monarchy and, therefore, our present monarchy, the Tudor monarchy owed a formal debt to the King in Parliament:

> Henry, by the grace of God, king of England and of France and lord of Ireland, at the parliament holden at Westminster . . .: be it ordained, established, and enacted by authority of this present parliament that the inheritance of the crown of the realms of England and of France, with all the pre-eminences and dignity royal to the same pertaining, and all other seignories to the king belonging beyond the sea . . . be, rest, remain and abide in the most royal person of our now sovereign lord, King Henry VII, and in the heirs of his body lawfully coming, perpetually with the grace of God so to endure, and in none other.[35]

[33] *Parliament Roll* of 1399; Stephenson & Marcham, p. 252.

[34] Hewart, *The New Despotism* (1929); Denning, *Freedom under the Law* (1949), Scarman, *English Law—the New Dimension* (1974), Hailsham, *Elective Dictatorship* (1976).

[35] *Act of Succession*, 1485; *Statutes of the Realm*, II, 499; Stephenson & Marcham, p. 298.

But, having recognised the King as King, Parliament in turn had to recognise that he possessed inherent special powers and privileges allowed by law:

> For besides that that he [a prince or sovereign governor of a realm] is the most excellentest and worthiest part or member of the common body of the wealth, so is he also (through his good governance) the preserver, nourisher and defender of all the people . . . For which cause the laws do attribute unto him all honour, dignity, prerogative and preeminence, which prerogative doth not only extend to his own person but also to all his other possessions, goods and chattels . . . [Describes the statute *Prerogativa Regis* as merely declaratory] Howbeit, this Parliament maketh no part of the king's prerogative but long time before it had his being by order of the common law . . .[36]
>
> [Lists examples of the king's prerogatives] Diverse other rights and preeminences the prince hath which be called prerogatives royal . . . which be declared particularly in the books of the common laws of England.[37]

So the King's status had the special prestige flowing from its multiple origins—the grace of God, Parliament, the common law. Parliament itself also gained prestige from its ambiguous status, as council and court. As one among the King's councils, it had the special pre-eminence of being in some sense representative of the kingdom.[38] As court, it had the pre-eminence of being the highest court.[39] Notwithstanding McIlwain's impressive presentation of the case for regarding Parliament as having been, in an important and even primary sense, a court, it is difficult to avoid the conclusion that, at least after the end of the medieval period, it is an idea which has been over-exploited as a source of mythical prestige. It is, perhaps, possible to detect a tone of disbelief, or at least an awareness of the risks he was running in saying such a thing, in Henry VIII's intervention in *Ferrers' Case* (1543):

> . . . And further we be informed by our judges that we at no time stand so highly in our estate royal as in the time of Parliament, wherein we as head and you as members are con-

[36] Stanford, *An Exposition of the King's Prerogative* (1569), quoted in Elton, *The Tudor Constitution* (1960), p. 18. *Cf.* Coke, I *Institutes* 2, v; Selden, *Table Talk*, s.v. *Prerogative* (prerogative is "the King's Law"); Wormuth, *op. cit.* (note 11).

[37] Smith, *De Republica Anglorum* (1565), quoted in Elton, *op. cit.*, p. 19.

[38] "Parliament represents the whole body of the kingdom": Y.B. 39 Ed. III Pasch. 7, *per* Thorpe C.J.; "The great corporation or body politick of the kingdom" (Coke, IV *Institutes* 2); Chrimes, *op. cit.* (note 12), pp. 76–80; Gierke, *op. cit.* (note 30), pp. 61–67; Smith, *De Republica Anglorum*, ed. Alston (1906), p. 49. Such an idea is a denial of another medieval monarchical conception, perpetuated by Louis XIV, that the sovereign in person embodies the realm: *cf.* Wilks, *op. cit.* (note 30), p. 41.

[39] Coke, IV *Institutes*, Preface; McIlwain, *op. cit.*, Chap. III; Holdsworth, *H.E.L.*, IV, 182 *et seq.*; Pollard, *op. cit.* (note 13), Chap. II.

joined and knit together into one body politic, so as whatsoever offence or injury (during that time) is offered to the meanest member of the House is to be judged as done against our person and the whole Court of Parliament. Which prerogative of the court is so great (as our learned counsel informeth us) as all acts and processes coming out of any other inferior courts for the time being cease and give place to the highest.[40]

The status of Parliament as a court is a complicating factor in determining the status of the ordinary courts in the period to 1600. Their status was once again enhanced by an ambiguous duality—as instruments of one aspect of the royal prerogative and as agents of the law which was above kings. A structure which included the courts of common law and equity, the Star Chamber, Justices of the Peace and the High Court of Parliament must have seemed a formidable structure, whatever its links of dependence on Parliament and the King. But, if it was true that the summit of the court system was to be found in the King in Parliament—deciding cases, advising the king, making new law, creating new courts—then it would be correspondingly difficult to perceive and promote the courts as an actual third force in the constitutional structure. The only possibility open to the courts for enhancing their independent status lay in the prestige of the common law. But it would have to be in a new age, under a new dynasty, with judges of the standing of Coke and his successors, that such a possibility could be explored. Under the Tudors, the prerogative and statute were in the ascendant.

The remaining perennial distribution-of-power issue, concerning the King's council and advisers, was submerged by the personal dominance of the later Tudor monarchs. But criticism of the king's ministers and the call for them to be appointed or approved by Parliament had been often heard in medieval parliaments.

> And whereas the king, as aforesaid, has been badly advised and guided by evil councillors, we ordain that all the evil councillors shall be put out and utterly removed, so that neither they nor other such persons shall be near him or shall be retained in any office under the king; and that other persons who are fit shall be put in their places. And the same shall be done in the case of domestics, officials, and other men in the king's household who are not fit.[41]
>
> Item, on the same Saturday the said commons prayed our said lord the king that, in the ordinance to be drawn up for the household of our same lord the king, nomination and appointment should be made of honest, virtuous, and reputable persons, concerning whom notice might be given to the said lords and commons in this parliament . . .[42]

[40] Holinshed, II, 824–826; Elton, *op. cit.*, p. 267.
[41] *Ordinance* of 1311; Stephenson & Marcham, p. 195.
[42] *Record of Parliament* (1404); *ibid.*, p. 259.

"The King can do no wrong," that medieval prototype of ministerial responsibility, concentrated attention on the deeds of the King's servants. But, under the later Tudors, the matter presented itself in a different way, with important implications for the future balance of the constitution. The commons asserted the idea that they were entitled to discuss the King's business. It was not merely a question of controlling his advisers, or forcing their grievances on his attention or of manipulating their power to consent to taxation. They began to assert as a fundamental privilege their freedom to discuss all matters, including the exercise of the king's prerogative powers outside parliament. Peter Wentworth, representative of the radical point of view in the matter and arguing that Parliament's privileges are conferred by the law and not by the Queen, asked—

> Whether this council be not a place for any member of the same here assembled, freely and without controlment of any person or danger of laws, by bill or speech to utter any of the griefs of this commonwealth whatever touching the service of God, the safety of the prince, and this noble realm.[43]

The customary royal reply was unlikely to resist the assault for very much longer:

> Next, if any speech undecent or matter unfit for that place be used, remember them of this lesson: your petitions . . . must be ruled, and that thus her majesty granteth you liberal not licentious speech; liberty therefore, but with due limitation. For even as there can be no good consultation where all freedom of advice is barred, so will there be no good conclusion where every man speaketh as he listeth, without fit observation of persons, matter, times, places and other needful circumstances. It shall be meet, therefore, that each man of you contain his speech within the bounds of loyalty and good discretion, being assured that, as the contrary is punishable in all men, so most of all in them that take upon them to be counsellors and procurators of the commonwealth.[44]

The Tudors thus left the instruments of governments full of power and potentiality—the King with his general responsibilities and his powerful prerogatives; Parliament as court, law-maker, source of revenue and council of "counsellors and procurators of the commonwealth"; the courts as agents of the law and arbiters of disputed powers. Subsequent constitutional history is the story of how the King, who had been personally and intrinsically present in all three instruments of government, was excluded from all three, and of how they came to establish their respective autono-

[43] (1587) *ibid.*, p. 372.

[44] (1593) *ibid.*, p. 372.

mous identities. The royal agents became royal principals, each using the royal coat of arms at the head of its formal acts, each using the monarch as its hereditary president-of-honour. It is also the story of the working-out of the horizontal relationship between them, including the question of which, if any, was to be master—the courts, because they have the last word concerning the law; or Parliament, because it makes the law and votes the money; or the executive, because it causes the law to be made and calls forth the revenue. Or was it to be, in the manner of the American Constitution, that there would be no master?

Bonham's Case thus takes its place as one of a series of notorious decided cases in which the potentialities of the post-Tudor constitutional situation were explored by the judges. It has been customary to regard the leading cases decided under James I and Charles I as incoherent or as reflecting varying responses to the conflict between King and Parliament. But it is also possible to see them as a concerted exploration of the puzzling relationship between the law, the prerogative and the power of Parliament.

> The king in his own person cannot adjudge any case, either criminal . . . or betwixt party and party . . . ; but this ought to be determined and adjudged in some Court of Justice according to the law and custom of England . . . [It] was answered by me . . . that the law was the golden metwand and measure to try the causes of the subjects; and which protected his majesty in safety and peace: with which the King was greatly offended, and said, that then he should be under the law, which was treason to affirm, as he said, to which I said that Bracton saith, *quod Rex non debet esse sub homine, sed sub Deo et lege*. (*The Case of Prohibitions 1607*).[45]
>
> . . . the King by his proclamation cannot create any offence which was not an offence before, for then he may alter the law of the land by his proclamation in a high point; . . . also the law of England is divided into three parts: common law, statute law, and custom; but the King's proclamation is none of them: . . . Also it was resolved, that the King hath no prerogative, but that which the law of the land allows him (*The Case of Proclamations 1610*)[46]
>
> Though the King of England hath a monarchical power and hath *jura summae majestatis* and hath an absolute trust settled in his crown and person for the government of his subjects, yet his government is to be *secundum leges regni* . . . By those laws the subjects are not tenants at the king's will, of what they have . . . They have a birthright in the laws of the kingdom. No new laws can be put upon them; none of their laws can be altered or abrogated without common consent in parliament . . . Mr. Holbourne [counsel for Hampden] sup-

[45] 12 Co.Rep. 64; 77 E.R. 1342.

[46] 12 Co.Rep. 74; 77 E.R. 1352.

> posed a fundamental policy in the creation of the frame of this kingdom, that in case the monarch of England should be inclined to exact from his subjects at his pleasure, he should be restrained, for that he could have nothing from them but upon a common consent in parliament. He is utterly mistaken herein. I agree the parliament to be a most ancient and supreme court, where the king and peers, as judges, are in person, and the whole body of the commons, representatively . . . But the former fancied policy I utterly deny. The law knows no such king-yoking policy. The law is itself an old and trusty servant of the king's; it is his instrument or means which he useth to govern his people by . . . There are two maxims of the law of England which plainly disprove Mr. Holbourne's supposed policy. The first is "That the king is a person trusted with the state of the commonwealth." The second of these maxims is that the king cannot do wrong. Upon these two maxims the *jura summae majestatis* are grounded, with which none but the king himself (not his high court of parliament without leave) hath to meddle . . . I confess, that by the fundamental law of England the Parliament is *commune concilium regis et regni*, that is the greatest the most honourable and supreme court in the kingdom; that no man ought to think any dishonourable thing of it: yet give me leave to say that it is but a *Concilium* . . . the King may call it, prorogue it, dissolve it, at his pleasure; and whatsoever the King doth herein is always to be taken for just and necessary (*Hampden's Case* 1637; *per* Berkeley J.).[47]
>
> The two houses of Parliament without the King cannot make a law, nor without his royal assent declare it; he is not bound to call it but when he pleaseth, nor to continue it but at his pleasure. Certainly there was a King before a parliament, for how else could there be an assembly of King, Lords and commons? And then what sovereignty was there in the kingdom but this? His power then was limited by the positive law . . . Acts of Parliament may take away flowers and ornaments of the crown, but not the crown itself; they cannot bar a succession . . . No Act of Parliament can bar a king of his regality . . . or bar him of the allegiance of his subjects . . . Therefore Acts of Parliament to take away his royal power in the defence of his kingdom are void . . . They are void Acts of Parliament to bind the King not to command the subjects' persons and goods . . . (the same: *per* Finch CJCP).[48]

It is meaningless to say that such cases were rightly or wrongly decided. They were the judicial contribution to a fundamental political process which was also taking place in parliament. The dialogue between the Commons and the two Kings, James and Charles, was a negotiation concerning the proper limits of the King's powers, within a constitutional structure which must also take account of the authority of "the law" and the power of the King in Parlia-

[47] Howell, *State Trials*, III, 1090, 1098, 1101.

[48] *Ibid.*, 1226, 1235.

ment. Not only in the cases but also in the petitions of the Commons and the replies of the Kings,[49] in the impeachment of Strafford and in the trial of Charles, there is a prolonged debate of exceptional intellectual distinction and within a framework of much that was agreed and taken for granted—

> . . . I have ever admired the wisdom of our ancestors who have so fixed the pillars of this monarchy that each of them keeps due measure and proportion with other, and have so handsomely tied up the nerves and sinews of the State that the straining of one may bring damage and sorrow to the whole economy. The prerogative of the Crown and the propriety of the subject have such mutual relations that this took protection from that, that foundation and nourishment from this; and as on the lute, if anything be too high or too low wound up you have lost the harmony, so here the excess of a prerogative is oppression, of a pretended liberty in the subject disorder and anarchy (Strafford).[50]
>
> It is the law that doth entitle a king to the allegiance and service of his people; it entitles the people to the protection and justice of the King. . . . The law is the boundary, the measure between the King's prerogative and the people's liberty. Whilst these move in their own orbs they are a support and a security to one another; the prerogative a cover and defence to the liberty of the people, and the people by their liberty are entitled to be a foundation to the prerogative; but if these bounds be so removed that they enter into contestation and conflict . . . mischiefs must ensue (Pym).[51]
>
> Charles Stuart . . . hath had a wicked design totally to subvert the ancient and fundamental laws and liberties of this nation and in their place to introduce an arbitrary and tyrannical government (Act of the Commons erecting a court to try King Charles, 1649).[52]
>
> And what hope of settlement is there so long as power reigns without rule of law, changing the whole frame of that government under which the kingdom hath flourished for many hundred years? (Charles I).[53]

With the abolition of the monarchy there was an opportunity to construct a constitution *de novo* and the opportunity was used to remarkable, if short-lived, effect. In the *First Agreement of the People* of 1647, it had been provided that "the power of this and

[49] *E.g.*, the King's message and the Apology of the Commons (1604), the Commons' Petition of Grievances to the King (1610), the Commons' Protestation (1621) and the Kings' letters to the Commons (1621 and 1626), the Petition of Right (1628) and the proceedings in the Commons on the Petition in the presence of the King.

[50] Kenyon, *The Stuart Constitution* (1969), p. 211.

[51] *Ibid.*, p. 214.

[52] Firth & Rait, *Acts & Ordinances*, I, 1253; Stephenson & Marcham, p. 516.

[53] (1649) Rushworth, *Historical Collections*, VII, 1403; Stephenson & Marcham, p. 517.

all future representatives of this nation is inferior only to theirs who choose them and doth extend . . . generally to whatsoever is not expressly or implicitly reserved by the representatives to themselves." [54] There were then listed five matters which were reserved as "our native rights." The *Act establishing the Commonwealth* of 1649 referred to the representatives of the people as "the supreme authority of this nation." [55] The *Instrument of Government* of 1653, the modern world's first written constitution, provided that "the supreme legislative authority" would reside in the Lord Protector and the people assembled in Parliament. Article 24 set a limit on the legislative power—Bills would become law "provided such bills contain nothing in them contrary to the matters contained in these presents." [56] The monarchy was very soon restored and the Interregnum became an historical curiosity. But it has a particular interest for our present purposes, as showing what was made of the status of Parliament when it became temporarily possible to fix that status explicitly and at its highest.

There remains to consider, as a matter of constitutional history, the significance of the Revolution of 1688–89 which, it has been repeatedly claimed and assumed, finally established the sovereignty of Parliament.

The parliamentary debates surrounding the Revolution were of an obsessive legalism. Although it was not in the end possible to square the circle of constitutionality, much effort was spent to stay as close as possible to constitutionality.[57] There was much debate on the appropriate verb to describe what had terminated James II's reign. Had he deserted or abdicated? At least it was clear that he could not be said to have been deposed, although there was much talk of the medieval precedents. In due course, the Commons house of the Convention resolved that James,

> having endeavoured to subvert the Constitution of the Kingdom, by breaking the Original Contract between King and People, and, by the Advice of Jesuits and other wicked Persons having violated the fundamental laws; and having withdrawn himself out of this Kingdom; has abdicated the Government, and that the Throne is thereby vacant.[58]

It was the drafting style of a committee, containing something for everyone. After much anxious debate in the Lords house and a

[54] Gardiner, *History of the Great Civil War*, ed. 1893, III, 392; Kenyon, *op. cit.*, p. 308.
[55] Firth & Rait, *Acts & Ordinances*, II, 122; Stephenson & Marcham, p. 523.
[56] *Ibid.*, pp. 813, 525.
[57] Macaulay, *History of England from the Accession of James* II, ed. Firth (1914), III, 1296 *et seq.*; Nenner, *By Color of Law: Legal Culture & Constitutional Politics in England 1660–1689* (1977), 173 *et seq.*
[58] *Commons Journal*. 28 January 1689, 14.

joint meeting of the two houses, the Lords in the end accepted the ideas of abdication and vacancy. Abdication was a tendentious description of James's departure from England. Vacancy was particularly difficult to accept, given the structure of an hereditary monarchy in which the King does not die. The two houses agreed that the throne should be offered to William and Mary on terms. It was decided to have a relatively simple instrument inviting them to take the throne, fixing the subsequent succession and then setting forth "in the most distinct and solemn manner, the fundamental principles of the constitution." [59] The Declaration of Rights was drafted and adopted by the Commons within a matter of hours, and approved by the Lords without significant amendment. The Prince and Princess accepted the throne in the light of, if not on the basis of, the Declaration, the substance of which was incorporated in the Bill of Rights formally adopted on 16 December 1689.

The provision in the Bill of Rights giving legal effect to the Declaration is as follows:

> . . . all and singular the rights and liberties asserted and claimed in the said declaration, are the true, ancient, and indubitable rights and liberties of the people of this kingdom, and so shall be esteemed, allowed, adjudged, deemed, and so taken to be . . . ; and all officers and ministers whatsoever shall serve their Majesties and their successors according to the same in all times to come.[60]

In the first place, it should be noted that, James II having dissolved Parliament in July 1688, the Convention which drafted the Declaration and offered the crown to William and Mary and the Convention Parliament which had declared itself to be a Parliament and had adopted the Bill of Rights were not Parliaments regularly constituted. It is for this reason, in particular, that they felt inhibited from going further to conclude a new constitutional contract with the new monarchs. Secondly, the thirteen articles of the Declaration set out in the Bill of Rights deal with the suspending power, the dispensing power, the creation of (prerogative) courts of commissioners, levying money without grant of Parliament, right of petition to the King, keeping a standing army without consent of Parliament, arming of protestants for their defence, free election of members of Parliament, freedom of speech in Parliament, excessive bail, the appointment of jurors, grants of fines and forfeitures, Parliaments to be held frequently. In other words, the Declaration was concerned to remove abuses of prerogative powers and not to define

[59] Macaulay, *op. cit.*, III, 1300.
[60] *Statutes of the Realm*, VI, 142; Williams, *The Eighteenth Century Constitution* (1970), 26.

the status of Parliament.[61] Needless to say, there is no mention of the supremacy or sovereignty of Parliament.

Thirdly, the operative clause of the Bill of Rights (above) binds the servants of the King, not the King himself.[62] The Declaration was the basis on which the throne was offered, but it remains to be seen, as a matter of constitutional theory, in what sense such a transaction can be said to bind the King. Finally, and above all, account must be taken of the attitude of those who made the Revolution and the constitutional significance which they themselves attached to it. That significance became a matter of political debate in the decades following the Revolution. Edmund Burke said:

> It rarely happens to a party to have the opportunity of a clear, authentic, recorded declaration of their political tenets upon the subject of a great constitutional event like that of the Revolution. The Whigs had that opportunity, or, to speak properly, they made it.[63]

The opportunity in question was the impeachment of Dr. Sacheverell for preaching against the revolution. At his trial, it was Lechmere who, in the words of Kenyon,[64] offered the most lucid summary of the Whig theory of the Revolution:

> The nature of our constitution is that of a limited monarchy, wherein the supreme power was—by mutual consent and not by accident—limited and lodged in more hands than one; and the uniform preservation of such a constitution for so many ages, without any fundamental change, demonstrates to your lordships the continuance of the same contract. The consequences of such a form of government are obvious: that the laws are the rule to both, the common measure of the power of the crown and of the obedience of the subject; and if the executive part endeavours the subversion and total destruction of the government the Original Contract is thereby broke . . . and that part of the government thus fundamentally injured hath a right to save or recover that constitution in which it had an original interest.[65]

[61] *Cf.* Hill, *The Century of Revolution 1603–1714*, Sphere ed. (1969), p. 238; Carter, "The Revolution & the Constitution," in Holmes, ed., *Britain after the Glorious Revolution* (1969), p. 42; Kemp, *King & Commons 1660–1832* (1957), p. 8; Holdsworth, *H.E.L.*, VI, 241.

[62] The Coronation Oath was altered to require government according to "the statutes in parliament agreed on." On the significance of the change, see Maitland, *Constitutional History of England* (1908, ed. Fisher 1968), p. 286. On the question of whether William assented to the Declaration, see the sources cited by Nenner, *op. cit.*, p. 199n.

[63] *Appeal from the Old to the New Whigs* (1791), *Works* (Bohn), III, 43.

[64] Kenyon, *Revolution Principles—the Politics of Party 1689–1720* (1977), p. 134.

[65] *The Tryal of Dr. Henry Sacheverell* (1710), p. 22; Burke, *Works* (Bohn), III, 46; Kenyon, *op. cit.*, p. 134. The Articles of Impeachment are set out as App. A. in Holmes, *The Trial of Dr. Sacheverell* (1973).

Burke himself, who was discriminating in his attitude to revolutions, said:

> What we did [in the Revolution] was in truth and substance, and in a constitutional light, a revolution not made but prevented. We took solid securities; we settled doubtful questions; we corrected anomalies in our law. In the stable, fundamental parts of our constitution we made no revolution, no, nor any alteration at all.[66]

And there is the evidence of Macaulay, the most notorious of Whig historians, who devoted some of his most fervent pages to explaining the significance of the Revolution and who believed that all the merits of nineteenth-century society stemmed directly from it:

> It was a revolution strictly defensive, and had prescription and legitimacy on its side. Here, and here only, a limited monarchy of the thirteenth century had come down unimpaired to the seventeenth century. Our parliamentary institutions were in full vigour. The main principles of our government were excellent. They were not, indeed, formally and exactly set forth in a single written instrument: but they were to be found scattered over our ancient and noble statutes; and, what was of far greater moment, they had been engraven on the hearts of Englishmen during four hundred years. . . . A realm of which these were the fundamental laws stood in no need of a new constitution. . . .
>
> Thus the Convention had two great duties to perform. The first was to clear the fundamental laws of the realm from ambiguity. The second was to eradicate from the minds, both of the governors and of the governed, the false and pernicious notion that the royal prerogative was something more sublime and holy than those fundamental laws. The former object was attained by the solemn recital and claim with which the Declaration of Right commences; the latter by the resolution which pronounced the throne vacant, and invited William and Mary to fill it.
>
> The change seems small. Not a single flower of the crown was touched. Not a single new right was given to the people. The whole English law, substantive and adjective, was in the judgment of all the greatest lawyers, of Holt and Treby, of Maynard and Somers, almost exactly the same after the Revolution as before it. Some controverted points had been decided according to the sense of the best jurists; and there had been a slight deviation from the ordinary course of succession. This was all; and this was enough.
>
> And yet this revolution, of all revolutions the least violent, has been of all revolutions the most beneficent. It finally decided the great question of whether the popular element

[66] *Speech on the Army Estimates* (1790): Works (Bohn), III, 279.

> which had, ever since the age of Fitzwalter and De Montfort, been found in the English polity, should be destroyed by the monarchical element, or should be suffered to develope itself freely, and to become dominant. The strife between the two principles . . . had lasted four reigns. . . . The King of Arms, who proclaimed William and Mary before Whitehall Gate, did in truth announce that this great struggle was over; that there was entire union between the throne and the Parliament; . . . that the ancient laws by which the prerogative was bounded would thenceforth be held as sacred as the prerogative itself, and would be followed out to all their consequences.[67]

There are still matters of controversy concerning the Revolution of 1688,[68] but there is broad support for the view that it was a conservative revolution, "a revolution in defence of law, not a revolution against law,"[69] that it marked "one more failure of the Crown to secure control over the legislature."[70] In other words, put at its highest, the Revolution decisively limited the prerogative power of the King. From that it in no way follows that it established the absolute pre-eminence of Parliament. It created the possibility of a rapid development of Parliament's status, a possibility which was not realised in the eighteenth century, or even in the nineteenth. On the contrary:

> The Revolution, however, strengthened the two processes, the development of oligarchy and the growth of the executive, which were in time not only to reduce the power of the independent Member, but also to secure single-party government, and this was to achieve that subjugation of the legislature that the Stuarts had frequently attempted but never achieved.[71]

How was it then that this modest, defensive revolution should have acquired the status of a legend,[72] as the moment when one of

[67] *Op. cit.* (note 57), III, 1306, 1309, 1310.

[68] Was the Revolution really necessary to prevent royal backsliding? Was it a victory for law or legal illusions? Was it a change of things or of men? Was it the victory of ideas or of a class? See Feiling, *A History of the Tory Party 1640–1714* (1924); Gooch, *English Democratic Ideas in the Seventeenth Century* (1929); Trevelyan, *The English Revolution 1688–89* (1938); Pinckham, *William III and the Respectable Revolution* (1954); Ogg, *England in the Reigns of James II and William III* (1955); Straka (ed.), *The Revolution of 1688, Whig Triumph or Palace Revolution?* (1963); Plumb, *The Growth of Political Stability in England 1675–1725* (1967); Jones, *The Revolution of 1688 in England* (1972); Nenner, *op. cit.* (note 57).

[69] Pinckham, *op. cit.*, p. 191. *Cf.* Trevelyan, *op. cit.*, p. 71: "It was the triumph of common law and lawyers over the King, who had tried to put Prerogative above the law" (a view described by Nenner, at p. 62, as "Whiggish and wrong").

[70] Plumb, *op. cit.*, p. 63. *Cf* Horwitz, *Parliament, Policy & Politics in the Reign of William III* (1977), pp. 85 *et seq.*

[71] Plumb, *op. cit.*, p. 65.

[72] Hill, *op. cit.*, p. 240. *Cf.* Burnet preaching before William of Orange in December 1688: "We have before us a work that seems to our selves a Dream, and that will appear to posterity a Fiction": quoted by Nenner, *op. cit.*, p. xix, who speaks of "the myth of 1688."

the organs of the constitution acquired absolute superiority over the other two, or finally established a superiority which had, however, not been recognised before—a superiority which apparently gave it a constitutional status *hors catégorie*, essentially different from that of the other two organs, and, what is more, a status which is said to give formal validity to the whole constitutional structure, in derogation from the " fundamental laws " of the " ancient constitution "? To answer that question, it is necessary to move, finally, to the level of constitutional theory.

Constitutional Theory

Accompanying the accumulation of positive law and the unfolding of constitutional fact, there has been a complex counterpoint of theory. Constitutional theory has had a special character in England compared with other constitutional systems. It has been fated to be more abstract and yet more pragmatic. Given the absence of a basic constitutional document to serve as the foundation of deductive theory, constitutional theory in England has been especially broad, diffuse and fundamental—with the most general theories about the origin and nature of political society playing a part in the effort to understand the day-to-day working of the constitution. At the same time, the content of constitutional theory has been notably purposive, radically affected by the facts of constitutional experience. That experience has called forth local and temporary superstructures of ideas built upon current patterns of political power, not only to explain them but also to justify them and to reinforce them. What the present study is intended to suggest is that the idea of the sovereignty of Parliament is one such superstructure and that it is the product of three things—an inadequate view of what had been achieved by our constitution before 1600, a distorted view of the outcome of the constitutional struggle of the seventeenth century in the Revolution of 1688–89 and now, finally, a distorting intrusion into British constitutional theory of a particular tradition of general political thought, namely sovereignty theory.

Sovereignty theory has had an important place in the general history of political thought, playing a major role in the conceptualisation of the Papacy, the Holy Roman Empire, the absolute monarchies of continental Europe, and the modern political revolutions (since 1776). In British constitutional theory, it has played a much more disorganised role—a reservoir of potent ideas to be drawn on, as and when necessary, to fulfil specific functions at different times. In particular, it has made itself useful variously to help to conceptualise the authority of "the law," the King, the people, and Parliament.

When all human existence was perceived as an integral whole within the unity of God's earthly creation under the supremacy of an omnipotent God, it was natural to believe that human authority was derived from divine authority. This descending theory of government, in Ullmann's phrase,[73] in turn meant that there was a hierarchical system of descending authority. Who exercised jurisdiction over whom was a central constitutional question at every level from the Pope and Emperor down to the last serf or lay-brother. And jurisdiction was a substantial relationship, supported by some sort of contractual bond of mutuality, implying control and protection, on the one side, and obedience and service, on the other.[74] Control included confused aspects of law-making and law-enforcement, ordering and deciding. Each intermediate level was itself subject to jurisdiction, and jurisdictions could overlap. Within the integrated structure of Christendom, the relative supremacies of Pope and Emperor were never finally settled, but their authority entitled them to intervene directly in national affairs.

> Then the lord Pope, after consultation with his Cardinals, Bishops and Wise Men, decided that King John should be deposed from his throne because of the desolation of his realm, and that another more worthy should succeed with Papal approval. To execute this sentence the Lord Pope wrote to the most powerful Philip, King of France, encouraging him to this good work for the remission of all his sins and so that, after John's expulsion, he and his heirs should possess the Crown of England for ever.[75]

As the new nations gradually established their jurisdictional independence, they were able to appropriate the intellectual framework built around the *plenitudo potestatis* of the Pope and the supreme authority of the Emperor in their own ideology of "supremacy," using that framework precisely to destroy the supranational power which it had sustained.[76] In another of the Acts of Parliament used to effect the Reformation in England, the Act of 1536 extinguishing the authority of the bishop of Rome, there was

[73] Ullmann, *Medieval Political Thought* (1965), p. 31; *Short History of the Papacy in the Middle Ages* (1972), p. 36; *Growth of Papal Government in the Middle Ages*, 2nd ed. (1962), Chaps. XII and XIII.

[74] Maine, *Ancient Law* (1865), Chap. 5; Pound, *Interpretations of Legal History* (1923), pp. 53 *et seq.*; Gierke, *op. cit.* (note 30), p. 88.

[75] Wendover, *Flores Historiarum (Chronica)*, p. 241; quoted in Jones, *King John & Magna Carta* (1971), p. 124.

[76] Figgis, *From Gerson to Grotius 1414–1625* (1907), pp. 37, 69 *et seq.*; *Divine Right of Kings* (1927), especially pp. 45 *et seq.* and 237 *et seq.*; Ullmann, *op. cit.* (1965), especially Chap. 5, and *op. cit.* (1972), p. 223; Gierke, *op. cit.*, p. 36.

reference to " the pretended power and usurped authority of the bishop of Rome, by some called Pope," who did " rob the King's Majesty, being only the supreme head of this his realm of England immediately under God, of his honour, right and pre-eminence due unto him by the law of God." St. Thomas More died because he could not accept that the supreme government of the Church in England could be taken over by a temporal prince by means of a mere Act of Parliament.[77]

Here then was a moment at which sovereignty theory, which had been explored and refined at the highest intellectual levels in the papal and imperial causes, began to flow into the English system. But, unlike the monarchies of continental Europe, in the English case it was by way of a narrow channel for a specific purpose and it had to meet a strong current of established constitutional ideas. It might be used to establish the external independence of England, but it would not be able to overturn the complex internal balance of forces of the late-Tudor period which we have already surveyed.

Bodin's *Six Books on the Republic* was published in 1576. An English translation by Knolles was published in 1606. We are told that it was at once used as a textbook in Cambridge.[78] The familiar characteristics of later British sovereignty theory (Hobbes, Bentham, Austin, Dicey) are already fully-fledged in Bodin. Sovereignty is treated as a condition for the existence of a state (commonwealth) by being included in its definition.

> A commonwealth may be defined as the rightly ordered government of a number of families, and of those things which are their common concern, by a sovereign power.[79]
>
> Sovereignty is that absolute and perpetual power vested in a commonwealth which in Latin is termed *majestas*. . . . The term needs careful definition, because although it is the distinguishing mark of a commonwealth, and an understanding of its nature fundamental to any treatment of politics, no jurist or political philosopher has so far attempted to define it.

If, in a given case, there is a commonwealth, then there *must* be a sovereign power, but this " must " is a methodological " must," depending on a definitional premise. Austin's notorious " law *properly* so called " is an example of the same procedure. Secondly, sovereignty is treated as a quasi-material substance.[80] But, like the

[77] Roper, *Life of More*, p. 87; Chambers, *Thomas More* (1935), p. 338.

[78] Figgis, *op. cit.* (1907), p. 126.

[79] Trans. Tooley (1960). The following quotations are from Chaps. I and VIII of Book I.

[80] de Jouvenel, *Sovereignty, an Inquiry into the Political Good*, trans. Huntington (1957), p. 183.

virtus dormitiva of medieval medicine and the " energy " of modern physics, it is a substance which is known only by its effects. And, like God, once it has been postulated, sovereignty may be explored deductively, even generating normative inferences. In particular, it is found to be the explanation, otherwise so much a matter of doubt, of the nature of " law." " Law is nothing else than the command of the sovereign in the exercise of his sovereign power." And this, in turn, means that the sovereign must be *absolute*.

> . . . it is the distinguishing mark of the sovereign that he cannot in any way be subject to the commands of another, for it is he who makes law for the subject, abrogates law already made, and amends obsolete law. No one who is subject to the law or to some other person can do this. That is why it is laid down in the civil law that the prince is above the law, for the word *law* in Latin implies the command of him who is invested with sovereign power.

Thirdly, such a structure of ideas gives rise to a problem as to the reason why the sovereign is sovereign—is it a mere matter of power, a matter of fact, or is it under a form of super-law system?

> It is far otherwise with divine and natural laws. All the princes of the earth are subject to them, and cannot contravene them without treason and rebellion against God.
>
> The constitutional laws of the realm, especially those that concern the king's estate, being, like the salic law, annexed or united to the Crown, cannot be infringed by the prince. Should he do so, his successor can always annul any act prejudicial to the traditional form of the monarchy, since on this is founded and sustained his very claim to sovereign majesty.

Fourthly, where there are phenomena which do not fit into the sovereignty framework, then either there cannot be said to be a sovereign State, or they must be reinterpreted.

> [concerning the argument that the authority of the Estates is superior to that of the prince] Such arguments serve only to encourage subjects to resist their sovereign rulers. . . . Although in the Parliaments of the kingdom of England, which meet every three years, all three orders use great freedom of speech, as is characteristic of northern people, they still must proceed by petition and supplication. . . . Moreover Parliaments in England can only assemble, as in the kingdom of Spain, under letters patent expressly summoning them in the King's name. This is sufficient proof that Parliaments have no independent power of counselling, commanding or determining, seeing that they can neither assemble nor adjourn without express royal command.

As Bodin's work was a response to what he saw as the anarchy of the wars of religion in France, so Hobbes, writing between 1640 and 1651, was frightened by the anarchy of the English civil war. What he did was to fuse together sovereignty theory and social contract theory (which also had an ancient and respectable background) to justify submission to established authority.

> A Common-wealth is said to be instituted, when a multitude of men do agree, and covenant, every one with every one, that to whatsoever man, or assembly of men, shall be given by the major part, the right to present the person of them all (that is to say, to be their representative) everyone, as well he that voted for it, as he that voted against it, shall authorise all the actions and judgments of that man, or assembly of men, in the same manner, as if they were his own, to the end, to live peaceably amongst themselves, and be protected against other men.
>
> From this institution of a common-wealth are derived all the rights and faculties of him, or them, on whom the sovereign power is conferred by the consent of the people assembled.[81]

Hobbes went on to draw a series of remarkably totalitarian inferences from these premises. But very much of modern democratic political theory has been developed from his ideas—the personalisation of the State, the general will, government by consent, representative democracy, the autonomy of law in relation to morality and social values. It was a specific part of his purpose to deny the possibility of an appeal from within the system to some standard or continuing source of validity outside the system. The subject, having exhausted his power in willing the sovereign, must obey the laws.

> To the care of the sovereign belongeth the making of good laws. But what is a good law? By a good law, I mean not a just law: for no law can be unjust. The law is made by the sovereign power, and all that is done by such power, is warranted, and owned by every one of the people; and that which every man will have so, no man can say is unjust. It is in the laws of a common-wealth, as in the laws of gaming: whatsoever the gamesters all agree on, is injustice to none of them.[82] A good law is that, which is needful, for the good of the people, and withal perspicuous.[83]

In particular, there can be no appeal against positive law to the so-called law of nature, which is law only so far as it has been incorporated in positive law.

> These dictates of reason, men use to call by the name of laws, but improperly: for they are but conclusions or theorems concerning what conduceth to the conservation and defence of themselves; whereas law properly is the word of him that by right hath command over others.[84]

[81] *Leviathan*, ed. Oakeshott (1955), Chap. XVIII, p. 113.
[82] *Cf.* Hart, *Concept of Law* (1961), p. 55.
[83] Hobbes, *op. cit.*, Chap. XXX, p. 227.
[84] *Ibid.*, Chap. XV, p. 104.

Biology and utility dictated the content of laws, but were not a test of formal validity, or its source. Bentham and Austin would have to add very little to this structure of ideas to complete modern sovereignty theory, once Hobbes' capital error is corrected and his "peculiar fiction" of the "imaginary covenant"[85] is removed.

If Bentham and Austin were to remove the contract theory from Hobbes, Locke removed the sovereignty theory. The fact that Locke's *Two Treatises of Government* were published in 1690 and his reputation as the apologist of the Revolution of 1688–89 have meant that his ideas, which are not easy to understand, have become confused with the principles of the Revolution, which, it has been suggested above, are often misunderstood. But it seems certain that his main ideas were formulated before the Revolution[86] and, on the other hand, the principles of the Revolution were of a different, more modest order than Locke's ideas. Locke's repeated insistence on the legislative as "the supreme power" seems so obviously to be a theoretical explanation of the parliamentary exclusion of a King and the parliamentary creation of another. And Locke's half-hearted references to the prerogative power and his notable failure to make a ritual genuflection before "the law" (as distinct from legislation) seem to suggest that his whole purpose was to vindicate the final triumph of the legislative branch of government.

But such conclusions are a wholesale distortion of Locke's main thesis—and it is that thesis which has been extracted by political experience and which has had a profound influence on the development of modern liberal democracy. What Locke did was to offer a non-theological, non-biological, non-utilitarian basis for believing that society has fundamental principles necessarily built into its very structure. They are principles which guide and constrain governors and governed, and which have been incorporated in modern written constitutions, as the source of their "higher law" validity and as express terms attaching to the distribution of political power.

Locke's contract theory, unlike Hobbes's, is a theory of continuing government by consent. It is in this sense that he is the apologist of the Revolution of 1688–89. Established authority does not have the right to govern when it forfeits the consent of the governed. Locke may be read as saying that all government tends to the

85 Austin, *Province of Jurisprudence Determined* (1832, ed. Hart 1955), pp. 276n.–288n.

86 Locke, *Two Treatises of Government*, ed. Laslett (1960), editor's Introduction, III; Dunn, *Political Thought of John Locke* (1969) p. 77. Figgis, *op. cit.* (1927), p. 242 describes Locke's treatises as an attack on the idea of sovereignty: "it is expressly directed against the notion that there is any sovereign power in the State, whilst realising that the legislature is supreme."

condition of legislation, because legislation is the continuing expression of the consent of the governed, through the medium of their representatives. But by "legislation" we should not understand merely "statute law," but law made by the legislative procedures ordained by the constitution of a given society. Law regularly made, regularly applied (by impartial judges) and regularly executed (by the executive) is the essence of a just society. In other words, Locke's is a theory of the supremacy of law regularly made, not a theory of parliamentary supremacy. This explains how Locke can regard the legislative authority as itself a limited power (limited, among other things, by the natural rights which we do not alienate by participating in society) and not an arbitrary or absolute power. It might also explain his reluctance to venerate the common law which, sometimes if not always, had been in the seventeenth century an accomplice of arbitrary power. It suggests, finally, that, no more than the makers of the Revolution, Locke would not have wanted to be an apologist for the transformation of absolute and arbitrary royal power into absolute and arbitrary parliamentary power.

Paradoxically, however, Locke did contribute to a further theoretical development of "the ancient constitution." He included a distinction of governmental powers in his fundamental structure of political society. This flowed methodologically from his specifying the three things lacking in the state of nature which caused men to participate in political society, deficiencies which are repaired respectively by establishing a legislative, a judicial and an executive power. Although the independence of the judicial power seemed to be regarded by Locke as necessary, the separation of the executive power (and its external, "federative" aspect) seemed to be largely a matter of convenience. But he had sown a seed which, fertilised by Bolingbroke and Montesquieu, would lead to the revival in the eighteenth century of the ancient constitutional idea that the relationship between the various holders of political powers is critical to the satisfactory working of the constitution, a new version of the idea of "the balanced constitution." [87] It was now possible to make explicit the particular kind of balance which, it has been suggested above, had emerged from the Tudor development of the constitution—of King in Parliament, King outside Parliament, and courts—and which had now been the resultant of the political forces acting and reacting in each stage of the seventeenth century constitutional struggle.

[87] Vile, *Constitutionalism & the Separation of Powers* (1967), Chaps. III and V.

> It is highly necessary for preserving the balance of the constitution, that the executive power be a branch, though not the whole of the legislative. The total union of them, we have seen, would be productive of tyranny; the total disjunction of them, for the present, would in the end produce the same effects, by causing that union against which it seems to provide. The legislative would soon become tyrannical, by making continual encroachments, and gradually assuming to itself the rights of the executive power.
>
> . . . To hinder therefore any such encroachments, the king is himself part of the parliament. . . . The legislative therefore cannot abridge the executive power of any rights which it now has by law, without its own consent; since the law must perpetually stand as it now does, unless all the powers will agree to alter it. And herein indeed consists the true excellence of the English government, that all the parts of it form a mutual check upon each other. . . . Like three distinct powers in mechanics, they jointly impel the machine of government in a direction different from what either, acting by itself, would have done; but at the same time in a direction partaking of each, and formed out of all; a direction which constitutes the true line of the liberty and happiness of the community.[88]

Blackstone's third power was the House of Lords. Elsewhere he recognises the necessity for an independent judiciary.

> In this distinct and separate existence of the judicial power in a peculiar body of men, nominated indeed, but not removable at pleasure by the Crown, consists one main preservative of the public liberty which cannot subsist long in any state unless the administration of common justice be in some degree separated both from the legislative and from the executive power.[89]

If the courts are substituted for the House of Lords in Blackstone's mechanical analogy, and if Dicey's analysis of the Rule of Law[90] is added to Blackstone's view on the independence of the judiciary, then, it is submitted, we at last have an appropriate picture of the fundamentals of our constitution.

Before we can allow ourselves to accept such a picture, however, we must face the withering scorn and the zeal of Jeremy Bentham and the cold dogmatism of Austin and Dicey. It was not difficult to demonstrate the contrast between the idea of the "matchless" British constitution and the murky reality of eighteenth-century

[88] *Commentaries*, 15th ed. (1809), I, 153.

[89] *Ibid.*, I, 268.

[90] Dicey, *Introduction to the Study of the Law of the Constitution* (1885, 10th ed. E. C. S. Wade 1959), Part II. *Cf.* Jennings, *The Law & the Constitution*, 5th ed. (1959), App. II. On the problem of reconciling Blackstone's views on parliamentary sovereignty and on division of powers, see Holdsworth, *Some Lessons from our Legal History* (1928), p. 130; Jones (ed.), *The Sovereignty of the Law* (1973), editor's Introduction, p. xliii.

British politics or between the ideals of the French Declaration of Rights—" the *ne plus ultra* of metaphysics "[91]—and the dreadful facts of the Revolution itself. Nor was it difficult to demonstrate the contrast between the idea of the " perfection of reason " [92] of the English common law and the grim realities of English justice, where the judges " kill men for not having guessed their dreams." [93] But Bentham's intellectual life, from the time when he listened to Blackstone as his tutor at Oxford almost to his dying day, was the product of exceptional energy and passion. Once accept the principle of utility as the ultimate principle governing the framing of institutions and the content of adjective and substantive law, once accept a simple definition of political society, requiring only a number of persons who are in a disposition to pay obedience to a person or an assemblage of persons who make laws in the form of commands,[94] then you will naturally have a legislation-centred view of the constitution, but, much more important, you will have the conceptual framework for unlimited reform of society by purposive action. Bentham did not follow through the extreme implications of sovereignty theory [95]; the practical task was more important than the intellectual problem.

In Bentham's favour, therefore, we may say that his importance lies in the stimulus which he gave to nineteenth-century radicalism and to the modern philanthropic theory of political action in a mixed economy, rather than in his contribution to legal theory—that his concern was to bring about what should be, not to understand what has been. The same cannot be said for Austin. Austin has been so often and so substantially criticised,[96] that it is surprising that he should retain any hold over our thinking.

> England was visited in the second and third quarters of the nineteenth century, by a combination of rising intellectual curiosity with a grossly defective training; and this made it possible for authors who knew a little political philosophy to impose the shallowest of dogmas upon lawyers who knew none.[97]

[91] Bowring, *Autobiographical Recollections* (1877), quoted in Halévy, *Growth of Philosophical Radicalism*, trans. Morris (1928), p. 174.
[92] Coke, II *Institutes*, p. 179.
[93] Bowring, *op. cit.*, quoted in Halévy, *op. cit.*, p. 77.
[94] *Of Laws in General: Collected Works of Jeremy Bentham*, ed. Hart (1970), pp. 18 *et seq.*
[95] See Pollock, *History of the Science of Politics* (1911), p. 104.
[96] Maine, *Early History of Institutions* (1875), Lec. XII; Sidgwick, *Elements of Politics* (1891); Bryce, *Studies in History and Jurisprudence* (1901), X; Pollock, *op. cit.*, Pt. IV; Stephen, *The English Utilitarians* (1912), III, Chap. 5; Hart, *Concept of Law* (1961), Chaps. II–IV. And see Merriam, *History of the Theory of Sovereignty since Rousseau* (1900), Chap. VII; Rees, "The Theory of Sovereignty Restated," 59 *Mind* (1950), p. 495.
[97] Pollock, *op. cit.*, p. 112.

Pollock was referring here especially to Austin, for whom he reserved some invective worthy of Bentham.[98] But Austin's significance for our present purposes is not on account of his own views of sovereignty,[99] but because of his influence on the influential Dicey. Dicey recognised that "the dogma [his doctrine of the sovereignty of Parliament] sounds like a mere application to the British constitution of Austin's theory of sovereignty." [1] But, in his mildest manner, Dicey insisted that his only concern was to show that the principle was "fully recognised by the law of England." His principle was simple enough to state:

> The principle of Parliamentary sovereignty means neither more nor less than this, namely, that Parliament . . . [defined as The Queen in Parliament] has, under the English constitution, the right to make or unmake any law whatever; and, further, that no person or body is recognised by the law of England as having a right to override or set aside the legislation of Parliament.[2]

(It may be noted in passing that, oddly enough, this double proposition could also be applied *mutatis mutandis* to the courts in their law-making capacity.) Dicey stressed that his was the view of "lawyers," who are only interested in strictly legal sovereignty and cannot concern themselves, as Austin seemed to have done, with the question of who may possess ultimate "political sovereignty":

> . . . we may assert that the arrangements of the constitution are now such as to ensure that the will of the electors shall by regular and constitutional means always in the end assert itself as the predominant influence in the country. But this is a political, not a legal fact. The electors can in the long run enforce their will. But the courts take no notice of the will of the electors. The judges know nothing about any will of the people except in so far as that will is expressed by an Act of Parliament.[3]

This is the moment at which Dicey wins lawyers to his side, by seeming to offer at long last a simple, self-contained, non-metaphysical, lawyers' theory of the constitution. Warmed by the general democratic benevolence of his class and his period and by his own faith in the power of public opinion, and leaving his readers to pursue or ignore the problem of reconciling parliamentary sovereignty with his own principle of the Rule of Law, he managed to give the impression that there was nothing very new or surpris-

[98] "Austin's manner is so repulsive (as even his admirers allow) that it is hard to be quite just to his matter." *Ibid.*, 109n.

[99] *Op. cit.* (note 85), especially Lec. VI.

[1] Dicey, *op. cit.*, p. 71.

[2] *Ibid.*, pp. 39–40.

[3] *Ibid.*, pp. 73–74.

ing about what he was saying. Dicey's own demonstration of the sovereignty of Parliament, remarkably brief when seen in the light of the long and tortuous story of English constitutional history and theory, rests on three bases—illustrations of how omnicompetent Parliament has been in practice, the rejection of three supposed limitations (morality and international law, the inviolability of the prerogative, and the binding of successor Parliaments), and a long quotation from Blackstone (which he calls " the classical passage " on the subject) who himself quoted from Coke and Hale. And there is a footnote reference to a well-known statement by Sir Thomas Smith. The four statements of Smith, Coke, Hale and Blackstone have, indeed, become the equivocal *loci classici* of the theory of the sovereignty of Parliament. Although it is not possible to analyse them fully here,[4] it is necessary to say something about their equivocal character.

Each of the classical statements must be put within its own specific context—the context of the constitutional circumstances in which it was uttered and the context of the other views of the writer in question. Coke was speaking of Parliament in a very special light, as a court or court/legislature, and not simply as a legislature in the modern sense. A substantial part of his idea of the " supremacy " of Parliament was as a final court, and was not intended to imply wholly unlimited power in the sense of sovereignty theory. His notorious views on the status of the common law, and on the law in general, would surely have made any such idea inconceivable to him, even in his most parliamentary moments.[5] Similarly, the statement by Smith must be read in the light of the context indicated in Alston's introduction to his edition of *De Republica Anglorum*:

> Smith, then, in declaring Parliament to be the most high and absolute power of the realm (in time of peace) is by no means bringing up for consideration the question of sovereignty in the modern sense, or making statements which have any direct bearing on the great controversy of the next century. The contrast upon which Smith's attention is focussed is not the contrast between the powers of the Prince and of the Parlia-

4 They are discussed in McIlwain, *High Court of Parliament* (1910), pp. 124 *et seq.*

5 " In this book in effect appeareth the whole frame of the ancient common laws of this realm. . . . This grave and learned author will show as in this Mirror the great antiquity of the said courts of common law, and particularly of the High Court of Parliament ever since the time of King Arthur [*sic*] who reigned about the year of our Lord 516." (9 Co.Rep., Preface.) " It is a dangerous thing to alter or shake any of the fundamental rules of the common law, which in truth are the main pillars and supporters of the fabrick of the commonwealth." (II *Institutes*, p. 71.) On Coke's view of the law, see Holdsworth, *H.E.L.*, V, 428, 454, 475, 491, 493.

ment, but between the powers of Parliament and of those other courts which he describes in later chapters.[6]

Anstey has sought to show[7] that Blackstone's quotation from Hale was simply a fraud, a posthumous invention by another hand. According to Yale, Hale's unHobbesian view of the sovereign power was as " a power within and not above the constitutional framework." [8] Hale, who emphatically opposed the idea that the sovereign power was in Parliament separately from the King, was another great believer in the ultimate character of law.[9]

So far as the passage from Blackstone himself is concerned, it is right to recall the notorious and erratic eclecticism of his thought. There is clear influence of pure sovereignty theory in the immediate context of the passage in question: "[parliament], being the place where that absolute despotic power, which *must* in all governments reside somewhere, is entrusted by the constitution of these kingdoms " [10] (emphasis added). This " must," as in the case of Hobbes, is the methodological " must " of *a priori* sovereignty theory, with no special claim to be an exclusive explanation of constitutional structures. But Blackstone, of course, also had Coke-ish views about the status of " the law " and, if emphasis is put on his views about the separation of powers in a balanced constitution, then it is possible to see him also as the advocate of a form of Lockeian limited sovereignty.[11]

But, in the end, Dicey's success must be attributed to his having combined an apparently " legal " view of the past history of the sovereignty of Parliament with an obscure appeal to Austin as the theoretical exposition of sovereignty. He did this by suggesting [12] that Austin's theory was itself merely a generalisation from English law and not a deduction " from abstract theories of jurisprudence." In saying this, he managed to import classical sovereignty theory in disguise into the minds of English lawyers.

Some more subtle modern variants of Diceyism reflect the complexities which have been found to underly the theory. The first variant is the idea that the omnicompetence of Parliament is a political fact which can only be changed by political decision and not

[6] Smith, *De Republica Anglorum*, ed. Alston (1906), ed.'s Intro., p. xxxiii.
[7] " Blackstone's View on the Omnipotence of Parliament " (1863–70), III *Juridical Society Papers*, 305.
[8] " Hobbes and Hale on law, legislation & the sovereign " [1972B] C.L.J. 121. See also Holdsworth, *op. cit.* (note 90), pp. 127 *et seq.*; McIlwain, *op. cit.*, pp. 162 *et seq.*
[9] Holdsworth, *H.E.L.*, V, 482 *et seq.*, 499: VI, 203 *et seq.*
[10] *Commentaries*, 15th ed. (1809), I, 160 (in the passage used by Dicey).
[11] See Holdsworth, *op. cit.* (note 90), p. 130; Jones, *op. cit.* (note 90).
[12] Dicey, *op. cit.*, p. 72.

by legislation.[13] The second is the idea that the rules about changing the ultimate constitutional rule are a "presupposed superior constituent ideology" whose alteration would be a "social-psychological fact outside the province of legal procedure."[14] The third is the idea that the rule underlying the legal system is a question of fact at any given time and that the presently accepted rule "is one of continuing sovereignty, so that Parliament cannot protect its statutes from repeal."[15]

Of such views, four things may be said, in addition to what has been said above. In the first place, such views fly in the face of one thousand years of talk about "fundamental law" by kings, judges, political men, and commentators.[16] If there is one thread which runs through the whole turbulent story of British constitutional development, it is the belief that we are the servants of fundamental constitutional rules which were there before us and will be there after we are gone. From the days when the King's subjects demanded respect for "the laws of King Edward (the Confessor),"[17] through the centuries in which legendary superiority attached to such acts as Magna Carta, the Petition of Right, the Bill of Rights, the idea of "our ancient rights and liberties" has determined the form of our endlessly progressive/conservative constitutional change.

> Society is indeed a contract. Subordinate contracts for objects of mere occasional interest may be dissolved at pleasure—but the state ought not to be considered as nothing better than a partnership agreement in a trade of pepper and coffee, calico or tobacco, or some other such law concern, to be taken up for a little temporary interest, and to be dissolved by the fancy of the parties. It is to be looked on with other reverence because it is not a partnership in things subservient only to the gross animal existence of a temporary and perishable nature. It is a partnership in all science; a partnership in all art; a partnership in every virtue, and in all perfection. As the ends in such a partnership cannot be obtained in many generations, it becomes a partnership not only between those who are living, but between those who are living, those who are dead, and those who are to be born.[18]

Secondly, political facts, facts in general and ideologies are matters of uncertainty. What happened in 1688–89? What was its signifi-

[13] Wade, "The Basis of Legal Sovereignty" [1955] C.L.J. 172.

[14] Ross, *On Law and Justice* (1958), p. 81.

[15] Hart, *Concept of Law* (1961), p. 146.

[16] Surveyed in Gough, *Fundamental Law in English Constitutional History* (1955) whose conclusions are, however, different from those of the present study.

[17] *E.g.*, in the *Waverley Annals* for 1214—"[John's barons] demanding from him the laws of St. Edward and the liberties granted by later kings:" quoted in Jones, *King John & Magna Carta* (1971), p. 130.

[18] Burke, *Reflections on the Revolution in France: Works* (Bohn), II, 368.

cance? What do people believe about its significance? Who can say for certain? Such things are also liable to change. Who can say whether the development since 1689 of cabinet government, the party system and executive control of Parliament amounts to a factual and political change so fundamental as to unsettle the accepted basis of the constitution?

Thirdly, the "internal aspect" (to adopt Hart's illuminating concept)[19] of constitutional rules is legal. In the celebrated passage from the judgment of Willes J., in *Lee* v. *Bude & Torrington Ry. Co.*[20] quoted above, there are words which are clearly stated as a legal rule: ". . . as long as [an Act of Parliament] *exists as law*, the Courts are *bound to obey* it" (emphasis added). Such a formula implies that there are not only rules about how courts recognise Acts of Parliament as existing and in force, but also rules about their duty to give effect to them. The task of the courts is to declare and apply the law, not to recognise facts. Mr. Justice Willes was stating a rule, not recollecting that his predecessors had recognised political facts

Fourthly, and finally, the supposedly ultimate principle of the sovereignty of Parliament is itself an impressive illustration of the danger of rejecting, after so many centuries, a "higher law" or "fundamental law" view of our constitution. In and since the nineteenth century, a notorious development has occurred at the level of constitutional fact. As in the late Tudor period, an enormous increase in the actual power of all three supreme organs of the constitution has occurred. Almost every detail of social existence has been regulated through legislation. The Executive has acquired powers which are vast in scope and scale and go far beyond anything ever claimed by the King as prerogative. The courts have been organised into a vast and complex machine for dispensing justice and, through statutory interpretation and the common law, for making law. Over the same period, the Executive has acquired an overall position of dominance, extending its authority in all three of the functional branches of government—legislative, executive and judicial. Above all, it has acquired a practical control over the House of Commons in Parliament, from which it has virtually excluded the House of Lords as a countervailing power.

It would be a painful irony if we had to conclude that the most fundamental principles of our constitution had led inevitably and unquestionably to an "elective dictatorship,"[21] in law as well as in fact, because those principles confer absolute and unlimited power

19 *Concept of Law*, p. 55.
20 (1871) L.R. 6 C.P. 576.
21 Hailsham, *Elective Dictatorship* (1976).

on a body which, in conformity with accepted conventions of the constitution, is now in the grasp of "the King outside Parliament." But it is not a necessary conclusion, if only we recall that the supremacy which our constitutional history has recognised is the supremacy of law, including law made in Parliament. Smith, Coke, Hale and Blackstone in paying their respect to the power of Parliament, did so out of respect for "the law" and not in order to honour anyone who at any given time happens to control Parliament, whether the King or his successors in fact. Paradoxically, it might actually increase the self-respect of Parliament if it were to see itself as formally co-ordinate with an Executive whose status had also been demystified.[22]

The consequences which flow from the view taken in the present study may be set out in the following schematic and tentative form [23]:

(1) There are fundamental laws of the British constitution.

(2) Those fundamental laws persist unless and until they are changed by agreement among the supreme organs of the constitution.

(3) The fundamental laws are made specific in the common conceptions of them held by the supreme organs of the constitution.

(4) Particular aspects of the fundamental laws may be manifested in documentary form when particular acts come to be regarded as fundamental according to such common conceptions.

(5) Leading examples of such fundamental acts are Magna Carta and its statutory confirmations, the Habeas Corpus Acts, the Petition of Right, the Bill of Rights, the Act of Settlement, the Acts of Union, the Statute of Westminster.

(6) Under established common conceptions of the fundamental laws, the supreme organs of the constitution (Parliament,

[22] On the demystification of the status of the Executive, see Allott, "The Courts & the Executive: Four House of Lords Decisions" [1977] C.L.J. 255.

[23] These conclusions, which will be elaborated in a further study, appear to go in the direction of the "new view of sovereignty," identified as such in Heuston, *Essays in Constitutional Law* (1961), Chap. 1, and Marshall, *Constitutional Theory* (1971), Chap. III. But they go further than that view, and are essentially a new-old view of the constitution as a whole. They are closest to the views of Anstey, *op. cit.* (note 7), and Dixon, "The Law and the Constitution" (1935) 51 L.Q.R. 590, who was following the views of Hearn, *The Government of England* (1867), a work referred to with appreciation by Dicey but which his own work completely eclipsed. See also Dixon, "The Common Law as an Ultimate Constitutional Foundation" (1957) 31 A.L.J. 240. On the growing need for a new view of the sovereignty of Parliament, see Williams, "The Constitution of the United Kingdom [1972B] C.L.J. 266, and Winterton, "The British Grundnorm: Parliamentary Supremacy Re-examined" (1976) 92 L.Q.R. 591.

executive, courts) could be regarded as being in a state of balance, with each having only the degree of power allowed by those common conceptions, and with none having an intrinsic and exclusive superiority over the others.

(7) It remains to be seen whether the European Convention on Human Rights and Fundamental Freedoms, the European Communities Act 1972, the Scotland and Wales Acts 1978 will come to be regarded as fundamental acts (having regard to the special circumstances attending their adoption and their exceptional content) and, in particular, whether the institutions of the European Communities will come to be regarded as co-ordinate with the established supreme organs of the constitution.

[6]

PARLIAMENTARY SOVEREIGNTY: LORD DENNING'S DEXTEROUS REVOLUTION

T. R. S. ALLAN*

The Court of Appeal in *Macarthys Ltd* v *Smith*[1] decided that where a directly effective provision of European Community Law conflicted with a subsequent United Kingdom statute, the European provision should prevail. It seems that the traditional theory of parliamentary sovereignty which prevents one Parliament from curtailing the unlimited sovereignty of its successors has been modified. The purpose of the present writer is to suggest that the decision presents an interesting challenge to both sides in the perennial debate about the nature of sovereignty. If the view of Professor H. W. R. Wade is accepted, parliamentary sovereignty is a continuing one.[2] Parliament has power to legislate by its ordinary procedures on any subject it chooses, with one exception: it cannot control the manner or form of future legislation, for that would be to impose fetters on the sovereignty of future Parliaments. The courts will not permit such fetters to be imposed. Alternatively, parliamentary sovereignty may be regarded as self-embracing.[3] On this view Parliament has power to legislate effectively about the manner and form of future legislation as about any other subject. Accordingly, the courts will give effect only to legislation which complies with whatever conditions are currently laid down as required for valid legislation on the matter in question. It will be argued that neither analysis is a satisfactory or helpful way of considering issues of sovereignty, and that Lord Denning has deftly overcome an apparent constitutional hurdle leaving the constitutional theorists on one side debating hotly in a vacuum.

The importance of Macarthys Ltd *v* Smith

The salient facts in *Macarthys Ltd* v *Smith* may be briefly rehearsed. The manageress of a stockroom claimed that she was entitled to be paid the same as her male predecessor, who had been paid £10 a week more. An industrial tribunal decided that Mrs Smith and her predecessor were employed on 'like work' within the meaning of section 1(2)(*a*) of the Equal Pay Act 1970 and that, since the difference in pay was not due to any material difference other than the difference of sex, Mrs Smith was entitled to be paid at the higher rate. The Employment

*Lecturer in Law, University of Nottingham.

1 [1979] 3 All ER 325; [1981] QB 180.

2 [1955] *Camb LJ* 172. See also P. N. Mirfield, 95 *LQ Rev* 36 (1979).

3 See especially R. F. V. Heuston, *Essays in Constitutional Law* 2nd ed, Chap 1; Sir Ivor Jennings, *The Law and the Constitution* 5th ed, Chap 4; G. Winterton, 92 *LQ Rev* 591 (1976), 95 *LQ Rev* 386 (1979). H. W. R. Wade refers to these writers as the 'manner and form school': *Constitutional Fundamentals* 28. The terms 'continuing' and 'self-embracing' are those of H. L. A. Hart, *The Concept of Law* 146.

Appeal Tribunal affirmed the decision of the industrial tribunal and Macarthys Ltd appealed to the Court of Appeal on the ground that the Equal Pay Act applied only where both employees were employed at the same time, and did not permit a female employee to compare her conditions of employment with a *former* male employee who had left the company.

The majority of the Court of Appeal (Lawton and Cumming-Bruce LJJ) held that the meaning of section 1 was clear: it only applied where the man and the woman were employed on like work at the same time. Since the meaning was clear, there was no need (or power) to look to Article 119 of the EEC Treaty as an aid to construction.[4] Article 119 requires each Member State to apply the principle that men and women should receive equal pay for equal work. It had, however, already been decided by the European Court of Justice that Article 119 was directly effective,[5] so that Mrs Smith could plead her rights under the Article in the English courts. Although Lord Denning thought that Article 119 applied where a woman was employed on like work in close succession to a man, Lawton and Cumming-Bruce LJJ were uncertain of its ambit and the Court therefore referred the question to the European Court for a preliminary ruling under Article 177. The European Court decided that Article 119 did permit comparison with a former employee.[6]

The result was that the Court of Appeal was faced with a United Kingdom statute which was subsequent to the European Communities Act 1972 (the Equal Pay Act came into force in December 1975 as amended by section 8 of the Sex Discrimination Act) and which was inconsistent with a provision of the Treaty of Rome which was directly effective as part of English law. Traditional constitutional theory might lead one to expect that the Court would be bound to give effect to the latest enactment of Parliament: since Article 119 could only derive its validity as part of English law from section 2(1) of the European Communities Act 1972 and since no Parliament can bind its successors, it would seem that the rights conferred by Article 119 had been restricted by the Equal Pay Act.[7] Such a result would, of course, be contrary to the doctrine of the primacy of

4 'I do not think that it is permissible, as an aid to construction, to look at the terms of the Treaty. If the terms of the Treaty are adjudged in Luxembourg to be inconsistent with the provisions of the Equal Pay Act 1970, European Law will prevail over that municipal legislation. But such a judgment in Luxembourg cannot affect the meaning of the English statute.' [1979] 3 All ER 335–6 per Cumming-Bruce LJ.

5 *Defrenne (Gabriele)* v *Société Anonyme Belge de Navigation Aérienne* [1976] ECR 455.

6 [1981] QB 180.

7 Lord Denning asserted that a UK Act would prevail over the Treaty of Rome in the event of inconsistency in *Felixstowe Docks and Railway Co* v *British Transport Docks Board* [1976] 2 CMLR 655. This was also the view of Lord Diplock, 'The Common Market and the Common Law' (First Lord Upjohn lecture) 6 *Law Teacher* 3, 8 (1972): 'It is a consequence of the constitutional doctrine of the supremacy of the Queen in Parliament that if a subsequent Act of Parliament were passed that was in conflict with any provision of the Treaty which is of direct application in the member states . . . the courts of the United Kingdom would be bound to give effect to the Act of Parliament notwithstanding any conflict.'

Community law consistently asserted by the European Court.[8] The Court of Appeal, apparently untroubled by the constraints of orthodox theory, simply asserted that Community law prevailed over the national legislation and Mrs Smith's claim succeeded. Lord Denning proclaimed: 'It is important now to declare and it must be made plain that the provisions of article 119 of the EEC Treaty take priority over anything in our English statute on equal pay which is inconsistent with article 119. That priority is given by our own law. It is given by the European Communities Act 1972 itself. Community law is now part of our law and, whenever there is any inconsistency, Community law has priority.'[9]

It may be observed that, strictly speaking, it was unnecessary to decide what should happen when a conflict occurred between Community law and subsequent national legislation. Since Article 119 was directly effective, it would have been sufficient to say that, although the Equal Pay Act did not permit comparison with a former male employee, the plaintiff could rely instead on the Article which (the European Court had decided) did permit such comparison. This was essentially a case of inconsistency in the sense that the ambit of Article 119 was wider than that of the Act, but not inconsistency in the sense of conflict. Nevertheless, the Court of Appeal did not appear to attach any particular significance to that.

The only exception to the new principle—that Community law prevails over subsequent national law which is inconsistent—applies where Parliament deliberately legislates inconsistently with Community law 'and says so in express terms'[10]: in these circumstances the court would apply the Act of Parliament. Although Lawton LJ asserts that he 'can see nothing in this case which infringes the sovereignty of Parliament',[11] he seems to be referring to *ultimate* sovereignty in the sense that Parliament retains the power to repeal the European Communities Act: 'Parliament's recognition of European Community Law and of the jurisdiction of the European Court of Justice by one enactment can be withdrawn by another. There is nothing in the Equal Pay Act 1970 as amended by the Sex Discrimination Act 1975, to indicate that Parliament intended to amend the European Communities Act 1972, or to limit its application.' Reassuring though this assertion of ultimate sovereignty may be to those who value traditional doctrines, it should not be allowed to disguise the remarkable innovation which has occurred. In the absence of clear evidence of a deliberate decision to legislate in conflict with prevailing Community law, future United Kingdom statutes will not be applied when they are inconsistent with pre-existing

8 *Costa* v *ENEL* [1964] ECR 585. In *Italian Finance Administration* v *Simmenthal* [1978] ECR 629 the Court held that provisions of the Treaty and directly applicable legislation not only take precedence over any conflicting provision of national law but also preclude the valid adoption of new national legislative measures to the extent to which they would be incompatible with the Community provisions.

9 [1981] QB 180, 200.

10 [1979] 3 All ER 329 d (Lord Denning).

11 [1979] 3 All ER 334 e.

Community legislation. The attempt to entrench section 2(1) of the European Communities Act by means of section 2(4) has to some extent succeeded: the effect of the decision seems to be to impose a requirement of form (express wording) on future legislation designed to override Community law. In short, Parliament in 1972 accomplished the impossible and (to a degree) bound its successors.[12]

It has been argued that, since there was no attempt to repeal the European Communities Act (as Lawton LJ pointed out), the decision of the Court of Appeal did not involve any departure from the orthodox theory of sovereignty.[13] The inconsistency was between Community law and a United Kingdom statute dealing with sexual discrimination: there was no conflict with the European Communities Act and therefore no question of implied repeal of that Act. Accordingly (it is argued) the principle stated in ***Ellen Street Estates Ltd*** v ***Minister of Health***[14] that 'it is impossible for Parliament to enact that in a subsequent statute dealing with the same subject-matter there can be no implied repeal'[15] remains unharmed. But this point conceals the significance of the Court of Appeal's decision. The fact remains that there was an inconsistency between the result stipulated by the European Communities Act and that stipulated by the Equal Pay Act, and the Court of Appeal chose to adopt the former. The essence of the traditional doctrine of parliamentary sovereignty is that the courts should give effect to the most recent expression of parliamentary intent: the rule protecting implied repeal is simply one consequence of that doctrine. The Court of Appeal in *Macarthys Ltd* v *Smith* decided, in effect, that the will of the Parliament of 1972 should prevail over that of the Parliament of 1975 (which, on the court's view of the Equal Pay Act, had legislated inconsistently with the legal results of the European Communities Act).

But it may be further objected that this view attributes too much importance to *Macarthys Ltd* v *Smith* by neglecting the special character of Community law as an element of our national law. Rather than treating Community law as a species of delegated legislation,[16] deriving its validity and effect under the European Communities Act, it should be perceived as a separate realm of law, recognized by the European Communities Act as effective in the United Kingdom, but operating alongside national law. Directly applicable Community law must be uniformly applied throughout the Community. For example, the European Court has held that the need for Community regulations to be uniformly applied prevents Member States from adopting measures for the implementation of a regulation

12 It is interesting to recall that Lord Denning has declined to decide, in advance of the point arising for decision, whether or not Parliament can repudiate the Treaty of Rome: ***Blackburn*** v ***Attorney-General*** [1971] 1 WLR 1037.

13 E. Ellis, 96 *LQ Rev* 511.

14 [1934] 1 KB 590.

15 Maugham LJ at 597.

16 Strictly speaking, only post-accession Community law need be regarded as 'delegated legislation': see Lord Diplock, op cit, 6–7.

which affect its scope.[17] The essence of such Community legislation is that it is directly applicable and its substantive content is entirely a matter of Community law.[18] On this view the court is free to follow the doctrine of the primacy of Community law espoused by the European Court and, subject to any amendment of the European Communities Act, it need not be concerned by any conflicts between Community and national law.

Attractive though the argument is, it must not be allowed to obscure the reality, which is that the present Parliament is precluded from legislating effectively (except by special wording) on a particular subject where there is inconsistent Community law.[19] The point is simply that either Parliament has succeeded in limiting its unbounded sovereignty by the European Communities Act (in the sense that the latest statement of Parliament's will—expressed in the usual manner—no longer automatically takes effect in priority to previously existing law on the relevant subject) or it has not done so (so that the most recent enactment of Parliament will automatically override any relevant pre-existing Community law which is inconsistent). If we accede to the European Court's view of the supremacy of Community law, then Parliament's authority to legislate in the ordinary way on any subject has been fettered.[20]

The fallacy of the fundamental rule

If the argument that *Macarthys Ltd* v *Smith* represents a significant development in English constitutional law is accepted, what does it tell us about the nature of sovereignty? The European Communities Act 1972 seems to have achieved a degree of entrenchment even without expressly imposing a requirement of any special manner and form. The Act itself does not stipulate that express wording is required to legislate inconsistently with current Community law. The decision of the Court of Appeal is that that is the *effect* of the bare assertion in section 2(4) that 'any enactment passed or to be passed . . . shall be construed and have effect subject to' Community law.

Lord Denning's interpretation of section 2(4) of the European Communities Act mirrors the wording of section 2 of the Canadian Bill of Rights 1960: 'Every law

17 Case 40/69 *Hauptzollamt Hamburg* v *Bollman* [1970] ECR 69.

18 See Ipsen, *CML Rev* (1964–65) 379, 396 and 401. In discussing conflicts between the law of the EEC Treaty and a subsequent municipal law, Ipsen argues: 'It cannot even be objected that the rules of the Treaty are no different legally from those in other multilateral treaties. They are different, at any rate to the extent that they create a specific norm, specific *because directly applicable in member States in their capacity as common law.*'

19 Even if the special character of Community law is accepted, there remains the problem of explaining how Community law acquired its unique authority as a matter of English constitutional law: see J. Usher, *European Community Law and National Law* 34.

20 In *Re an Absence in Ireland* [1977] 1 CMLR 5, the National Insurance Commissioner decided, without discussion, that the Social Security Act 1975 s 82(5)(*a*), which disqualifies a claimant of invalidity benefit for periods of absence from Great Britain, was overridden in the circumstances by Articles 38 and 39 of EEC Regulation 1408/71 which were inconsistent. To ensure that s 82(5)(*a*) was to take effect without such qualification, Parliament would (presumably) have had to say so expressly.

of Canada shall, ***unless it is expressly declared by an Act of the Parliament of Canada that it shall operate notwithstanding the Canadian Bill of Rights,*** be so construed and applied as not to abrogate, abridge or infringe, or to authorize the abrogation, abridgement or infringement of any of the rights or freedoms herein recognized and declared.' (My italics.) In *R* v *Drybones*[21] the majority of the Canadian Supreme Court held that section 94(*b*) of the Indian Act 1952 was rendered inoperative by the Bill of Rights since it infringed the respondent's right to equality before the law. Since it could only be sensibly construed so that its application would operate to infringe the right to equality declared by the Bill of Rights, and in the absence of express declaration by Parliament that it should operate notwithstanding the Bill of Rights, section 94(*b*) must be held inoperative. Though concerned with a pre-1960 statute, the reasoning of the majority judgment would apply equally to a statute passed subsequently to the Bill of Rights. (The Bill is stated in section 5 to apply to Acts of Parliament enacted before or after the coming into force of the Bill.) The decision is a good parallel since, equally with *Macarthys Ltd* v *Smith,* it represents a decision by the judges to recognize a special requirement of form in the case of legislation for certain purposes. Moreover, in neither case was the court compelled to do anything so constitutionally dangerous as to declare an Act of Parliament invalid: the offending rule (or in *Macarthys Ltd* v *Smith,* the offending restriction) was simply not applied. Ritchie J stated (at 294–5): 'I think a declaration by the courts that a section or portion of a section of a statute is inoperative is to be distinguished from the repeal of such a section and is to be confined to the particular circumstances of the case in which the declaration is made. The situation appears to me to be somewhat analogous to a case where valid provincial legislation in an otherwise unoccupied field ceases to be operative by reason of conflicting federal legislation.'

Adherents of the 'self-embracing' theory of parliamentary sovereignty could no doubt argue that in 1972 Parliament successfully changed the law about what counts as a valid Act of Parliament for the purpose of legislating inconsistently with existing Community law. The consequences of this view would be exciting indeed. If the courts can decide (in effect) that a former statute can prevail over a later statute except where the later one expressly provides otherwise, they could presumably take the next step of deciding that an earlier statute prevails over a later one except where any special procedure stipulated by Parliament in the earlier Act is duly complied with in enacting the later one. It would, for example, be possible to enact a Bill of Rights and preclude future Parliaments from legislating inconsistently with its provisions by an ordinary parliamentary majority. The problem with this theory, however, is that it would seem to *require* the court to reach such a decision. Parliament would have changed the law defining the proper procedure for certain types of enactment and any such 'Act' whose passage failed to comply with the new procedure could not be recognized as

21 [1970] SCR 282.

valid.[22] This would seem to enable a government with a strong majority so to entrench its own legislation as to make future repeal or amendment extremely difficult or even impossible. The self-embracing theory of sovereignty appears to compel the court—as a matter of law—to decide in such a case that future Parliaments have been fettered by one of their predecessors.[23] The theory may therefore have most undesirable (and undemocratic) results.[24]

Advocates of the theory of 'continuing' sovereignty, if they accepted that Parliament's power to legislate freely in the ordinary way for all purposes has been fettered, would presumably say that a revolution has occurred. The courts may now have withdrawn their unquestioning allegiance to the enactments of the present Parliament: all future legislation will be read subject to, and held inapplicable insofar as it is inconsistent with, any directly effective Community provision, except where Parliament expressly indicates that it wishes to override Community law. This is not a change which Parliament itself could have brought about because the degree of authority accorded by the courts to statutes is a fundamental rule of the legal system preceding the legislative power of Parliament. As Wade explains[25]: 'the rule of judicial obedience is in one sense a rule of common law, but in another sense—which applies to no other rule of common law—it is the ultimate *political* fact upon which the whole system of legislation hangs. Legislation owes its authority to the rule: the rule does not owe its authority to legislation.'

This view of the problem would seem to permit the court the freedom to accord priority to Community law without requiring that the court should, in consistency, accept any other statutory amendments of the legislative process for particular purposes which may be attempted in the future. But the decision of the Court of Appeal in *Macarthys Ltd* v *Smith* highlights the artificiality of analyses which seek to explain such developments in terms of revolutions. For, it must be admitted, the judgments, though significant, hardly look revolutionary. They expressly affirm the ultimate sovereignty of the contemporary Parliament and Lawton LJ denies any infringement of the doctrine. Indeed, the reasoning is essentially that, in according priority to Community law, the court was giving effect to Parliament's (present) intention. The object of the Equal Pay Act was to implement the United Kingdom's obligations under the Treaty of Rome to ensure the equality of the sexes in terms and conditions of employment. Parliament could

22 For example, it is sometimes argued that the Parliament Acts 1911 and 1949 have 'redefined' Parliament for the purposes of legislation permitted by those Acts (though here, of course, the alternative legislature is an optional alternative).

23 See, e.g., Jennings, op cit, 152: '"Legal sovereignty" is merely a name indicating that the legislature has for the time being power to make laws of any kind in the manner required by the law . . . the "legal sovereign" may impose legal limitations upon itself, because its power to change the law includes the power to change the law affecting itself.'

24 G. Winterton recognizes this problem but suggests that a court might abandon the notion of self-embracing sovereignty (in a procedural sense) at this point, relying on the maxim that 'what cannot be done directly cannot be done indirectly': 92 *LQ Rev* 591, 605 (1976).

25 [1955] *Camb LJ* 188.

not, therefore, have intended there to be any conflict or incompatibility between the United Kingdom statute and Community law.

One might have expected that the simplest way of arriving at this conclusion would have been to explain that, as a matter of *interpretation*, the Equal Pay Act should be construed so as to be consistent with Article 119. Is this not envisaged by section 2(4) of the European Communities Act? However, as we have seen, the majority held that it was not appropriate to have regard to Article 119 when construing section 1 of the Equal Pay Act. But it hardly seems sensible to attribute the description 'revolutionary' to the decision merely because the Lords Justices chose one line of argument rather than another. Instead of explaining their decision as a matter of statutory interpretation, they preferred to rely on a wider notion of Parliament's intention in order to defeat an inescapable interpretation. Can revolutionary alterations of the fundamental rule, shifts of grundnorm, really be held to turn on such (comparatively) delicate shading?

It is suggested that *Macarthys Ltd* v *Smith* reveals the fallacy underlying both views of parliamentary sovereignty. Each school of theorists has proceeded on the assumption that at the root of the legal system there is a fundamental rule or ultimate principle,[26] and the object of debate has been to identify it precisely and to state its nature. Is the sovereignty accorded by the fundamental rule to Parliament a self-embracing or a continuing one? That has been the mystery to be solved. It is accepted by all sides in the dispute that sovereignty is a concept explaining the relationship between the courts and Parliament. For Professor Wade it is simply a matter of political fact that the courts will recognize a statute enacted in the usual form and adopted in the customary manner. For adherents of the self-embracing doctrine the rule is that the courts will recognize only statutes enacted by whatever procedures governing the legislative process are currently in force. The present writer's contention is that neither interpretation can be accepted: the so-called 'fundamental rule' is simply indeterminate.

The notion of a rule implies that, at least in some cases, a problem requires a particular solution. If it cannot be stated in advance that one result rather than another is in some sense required, there is no rule to be applied. Yet this is precisely the situation confronted by the court in those rare cases where problems of sovereignty arise. It is the nature of problems of sovereignty to raise questions which cannot be answered *as a matter of law*.[27] As Wade explains, it is question-begging to assert that Parliament can change the law defining an Act of

26 This idea corresponds to Hart's 'rule of recognition' and Kelsen's 'grundnorm'.

27 Wade makes this point clearly. In commenting on *Harris* v *Minister of the Interior* he observes: 'It is perhaps not surprising that the whole case was argued as if there was a right or wrong legal answer. In fact, if the foregoing argument is sound, there was no such necessary legal answer: the court had reached the ultimate boundary of the legal system, and had in substance to make a political decision.' [1955] *Camb LJ* 192. See also H. L. A. Hart, *The Concept of Law* 147. Hart observes of arguments concerning Parliament's ability to entrench legislation: 'None of them can be ruled out as wrong or accepted with confidence as right; for we are in the area of open texture of the system's most fundamental rule. Here at any moment a question may arise as to which there is no answer—only answers.'

Parliament for it is the legislative authority of Parliament which is itself under discussion. Even if the court accepts that there has been a limited modification of the rule protecting implied repeal in one case (as seems to have happened in *Macarthys Ltd* v *Smith*) it does not follow that the court has thereby endorsed a doctrine of self-embracing sovereignty to govern future cases. Future cases may involve more serious limitations on Parliament's legislative capacity and raise different problems justifying a more conservative political choice by the courts.

Constitutional development without revolution

Both schools of theorists make, it is suggested, the same error. Recognizing that the idea that the courts obey Acts of Parliament is ambiguous, they each seek to establish that one conception of that idea is the true conception and valid for all purposes. Either parliamentary sovereignty is continuing or it is self-embracing, and the legal consequences of any particular legislative attempt at entrenchment follow from whichever view one adopts. But both views seem to overlook the elasticity inherent in the simple idea that what the Queen in Parliament enacts will be recognized by the courts as law. Even before any question of conflict between the enactments of former and subsequent Parliaments can arise, the courts must grapple with their more immediate task—the interpretation of parliamentary intent.[28] The ease with which in *Macarthys Ltd* v *Smith* Lord Denning escaped from the apparent shackles of orthodox theory illustrates above all the flexibility inherent in the process of interpreting and applying statutes.

It is well known and obvious that, in applying statutes to particular situations, the courts must fall back on principles of construction and interpretation of their own devising. Appeals to parliamentary intent of themselves can decide nothing. Parliamentary intention is necessarily a constructive intention. Even when applying the 'literal' rule of statutory interpretation, the court may consciously depart from the result that it recognizes the relevant parliamentary majorities would have wanted.[29] As Lord Reid explained in *Black-Clawson International Ltd* v *Papierwerke Waldhof-Aschaffenburg AG*[30]: 'We often say that we are looking for the intention of Parliament, but that is not quite accurate. We are seeking the meaning of the words which Parliament used. We are seeking not what Parliament meant but the true meaning of what they said.'

But, in addition, the courts rely on principles of interpretation which possess varying degrees of strength. One such principle is the 'prima facie presumption that Parliament does not intend to act in breach of international law'.[31] It may be

28 Note Hart's interesting observation: 'The distinction between the uncertainty of a particular rule, and the uncertainty of the criterion used in identifying it as a rule of the system, is not itself, in all cases, a clear one.' (*The Concept of Law* 144.)

29 See, e.g., *IRC* v *Hinchy* [1960] AC 748 per Lord Reid at 767.

30 [1975] AC 591, 613.

31 *Salomon* v *Commrs of Customs and Excise* [1967] 2 QB 116, 143 (Diplock LJ). Professor R. Cross observes that there is some uncertainty whether the presumption operates only in cases of ambiguity or whether clear words are needed to exclude its operation: *Statutory Interpretation* 143.

that clear statutory words are necessary to exclude its operation. Lord Denning's interpretation of section 2(4) of the European Communities Act results in an even stronger principle of interpretation: Parliament must state expressly that inconsistent Community law is not to prevail if the presumption against conflict between Community law and national legislation is to be rebutted. But, of course, that is in effect to impose a special requirement of legislative form for a particular purpose. There is no sharp conceptual division between a strong presumption, requiring the use of clear words to defeat it, and an even stronger principle of interpretation, which Parliament can override only by stating its intention to do so in so many words. The difference is only one of degree. In either case the court may be said to be giving effect, as best it can, to the (real) 'intention' of Parliament.[32] And if in *Macarthys Ltd* v *Smith* the Court of Appeal could say that, in the absence of express words, Parliament must be taken not to have intended any conflict with Community law, why should not some future Court of Appeal decide that, in the absence of some special procedure having been followed (say a two-thirds majority obtained), Parliament must be taken not to have 'intended' (say) to legislate contrary to a Bill of Rights? If the court can recognize (or require) a limitation of form, it can presumably accept a limitation of 'manner and form'. Once it is recalled that Parliament's intention is necessarily a constructive one, it can be seen that no water-tight conceptual divide exists between principles of interpretation, on one hand, and limited forms of entrenchment, on the other. Just as there are many degrees of entrenchment, ranging from the stipulation of special forms of wording to the need for adoption by special majorities or plebiscites, so there are many degrees of creative interpretation, ranging from the literal rule of construction to strong presumptions of legislative intent.[33]

The point is that bold and creative statutory interpretation may at some point embrace acceptance of a limited degree of entrenchment. It is one and the same judicial process. When the stage is reached where the court can insist on a certain stipulated form for legislation on a particular question, the political[34] nature of the

32 In *Birdi* v *Sec of State for Home Affairs, The Times*, 12 February 1975, Lord Denning suggested that an Act of Parliament which did not conform to the European Convention on Human Rights might be held invalid. He resiled from this view in *R* v *Sec of State, ex p Bhajan Singh*, [1976] QB 198, but, in holding that the Immigration Act 1971 should be construed so as to conform to the Convention, said: 'It is to be assumed that the Crown, in taking its part in legislation, would do nothing which was in conflict with treaties.' He referred to Lord Reid's statement in *Waddington* v *Miah* [1974] 1 WLR 683, 694, in relation to the European Convention: 'So it is hardly credible that any government department would promote or that Parliament would pass retrospective criminal legislation.' It may be commented that extremely clear words are likely to be needed to achieve a result that the courts think is 'hardly credible'.

33 In the same way, the distinction between fettering the 'area of power' of future Parliaments and changing only the 'manner and form' of legislation breaks down, since a sufficiently radical change of manner and form could, in practice, render legislation immune from repeal. See Hart, op cit, 147; Winterton, 92 *LQ Rev* 605 (1976).

34 I use the term 'political' in Wade's sense: we are concerned with the relationship between the courts and Parliament, which must, in the final analysis, be a matter of politics rather than law.

court's decision has become more obvious. But the whole enterprise was 'political' all along—the task of statutory interpretation represents an aspect of the relation between the courts and Parliament quite as much as questions of parliamentary supremacy. The point at which the courts have stepped sufficiently beyond the traditional limits of statutory construction, imposing more ambitious restraints on legislation, as to justify use of the term 'revolution' is surely a matter of taste. It certainly defines no point of special legal significance—the legal order has, perhaps, been modified one more degree, but it is the same legal order. To insist that, at some magic moment, the old legal order passes away and a new one comes into being is to insist on an arbitrary division and to hinder the natural process of legal evolution and development by raising non-existent theoretical obstacles.

The importance of Lord Denning's judgment in *Macarthys Ltd* v *Smith* lies in the degree of strength of the principle of construction adopted: statutes will be presumed to be intended not to conflict (nor to be applied in case of conflict) with Community law unless Parliament states the contrary. For the future, then, the court has departed from the ordinary rule of implied repeal in such cases. Although as a matter of strict construction, section 1 of the Equal Pay Act was in conflict with Community law, the court complied with the (assumed) governing intention of Parliament that no such conflict should be allowed to defeat the plaintiff's rights in Community law. This is an overriding (or higher-order) principle of interpretation which gives way only in the face of express wording to the contrary. Once it has been recognized that such restraints of form may be imposed, there can be no *legal* barrier to more ambitious procedural restraints on the legislature for certain purposes, since the doctrine of automatic implied repeal by ordinary enactment will (ex hypothesi) have been abandoned. Since the principle of implied repeal by ordinary enactment is not enshrined in any written constitution, but exists simply as a constitutional practice, it is open to the courts to depart from the principle (for certain purposes) by changing the practice.[35]

The error of the theory of continuing sovereignty, it is suggested, lies in the failure to see that questions concerning the ability of one Parliament to fetter another are not fundamentally different *in nature* from other, more usual, questions of statutory interpretation: they are simply more serious and more dramatic. The error of the theory of self-embracing sovereignty lies in its attempt to provide a solution, as a matter of law and in advance, to any questions concerning the possibility of entrenchment of legislation which may arise in the future. Since, as Wade has explained, such questions are fundamental questions

35 Much of the confusion over the question of revolution stems from Kelsen's theory of legal discontinuity which cannot account satisfactorily for the role of custom in unwritten constitutions. See G. Maher, 1 *Oxford J of Legal Stud* 167 (1981). Kelsen's theory has no place for the gradual evolution of the basic norm. J. W. Harris attempts to apply Kelsen's theory to the UK constitution but is driven to argue that where a constitution is custom-based, a change in the basic norm will occur only if a written constitution is substituted: [1971] *Camb LJ* 103. It is evident that constitutional theorists who believe that the doctrine of Parliamentary supremacy in its present form can be changed only by revolution can derive little support from Kelsen's theory.

concerning the relation between the courts and Parliament, they require the exercise of political, rather than legal, judgment for their solution. It may well be a form of judgment which the judges, distanced as they are from more immediate political pressures, are ideally suited to make. This view, if it is accepted, should not, however, be allowed to obscure the nature of the judicial process at this high constitutional level. And political judgments must be made at the time the relevant questions arise. The judges might well come to decide that Parliament and people were ready to accept unfamiliar limitations on parliamentary sovereignty in the interests of fulfilling United Kingdom obligations under the Treaty of Rome. It would not necessarily follow that similar limitations would be acceptable in the interests of restraining an elected government which wished to legislate in contravention (in the courts' view) of a previously enacted Bill of Rights. These are separate questions and must be considered separately when (and if) they arise. They are questions of immense constitutional importance and cannot, and must not, be determined in advance.[36]

A variety of means of securing a new form of constitution have been suggested by those who think that some sort of political revolution is needed for change. H. W. R. Wade has recently argued that a change in the judicial oath, binding the judges to uphold a new fundamental law, is 'the one and only way in which we can take command of our constitution without having to wait for some sort of political revolution, which is most unlikely to arrive just when we want it, and without having to contrive some artificial legal discontinuity'.[37] If the present argument is accepted, the decision in *Macarthys Ltd* v *Smith* demonstrates that a creative-minded judge, intent on constitutional reform, can achieve remarkable success without revolution. The process is likely, of course, to be a gradual one. Moreover, it requires the judges to follow the timely lead given by the Master of the Rolls before his retirement. They have to combine a cautious wisdom in estimating the readiness of the political climate for change with the courage and dexterity of Lord Denning in achieving it. Wade concludes his discussion with the remark: 'It is in the breasts of the judges that the problem lies and it is in their breasts that we must contrive the solution.'[38] Lord Denning, at least, has shown that he could be trusted to provide one.

36 It is not, of course, contended that such questions should not be argued in advance as matters of political principle. The contention is simply that it is neither possible nor prudent to give in advance (by selecting a particular conception of sovereignty) a single answer to the many different issues which may arise for consideration in the future.

37 *Constitutional Fundamentals* 39.

38 Ibid., 40.

[7]

Coherence, Hypothetical Cases, and Precedent

S. L. HURLEY*

Coherence accounts of practical reasoning in general, of which legal reasoning is a particular case, postulate the existence of a theory, sought in deliberation, which best displays as coherent the relationships among specific reasons for action which conflict in application to the case to be decided. These relationships are discovered in part by consideration of the way in which the same conflicting reasons apply in other cases, the resolution of which is settled. Ronald Dworkin's account of legal reasoning in *Law's Empire* is an example of a coherence account. Coherence accounts provide elements of various familiar conceptions of practical reasoning, such as the Rawlsian conception of reflective equilibrium as the outcome of a process of mutual adjustment between theory and intuition, and the decision-theoretic conception of rationality in terms of adjustment between data about preferences, criteria of choice, and principles of consistency.[1] I have elsewhere discussed the general rationale and motivation for coherence accounts of practical reasoning, illustrated the process of seeking coherence through deliberation with both legal and ethical examples, abstractly characterized the search for coherence, and considered various problems to which the abstract characterization gives rise.[2] In this paper I shall:

First, briefly set out my abstract characterization of deliberation as a search for coherence;

Second, consider various further examples of legal and ethical reasoning and indicate briefly the way in which they provide instances of my general coherentist characterization of deliberation;

Third, point out the generally similar roles within coherentist accounts of practical reasoning of settled actual cases and settled hypothetical cases as data to be accounted for by the sought-after theory or principles;

Fourth, present an objection to coherence accounts of legal reasoning in particular discussed by Kenneth Kress, who argues that they may give rise to

* Fellow in Philosophy and University Lecturer, St. Edmund Hall, Oxford. For helpful suggestions and comments on earlier drafts that saved me from various errors and unclarities, I am grateful to Ronald Dworkin, Mark Greenberg, and Joseph Raz; needless to say, responsibility for all remaining errors is entirely my own.

[1] See John Rawls, *A Theory of Justice* (Cambridge, Mass, Belknap Press of Harvard University Press, 1971); and Ralph L. Keeney and Howard Raiffa, *Decisions with Multiple Objectives: Preferences and Value Tradeoffs* (New York, Wiley & Sons, 1976).

[2] See my *Natural Reasons* (New York, Oxford University Press, 1989), chapters 4, 10, 11, 12, etc. Many background issues about the nature and objectivity of coherentist practical reasoning are raised by the argument of this article which I cannot here address but do address at length in *Natural Reasons*. They include: the need for substantive constraints on the description of the problem in terms of conflicting reasons, the relationships of these constraints to the structure and process of coherentist deliberation and the explanatory character of the resulting theories, the nature and limitations of the authority of theories about conflicting reasons, and many others.

 Oxford Journal of Legal Studies Vol. 10, No. 2

retroactive application of legal principles when new cases are decided between the occurrence of the events litigated and the litigation of them (the problem of intervening cases); and

Finally, consider various possible responses to Kress's argument. I shall briefly evaluate and put aside the possible responses of giving intervening cases prospective effect only, and of accepting intervening case retroactivity as not so bad. I shall then go on to diagnose the source of the problem by evaluating the relationships among concept of coherence, hypothetical cases, and the doctrine of precedent. I will show that the weaker coherentist requirement of treating like cases alike within practical reasoning in general is not sufficient to give rise to the problem of intervening cases, but that the stronger requirement imposed by the doctrine of precedent within legal reasoning in particular is necessary for the problem to arise. The distinction between the weaker and stronger requirements turns on the asymmetrical treatment of actual and hypothetical cases by the doctrine of precedent, by contrast with their symmetrical treatment in coherentist practical reasoning in general. However, I shall then argue that, when this asymmetry is properly understood, neither is the doctrine of precedent by itself sufficient to give rise to the problem of intervening cases, but only does so when the intervening legal decision is not *ex ante* correct, and that the role of hypothetical cases in coherentist practical reasoning in fact limits the problem of intervening case retroactivity. I shall conclude, following suggestions made by Dworkin, that intervening case retroactivity does not present a problem for coherence accounts such as his in particular.

1. An Abstract Characterization of Deliberation, and Coherence Functions

Our subject matter is deliberation about what to do when the reasons that apply to the alternatives conflict. The alternatives may be possible individual actions (eg, keeping one's promise and risking someone's life, or breaking it and avoiding risk to life), or possible judicial actions (eg, holding that a statute violates the Equal Protection Clause, or that it does not). The reasons that apply to the alternatives may be of various kinds, depending on the context of deliberation. An individual may deliberate about his own conflicting self-interested reasons, when no one else is significantly affected by the alternatives, or about a conflict involving the interests of others; the applicable reasons may be ethical, aesthetic, etc. A judge deliberates about conflicting legal reasons: legal doctrines, precedents, rights, principles, policies, as expressed within various legal practices and institutions, by cases, statutes, a constitution, legal scholarship, etc.

Coherence accounts claim that to say a certain alternative ought to be done is to say that it is favoured by the theory, whichever it may be, that gives the best account of the relationships among the various specific reasons that apply to the alternatives in question. Which theory is in fact the best theory, which best displays the applicable reasons as coherently related, is not specified by a coherence account *per se*. Rather, it is left to deliberation to discover what the best theory is. A coherence account merely claims that what ought to be done is whatever alternative the best theory, whatever that is, favours. Thus the deliberator's task is to discover the theory that best displays coherence. Deliberation involves a process of constructing hypotheses about the content of what I call a 'coherence function', which represents the theory sought and which takes us from alternatives ranked by specific reasons to all-things-considered rankings of alternatives. Of course the coherence function must meet certain conditions, and the all-things-considered ranking must meet certain conditions. For example, the latter ranking should not be intransitive. However, I shall not be considering the full range of these conditions in this article, but only those embodied in the requirements of treating like cases alike and of the doctrine of precedent.[3]

The process of deliberation can be analysed into five stages. At the *first* stage, we specify the problem. We try to arrive at a characterization of the alternatives at issue, and to determine what various specific reasons apply and how they rank the alternatives. We here exercise our abilities to perceive the world in terms of ethical, or legal, or other reason-giving concepts. (This is the issue spotting stage familiar to law students; however, there is much more to legal deliberation than issue spotting.) Assuming the reasons that apply conflict, that is, rank the alternatives at issue differently, we proceed to the *second* stage, and examine more carefully the various specific reasons that apply. Perhaps when we consider the purpose of one reason, it will turn out to have a rather different import than we originally thought in this particular case. At any rate, at this stage we develop and firm up our local conceptions of the various specific reasons that apply, without yet trying to arrive at a global conception of their relations to one another.

At the *third* stage we begin gathering data, by looking for other issues to which the conflicting reasons examined at stage two apply. In particular we are looking for settled cases. They may have actually been decided, or may be posed as hypothetical issues, the resolution of which can be taken as evident. By a 'settled' case, I mean a case which, if actual, is such that its resolution is clear to the relevant decision-maker or decision-makers, and which, if hypothetical, is such that its resolution would be clear to the relevant decision-maker or decision-makers were the case to be considered. (That a resolution of a particular case is or would be clear does not mean that it cannot be mistaken; settledness in particular cases is a matter of what is or would be believed to be correct, not necessarily of what is correct. However, it is of the nature of a coherentist account of what should be done, in terms of coherence with settled cases in general, that not all settled cases can be mistaken. I will return to this point below.) Thus, at least as a conceptual matter, not all actually decided cases are settled, and some settled cases are hypothetical, not actual (see section 8 below for more on this use of 'settled'). We may give settled actual cases more weight than settled hypothetical cases, or we may give them equal weight. The doctrine of precedent in law gives settled actual cases more weight than settled hypothetical cases, though usually only when the settled cases

[3] For discussion of such conditions, see my *Natural Reasons*, ibid, ch 12.

are those of the same court or higher courts of the same jurisdiction; actual cases of lower courts or courts of other jurisdictions may be treated on a par with settled hypothetical cases. However, as we shall see, this difference in weight may only be significant under certain circumstances.

The *fourth* stage is the heart of the deliberative process. At this stage we engage in all-out theorizing, looking for hypotheses which account for the resolutions of issues we found at stage three. That is, we are trying to formulate hypotheses about the relationships between the conflicting reasons under various different circumstances present in the stage three cases, which account for those resolutions. To this end we examine the stage three cases for distinctive circumstances or dimensions which seem to enhance or diminish the weight of one of the conflicting reasons in relation to the other. When we have formulated such an hypothesis, we try to test it, by going back to stage three and looking for further settled cases in which the same reasons apply and in which the circumstances identified by the hypothesis are present. We thus go back and forth between stages three and four, looking for settled actual and hypothetical cases that help us to refine our hypotheses about the relationships between the conflicting reasons in various circumstances.

Finally, at the *fifth* stage, we work out the consequences of the best hypothesis we have arrived at for the original case at issue. That is, we apply that hypothesis about the relationships between the applicable reasons to the circumstances present in the case at issue. This hypothesis is a partial specification of a coherence function, which takes us from the rankings of alternatives involving various circumstances or dimensions by the conflicting reasons to an all-things-considered ranking.

This characterization of deliberation can be pictured in terms of a *deliberative matrix*. The data gathered at stage three can be represented as follows, where in each row, alternatives are ranked above or below one another by the applicable reasons.

	Reason X	Reason Y	Resolution, all-things-considered
case at	alt a	alt b	?
issue:	alt b	alt a	
settled	alt d	alt c	alt c
actual	alt c	alt d	alt d
cases:	alt e	alt f	alt e
	alt f	alt e	alt f
settled	alt g	alt h	alt h
hypothetical	alt h	alt g	alt g
cases:	alt j	alt i	alt j
	alt i	alt j	alt i
	etc		

I present the matrix with only two conflicting reasons, X and Y, merely for convenience; there is no restriction on the number of reasons that may be represented. (Indeed, multi-dimensional conflicts give rise to interesting theoretical questions.[4]) During stage four the alternatives are analysed and more fully characterized in terms of various circumstances and dimensions of the cases which may help to explain their resolution. These circumstances may be represented by adding propositions, p, q, etc, to the alternatives in each row. The content of such a proposition may be quantitative or non-quantitative. A hypothesis would then take the form: 'Reason X tends to outweigh Reason Y when it is the case that p, while Reason Y tends to outweigh Reason X when it is the case that q; when it is the case that both p and q, but not r, Reason X has more weight, but when r is present as well, Reason Y has more weight', and so on.[5]

Two points of clarification may be helpful. First, I do not in this article aim to give a full account of what is distinctive about legal reasoning in particular, but rather to consider what follows about legal reasoning from the fact that it has the general features of practical reasoning, understood along coherentist lines. My examples in the next section are intended to illustrate the application of the coherentist account of practical reasoning in general to legal problems, rather than to illuminate what is distinctive about legal reasoning in particular. I will go on to consider the distinctively legal doctrine of precedent in the context set by a view of legal reasoning as having the general features of coherentist practical reasoning. This is important to understand for purposes of my discussion below of the problem of intervening cases, since my eventual response to Kress in sections 7 and 8 turns on the features that legal reasoning shares with practical reason in general, on a coherentist view of it, with respect to the role of hypothetical cases. Such general features of coherentist practical reasoning limit the effects of the distinctively legal doctrine of precedent in giving rise to intervening case retroactivity,

[4] Which I pursue in *Natural Reasons*, ibid, chs 12 and 13.

[5] This schematization, applied to legal deliberation, may be compared to that employed by the programme HYPO, developed by Edwina Rissland and her student Kevin Ashley, and discussed in a Harvard Law School seminar conducted by Rissland on artificial intelligence and legal reasoning, Autumn Term 1987. See Kevin D. Ashley, *Modelling Legal Argument: Reasoning with Cases and Hypotheticals*, PhD dissertation, 1987, University of Massachussetts, Dept of Computer and Information Science. While there are many differences in detail between the two approaches, I do not believe there is any incompatibility in principle between them. The role of HYPO's 'dimensions' is similar to the role of my propositions p, q, etc in the analysis of actual and hypothetical settled cases at stage four. Perhaps I try to say a bit more than Rissland and Ashley do about the role of hypotheticals in reaching legal conclusions, in that the answers to hypothetical questions feed back into the resolution of the case at issue via the coherence function, but again I do not believe that what I say is incompatible with their approach. Perhaps the most striking difference is that over whether to use favourableness to conflicting legal doctrines or favourableness to plaintiff as opposed to defendant, as the basic means of organizing the data. Often, within a narrowly limited area of the law, such as trade secrets law, plaintiffs will typically represent one legal doctrine, and defendants another, so that the two approaches are in principle quite similar. However, the doctrine-oriented rather than party-oriented method of organization may have advantages when one comes to generalize beyond a narrowly limited area of the law, so that plaintiff and defendant no longer typically represent particular legal doctrines. By organizing the cases according to legal doctrines directly rather than by plaintiffs' and defendants' positions, one may hope to keep theoretical score as one moves from one area of law to another in which the same doctrines apply, and to bring insights about the relationships between legal doctrines from one area to the next.

Of course, different ways of perceiving what legal doctrines apply will yield different analyses, but that is the way the law is, and an analysis which reflects this relativity of conclusion to starting point may be illuminating. Moreover, we can in principle start with as many different legal doctrines as we think may be relevant; again, there is no need to restrict the number of reasons weighed against one another by the coherence function to two.

and thus illuminate the source of the problem. But I would certainly not claim that the generally coherentist character of legal reasoning as a kind of practical reasoning plus the features of precedent I consider provide a full account of what is distinctive about legal reasoning in particular; this is not my purpose. Second, I would expect the account and illustrations of practical reasoning to be controversial to the extent they represent a kind of deliberative rationality with respect to conflicting ends, values or reasons, the possibility of which has often been denied, for example, in favour of a view of practical reasoning as exclusively instrumental, or in favour of more radically sceptical or nihilistic views about practical rationality (in the legal context, consider certain views associated with the critical legal studies movement, or parodies thereof). However, I cannot join these issues here.

2. Some Examples of Legal and Ethical Deliberation Analysed

I have elsewhere considered in detail and at length a legal illustration of this general account of practical reasoning, the stages of deliberation, and the deliberative matrix. That discussion involved deliberation about the relationships between the conflicting legal doctrines of estoppel and of consideration in cases now usually covered by the doctrine of promissory estoppel.[6] I will not here give another lengthy and detailed illustration, but rather will give several sketchy illustrations. I hope in the former discussion to have persuaded readers that my account can be made to work in detail. In this discussion I rather aim to persuade readers that the account applies readily and intuitively in a wide range of cases. Accordingly I shall not work out the details of my applications here, but shall merely briefly indicate how the framework of my account would fit the examples.

Let us begin with the case of *California* v *Carney*.[7] In *Carney*, Fourth Amendment issues were raised by a warrantless police search of a motor home, parked in a downtown San Diego parking lot. The police had reason to believe that Carney, the owner of the motor home, was exchanging marijuana for sex acts. They observed a young boy enter the motor home and leave again an hour and a quarter later. On questioning by the police, the boy said that such an exchange had just occurred. The police then knocked on the door, and when Carney came out they entered the motor home without a warrant and found marijuana. A further search of the vehicle at the police station revealed more marijuana, in cupboards and in the refrigerator. The parking lot where the warrantless search occurred was a short distance from a courthouse where a warrant could easily have been obtained.

The case and its oral argument, rich in hypothetical cases, have been analysed by Edwina Rissland to illustrate the idea of a 'dimension', which is used by the case-based reasoning programme HYPO to generate hypothetical cases.[8] My treatment of the case essentially adapts her analysis to my framework, and illustrates, I believe, the compatibility of my framework and the notions of a deliberative matrix

[6] See *Natural Reasons*, op cit, ch 11.
[7] *California* v *Carney*, 105 SCt 2066 (1985).
[8] Op cit n 3.

and a coherence function, with Rissland's dimension-based analysis. As she points out, *Carney* is a case in which there is a conflict between a citizen's expectations of privacy, protected by the Fourth Amendment's prohibition of unreasonable searches and seizures, and the responsibilities and desires of the police to investigate and control drug use and other prohibited activities. Thus, the first row of our matrix for the case at issue involves at least two kinds of legal reasons: I shall refer to them as reasons of Privacy, and reasons of the Police Power. The alternatives in the case at issue are to allow or to disallow the warrantless search of the motor home in *Carney* under the Fourth Amendment. Reasons of Privacy would favour disallowing the search, while reasons of the Police Power would favour allowing it. We want to discover how reasons of Privacy and reasons of the Police Power are related to one another with respect to warrantless searches. Settled actual cases at the next several rows of the matrix tell us that reasons of Privacy are augmented relative to those of the Police Power in circumstances in which the warrantless search at issue is of someone's home; if we sum up these circumstances in proposition p, we can hypothesize that Privacy is augmented relative to the Police Power when it is the case that p. By contrast, settled cases tell us, the Police Power is augmented relative to Privacy when the warrantless search at issue is of a vehicle; if we sum up the latter circumstances in proposition q, we can hypothesize that Privacy is diminished relative to the Police Power when it is the case that q. We have thus begun to specify a coherence function which weighs Privacy against the Police Power in various circumstances.

While these hypotheses about the relations between Privacy and the Police Power are well supported by settled cases, they really only set the stage for the *Carney* problem, since the motor home in *Carney* is both a home and a vehicle. We need a finer analysis of relevant circumstances in order to resolve the conflict in this case. Thus we look for other settled cases, actual or hypothetical, in which these two reasons come into conflict, in circumstances in which the home–vehicle distinction is difficult to draw. On the basis of such cases, we try to arrive at a hypothesis that will help police to draw the home–vehicle distinction in a reliable and straightforward way in cases in which aspects of both home and vehicle are present; that is, we would like to find a 'bright-line' distinction, which will not require police officers to make excessively subtle or difficult determinations. We will try various hypotheses about the relevant circumstances, or dimensions of cases, and will test them against various actual and hypothetical cases.

The fact that the thing to be searched is a vehicle seems to augment the Police Power reasons relative to those of Privacy in part because it is inherently mobile, such that requiring a warrant would leave it time to 'get away' and would greatly frustrate legitimate exercises of the Police Power, and also because vehicles are not usually used as homes, and thus not the objects of normal expectations of privacy. These hypotheses are developed and tested in oral argument by reference to hypothetical cases in which vehicles are also homes, but some of which are more inherently mobile, or more home-like than others, owing to varying circumstances and dimensions. The presence of wheels is obviously dispensable to inherent mobility in the case of most boats, with respect to which presumably reasons of the Police Power predominate. Nor is the presence of wheels decisive in the case of motor homes with wheels but which are not self-propelling and which are permanently connected to utilities supplies, with respect to which presumably reasons of Privacy predominate. Location in a temporary parking lot as opposed to a permanent motor home park strengthens the case with respect to inherent mobility and hence with respect to the weight of Police Power reasons. But a counter-example to that hypothesis would seem to be the case of someone very poor who cannot afford a permanent spot for his vehicle but lives in it behind curtains, on the move from day to day. The presence of the normal accoutrements of a home, such as a refrigerator, in a vehicle, may strengthen reasons of Privacy; but again we would seem to have a counter-example when the refrigerator is used solely to store marijuana, as seemed to be the case in *Carney*, and not for home-like purposes.

From among these various circumstances and dimensions of hypothetical cases, the best hypothesis will focus on objective factors that are straightforward for the police to ascertain before deciding whether to search without a warrant or not (as the contents of a refrigerator are not), so as to provide police with 'bright-line' guidance. This is because the investigation needed to apply an excessively subtle distinction will make for a prior, unprincipled defeat of reasons of Privacy, while a strong presumption in favour of home-likeness to accommodate all unusual uses of vehicles as homes would in effect eliminate the vehicle exception to the warrant requirement and would thus excessively compromise the Police Power. Thus the need for bright-line guidance in effect provides a way for the theory to get around the apparent counter-example to inherent mobility hypothesis provided by the poor person who lives in his car. The case does not really provide a counter-example, after all, since the police cannot tell that such unusual vehicles are homes without privacy-infringing investigation; and it is already settled by the vehicle exception that the alternative of disallowing searches of *any* vehicles which might possibly be homes has been ruled out. The majority opinion in *Carney* indicates in effect that the best hypothesis makes the relation between reasons of Privacy and those of the Police Power in cases involving vehicles that may be homes turn on objective indications of mobility and use for transportation, rather than on the more difficult-to-ascertain home-like uses of the vehicle. If the presence of the former characteristics is expressed by proposition r, the majority's hypothesis, which they implicitly regard as supported by the hypothetical cases considered, in light of the need for bright-line guidance, is that when it is the case that r, as it was in *Carney*, reasons of the Police Power outweigh reasons of Privacy, and thus support the warrantless search at issue. By contrast, the dissenting opinions seem to prefer a hypothesis which gives more of a role to the home-like character of the place in strengthening reasons of Privacy.

Equal Protection cases raised under the US Constitution are a fertile source of illustrations of the coherentist framework, as the jurisprudence of varying degrees of relationship to various state interests served by challenged classifications lends itself immediately to representation within a deliberative matrix. In discussing several such cases I shall not stop to assign labels, p, q, etc, to the propositions employed in hypotheses about the relationships among the conflicting reasons in various circumstances. I shall merely identify the general categories of reasons in play, and try to draw out the hypotheses about the relations between the reasons in play that are implicitly tested by appeal to various settled cases. It should be evident, however, how labels could be assigned and hypotheses located within a deliberative matrix. In Equal Protection cases one category of legal reasons is provided by the Equal Protection Clause itself: reasons of Nondiscrimination, which oppose legal classifications which fail to treat similarly situated citizens in similar ways. Further categories of reasons are provided by whatever state interests are supposed to be served by the challenged classification.

In *Parham* v *Hughes*[9], for example, the father of an illegitimate child challenged a law which prevented him from recovering for the wrongful death of his child, where an unmarried father who had filed papers to legitimate the child, or the mother of the illegitimate child, would have been allowed to recover. If he could be regarded as similarly situated with other parents of illegitimate children who were allowed to recover for wrongful death, then reasons of Nondiscrimination would favour striking the statute down. However, the state considered that it had an interest in promoting the integrity of the legitimate family unit, and that reasons of Legitimacy favoured restricting recovery for wrongful death to unmarried fathers who had filed to legitimate their children and unmarried mothers. The implication seems to be that such a restriction would provide incentives to unmarried fathers to file to legitimate their children. Moreover, the state also claimed to have an interest in avoiding difficult problems of proof of paternity, and that reasons of Provability favoured the restriction of wrongful death suits for the death of children born illegitimate to fathers who had filed to legitimate and mothers, whose identity would rarely be in doubt. Thus we seem to have a conflict between reasons of Nondiscrimination, on the one hand, and reasons of Legitimacy and of Provability, on the other.

The court held that this state scheme did not violate Equal Protection or Due Process by discriminating against unmarried fathers relative to unmarried mothers, because fathers and mothers of illegitimate children are not similarly situated since, under Georgia law, only fathers *can* by voluntary unilateral action make an illegitimate child legitimate. That is, the plurality opinion seems implicitly to support the hypothesis that when it is the case that men and women are not similarly situated *owing to a difference in their legally imposed abilities and status*, that difference may provide a basis for a statutory classification which does not constitute invidious discrimination, such that, when such a classification is related in the right way to the right kinds of state interests, the latter outweigh reasons of Nondiscrimination.

[9] 441 US 347, 99 SCt 1742 (1979).

The dissent appeals to a hypothetical case to refute the plurality's hypothesis. Justice White writes:

> There is a startling circularity in this argument. The issue before the Court is whether Georgia may require unmarried fathers, but not unmarried mothers, to have pursued the statutory legitimization procedure in order to bring suit for the wrongful death of their children. Seemingly, it is irrelevant that as a matter of state law mothers may not legitimate their children, for they are not required to do so in order to maintain a wrongful-death action. That only fathers *may* resort to the legitimization process cannot dissolve the sex-discrimination in *requiring* them to. Under the plurality's bootstrap rationale, a State could require that women, but not men, pass a course in order to receive a taxi license, simply by limiting admission to the course to women.

In the taxi licence hypothetical, men and women would not be similarly situated, owing to their differing legally imposed abilities, ie their differing abilities to enroll in the course. But here it is clearly absurd to suppose that this prior discrimination, unscrutinized, could provide a justification for further discrimination in the form of a statutory classification requiring only women to pass the course in order to get a licence. Thus the hypothetical case provides a counter-example to the plurality's hypothesis. The implication of the dissenting opinion is that the embedded distinction must itself be scrutinized, and not merely taken as given. In *Parham*, the embedded distinction was one with respect to the ability to file papers to legitimate: only men were able to do so. It is hard to see how a rule making it impossible for women to file papers to legitimate children serves either the state interest in promoting the legitimate family unit or in avoiding proof of paternity issues. Permitting women to file as well as men would have no adverse effects whatsoever on either of these state interests.

The dissent goes on to appeal to another counter-example, this time a type of actual rather than hypothetical case, to the hypothesis that reasons of Legitimacy outweigh those of Nondiscrimination if allowing members of one class but not another to sue for wrongful death serves the state interest in promoting the integrity of the legitimate family unit. The dissent points out that unmarried mothers and fathers who file to legitimate but remain unmarried defy the integrity of the legitimate family unit, just as do fathers who fail to file, but the former are allowed to sue for wrongful death while the latter are not.

In *Craig* v *Boren*, the question was whether a statute prohibiting the sale of weakly alcoholic beer to males under 21 and females under 18 constituted denial to males aged 18 to 21 of equal protection of the law. On behalf of the statute it was urged that statistical evidence about the relative tendencies of males and females aged 18 to 21 to drink and drive supported the gender line. Thus we have a conflict between reasons of Nondiscrimination and the state interest in Preventing Drunk Driving. The Court rejects the hypothesis that reasons of Nondiscrimination can be overcome by the interest in Preventing Drunk Driving when the latter is served by 'statistically measured but loose-fitting generalities concerning the drinking tendencies of aggregate groups'. In doing so it appeals to hypothetical variations on the *Craig* v *Boren* statute involving statistically supported ethnic or racial lines instead of gender lines aimed at alcohol regulation. The assumption made is that such ethnic or racial lines would not be acceptable, despite statistical support, and that reasons of Nondiscrimination would predominate in such cases: 'In fact, social science studies that have uncovered quantifiable differences in drinking tendencies dividing along both racial and ethnic lines strongly suggest the need for application of the Equal Protection Clause in preventing discriminatory treatment that almost certainly would be perceived as invidious.' The Court illustrates its comments with reference to statistical evidence to the effect that Jews, Italian Catholics, and black teenagers tend not to be problem drinkers, in contrast to whites and North American Indians.

Finally, consider the uses of hypothetical and actual cases in ethical argument, as illustrated by the debate between Stephen Pepper and David Luban over whether lawyers in an adversary system should help their clients to do legal but unethical acts. Pepper argues that under many circumstances the answer is 'yes'. He argues roughly as follows. We hold the value of individual autonomy to be more important than getting people to do the ethically right act in a wide range of cases; for example, we allow that people should have the legal power to disinherit a child for marrying outside the faith, even though we may agree that it would be wrong to do so. Individual autonomy in our complex society requires, in many cases, legal assistance; only with the help of lawyers can people, in many circumstances, be 'first class citizens'. Therefore lawyers should give their clients the legal help required for individual autonomy even when it permits them to do unethical acts.

Luban replies by arguing that, while it is true that, since exercising autonomy is good, helping people exercise autonomy is good, this is only half the story. 'The other half is that since doing bad things is bad, helping people do bad things is bad. The two factors must be weighed against each other, and this Pepper does not do'. That is, Pepper's general hypothesis that when helping someone to do a legal but unethical act is favoured by reasons of autonomy, reasons of autonomy prevail, is too crude. Luban appeals to an analogous hypothetical case to defeat the unqualified hypothesis:

> Compare this case: The automobile, by making it easier to get around, increases human autonomy; hence, other things equal, it is morally good to repair the car of someone who is unable by himself to get it to run. But such considerations can hardly be invoked to defend the morality of fixing the getaway car of an armed robber, assuming that you know in advance what the purpose of the car is. The moral wrong of assisting the robber outweighs the abstract moral goodness of augmenting the robber's autonomy.[10]

Not only may reasons of autonomy sometimes be outweighed by the wrongness of the act in question, but even if the balance of reasons favours allowing the agent to do the unethical act himself, it does not necessarily follow that it will also favour helping him to do it. The balance between autonomy and conflicting reasons may

[10] David Luban, 'The Lysistratian Prerogative: A Response to Stephen Pepper', [1986] *American Bar Foundation Research Journal*, at 639.

be struck differently in different circumstances, ie with respect to omitting to prevent as opposed to positively aiding.

Another argument Pepper makes is that allowing lawyers to weigh the wrongness of acts and thus act as screens to filter out certain legally permissible acts is to submit individuals to 'rule by an oligarchy of lawyers'.[11] The implication of the term 'oligarchy' is that such weighing and screening by lawyers would constitute an elitist centralization of ethical decision-making highly threatening to the value of individual autonomy, and that, when this would be the result, reasons of autonomy should prevail. Luban offers a counter-example to this implied hypothesis:

> . . . there is no oligarchy of lawyers, actual or potential, to worry about. An oligarchy is a group of people ruling *in concert*, whereas lawyers who refuse to execute projects to which they object on moral grounds will do so as individuals, without deliberating collectively with other lawyers. The worry about a hidden Central Committee of lawyers evaporates when we realize that the committee will never hold a meeting, and that its members don't even know they are on it. An analogy will clarify this. No doubt throughout history people have often been dissuaded from undertaking immoral projects by the anger, threats, and uncooperativeness of their spouses. It would scarcely make sense, however, to worry that this amounts to subjecting autonomous action 'to rule by an oligarchy of spouses'. There *is* no oligarchy of spouses.

Luban seems to accept for the sake of argument that screening by a true Central Committee might well be intolerable. But if weighing and screening by spouses does not constitute an elitist centralization of ethical decision-making highly threatening to the value of individual autonomy, it is not clear how this can be regarded as the result when we substitute 'lawyers' for 'spouses'. Indeed, Luban suggests that informal social pressures are an essential complement to legal rules in regulating harmful behaviour. (Note that I am not here endorsing Luban's conclusions, but only using his arguments to illustrate certain characteristic features of deliberation.)

3. *Hypothetical Cases as Thought Experiments*

The role of the settled cases appealed to in the above examples of deliberation is analogous in some respects to the role of data in scientific theorizing. In both areas, that is, one looks both for relevant data, or clear cases, and for generalizations that account for what seems to be clearly the case (though of course such apparent clarity is not infallible in either area), and uses the latter generalizations to make determinations about further cases. In neither area is the best account of the data deductively entailed by the data. Nevertheless, in both areas the data in some sense determines the best theory (or theories, in the case of a tie or moderate degree of underdetermination of theory by data). The best theory (or theories—I will hereafter omit the qualification, but it continues to apply) is some function of the

[11] Stephen Pepper, 'The Lawyer's Amoral Ethical Role: A Defense, A Problem, and Some Possibilities', [1986] *American Bar Foundation Research Journal*, at 617.

data, in the sense that if the best theory were other than what it is, the data would have to be different in some way. This is just another way of saying that situations that are relevantly similar in respect of data must be treated consistently in theoretical respects, or, more briefly, that like cases should be treated alike. With respect to legal deliberation, this general consistency requirement is that cases relevantly similar, in respect of applicable legal doctrines and distinguishing circumstances, should be similarly resolved.

Of course, the analogy should not be strained; some of the general roles of ethical and legal deliberation and theorizing are very different from those of scientific theorizing. Scientific theories are used to predict what will happen on the basis of causal theories that account for what has happened in well-designed experiments, and sometimes also for what it is thought would have happened under significant counterfactual circumstances. The basis for scientific hypotheses are thus experimental data and sometimes intuitions gathered in 'thought experiments', such as Einstein's famous thought experiments about flashlights emitting beams of light in trains travelling at close to the speed of light. Scientific hypotheses generate predictions which are then tested against the results of further experiments.

By contrast, ethical and legal deliberation can hardly be described as having the role of predicting what will be done on the basis of causal theories. Rather, it has a normative role: to give guidance in extending consistently to the case at issue a series of settled ethical or legal judgments about what should be done when the applicable ethical or legal reasons conflict. Its normative hypotheses thus aim to account for clear resolutions of past cases in which the relevant reasons stood in conflict, and also for clear resolutions of significant hypothetical cases, designed to test the relationships between the conflicting reasons. Deliberative hypotheses are used to generate not mere predictions of decisions and actions, but decisions and actions themselves; hypotheses cannot be tested against the very decisions and actions they generate. Rather, they are tested against cases, both actual and hypothetical, in which the right answer about how a conflict of reasons should be resolved is settled.[12]

Despite the differences between scientific, causal theorizing, and deliberative, normative theorizing, it is important to recognize the way in which both kinds of theorizing are responsible to the data to be explained. The requirement that the sought-after hypothesis explains the data can be seen as the source of the deliberative requirement of consistency, the general requirement that like cases be treated alike. Some philosophers have regarded it as puzzling how one could hold that both:

[12] I do not suggest that scientific, ethical or legal deliberation are to be understood instrumentally rather than realistically; it is common ground between instrumentalism and realism that theoretical propositions should be able to be used in practical roles, eg to predict, explain or guide. I am concerned here to avoid overstating the analogy between the practical roles of scientific and deliberative theorizing rather than to take a position on the further issues that divide instrumental and realistic views of theories.

(1) the right answer about which alternative should be done is not entailed by the nonevaluative facts about the alternatives (*nonreductionism*: what should be done does not reduce to nonevaluative facts about the alternatives)

and:

(2) one must treat cases alike in respect of nonevaluative facts alike, so that if there is a difference between two cases in respect of what should be done, there must be some difference between them with respect to the nonevaluative facts about the alternatives as well (*supervenience*: what should be done supervenes on nonevaluative facts about the alternatives).

While there is no logical incompatibility between (1) and (2), the puzzlement about how they can both hold can be expressed by asking: If the right answer is not entailed by the nonevaluative facts, then what is the source of the requirement that cases alike in nonevaluative respects be treated alike?[13] However, recognition of the way in which right answers to questions about what should be done reflects hypotheses that are required to explain the data about settled cases provides a response to this puzzlement. The best theory about the data is not entailed by—cannot be deduced from—the data. Nevertheless, it is essential to the notion of a theory responsible to data that the best theory, whatever it may be, treats like cases alike. The source of this requirement is the essential explanatory aspirations of theories: a theory the content of which varies independently of the data it purports to account for to that extent does no explanatory work. This remains true even though the best theory is not entailed by the data.[14]

Thus, the requirement that like cases be treated alike has its source in the theoretical nature of judgments about what should be done when reasons conflict, which is highlighted by coherence accounts. Moreover, the data to which theories about what should be done are responsible are settled cases, both actual and hypothetical. If in general the role of settled cases in deliberation is somewhat analogous to that of experimental data in scientific theorizing, then the role of hypothetical cases in particular may be regarded as somewhat analogous to that of thought experiments.[15] It is important for our understanding of the requirement that like cases be treated alike that we include settled hypothetical cases, cases the answer to which would be clear were they to arise, as well as settled actual cases among the data to be explained. For reasons that will emerge in what follows, this is particularly important in the case of legal deliberation, where the general requirement that like cases be treated alike must be distinguished from the further specific requirement imposed by the doctrine of precedent. My examples in the previous section make clear that, since legal deliberation and argument often turn not merely on settled actual cases but also on settled hypothetical cases, effective legal reasoning often requires one to discover or construct revealing hypothetical

[13] See, for example, Simon Blackburn, *Spreading the Word* (Oxford, Clarendon Press, 1984), ch 6.

[14] For further discussion of supervenience, irreducibility and explanation, see my *Natural Reasons*, op cit, ch 14.

[15] The effective postulation of hypothetical cases thus has something in common with effective experimental design.

cases[16]; a coherence account provides a framework for understanding the function of hypothetical cases in legal reasoning. Hypothetical cases are not merely *posed* by lawyers and judges, but *answers* to questions about how they should be resolved are often taken for granted in a way which the argument of the case at issue depends on. The answers to hypothetical cases may be implicitly assumed rather than explicitly stated, but nevertheless they are often depended on in the reasoning of opinions, in a way that may be explicitly represented within a deliberative matrix. This is to say that legal hypotheses are responsible to data about settled hypothetical cases as well as settled actual cases; both are among the cases with respect to which the requirement that like cases be treated alike must be understood. Nevertheless, as we shall see, the doctrine of precedent imposes a further constraint on legal deliberation in giving actual settled cases *more weight* than that of hypothetical settled cases for purposes of determining what counts as treating like cases alike.

4. *Kress on Coherence Accounts and Retroactivity: the Problem of Intervening Cases*

In an interesting article entitled 'Legal Reasoning and Coherence Theories: Dworkin's Rights Thesis, Retroactivity, and the Linear Order of Decision', Kenneth Kress argues that the role within coherence theories such as Dworkin's of coherence with past decisions and deference to precedent makes for retroactive applications of the law. In Kress's view, retroactivity may occur if settled law changes between the occurrence of the events being litigated and the adjudication of them, since at adjudication the most coherent account of settled cases will be responsible to actual cases decided after the occurrence of the events litigated. What Kress calls the 'ripple effect'

> . . . depends upon legal rights being a function of settled law and upon the temporal gap between events being litigated and their eventual adjudication. Judicial decisions often change the settled law. Often, if not always, the settled law will be changed between the occurrence of events being litigated and their eventual adjudication. In consequence, a litigant's rights will sometimes also be changed. If changes in the settled law change the dispositive legal right, a litigant who would have prevailed given the legal rights existing at the time of the occurrence will lose because he no longer has that right at the time of adjudication. The opposite is true of the opposing litigant.
> This is retroactive application of the law.[17]

I shall refer to the problem Kress identifies as *the problem of intervening cases.* Kress regards this as a particularly serious problem for Dworkin's rights-oriented version of a coherence account of legal reasoning, since Dworkin works his account

[16] I do not suggest the existence of a positive professional obligation imposed on court or counsel to discover or construct hypothetical cases, but of a normative requirement that arises from characteristic features of legal reasoning as a species of practical reasoning. It may be that my account of the latter is particularly influenced by characteristic features of the legal system in the United States, such as the prominent role of the posing of 'hypos' in Supreme Court oral argument, in legal education, etc.

[17] (1984) 72 *Cal LR* 369, at 380.

up in the course of criticizing Hart's account for the scope it gives to judicial discretion and for the retroactive applications of the law which judicial discretion involves.

However, Kress regards the problem as generalizable: it applies to any coherence account which is conservative in the sense that it adheres to the dominant conception of precedent. According to the latter, legal truths depend in part on prior legal decisions. The general form of the problem is that the best theory about settled law may change between the time the events occurred and the time they are litigated, owing to intervening legal decisions. 'The mere historical fact of a prior decision influences the decisions in later cases, and thus the law, because it enlarges the settled law with which later decisions must cohere.'[18] This is in effect just to say that the prevalent conception of precedent gives more weight to settled actual cases than to settled hypothetical cases for purposes of determining what counts as treating like cases alike.

5. *A First Response: Prospective Application*

What is the correct response to or diagnosis of the problem of intervening cases? Let us first briefly consider and dismiss, with Kress, the possibility that present legal practice should be changed so as to base legal decisions on law settled at the time the events adjudicated occurred rather than at the time of adjudication. Kress suggests that to give decisions only prospective effect in this way is particularly appropriate when decisions are legislative in character; as he puts it: 'The doctrine of prospective overruling is the legacy of legal realism, the doctrine that maintains that judges legislate'. However, Kress considers and rejects this possible response to his problem, on theoretical grounds and on pragmatic grounds (such as the difficulties of determining which events are relevant for purposes of dating the law to be applied). I find his pragmatic arguments against this line of response fairly persuasive.[19]

[18] Kress, ibid, at 400.

[19] At 386–7: 'It is unlikely that the revised . . . theory could be developed in detail, or utilized by judges if it could, for several reasons. First, the possibility of temporally extended events and transactions raises difficult problems in determining the date of the law to be applied. These problems are compounded if several related but separable transactions are being litigated and there are multiple issues. The prospect of applying the law at different times to different but related aspects of a complicated transaction raises unappealing complexity. Further and perhaps insuperable complexity arises if it is possible to analyze the overall transaction in multiple ways into different temporal components. Unless we can be sure that one temporal analysis will be superior to all others, we will need rules to choose among the various analyses. More important, it is unclear what precedential effect should be given to a decision that applies law from many time periods, law that by definition differs from the law that would be applied to an event that occurred at the time of adjudication if litigated at that time.'

See especially Kress's note 77, commenting on the line of criminal procedure cases involving prospective-only application. Kress distinguishes the 'more common form' of prospective-only application, which nevertheless applies intervening decisions to pending cases, from the more extreme form that would be necessary to avoid ripple effect retroactivity, which would deny the 'new' rule to pending cases as well. For the 'more common form', see *Linkletter* v *Walker*, 381 US 618 (1965), which did apply the intervening decision to pending cases.

It may be objected to Kress that he has not addressed the line of criminal procedure cases subsequent to *Linkletter* which explicitly discuss the application of intervening decisions to pending cases. See *Stovall* v *Denno*, 388 US 293 (1967); *Desist* v *US*, 394 US 244 (1969), especially Justice Harlan's dissent; *Shea* v *Lousianna*, 470 US 51 (1985), especially Justice White's dissent. The Court divides over the problem of intervening cases, and moreover, seems to change its own position. *Stovall* and *Desist* come down in favour of nonretroactivity by refusing to apply the

continued on page 237

However, if Kress's own objections to giving intervening cases prospective effect only are persuasive, his problem is not just a problem for coherentists; it cannot be avoided by 'frank' assimilation of adjudication to legislation. Moreover, even if we assume for the sake of argument that the correct response to the problem of intervening cases is to give them prospective effect only, I am not persuaded that this response would be inconsistent with a coherence account. To the extent that retroactivity is the concomitant of a conception of precedent that gives more weight to actual than hypothetical cases, a coherentist could argue that it is the fact that actual decisions may change the law, through the operation of precedent, that makes prospective application appropriate. But this law-changing effect of precedent should not be confused with 'legislative' discretion to make law for the case at hand; these are two logically distinct issues. That is, the occurrence of a judicial decision may change what the law requires from that point on, through the operation of precedent, even though the judge had no antecedent discretion as to how that case should be decided.[20] Even if only mistaken intervening decisions can change the law, as Dworkin urges (see section 8) below, nevertheless a mistaken decision that changes the law through the operation of precedent is logically distinct from quasi-legislative discretion to make new law.

So, if the correct response to the problem of intervening cases is prospective-only application, a coherence account is not thereby defeated, since there is no inconsistency between a coherence account and this response. On the other hand, Kress's pragmatic reasons against this response to the problem are equally valid given legislative accounts of judicial reasoning. So if this response is ruled out, it is not only coherence accounts that are left with a problem. Let us thus suppose, for the sake of argument, that the prospective-only response to the problem of intervening cases is to be ruled out (but for a qualification relating to changes in settled cases with extra-judicial sources, see the end of section 7 below).

6. *A Second Response: It Is Not So Bad*

Consider a second possible response envisaged by Kress to the problem of intervening cases, namely, that of accepting the retroactivity in question as, for one reason or another, not all that bad. And at any rate, a coherentist might add, the

continued from page 236
intervening decisions to pending cases in which the relevant events of police conduct occurred prior to the intervening decisions. However, Justice Harlan's dissent in *Desist*, favouring precedent over nonretroactivity, becomes the Court's position in *Shea*, where Justice White dissents, arguing on nonretroactivity grounds. A nice self-referential problem of intervening cases about the problem of intervening cases, the logic of which I will not even attempt to untangle!

In reply, it should be kept in mind that the degree to which the Court is willing to consider and countenance intervening case retroactivity in the criminal procedure context, where police reliance on earlier cases is in question, may well not generalize. That is, an acceptable degree of retroactivity with respect to police reliance, which cuts in *favour* of criminal defendants, may not be acceptable in general, that is, where the intervening case might cut *against* criminal defendants and undermine *their* reliance rather than police reliance, or where it might change the positions of civil litigants. It would be interesting to develop an integrated view of retroactivity doctrine within and without the criminal procedure context, and to try to isolate the special effects of the criminal procedure context on retroactivity doctrine, but I cannot do so here.

[20] Kress does allow for this type of view, at 386; he does, at 382, distinguish judicial discretion from judicial creation of law.

problem of intervening cases is not a problem for coherence accounts in particular, since they will still involve less retroactivity than accounts of adjudication as *ex ante* discretionary do.[21]

Just how objectionable would intervening case retroactivity be? Perhaps coherentists should not regard it as a matter for particular concern. Kress offers Dworkin something like this possible position in a footnote (though in fact this is not Dworkin's response to the problem):

> Dworkin believes that the unfairness of retroactive application of law is not fully explained by the rule of law requirements to give prior notice, satisfy justified expectations, and the like. . . . Dworkin must take this position because the controversial nature of right answers even when they exist means, as Dworkin admits, that right answers often cannot be demonstrated and therefore often are not known in advance. . . . Dworkin's objection to retroactivity appears to focus on the importance of giving a principled justification for enforcing judicial decisions. Dworkin's concern with retroactivity derives from the belief that creating and applying new rights at the time of adjudication cannot be given a principled justification. . . . Arguably, therefore, ripple effect retroactivity with its consequential disruption of expectations and failure to provide notice is not the kind of retroactivity that would concern Dworkin.[22]

Though Kress's article was published before *Law's Empire*, this suggestion seems reasonably consistent with Dworkin's views in *Law's Empire* about respect for precedent and coherence as expressing the integrity and personification of the community. On the above suggestion, people would simply be on notice that their claims were subject to requirements of coherence with possible intervening precedents. Perhaps one could justify the retroactivity to people on the grounds of their membership in a community with the virtues of integrity, which unfortunately entail such retroactivity. People could of course try, perhaps through their lawyers, to anticipate intervening precedents as best they could, by identifying any relevant settled hypothetical cases. But the possibility would remain that an unsettled hypothetical case might become a decided actual case and thus create an unanticipated intervening precedent.

We might fill out this possible line of response further. I claimed there is no inconsistency between admitting that the mere fact that a judge has decided a case may change the law and claiming that in deciding it he has no discretion. Perhaps the mere fact that the judge has decided the case changes the law, not through an exercise of discretion, but as a result of his efforts to discover the right answer. The retroactivity problem may arise because in law, as is not the case in science, the mere fact of theorizing by a judge itself counts as a further piece of data for later theorizing. But perhaps so long as the judge can give a principled justification for his decision, even if it was not reliably predictable, the change to the law represented by his decision is not arbitrary. Recognizing such changes, it might be argued, is itself supported by the considerations of coherence and community

[21] This *tu quoque* on behalf of coherence accounts seems to be borne out by the Court's oscillation between precedent and nonretroactivity in *Stovall*, *Desist* and *Shea*, op cit, where the issues do not arise as a consequence of any particular theory of adjudication.

[22] Kress, op cit, at 384.

integrity that support respect for precedent. People know that the legal system gives weight, in this timeless sense, to intervening precedents, even if they do not know that they are ahead of time. Is this really any more objectionable than not knowing the right answer itself ahead of time?

Of course, we accept that it may be hard to determine what the best account of settled cases would say about the case at issue, before it is decided. What the best theory really is, and how it bears on the case at issue, may be quite controversial.[23] But these are epistemological problems, not problems of true retroactivity; changes in our knowledge of the law should be distinguished from changes in the law. It simply is often extremely difficult to know what the law requires; perhaps only the best lawyers know for sure, and we cannot afford them. But nevertheless we are held to the law, and we must do the best we can to understand what it is. It is unfortunate, and gives rise to unfairness, that the law is so complex and difficult, and that access to it so expensive and restricted; but again these are not problems of true retroactivity. It might be objected that if from a litigant's practical point of view the effects of the 'mere' epistemological problem and those of 'true' retroactivity are much the same, and we can live with the former, then the latter cannot be so bad. But the stubborn intuition remains that true retroactivity is somehow more profoundly unfair than are the effects of the epistemological problem. Let us therefore, for the sake of argument, also put the 'not-so-bad' response aside.

7. The Source of the Problem: Coherentism vs Precedent

Consider what features of a system of decision-making are necessary or sufficient to give rise to the problem of intervening cases. As we have seen, coherence accounts of practical reasoning give settled cases an important role as the data, so to speak, to which the theories or principles sought in deliberation are responsible. Moreover, coherence accounts impose a general requirement with respect to settled law of treating like cases alike (which I will sometimes refer to as 'the weaker requirement'). That is, legal truths are a function of, among other things, settled law;[24] resolution of the actual case at hand must be consistent with the resolution of comparable settled cases. While, concerning any particular settled case, it is possible that the best theory of settled cases may show that it is mistaken, if theoretical coherence overall with settled cases is the standard, then it is not possible for all settled cases to be mistaken; hence coherentist consistency involves a certain element of conservatism. However, while these elements are present in coherence accounts of legal reasoning in particular, they are not sufficient to give rise to the problem of intervening cases or any distinctive issues about retroactivity. The latter only arise in virtue of a further requirement (that I will sometimes refer to as 'the stronger requirement', since it is not entailed by the weaker requirement),

[23] This paper is not intended to address the problem of whether systematically wicked law is really law; on this see, for example, Ronald Dworkin, *Law's Empire* (London, Fontana Press, 1986), at 102–8.

[24] Kress, op cit, at 380.

imposed by the doctrine of precedent in the legal context in particular, namely, that actual settled cases are to be given more weight, in virtue of having actually been decided by a court, than hypothetical settled cases, or, in Kress's words, that 'prior decisions are to be accorded weight which may influence the outcomes in later cases merely by virtue of the fact that the decisions have occurred'.[25] Since the stronger requirement imposed by the doctrine of precedent is not a necessary feature of all coherence theories, Kress is wrong to the extent that he suggests that the prospect of intervening case retroactivity arises for all coherence theories.[26]

Decision theory provides one illustration of coherentist reasoning minus the stronger requirement of precedent; within decision theory, coherence with settled preferences provides a standard for the determination of problematic preferences, but settled preferences about actual alternatives that have issued in actual decisions are not given greater weight in principle than settled preferences about hypothetical cases. Consideration of decision theory, in which no problem of intervening cases arises, will thus help to bring into focus the way in which the problem depends on the stronger requirement of precedent.

Suppose a decision theorist is trying to help a decision-maker arrive at decisions about certain difficult issues where his criteria of choice or goals conflict. The decision theorist aims to discover the decision-maker's indifference curves with respect to those conflicting criteria or goals in order to help him to make the decision among the actual alternatives that places him on his highest indifference curve. To do this the decision theorist must depend on data provided by the decision-maker about what his preferences clearly are or would be in various cases which are easier for him to decide about than the case at issue is. These cases need not all involve feasible alternatives; some may be purely hypothetical. The exercise is one of extrapolating consistently from the set of settled preferences to a determination of the case at issue. Perhaps some of the settled preferences of the decision-maker are outliers and cannot be regarded as consistent with the rest within any theoretically acceptable representation of the decision-maker's preference space; such settled preferences may be disregarded as 'mistakes'. But it is of the nature of this exercise that there cannot be too many such mistakes. Settled preferences are here the data for which the decision theorist's representation of the decision-maker's preference space must account. Theories may tell us that some of the data they aim to account for are suspect or corrupt, and must be disregarded, but ultimately theories are supported by data. The basis for regarding some settled preferences as mistaken is their failure to cohere with the rest; thus

[25] Kress, op cit, at 400.

[26] At 398: '. . . since nothing in the argument has relied on the details of any coherence theory, it should be clear that ripple effects will occur in all coherence theories. . . .'. See also 371: 'The ripple effect will occur in any coherence theory with a principle of conservation. In adjudication, precedent provides the conservative element.' However, compare his concessions to the distinction between coherence theories in general and the legal doctrine of precedent in particular at the very end of the article, 401–2. It is possible that, despite the way Kress introduces his problem by reference to coherence theories in general, not just in law (369–70), the remarks quoted above should be interpreted as restricted to legal contexts, which involve the doctrine of precedent in particular. But my primary purpose is to address Kress's interesting problem on the merits, and the substantive issues I consider arise however Kress's remarks are interpreted.

there cannot be a basis for regarding too many of them as mistaken (though, of course, just what counts as 'too many' is difficult to specify).

The conservatism of this interpretative exercise is also attributed by a coherence account to legal reasoning: not too many settled cases can be regarded as mistakes, or the basis for regarding them as mistaken is itself undermined. However, these elements of conservatism do not entail that settled actual cases should be given more weight than settled hypothetical cases, and hence they are not sufficient to give rise to the problem of intervening cases. The mere fact that a decision-maker actually makes an intervening decision between the time at which certain events occur and the time at which he must face a further problematic decision about those events does not alter the set of settled cases with which his second problematic decision must cohere. (Of course a change of mind does alter the set of settled cases; but this is a different matter.) A settled case may be equally settled, whether actual or hypothetical. More generally, the set of settled cases does not coincide with the set of actual cases. Not all actual cases are settled (some are problematic), and not all settled cases are actual (some are hypothetical).[27]

If the stronger requirement of adherence to precedent were not imposed on legal reasoning in addition to the weaker elements of conservatism imposed by a coherence account and shared with decision theory, no problem of intervening cases would arise in law either. To see this, consider a revisionary conception of the law as equally responsible in principle to both settled actual and settled hypothetical cases, so that the change of a settled case's status from hypothetical to actual between occurrence of the events litigated and their adjudication cannot via precedent change the law about the later case. Such a revisionary conception of the law is compatible with a generally coherentist approach to practical reasoning, but it omits the distinctively legal doctrine of precedent. Now whether a case is settled or not does not depend on whether it has actually been decided; a settled case is equally settled whether its current status is actual or hypothetical, and retroactivity does not arise in the way Kress envisages.

Kress considers the possibility that the law does not change purely in consequence of legal decisions, but points out that this would be to purchase unchanging right answers at the cost of dispensing with the doctrine of precedent. He writes: 'Judicial decisions change the settled law' and: 'To deny that law and legal rights change at all in response to new decisions is to deny that legal rights are, at least in part, determined by settled law.'[28] While I think he is correct to regard the denial of any change of law in response to new actual decisions as giving up the doctrine of precedent, nevertheless, it is logically possible to hold that legal rights are, at least in part, determined by settled law, without holding that a change in a case's status from hypothetical to actual is *per se* a change from unsettled to settled. It is just this logical space that is occupied by the revisionary conception of law we are now

[27] Compare Kress on the analogy between legal and scientific theorizing, at 392n, and on the character of settled law, at 278. My use of the term 'settled' here does not coincide with his, but I believe that something like my use is essential to convey what is distinctive about coherentist views of practical reasoning, and of legal reasoning in so far as it is a species of practical reasoning.

[28] At 380, 393.

considering, which in effect does not incorporate the doctrine of precedent as we know it. Of course, new legal decisions may reflect extra-judicial changes in the settled law. But absent extra-judicial changes, under the revisionary conception new legal decisions would not change settled law, though they might change our awareness of it.

Kress further points out that, within Dworkin's theory at least, 'While at each point in time, there are right answers to all or nearly all legal issues, the right answer that is given may not be the same as that which would be given at another point in time, in consequence of changes in institutional history'. However, giving hypothetical and actual settled cases equal weight would *not* mean that the law cannot develop and change, but merely that such developments and changes, in *both* actual and hypothetical cases, would reflect *extra-judicial* developments and changes in institutional history, social practices, etc.[29] Cases that were unsettled might become settled as the law develops, in response to extra-judicial developments. But under the revisionary conception a case would not change from unsettled to settled *merely* by becoming the subject of a judicial decision and changing status from hypothetical to actual.

I emphasize that I have invoked this revisionary conception of law not in order to endorse it, of course, but merely to illustrate my claim that the problem of intervening cases does not arise from the coherentist character of legal reasoning *per se*, but rather from the further distinctive asymmetrical treatment of actual and hypothetical cases by the doctrine of precedent in particular. The point of the distinction between coherentist practical reasoning absent the doctrine of precedent and legal reasoning with the doctrine of precedent is not to suggest we should respond to Kress's problem by doing away with precedent, but rather to contribute to diagnosing the source of the problem. This distinction is important because it is the general character of consistency and conservatism with respect to hypothetical as well as actual cases in coherentist practical reasoning, which legal reasoning shares and which the doctrine of precedent does not eliminate but rather supplements, that supports the view I go on to assert in section 8 below, namely, that the special role of precedent in legal reasoning only makes a difference when the decided cases appealed to as precedent were not *ex ante* correct.

It may be objected that intervening case retroactivity would occur even under the revisionary conception of law, so long as the law is subject to change such that coherence with intervening, newly settled cases may be invoked to justify legal decisions about events that occurred before the change. Perhaps the objector will admit at this point that it would not matter whether the change in settled cases occurs within the category of actual or hypothetical cases; it need not be the result of a change in status from hypothetical to actual. But so long as the possibility of change in the set of settled cases is admitted, even though the initiation of change is distributed across actual and hypothetical cases, it may be claimed that the problem of intervening cases would remain.

[29] See and compare Kress, op cit, at 392–4.

Advocates of coherence accounts are not committed to denying that the law may change. However, they may wish, as Dworkin does, to deny that judges should initiate such changes, as opposed to trying to discover what the best theory of settled law requires. (There is nothing analogous to this division of labour between the judiciary and other, law-making, branches of government, in the ethical and decision-theoretic versions of the pursuit of coherence. In these latter cases, the deliberator plays the legislative as well as the judicial role; his decisions may reflect changes of mind that originate changes in the set of settled cases. At the same time, there is no problem of retroactivity, although if someone changes his mind about what he should have done after doing it, he may well regret having done it.) On the view that the judicial role is to discover the law, not to make it, changes in judicial perception of the content of settled cases, whether actual or hypothetical, *ought* to reflect extra-judicial legal developments, such as changes in social practices and customs with constitutive bearing on the law,[30] or in legislative or administrative background. Such extra-judicial developments put members of society on fair notice, and changes in legal theory which reflect such intervening changes should in principle be applied prospectively only.[31] However, legislative and administrative changes usually *are* applied prospectively only. Moreover, changes in social practices usually occur gradually enough that worry about such a change intervening between the time of the events litigated and their adjudication may often seem contrived and artificial. Perhaps there are occasionally abrupt, revolutionary changes in social practices, but they are surely unusual. Perhaps in these unusual cases changes in settled hypothetical cases which reflect the change in social practice should in theory be given effect prospectively only (although there may be practical difficulties in identifying such cases and the time of the change of social practice involved). Such exceptions would have a rationale in the extra-judicial source of the change, and could be admitted without threatening the normal judicial practice to the contrary. Thus, extra-judicial changes in law do not threaten my claim that the problem of intervening cases does not arise from the coherentist character of legal reasoning *per se*, but rather from the distinctive

[30] See Ronald Dworkin, *Taking Rights Seriously*, (London, Duckworth, 1977), at 40–2.

[31] An example would be given by a slight variation of the sequence of events in *California Federal Savings and Loan Association* v *Guerra*, 107 SCt 683 (1987). In *Cal Fed*, a pregnant worker's employer brought suit seeking a declaration that a California statute requiring employers to provide leave and reinstatement to employees disabled by pregnancy was preempted by the federal statute, Title VII, which prohibited sex discrimination. The court upheld the California statute, although in the 1976 case of *General Electric Co* v *Gilbert*, 429 US 125, 97 SCt 401, it had interpreted Title VII in a different manner, reasoning that discrimination against pregnant persons was not sex discrimination because many non-pregnant persons are female. In 1978 Congress expressed its disapproval of the *Gilbert* reasoning by amending Title VII to make clear that it intended sex discrimination to include discrimination against pregnant persons. The disputed events in the *Cal Fed* case occurred in 1982: the employee took a pregnancy leave, and when she informed her employer she was ready to return to work she was told her job had been filled and there was no available positions. She filed a complaint under the California statute, and her employer brought a suit seeking a declaration that the statute was preempted by Title VII's ban on sex discrimination. The case was decided in 1987.

Now suppose that between the *Gilbert* decision in 1976 and the 1978 amendment to Title VII events like those disputed in *Cal Fed* occurred, but only came to trial after the *Cal Fed* decision. Then *Cal Fed* would have the status of an intervening case. However, it would have been following an extra-judicial initiation of an addition to the settled law, namely, the amendment of Title VII in 1978. Under these circumstances it would seem that the legislative change should be given prospective effect only.

asymmetrical treatment of actual and hypothetical cases by the doctrine of precedent in particular.

In summary, the purely coherentist revisionary conception of law as lacking the stronger requirement, imposed by the doctrine of precedent, would support the following argument. Either cases intervening between the occurrence of events and their adjudication reflect intervening extra-judicial changes in settled law or they do not. If they do, the prospective-only application of the new legal hypotheses supported by the newly settled law is appropriate for the same reason that prospective-only application is appropriate for legislative decision-making, namely to avoid the unfairness of retroactivity. In such circumstances, we have judicial reflections of extra-judicial legal developments, not judicial law-making.[32] Cases that articulate such developments and incorporate them within a coherent legal theory may change what we believe the law to be, but they do not in themselves change the law, any more than an illuminating new scientific theory changes the truth about what the best theory is merely by changing our beliefs about what it is. On the other hand, if the intervening cases do not reflect extra-judicial changes, then either they are settled or they are not. The mere fact that they have been actually decided does not resolve this question. If an intervening case is not settled, the fact that it has been decided between the occurrence of events and their adjudication does not change the settled law. The fact that the case has been explicitly considered and decided *per se* does not make it a case that is clear to the relevant decision-makers. Moreover, it may have been a settled case before it was decided, if its resolution would have been clear had it been considered. That is, either the intervening case is not settled, despite being actual, or is settled, and was before it was decided. Either way, there is no retroactivity. Thus the coherentist character of the revisionary conception of law as merely requiring that like cases be treated alike and that hence not too many settled cases be regarded as mistaken is not sufficient to give rise to the problem of intervening cases; in addition, the doctrine of precedent is necessary.[33]

8. *The Source of the Problem: Precedent vs Mistake or Underdetermination*

There thus seems to be a—perhaps surprising—tension between the doctrine of precedent, on the one hand, and the requirements of fairness which make retroactivity objectionable, on the other. But perhaps the doctrine of precedent is not sufficient to give rise to the problem of intervening cases either, though necessary. It seems clear that the revisionary coherentist conception of law I sketched in the last section, under which no distinction of weight at all is drawn between settled actual and settled hypothetical cases, involves a substantial departure from the doctrine of precedent as we know it. Nevertheless, the doctrine of precedent as we know it is compatible with the significant influence of settled

[32] As in the variation on *Cal Fed*, ibid.

[33] Cf Kress, op cit, at 401–2.

hypothetical cases; it does not require that status as actual and status as settled coincide. Because of this, the argument that applied to the revisionary conception of law to show that intervening case retroactivity would not arise may be available, at least under certain circumstances, in a legal system that does incorporate the doctrine of precedent. I will briefly consider some cases to illustrate the point that status as actual and status as settled do not in fact coincide. I will then go on to try to sharpen the diagnosis of the intervening case retroactivity. I shall argue, largely following suggestions made by Dworkin, that only actual intervening decisions that are *ex ante mistaken*, or at least not uniquely correct (in cases of underdetermination), but which the doctrine of precedent nevertheless presumptively constitutes as judicially-initiated changes in the law, give rise to retroactivity.

Not all actually decided cases are settled; indeed, some actual cases, even some that are settled, may be mistaken,[34] in virtue of their failure to cohere with other settled, including actual, cases. Dependence on some actual cases, is avoided, even if they have not been explicitly overruled as mistaken, because they are highly controversial, and/or considered uncertain, dubious, or poor authority. Moreover, the doctrine of precedent may not treat actual cases of courts of other jurisdictions as settled. An example of an intervening actual case which was nevertheless not settled is that of *Brown* v *Porcher*.[35] In *Brown*, the US Court of Appeals held that the construal of a South Carolina statute to disqualify any claimant who voluntarily left her most recent employment because of pregnancy violated a federal statute providing that no person shall be denied unemployment compensation under state law solely on the basis of pregnancy. *Brown* was decided in 1981; the US Supreme Court denied certiorari in 1983. In 1980, however, events had already occurred which gave rise to the closely related case on the same issue of *Wimberly* v *Labor and Industrial Relations Commission*, which went up on appeal through the Missouri court system to the Missouri Supreme Court (in 1985), and eventually reached the US Supreme Court (in 1987).[36] The Missouri Court of Appeals had followed *Brown*, despite reservations concerning the soundness of its reasoning; but the Missouri Supreme Court reversed, declaring that it had never subscribed to the notion that Missouri state courts were bound to follow the decisions of lower federal courts in construing federal statutes.[37] The Missouri Supreme Court declined to follow *Brown*. 'We do not mean to suggest that a lower federal court's construction of a federal statute is wholly irrelevant. The courts of this state should "look respectfully to such opinions for such aid and guidance as may be found therein". . . . In some circumstances it may be appropriate for a state court to defer to long established and widely accepted federal court interpretations of federal statutes'. But it evidently felt that *Brown* was not a settled case in this sense. The US Supreme Court eventually resolved *Wimberly* in favour of the Missouri

[34] As Kress admits, at 378.

[35] 660 F2d 1001 (1981), cert denied, 459 US 1150, 103 SCt 796 (1983). Perhaps various abortion cases provide other current examples.

[36] 107 SCt 821 (1987).

[37] Justice Donnelly, concurring in the result, denied that US Supreme Court decisions interpreting the US Constitution are binding on the states.

view and against *Brown*. But the point to be made here is not that *Brown* was mistaken; perhaps it was correct. It is rather that *Brown*, the intervening case, did not change the settled law because it was not a settled case, from the perspective of the Missouri Supreme Court. Thus, whether or not *Brown* was correct, the best theory about settled law, which should determine the outcome in the similar case which comes to trial after *Brown*, was not altered by the intervening case. If the result in *Brown* were to have been upheld as the correct result, there would have nevertheless been no retroactive application of the decision in the intervening case, since, as the Missouri Supreme Court implied, it was not a settled case. Continuing uncertainty about the right answer is just that, not retroactivity.

Furthermore, there are many settled hypothetical cases which are more deeply entrenched and would be more difficult to justify regarding as mistaken than many actual cases: we are lucky that such cases have remained hypothetical rather than actual. They have not become actual, in some cases, because the flagrant violations of rights they would involve luckily have not occurred in our communities. But they are nonetheless clearly settled for being hypothetical. A good example is found in Justice Marshall's eloquent dissent in the recent case of *US* v *Salerno and Cafaro*. The majority had upheld a statute permitting the denial of bail altogether in certain cases against Due Process and Excessive Bail Clause challenges, on the grounds in part that the statute is a regulatory rather than a punitive measure. Justice Marshall writes:

> The ease with which the conclusion is reached suggests the worthlessness of the achievement. The major premise is that '[u]nless Congress expressly intended to impose punitive restrictions, the punitive/regulatory distinction turns on "whether an alternative purpose to which [the restriction] may rationally be connected is assignable for it, and whether it appears excessive in relation to the alternative purpose assigned [to it]."' The majority finds that 'Congress did not formulate the pretrial detention provisions as punishment for dangerous individuals', but instead was pursuing the 'legitimate regulatory goal' of 'preventing danger to the community'. . . . Concluding that pretrial detention is not an excessive solution to the problem of preventing danger to the community, the majority thus finds that no substantive element of the guarantee of due process invalidates the statute.

Justice Marshall produces a settled hypothetical case as a counter-example to the majority's hypothesis about the punitive/regulatory distinction. He goes on:

> This argument does not demonstrate the conclusion it purports to justify. Let us apply the majority's reasoning to a similar, hypothetical case. After investigation, Congress determines (not unrealistically) that a large proportion of violent crime is perpetrated by persons who are unemployed. It also determines, equally realistically, that much violent crime is committed at night. From amongst the panoply of 'potential solutions', Congress chooses a statute which permits, after judicial proceedings, the imposition of a dusk-to-dawn curfew on anyone who is unemployed. Since this is not a measure enacted for the purpose of punishing the unemployed, and since the majority finds that preventing danger to the community is a legitimate regulatory goal, the curfew statute would, accord-

> ing to the majority's analysis, be a mere 'regulatory' detention statute, entirely compatible with the substantive components of the Due Process Clause.[38]

He regards the absurdity of this conclusion as a settled aspect of the law, and nonetheless settled for the fact that the case envisaged is merely hypothetical. Here is a settled hypothetical case that is more entrenched, and less likely to be regarded as mistaken by the best legal theory, than many actual cases.

We have considered two cases in which the dissenting opinions appeal persuasively to hypothetical cases to defeat hypotheses on which the majority opinion seems to turn, *Parham* and *Salerno*. Suppose for the sake of argument that these decisions were mistaken up to the time of the decision, or *ex ante mistaken*. Nevertheless, the doctrine of precedent tells us we cannot assume them to be *ex post mistaken*; we cannot infer an *ex post* mistake from an *ex ante* mistake because the fact of the actual decision may change the law. It is possible that an *ex ante* mistake is so serious that the enormity of the mistake outweighs its precedential force, and it remains a mistake even *ex post*; but the mere fact of the decision has loaded the balance against this possibility. A mistake must be more serious, must be more deeply incoherent with the settled law, including hypothetical as well as actual cases, to be an *ex post* mistake than to be an *ex ante* mistake; the difference is a matter of degree, a matter of how much must be uprooted to accommodate the law to the mistake.

We see then that the doctrine of precedent permits determinately *ex ante* mistaken decisions to change the law;[39] such decisions, as intervening cases, may give rise to retroactivity. Of course, the doctrine of precedent is not addressed to mistakes in particular; it does not perversely dignify *ex ante* mistaken actual decisions as opposed to *ex ante* correct actual decisions by presumptively constituting only the former as law henceforward. But precedential force is not needed to constitute an *ex ante* correct decision as correct *ex post*; in this respect it is redundant (though of course it may feature nonredundantly in the reasoning from previous precedents that makes the decision *ex ante* correct). No special method of transition between *ex ante* standing and *ex post* standing is needed in the case of correct decisions; precedent has no law-changing work to do in these cases. Since resolutions that are *ex ante* correct all things considered do not conflict with one another to begin with, increasing the weight of a correct settled case as it changes from hypothetical to actual makes no difference. Of course, courts may not *know* whether the actual cases they defer to as having precedential force were *ex ante* mistaken or not. Nevertheless, we may issue a challenge: how, on coherentist assumptions, could the precedential force of a decision, other than one reflecting extra-judicial legal developments, change the *law* itself, as opposed to our *beliefs* about it, if that decision were *ex ante* correct?

[38] *US* v *Salerno* 107 SCt 2095, 2107–2108 (1987).

[39] Compare Kress's claim at 394 that 'wholesale and final determination of the truth or falsity of all possible legal propositions leaves no room for the operation of the dominant notion of precedent'.

This in effect is Dworkin's response to the problem of intervening cases. He argues as follows.[40] He does consider that integrity requires us to give weight to the fact that a case was actually decided so, even if it was decided wrongly. Either an intervening case is wrongly or rightly decided. Suppose it is wrongly decided. Then it will indeed change the law retroactively, and for the worse, since it was wrongly decided. That is one reason it is so important for judges to reach the right answer! We can accept that there is objectionable retroactivity in this case, but that is not a consequence of the coherentist account of adjudication, or of the doctrine of precedent, but rather of the fact that the wrong answer was reached. Suppose, on the other hand, that the intervening case was rightly decided; then we are presented with a challenge. How could a correct decision in an intervening case make for retroactive change of the law?[41] How could the affirmation of a correct hypothesis itself change hypotheses in subsequent cases from right to wrong or vice versa? It might make the correct answers to later cases more evident or predictable, but this is not what Kress needs for his claim; retroactivity involves a change in the law, not merely a change in our beliefs about the law.

For the moment put aside the possibility, which I will return to, that the correct decision (not merely our beliefs about it) was *ex ante* underdetermined, rather than mistaken. To claim, following Dworkin, that precedent only makes a difference given an *ex ante* mistake does not amount to saying that precedent does not make any difference to the way people *should* reason about the law. One can hold that decided cases do and should make a difference to the way people should reason, via the doctrine of precedent, *though they are ex ante mistaken*, even if one also holds that they make a difference only when they are *ex ante* mistaken, since they must be either correct or mistaken, and if they are correct their actually being decided makes no difference. The argument for the latter qualification derives from the role of hypothetical cases in coherentist practical reasoning in general; precedent is an additional special feature of legal reasoning, but it does not eliminate the general

[40] In discussion.

[41] Kress gives an example, in which the force of precedent is conceived in a mechanical way to involve counting the number of steps required for privity of contract, which he claims is a paradigm case of coherentist reasoning. See 382–3. However, it can be dismissed as not an example of Dworkinian, or more generally, coherentist reasoning at all, since it does not involve consideration of the reasons or principles that support particular results.

Some implicit support is found in Supreme Court cases for Dworkin's view that a correct decision in an intervening case does not change the law. In the criminal procedure context, see in particular the dissents by Justice Harlan and Justice Fortas in *Desist*, op cit. Justice Harlan writes: '. . . If a "new" constitutional doctrine is truly right, we should not reverse lower courts which have accepted it; nor should we affirm those which have rejected the very arguments we have embraced. Anything else would belie the truism that it is the task of this Court, like that of any other, to do justice to each litigant on the merits of his own case. It is only if each of our decisions can be justified in terms of this fundamental premise that they may properly be considered the legitimate products of a court of law, rather than the commands of a super-legislature'. See also H. Schwartz, 'Retroactivity, Reliability, and Due Process', (1966) 33 *U Chi LR* 719 at 748–9. In *Hanover Shoe* v *United Shoe Machinery Corp*, an antitrust case, the US Supreme Court discussed the intervening case issue explicitly, writing: 'The theory of the Court of Appeals seems to have been that when a party has significantly relied upon a clear and established doctrine, and the retrospective application of a newly declared doctrine would upset that justifiable reliance to his substantial injury, considerations of justice and fairness require that the new rule apply prospectively only.' The Supreme Court, however, did not find before it a situation in which there was a clearly declared judicial doctrine upon which a party had relied and which was overruled in favour of a new rule. The intervening cases in question did not indicate that the issues they decided were novel, or that they involved a departure from an earlier line of cases or the need for innovative principles. 'Whatever development in antitrust law was brought about was based to a great extent on existing authorities and was an extension of doctrines which had been growing and developing over the years.' See *Hanover*, 392 US 481, at 496–9 (1968).

role of hypothetical cases in legal reasoning as a special case of practical reasoning. Precedent does and should make a difference to correct reasoning about what the law is, and this is why, in part, the problem of retroactivity does arise. Reasoning from an *ex ante* mistaken precedent is not itself mistaken simply because of the *ex ante* mistake.

The argument as to under what circumstances an intervening precedent can change the law may be elaborated as follows. Either the intervening decided case was *ex ante* correct or *ex ante* mistaken; moreover, either the corresponding hypothetical case was settled in the same way as the actual case was decided, or it was not so settled. Then there are four cases to consider. Suppose first that the decision was *ex ante* (but not *ex post*) mistaken in fact, but nevertheless settled, ie it was, or would have been, wrongly believed of the corresponding hypothetical case that the (in fact) mistaken decision would be the correct decision for such a case. False beliefs about the *ex ante* law have been replaced by true beliefs about the *ex post* law, made true because the law has changed, in virtue of an *ex ante* mistaken precedent that is good *ex post* law. The retroactivity problem arises with respect to what the law is (though not with respect to beliefs about the law), but that is due to the *ex ante* mistaken decision. Second, suppose that the decision was *ex ante* (but not *ex post*) mistaken, though not settled as a hypothetical case. In this case the law and beliefs about it may change as a result of the decision, but again retroactivity is associated with an *ex ante* mistaken decision. Third, suppose the decision was *ex ante* correct and settled. In this case there is change neither in the law nor beliefs about it, so no retroactivity problem can arise.

The fourth case is the interesting case: here the decision was *ex ante* correct, but the corresponding hypothetical case was not settled in accord with the correct decision. The truth about the law has not changed as a result of the correct decision, though what is believed about it *may* have changed (again, the change from hypothetical to actual does not *necessarily* entail a change from unsettled to settled, since a decided case may remain unsettled). If beliefs about the law do not change as a result of the correct decision, neither the law nor beliefs about it have changed, so it is hard to see how the correct decision in a subsequent case could change. If beliefs about the law do change, it may be in one of (at least) two ways. On the one hand, they may have been undetermined before, and may now be settled in accord with the correct decision. Could this change in belief, absent a change in the law, be sufficient to change what the law is in a subsequent case? Whatever considerations they were in virtue of which the intervening decision was correct still obtain, and, to the extent they ever applied to the subsequent case, apply equally after the intervening case is decided. How could the mere addition of true beliefs about these unchanged considerations change the correct decision in the subsequent case, as opposed to making it more evident? On the other hand, beliefs about the law may have been mistaken before the intervening case, and they may have changed to accord with the correct decision in the case. How could this change from false to true beliefs about the intervening case change the law, as opposed to beliefs about it, in the subsequent case? It does not help to point out that according to a coherence account not too many settled cases can be mistaken, because we are now supposing the prior beliefs were false; if they were true, we are back to case three above, and there is no retroactivity. Whatever considerations they were in virtue of which the prior beliefs about the hypothetical version of the intervening case were false would apply also to the subsequent case, to the extent relevant. If we continue to assume that the law in the subsequent case was either determinately one thing or another at each point, and no change of law with respect to the intervening case was brought about by its correct decision, the challenge on coherentist assumptions still stands: how could a decision in the subsequent case be changed from correct to mistaken or vice versa merely as a result of a change in beliefs about the law in the intervening case from false to true, given no change in the law itself with respect to that case? Note that it is incorrect to object here that the determinacy assumption leaves no room for the operation of precedent, since we have seen that it does leave room for it in cases of mistaken decisions. What is at issue is whether precedent can make a difference given correct intervening decisions.

At this point we should consider the consequences of suspending the assumption of determinacy. If we allow that prior to a decision the right answer (not merely beliefs about it) may be underdetermined, then precedent may make a difference not just as a result of *ex ante* mistake, but also as a result of resolving *ex ante* underdetermination. Dworkin, of course, would resist the possibility of underdetermination in arguing for his right answer thesis, so it does not, in the absence of an independent argument against the right answer determinacy thesis, help Kress make a case against Dworkin in particular. But some coherentists might accept the possibility of underdetermination, so it is relevant to the general discussion with respect to coherentism.

Thus, from a theoretical point of view at least, intervening case retroactivity can be laid at the feet, not of coherentist legal reasoning, or even of the doctrine of precedent, but rather of mistaken decisions, and perhaps also of underdetermination of the law, to the extent a given version of coherentism admits this possibility. That legal mistakes are unfair to people is hardly news; the theoretical novelty and interest of the problem of intervening cases thus looks to diminish to the extent mistakes are its source. Moreover, the use of the problem as a means of criticizing Dworkin's version of coherentism in particular is limited by his rejection of the possibility of underdetermination. The general shape of my response to Kress with respect to the problem of intervening cases has been to draw out the consequences of a coherentist view of practical reasoning in general for legal reasoning and the doctrine of precedent in particular, which consequences limit intervening case retroactivity. The argument has proceeded by presenting a challenge to show how, *given the role of hypothetical cases within coherentist views of practical reasoning*, a correct, as opposed to *ex ante* mistaken or indeterminate, intervening case could give rise to retroactivity. Of course we may reject coherentist views and their consequences with respect to the doctrine of precedent altogether, but then we depart from Kress's subject matter. Note that my aim has not been to dispute the interest of the retroactivity problem which Kress has highlighted, but rather his conception of coherentism in general and Dworkin's version thereof in particular as the proper targets of the argument.

In pursuing my course of argument, however, I have at several points had to put considerable weight on the distinction between changes in the law and changes in our beliefs about the law in particular cases. Coherentism admits this theoretical distinction on a case by case basis, even though it ties right answers and beliefs about them together globally in the way indicated in section 7 above, in that not too many settled cases can be mistaken. However, perhaps from a more pragmatic point of view, one more concerned with matters of notice and predictability, which may be closer to that of litigants and potential litigants, this distinction has been strained even so. Perhaps it is from this more pragmatic point of view that a distinctive problem about intervening cases arises.

[8]

CONSTRAINED BY PRECEDENT*

LARRY ALEXANDER**

I. INTRODUCTION

The notion that courts ordinarily should follow precedent in deciding cases is one of the core structural features of adjudication in common-law legal systems. Indeed, there is probably no experience more emblematic of legal education in America than the first year (and frequently upper division) emphasis on the case method: the task of training students to discern the "holdings" of cases and to determine whether those precedent cases have been followed, appropriately distinguished, or overruled in subsequent cases.

Despite the centrality of the practice of following precedent to common-law legal systems and its adjunct, the case method of instruction, I think it is fair to say that our theoretical understanding of the practice is still at a very primitive stage. Although what it means to follow precedent has been debated for hundreds of years by some of the top minds in legal theory,[1] and still receives regular attention in contemporary literature,[2] if one were to ask law students, lawyers, judges, or legal academics what following precedent entails, one would almost surely get a variety of inconsistent answers.

** Professor of Law, University of San Diego. B.A., 1965, Williams Coll.; LL.B., 1968, Yale University. I received helpful comments, some of them extensive enough to count as articles, from a large number of people: Elaine Alexander, Ron Allen, Carl Auerbach, Randy Barnett, Myke Bayles, Kevin Cole, Tony D'Amato, John Garvey, Paul Horton, Heidi Hurd, Bob Klonoff, Gary Lawson, Evan Lee, Bill Marshall, Michael Moore, Michael Perry, Joseph Raz, Martin Redish, Carol Rose, Henry Schwarzschild, Steven Schwarzschild, Fred Schauer, Rod Smith, Tim Terrell, Richard Warner, Chris Wonnell, and members of the faculty at Northwestern University School of Law who attended a forum at which I presented a version of this Article. Those who believed I was on the right track gave me confidence in my thesis. Those who thought my views on precedent entirely wrongheaded helped me to see which of my arguments needed strengthening or clarification. Thanks to all of you.

1. *See, e.g.*, 2 J. AUSTIN, LECTURES ON JURISPRUDENCE 290-378 (1861); 1 W. BLACKSTONE, COMMENTARIES *70-71; B. CARDOZO, THE NATURE OF THE JUDICIAL PROCESS (1921); O.W. HOLMES, THE COMMON LAW (1881); K. LLEWELLYN, THE COMMON LAW TRADITION 62-212 (1960).

2. *See, e.g.*, PRECEDENT IN LAW (L. Goldstein ed. 1987); Maltz, *The Nature of Precedent*, 66 N.C.L. REV. 367 (1988); Monaghan, *Stare Decisis and Constitutional Adjudication*, 88 COLUM. L. REV. 723 (1988); Perry, *Judicial Obligation, Precedent and the Common Law*, 7 OXFORD J. LEGAL STUD. 215 (1987); Schauer, *Precedent*, 39 STAN. L. REV. 571 (1987).

In this Article I hope to advance the theoretical understanding of precedent following through an elucidation of three different models of the practice. More particularly, I intend to explore the distinctive contribution each model makes to the understanding of why a decision by a prior court might constrain a subsequent court of lesser or equal authority to reach a decision different from the one the latter court would have reached in the absence of the precedent case. In other words, I shall focus on those situations, however frequent or rare, in which a subsequent court believes that, though a previous case was decided incorrectly, it must, nevertheless, through operation of the practice of precedent following, decide the case confronting it in a manner that it otherwise believes is incorrect. In short, *I shall be dealing with constraint by incorrectly decided precedents*.

A few comments on my choice of focus are in order. First, when I speak of precedents that are "incorrect" in the eyes of the subsequent court, I am referring to cases of first impression, cases that were directly governed by principles of political morality (or policies derived therefrom) and in which those principles (or policies) were misapplied (in the view of the subsequent court). I reserve to Appendix B my discussion of precedential constraint by cases that are "incorrect" because of the different problem of the precedent courts misapplying applicable precedents.

Second, I shall not deal directly with a court's use of precedent cases that it believes were *correctly* decided. Frequently courts use precedents as authoritative support for decisions they would deem correct (on the basis of political/moral principles) in the absence of those precedents. The principal reason that I shall not address explicitly this use of precedents is that the power of precedents to *support* decisions a court believes are otherwise justifiable depends upon the power of precedents to *constrain* a court from reaching decisions it believes are justifiable. Thus, *until we understand how and to what extent precedents can constrain a subsequent decision, we cannot understand how and to what extent they can support one*. In addition, I shall not deal with the use of precedents to support decisions because the principles governing such use are easily deducible from the discussion of precedential constraint.

Third, I shall not deal directly with the overruling of incorrect precedents. What I say, however, will be relevant to an understanding of what overruling is and whether and how it can be justified.

Finally, I shall assume throughout this Article a pure common-law decisionmaking context and reserve to Appendix A the discussion of precedent following where the meaning of statutes or constitutional provisions is at issue.

The three models of precedent following that I shall describe are, I believe, exhaustive of the possibilities. The first, the *natural model*, does not admit of any variation. The second, the *rule model*, has quite a few possible variations depending upon how the rules are identified. Each of these variations, however, have sufficient features and problems in common to allow them to be dealt with as one model. The third, the *result model*, has both a pure and an impure version, each of which shall be discussed separately. As far as I can determine, both from reading the literature and from thinking about other possibilities that might be plausible, there are no other models of precedent following worthy of consideration.

In the final analysis, I conclude that the natural model of precedent, however normatively attractive, is not really a model of precedential constraint at all. I also conclude that the result model, in both its forms, is quite unattractive and perhaps ultimately incoherent. That leaves the rule model, with all of its variations and problems, as the only reasonable alternative. But that is to get ahead of myself.

II. THE FIRST MODEL: GIVING PRECEDENT ITS NATURAL WEIGHT

A. The Natural Model of Precedent Described

The first model of precedent following is what I call the natural model. Under this model the court in deciding a case gives prior judicial decisions the weight that those decisions carry independently of any formal requirement that precedent be followed. In other words, the constrained court looks to the "precedential" effects of the prior decision and assigns them a moral weight, which it then factors into its overall decisionmaking calculus.

To understand the natural model better, let us look at an instance of nonlegal decisionmaking where the model clearly does operate. Suppose that when my daughter reaches the age of thirteen, she requests permission from me to attend a rock concert. I weigh the possible risks involved in her going and the potential benefits to her and to our relationship, and I decide to grant her permission to go. When my son reaches the age of thirteen and also seeks permission to attend a rock concert, he predictably will cite my previous decision granting permission to his sister as a reason for a decision in his favor, a reason in addition to the risks and benefits I would normally consider. The natural model of precedent requires that I give the previous decision its true weight as an independent reason.

The natural model would have the same features in the legal system. In the precedent case, which I am assuming is not governed by any statute or constitutional provision that speaks to its substantive merits, and which I shall also assume is not itself governed by an applicable precedent case, the court—which I shall hereafter call the "precedent court"—will assess the reasons why the dispute should be resolved in one party's favor or the other's. Those reasons might primarily be the parties' relative moral desert or some other deontological consideration—a sort of "What if these parties were alone on a desert island?" inquiry. Alternatively, those reasons might primarily be the social consequences of the alternative decisions.[3] Although it is interesting to reflect upon how a court should resolve a dispute in the absence of controlling statutory rules or precedent, we do not need to assume anything beyond the fact that the precedent court does in fact resolve the dispute based on reasons—deontological, consequentialist, or some mixture—that it believes correct political/moral theory approves.

The important point here is that once the precedent court decides the case, the existence of that decision can be invoked as an independent reason for subsequent courts to decide "similar" disputes in the same way. This is true even in the absence of a formal practice of precedent following. Similarly, my decision to allow my daughter to attend a rock concert at age thirteen can (and will) be invoked by my son as a reason for permitting him to attend a rock concert at the same age. The earlier decision is invoked as a reason for a similar decision, a reason that did

3. Of course, the distinction between justice in the case and the long-range consequences of a decision may be quite subtle and slippery, given that the location of the line between what norms are morally ideal and what norms are concessions to real world limitations is quite controversial. *See* Alexander, *Pursuing the Good—Indirectly*, 95 ETHICS 315, 317-30 (1985); Wonnell, *Problems in the Application of Political Philosophy to Law*, 86 MICH. L. REV. 123, 123-30 (1987); *see also* Perry, *Second-Order Reasons, Uncertainty and Legal Theory*, 62 S. CAL. L. REV. 913, 984-85 (1989) (discussing the role of forward-looking considerations in common-law adjudication); Raz, *Facing Up: A Reply*, 62 S. CAL. L. REV. 1153, 1209-12 (1989) (discussing Perry's use of forward-looking precedents); *infra* text accompanying notes 13-17 (discussing the value of general rules). Nonetheless, let us assume the distinction can be drawn. If the precedent court determines cases based on the long-run social consequences of its decisions, then it primarily will be interested in how others will modify their behavior in reaction to that decision. Moreover, even without a formal practice of precedent following, people can and will draw inferences from decisions in earlier cases about how future cases will be decided.

not exist in the precedent case and that is to be added to the other reasons for such a decision. More precisely, the precedent decision gives rise to reasons for a similar decision, such as equality and reliance, that did not exist in the precedent case.

Moreover, even if the subsequent court—which I shall hereafter call the "constrained court"—believes the precedent case was decided incorrectly because the balance of reasons favored the losing party, the constrained court might believe that the new reasons generated by the precedent decision tip the balance in favor of the party who would have lost had the constrained court decided the precedent case. Similarly, I might decide that although I should not have let my daughter attend the rock concert, and should not let my son attend were this my first decision on the point, the decision in my daughter's case now tips the balance of reasons in favor of permitting my son to go.

B. The Rationale Behind the Natural Model of Precedent

I suspect that we all recognize the natural model, if not in the legal system, at least in other areas of our lives. But how can a past decision that we now believe was incorrect convert a present decision that would otherwise be incorrect into a correct decision? The arguments on behalf of following incorrect decisions on the natural model of precedent boil down to two reasons: furthering equality of treatment and respecting justified expectations on which people have relied.

It is easy to see why one might argue that equality supports the constrained court's decision that, but for the precedent court's decision, would be incorrect. If I tell my son that I will not permit him to attend the rock concert and that I should not have permitted his sister to go, he predictably will claim that I have not treated him equally with respect to her. By saying so, he will be making more than the obvious descriptive point that my treatment of his sister and him with respect to attending rock concerts at age thirteen is dissimilar. Rather, he will be making the normative claim that such dissimilarity in treatment is wrong in the absence of countervailing considerations of substantial moral weight. In other words, he will be asserting that the value of equality is a sufficiently weighty reason in support of letting him go to the concert that it tips the balance of reasons in his favor.

The role of the justified reliance argument in support of a decision in favor of the present analog to the party who won in the precedent case is also fairly easy to understand. Even if there is no formal requirement that courts follow precedent, people frequently will look to judicial decisions and the expressed reasons on which they are based in order to predict how their contemplated courses of action will be treated by the courts should a legal dispute arise.[4] Similarly, my son may undertake action based upon his reasonable expectation that because I allowed his sister to attend a rock concert at age thirteen, I will allow him to do the same. These expectations become reasons that may justify decisions that would otherwise (in the absence of the expectations) be regarded as erroneous.

The natural model of precedent has had and continues to have its supporters. Michael Moore's recent contribution to the literature is perhaps the most sophisticated defense of the model.[5] Moore argues that, for separation of powers reasons, courts should not be deemed to have authority to lay down general rules. Rather, their authority should be limited to deciding cases. Thus, the force of the precedent case qua precedent is exhausted by the fact that the precedent court decided that case with its particular facts in favor of the plaintiff or the defendant.[6] Moore concludes that the force of the precedent case qua precedent is not found in the court's opinion or in any canonical rule laid down by the court. Rather, its precedential force comes from the value of equality and the rule of law virtues that center on the predictability of legal rules.[7]

C. Is the Natural Model of Precedent Really a Form of Precedent?

In one sense, the natural model of precedent is not a model of precedential constraint at all. The constrained court need do nothing more than decide the case before it as it believes is morally correct, even if it knows that the precedent court would strongly disagree with its decision. What is morally correct, of course, will be a function of facts about the parties and the world. Importantly, these facts might include the equality and reliance effects of earlier court decisions. This same concern for equality of treatment, however, might also arise from a decision by a court inferior in rank to the constrained court or from a decision by a

4. *See* Perry, *supra* note 2, at 248-50; Perry, *supra* note 3, at 963-80.

5. Moore, *Precedent, Induction, and Ethical Generalization*, in PRECEDENT IN LAW, *supra* note 2, at 183. I also argue that Melvin Eisenberg should be read as a proponent of the natural model, at least as the most accurate *description* of common-law methodology. *See* M. EISENBERG, THE NATURE OF THE COMMON LAW (1988); *infra* text accompanying notes 82-90 (Appendix C).

6. Moore, *supra* note 5, at 187.

7. *Id.* at 200-05.

nonjudicial official or body. Likewise, people may have present expectations that should be given weight by the constrained court even though they are not based on the decisions of precedent courts and perhaps not based on the decisions of any courts. Thus, equality and reliance concerns founded on an earlier decision within the jurisdiction by a court of equal or superior rank are simply items that the constrained court must factor into its deliberations along with many other relevant considerations, including not only constitutional, statutory, and other authoritative rules beyond the power of the constrained court to affect but also equality and reliance concerns traceable to sources other than precedent decisions. It is perhaps misleading, therefore, to label the method of the natural model of precedent as precedent following at all.

Nevertheless, this is a semantic point, not a normative or descriptive one. The natural model may be the model our courts (or some of them) actually employ, or it may be the model they should employ. Whether it is properly labeled a model of precedent is unimportant if the model is otherwise descriptively accurate and/or normatively attractive.

D. The Normative Case for the Natural Model of Precedent

It is difficult to assess the descriptive accuracy of the natural model of precedent before the other two models—the rule model of precedent and the result model—have been fleshed out and analyzed. This difficulty arises because the differences between the models can be quite subtle. Until we are clear as to what the other forms of precedential constraint look like, it will be very difficult to determine whether a court's use of precedent conforms to the natural model or to some other model of precedent.

We can, however, assess the natural model's normative underpinnings. What we find is that the model, correctly applied, either gives too little weight to precedent following, or, put differently and paradoxically, itself dictates the adoption of another model.

1. *The Equality Value*

Under the natural model of precedent, the constrained court should look to what the precedent court did in order to further the value of equality. Even if the constrained court disagrees with the earlier decision, the value of equality requires the constrained court to consider the precedent case when making its decision about what is the morally correct solution to the present dispute (or so the argument goes). Equality likewise makes my decision to allow my daughter to attend a rock concert relevant to whether I ought to let my son attend.

Yet the value of intertemporal equality does not in fact carry this much weight. If the past decision was, as I am hypothesizing throughout, morally incorrect, intertemporal equality cannot render a similar decision now either correct or less incorrect. To take an extreme example, if most members of a particular group of people have been subjected to grossly unjust treatment—say, slavery or genocide—seeing that the rest of the members are subjected to the same treatment is no less wrong despite its furtherance of "equality." Neither two nor two million wrongs can make a right, however much they equalize situations. Nor is the two millionth wrong somehow less wrong than the first.

Furthermore, unless we assume the universality of immoral treatment, treating someone equally with another who was treated immorally is to deny that person equality with those who have been treated morally correctly. The member of the persecuted group who is spared genocide is treated equally with all who rightfully have been allowed to live.[8]

Even the case of deciding whether to allow my children to attend a rock concert is misleading on this point. If the dangers of allowing a thirteen-year-old to attend the concert outweigh the pleasures, and if my responsibility as a parent is such that I should not allow my children to attend under those circumstances, then my mistake regarding my daughter should carry no weight in deciding whether to grant my son's request. It would be a perversion of the role of equality as a moral value to invoke it as a reason to endanger my son's welfare. My response to my son's predictable complaint of unequal treatment is that it is his sister who has the true grievance, namely, that I endangered her by permitting her to attend. In sum, the sense of equality that carries moral weight cannot require perpetuation of otherwise immoral conduct.

I realize—due in large measure to the response my minimization of intertemporal equality provoked among several readers of an earlier draft—that this argument is controversial. Nonetheless, I believe that there is no intertemporal equality value of sufficient weight to support precedential constraint; intertemporal equality cannot convert an otherwise morally erroneous decision into a correct one.

8. *See id.* at 204.

I am not attacking mere formal equality, the empty injunction to treat like cases alike. No one believes that formal equality can constrain.[9] Rather, I am attacking a form of substantive equality: the injunction to treat present cases like past cases, even where the past cases were decided incorrectly from a moral standpoint. I am claiming that, to use the terminology of moral philosophy, intertemporal comparative justice claims cannot displace noncomparative justice claims.

There are several ways to make this claim convincing. First, if intertemporal equality claims have weight capable of displacing other moral considerations, then wrongs to cavemen should carry weight in our current deliberations. Indeed, there is no apparent reason other than epistemic uncertainty for discounting equality claims that are generated by temporally remote events.

Second, we naturally think that the more grievous the moral wrong that resulted from the past incorrect decision, the less reason there is to follow that decision in the present case. Yet the comparative justice claim is actually stronger for following a decision that is seriously wrong than for following a decision that is only minimally wrong. If we do not follow the seriously wrong decision, the present winning party will be much better off than her equally deserving but losing analog in the earlier case. The strength of comparative justice claims generated by a past incorrect decision should vary inversely with the strength of the noncomparative justice claims present in both the past and present cases. The greater the past (noncomparative) injustice, the greater the claim of noncomparative justice to depart from the past decision, but the greater the claim of comparative justice to follow it. Thus, if intertemporal equality—intertemporal comparative justice—is a substantive value of more than de minimis weight, we should have the same balance of reasons for following seriously wrong decisions as we do for following minimally wrong past decisions. Because we do not believe that seriously wrong past decisions are that compelling, we must not believe that intertemporal equality is a true (or at least weighty) substantive value.

The sense of equality used by Moore and others who find erroneous decisions by precedent courts to be morally constraining is, thus, an extremely weak moral value. In fact, I would argue that it operates, if at all, only as a tie breaker. The only possible exceptions would be two situations, though neither squarely applies to the issue of precedential constraint. First, equality generates precedential effects where the good

9. *See, e.g.*, Westen, *The Empty Idea of Equality*, 95 HARV. L. REV. 537 (1982).

at issue is a discretionary benefit. The reason is that the distribution of these goods violates no rights and harms no legitimate interests of anyone beyond its effect on equality among recipients. Significantly, therefore, in such cases the precedent decision cannot be "wrong." Second, equality also operates where the good at issue is competitive, so that inequality is tantamount to deprivation. An example of a competitive good might be the right to vote, where, for example, giving extra votes to the members of one political party is the equivalent of taking away votes from members of the competitor party. Even here, however, the deprivation results from unequal treatment at a given time, not intertemporal inequality such as that involved in departing from precedent. Only rarely does intertemporal inequality of this type result in a present competitive disadvantage.

Beyond those two situations, equality as a moral value does not appear to carry any weight in terms of constraining a court to reach a decision that it believes would otherwise be morally incorrect merely because the precedent court reached a similar decision.[10] Whether or not equality carries any weight intratemporally—and some have denied that it does[11]—it almost certainly does not do so intertemporally, which is the relevant framework for assessing the decision whether to follow precedent. If a correct weighing of moral values would have led to a decision for the losing party in the precedent case, or to a decision refusing my daughter permission to attend the rock concert, "equality" cannot now require decisions that replicate the incorrect precedent decisions.

* * * * *

A final point that must also be considered is that if equality is a value that supports constraint by a precedent decision, then it becomes necessary to ascertain if the constrained case is factually similar to the precedent case. Yet access to the facts of the precedent case is extremely limited. For one thing, the opinion in the precedent case only reveals those facts that the precedent court thought important. Moreover, those facts will be described at the level of generality thought relevant by the precedent court. Thus, although there could be an indefinite number of

10. If equality were a reason for a constrained court to follow an erroneous decision by a precedent court of equal or superior rank within its jurisdiction, then it would also be a reason to follow an erroneous decision by courts of lower rank within the jurisdiction. Indeed, it would be a reason to follow erroneous decisions from courts outside the jurisdiction, including decisions of unlimited remoteness in time and space. Does one really believe that an unjust act toward a caveman or in Indonesia creates a reason for similar treatment of a twentieth century American?

11. *See, e.g.*, Coons, *Consistency*, 75 CALIF. L. REV. 59 (1987); Westen, *supra* note 9.

facts about the precedent case that the constrained court would find relevant to deciding what resolution effects equality with the precedent case, many, if not all, of those facts might not be revealed by the precedent court's opinion. Even the factual record of the precedent case will reveal only what the trial court thought were the relevant facts and the relevant level of generality of description. Thus, if the precedent court believes that all promises should be legally enforced, and writes its opinion in favor of the promisee revealing only that there was a promise made by defendant promisor to plaintiff promisee—and if the trial court's record reveals only those same facts—the constrained court, if it disagrees, will have no access to the facts that would determine whether equality pointed to a decision for the promisee in the subsequent case. (If the constrained court views equality as turning on the facts identified by the precedent court and not on all the facts about the precedent case, it will in effect have given the precedent court the ability to constrain by rules,[12] though the constraint will not be absolute if equality is not always an overriding value.) My point is that true equality would turn on the similarity of all relevant facts, not just on the similarity of the facts thought relevant by the constrained court.

I conclude that equality cannot account for any force that a decision in a precedent case naturally carries in subsequent cases.

2. *The Reliance Value*

The reliance value is the second value under the natural model of precedent that may justify a constrained court deciding a case differently from how it would decide in the absence of the precedent case. The reliance value is defined as the value of fulfilling expectations on which people have acted otherwise to their detriment. The argument runs as follows: If the decision in the precedent case has generated expectations of similar future decisions on which people have relied, particularly if the parties now litigating before the constrained court were among those who relied, and a decision that the constrained court would otherwise find correct would dash those expectations, then the opposite decision may in fact be the correct one. Thus, the value of reliance illustrates how, even under the natural model where a court merely has to decide its case morally correctly, an incorrect precedent can constrain.

An immediate problem with the expectations argument for natural constraint is that, because precedent courts on the natural model have

12. *See* K. LLEWELLYN, THE BRAMBLE BUSH: ON OUR LAW AND ITS STUDY 48-49 (1960).

authority only to decide cases and no authority to legislate rules binding on other courts, it might at first glance be difficult to see how the parties before the constrained court could have formed justifiable expectations that the constrained court would follow the precedent court. The answer to this is that even if the precedent court's decision was (in the constrained court's view) incorrect, and even if the precedent court had no authority to lay down general rules binding on future courts, rational people will take into account the precedent court's decision and its opinion in predicting what other courts will do. Thus, some people, despite the lack of any formal practice of precedent following, will justifiably rely on the precedent court's opinion and will modify their behavior in response to it. A constrained court, therefore, should take that behavior into account when determining what decision to reach.

Therefore, even in the absence of the precedent court's power to legislate and a correlative formal duty of the constrained court to follow precedent, an incorrect decision in a precedent case can dispositively affect the decision of the constrained court. Moreover, the predicted decision of a court will sometimes become normative for that court. In addition, a judicial opinion may give one course of conduct a salience that makes the opinion the most eligible basis on which to establish a convention, which, once established, has normative bite. (Of course, the constrained court should announce, for the purpose of affecting future behavior, that no one should henceforth rely on the precedent court's decision, unless the reliance has become so solidly entrenched in patterns of behavior that the costs of eliminating it outweigh the gains from doing so.)

3. *The Value of General Rules*

Although under the natural model of precedent the precedent court cannot legislate for the constrained court, it can, in deciding each case "on the merits," take into account the rule of law virtues that are served by formal rules. Moore is quite clear, for example, that if it is morally best that there be a general rule rather than case-by-case particularized decisionmaking, then it is part of deciding the true moral merits of a case that it be decided "as if" there were such a rule.[13]

13. *See* Moore, *supra* note 5, at 201-04. One virtue of general rules associated with their clarity and predictability is that they make invidious discrimination by officials easy to detect and hence difficult to accomplish. In this way, general rules serve a value associated with "equality," though one that is quite distinct from the value of equality invoked on behalf of precedential constraint per se.

This is an important point for several reasons. First, it shows how complex the notion of a morally correct decision is. It may well be the case that, looked at one way, A ought to prevail over B in a dispute, but looked at another way, there ought to be a rule that mandates a decision for B over A. This divergence between the optimal rule and the optimal result in the particular case is a familiar theme in political and moral theory.[14] It points out the deep difficulty we have in identifying the correct moral decision in any situation.[15] Moreover, there are probably more than just the two levels of the individual merits and the general rules, with the rules being a concession to institutional, motivational, and epistemological imperfections that make aiming directly at the individual merits less protective of individual merits in the overall run of cases. Instead, even our conception of the individual merits is probably shaped by rule-like, strategic considerations dictated by human limitations.[16] For example, if one were able to pick any moral ideal, would it be the ideal if humans were completely altruistic? incorporeal? omniscient?

---

14. *See* Alexander, *supra* note 3, at 317-30; Schauer, *supra* note 2, at 588-91; Wonnell, *supra* note 3, at 138-43. It may be true that one's set of political/moral principles P is best furthered by promulgation of a rule R that proclaims regarding situation S, "You are P-justified in following R in S, and you shall be punished for not following R in S, even if you believe P is best furthered by not following R in S." What can we say of X's "reasons" when X believes the above statement but also believes that P is best furthered by not following R in a particular instance of S, and/or P is in fact best furthered by not following R in that situation. For a discussion of this general issue, see Moore, *Authority, Law, and Razian Reasons*, 62 S. CAL. L. REV. 827 (1989); Perry, *supra* note 3; Raz, *supra* note 3, at 1154-1212; Regan, *Authority and Value: Reflections on Raz's Morality of Freedom*, 62 S. CAL. L. REV. 995, 1001-40 (1989).

15. *See* Kennedy, *Freedom and Constraint in Adjudication: A Critical Phenomenology*, 36 J. LEGAL EDUC. 518, 559-62 (1986).

16. The ability of general rules to play a significant role in the natural model creates one more problem for anyone who believes equality figures in any explanation of constraint by precedent. Assume, for example, the following situation. First, the constrained court believes that a certain case ought to be governed by a general rule that focuses on only a few of the larger number of otherwise morally relevant facts. Its reasons are the standard ones for preferring bright-line rules over case-by-case determinations. Second, the precedent case came out the wrong way under the rule the constrained court thinks should govern; a bona fide purchaser lost, but the ideal rule would be that bona fide purchasers always win. Third, on the full merits, that is, taking into account all the morally relevant facts and not just the facts the rule makes relevant, the precedent case is distinguishable; the bona fide purchaser in the precedent case was a quite unsavory and undeserving sort, unlike the bona fide purchaser in the constrained case. If the constrained court repudiates the precedent case, announces the rule that bona fide purchasers always win, and decides for the bona fide purchaser, has the constrained court offended equality given that some unsavory bona fide purchasers will win under the new rule and some litigants more deserving than the winner in the precedent case will lose? The parties in the constrained case (and subsequent cases as well) have been treated "unequally" with respect to the parties in the precedent case on the factors the rule deems to be relevant. In addition, the parties sometimes have been treated "equally" and other times "unequally" with respect to the totality of morally relevant factors, i.e. the nonrule merits.

Alternatively, would it be the ideal if one had fallen in among brigands, or lived in a time of war, revolution, anarchy, or impending holocaust?

The second reason why it is important that, under the natural model of precedent, the courts should decide cases as if the best rule were in place is that it exposes the instability of the natural model itself. If on the natural model courts can recognize the moral superiority of rules, why can they not lay those rules down? Why can they not legislate for future courts? Moore claims that precedent courts should not lay down rules for future courts, yet he admits that they can decide the moral merits of cases as if such ideal rules existed.

The principal difference between the natural model and a model of precedential constraint under which courts could legislate rules is that under the natural model, the constrained court is not constrained by the rule announced by the precedent court but only by the rule that the constrained court takes to be the ideal rule. *But it may very well be the case that one such ideal rule that a constrained court should follow as if it had been authoritatively promulgated is a rule requiring it to follow nonideal rules laid down by precedent courts.* If so, the natural precedent model paradoxically dictates its own replacement by another model.

But here I am getting ahead of myself. I shall deal with how the model of natural precedent might paradoxically dictate its own abandonment in favor of a different model after I have discussed the remaining models of precedential constraint.[17] I will conclude by summarizing the features of the natural model and assessing its strengths and weaknesses.

E. An Assessment of the Natural Model of Precedent

The natural model of precedent leaves the constrained court free to decide the case before it in the way that, all things considered, it believes is morally correct. Among the considerations the model looks to are the advantages of formal rules, advantages that might outweigh the costs of some decisions under the rules that would be incorrect in the absence of the rules. Among the factors that would incline the constrained court to follow an erroneous decision by the precedent court are equality and reliance. Equality, however, is a very weak reason at best, and more plausibly no reason, for following an incorrect decision. Reliance is a more plausible reason, but the constrained court is never bound to adhere to any rule announced in the precedent case merely because it was so

17. *See infra* text accompanying notes 59-68.

announced. No court can legislate under the natural model, though any court can "discover" and follow rules it believes are appropriate.

In one sense, the natural model of precedent cannot be criticized because it never requires of any court a decision other than the decision that the court deems best, all things considered, including the virtues of rules. In another sense, however, the model seems defective. Because each court is free to reject the rules announced in prior decisions, inferior courts and people generally will be unable to predict future decisions with much security. Although they will know that their acts in reliance on past decisions will be considered along with everything else that is morally relevant, this knowledge will not generate the predictability and concomitant security that a stronger doctrine of precedent will generate. The fear is that reliance may be outweighed—or more to the point, may be mistakenly believed outweighed—by other values. This unpredictability and insecurity may produce a state of affairs that is morally inferior to the state of affairs a stronger doctrine of precedent would produce.[18] Paradoxically, if the courts always attempt to do what is morally best it may in the end be morally worse than if the courts had acted under greater constraint (and occasionally followed an incorrect precedent).

Thus, although the model of natural precedent will generate some impetus in the direction of following precedents, even incorrect ones, its very freedom to achieve the morally best result and the weakness of its precedential constraint is a source of great, perhaps fatal, disvalue.

III. THE SECOND MODEL: THE RULE MODEL OF PRECEDENT

A. The Rule Model of Precedent Described

The second model of precedential constraint is the rule model of precedent. Under the rule model, the precedent court has authority not only to decide the case before it but also to promulgate a general rule

18. *But see* Kaplow, *An Economic Analysis of Legal Transitions*, 99 HARV. L. REV. 508 (1986) (arguing generally against taking into account reliance on nonideal legal rules). In my opinion, however, Kaplow overstates the ability to predict transitions from less ideal to more ideal legal rules, and understates the costs associated with his proposal.

I do not deal in this Article with the practice of prospective overruling. Prospective overruling may or may not be warranted in particular cases under the natural model of precedent. If, however, prospective overruling is chosen for reliance reasons in any case where the natural model would prescribe ordinary overruling, we are dealing with a stronger model of precedential constraint than the natural model. For a more general discussion of prospective legal change and its relation to the models of precedential constraint, see the discussion *infra* note 65 and accompanying text.

binding on courts of subordinate and equal rank. The rule will operate like a statute and will, like a statute, have a canonical formulation.

Versions of the rule model can vary along two dimensions. First, they can vary according to the strength by which the precedent court's rule binds the constrained court. On some versions, the constraint may be absolute, like that of a statute or constitutional rule on a court. On those versions, the constrained court may never overrule a precedent rule. On other versions, the constraint may be much weaker. On no version, however, is a constrained court as free to disregard a precedent rule as it is on the natural model. The constrained court cannot decide to overrule merely because, having weighed equality and reliance against the advantages of a different rule or decision, it has found the balance slightly tilted in favor of the latter.

The second dimension along which versions of the rule model vary is in their methodologies for identifying the precedent rule. Some versions try to locate a statement of a canonical rule in the opinion of the precedent court.[19] Other versions look for rules that the precedent court implicitly as well as explicitly used as necessary steps in reaching its decision[20] or facts that it deemed material to its decision.[21] On all versions of the rule model, however, the identification of the rule must meet three

19. *See, e.g.*, 26 HALSBURY'S LAWS OF ENGLAND 292-93 (4th ed. 1977); E. MORGAN & F. DWYER, INTRODUCTION TO THE STUDY OF LAW 154-56 (2d ed. 1948); J. SALMOND, SALMOND ON JURISPRUDENCE 177 (P. Fitzgerald 12th ed. 1966); R. WASSERSTROM, THE JUDICIAL DECISION 35-36 (1961); Hardisty, *Reflections on Stare Decisis*, 55 IND. L.J. 41, 53-55 (1979); Postema, *Some Roots of our Notion of Precedent*, in PRECEDENT IN LAW, *supra* note 2, at 9, 14-15. Hardisty is the source for the names I give my second and third models.

20. *See, e.g.*, R. CROSS, PRECEDENT IN ENGLISH LAW 75-76 (1977). For a striking example of the position that a judge may be bound by a narrow, but still general, rule with which he disagrees, but not be bound by the broader rule that the previous court endorsed and from which it derived the narrow rule, see the dissenting opinion of Justice Harlan in Duncan v. Louisiana, 391 U.S. 145, 181 n.18 (1968) (Harlan, J., dissenting). That position, unlike most that Justice Harlan held, is theoretically indefensible.

21. There is a lengthy and infamous debate in the literature over the "material facts" version of the rule model and whether it is sufficiently determinate to be constraining or whether it is completely indeterminate. *See* J. STONE, LEGAL SYSTEM AND LAWYERS' REASONINGS 267-80 (1964); J. STONE, THE PROVINCE AND FUNCTION OF LAW 185-89 (1950); Goodhart, *The Ratio Decidendi of a Case*, 22 MOD. L. REV. 117 (1959); Goodhart, *Determining the Ratio Decidendi of a Case*, 40 YALE L.J. 161, 169-83 (1930) [hereinafter Goodhart, *Determining the Ratio Decidendi*]; Simpson, *The Ratio Decidendi of a Case*, 20 MOD. L. REV. 413 (1957); Simpson, *The* Ratio Decidendi *of a Case*, 21 MOD. L. REV. 155 (1958); Stone, *The* Ratio *of the* Ratio Decidendi, 22 MOD. L. REV. 597 (1959); *see also* MacCormick, *Why Cases Have Rationes and What These Are*, in PRECEDENT IN LAW, *supra* note 2, at 155, 181 (briefly outlining the debate over the determinacy of Goodhart's "material facts method" for determining the *ratio decidendi* of a case). If the "material facts" are those facts in the precedent case that the precedent court, either explicitly or implicitly, and under a particular description at a particular level of generality, deems to be relevant facts under the norm the precedent court wishes to promulgate, then the "material facts" view of precedent is consistent

conditions. First, the rule must have a canonical formulation, even if that canonical formulation does not appear in the original opinion, such as, "Whenever facts A, B, and C, and not fact D, decide for P." Second, the rule must be treated as separate from the reasoning that led to its adoption by the precedent court; it is only the rule, and not the reasoning, that binds the constrained court. Third, the formulation of the rule must be fixed at the time of the precedent decision; that is, it must not be dependent on what any court other than the precedent court did.

As long as these three conditions are met, coupled with the condition that the constraint be greater than under the natural model of precedent, we are dealing with the rule model. Thus, issues such as whether an announced rule can be a precedent when the precedent court (mistakenly) reached a decision opposite from that which its rule dictates or, relatedly, whether rules intended to apply prospectively only can be binding are issues that arise within the rule model of precedent.[22] The resolution of these questions as well as the resolution of the general debate over how to identify the precedent rule do not affect the general points that I wish to make about the rule model. If the model is otherwise attractive, however, their resolution will become necessary.

B. Modifying or Narrowing the Rule

Under the rule model, the constrained court faces a binary choice: it can either follow the precedent rule in its canonical form or overrule it. All modifications of the rule, like subsequent amendments of a statute, amount to overruling the precedent rule and replacing it with a new rule. *Any practice of precedential constraint that distinguishes between overruling a precedent and narrowing/modifying a precedent is not a practice of the rule model of precedent.*

---

with the rule model. If the level of generality of description of the "material facts" has not been fixed by the precedent court, then the "material facts" view describes a different model.

22. Another problem faced by the rule model of precedent is working out the theoretical relationship between the precedent court's decision in a case of first impression and its laying down a rule in such a case to constrain future courts. Put in the form of a question, must the precedent court decide its case in the same way that the rule it lays down would have future courts decide such cases? If so, why? Rules almost always have a range of applications that includes applications that are incorrect from the standpoint of the more general policies or principles that the rules seek to implement. *See* Schauer, *supra* note 2, at 588-91. Must the precedent court apply its rule to its own case if to do so disserves the policies or principles behind the rule? Must it do so if all forward-looking gains the rule produces will be produced merely by its promulgation for the future, with no further gains achievable through its application to the case at hand? *See* Perry, *supra* note 3, at 984-85; Raz, *supra* note 3, at 1209-12.

1. *Narrowing the Rule to the Facts of the Precedent Case*

It is easy to see that restricting a rule to the facts of the precedent case is inconsistent with constraint by precedent. No matter how broad the precedent rule and how brief the description of the facts in the precedent case, there will always be some factual distinctions between the precedent case and all other cases. At a minimum, the precedent case will almost always involve different parties. Even if the parties are identical, the time of the transaction will be different. Thus, if a constrained court could escape the constraint of a precedent rule by citing *any* factual distinctions between the precedent case and the constrained case—whether or not those factual distinctions are relevant under the rule announced in the precedent case or are relevant under any plausible moral principle—a precedent case and its rule could never constrain, and the distinction between distinguishing a case and overruling it would collapse.

2. *Narrowing the Rule Based Upon the Reasons Behind It*

Allowing the constrained court to distinguish a precedent case on any factual grounds whatsoever amounts to eliminating precedential constraint altogether. Nevertheless, some urge that allowing the constrained court to modify the rule of the precedent case based on the reasons behind the rule is consistent with and the appropriate form of such constraint.[23]

There are two points worth making about this version of precedential constraint. First, as noted earlier,[24] any modification of a canonical rule overrules that rule. On the version of precedential constraint now being considered, the overruling of the announced rule is constrained by the reasons behind the rule. These reasons can be overruled, if at all, only in restricted circumstances, which depend upon the strength that we assign to precedential constraint. The rule itself, however, as opposed to its reasons, has, on this version, no real constraining power.

The first point leads to the second point: What this version really amounts to is constraint by the reasons of the precedent court, not constraint by its rule. This identification of the constraining rule with its underlying reasons threatens to take this version completely outside the rule model of precedent, where the rule stands apart from its reasons, and turn it into one of the other two models of precedent. Whether this

23. *See, e.g.*, Monaghan, *supra* note 2, at 764-65; Summers, *Two Types of Substantive Reasons: The Core of a Theory of Common-Law Justification*, 63 CORNELL L. REV. 707, 730-35 (1978).

24. *See supra* text accompanying note 22 (Section III, subsection B).

version can be made consistent with the rule model depends upon how it identifies the reasons (for the announced rule) that constrain. If the constraining reasons behind the rule are identified as the constellation of correct political/moral reasons with their correct weights, as assessed by the constrained court—and at the highest level of generality, all courts are attempting to do what correct political/moral reasons require of them—then this version simply amounts to the natural model of precedent previously discussed.

On the other hand, if the constraining reasons are (incorrect) political/moral reasons that "justify" the decision of the precedent court but that the constrained court does not agree with, then constraint by the precedent court's reasons amounts to the result model, the third model of precedential constraint that I shall discuss. Because I have not described that model yet, however, I will go no further at this point than to assert that constraint by (incorrect) political/moral reasons that "justify" the decision of the precedent court is in fact one way to describe that model.

Constraint by the precedent court's reasons can be a version of the rule model of precedent, however, if, but only if, the reasons meet the following criteria: (1) they are expressible in canonical form; (2) they are reasons the precedent court actually considered; and (3) they are reasons the precedent court wanted to override its stated rule in cases of conflict. In such cases, the precedent court's reasons really are its rule.

3. *Narrowing the Rule to the Facts of the Precedent Case While Limited to Factual Distinctions that Point to a Different Outcome*

A third version of precedential constraint is as follows. The constrained court should begin with the rule announced in the precedent case. If, however, the constrained court believes (1) that the factual differences between the constrained case and the precedent case make the constrained case a *weaker* case for the party analogous to the winner in the precedent case, and (2) that the party in the constrained case analogous to the winner in the precedent case should, all things considered, lose the case, then the constrained court may decide in favor of the other party and will not be deemed to have overruled precedent, even if the rule in the precedent case by its terms dictates a similar decision in the constrained case (a decision for the party analogous to the winner in the precedent case).[25]

This version of precedential constraint, which allows the constrained court to make factual distinctions between the constrained case and the precedent case even if they are not factual distinctions picked out by the precedent rule, is a version of precedent that does constrain, unlike the version that allows the constrained court to seize upon *any* factual difference. Moreover, this version does preserve the distinction between overruling and distinguishing precedent. Thus, so long as the constrained court (whether it likes it or not) follows the precedent court in situations where all factual distinctions between the cases indicate that the constrained case is a stronger case for the result in the precedent case than was the precedent case itself and departs from the precedent court only when the factual distinctions point the other way, the constrained court is following/distinguishing the precedent decision, but not overruling it.

Nonetheless, this version of precedential constraint is not a version of the rule model. Rather, just as was one version of restraint by the precedent court's reasons, it is one of the forms of the result model of precedent that I shall fully analyze in Section IV below. The reason I characterize it as a form of the result model is that the rule model requires following the rule as found in the precedent case. Any departure from that rule amounts to overruling it, just as a limiting amendment to a statute is equivalent to repealing the supplanted portion. In the version of precedential constraint just described, however, the constraint comes not from the precedent court's rule but from the facts of the precedent case. Under the rule model of precedent, by contrast, the constraint comes not from the facts of the precedent case but from the precedent court's rule.[26]

25. *See, e.g.*, R. CROSS, *supra* note 20, at 76-78; K. LLEWELLYN, *supra* note 12, at 52, 66-67; J. SALMOND, *supra* note 19, at 178; Hardisty, *supra* note 19, at 57-60; Kress, *Legal Indeterminacy*, 77 CALIF. L. REV. 283, 298-301 (1989).

26. It follows from this that where the precedent court's rule does not cover the constrained case, the constrained court can decide the case as it believes is morally correct. Even if the constrained court's case is a stronger case on its facts for the same result as in the precedent case, the court is not constrained to reach the same decision. On the pure version of the result model of precedent, however, which I discuss in Section IV, *see infra* text accompanying notes 42-56, the court is so constrained in that manner, though not by the rule.

4. *Narrowing the Rule Based Upon Its Inconsistency With Other Rules, or Based Upon Clear Inadvertent Mistake*

Unlike the previous three versions of precedential constraint, which were deemed to be inconsistent with the rule model of precedent because they allowed the constrained court to narrow the precedent court's rule, the version here described is consistent with that model. On this version, the constrained court must generally follow an applicable precedent rule, except that it can narrow the scope of the rule to eliminate inconsistencies between it and other rules that it does not believe were intended to be overruled by the precedent court. The constrained court can also narrow the precedent rule to exempt the following three situations: (1) those that were not adverted to by the precedent court; (2) those where application of the rule is (in the constrained court's view) undesirable; and (3) those in which the constrained court is confident that the precedent court would not wish to have its rule applied. This version is consistent with the rule model of precedent because the instances in which the constrained court can modify the precedent court's rule parallel the instances in which a court can depart from the literal command of a statute.[27] Because the rule model of precedent treats following the canonical rule of the precedent case as being similar to following a statutory rule, this version is within the model.

5. *Narrowing the Rule to Make an Ideal Rule*

Throughout this section I have been assuming that the constrained court disagrees with the precedent court's result and, thus, disagrees with its rule (because the rule presumably supports the result). The question has been to what extent on the rule model of precedent can the constrained court narrow the rule to avoid reaching another result that it believes is wrong and yet deny that it is overruling the rule. The answer is "not at all," except when overruling is unavoidable to eliminate inconsistencies with other rules (that have not been overruled) or to remedy clear, inadvertent mistakes.

When the constrained court *agrees* with the precedent court's result, but disagrees with its rule, may the constrained court alter the rule without being deemed to be escaping precedential constraint? The answer on

27. *See, e.g.*, Cernauskas v. Fletcher, 211 Ark. 678, 201 S.W.2d 999 (1947). *But see* United States v. Locke, 471 U.S. 84, 96 (1985) (following the literal meaning of a statute despite obvious contrary legislative intent).

the natural model is, of course, "yes," but the answer is not so clear on the rule model.

It is clear that even where the constrained court approves of the precedent court's result, tampering with the precedent court's rule amounts to abandoning the rule model of precedent in favor of the natural model. Of course, it is possible to have one model—the rule model—apply to precedent results believed wrong by the constrained court and another model—the natural model—apply to precedent results believed correct by the constrained court.[28] But the rule model of precedent as a distinct model tolerates only very limited tampering with rules, whether the rules originated in cases with correct or incorrect decisions. Beyond this limited tampering, a court must follow the precedent rules or, depending upon the strength of precedential constraint that we attribute to our practice of following precedent, overrule them.

6. *Broadening the Rule*

If the precedent court declares that in all cases with facts A, B, and C the decision shall be X, then narrowing the rule takes the form of amending it to hold that, for example, in all cases of A, B, C, and not D the decision shall be X. Broadening the rule, by contrast, would be amending it to hold that in all cases of A and B, the decision shall be X. Broadening the rule, unlike narrowing the rule, does not ordinarily overrule it, for the rule "A, B, C, then X" does not speak to situations involving A, B, and not C at all. It is quite consistent with acceding to precedential constraint under rule precedent for the constrained court to decide "A, B, then X" where the precedent rule is "A, B, C, then X."

Of course, because our inquiry is concerned with constraint by incorrect precedents, and a rule that is too narrow may be correct as far as it goes, cases dealing with broadening such rules are really outside of our inquiry. Put differently, a court that confronts a rule "A, B, C, then X" in a case of A and B is not constrained by the rule even if it believes the rule is too narrow and that the correct rule should be "A, B, then X." *This is because the rule "A, B, C, then X" does not cover the case of A, B.*[29]

28. It might seem more plausible to have the natural model apply to precedent results believed wrong by the constrained court and the rule model apply to precedent results believed correct by the constrained court. However, this would in fact be highly unstable: an erroneous rule attached to a correct result would produce incorrect results in the future, which would then make the rule no longer binding.

29. *See* J. RAZ, THE AUTHORITY OF LAW 185 (1979).

Occasionally, however, broadening the rule *will* mean overruling it. If the precedent court held "if and only if A, B, and C, then X," the constrained court's holding "A and B, then X" would be tantamount to a partial overruling. Thus, unless the situation justified overruling, broadening the rule would be inconsistent with precedential constraint under the rule model of precedent.

It is no objection to rules that contain an "if and only if" and, thus, preclude broadening that they purport to resolve issues that need not be resolved to decide the case at hand. *All* rules resolve issues not before the court. In principle there is no difference between narrowing a broad rule and broadening a narrow rule that by its terms precludes broadening. Both amount to amending and, hence, overruling a portion of the rule.

I should add a word about the distinction between holding and dictum, the existence of which all lawyers are trained to acknowledge, but the determination of which proves in practice to be quite controversial. The distinction cannot apply to the natural model of precedent, nor can it apply to the result model of precedent that I shall discuss in Section IV. It cannot apply to those models for the simple reason that on both of them, what the court *says*, as opposed to what it *does*, is irrelevant to the constrained court.

The distinction, however, does apply to the rule model. Under the rule model, the "holding" of the precedent court is nothing other than its rule. "Dicta," in turn, are those portions of the precedent court's opinion that are not part of its rule. The distinction between holding and dicta will be as controversial as the content of the precedent court's rule, no more and no less. The distinction is not synonymous with the division between issues necessarily decided by the precedent court in reaching its result and other issues on which it opined. *Every rule, by virtue of being a rule, decides issues that are broader than the particular facts of the cases in which they are announced.* Indeed, any model of precedent stronger than the natural model, which is arguably not a model of precedent at all, will legitimate the precedent court's deciding a range of cases beyond the precedent case itself. Rules are always to some extent general, while cases always involve particulars.

C. Advantages of the Rule Model of Precedent

The rule model of precedent has several advantages over the natural model. If one considers equality to be a value supporting precedential constraint—a value that I, for one, discount heavily[30]—then the rule model has the advantage of providing access to all the facts of the precedent case relevant to equality. All one needs to know about the precedent case is its rule, which establishes the relevant criteria of equal treatment.[31]

The most important advantage of the rule model, however, is that lower courts (and people in general) derive much more guidance from constraining general rules than they do from constraining particular decisions, even when the particular decisions take the value of rules into account. In claiming this, I am making three assumptions. First, I am assuming a practice of precedent following—precedent here consisting of the rules laid down in precedent cases—that is at least moderately strong. In other words, the constrained court cannot overrule the precedent merely because it can think of a rule that is slightly superior to the precedent court's rule. The rule model collapses into the natural model if the precedent can be so easily overruled. The advantage that the rule model provides in terms of guidance does not require that precedential constraint be absolute, but it does require that it be greater than zero.

Second, I am assuming that rules provide greater predictability than do other factors to which people might resort in order to predict courts' decisions—factors such as the judges' politics, economic class, and so forth.

Third, I am assuming that an improvement in legal predictability can be a net gain in terms of whatever political morality we hold, even when it comes at the cost of setbacks under that same political morality in particular cases and to particular litigants. This assumption holds up, I believe, despite its paradoxical quality, at least for any political morality that seems at all plausible.[32]

Finally, there is one additional "advantage" of the rule model: the third model of precedential constraint, the result model, is undesirable

30. *See supra* text accompanying notes 8-12 (Section II, subsection D.1).

31. There is a value furthered by constraint by general rules that is often confused with "equality": the value of preventing invidious discriminations and other abuses of authority by officials. It is easier to monitor compliance with general rules that pick out only a few factors as relevant to a decision—especially if the existence or nonexistence of those factors is not particularly controversial—than it is to monitor compliance with the standard "do justice in each particular case." *See* Alexander, *supra* note 3, at 319-21; Schauer, *Formalism*, 97 YALE L.J. 509, 532-35 (1988). Or, put negatively, it is more difficult for officials to hide their abuses if they operate under mechanical rules rather than under nonmechanical standards.

32. *See also* Alexander, *supra* note 3, at 319-21; Wonnell, *supra* note 3. *See generally infra* notes 61-63 and accompanying text (discussing this paradox under the natural and rule models of percedent).

and perhaps incoherent. Therefore, it is not a tenable alternative to the rule model.

D. Problems with the Rule Model of Precedent

1. *Cases with No Discernible Rules*

One problem with the rule model of precedent is its requirement that cases contain discernible rules in order to operate as precedents. This is a problem because many cases clearly fail this condition.[33] For instance, some cases lack discernible rules because the court's opinion is particularly opaque, cryptic, or self-contradictory. Other cases lack discernible rules because the majority of the court is divided into factions, each of which offers a different rule, and no rule justifies the decision that commands a majority of the court.

If the rule model of precedent is an otherwise attractive model of precedential constraint, then cases that lack discernible rules are undesirable. Courts should be encouraged to write opinions that clearly identify the rule that the court wishes to promulgate, and to do everything possible to garner majority support for that rule and not just a particular result.

Nonetheless, the failure of some cases to reveal their rules is not fatal to the model. Those particular cases will just have to be treated under one of the other two models of precedential constraint if they are to be treated as constraining at all. For reasons that will be clear once I have discussed the result model of precedent, the default model for the rule model applicable to cases without rules will have to be the natural model of precedent.

2. *The Precedent Court as Legislature*

The central problem with the rule model of precedent is the tremendous power that it gives the precedent court vis-à-vis the constrained courts. While the rule that the precedent court lays down may be quite narrow, it may also be quite sweeping. If it is sweeping, then no matter how misguided the rule is, and no matter how poorly the precedent court anticipated the rule's future applications, the constrained court must follow the rule unless and until the legislature steps in. To do otherwise

33. Many opinions contain no statement or clear implication of the rule adopted by the court. Many cases contain conflicting statements, either in the same opinion or in the multiple opinions of the judges who make up the majority. *See* Goodhart, *Determining the Ratio Decidendi*, *supra* note 21, at 165-68.

would be the antithesis of precedential constraint, because to limit the rule in any way is to overrule it. Thus, so long as the constrained court is constrained at all by the precedent—and our focus is primarily on precedential constraint, not overruling—it may be constrained quite strongly under the model.

A related objection to the rule model that Michael Moore raises is that rule precedent quite explicitly grants authority to courts to legislate and not just to decide particular disputes.[34] Moore argues that this is a mistake because, for institutional and other reasons, the judiciary should not be given the power and right to legislate. On the natural model, which Moore favors, the influence that courts' decisions would have over other courts' decisions would be limited to equality and reliance concerns. In addition, courts could decide cases "as if" particular rules existed in order to further the "rule of law" values. No court could however, legislate for subsequent courts. Rather, legislation under the natural model is reserved for the legislature, with its superior resources and its electoral accountability. (Even under the third model that we shall take up, the result model, courts cannot legislate for future courts, even though the constraint of their decisions is greater than under the natural model.)

It is these criticisms of the rule model of precedent, particularly its strong version of what precedential constraint entails, that has led commentators like Moore to reject it and to advocate other models. I have already examined the natural model and its advantages and problems. I shall now turn to the third model, which I have already previewed, the result model. It has perhaps the most heavyweight supporters. It also, however, has the most serious problems.

IV. THE THIRD MODEL: THE RESULT MODEL OF PRECEDENT

Many readers will feel that I have as yet failed to describe the model of precedential constraint with which they are most familiar. Like Goldilocks and the bowls of porridge and beds, they will complain that the natural model of precedent is too weak to capture their sense of how precedents operate and that the rule model of precedent is too strong. I have not described a model that is "just right."

34. *See* Moore, *supra* note 5, at 186-87; *see also* M. DETMOLD, THE UNITY OF LAW AND MORALITY 191 (1984) (discussing the authority of courts to lay down binding rules).

The third model of precedential constraint appears to meet this complaint. It seems stronger than the natural model in that an incorrect decision has more power to constrain subsequent courts than just reliance or equality values would explain. Yet it also seems weaker than the rule model in that the precedent court's stated rule is not itself binding.

Moreover, it is by far the favorite model of modern commentators. It is endorsed in one form or another by such otherwise jurisprudentially diverse types as Edward Levi,[35] Steve Burton,[36] Brian Simpson,[37] Joseph Raz,[38] and perhaps Ronald Dworkin.[39] Also, although he is not totally clear on this point, Fred Schauer also appears to favor the result model.[40] Finally, even Michael Moore, whom I have described as a proponent of the natural model, can be read as endorsing the result model instead.[41]

There are two versions of the result model. I shall deal with the more powerful (more constraining) pure version first. I shall then deal with the impure or hybrid version.

A. The Pure Result Model of Precedent Described

What are the major structural features of the pure result model of precedent, and how specifically does it differ from the other two models? To answer that question I will give three different formulations of precedential constraint that appear to describe three different models. I will then demonstrate that these three different formulations are functionally equivalent formulations of a single model of precedential constraint.

1. *First Formulation: Incorrect Precedents Control A Fortiori Cases*

The simplest formulation of the pure result model is as follows: To follow precedent, a constrained court must decide its case for the party analogous to the winner in the precedent case if the constrained case is as strong or stronger a case for that result than the precedent case was for

35. E. Levi, An Introduction to Legal Reasoning 1-27 (1963).

36. S. Burton, An Introduction to Law and Legal Reasoning 27-40, 59-64 (1985).

37. Simpson, *The* Ratio Decidendi *of a Case and the Doctrine of Binding Precedent*, in 1 Oxford Essays in Jurisprudence 148, 164-75 (A. Guest ed. 1961) [hereinafter Simpson, *Precedent*]; Simpson, *The Common Law and Legal Theory*, in 2 Oxford Essays in Jurisprudence 77, 87-88 (A. Simpson ed. 1977) [hereinafter Simpson, *Common Law*].

38. J. Raz, *supra* note 29, at 183-89.

39. R. Dworkin, Law's Empire 240-50 (1986) [hereinafter R. Dworkin, Empire]; R. Dworkin, Taking Rights Seriously 110-15 (1977) [hereinafter R. Dworkin, Rights].

40. Schauer, *supra* note 2, at 579-82, 593-95.

41. Moore, *supra* note 5, at 201. I leave to a footnote at the conclusion of Section IV, when I have fully explicated the result model, my reasons for placing these scholars and others in the camp of the result model of precedent. *See infra* note 57.

its result. The constrained court must do so even if under the natural model it would have decided its case differently and regardless of any rule stated in the precedent case.[42] Conversely, however, the constrained court may depart from the precedent court's result if the constrained case is a weaker case for that result than was the precedent case, even when the stated rule of the precedent case covers the constrained case and demands a similar result. Put differently, under the pure result model the constrained court must depart from what the natural model requires if and only if its case is an a fortiori case for the same (incorrect) result as in the precedent case.

This formulation of the pure result model of precedent can be presented schematically as follows: Assume that the relevant facts of the precedent case are A, B, C, and D and the precedent court holds for P, declaring as its rule that in all cases of A and B, the decision must be for P. In the constrained case the facts are A, B, C, and E (rather than D) plus N, the natural weight (equality and reliance) of the precedent case. If the absence of D and the presence of E and N make the constrained case a weaker case for P than the precedent case, the constrained court may ignore the rule of the precedent case ("if A and B, decide for P") and decide against P. On the other hand, if the presence of E is a stronger reason for deciding for P than was the presence of D, then even if the constrained court believes that, giving precedent its natural weight, P ought not prevail, the pure result model of precedent constrains it to decide in favor of P.

The a fortiori case formulation of the pure result model of precedent is a way of giving meaning to the injunction "treat like cases alike." That injunction is either empty, because all cases are alike in some respects and not in others, or it translates into "reach the same result as in the precedent case in any case that is as or more morally compelling for the result reached in the precedent case than was the precedent case itself, even if that result is not on balance compelling in either case." In other words, a case is "like" the precedent case if the facts point at least equally as strongly toward a decision analogous to the decision in the precedent case.

42. The stated rule is completely irrelevant under the pure result model of precedent. It does not bind the constrained court within the ambit of cases that it purports to control. Moreover, the outer boundaries of the stated rule do not mark the outer boundaries of the constraining force of the precedent case. Thus, on this model, any a fortiori cases are controlled by the precedent case even if they fall outside of its stated rule.

2. *Second Formulation: General Principles Constructed from Legal Materials that Include Incorrect Precedents Bind Constrained Courts*

Readers familiar with the legal philosophy of Ronald Dworkin will recognize the second formulation of the pure result model as Dworkin's recipe for discovering the law applicable to a given dispute. Briefly, Dworkin argues that to reach a correct decision according to "the law," a court should first collect the basic legal material such as statutes, constitutional provisions, and court decisions not yet overturned. The court should then ask which set of political/moral principles offers the best—the politically/morally most attractive—justification for most of the legal materials. (Some legal materials can be treated as mistakes and ignored in constructing the justifying principles, but such mistakes cannot be too numerous; all eligible sets of principles must meet a threshold of "fit" with the primary legal materials.[43])

One problem with this methodology is that Dworkin is ambiguous on the question of whether the "precedents" from which the justifying principles are to be constructed are just the decisions of courts in particular factual settings or whether they also include the rules those courts have promulgated. It is possible to read Dworkin as accepting the rule model of precedent and as principally describing what courts should do in cases that are not covered by the rules. Some evidence for this reading is provided by Dworkin's distinction between a precedent's gravitational force and its enactment force, with precedents that are "mistakes" under the constrained principles having only the latter force.[44] Enactment force looks like it refers to the explicit rule of the case. On this reading, Dworkin is dealing with the constraint decisions in cases impose in situations that their rules do not explicitly cover.

There is another way of reading Dworkin, however, on which the force of any precedent is dependent upon the principles that support it, whether that force operates to narrow the explicit rule of the precedent or to extend the scope of the precedent beyond the ambit of the explicit rule. On this reading, the distinction between a precedent's gravitational force and its enactment force collapses. This reading is more consistent with Dworkin's insistence that courts do not legislate but merely decide cases on the basis of either preexisting rules or principles, because if

43. Dworkin's approach to adjudication is set forth in the books cited *supra* note 39. *See also* Alexander, *Striking Back at the Empire: A Brief Survey of Problems in Dworkin's Theory of Law*, 6 LAW & PHIL. 419, 420-21 (1987) (surveying Dworkin's theory of legal doctrine).

44. *See* R. DWORKIN, RIGHTS, *supra* note 39, at 110-15.

courts could "enact" rules for future cases, those rules would either be based on policy considerations, which Dworkin rejects for courts, or on principles that would be paramount to and render superfluous any judicial enactments based upon them.

I am going to take the liberty of reading Dworkin in a way that allows a constrained court to narrow the rules enacted by precedent courts. Because many of my criticisms of the pure result model also cover the alternative reading of Dworkin—the rule model coupled with precedent-generated gravitational force for cases ungoverned by rules—it is not crucial that I have correctly interpreted his doctrine of precedent.

Dworkin's theory of adjudication, in which a precedent case is a datum that the constrained court must "justify" by constructing as attractive a political/moral theory as it can, draws much of its appeal with legal scholars from its theoretical account of, and justification for, a popular form of doctrinal analysis. The popularity of this methodology can be seen in the law reviews, which are full of articles that examine a line of cases, the opinions in which are unsatisfactory, and that construct a moral theory that reconciles all or almost all of the cases. The theory need not be, and frequently is not, expressed in any of the opinions and may even be opposed to the theories that are expressed in the cases. Moreover, the theory need not be, and frequently is not, one that the author regards as morally ideal.

It is plain that this type of doctrinal analysis is Dworkinian in nature and explains why Dworkin's jurisprudential views resonate as strongly as they do with lawyers and legal academics. This form of doctrinal analysis is, therefore, another way of describing the methodology of the pure result model of precedent. Thus, my criticism of Dworkin's formulation of the model is equally applicable to it.

3. *Third Formulation: The Precedent Court's Reasons, Not Its Rules, Control*

Another way to describe the pure result model of precedent is in terms of constraint by the precedent court's reasons for its decision rather than its rule. There are various denotations of the precedent court's "reasons." First, the precedent court's "reasons" might refer to some sort of algorithm endorsed by the precedent court that generates subsidiary rules and that itself can be canonically stated and applied as a rule. "Reasons" thus refer to a meta-rule to which the precedent court adheres. This meaning of constraint by the precedent court's "reasons" is a particular form of the rule model, one distinguished from other forms by its means of identifying the "rule" of the precedent case.

Second, the precedent court's "reasons" might refer to a set of principles that it believes supports its decision (and rule) in the precedent case but that cannot be stated algorithmically. The precedent court obviously believes its principles are consistent with correct political/moral theory; thus, it believes that there is no conflict between its more basic and less basic principles. The constrained court, therefore, believing the precedent court to have misapplied or misgauged the principles of correct political morality, and thus the precedent case to have been wrongly decided, would have no reason not to decide its case as *it* deemed correct, because the principles of correct political morality that *it* would invoke to support the correctness of its decision would be principles it could also attribute to the precedent court at the highest level of generality. The "reasons" of the precedent court, like the "reasons" of the constrained court, would be correct reasons (as necessarily interpreted from the point of view of the constrained court).

Put differently, because both the precedent court and the constrained court are trying to decide as truly correct reasons dictate, there is no inconsistency between the precedent court's "reasons," which were just erroneously applied, and the constrained court's reasons. There is no logical stopping place between the incorrect precedent decision (and rule) and the level of generality at which the constrained court and precedent court agree. On this interpretation of "reasons" we get the natural model of precedent, where the constrained court just does what is right from its point of view.

Third, the precedent court's "reasons" might refer, not to metarules, and not to correct principles that are applied incorrectly, but to that set of reasons—principles and their weights—that best justifies the (unjustifiable) decision of the precedent court. "Reasons" on this interpretation are, thus, not capable of rule-like application, nor are they as unconstraining of the constrained court (because nondissonant) as the correct reasons of the natural model of precedent. They constrain, though not like rules.

4. *The Equivalence of the Three Formulations*

I now want to show that the three formulations of the pure result model of precedent are in fact equivalent. It is obvious that the second and third formulations are equivalent, because the third formulation—the "reasons" of the precedent court—either translates as the natural model or rule model of precedent, in which case it is not the formulation of a new model, or else it translates as those principles that best justify the precedent decision, the latter simply being the second formulation of the pure result model.

It is more difficult to see the equivalence of the first formulation—the a fortiori case formulation—and the second and third formulations. I shall argue that while the a fortiori case formulation can be construed as different from the Dworkinian (second and third) formulations, it runs into deep problems that the alternative, Dworkinian, construal avoids. It will be easier to show how the a fortiori case version relates to the "best justification" version if we examine the problems with the entire pure result model.

B. Problems with the Pure Result Model of Precedent

1. *Incorrect Weighings and A Fortiori Cases*

The first problem with the pure result model is how to determine whether the constrained case is an a fortiori case for the result in the precedent case. By the hypothesis we are using to compare the models, the constrained court believes that by taking into account correct political/moral principles, including the correct natural weight of the precedent decision, the constrained case should be decided differently from the precedent case (which should have been decided differently itself). The issue is how a case that on its merits ought to be decided one way can be an a fortiori case for the opposite decision?

The most tempting answer is as follows: Assume the precedent case was composed of facts A, B, and C on the plaintiff's side and facts X, Y, and Z on the defendant's side. A, B, and C, correctly weighed, outweigh X, Y, and Z. Therefore, the precedent case should have been decided for the plaintiff. It was, however, mistakenly decided for the defendant. In the constrained case there are again facts A, B, and C for the plaintiff. For the defendant, however, there are facts W, Y, and Z, plus fact N, the natural weight of the precedent decision (reliance and perhaps equality). If fact W is a stronger reason for defendant than fact X, then facts A, B, and C might still outweigh facts W, Y, Z, and N, but by less than they outweighed X, Y, and Z alone. Because the balance tips in favor of plaintiff by less in the constrained case than in the precedent case, the constrained case is an a fortiori case for the defendant.

The major difficulty with this methodology for determining if a constrained case is an a fortiori case is that it requires a single metric on which the facts of two cases can be compared and weighed. In other words, the methodology must assume a single master principle that assigns weights in a common currency to various facts. Actual moral reasoning, however, is much more complex than this metaphor depicts. Facts that help the plaintiff or the defendant might represent distinct principles or policies that a decision for a particular party will further. A decision in the constrained case that parallels the decision in the precedent case may further some principles or policies to a greater extent than in the precedent case and others to a lesser extent. Under such circumstances, therefore, what is an a fortiori case?

The choice that is presented here is stark. If we assume that there *is* a master principle, a common metric for weighing values, such as utility, equal welfare, etc., then the pure result model on the first (a fortiori) formulation tells the constrained court something like this: If there is a precedent case where the balance was in favor of the plaintiff by, say, ten utiles, but the precedent court decided for the defendant, then in *all* cases where the balance of utility comes out in favor of plaintiff by ten or fewer utiles, decide for the defendant, *no matter how unrelated the cases might seem at first blush*. If there is but one metric, then a torts case can be a precedent for contract or agency cases that bear no resemblance to it at all. Thus, the determination of whether a case is a fortiori given another case is nothing more than comparing, on that single metric, the balance in the two cases in favor of the plaintiff or defendant.[45]

A further difficulty with the a fortiori constraint given a single metric of value is that there will undoubtedly be cases that are correctly decided according to this metric as well as cases that are incorrectly decided. *If this is so, then every constrained case will be constrained in opposite and irreconcilable directions.* If there is a case where the balance

45. One cannot escape this far-reaching consequence of the single metric view by arguing that there may be positive value (according to our metric) in keeping classes of cases distinct, even if they are otherwise commensurable on that metric. That may be true, but the a fortiori formulation of the pure result model of precedent already contemplates, and indeed demands, that the constrained court knowingly decide in a way that sacrifices value as long as the sacrifice is no greater than in the precedent case. If we wanted to maximize value according to our metric, why require that the constrained court sacrifice value at all?

This response to the value of distinguishing cases applies as well to the value of rules that distinguish classes of cases. In moving from the rule model of precedent to the result model, we have dispensed with constraint by rules and the utility of that constraint. The a fortiori formulation of the result model cannot reintroduce a concern with the utility of rules, even rules defining classes of cases, because it directs courts to sacrifice utility up to the level of sacrifice in the precedent case. To state this point differently, we must distinguish between the disutility of a particular decision and the disutility of following a particular method, here, the method of the pure result model of precedent. That method cannot take into account its own disutility without collapsing as a method.

of utilities favoring plaintiff is one utile, and the plaintiff won, that case will be an a fortiori case for the constrained case we have been imagining, where the balance of utilities favors plaintiff by ten. But so was the precedent case, where plaintiff was similarly favored but where the defendant won.

This point can be illustrated by reference to those numerous "criminal" cases where the Supreme Court held that one suspected of a crime *may not* be induced to make self-incriminating statements through threat of a civil sanction, such as loss of employment, attached to remaining silent,[46] and those also numerous "administrative" cases where the Supreme Court held that one *may* be compelled through threat of sanction, including criminal sanction, to file reports and statements even if self-incriminating.[47] The "criminal" cases make the "administrative" cases a fortiori cases in favor of the defendants. The "administrative" cases make the "criminal" cases a fortiori cases in favor of the state. The rule model of precedent could keep the cases from clashing through the device of simply limiting the rules governing the two sets of cases. The pure result model of precedent, however, does not respect rules announced in cases; it only acknowledges results.

Moreover, an incorrect decision on the pure result model of precedent throws everything out of kilter. If the precedent court incorrectly decided that facts A, B, and C outweigh facts X, Y, and Z, then consider the case of facts D, E, and F versus facts U, V, and W. If the latter outweigh the former, the court may still be constrained to hold otherwise if facts D, E, and F outweigh facts A, B, and C, and facts X, Y, and Z outweigh facts U, V, and W.

If we have a common metric for weighing facts and comparing cases across the entire corpus juris, then an incorrect result under the result model is like a piece of a jigsaw puzzle that is misshaped. If the other pieces must be conformed to it, they will not fit with each other. No matter how one makes adjustments, the puzzle cannot be pieced together coherently.

Alternatively, if there are multiple principles that cannot be reduced to a common metric, how do we determine whether an incorrectly decided case controls a factually distinct case in the sense that the latter is an a fortiori case given the former? If only a single principle is involved in both cases, or if one principle is lexically prior to the others, we are

46. *See, e.g.*, Garrity v. New Jersey, 385 U.S. 493, 496-500 (1967).

47. *See, e.g.*, California v. Byers, 402 U.S. 424, 427-34 (1971).

back to the preceding explanation: any case that damages that principle less than the precedent case did is an a fortiori case, regardless of the subject matter. But if the principles at stake are multiple and are not lexically ordered or reducible to a common master principle, determining whether the constrained case is an a fortiori case is impossible. (The only exception would be if the constrained case is an a fortiori case under every principle.) The one thing we do know is that the constrained court does not decide its case correctly merely because it applies this complex set of principles correctly.

2. *The "Best Justification" Version and the Problem of Incorrect Principles*

It is here that Dworkin's approach, the second and third formulations of the pure result model, solves the puzzle of the a fortiori case. We have been struggling with the a fortiori case because we have been operating with that principle or set of principles that we think is correct. We have been trying to measure the strength of an incorrect decision under a correct set of principles, which strength must be greater than its natural strength to fit the model we are exploring. But because an incorrect precedent can be given a weight on correct principles greater than the weight it in fact has on those principles, we are getting nowhere.

The problem can be illustrated from a slightly different perspective. The pure result model requires that incorrect decisions be extended to (as well as limited to) their logical limits. But their extension will run up against the extensions of other decisions, both correct ones and incorrect ones. Moreover, the conflict of precedents will not be an occasional result. Each decision can be viewed as implying a complete moral calculus, one that entails answers to all future cases. Thus, any two decisions, if not based on correct application of the same political/moral theory, are in actual conflict. Put differently, the notions of what is a morally a fortiori case and what is a morally distinguishable case are theory dependent. Two decisions embodying two different theories will produce irreconcilable conflicts, even if the decisions appear to apply only in quite separate domains. Once we dispense with rules and the opinions in which they are contained and look only to results, the law really does become not only a seamless web but an unmappable one as well.

Dworkin solves these problems of the a fortiori case by jettisoning the correct political/moral principles and replacing them with principles that are not necessarily correct but that do best explain the existing precedents. Dworkin's formulation of the method of the pure result model of precedent has the constrained court applying, not the principles of correct political morality and their correct weights, but the principles and weights of a political morality that is constructed from results reached by precedent courts. As we saw in the previous section, trying to allow an incorrect weighing to constrain other weighings in a moral universe governed by correct principles and their correct weights leads to indeterminacy or incoherence. Dworkin's alternative is to reformulate the governing principles and weights, adjusting them to the results with which they must cohere.

The first problem that confronts Dworkin is underdetermination.[48] Dworkin is asking us to imagine a possible moral world that is like ours except that certain results that are wrong in our world are correct in this possible world. If the precedent court has, for instance, held that facts A, B, and C outweigh facts X, Y, and Z, and the constrained court believes that correct application of correct political/moral principles leads to the opposite conclusion, its task, per Dworkin, is to imagine the possible world and its associated political/moral principles in which A, B, and C really do outweigh X, Y, and Z. The principles of *that* world then dictate the results the constrained court should reach.

The problem, however, is that there is an indefinite number of possible worlds and possible sets of principles that can "justify" the results in the precedent cases, assuming that we can really imagine these possible worlds and possible incorrect sets of principles. Once we are freed from the constraint of correct political/moral principles, our construction of alternative sets is unguided and unconstrained. Any given set of data, no matter how large, always underdetermines the theory constructed to explain it; likewise, any set of case results, no matter how large, will underdetermine the political/moral principles that would justify that set.

Dworkin, perhaps in recognition of this point, adds an additional constraint in the construction of the constrained court's principles to the constraint that those principles justify the results in the precedent cases (the constraint of "fit"). This additional constraint is that the set of principles constructed be the "best" or "most acceptable" set from among those sets that fit the results.

While this additional constraint on the construction of justificatory principles and their weights removes the bogey of indeterminacy, it does

48. The following discussion is a shortened version of that found in Alexander, *supra* note 43, at 426-34.

so at the cost of plunging Dworkin's enterprise into incoherence. For what is the meaning of "best" or "most acceptable" here? Their meaning must be dependent upon some normative theory, but what is it? It cannot be the political/moral theory to be constructed from the precedents, for then each theory would judge itself "best" or "most acceptable," and we would not have constrained our choice from among the indefinite number of such theories that can be constructed from the same data.

On the other hand, if the meaning of "best" or "most acceptable" is derived from correct political/moral theory (from the constrained court's point of view), the question for the constrained court becomes: "Which incorrect political/moral theory is 'best' from the point of view of correct political/moral theory?" But no political/moral theory can answer such a question because the question is so bizarre. A political/moral theory will perhaps determine for us a scale on which to rank and compare evils. But evils just remain evils, decisions that should not have been taken according to correct political/moral theory. Evil results are not translatable into more or less pernicious political/moral principles, *which are then to be substituted for correct political/moral principles and extended into new decisions*.[49] I deny that we could ever devise a set of principles that was the "best incorrect set" that would ever prescribe a result different from the result the correct set would prescribe taking incorrect results into account—that is, the result we would reach under the natural model of precedent. No political/moral theory will ever dictate its own abandonment in favor of another political/moral theory that is erroneous (from the former's perspective).[50]

Dworkin believes that the value of Integrity supports his approach to precedent in that the parties in the precedent case and in the constrained case will all be treated according to the same set of political/moral principles, though not the correct set. Integrity, for Dworkin, is a particular conception of the value of equality, one that requires that everyone be treated by government in accordance with the same set of principles, even if that set of principles is constructed from past and contemporary instances of governmental treatment of which none were

49. I doubt it is possible for a court sensitively to weigh and apply principles that it believes are mistaken. The reader might consider how sensitively to weigh and apply Nazi principles or the principles that best "justify" apartheid.

50. That is not to say, however, that a political/moral theory will not prescribe the adoption of rules that operate opaquely with respect to the theory and that will in some cases produce results different from those warranted by direct application of the theory. In other words, a political/moral theory may best be furthered by indirect means. *See* Alexander, *supra* note 3; Wonnell, *supra* note 3.

intentional invocations of that set of principles. Given instances of governmental treatment that cannot be justified by correct political/moral principles, equality as Integrity requires that we construct the "best" incorrect set of political/moral principles that cover and, hence, "justify" those instances. Because we will then have treated everyone in accordance with the same set of principles, we will have treated them "equally."

A correct account of equality, however, cannot be detached from a correct account of political morality in general. It makes no sense to further one correct principle of political morality in adjudication and disregard the others with which it is linked. Moreover, even if equality (of something) is the supreme value from which all others are derived, and furthering that conception of equality *is* acting in accordance with correct political/moral principles, it cannot have the kind of intertemporal implications that Dworkin requires. For if that conception of equality is the only value a court need consider, and if the precedent case was *wrongly* decided, then it must be because the decision offended that correct conception of equality. If the precedent is to operate on the constrained court in the way Dworkin envisions, it will do so because the correct conception of equality dictates extension of an incorrect conception of equality. But that conclusion is nonsense.

Dworkin's version of the pure result model also generates peculiarities with respect to the overruling of precedents. Under the natural model of precedent, there is really nothing for a constrained court to overrule: there is only the ineluctable historical record of what the precedent court did and its equally ineluctable present effects in the world. The rule model dictates that overruling is the express repudiation of a precedent rule or the promulgation of a rule inconsistent with the precedent rule in whole or in part. Under Dworkin's theory, however, a decision that is inconsistent with the political/moral principles generated by all of the preceding cases overrules the principles but not the cases. It becomes a datum for the construction of a new set of principles. Thus, precedents cannot themselves be overruled for the same reason that there is no overruling of precedents under the natural model, namely, the ineluctability of the historical facts. (Indeed, as I argue elsewhere, a Dworkinian court logically should look at repealed statutes and constitutional provisions as well as presently operative ones in constructing the set of political/moral principles to use in adjudication.[51]) But although

51. *See* Alexander, *supra* note 43, at 422. Briefly, the argument is this: If courts could overrule precedents and then ignore them, and if courts could ignore repealed statutes or constitutional provisions, Integrity would operate only intratemporally, not intertemporally. But the vice of

precedents cannot be overruled, the legal rights of people arising from particular transactions are being changed retroactively by the subsequent changes in the set of political/moral principles that is to govern those transactions.[52]

To sum up this discussion, Dworkin does not want the constrained court to be constrained by either the precedent court's rule (as under the rule model of precedent) or by correct political/moral principles (as under the natural model of precedent). Rather, he wants the constrained court to consult correct political/moral principles in order to determine which set of incorrect political/moral principles among those that would "justify" the incorrect precedents is the "best" set, and then to jettison correct political/moral principles in favor of applying this best incorrect set in future cases. Dworkin's enterprise has neither the virtues of moral correctness nor the rule-of-law virtues of rule-following. If it is coherent at all, which I deny, it is so normatively unattractive that it cannot be a tenable option for a model of precedential constraint.

(I should point out parenthetically that perhaps the most powerful aspect of Dworkin's theory of adjudication is how well it seems to resonate with—and indeed seems to be a more sophisticated rendition of—a very common version of precedential constraint, which I call the "inducing a covering rule" formulation of the pure result model of precedent. In brief, on this formulation, the precedent cases are viewed as a collection of particulars, and the constrained court must decide its case under a general rule, the consistent application of which would explain the pattern of precedent decisions. In other words, a general rule is induced from the collection of precedent cases and then applied in the constrained case.

Because an indefinite number of such general rules can be induced from any set of precedent cases, no matter how large the set, this version faces the following dilemma. If the constrained court wishes to decide as it deems correct—pursue the method of the natural model—it need only formulate the rule it has induced as the correct rule, but with exceptions for any cases identical to those precedent cases that came out the wrong

unprincipled action that Dworkin represents through his hypothetical checkerboard statutes is one that can only occur over time, not instantaneously. Although all the parts of the checkerboard statute may exist at the same time, they apply to people—and thus produce their checkerboard effect—only over time. Thus, a concern with Integrity must necessarily be a concern with intertemporal treatment. Precedents, statutes, and constitutional provisions that had past effects on people cannot be ignored in the present even if formally overruled or repealed.

52. *See* Kress, *Legal Reasoning and Coherence Theories: Dworkin's Rights Thesis, Retroactivity, and the Linear Order of Decisions*, 72 CALIF. L. REV. 369, 398-402 (1984).

way according to the correct rule. Because no future case will be identical to past cases, the exceptions will not constrain. To build in constraint on this version—and here is the other horn of the dilemma—the rule induced must be one that "justifies" the precedent decisions. However, because some of the precedent decisions were not really justified from the constrained court's point of view, the constrained court must ask itself the counterfactual: "If the precedent decisions were justifiable, what covering rule would justify them?" Because this is essentially the same incoherent question Dworkin's theory has the constrained court ask, I do not treat the "inducing a covering rule from particular cases" version as a distinct formulation of the pure result model of precedent.[53])

3. *The Problem of Access to the Facts of the Precedent Case*

A further problem with the pure result model is that it requires the constrained court to have access to those facts of the precedent case that bear on the constrained court's assessment of whether its case is or is not an a fortiori case given the precedent. The precedent court might be quite obliging and recite volumes of facts in its opinion regardless of *its* view of their relevance. On the other hand, the precedent court may believe that its case and future cases should be governed by a very broad rule, which in turn may lead it to recite only those facts pertinent to the rule and only at the level of generality at which the rule operates. For example, it may reveal only that defendant is a promisor and plaintiff a promisee if it believes that the appropriate rule is that all promises should be legally enforced.

The problem raised by a spare recitation of facts characterized at a high level of generality is that it seriously impedes the constrained court's determination of whether the constrained case is an a fortiori case or is instead distinguishable on its facts from the precedent case. If all the constrained court knows about the precedent case is that the plaintiff was a promisee, the defendant was a promisor, and the plaintiff won, then if it believes its plaintiff-promisor should not win (in the absence of the precedent case), it will be unable to determine whether its case is factually

53. Both inducing a covering rule to "justify" unjustifiable precedent decisions and narrowing stated rules so that they do not cover the constrained case but still "justify" the unjustifiable precedents, *see supra* text accompanying note 28, run afoul of the same problem of "justifying" the unjustifiable. No rule that purports to justify a precedent that the constrained court believes was wrongly decided will be a justifiable rule. Thus, no such induced or narrowed rule will be any more justifiable than a rule that covers only the precedent cases and hence does not constrain at all! For an example of a recent discussion of precedent that assumes the contrary, see Kress, *supra* note 25, at 298-301.

different from the precedent case in a way that supports the defendant (that is, that it is not an a fortiori case for the plaintiff).

If this lack of access to the facts of the precedent case causes the constrained court to follow the precedent decision and to decide, contrary to its natural model judgment, for the party analog to who won in the precedent case, the pure result model of precedent all but collapses into the rule model. At least it does so if the precedent court is clever and reveals only that the facts picked out by its rule obtain. In other words, the advantage that the pure result model purports to have over the rule model—the absence of judicial legislation—is quite fragile and easily defeated by a clever court.

Joseph Raz, in response to this problem, argues that the constrained court should be free to assume that any fact not mentioned by the precedent court was not present in the precedent case.[54] Thus, if (1) the precedent court reveals facts A, B, and C and announces as its rule, "A, B, then X"; and (2) the constrained case has facts A, B, C, and D, D being a fact that supports non-X; then (3) the constrained court may assume that D did not exist in the precedent case and, under the pure result model of precedent, decide for non-X (assuming it favors non-X on the natural model).

Raz's solution to the problem of access to facts saves the pure result model from collapsing into the rule model. It does so, however, at the price of collapsing it into the natural model. This is so because if *anything* in the constrained case points to an opposite decision—and there always will be in the cases we are considering, the cases where the precedent decision is viewed as incorrect by the constrained court—then, unless that fact also clearly exists in the precedent case, the precedent case will not constrain beyond its natural model strength. Suppose that the precedent case involved snail remains in a bottle of ginger beer,[55] as revealed in the precedent opinion, and the constrained case involves particularly ugly snail remains in a bottle of high priced ginger beer. If the precedent court decided for the defendant, and the constrained court wishes to decide for the plaintiff, on Raz's argument the constrained court need only assume that the facts "ugly" and "high priced" did not exist in the precedent case because the precedent opinion did not mention them. Moreover, the constrained court does not need to find the ugliness of the snail remains or the price of the ginger beer relevant under the rule

54. J. RAZ, *supra* note 29, at 187.

55. *Cf.* Donoghue v. Stevenson, [1932] App. Cas. 562 (deciding for plaintiff with same facts of snail remains in a bottle of ginger beer).

it would favor.[56] Rather, it need only find that these facts point more strongly toward a decision for plaintiff.

Thus, the pure result model is, because of lack of direct access to the facts of the precedent case, threatened with collapse into either the rule model or the natural model. Neither of these models, however, are hampered by the problem of the precedent court's characterization of the facts of the precedent case. The rule model clearly is not; the natural model merely asks the constrained court to do the best it can with whatever facts it has. On the natural model, limitations on the constrained court's knowledge about the facts of the precedent case are no more significant than other limitations on its information about the world, limitations that are the hallmark of the human condition generally.

* * * * *

The pure result model in all its formulations, to the extent it avoids collapse into and differentiates itself from the natural model and the rule model, faces either indeterminacy or incoherence. This is not surprising because the normative enterprise it describes, having neither the virtue of moral correctness nor the virtues of rule-following, lacks any normative appeal whatsoever.

C. The Impure Result Model of Precedent: A Rule/Result Hybrid and One-Way Ratchet

The impure result model is a hybrid of the rule model and the pure result model. It is another model of constraint by erroneous precedent. On this model, the rule announced in the precedent case acts as a limit on the precedent court's constraint; the constrained court need not extend the result of the precedent case to a fortiori cases that are not covered by the rule of the precedent case (as it must on the pure result model). On the other hand, the precedent rule can be narrowed in the constrained case if the latter is not an a fortiori case for the same result as in the precedent case; within the ambit of the precedent rule, only the precedent result, not the rule itself, constrains.

The impure result model avoids the pure result model's problem of extending incorrect results so that they are perpetually in conflict with other incorrect and correct results, a conflict avoidable only by the construction of a complete but incorrect political/moral theory. If the

56. Otherwise, a rule that selected the criteria that it should select but then dictated the opposite result from what it should would be more constraining than a less perverse rule.

notion is coherent that a case can be an a fortiori case for result X even though both it and its precedent case should really have result Y, then the impure result model may be capable of application. (The governing assumptions for both result models are that the precedent rule can be treated as erroneous but the precedent result must be treated as correct, though only within the limits of the rule on the impure model. The question for the constrained court on both models is, given these assumptions, are the constrained and precedent cases distinguishable?) Nonetheless, the impure result model is extremely curious, even bizarre. The main question is why should rules count as marking the outer limits of constraint of an incorrect precedent but not count as rules within those limits.

Not only does the impure result model face the problem of all hybrids—lack of a principled rationale—but it shares with the pure model several unattractive features. First, unlike the natural model of precedent, it requires the constrained court to decide some cases contrary to the way it believes those cases ought to be decided. Second, unlike the rule model, it does not offer the predictability and stability that decisions based on rules provide. Thus, it has the virtues of neither of the non-result models and the vices of both. Moreover, like its purer cousin, it also faces the "access to the facts of the precedent case" problem. All in all, it is an ugly model, conceptually and normatively. If it accurately describes our practice of precedential constraint, then changing that practice is surely in order.

D. The Curious Attraction of the Result Model of Precedent

I hope that my attack on the result model of precedent in both its pure and impure versions will be universally assessed as, not only devastating, but fatal. But if I am correct about the seriousness of the result model's problems, what can account for its attraction among the commentators?[57] I have three hypotheses to offer that may explain this phenomenon.

57. The following are my reasons for placing various commentators either firmly or tentatively in the result model of precedent camp.

Edward Levi: Levi is an advocate of the view that rules in cases do not bind, but instead precedent cases are continually susceptible to reinterpretation under covering rules induced from them. This is clearly one formulation of the pure result model of precedent. *See* E. LEVI, *supra* note 35, at 1-27.

Steve Burton: Burton, in his discussion of analogical reasoning, like Levi, adopts the view that "the rule" of the precedent case is not fixed by the court in that case but is continually subject to

First, in cases where the precedent court reaches the correct result but promulgates an unfortunate rule, both the result model and the natural model prescribe the same course of action for the constrained court:

reformulation in future cases. His position is, in all respects relevant to our topic, the same as Levi's. *See* S. BURTON, *supra* note 36, at 27-40, 59-64.

Brian Simpson: Simpson explicitly rejects the rule model of precedent and says that language in the precedent case that purports to be canonical need not be treated as such. Because he believes precedents constrain beyond the minimal force they have on the natural model, he can be read as endorsing the result model. *See* Simpson, *Common Law*, *supra* note 37, at 87-88; Simpson, *Precedent*, *supra* note 37, at 164-75.

Joseph Raz: Raz believes that the rule stated in the precedent case can be narrowed by the constrained court and that such narrowing differs from overruling. Narrowing and (partial) overruling are synonymous on the rule model of precedent, so it appears that Raz rejects that model. In cases where the precedent case was correctly decided, the natural model of precedent and the result model of precedent give the constrained court the same latitude to reformulate and improve the rule of the precedent case. In the cases pertinent to our inquiry—cases the constrained court believes were decided incorrectly by the precedent court—both the natural model and the result model allow the constrained court to modify the precedent rule. However, the result model imposes the a fortiori constraint while the natural model does not. Raz says that the modified rule must "justify" the precedent decision and must "improve" the precedent rule. J. RAZ, *supra* note 29, at 185-86. That could be read as a natural model injunction, in which case it translates into the correct rule plus an exception for all cases (of which there will be none in the future) absolutely identical to the precedent case. However, that is a very strained reading of Raz because Raz later says that the modified rule must have the same essential rationale as the precedent rule. *Id.* at 189. This only fits the natural model at the highest level of generality, where the essential rationale of all rules is to do what is right and good. (Raz can also be read as endorsing a version of the rule model if the real rule, the one that cannot be modified by the constrained court, is the "essential rationale" stated in canonical, rule-like form. Again, this is a very strained reading.) The most straightforward reading of what Raz says about modifying precedent is the Dworkinian one: one "justifies" an incorrect precedent by constructing a set of principles with which it and other principles cohere. This is, therefore, one formulation of the result model of precedent. Nonetheless, I place Raz in this camp rather tentatively since he is in all other areas very critical of Dworkin's approach to adjudication.

Fred Schauer: I hesitate to place Fred Schauer with the proponents of the result model of precedent because most of his focus is on the precedent court's formulation of rules and on the virtues of constraint by rules. Indeed, this latter focus would seem to indicate that Schauer would endorse the rule model of precedent. Yet Schauer argues that precedents can be distinguished without being overruled, which is not possible under the rule model. *See* Schauer, *supra* note 2, at 579-82, 593-95.

Michael Moore: In Section II, *see supra* text accompanying notes 5-7, Michael Moore was characterized as a proponent of the natural model of precedent. Yet Moore can also at times sound like Dworkin. For example, he states, citing Dworkin: "We know how to justify . . . truths of the common law. We take . . . all . . . legal decisions in our jurisdiction . . . and construct the most coherent theory that we can think of that has those decisions as its deductive implications." Moore, *supra* note 5, at 201 (citations omitted).

Treating incorrect precedents as if they were correctly decided is the hallmark of the result model of precedent, not the natural model, where incorrect decisions are taken into account but not "justified." Unless Moore is dealing only with correctly decided precedents, where the natural and result models have the same implications, the quoted passage is a recipe for the result model.

Others: There are a large number of legal theorists who reject the rule model of precedent in that they do not view the constrained court as bound to apply the precedent rule as stated, but who also view precedential constraint as stronger than it would be on the natural model. For example, Felix Cohen argues for precedential constraint that is stronger than *logical* consistency (which is no

ignore the precedent court's rule and do what is right. Because the precedent court reached the correct result, there is nothing in the precedent case to stand in the way of the constrained court's doing justice in its case once the precedent court's rule is jettisoned. *If commentators focus only on precedents that reached correct results, they will not see any difference between the result model and the natural model.* Seeing no difference, they will be deceived about the efficacy of the result model because of the coherence of the natural model.[58]

Second, commentators may be attracted to the view that courts do not "legislate," and they may fail to notice that on any model of precedent stronger than the natural model—which may be tantamount to saying on any model of precedent rightly so called—the precedent court perforce legislates (makes law) for future courts. As the result model may appear to sanction a weaker form of judicial legislation than the rule model, it may, therefore, appear attractive to commentators. But appearances are deceiving. In reality, the result model's form of judicial legislation is, in its own way, just as strong as the rule model's. Moreover, it has none of the redeeming virtues of the latter.

Third, many precedents contain no clear articulation of a canonical rule. Under the rule model, the constrained courts in such situations may follow a convention that identifies the rule of such precedents as the narrowest rule that can reasonably be intended by the precedent court in light of what it said in its opinion. (The narrowest rule that can reasonably be intended does not mean, of course, a rule that is actually justifiable. If it did, we would be outside the rule model of precedent, where rules constrain because they are the precedent court's rules and not because they are justifiable. Moreover, justifiable rules cannot be inferred from those precedents that are incorrectly decided.)

This method of finding the precedent court's rule might appear to some commentators to sanction the constrained court's narrowing the precedent court's rule and, thus, to be inconsistent with the rule model Thinking that precedent must be stronger than the natural model would

constraint at all), a concept he calls "ethical consistency." F. COHEN, ETHICAL SYSTEMS AND LEGAL IDEALS 33-37 (1933). "[A]ssuming that the decision in the earlier case was a desirable one, is it desirable to attach legal weight to any of the factual differences between the instant case and the earlier case?" *Id.* at 37. This, again, is similar to Dworkin's formulation of the result model of precedent.

Likewise, R.W.M. Dias argues for limiting precedent decisions to their facts as long as they are "reasonably" distinguishable from the constrained case. R. DIAS, JURISPRUDENCE 145-46 (5th ed 1985).

58. This may explain Moore's apparent endorsement of the result model. *See supra* note 57.

have it, and construing the method in question as inconsistent with the rule model, the commentators might be drawn to the result model by default. But, of course, the method is *not* inconsistent with the rule model. To the contrary, it is a method for finding the rule of those precedent cases in which the opinions do not contain readily identifiable rules.

In the end, I do not know why the commentators have been attracted to the result model. I offer these three hypotheses merely as possibilities. Whatever the explanation for its attraction, the result model in both its pure and impure versions surely must be rejected. Because of its internal incoherence, it cannot be the model courts in fact employ. Even if it were not internally incoherent, however, it is so normatively unattractive that it could not be recommended as the model for courts to adopt.

V. THE NATURAL AND RULE MODELS OF PRECEDENT REVISITED

I have shown that the result model of precedent in both its pure and impure versions lacks both internal coherence and normative appeal. That leaves the natural and rule models as the only possible models for an attractive method of precedential constraint.

I now return to an earlier suggestion and argue that the natural model and the rule model might complement each other in the sense that the former might endorse the latter. Here is how the argument goes.

The natural model recognizes the value of bright line rules and the propriety of courts' deciding cases as if the ideal bright line rules had been judicially promulgated. What the natural model denies and the rule model affirms, however, is that the precedent court can bind the constrained court to the rule the precedent court believes is ideal as opposed to the rule the constrained court believes is ideal.[59]

The problem the natural model of precedent faces with its injunction to "get it right" is that such an injunction may create, through unpredictability and uncertainty, more disvalue (under correct political/moral principles) than the injunction "follow the precedent rules even if they are incorrect." That is so even though the natural model instructs

59. Of course, even on the natural model, the announcement of a rule in the precedent case may be constraining, not because the rule is binding per se, but because of reliance. Still, reliance may not outweigh other reasons for departing from the precedent court's rule in the constrained case and is even less likely to outweigh reasons for announcing a new prospective rule (though it could).

the constrained court, in its attempt to "get it right," to consider the unpredictability and instability its decisions will cause.

The point is the familiar one about how direct pursuit of political/moral values may achieve less in terms of those values than the indirect pursuit of those same values, that is, pursuit through norms, such as general rules, that are to be followed without reference to those values.[60] The point is highly paradoxical; yet I believe it accurately describes the normative universe we inhabit. For various reasons, primarily those concerned with the informational and motivational limitations human decisionmakers face, adherence to rules even when the rules dictate incorrect results—as they inevitably will in some cases—may achieve more value and thus be more "correct" than deciding each individual case "correctly."[61]

While the natural model of precedent recognizes the value of rules, it doesn't carry this insight far enough. The natural model admits that an ideal rule may produce results contrary to the results produced by (correct) direct application of the governing political/moral principles. In such cases, the constrained court should abide by the constraint of the ideal rule. What the natural model of precedent denies and the rule model affirms, however, is that the constrained court must also abide by nonideal rules announced in precedent decisions.

The relationship between an ideal rule and those applications of the rule that diverge from (correct) direct application of the governing political/moral principles is exactly parallel to the relationship between the (perhaps) ideal meta-rule—"follow the rules laid down in precedents"—and *its* nonideal applications (those instances where the precedent rules are nonideal). If the natural model of precedent envisions that constrained courts will decide cases according to ideal rules even where the decisions diverge from direct application of the governing political/moral principles, there is no reason for it to preclude the constrained courts from deciding cases according to an ideal meta-rule. If the ideal meta-

60. *See* Alexander, *supra* note 3; Wonnell, *supra* note 3.

61. This is a familiar theme in the literature on rules. *See* Alexander, *supra* note 3; Alexander, *supra* note 43, at 432-33; Schauer, *supra* note 31, at 538-44; Schauer, *supra* note 2, at 595-602; Wonnell, *supra* note 3; Schauer, *The Jurisprudence of Reasons* (Book Review), 85 MICH. L. REV. 847, 863-70 (1987) (reviewing R. DWORKIN, LAW'S EMPIRE). It has also been a favorite topic in the scholarship of members of the Critical Legal Studies movement, though they tend to regard rules less sympathetically than the other authors mentioned. *See, e.g.*, M. KELMAN, A GUIDE TO CRITICAL LEGAL STUDIES 15-63 (1987); Kennedy, *Form and Substance in Private Law Adjudication*, 89 HARV. L. REV. 1685, 1687-1713 (1976); Kennedy, *Legal Formality*, 1 J. LEGAL STUD. 351 (1973); *see also* Schlag, *Rules and Standards*, 33 UCLA L. REV. 379 (1985) (discussing problems with certainty and flexibility in rules versus standards).

rule is one that makes precedent rules binding even where the constrained court can do better in terms of the governing political/moral principles by departing from the precedent rule—and that paradoxical possibility is quite likely—then the natural model itself dictates the adoption of that ideal meta-rule by the constrained courts. In other words, once a proponent of the natural model, such as Moore, admits that courts may decide cases under optimal rules that will produce non-optimal results in some cases, he can have no principled objection to courts legislating for other courts if such a meta-rule is optimal. But this meta-rule constitutes the rule model of precedent.[62]

We can then see how this paradoxical relation between reasons and rules, between direct and indirect applications of the same political/moral principles, can lead to the natural model's endorsing the rival rule model. I believe that any set of political/moral principles that is a plausible candidate for the correct set will be best implemented indirectly. Moreover, I believe it very likely that the indirect strategy for implementing political/moral principles not only warrants binding rules that are legislatively-authored but also binding rules that are "legislated" by courts in the gaps left by legislation. Thus, I believe that the natural model of precedent, correctly applied, quite plausibly requires adoption of the rule model of precedent.

A natural model of precedent gives the precedent case no authority.[63] Rather, the precedent case generates some gravitational pull

62. Moore clearly concedes the legitimacy of courts deciding cases under rules. Moore, *supra* note 5, at 201-04. The core of his argument against the rule model is one of institutional inappropriateness:

> Courts deciding individual cases do not have the information before them (nor the means to get it) either to issue rules in the linguistically precise form of a statute or to give authoritative statements of policy objectives. They do not know precisely what the reach of a rule or goal should be when deciding cases. Attaching precedential weight to their statements of rules or reasons may thus put a burden on them that they are not equipped to meet.

Id. at 187. However, since all general rules are formulated with an eye toward their consequences, and therefore resemble statutes in that respect, Moore's "separation of powers" argument is too strong. It is, in fact, an argument against all common-law decisionmaking by courts, as distinct from decisionmaking under statutes and constitutional provisions. But, since Moore otherwise supports common-law decisionmaking and the employment of general rules in that process, his argument really boils down to one about the relative competence of the precedent and the constrained courts. There is reason to believe that we learn from experience, which is, at the extreme, an argument against any entrenchment of choices in rules. *See* Eule, *Temporal Limits on the Legislative Mandate: Entrenchment and Retroactivity*, 1987 AM. B. FOUND. RES. J. 379, 384-427; Schauer, *Rules, the Rule of Law, and the Constitution*, 6 CONST. COMMENTARY 69 (1989). However, the value of rules on the other side of the balance is quite considerable, a point that Moore himself recognizes and indeed must find compelling, given his support for general rules.

63. *See* J. RAZ, *supra* note 29, at 19-27.

toward an analogous decision because of the values of reliance and (controversially) equality. But the goods associated with the reliance value may be more realizable under a stronger model of precedent, one in which the precedent case has authority—that is, the rule model. Moreover, these reliance goods may outweigh the negative aspects of constraining courts to follow rules that they believe are wrong, even though the constrained courts are as wise as precedent courts and have the advantage of more experience, or so the argument runs.

This argument is probably correct if the rule model of precedent has a moderate but not absolute strength in the area of common-law decisionmaking that is our area of concern. Thus far, I have said nothing about the strength of precedential constraint under the rule model of precedent. On the natural model, the constraint of a precedent decision is equal to the strength of the reasons it generates in favor of a like decision. On the rule model, the strength of precedential constraint is the greater of either its strength on the natural model or the constraint of the meta-rule that defines the rule model. That meta-rule could be "always follow the precedent rule," in which case the constraint is absolute, or it could be "always follow the precedent rule, except under certain (specified) conditions," in which case the constraint is less than absolute. The limiting case, where the rule model disappears and is replaced by the natural model, is the meta-rule "always follow the precedent rule except when the reasons for *not* doing so outweigh the reasons *for* doing so."

* * * * *

If precedential constraint is too weak—if the constrained court can overrule the precedent with little more reason than mere disagreement with it—the "ruleness" of the precedent is undermined and the model virtually collapses into the natural model. If precedential constraint is too strong and approaches absolute constraint, many bad rules (some of them *really* bad) will become entrenched over time. Only the legislature will be able to get rid of those precedents.[64] The optimal form of the rule model will most likely be one that gives the precedent rule absolute constraining power over lower courts and parties and, with respect to co-

64. Interestingly, legislation operates analogously to the natural model of precedent. That is, no legislative rule can be entrenched against future legislative repeal. *See* Eule, *supra* note 62, at 403-05. Nor can any judicial rule of nonconstitutional status be entrenched against repeal. Of course, promiscuous legislative repeals of legislative and judicial rules are limited to some extent by constitutional doctrines relating to ex post facto laws, takings of property, impairments of contracts, and vested rights. (Courts would be so limited even if they operated on the natural model and not under

equal courts, strong constraining power (beyond the constitutional constraints that exist) to limit overrulings that would apply retrospectively and weaker constraining power to limit prospective overrulings.[65]

There are a couple of final points that need to be addressed. First, I have criticized the result model of precedent in several places on grounds that might be construed as inconsistent with what I am claiming is true for the natural model, namely, that it leads to its own abandonment. For example, I pointed out in criticizing Dworkin that a correct political/moral theory would never endorse following an incorrect political/moral theory no matter how well the latter fit with past decisions.[66] I also pointed out that application of the result model could not take into account its own disvalue when it is not constrained by disvalue in particular cases.[67]

Here, however, I am not arguing that correct political morality, the natural model of precedent, be abandoned in favor of an incorrect political morality. The relation between the natural and rule models is one of direct versus indirect application of the same political morality. Nor is there any "indirect" version of the result model of precedent, for it is a model that eschews the pursuit of correct value altogether, whether directly or indirectly.

A second point that needs to be made is that the result model of precedent cannot be justified as an indirect method for implementing correct political/moral principles, one that is a plausible alternative to the rule model in this role. The result model, besides being internally incoherent, lacks the determinateness and predictability that are the *sine qua non* of indirect methods of implementing political/moral principles.[68]

---

the stronger constraints of the rule model.) But the primary check on legislative upsets of reliance is undoubtedly inertia.

The question then is, why do we need courts to be constrained by a formal practice of following precedential rules when ultimately those rules can be repealed legislatively by a body not so constrained? In other words, if the natural model is appropriate for the legislature, why is it not also appropriate for courts, at least for those of co-equal status with the precedent court? The best answer may be that the courts are not as well-equipped in a variety of ways to legislate as are legislatures and that courts function best when they take one stab at promulgating a rule and then leave matters to the legislature. I believe that answer is probably correct.

65. Even prospective overrulings, like statutes that apply prospectively, have retrospective, reliance-upsetting effects. *See generally* Munzer, *Retroactive Law*, 6 J. LEGAL STUD. 373 (1977) (discussing retroactivity and legal validity).

For an interesting discussion of the strength of precedential constraint, see Perry, *supra* note 3, at 963-90; Raz, *supra* note 3, at 1206-09.

66. *See supra* text accompanying notes 48-49.

67. *See supra* note 45.

68. *See* Alexander, *supra* note 43, at 434.

Because we have reasons for having a rule model of precedent, we have reasons for doing other than what the balance of reasons requires. We have reasons to have rules that preclude resort to reasons. This is surely paradoxical, but it is equally surely true. Even if the existence of rules adds to the balance of reasons in favor of doing what the rules require in all cases, there is still a gap between following the rules *qua* rules and acting on reasons, including the reasons for having rules. It is always possible that we have reasons to follow rules that produce results at odds with those reasons.

VI. CONCLUSION

In this Article I have discussed three models of precedential constraint. I have demonstrated that two of these, the natural and rule models, are tenable, and one, the result model, is not. Moreover, I have argued that if the value of rules is admitted even when they do not "get it right" in every application, there is no reason to deny the possibility that the rule model of precedent may be superior to the natural model on the latter's own terms.

Which of these models are we likely to discover when we examine the case law? Although some formulation of the result model is frequently asserted to capture how courts in fact view precedential constraint, the internal incoherence of the model leads me to believe that the courts cannot really be following it. Moreover, I think we will find the courts paying far more attention to the opinions in precedent cases than either the result model or the natural model would warrant and surely viewing themselves as more constrained than the latter model would suggest. While I suspect that the data would be messy, I imagine they would reveal that constrained courts of lower rank than the precedent courts follow a strong version of the rule model,[69] constrained courts of equal rank follow weaker versions of the rule model, and unconstrained courts—those of higher rank than the precedent court,[70] or those in

69. Lower courts surely follow some version of the rule model. They pay careful attention to the opinions of courts superior to them in the judicial hierarchy. Indeed, they frequently have nothing else from the higher courts but opinions, as when the higher court remands a case to the lower court for further proceedings not inconsistent with what the higher court has said. In these cases, there are only rules, not results, for the lower courts to follow. But even where there are "results" from higher court decisions and not just rules, imagine the chaos that would result if the lower courts felt free to disregard the higher courts' rules.

70. Because the constraint of precedent is not absolute for constrained courts of equal rank, the potential breadth of the precedent courts' rules is less of a problem than might be feared. Still, it is a problem, and the "solution" of weakening precedential constraint is really no solution at all, being, in essence, an anti-precedent tack. The real solution is for precedent courts to exercise restraint and

other jurisdictions—follow the natural model. (Much of the messiness in the data would be traceable to disagreements over what part of a precedent opinion contains the rule and how the rule is properly formulated; much would also be traceable to partial overrulings—amendments—by courts that are not absolutely constrained.) Finally, in cases not covered by precedent rules, all courts would follow the natural model, though in attempting to reach the correct decision and to promulgate the correct rule, they would take into account, as relatively fixed parts of the environment, not only the statutory and constitutional rules governing other areas of the law but also the judicial rules that do so.

Finally, the debate over models of precedential constraint tracks the more general debate over the nature of law. In *Law's Empire*, Dworkin gives the name "Pragmatist" to the natural law position that "the law" in adjudication is whatever is morally correct for courts to do, the name "Conventionalist" to the legal positivist position that "the law" is a set of formal rules or conventions, and the name "Integrity" to the middle-ground jurisprudential position that he proposes.[71] In criticizing Dworkin, I wrote the following:

> Now the Pragmatist will realize that in any community of more than a few people, it will be morally correct to establish conventions and institutions for deciding authoritatively what is morally correct. Those conventions and institutions, which are themselves decisions about what is morally correct, plus the more substantive decisions they produce regarding what is morally correct, make up the Conventionalist's "law." Thus, the Pragmatist's "law" (what it is best to do) leads inevitably to the Conventionalist's "law" (what we have already decided it is best to do in accordance with conventions and through institutional mechanisms that we have decided it is best to have). The Pragmatist, or as I would call her, the Sophisticated Natural Lawyer, may claim that the term "law" properly applies to her broad, practical question. The Conventionalist, or Legal Positivist, may claim that "law" properly applies only to her narrower question regarding the content of authoritative decisions. But this dispute is at bottom terminological, not substantive. The two positions can be viewed as complementary parts of one coherent moral enterprise.
>
> Although Pragmatism and Conventionalism are complementary parts of the same enterprise, there is a quite paradoxical relation between them. Although the Pragmatist, to do what is morally right,

to formulate rules rather narrowly. While the desirability of rules stems from the fact that every rule decides cases not before the court, one can still have much of the benefit of a regime of rules if the courts formulate the rules with caution and modesty.

71. *See* R. DWORKIN, EMPIRE, *supra* note 39, at 94.

needs authoritative conventions—conventions that should be treated as binding—these conventions may produce answers that are not morally right. Morality requires us to make binding decisions, and those decisions can be morally wrong. I have explored this paradox elsewhere. What I wish to say here is that there is no middle ground within the paradoxical relation between Pragmatism and Conventionalism for Dworkin to occupy with Integrity. And Pragmatism/Conventionalism, unlike Integrity, is coherent and attractive. Its paradoxes are paradoxes born of features of reality, not unattractive, theory-discrediting blemishes.[72]

If one substitutes the natural model of precedent for Pragmatism, the rule model of precedent for Conventionalism, and the result model of precedent for Integrity, one has a restatement of the conclusions of this Article.[73]

---

72. Alexander, *supra* note 43, at 432-34 (citations omitted); *see also* Posner, *The Jurisprudence of Skepticism*, 86 MICH. L. REV. 827 (1988) (defining a moderately skeptical approach to law and judging).

73. A thoroughgoing natural law position denies practical authority to all humanly posited rules and thus to those institutions, such as courts and legislatures, that owe their existence to such rules. A thoroughgoing legal positivist position leads to Eichman. But because I see these positions as the two sides of a paradoxical relation, I deny that there is a "middle," "compatibilist" position for theorists like Dworkin to occupy. *See* Alexander, *supra* note 43, at 433-34; *see also* Alexander, *Personal Projects and Impersonal Rights* (1989) (publication forthcoming in Harvard Journal of Law & Public Policy) (discussing the positivism/natural law relationship).

The interpretivist/noninterpretivist debate in constitutional law is itself a version of the positivism/natural law debate. *See* Alexander, *The Constitution as Law*, 6 CONST. COMMENTARY 103 (1989). Noninterpretivism carried to its logical limits, like the strong natural law position with which it is affiliated, undermines the authority of the courts' noninterpretive decisions themselves. For, given noninterpretivism, why should any court be bound to interpret an earlier court's decision that it disagrees with if neither it nor the earlier court is bound by correct interpretation of legally authoritative sources? Indeed, given noninterpretivism, how do we even recognize courts, legislatures, or other legally authoritative institutions and their products?

Finally, the positivism/natural law debate is part of a more general problem of practical rationality, the problem of decisionmaking. Practical rationality requires that we make decisions based on the balance of reasons as it appears to us at the time of the decision. But to make a decision means that we are not open thereafter to reconsideration based on the balance of reasons as it appears to us later. If we were so open, then we would not have "decided." Decisions, as the etymology of the word suggests, "cut off" this type of reconsideration. Yet, reconsideration might reveal that we misassessed the balance of reasons and thus that our decision was incorrect. In other words, reconsideration might lead to a more reasonable decision. If that is so, decisions, which rationality requires that we make, appear also to conflict with rationality. In other words, practical rationality is itself paradoxical. *See* M. BRATMAN, PERSONAL POLICIES (Center for Philosophy and Public Policy Working Paper No. RR-8, March, 1987); Raz, *Reasons for Actions, Decisions and Norms*, in PRACTICAL REASONING 128-42 (J. Raz ed. 1978). One example of this paradox is in the free speech area; we cannot know whether a bar to acquiring information is good or bad without knowing the information we are barred from acquiring.

In jurisprudence, the decisions we are concerned with are those that determine what people are obligated to do and that claim practical authority. Once such a determination is made, the claim of practical authority means that the legal rule that issues from the determination—the Constitution, the statute, the judicial decision—supplants the balance of reasons that underlies the determination. The paradox here is that we must determine, both in general and in particular cases, whether to abide by these legal rules without revisiting the balance of reasons behind the rules or their particular application. For if we so pierce the rules, we have already failed to give them the practical authority they claim and that rationality requires we give them. On the other hand, how can it be rational not to examine how good or bad they are?

APPENDIX A: PRECEDENTIAL CONSTRAINT IN STATUTORY AND CONSTITUTIONAL INTERPRETATION

A. The Rationale

Some commentators believe that the whole notion of being constrained by precedent is problematic when the subject is statutory and/or constitutional interpretation rather than common law decisionmaking.[74] After all, if the constrained court believes the precedent court has misinterpreted a statutory or constitutional provision, does it not defeat the purpose of lawmaking through statutes and constitutional provisions for the constrained court to follow the precedent rather than the correct meaning of the provision at issue?

The answer is that precedential constraint in statutory and constitutional cases *does* fit uneasily with a pure statutory/constitutional regime, but that our statutory/constitutional regime is an impure one, and for good reason. First, we have statutes and constitutions rather than a mere general injunction to decide cases as justice dictates. This is because the indeterminacy of "do justice" leads to less justice overall than the more determinate directions of statutory and constitutional rules, even when what the rules prescribe is not just in every case. Rules, even nonideal rules, lead to more justice than doing justice directly, case by case.

Second, we have the institution of judicial review in constitutional cases because having some institution whose interpretation of the Constitution is authoritative and final within the legal system furthers the value of determinateness in law. We have, at least since *Marbury v. Madison*,[75] accepted the risk of making an incorrect judicial interpretation final in exchange for the benefit of settling disputes over constitutional meaning. The same argument for rules instead of direct application of political/moral principles supports judicial finality in constitutional interpretation rather than institutional anarchy, even if in some cases this means that the judicial interpretation in effect displaces the authority of the Constitution, correctly interpreted.

It is this argument for judicial finality—for making the courts' interpretations supreme over the correct interpretations as assessed by other actors—that also supports making the precedent court's interpretation of a statute or constitutional provision supreme over the constrained court's

74. *See, e.g.*, Brilmayer, *The Conflict Between Text and Precedent in Constitutional Adjudication*, 73 Cornell L. Rev. 418 (1988).

75. 5 U.S. (1 Cranch) 137 (1803).

interpretation. Statutes and constitutions are means to justice. So, too, is judicial finality. And so, too, is precedential constraint. There is no reason why these three means to justice cannot coexist as complements.[76]

B. THE FORM

The model of precedential constraint in statutory and constitutional cases must perforce be the rule model, with a qualification that I shall discuss in a moment. What the precedent court is doing in each case is translating the language of the provision in question into language of its own. It is the latter that is "the rule" and that constrains later courts. In other words, a precedent in statutory and constitutional cases is a canonical translation of a canonical text.

If the precedent court interprets the statutory or constitutional provision as a mechanical rule, then it will merely convert the language of that rule into different language. That language will thereafter also have the characteristics of a mechanical rule.

On the other hand—and this is the qualification I mentioned—if the precedent court interprets the provision as a correct political/moral principle, case-by-case implementation of that principle will proceed as if under the natural model of precedent, because the natural model is characterized by the case-by-case implementation of correct political/moral principles. Of course, once a court decides to implement the correct principles of the governing text through subsidiary mechanical rules,[77] the rules could then bind constrained courts as they would under the rule model of precedent.

If the precedent court interprets the statutory or constitutional provision as an *incorrect* political/moral *principle*—that is, as neither a mechanical rule nor a correct principle—that court and subsequent courts will inevitably convert the provision into either a correct principle or into a mechanical rule. Incorrect principles cannot be applied as such because they lack real weight as well as determinate form.[78] Moreover, as normative prescriptions they have no virtues, being neither correct nor clear.[79]

76. *See* Easterbrook, *Stability and Reliability in Judicial Decisions*, 73 CORNELL L. REV. 422 (1988); Monaghan, *supra* note 2, at 744.

77. *See* Monaghan, *Foreword: Constitutional Common Law*, 89 HARV. L. REV. 1, 10-34 (1975).

78. *See* Alexander, *supra* note 43, at 431-32 n.20.

79. *See* Alexander, *Modern Equal Protection Theories: A Metatheoretical Taxonomy and Critique*, 42 OHIO ST. L.J. 3, 15-16 (1981).

C. The Strength

The strength of precedential constraint in statutory and constitutional cases will be determined by what factors the constrained court must find, other than finding the precedent interpretation incorrect, to justify overruling. The precedent interpretation's incorrectness is perforce a necessary but not a sufficient condition for overruling. If incorrectness were *not* a necessary condition for overruling—if the constrained court were able to overrule the precedent merely because it believed that the precedent caused mischief—the authority of statutory and constitutional texts themselves would be undermined. On the other hand, if incorrectness were a sufficient condition for overruling, there would be no precedential constraint in statutory and constitutional cases. Thus, to preserve both the authority of texts and precedential constraint, the constrained court must find a precedent under a statute or constitutional provision to be both incorrect and something else. That something else might be that the precedent causes mischief, is egregiously incorrect as an interpretation, is very recent and yet to be relied upon, or is very old and eroded and, hence, no longer relied upon. The strength of the precedential constraint will be determined by what that something else is.[80]

80. For some of the implications of a practice of precedent in constitutional cases that treats the precedential constraint as real but less than absolute, see Bittker, *The Bicentennial of the Jurisprudence of Original Intent: The Recent Past*, 77 CALIF. L. REV. 235, 278-80 (1989).

APPENDIX B: THE RULE MODEL OF PRECEDENT AND LINES OF PRECEDENT

What should happen on the rule model of precedent when the precedent court's "rule" purports to be the correct interpretation of a still earlier precedent court's rule, but the constrained court believes that the precedent court misinterpreted the earlier court? Should the constrained court follow the precedent court's interpretation, or should it follow what it believes is the correct interpretation of the earlier court's rule?

Although my thoughts on this are somewhat tentative, I believe that the proper analysis of these situations goes like this: If the second court has the authority to overrule the precedent rule of the first court, which will generally be the case where the second court is equal in rank to the first court, then whether or not the second court intended to overrule the first court, and whether or not it should have overruled the first court, the third court should follow the second court. At least it should do so unless it is equal in rank to the second court and has reasons for overruling stronger than merely that the second court made an interpretive mistake. This analysis parallels the analysis given in Appendix A of the practice of following precedent in cases of statutory or constitutional interpretation, except that the egregiousness of the second court's mistake in interpreting the first court can never be a reason for the third court to overrule the second court.[81]

Again, I have nothing to offer on the question of how precedent rules are correctly identified and interpreted beyond the conditions that circumscribe the enterprise that I mentioned in Section III. The nub of that discussion is that precedent rules are best conceptualized as judicial statutes, with all that implies for their identification and interpretation. Nor do I have anything to offer here on the question of the strength of precedential constraint, except, as I have said before, that it should be less than absolute but more than the precedent's natural strength for courts of equal rank. What is clear is that the reasons for constraining a court to follow a precedent court's rule even when the constrained court

81. The reason for this possible distinction between the constraint of a precedent that misinterprets a statute and the constraint of a precedent that misinterprets a prior case is that mere misinterpretation of an institution of equal authority (like a predecessor court) is, unlike the substance of a particular interpretation or misinterpretation, not in itself an evil, especially where the misinterpreting body has authority to overrule. In the case of a precedent that misinterprets legislation or the Constitution, the precedent court lacks that equality of status with the interpreted institution. Therefore, even with a practice of precedent following in statutory and constitutional cases, the egregiousness of the precedent court's misinterpretation could be a reason for overruling that misinterpretation.

believes the rule is ill-advised apply with no less force in situations where the constrained court thinks the precedent court's rule is a misinterpretation of an earlier court's rule.

APPENDIX C: MELVIN EISENBERG ON THE COMMON LAW: A FURTHER COMPARISON OF THE NATURAL AND RULE MODELS OF PRECEDENT

In a recent book devoted to the common law and the processes of judicial decisionmaking associated with the common law, Melvin Eisenberg distinguishes different ways that a constrained court might establish the rule of the precedent case.[82] One approach, the minimalist approach, allows the constrained court to cut back the precedent court's announced rule to the bare minimum necessary for producing the result in the precedent case. The constrained court can then treat the resulting rule as the only constraint it faces. Another approach, the result-centered approach, disregards the precedent court's announced rule altogether and merely requires the constrained court to make its result consistent with the result in the precedent case. Eisenberg admits that neither approach provides much precedential constraint. I would add that this is especially the case if particulars such as the names of the parties and the dates of the transaction at issue are regarded either as parts of the necessary rule or as parts of the result. (If they are not so regarded, then, as I have pointed out, the precedent court can produce considerable constraint through a very general characterization of the facts.[83])

In any event, neither approach attributes to the precedent court's announced rule the force common law courts characteristically grant both verbally and behaviorally to announced rules in precedent cases. Under a third approach, however, what Eisenberg calls the announcement approach, the constraining aspect of a precedent case *is* the announced rule in that case. It is the announcement approach that is most characteristic of common-law judicial behavior.

It would appear that Eisenberg is endorsing what I have called the rule model of precedent, at least as the most accurate general description of common law methodology. But when Eisenberg turns his attention from establishing precedent rules to overturning them in whole or in part (transformation), his model of common law methodology deviates from the rule model.

The deviation does not consist in his recognition that courts do in fact overrule announced precedent rules or, what is in fact the same thing, narrow them through techniques such as the minimalist and

82. M. EISENBERG, *supra* note 5, at 52-55.

83. *See supra* text accompanying notes 54-56 (Section IV, subsection B.3).

result-centered approaches. After all, the rule model does not entail giving any particular weight, much less absolute weight, to precedential constraint. Thus, the rule model is consistent with a considerable amount of total and partial overrulings.

Where Eisenberg deviates from the rule model—and in fact adopts the natural model—is in his discussion of the proper bases for overruling.[84] For Eisenberg, the key to determining when total or partial overruling is proper lies in what he calls social congruence and systemic consistency.[85] Basically, social congruence refers to the compatibility between the precedent rule and what Eisenberg calls background social propositions, which function for Eisenberg essentially the same way as what I have been calling principles of political morality.[86] Systemic consistency refers to the compatibility among legal rules themselves, though that compatibility I would argue must ultimately be cashed out as well in terms of background principles.[87]

Eisenberg argues that total or partial overruling is justified when the announced precedent rule does not substantially satisfy the standards of social congruence and systemic consistency and when the reliance costs brought about by overruling—costs that are themselves made relevant by the same background principles that determine social congruence—are not great relative to the costs of following the precedent.[88] Put differently, background principles of political morality provide the bases both for the substantive critique of the precedent rules and also for the decision whether to overrule them wholly or partially.

It is here that the real though subtle difference between the rule and natural models emerges. The weight of precedential constraint in both models is a product of background political/moral principles. Under the natural model, overruling or modifying a precedent rule is governed directly by these principles. As I have pointed out,[89] these principles often will dictate that the constrained court continue to follow a nonideal precedent rule in order to avoid reliance costs. Under the rule model, however, these background principles dictate adoption of a second-order rule or meta-rule regarding when and when not to overrule or modify first-order precedent rules. That second-order rule—the rule that determines the weight of precedential constraint—is itself to be applied

84. M. EISENBERG, *supra* note 5, at 62-76.
85. *Id.* at 64-76, 104-06.
86. *Id.* at 43-47.
87. *Id.* at 44-46.
88. *Id.* at 68-74, 110-15, 130-36.
89. *See supra* text accompanying notes 13-18.

by constrained courts absolutely (without resort to its progenitor principles) though it is a product of reasoning from the background principles of political morality. I have already shown that the argument for first-order rules—an argument that proponents of the natural model accept—can support second-order rules such as a rule prescribing when first-order rules may be overruled or modified.[90] Eisenberg would base overruling and modifying on direct application of background principles and thus is urging a natural model of precedent. He nowhere denies the possibility nor gainsays the desirability of second-order rules, including a rule determining precedential constraint.. And the combination of first-order precedent rules and a second-order rule of constraint defines the rule model of precedent.

In short, the difference between the natural model of precedent and the rule model does not lie in the recognition of the importance of first-order rules, rules that might dictate some outcomes at odds with those produced by (correct) direct application of background political/moral principles. The proponents of the natural model such as Moore and Eisenberg recognize the value of first-order rules. Nor does the difference lie in the recognition of the role of political morality. Even the proponents of the rule model, like most legal positivists, acknowledge the connection at some level between legal rules and the political/moral principles from which their justifiability must ultimately be derived. Rather, the difference lies primarily in the area of second-order rules of stability and change, the level at which the practice of constraint by precedent is defined. For the proponent of the natural model, the principles of political morality operate at this level and apply directly to first-order rules. For the proponent of the rule model, those principles of political morality produce second-order as well as first-order rules. They thus apply to the latter only indirectly, that is, through the filter of those second-order rules.

90. *See supra* text accompanying notes 59-68.

[9]

THE HORWITZ THESIS AND COMMON LAW DISCOURSE IN ENGLAND

R. B. FERGUSON*

THE HORWITZ THESIS

It is the view of an appreciable number of American legal historians[1] that the character of judicial discourse in nineteenth century America underwent a discernible and significant change. There is rough agreement among them as to the timing of this change, and as to how American judicial discourse should be characterized both before and after it.

They locate the *grand* or *instrumentalist* style of discourse in the period up to 1840 or 1850 or even the Civil War. In this period, it is said, judicial opinions were marked by a relatively free-wheeling style of argument. Judges adopted a critical approach to precedents: precedents were regarded as more or less persuasive depending on the reputation of the judge who set the precedent, but were to be followed only if in conformity to 'principle' and embodying 'sound policy'. 'Sound policy' was regarded as the promotion of commercial prosperity and economic development. So judicial opinions had an overtly instrumentalist dimension: judges openly resorted to arguments which were 'utilitarian' or 'policy-oriented' or 'political'.[2]

Then, in the later decades of the nineteenth century, came the *formalistic* style of judicial opinion. It was characterized by a *closure* of the sphere of discourse, the reduction of judicial argument to appeals to the authoritative. Precedents were treated as giving rise to binding rules by a process of induction; the application of these binding rules was treated as a matter of pure deduction. Judicial logic thus presented itself as inexorable, ineluctable. Meanwhile policy considerations were suppressed as extraneous and irrelevant.[3] In Llewellyn's sketch of formalism: '. . . the rules of law are to decide the cases; policy is for the legislature, not for the courts. . . . Opinions run in deductive form with an air or expression of single-line inevitability. "Principle" is a generalization producing order which can and should be used to prune away those "anomalous" cases or rules which do not

*Lecturer in Law, University of Dundee.

1 K. N. Llewellyn, *The Common Law Tradition* (1960); K. N. Llewellyn, *Jurisprudence* (1962) esp 178–92; W. J. Chambliss and R. B. Seidman, *Law, Order, and Power* (1971) 125–31; Nelson, 'The Impact of the Antislavery Movement upon Styles of Judicial Reasoning in Nineteenth Century America' 87 *Harvard L Rev* 513 (1974); M. J. Horwitz, *The Transformation of American Law, 1780–1860* (1977) Chaps I, VIII; G. Gilmore, *The Ages of American Law* (1977).

2 Llewellyn, *The Common Law Tradition* 36; Chambliss and Seidman, op cit, 127; Nelson, op cit, 513–14, 548, 562; Horwitz, op cit, 255.

3 Chambliss and Seidman, op cit, 128; Nelson, op cit, 514–15; Horwitz, op cit, 254.

fit . . . [S]ense is no official concern of a formal-style court.'[4] The corresponding theoretical stance stressed the 'scientific' nature of juridical discourse.[5]

The idea of a transition from instrumentalism to formalism has not, however, gained universal adherence. Scheiber argues that Nelson exaggerates and oversimplifies the contrast between the periods of instrumentalism and formalism.[6] Tushnet in his study of slavery decisions documents a shift from an 'analogical' to a 'categorical' style *during* the antebellum period.[7] And Cover, also in a study of slavery cases before the Civil War, describes a transition from a routine, taken-for-granted formalism ('positivism') to a defensive, self-conscious formalism in which the judges took to advancing moral and political justifications of their formalistic approach. It is therefore clear that Cover does not regard formalism and instrumentalism as mutually exclusive categories.[8]

Among those who do adhere to the thesis of a shift from instrumentalism to formalism no uniform explanation is advanced. Here we shall address only the explanations furnished by Chambliss and Seidman and, above all, by Horwitz. For these, I shall argue, are of more than local interest; they have implications regarding the development of common law discourse in England.

Translating the movement from a grand style to a formal style into Weberian language as one from substantively rational to formally rational adjudication, Chambliss and Seidman argue that it

> reflected the great shift in economic and political power, from the aristocratic government of the eighteenth and early nineteenth centuries to the admission of the middle classes into the corridors of power during the fourth decade of the last century. A variety of different social currents carrying the political and economic demands of the new rulers reached confluence in the demand for law of Weber's logically, formally rational sort.

In particular, entrepreneurs demanded 'above all else . . . advance and certain notice of the legal climate in which they hazard their capital'. At the same time the new democratic dogma of the separation of powers relegated the judiciary to a passive role, as did Austinian analytical positivism.[9] It is beyond question that this account is meant to apply to England as much as to America. One of Chambliss and Seidman's examples of the grand style at work is an English case, *Priestley* v *Fowler* (1837).[10] And, with the exception of the separation of powers doctrine, the

4 Llewellyn, *The Common Law Tradition* 38.

5 Nelson, op cit, 562–63; Horwitz, op cit, 258.

6 Scheiber, 'Instrumentalism and Property Rights: A Reconsideration of American "Styles of Judicial Reasoning" in the 19th Century' 1975 *Wisconsin L Rev* 1.

7 Tushnet, 'The American Law of Slavery, 1810–1860: A Study in the Persistence of Legal Autonomy' 10 *Law & Soc Rev* 119 (1975).

8 R. M. Cover, *Justice Accused* (1975). For criticisms of the conceptual viability of the distinction between formalism and instrumentalism, see Paine, 'Instrumentalism v. Formalism: Dissolving the Dichotomy' 1978 *Wisconsin L Rev* 997, and Pratt, 'Rhetorical Styles on the Fuller Court' 24 *Am J of Legal Hist* 189 (1980).

9 Chambliss and Seidman, op cit, 130–31.

10 3 M & W 1; Chambliss and Seidman, op cit, 126–27.

factors by reference to which they explain the rise of formalism must surely have been operative in England as much as America.

Horwitz also relates the rise of formalism to the pressure of nineteenth century capitalistic interests, though not in exactly the same way. In Horwitz's account the eighteenth century common law is seen as precommercial and anti-developmental. In eighteenth century property law a 'static agrarian' conception of property held sway. Eighteenth century commercial law contained 'anti-commercial' legal rules. Eighteenth century contract law was 'essentially antagonistic to the interests of commercial classes'. But in Horwitz's eyes all this law just corresponds to what was after all a 'premarket' economy.[11] At the same time, common law discourse was based on the prevailing conception of the common law as founded upon custom and natural law. Judges saw their job as being to discover and apply pre-existing legal rules. This entailed, Horwitz says, a strict conception of precedent: '. . . the rule of strict precedent was derived from the very conception of common law principles as pre-existing standards discoverable by judges'.[12]

After the Revolution things quickly changed. The substantive doctrines of private law underwent a far-reaching transformation which adapted them to meet the needs of capitalist interests in a capitalist society. This transformation of American law was effected by flexible, instrumentalist judicial discourse for seven or eight decades after the Revolution. This instrumentalist style of discourse was used to rewrite the doctrines of American private law in such a way that they came to serve bourgeois interests and demands. By about 1850 instrumentalist judicial method had established new 'rules of law . . . to implement a market regime, primarily new rules of contract, property, and commercial law, now thoroughly exorcised of earlier protective or paternalistic doctrines and reshaped to serve the interests of the wealthy and the powerful'.[13]

By 1850, therefore, the way was clear for the entrenchment of formalism. Horwitz assigns formalism two functions. First, it stabilized the substantive law established by instrumentalism in the interests of the bourgeoisie and their economic order. An instrumentalist approach was now redundant; the function of formalism was to crystallize the doctrinal gains of the period of transformation. Formalism served to 'freeze' legal doctrine and thereby 'sharply curtail the ability of the legal system to bring about further redistributions of wealth'.[14] Secondly, formalism was a vehicle of obfuscation and mystification. Industrialists and entrepreneurs could only benefit from the transformation 'if both the recent origins and the foundations in policy and group self-interest of all newly established legal doctrines could be disguised'. Indeed, 'the paramount social condition that is necessary for legal formalism to flourish in a society is for the

11 Horwitz, op cit, 31, 212, 167, 169.

12 Horwitz, op cit, 7–9. This is a controversial claim. Contrast Holdsworth, 'Case Law' 50 *LQ Rev* 180 (1934) with C. K. Allen, *Law in the Making* 7th ed (1964) 210–32, esp 219 n 1.

13 Horwitz, op cit, 259.

14 Ibid., 258, 259.

powerful groups in the society to have a great interest in disguising and suppressing the inevitably political and redistributive functions of law'.[15] In mid-nineteenth century America the powerful groups in question were the elite of the legal profession and the newly powerful commercial and entrepreneurial interests, and their alliance with each other ensured the triumph of legal formalism.[16]

Thus Horwitz skilfully interweaves Marxist and Weberian themes into a coherent account of the relations between substantive law, modes of judicial discourse and the economy in eighteenth and nineteenth century America. That account may be summarized schematically as follows:

Period	Economy	Substantive law	Opinion style
Pre-Revolution	premarket	anti-commercial	declaratory/ strict doctrine of precedent
Post-Revolution —1840/50	emergent market	procommercial (dynamic)	instrumentalist
Post-1840/50	established market	procommercial (static)	formalistic

Clearly Horwitz's account is by no means identical to Chambliss and Seidman's. In particular, while Horwitz connects the grand or instrumentalist style with the ascent of capitalist groups, Chambliss and Seidman link it to aristocratic rule.[17] For us, however, the cardinal question is whether the logic of Horwitz's account is such that it implicitly but necessarily entails a hypothesis about the development of judicial discourse in England. I shall argue, albeit with a measure of diffidence, that Horwitz's account as it stands cannot plausibly be confined to American developments alone.

The crux of the matter is that the Horwitz thesis is in essence about the transformation in America of the eighteenth century common law under the pressure of industrial capitalism. But England was the home of Horwitz's pretransformation common law, and England as much as America was transformed by industrial capitalism. Therefore on the *logic* of the Horwitz thesis the English common law should have gone through an adaptive transformation effected by judicial instrumentalism, and should then have been stabilized by the onset of legal formalism.

This follows unless there is some uniquely American element in Horwitz's account. But what might that element be? It is clear that Horwitz's supposedly

15 Ibid., 254, 266.
16 Ibid., 258, 259.
17 Chambliss and Seidman, op cit, 125–27.

anti-commercial pretransformation American law is by and large the English common law.[18] So it cannot be argued that it was exclusively American law which stood in need of a transformation to bring it into line with commercial needs. Again, it is impossible to read the Horwitz thesis as an account of the *Americanization* of the common law; Americanization is no doubt a secondary theme, but the dominant theme is unquestionably that of the *embourgeoisement* of the common law.[19] Lastly, it seems far-fetched to suggest that there was nothing in England to correspond to the American 'alliance' between the elite of the legal profession and commercial interests.[20]

A more serious objection to the claim that the underlying logic of the Horwitz thesis extends it to England is that Horwitz himself says that the instrumental perspective on law 'did not simply emerge as a response to new economic forces in the nineteenth century'. Rather the explanation for its emergence 'can be found in more general changes in the political theory of the period'.[21] The crucial ideological development was the rise of the 'will theory of law'. Jurists 'began to conceive of the common law as an instrument of will'; judges 'began to conceive of themselves as legislators'. In short, common law rules came to be conceived of as made and not discovered.[22] This new conception was a *sine qua non* of instrumentalism. Again it must be observed that there is nothing uniquely American about all this. In England the idea that the common law was man-made, or at any rate judge-made, was vigorously propagated by Bentham and became part of the nineteenth century orthodoxy of Austinian analytical positivisim.[23] So the ideological element in Horwitz's account also has its counterpart in English history.

The suggestion is, then, that the course of English legal development may be regarded as a *test* of the Horwitz thesis. At first glance Atiyah's work on *The Rise and Fall of Freedom of Contract* in England might be construed as an indication that the Horwitz thesis can pass that test. Atiyah ascribes a long reign to legal

18 See Horwitz, op cit, 4–5; see also L. M. Friedman, *A History of American Law* (1973).

19 E.g. Horwitz, op cit, xvi, 253–54.

20 Thus a section of the legal profession specialized in commercial business. See, e.g., J. Hollams, *The Jottings of an Old Solicitor* (1906). And law reformers were sensitive to commercial needs, though they tended to define them in legalistic terms. See Ferguson, 'Legal Ideology and Commercial Interests' 4 *Brit J Law & Soc* 18 (1977) and Ferguson, 'The Adjudication of Commercial Disputes and the Legal System in Modern England' 7 *Brit J Law & Soc* 141 (1980).

21 Horwitz, op cit, 4.

22 Ibid., 19, 22, 23, 27.

23 Horwitz himself describes the will theory of law as Blackstonian: ibid., 21. In one instance (p 25) Horwitz's evaluation of his evidence seems questionable. He quotes Zephaniah Swift: 'If a determination has been founded on mistaken principles, or the rule adopted by it be inconvenient, or repugnant to the general tenor of the law, a subsequent court assumes the power to vary from it or contradict it. In such cases they do not determine the prior decisions to be bad law; but that they are not law.' Horwitz concludes: 'Swift thus came as close as any jurist of the age to maintaining that law is what the courts say it is.' But this seems to be a mere paraphrase of what Blackstone says in the course of his exposition of the *declaratory* theory of the common law: William Blackstone, *Commentaries on the Laws of England* Vol 1 (1765) 69–71.

formalism in the history of English contract law. For Atiyah, as for Horwitz, formalism reflected the rise of the market economy, and gave the impression that the rules of contract law were inexorable deductions from neutral principles, 'while in reality they were no doubt broadly in the interests of the new industrial and commercial classes'. Admittedly Atiyah has reservations about the nexus between legal formalism and class interest: '. . . it is too simplistic to see this whole process [the rise of legal formalism] in class terms. English judges almost certainly believed their own dogmas. Moreover, they were never wholly successful in creating this new body of value-free law, for they were engaged upon an impossible exercise.'[24] But it is hard to regard these as major reservations. The objective social and economic functions of legal formalism do not depend on whether the judges were sincere or not. And of course one of Horwitz's own points is that the formalistic image of judicial decision-making as value-free deduction is a misrepresentation; indeed for Horwitz this misrepresentation is a characteristic of formalism which helps to account for its emergence and persistence.[25]

Nevertheless there are decisive divergences on the question of legal formalism between the work of Atiyah and that of Horwitz. First, there is the matter of timing. English legal formalism, says Atiyah, gathered strength from 1770 onwards, though until the middle of the nineteenth century 'English law and lawyers were receptive to influences from outside the law, and in particular were much influenced by utilitarianism and political economy'. From about 1850 onwards, 'the phenomenon of formalism took an increasing hold upon English legal thought'. Even so, Atiyah discerns evidence that 'the full flowering of formalism did not take place until after the First World War'. It is impossible to be certain that the age of formalism is over even now.[26] It appears, therefore, that Atiyah is unable to find room for the period of full-blooded judicial instrumentalism that plays such an important part in Horwitz's story.

And then there is the question of what is to count as evidence of formalism. For Horwitz, legal formalism is something which is objectivated in judicial opinions; formalistic opinions have their own style.[27] For Atiyah, on the other hand, formalism is nothing more than a state of mind;[28] written judicial opinions are not a reliable indicator of instrumentalism or formalism:

> It would . . . be wrong to suggest that the rise of formalism was a simple or clear-cut process, especially as the traditional style of the English judgment has changed little over the centuries. This means that the differences between the formalist and the realist judges are not always easy to draw merely by looking at the cold printed page of the Law Reports. Both formalists and realists tend to justify their decisions by a similar judicial process; both generally accept the conventions of the judicial style. And if the realist is more willing on some occasions to declare his open allegiance to some policy, the formalist

24 P. S. Atiyah, *The Rise and Fall of Freedom of Contract* (1979) 389–90.
25 *Supra*, 36–37.
26 Atiyah, op cit, 660, 661, 664.
27 Horwitz, op cit, 2–4.
28 Atiyah, op cit, 388.

is just as likely to be influenced by the same policy in an unconscious manner. Then, too, the realist judge may often use the formalist approach in order to make his conclusions more palatable to his colleagues in an appellate court. And even with the formalist, appeals to 'justice', 'equity' and notions of 'fairness' are perfectly in order, although overt discussion of policy or moral principles is avoided. The result is to make it exceedingly difficult to assess the influence of formalism, so much so that even today it is not possible to assert with any confidence that formalism is dead or that a majority of the English judiciary subscribe to a more realist vision of the legal process. All this means that the true history of formalism in English law requires a great deal of research about the non-judicial utterances and beliefs of the judges, and such a history remains to be written.[29]

From this it emerges that in Atiyah's view English judicial discourse has been more or less unchanging in style. By no means, therefore, can Atiyah's work be regarded as a direct application of the Horwitz thesis to England.

Nor is it evident that Atiyah's subjectivistic concept of legal formalism is preferable. According to Atiyah the 'true history' of formalism must be based on the judges' extra-judicial utterances, the reason being that when they speak in their judicial capacity judges may dissemble. Perhaps so, but the assumption that judges cease to dissemble when speaking of their roles extra-judicially is unwarranted: the judge may also dissemble in his public lectures, essays, conversations, memoirs etc. Besides, judicial dissimulation may actually be regarded as a testimony to the strength of the current methodological orthodoxy. Why should the realist judge use the formalistic approach to win over his colleagues, unless formalistic justification is the norm? Why should the formalist judge appeal to justice, equity and fairness—considerations which, on Atiyah's account, he regards as extraneous and irrelevant—unless the dominant mode of discourse requires or at least permits this? What Atiyah dismisses as the 'conventions of the judicial style' may exact tribute even from those whose inclinations are at variance with them. These 'conventions' are just as real as judges' personal beliefs about the judicial process, and an equally worthy object of our attention.

Also of relevance to the question of legal formalism in England is Stevens' study of the House of Lords as a judicial body in the nineteenth and twentieth centuries.[30] Stevens' position is that substantive formalism ('the belief in legal formalism as an end in itself') in the House of Lords reached its apogee between 1940 and 1955. This development reflected the depoliticization and professionalization of the Law Lords, and political circumstances in which 'The need to play possum was obvious even to the least politically minded of the judges.' For the most part, says Stevens, the English judges in the House of Lords 'moved from a stage of political amateurism to a style of high formalism without the intervening stage of the Grand style'. This hardly squares with the implications which the Horwitz thesis has for England; but it is important to note that Stevens also flirts with the suggestion that a 'Weberian' concept of formalism

29 Ibid., 660–61.

30 Robert Stevens, *Law and Politics* (1979).

might be applicable to lower courts by the mid-nineteenth century, and that a 'Weberian' explanation—viz that formalism facilitated capitalism by entrenching vested interests in established doctrines—might be appropriate. But Stevens does not commit himself.[31]

JUDICIAL DISCOURSE IN ENGLISH SALE OF GOODS CASES

What follows is a report of a limited study of the character of judicial discourse in England based on a number of samples of reported sale of goods cases. The object was to determine whether the samples drawn disclosed any evidence of change in the character of English judicial discourse. In particular, was there any evidence of such a transformation as seems to be implied by the ideas of Chambliss and Seidman and Horwitz? A selective or impressionistic approach to the available evidence might lend itself merely to the affirmation of preconceived notions or wishful thinking. In an effort to avoid this pitfall a sampling procedure was adopted as follows.

Periods of time and series of law reports from which to take samples were chosen:

Sample A—1801–05—East's Reports. An attempt to take an earlier sample was abandoned: sale of goods cases are too thin on the ground in the last few decades of the eighteenth century. East's are common law reports from the King's Bench; this rules out cases from the courts of Exchequer and Common Pleas as well as equity cases. This sample comes from a period at which we might expect to find a grand or instrumental style of discourse.

Sample B—1881–90—Queen's Bench Reports. Here the sample was extended to ten years in order to catch a similar number of cases to that in *Sample A*. *Sample B* just predates the codification of the English law of sales by the Sale of Goods Act 1893. The question was whether a formalistic style of discourse would be discernible.

Sample C—1896–1905—Queen's Bench and King's Bench Reports. Again it was necessary to extend the sample to ten years. This sample too belongs to what is to be anticipated as an epoch of legal formalism, but this time we have to do with codified law.

Sample D—1971–75—All England Reports. The shift to the All England Reports was made to get a sample of comparable size. It would have been possible to shift to a specialist series of commercial reports, but it seemed preferable for the sake of continuity with the earlier samples to stick to a general series. *Sample D* was taken to bring the picture more or less up to date, and also to get an idea of judicial discourse in the context of an aging code.

31 Ibid., 101–04, 283, 320.

Confining the samples to the above series of law reports means that *Sample A* is composed of cases from the King's Bench; *Samples B* and *C* of cases from the Queen's/King's Bench and the Court of Appeal. All three samples contain cases at first instance and at appellate levels—mainly the latter. Being drawn from a series of law reports with general coverage, *Sample D*, as initially constituted, additionally contained two House of Lords decisions and one Chancery Division decision. To eliminate this source of discontinuity with the earlier samples these three cases were discarded.

Apart from that, every sale of goods case found in the designated reports in the designated years was analysed.[32] This approach produced samples of the following sizes: *Sample A*—18 cases, 18 reports; *Sample B*—16 cases, 17 reports; *Sample C*—18 cases, 19 reports; *Sample D*—14 cases, 15 reports.[33] It must be stressed that the analysis undertaken did not purport to throw any light on judges' *states of mind*; nor was any attempt made to assess the *quality* or *cogency* of the arguments used in judicial discourse. Our interest is in how judges *keep up appearances*—in other words, in the character of judicial discourse conceived of as a publicly accessible objectivation.

In the space of a few pages it is impossible to do more than sketch the general conclusions prompted by this analysis, and adduce by way of illustration some of the material upon which they were founded. The heart of the matter is that no transformation of English judicial discourse could be traced from the four samples analysed. On the contrary judicial discourse in these samples displayed marked stability over time. The same types of argument were used in much the same way throughout. Even codification seems to have made scant difference to the characteristic mode of discourse in the long run. That mode of discourse can aptly be termed *open formalism* (in contradistinction to the *closed* formalism envisaged by Chambliss and Seidman and Horwitz) or *ranked eclecticism*. To see why these terms fit, we must appreciate the different types of argument that recur in each of the samples, and their relationship to each other.

Axiomatic argument

Axiomatic argument transcends merely formal argument in the sense that its presupposition is that no specific 'authority'—i.e. no specific precedent or statute—need be cited to validate the authority of the norm propounded. Axiomatic argument proceeds from what purports to be established law, trite law. The judge *takes for granted* the legal validity of his principle; he treates it as too

32 By and large the 'sale of goods' criterion of inclusion/exclusion proved easy to apply. I chose to exclude sale of goods cases turning on a criminal statute (food and drugs legislation, trade descriptions legislation, road traffic legislation etc.) in order to ensure that all the cases both before and after codification are civil cases, and hence to facilitate comparison. I included hire-purchase cases: legally speaking, a hire-purchase includes a sale. In *Sample A* I included all sale of goods cases irrespective of the form of action: thus actions of case and trover are to be found as well as actions of assumpsit.

33 For an enumeration, see Appendix, *infra*, 56–58.

well settled to require the buttress of precedent. No doubt precedent *could* be adduced in support of the principle; but this would be redundant. Sometimes an axiomatic argument incorporates an allusion to its taken-for-granted authoritative status. For example:

1. [*Sample A*] *Coxe* v *Harden* (1803) 219–20, Lawrence J:

> Upon the shipment of the goods on account and at the risk of Oddy and Co the property became vested in them, and so it continued from that time, subject only to the consignors' right of stopping it in transitu. *That is so clear that no authority is wanted to establish it.* Then the right of stopping them not having been exercised while the goods were in transitu, when Oddy and Co got possession of them they had a right to transfer them to the defendants.

2. [*Sample B*] *Sanders* v *Maclean* (1883) 334, Brett MR:

> . . . it is *plain and known law* that . . . and it is also *known law* that. . . .

3. [*Sample D*] *The Albazero* (1975) 25, Cairns LJ:

> This appeal involves a conflict between two legal principles—one of a broad and general character, the other of a special nature and of a comparatively narrow compass. The general principle is that in an action for damages for breach of contract the plaintiff can only recover such damages as he has actually suffered. The special rule is that a plaintiff who has made a contract with a shipowner, under which goods are carried by sea can recover damages from a shipowner for the loss of or damage to the goods caused by the shipowner's breach of contract, whether or not he has himself been damnified.
>
> The broad principle is *so fundamental to our law that nobody in this case has thought it necessary to cite authority for it.*

Axiomatic argument does not necessarily take the form of abstract statements of principle; it not infrequently assumes the guise of legal 'analysis', the raw facts of the case being restated in terms of legal categories from which definite legal consequences flow. Example 1 above is an instance; others follow:

4. [*Sample A*] *Walley* v *Montgomery* (1803) 591–92, Grose J:

> In order to sustain this action the plaintiff must prove the property in himself, and a conversion by the defendant. The property of the goods was once in Schumann and Co: but by the bill of lading and invoice sent to the plaintiff, and the delivery to the captain, the property passed from them to the plaintiff to every purpose except as to the right of stopping the goods in transitu to the vendee: there is no pretence, however, for saying that they were stopped in this case under an exercise of that right. For as far as concerns the acceptances of the bills of exchange drawn on him the plaintiff was ready and offered to give them; and as to the payment of the freight, that was a question between the captain and the plaintiff, with which the defendant had no right to concern himself. The defendant must either have been a purchaser for a valuable consideration, or the agent of Schumann and Co. As a purchaser for a valuable consideration, the captain could not be considered as his

agent under the bill of lading, so as to entitle him to claim what was due to the captain. But in truth there is no pretence for saying that he was a purchaser for a valuable consideration. He was the mere agent of Schumann and Co, out of whom the property was devested by the bill of lading and invoice, and the delivery to the captain for every purpose except that of stopping in transitu. The defendant therefore had no title.

Here, for example, it is axiomatic that transmission of the bill of lading and invoice transfers ownership of the goods.

5. [*Sample C*] ***Braithwaite*** v ***Foreign Hardwood Co*** (1905) 551, Collins MR:

> The obligation upon the plaintiff was to deliver the rosewood by instalments. Where such an obligation exists, as each instalment is tendered under the contract, the buyer must be ready and willing to perform the contract as well as the seller, and if he is not willing to perform it he may by his conduct or by express words absolve the seller from his obligation. In the present case, after there had been a general repudiation of the contract by the defendants, the plaintiff's agent informed them that he had received the bill of lading for the first instalment; but the defendants again wrote refusing to take the bill of lading on the ground that they had previously repudiated the whole contract and refused to be bound by it. In my opinion that act of the defendants amounted in fact to a *waiver* by them of the performance by the plaintiff of the conditions precedent which would otherwise have been necessary to the enforcement by him of the contract. . . .

6. [*Sample D*] ***Alan*** v ***El Nasr*** (1972) 143, Megaw LJ:

> The confirming bank's *offer*, made to the sellers with the knowledge of, and on the instructions of, the buyers, was an *offer* which involved sterling; not merely as the currency of payment, but as the currency of account, in respect of that transaction. The sellers *accepted* the confirming bank's *offer*, including its terms as to currency, by submitting invoices and drafts with the form and contents which I have already described.
>
> As I see it, the necessary consequence of that *offer and acceptance* of a sterling credit is that the original term of the contract of sale as to the money of account was varied from Kenyan currency to sterling. The payment, and the sole payment, stipulated by the contract of sale was by the letter of credit. The buyers, through the confirming bank, had opened a letter of credit which did not conform, because it provided sterling as the money of account. The sellers *accepted that offer* by making use of the credit to receive payment for a part of the contractual goods. By that *acceptance*, as the sellers must be deemed to have known, not only did the confirming bank become irrevocably bound by the terms of the *offer* (and by no other terms), but so also did the buyers become bound.

In each of these passages an axiom is evoked by the legal language in terms of which the facts are characterized (waiver, offer, acceptance); but it is not explicitly stated.

But axiomatic argument may be 'pure' as well as 'applied' as in Example 3 above, and also

7. [*Sample B*] *Bethall* v *Clark* (1887) 561, Cave J:

> In all cases of stoppage in transitu it is necessary first of all to ascertain what is the transitus or passage of the goods from the possession of the vendor to that of the purchaser. The moment the goods are delivered by the vendor to a carrier to be carried to the purchaser the transitus begins. When the goods have arrived at their destination and have been delivered to the purchaser or his agent, or when the carrier holds them as warehouseman for the purchaser, and no longer as carrier only, the transitus is at an end. The destination may be fixed by the contract of sale, or by directions given by the purchaser to the vendor. But, however fixed, the goods have arrived at their destination, and the transitus is at an end, when they have got into the hands of someone who holds them for the purchaser and for some other purpose than that of merely carrying them to the destination fixed by the contract or by the directions given by the purchaser to the vendor. The difficulty in each case lies in applying these principles.'

Where, as here, the axiom is pure it may be used as the major premise in a syllogism; equally, however, it may be no more than a device for locating and defining the issue at stake in the case.

Argument from precedent

Needless to say, argument from precedent dominates all four samples. Its basic methodological imperative is mutual reconciliation of the precedents. Argument from precedent assumes contrasting forms. On the one hand, a precedent might be represented at a very low level of abstraction and generality, as a *concrete example*, with a highly circumstantial account of its facts. At this level, argument from precedent tends to be analogical, the precedent being assimilated to or differentiated from the instant case. On the other hand, a precedent might be treated as a *warrant for a statement of principle*. At this level, argument from precedent purports to be deductive. But there are intermediate forms, as where a broad principle is stated and the facts of a precedent are recounted in circumstantial detail by way of 'illustration'. So, in terms of the level of generality and abstraction, argument from precedent is pretty fluid. This quality is evident in the later samples as much as the first.

In the present context the level of respect shown for precedents is of particular concern.[34] In fact, in each of the four samples it is a rare event for a precedent to suffer outright rejection. When it does occur, rejection seems to proceed on the basis of supposed incompatibility with axiom or authority,[35] rather than by reference to informal arguments. It is more common for a precedent to undergo 'explanation', involving acceptance of a prior decision coupled with rejection of a dictum accompanying it. But whether one focuses on outright rejection or mere

34 *Supra*, 34.

35 [*Sample A*] *Dixon* v *Baldwen* (1804) 184 (inconsistency with other precedents); *Mussen* v *Price* (1803) 150–51 (inconsistency with axiom); [*Sample B*] *Grebert-Borgnis* v *Nugent* (1885) 94 (irreconcilability with precedent); [*Sample D*] *Lewis* v *Averay* (1971) (irreconcilability with precedent), *The Albazero* (1974) 923 (inconsistency with precedents).

explanation of precedents, it is far from easy to point out tangible differences in the treatment accorded to them from one sample to another.

Common sense argument

Implicit in axiomatic argument is the claim that 'This *is* the law.' In common sense argument the implicit claim is 'This *must* be the law; *surely* this is the law.' This sort of argument can also take a negative form: 'This *cannot* be the law.' It thus involves an appeal to what is taken to be *self-evident*. Common sense argument can assume a number of forms:

(*i*) *Stigmatization* of a proposition as 'ridiculous', 'absurd' or the like. Three illustrations follow:

8. [*Sample A*] *Rawson* v *Johnson* (1801) 208, Lord Kenyon CJ:

> However technical, rules are to be attended to, and in some cases cannot be dispensed with, yet in administering justice we must not lose sight of common sense, and the common sense of this case will not be found to militate against any rule of law. No doubt can be entertained how this case should be decided; one man agrees to do a certain act in consideration of another man doing another act; the acts are to be done at the same time and place; one of the parties goes there intending to do his part, and the other stays away altogether; the former is obliged to bring his action for this breach of the agreement, and he pleads according to the truth of the fact, that he was at the time and place appointed ready to have received the other's goods and to have paid the stipulated price for them, which is all that he was bound to do, and that nobody was there on the part of the defendant, or that the goods were not there ready to be delivered: *would it be any answer* to say that he ought to have pleaded a tender of the money? Now this case is the same in effect: the defendant undertook to deliver the malt when he should be requested, and the plaintiffs plead that they made the request to him, and were ready and willing to have accepted and paid for it, but that he did not deliver it when requested, or at any other time, but refused so to do. To be sure under this averment the plaintiffs must have proved that they were prepared to tender and pay the money if the defendant had been ready to have received it and to have delivered the goods: but it cannot be necessary in order to entitle them to maintain their action that they should have gone through the useless ceremony of laying the money down in order to take it up again. It would be *repugnant to common sense* to require it.

9. [*Sample C*] *Agius* v *Great Western Colliery Co* (1899) 419, Earl of Halsbury LC:

> *It would be a strange thing*, in my opinion, if the success of the defence, by which the damages were so reduced, prevented the plaintiff's recovering from the defendants the costs which he has incurred therein.

10. [*Sample D*] *Woodhouse* v *Nigerian Produce* (1971) 672, Lord Denning MR:

> If the judge be right, it leads to this *extraordinary consequence*: a letter which is not sufficient to vary a contract is, nevertheless, sufficient to work an estoppel, which will have the same effect as a variation. It would mean that the court would give the

letter a different meaning according to the legal use made of it. Thus in seeing whether the letter amounts to a variation of the contract by agreement, the court would construe it according to its ordinary meaning as found by the judge; but in seeing whether the letter is a representation such as to found an estoppel, the court would construe it according to the meaning put on it by the person who receives it, so long as he is reasonable in putting that meaning on it.

I *cannot believe* this is correct.

(*ii*) Common sense argument may also proceed by the device of the *rhetorical question*. For instance:

11. [*Sample A*] *Bohtlingk* v *Inglis* (1803) 396, Lawrence J:

If a man contract with the owner of a general ship to take goods, which are equal to half the tonnage of the ship, and the master complete the loading of his ship with the goods of others, there would be no question that there might be such stoppage: and *surely it will not be said* that the right of stoppage depends on the quantity of the goods consigned.

12. [*Sample B*] *Hutcheson* v *Eaton* (1884) 868–69, Bowen LJ:

Is a dispute as to the existence of the custom a dispute 'arising on the contract'? First of all, be it observed that no such custom exists at all. That has been decided by the jury. What, therefore, the defendant must maintain is this, that the arbitrators had power to read into the contract a non-existing custom, on the ground that they thought it did exist, and then on the faith of that supposed custom to discharge the defendants from the contract. Is that a decision of any dispute or question 'arising on the contract'? . . .

. . . can it be said that this clause is to be interpreted so as to read into the contract a wholly non-existent custom? If arbitrators might decide that, I do not know why arbitrators might not read anything into a contract, in order to give themselves jurisdiction, and by that means they might decide anything on the ground that there was a custom which governed the matter, though in fact there was none. The question is, can an arbitrator find a custom that does not exist, in order to give himself jurisdiction, and to discharge parties who have entered into the contract on the assumption that no custom is to be read into it?

(See also Example 8 above.)

(*iii*) Argument from a *suppositious example* often has a common sense basis. A hypothetical case is put to which common sense supposedly supplies a clear answer; then an analogy is drawn between the hypothetical case and the case in hand. This happens in Example 8 above, and again in

13. [*Sample B*] *Honck* v *Muller* (1881) 98–99, Bramwell LJ:

Suppose it was a purchase of 100 yards of silk at so much a yard, and the buyer came for fifty only, could he insist on it? Would it make any difference that fifty yards were to be taken and paid for on Monday and fifty on Tuesday and the Monday's delivery was not taken but refused, and then the Tuesday's was demanded? If there was a charter for an out-and-home voyage, and the charterer refused to load for the outvoyage, could he insist on the ship taking his cargo for the home voyage? Suppose 10,000 tons of coal bought to be delivered at Gibraltar, Aden, and Bombay, in equal quantities—at Bombay in January, at Aden in February, and at Gibraltar in March, and no delivery at Bombay, could the buyer be made to take the other deliveries? Suppose a contract to supply bread to a workhouse for a year from the 1st of January, and the contractor says he will supply and does supply none in January, can he insist on supplying in the other eleven months? Suppose he does not supply for eleven months, can he insist on supplying in December? Would it make any difference if he was paid monthly? I hope not—I think not. Suppose a man orders a suit of clothes, the price being 7 *l*—4 *l* for the coat, 2 *l* for the trousers, and 1 *l* for the waistcoat, can he be made to take the coat only, whether they were all to be delivered together, or the trousers and waistcoat first?

Contextual and instrumental argument

Contextual and instrumental arguments both presuppose an orientation to the needs of the business world. In contextual argument the judge purports to proceed from a 'business point of view' or to found a legal norm on the basis of commercial practice. The judge thus lays claim to some knowledge of the business context in which the dispute arose. The underlying assumption of contextual argument is that it is proper to give legal recognition to normal business expectations. Example 14 combines elements of contextual ('it happens for the most part . . .') and axiomatic ('It was never doubted but that . . .') argument:

14. [*Sample A*] *Feise* v *Wray* (1802) 101, Lawrence J:

> It has been contended . . . that the right of stopping in transitu does in point of law apply solely to the case of vendor and vendee. If that were so, it would nearly put an end to the application of that law in this country; for I believe it happens for the most part that orders come to the merchants here from their correspondents abroad to purchase and ship certain merchandize to them; the merchants here, upon the authority of those orders, obtain the goods from those whom they deal with; and they charge a commission to their correspondents abroad upon the price of the commodity thus obtained. It never was doubted but that the merchant here, if he heard of the failure of his correspondent abroad, might stop the goods in transitu.

Example 15, on the other hand, is a fairly pure instance:

15. [*Sample B*] *Sanders* v *Maclean* (1883) 341–43, Bowen LJ:

> By inveterate practice among most of the commercial nations of Europe, bills of lading have long been drawn by the shipowner in sets of three or more. Sometimes one of the set is retained by the captain, the others being transferred by the captain to the shipper. Sometimes the whole of the set are handed, upon shipment, to the merchant, the captain retaining a copy only. This practice of drawing bills of lading in triplicate may be at the present day, and under the altered conditions of communication between one part of the world and another, less valuable than it was when originally introduced. But it certainly had its distinct uses in the early stages of European commerce, and it still survives. If it survives it is probable that the

commercial world still finds it more convenient or less troublesome to preserve it than to change it.

And it is plain that the purpose and idea of drawing bills of lading in sets—whatever the present advantage or disadvantage of the plan—is that the whole set should not remain always in the same hands. The possibility of its separation is intentionally devised for the purpose not of fraud, but of protecting honest dealing. The separation may conceivably afford opportunities of fraud, if the holders chose to be dishonest, but on the whole the commercial world is satisfied to run the risk of this contingency for the sake of the compensating advantages and conveniencies which merchants rightly or wrongly have, till lately at all events, believed to be afforded by the system of triplicates or quadruplicates. The shipper or his vendees may prefer to retain one of the originals for their own protection against loss, or to transfer it to their correspondents. In such cases they are in the habit of treating the remainder of the set as the effective documents and as sufficient for all purposes of negotiating the goods comprised in the bill of lading. The question we have to decide is whether the tender to the vendee of the only effective originals of the set is a sufficient tender under their contract, notwithstanding the absence of a third original, which is outstanding in the hands of the shipper; but which it is admitted in the present case has been in no way dealt with by him, and which has always remained in his hands as an ineffective and innocent triplicate.

If we were to hold that such a tender is not adequate, we must, as it appears to me, deal a fatal blow at this established custom of merchants, according to which, time out of mind, bills of lading are drawn in sets, and one of the set is habitually dealt with as representing the cargo independently of the rest. If the set, for purposes of contracts like the present, must always be kept together, the whole object, be it wise or unwise, of drawing bills of lading in triplicate is frustrated. For if one of the set were lost, or had been forwarded by the shipper or any subsequent owner of the cargo to his correspondent by way of precaution, the cargo becomes unsaleable. The only possible object of requiring the presentation of the third original must be to prevent the chance, more or less remote, of fraud on the part of the shipper or some previous owner of the goods. But the practice of merchants, it is never superfluous to remark, is not based on the supposition of possible frauds. The object of mercantile usages is to prevent the risk of insolvency, not of fraud; and any one who attempts to follow and understand the law merchant will soon find himself lost if he begins by assuming that merchants conduct their business on the basis of attempting to insure themselves against fraudulent dealing. The contrary is the case. Credit, not distrust, is the basis of commercial dealings; mercantile genius consists principally in knowing whom to trust and with whom to deal, and commercial intercourse and communication is no more based on the supposition of fraud than it is on the supposition of forgery.

In the same case (p 337) Brett MR employs the same type of argument ('merchants could never have contemplated . . .'). The unstated premise is that commercial custom ('inveterate practice', 'established custom of merchants') founds expectations, and that the law's job, *ceteris paribus*, is to reinforce these expectations, not to undermine them ('deal a fatal blow'). Law is to reflect mercantile usage.

A final example of contextual argument comes from Lord Denning, who mixes it with argument from precedent:

16. [*Sample D*] *Cehave NV* v *Bremer* (1975) 749, Lord Denning MR:

> In these circumstances, I should have thought a fair way of testing merchantability would be to ask *a commercial man*: was the breach such that the buyer should be able to reject the goods? In answering that question the commercial man would have regard to the various matters mentioned in the new statutory definition. He would, of course, have regard to the purpose for which goods of that kind are commonly bought. If a buyer buys 'waste silk' and it is of no use for the purpose of 'waste silk', he can reject it: see *Gardiner* v *Gray*. If he buys dates for food and they are of no use for food, he can reject them: see *Asfar & Co* v *Blundell*. But if he buys groundnuts for cattle food, and they can reasonably be used for cattle food, he may not be able to reject them, even though they are not suitable for poultry; see *Kendall* v *Lillico*. The commercial man would also, of course, have regard to the description applied to them. If motor horns are sold, expressly or impliedly, as 'new' and then the buyer finds that they are dented and scratched, he ought to be able to reject them: see *Jackson* v *Rotax Motor and Cycle Co*. If they are sold as 'secondhand' or 'shop soiled', then he must take them as they are (see *Bartlett* v *Sidney Marcus Ltd*), unless there is something radically wrong with them. He would also have regard to the price. If they are sold at the market price, the buyer would expect them to be of good quality and condition; and, if they were not, he would be able to reject them: see *Jones* v *Just* and *Brown* v *Craiks* by Lord Reid. But, if they are sold at a 'cut' price or 'bargain' price, or a lower price, he would have to put up with something less. He would not be entitled to reject them simply because they were not perfect. The commercial man would also have regard to any other relevant circumstances. If there was a clause, express or implied, which would give the buyer an allowance, off the price for the particular shortcomings, such that a commercial man would say: 'The buyer is entitled to a price allowance but not to reject them'—again the goods would be of merchantable quality. The buyer would be entitled to an allowance or damages in lieu, but not entitled to reject the lot.

Instrumentalism is not a wholly precise term. An argument may be instrumental in the sense that it imputes a purpose to a statutory text. This sort of approach to statutes is fairly common in our samples. Alternatively an argument may be instrumentalist in the sense that the anticipated practical results of the proposition under consideration are assessed by the criterion of the well-being of commerce: here the argument is genuinely consequentialist. The later samples disclose one or two instances:

17. [*Sample C*] *Farquharson Bros* v *King* (1901) 709, A. L. Smith MR quoting Savage CJ (NY):

> A contrary principle would endanger the security of commercial transactions, and destroy that confidence upon which what is called the usual course of trade materially rests.

18. [*Sample C*] *Weiner* v *Gill* (1905) 182, 183, Bray J:

> Why should mere parting with possession create an estoppel? Why should the defendants assume that because Longman had possession he had authority to pledge, when every one must know that in the ordinary course of business owners of goods are every day parting with possession without authorising the person to whom possession is given to pledge? Business could not go on if it were so. No one would be safe in parting with the possession of anything. . . .
>
> It would certainly not be to the advantage of the community that pawnbrokers should be encouraged to make advances on goods without having first made most careful inquiries.

19. [*Sample D*] *Reid* v *Metropolitan Police Commissioner* (1973) 100, Phillimore LJ:

> Indeed to suggest otherwise would create a ridiculous situation since the safeguards would still apply to all the old markets whereas in the case of the statutory markets there would be none. It would not be long before they were indeed thieves' kitchens.

Moralistic argument

Moralistic argument might be regarded as a subset of common sense argument, but this time the appeal is not to our sense of the absurd or the obvious, but to our sense of right and wrong. Nevertheless moralistic argument has the same intuitive basis. While moralistic argument was not completely unheard of in the first three samples, its incidence in *Sample D* is markedly greater. There are two variants. The first is overt moralism, in which legalism is not a virtue but a vice:

20. [*Sample D*] *R. Pagnan* v *Corbisa Limitada* (1971) 169, Salmon LJ:

> . . . counsel for the buyers' argument, however attractively he puts it, on analysis comes to this—that the buyers, who in reality have made a handsome profit, are, in law, entitled to recover damages for a fictitious loss. I should be reluctant to come to such an absurd and ***unjust*** conclusion unless compelled to do so by the clearest authority.

21. [*Sample D*] *The Albazero* (1975) 41, 44, Roskill LJ and Ormrod LJ:

> No possible ***commercial injustice*** can follow from upholding the plaintiffs' right to recover full damages and in a case such as the present where the time charter was being used by the plaintiffs for the carriage of their own cargo it may be said to be ***legalistic in the extreme*** to deprive them and their underwriters of their rights, merely because it was decided to transfer title to the cargo to another company in the group rather than allow that title to remain vested in the plaintiffs. . . .
>
> If the defendants succeed on this appeal they will escape liability on what on the facts of this case is the ***merest technicality***.

The second variant of moralistic argument may be called ***tendentious reconstruction*** of the facts. It involves a loaded account of the circumstances of the case:

22. [*Sample D*] *Cehave NV* v *Bremer* (1975) 743–44, Lord Denning MR:

It is to be noticed that by this time the market price had fallen greatly. The contract price for these 3,400 tons was (when converted into sterling) about £100,000. But the market price on 24th May in Rotterdam was, for sound goods, only £86,000. This may give an explanation of subsequent happenings.

The cargo ex no 2 hold (2,053 tons) was in good condition. But some of the cargo ex no 1 hold (1,260 tons) was found to be damaged. On 24th May the buyers rejected the whole cargo (both no 2 and no 1 holds) on the grounds that it was not shipped in good condition and they claimed repayment of the purchase price of £100,000. On the next day the sellers refused, saying that the goods were shipped in good condition and that the damage must have occurred at sea and that the buyers ought to lodge their claim with the insurers. So there it was. The goods were in the lighters with both sellers and buyers disclaiming ownership. Now comes *an astonishing sequence of events*. There was a Mr Baas in Rotterdam who was an importer of feeding products (including citrus pulp pellets). On 29th May, if not before, he inspected the cargo in the lighters. On 1st June the lighter owners applied ex parte to the Rotterdam County Court, the commercial court I expect, asking it to authorise a sale of the goods. They applied by their lawyer, a Mr Driessen. The sellers were not told of this application. But the buyers were. They were represented by the same lawyer as the lighter owner, Mr Driessen. On the same day this court granted the application and authorised the sale. It appointed agents to make the sale. The agents approached Mr Baas. They did not approach any other possible bidders. They sold the whole cargo to Mr Baas (out of both no 2 and no 1 holds) for a sum equivalent to £32,720. The expenses of sale were deducted, leaving the net proceeds at £29,903. These were paid into a Dutch bank 'to the order of whom it may concern'. On the same day Mr Baas sold the whole cargo to the buyers (i.e. the original buyers under the two contracts) at the same price and on the same terms as he had himself bought them from the agents of the court. The Board of Appeal found 'as a fair inference' that the buyers and Mr Baas intended from the beginning 'that he (Baas) should acquire the cargo for their (the buyers') benefit, or on their behalf'. Having bought the whole cargo from Mr Baas, the buyers transported it in the same way as they would have done if it had never suffered any damage. They took the lighters by canal to their plant at Veghel, a journey of some 60 miles. The buyers then used the entire cargo to manufacture cattle food at their processing plant at Veghel. They used it in the self-same way as they would sound goods except that they used 'smaller percentages in their compound feeds than would be normal with sound goods'. This difference in manufacture did not cause them any loss. At any rate, there is no finding that it did. And it was surely for them to prove it.

The upshot of it all was, therefore, that the buyers took the whole cargo and used all of it for their business just as if they had never rejected it save for the small percentages. So the *ubiquitous* Mr Baas had helped them greatly. They paid only £32,720 for it instead of the contract price of £100,000. The Board of Appeal felt it necessary to make this comment: 'We wish to record that we are not satisfied that we have been presented with a full account of how the goods were disposed of in Rotterdam after rejection by the buyers. The witnesses produced by the buyers gave contradictory evidence on this question, as well as on other less vital issues.'

> *That is a devastating comment.* The buyers must have known the truth. But they did not tell it to the Board of Appeal. At any rate, not the whole truth.
>
> Nevertheless, despite that devastating comment, the Board of Appeal made their award in favour of the buyers. They ordered the sellers to repay to the buyers the £100,000 with interest, and directed the proceeds of sale (£29,903) to be repaid to the sellers.
>
> *So the buyers have got the entire cargo and used it for their cattle food, but instead of paying £100,000 for it, they have only paid £30,000.*

This is far from being a dry and dispassionate summary; moral indignation pervades the whole passage.

• • •

These are the types of argument from which common law discourse is constructed in the cases analysed.[36] Quantitatively, argument from precedent predominates. Qualitatively, argument from precedent and axiomatic argument are pre-eminent. By that it is to be understood that the other, informal types of argument perform a subordinate function: they are used where authority is absent or equivocal, but they are not set up against precedents. They are almost always used in conjunction with precedent; almost never in competition with it. So the discourse observed was *formal* in that appeals to precedents and axioms took precedence, but also *open* insofar as other types of argument performed a supplementary role. The openness of the discourse differentiates it from the *closed,* exclusive formalism depicted by Horwitz and Chambliss and Seidman. To put it another way, the cases in the samples display an *eclectic* mode of discourse, a variety of different types of argument being invoked; but it is *ranked* eclecticism in the sense that some types of argument are treated as better than others. By themselves, the labels 'formalism' and 'instrumentalism' would both be inapposite in this connection. And most decidedly, no transition from instrumentalism to formalism is discernible.

IMPLICATIONS

It may be that these observations have no implications at all. It is conceivable that the cases in *Sample A,* for example, represent nothing more than a freakish aberration from a generally instrumental mode of discourse typical of the sale of goods cases of the late eighteenth and early nineteenth centuries as a whole; or that the cases in *Sample B* add up to no more than a chance departure from the closed formalism characteristic of sales cases in the latter half of the nineteenth century. But this seems somewhat improbable.

More plausibly the point might be pressed that it is impossible to extrapolate from findings based on sale of goods cases to other branches of the law. This point

36 Goutal, 'Characteristics of Judicial Style in France, Britain and the U.S.A.' 24 *Am J of Comp L* 43, 46–51 (1976) reports broadly similar but not identical findings.

is well made. Nevertheless sale of goods transactions are at the heart of trade and commerce; surely, therefore, sale of goods law is a suitable arena in which to examine the impact of capitalist development upon judicial discourse? In any case, sales law is not obviously unrepresentative of commercial law and contract law.

Again, it is clear that the four samples throw no direct light on the mode of judicial discourse characteristic of periods not sampled. The fact that each sample looks very much like the others, however, raises the inference that any other sample taken between 1800 and 1975 would have yielded broadly similar results. But, of course, it would not be safe to draw the same inference in respect of judicial discourse before 1800. Accordingly this study is not inconsistent with the suggestion which might be advanced that English capitalism enjoyed prior to 1800 the benefit of a transforming phase of judicial instrumentalism, a phase which was over by 1800. But this suggestion is hard to reconcile with the chronology of the Horwitz thesis, which has it that a strict approach to precedent constrained common law discourse as late as the time of the American Revolution. This would leave only a couple of decades for the rise and fall of judicial instrumentalism in England—surely not long enough.

Finally, it might be urged that obvious evidence of movement in the direction of closed formalism has been disregarded—viz the codification of the law of sales in the Act of 1893. It is indeed the case that the promoters of the sale of goods code were animated by a formalistic conception of juridical discourse.[37] But this does not necessarily mean that in practice the Act was able to effect a closure of the sphere of judicial discourse. In fact, it did not. Despite the Act's pretensions, judicial discourse in sales cases remains as open and eclectic as ever.[38]

The upshot of these considerations is that the findings of this study must be viewed with circumspection, but cannot be dismissed out of hand as the mere artefact of a defective methodology. Nor are the findings vitiated by the codification of the law of sales. This being so, it must be recognized that the implications for the Horwitz thesis (as well as for Chambliss and Seidman) are adverse. The factors in Horwitz's explanation are replicated in England, but the phenomena they are said to have produced are not evidenced in our samples of English judicial discourse. This does not by any stretch of the imagination amount to a conclusive refutation, but it does cast doubt on the soundness of the accounts proffered.

37 Ferguson, 'Legal Ideology and Commercial Interests' 21–26.

38 This is not to say that the Act made no difference. Clearly it constitutes an additional source of authoritative materials with which the judges must contend. In the early days of the Act they sometimes confined themselves to this source alone. In the long run, however, the traditional mode of discourse has retained its vitality. Over thirty years ago Lawson could rightly say that 'the Sale of Goods Act seems to operate almost as a part of the common law, hardly checking the judges in their stride . . .': F. H. Lawson, *The Rational Strength of English Law* (1951) 18. More recently Lord Diplock has observed, in connection with the Sale of Goods Act, that 'Naturam expellas furca is a maxim which tends to apply to codifications': *Christopher Hill Ltd* v *Ashington Piggeries Ltd* [1972] AC 441, 496.

Horwitz's account is suspect at three main points. First there is his identification of modern industrial capitalism with capitalism in general. Only on this basis is it possible to assert that the eighteenth century common law corresponded to a premarket economy. The eighteenth century economy may have been by and large preindustrial, but to label it precapitalist is highly problematic.[39] Then there is the question of the historicity of the transformation of the substantive law described by Horwitz. Simpson has argued that many of the supposedly procommercial developments in the field of contract law, e.g. legal recognition of the executory contract, which Horwitz assigns to the period of transformation, in fact occurred a century or two earlier.[40] This has serious consequences for Horwitz's formalization hypothesis: for how can it be maintained that formalism's historic mission was to freeze the legal norms generated by the transformation, if in fact there was no such transformation as is posited by Horwitz, or if it substantially occurred long before? Finally, the 'freezing' hypothesis is plainly predicated upon the assumption that formalism is more resistant to substantive legal change than instrumentalism. But this supposition is ingenuous. Formalism conceals rather than stops the process of incremental growth and change characteristic of systems of case law. Nineteenth century America is no exception: '. . . the process of change continued unabated during the formalist period', says Gilmore, 'despite the anguished efforts of the formalist theorists to make it appear that the law had, at long last, reached a point of stable equilibrium'.[41] Turning briefly to Chambliss and Seidman's argument, one wonders whether it is not a gross oversimplification to locate the transition from aristocratic to bourgeois rule in such a short span of time as the 1830s.[42] Yet this is what their rise of legal formalism is supposed to reflect.

CONCLUDING REMARKS

The evidence of judicial discourse in the law of sales reviewed in this study lends no support to the hypothesis that an 'age' of instrumentalism was succeeded by one of formalism in the sense that these terms are understood by Horwitz. It may be, of course, that unalloyed legal formalism might be found in some other branch of the law; but such a find would only suggest that a retreat to pure formalism is (as Cover puts it) 'more issue-related than time-bound'.[43] Even the *open* formalism discerned in the present study cannot be regarded as little more than the product of the development of modern capitalism. Rather the emergence of common law

39 Simpson, 'The Horwitz Thesis and the History of Contracts' 46 *U of Chi L Rev* 533, 538–40 (1979).

40 Ibid., 542–99.

41 Gilmore, 'From Tort to Contract: Industrialization and the Law' 86 *Yale LJ* 788, 797 (1977).

42 Cf the debate over whether the English Revolution of 1641 was a 'bourgeois revolution'; see, e.g., Christopher Hill, 'A Bourgeois Revolution?' in J. O. A. Pocock, ed, *Three British Revolutions* (1980) 109–39.

43 Cover, op cit, 200.

discourse thus defined is best viewed as a process spanning several centuries. Among the milestones in this development are the emergence of the common law as a body of substantive (not merely procedural) norms conceived of as distinct from notions of justice,[44] the regularization of equity[45] and the refinement of law reporting in the mid-eighteenth century.[46] If any further formalization occurred in the nineteenth century it was by comparison just a tidying-up operation. This is not to deny that the closure of the sphere of legal discourse was a strong current in later nineteenth century legal thought, but it is necessary to distinguish between closed, exclusive formalism at the level of judicial *discourse* and at the level of jurisprudential *ideology*. Formalistic legal ideology refracted common law discourse but it has yet to be shown that it managed to transform it in practice.

APPENDIX

Sample A

Rawson *v* Johnson (1801)	1 East 203
Eland *v* Karr (1801)	1 East 375
Inglis *v* Usherwood (1801)	1 East 515
Penny *v* Porter (1801)	2 East 2
Neate *v* Ball (1801)	2 East 117
Parkinson *v* Lee (1802)	2 East 314
Williamson *v* Allison (1802)	2 East 446
Feise *v* Wray (1802)	3 East 93
Buxton *v* Bedall (1803)	3 East 303
Bohtlingk *v* Inglis (1803)	3 East 381
Walley *v* Montgomery (1803)	3 East 585
Swancott *v* Westgarth (1803)	4 East 75
Mussen *v* Price (1803)	4 East 147
Coxe *v* Harden (1803)	4 East 211
Dixon *v* Baldwen (1804)	5 East 175
Egerton *v* Mathews (1805)	6 East 307
Siffken *v* Wray (1805)	6 East 371
Hanson *v* Meyer (1805)	6 East 615

Sample B

Honck *v* Muller (1881)	7 QBD 92
Johnson *v* Raylton, Dixon (1881)	7 QBD 438
Sanders Bros *v* Maclean (1883)	11 QBD 327
Kendal *v* Marshall Stevens & Co (1883)	11 QBD 356

44 S. F. C. Milsom, *Historical Foundations of the Common Law* 2nd ed (1981) 82–88.

45 Ibid., 93–96.

46 J. P. Dawson, *The Oracles of the Law* (1968) 72–80; cf Simpson, 'The Common Law and Legal Theory' in A. W. B. Simpson, ed, *Oxford Essays in Jurisprudence* (1973) 77–99.

Stock *v* Inglis (1884)	12 QBD 564
Hutcheson *v* Eaton (1884)	13 QBD 861
Ex parte Miles (1885)	15 QBD 39
Grébert-Borgnis *v* Nugent (1885)	15 QBD 85
Page *v* Morgan (1885)	15 QBD 228
Pike *v* Ongley (1887)	18 QBD 708
Bethell *v* Clark (1887)	19 QBD 553
Hammond & Co *v* Bussey (1887)	20 QBD 79
Bethell *v* Clark (1888)	20 QBD 615
Chapman *v* Withers (1888)	20 QBD 824
Lucas *v* Dixon (1889)	22 QBD 357
Hugill *v* Masker (1889)	22 QBD 364
Jones *v* Padgett (1890)	24 QBD 650

Sample C

Kirkham *v* Attenborough (1896)	[1897] 1 QB 201
Gillespie Bros & Co *v* Cheney, Eggar & Co (1896)	[1896] 2 QB 59
Cahn *v* Pockett's Bristol Channel Steam Packet Co (1898)	[1898] 2 QB 61
Norton *v* Davison (1899)	[1899] 1 QB 401
Agius *v* Great Western Colliery Co (1899)	[1899] 1 QB 413
Ashmore & Son *v* C. S. Cox & Co (1899)	[1899] 1 QB 436
Cahn *v* Pockett's Bristol Channel Steam Packet Co (1899)	[1899] 1 QB 643
Varley *v* Whipp (1900)	[1900] 1 QB 513
Vigers Bros *v* Sanderson Bros (1901)	[1901] 1 QB 608
Taylor *v* Great Eastern Railway (1901)	[1901] 1 QB 774
Farquharson Bros & Co *v* King & Co (1901)	[1901] 2 KB 697
Clarke *v* Army and Navy Co-operative Society (1903)	[1903] 1 KB 155
Wren *v* Holt (1903)	[1903] 1 KB 610
Preist *v* Last (1903)	[1903] 2 KB 148
Bostock & Co Ltd *v* Nicholson & Sons Ltd (1904)	[1904] 1 KB 725
Re Walkers, Winser & Hamm and Shaw, Son & Co (1904)	[1904] 2 KB 152
Frost *v* Aylesbury Dairy Co (1905)	[1905] 1 KB 608
Weiner *v* Gill (1905)	[1905] 2 KB 172
Braithwaite *v* Foreign Hardwood Co (1905)	[1905] 2 KB 543

Sample D

R. Pagnan *v* Corbisa Limitada (1971)	[1971] 1 All ER 165
Woodhouse *v* Nigerian Produce (1971)	[1971] 1 All ER 665
Eshun *v* Moorgate Mercantile Co Ltd (1971)	[1971] 2 All ER 402
Barker *v* Bell (1971)	[1971] 2 All ER 867

Worcester Finance *v* Cooden Engineering (1971)	[1971] 3 All ER 708
Lewis *v* Averay (1971)	[1971] 3 All ER 907
W. J. Alan Ltd *v* El Nasr Co (1972)	[1972] 2 All ER 127
Sainsbury Ltd *v* Street (1972)	[1972] 3 All ER 1127
Chelmsford Auctions Ltd *v* Poole (1973)	[1973] 1 All ER 810
Reid *v* Metropolis Police Comr (1973)	[1973] 2 All ER 97
The Albazero (1974)	[1974] 2 All ER 906
Crowther *v* Shannon (1975)	[1975] 1 All ER 139
Microbeads *v* Vinhurst (1975)	[1975] 1 All ER 529
The Albazero (1975)	[1975] 3 All ER 21
Cehave NV *v* Bremer (1975)	[1975] 3 All ER 739

[10]

THE COMMON LAW PROCESS AND THE SELECTION OF EFFICIENT RULES

*GEORGE L. PRIEST**

THIS comment simplifies and extends the important insight of the preceding paper by Paul H. Rubin.[1] I shall argue that the tendency of the set of all legal rules to become dominated by rules achieving efficient as opposed to inefficient allocative effects is substantially more pervasive than might be thought. It will be shown that efficient rules will be more likely to endure as controlling precedents regardless of the attitudes of individual judges toward efficiency, the ability of judges to distinguish efficient from inefficient outcomes, or the interest or uninterest of litigants in the allocative effects of the rules. Furthermore, it will be shown that this tendency toward efficiency is a characteristic of the common law process so that the content not only of the common law itself, but also of the legal interpretation of statutes or of the Constitution, is subject to forces pressing toward efficiency. The only assumption necessary for the hypothesis is that transaction costs in the real world are positive. It follows from this assumption that inefficient legal rules will impose greater costs than efficient rules on the parties subject to them. Since litigation is more likely than settlement where, *ceteris paribus,* the stakes of a case are greater, disputes arising under inefficient rules will be more likely to be relitigated than disputes arising under efficient rules.[2] It will be shown that, as a consequence, judges will be unable to influence the content of the law to fully reflect their attitudes toward efficiency. The set of legal rules will always contain a greater proportion of efficient rules than judges themselves would prefer.

* Fellow in Law and Economics, University of Chicago Law School; Associate Professor of Law (on leave), University of Puget Sound.

I am grateful to Gary S. Becker, Edmund W. Kitch, Anthony T. Kronman, William M. Landes, B. Peter Pashigian, Wallace M. Rudolph, Robert Sherwin, Kenneth I. Wolpin and to the participants of the Law and Economics Workshop of the University of Chicago Law School for helpful comments on an earlier draft.

[1] Paul H. Rubin, Why is the Common Law Efficient?, 6 J. Leg. Studies 51 (1977) [hereinafter cited as Rubin].

[2] For this conclusion it is necessary in addition to abstract from wealth effects on the "consumption" of litigation. See note 20 *infra*.

The hypothesis builds on a model of litigation and an assumption about transaction costs that are simple and realistic. It is unnecessary to assume, as might have been implied by Professor Rubin's discussion, for example, that the parties agree on the probability of a given verdict, that transaction costs are greater than the savings from voluntary shifts in liability, or, as was crucial to Professor Rubin's results, that both parties to the dispute have a continuing interest in the legal outcome.[3]

My analysis provides a foundation for the more general theory that common law decision making facilitates over time the efficient allocation of resources. This theory has been developed in recent years in a growing literature on the apparently efficient consequences of the common law system.[4] This literature has been less successful, however, in explaining *why* the common law has developed in this manner. The most persuasive explanation has been that common law rules of evidence and procedure tend to emphasize those characteristics of legal disputes important to a determination of efficiency,[5] but to conclude that the rules that are promulgated will, in fact, achieve efficiency has required two additional (often implicit) assumptions: that judges prefer efficient outcomes, and that judges can devise with at least some success legal rules to achieve such outcomes.[6] These assumptions have been criticized as fragile reeds on which to build a theory, because the intent and motivations of judges are difficult to infer and are frequently ambiguous and because the consistent and accurate determination of efficient results is a very difficult task.[7] The analysis in this paper, however, shows that even if judges prefer *inefficiency* or prefer efficiency but are unable to achieve it, the common law process will restrain and channel judicial discretion so that the legal rules in force will consist of a larger proportion of efficient rules than the bias or the incapacity of judges might otherwise permit.

I.

Various recent articles have developed a model in which the major determinants of the decision of two parties either to settle their dispute

[3] Rubin §§ I-II. Professor Rubin necessarily assumes that legal rules possess some precedential influence on future judicial decisions, for otherwise, legal rules would have no allocative effects whatever.

[4] Ronald H. Coase, The Problem of Social Cost, 3 J. Law & Econ. 1 (1960); Richard A. Posner, Killing or Wounding to Protect a Property Interest, 14 J. Law & Econ. 201 (1971); *id.*, A Theory of Negligence, 1 J. Leg. Studies 29 (1972), and *id.*, Economic Analysis of Law (1973) [hereinafter cited as Posner, Economic Analysis].

[5] Posner, Economic Analysis 321-27.

[6] For specific discussion of Posner's various explanations of judicial behavior see text surrounding notes 43-49, *infra*.

[7] For a discussion of criticisms of the efficiency theory of the common law see text surrounding note 49 *infra*. For an illustration of the ambiguity of inferences of judicial intent see Morton J. Horwitz, The Transformation of American Law, 1780-1860, at 61 (1977).

out of court or to litigate are the difference between the parties' attitudes toward risk, the combined expenses of litigation versus settlement, and the stakes of the case, that is, the gain or loss to the parties from a particular judgment. An implication of this model is that, if all other factors are held constant, those cases in which the stakes are higher are more likely than those in which the stakes are lower to be litigated rather than settled.[8]

For the set of all legal disputes, the stakes will be greater for disputes arising under inefficient rules than under efficient rules. Inefficient assignments of liability by definition impose greater costs on the parties subject to them than efficient assignments. For example, where the marginal cost of reducing the likelihood of an accident by a given amount is greater for one party than for the other, to place liability on the party whose cost is greater will lead in general to more accidents or more severe accidents than if the assignment were reversed. Where the cost of avoidance is made greater, the amount invested in avoidance generally will be lower. Even where it is possible for the party legally liable to pay the other party to assume the burden of prevention, it will be necessary to invest resources to achieve this reallocation. Thus the costs imposed by inefficient rules will always be higher than the costs imposed by efficient rules.[9]

It follows, therefore, that other factors held equal, litigation will be more likely for disputes arising under inefficient rules than for those arising under efficient rules. Once promulgated, inefficient rules are more likely than efficient rules to be reexamined by courts because they will come up in litigation more often. This conclusion follows directly from the fact that inefficient rules impose higher costs than efficient rules on the parties subject to them, and thus that the value to the parties from overturning the judgments that result—which is what I call the stakes of the litigation—is higher.[10]

Other characteristics besides the stakes that influence the litigation-settlement ratio—such as differences between the parties' expectations of success, aversion to risk, litigation costs, settlement costs, and even characteristics ignored by the economic model of litigation such as differences in the

[8] William M. Landes, An Economic Analysis of the Courts, 14 J. Law & Econ. 61 (1971); Richard A. Posner, An Economic Approach to Legal Procedure and Judicial Administration, 2 J. Leg. Studies 399 (1973). Greater litigation follows because for a given distribution of the parties' subjective probabilities of winning, greater stakes lead to greater differences between plaintiffs' minimum settlement offers and defendants' maximum settlement offers.

[9] If this were not true, then the rules would not be inefficient. Where there are no transaction costs, there are no inefficiencies.

[10] This conclusion does not follow where the parties subjected to the costs of a given rule, including the higher costs of the rule's inefficiency, are denied legal standing or where the parties have no continuing interest in the class of disputes and the optimal response to the liability rule is to reduce the scope of the activity so that the level of disputes weighted by intensity declines.

"litigiousness" of the particular individuals or differences in the "litigation skill" of the respective attorneys—can be ignored because they are unlikely to differ systematically between disputes arising under inefficient and those arising under efficient rules. The parties' expectations of success may be affected by the clarity of given legal rules, but there is no reason to believe that inefficient rules are any more or less clear in general than efficient rules. If these empirical judgments are correct, then regardless of the distribution within society of the various characteristics—ability to predict, aversion to risk, even litigiousness—inefficient rules as a class will be more likely than efficient rules to generate litigation and thus to be subjected to judicial reexamination.

It follows, therefore, that if the disputes that proceed to judgment consist of a disproportionately large share which contest the appropriateness of inefficient rules, then the set of rules not contested, those remaining in force, will consist of a disproportionately large share of efficient rules. It is this consequence that limits the power of the judiciary to influence the character of the law. The set of all legal rules in force at a given time will consist of the sum of the rules not contested and the rules newly promulgated by the judiciary. The newly promulgated rules, of course, will reflect judicial preference for or hostility to efficiency. But since the effects of the rules not contested will be predominantly efficient, the allocative effects of the total set of rules will be systematically more efficient than the allocative effects of the subset of newly promulgated rules. Even where the judiciary exercises a strong hostility to efficient outcomes, it will be unable to fully impose its bias on the total set of legal rules in force.[11] In fact, as we shall see, it is possible for the total set of rules to be predominantly efficient, despite a preference of the judges promulgating the rules for inefficient outcomes.

An arithmetical example will illustrate the point. Imagine that judges decide cases on some basis unrelated to efficiency of outcome, so that, with respect to allocative effects, judicial decisionmaking may be described as random. Assume for simplicity that all rules can be characterized as (equally) efficient or inefficient.[12] The likelihood in any given case of the rule being efficient or inefficient then will be .5. Imagine that 100 disputes go to judgment. By definition, the rules announced for 50 of these cases will be inefficient and for 50 will be efficient. Now assume that further litigation ensues concerning some of these rules. It is unnecessary to place any restrictions on the distribution of the other characteristics that determine the litigation-settlement ratio, but imagine that they are distributed so that 30 of the initial 50 inefficient rules are relitigated. By our previous finding (and

[11] For a consideration of those most implausible conditions when no newly promulgated rules are efficient see text following note 14 *infra*.

[12] This assumption is not essential and is relaxed in text following note 13 *infra*.

this is essential to the theory), it follows that a smaller proportion of efficient rules will be relitigated, say 20 of the initial 50.[13] By assumption, the judges will decide the 50 relitigated cases again randomly with respect to allocative effects. Thus 25 of the new rules will be inefficient and other 25 efficient. But when the new rules are added to the uncontested rules, it is clear that the stock of legal rules has become in sum more efficient. The number of inefficient rules has declined from 50 to 45, and the number of efficient rules has increased from 50 to 55. (See Table 1.)

TABLE 1
TENDENCY TOWARD EFFICIENCY WITH RANDOM DECISIONS
(.5 inefficient)

	inefficient				efficient				
	in litigation		in force		in litigation		in force		
period 1				**50**				**50**	
	30	(.6)	20		20	(.4)	30		50 in lit.
50 in lit.	25		25		25		25		
period 2			45	total			55	total	

N.B.: Equilibrium = 60 rules.

The tendency of the proportion of efficient rules to increase does not depend on the assumption of decision making that is random with respect to allocative effects. The proportion of efficient rules may increase over time even where each judge has a strong bias against efficient outcomes. Amend the previous example by assuming that judges promulgate inefficient rules in 90 percent of all cases, so that at period 1, 90 of the rules are inefficient, 10 efficient. Assume even greater relitigation: 80 of the 90 inefficient rules are relitigated and 7 (again a smaller proportion) of the 10 efficient rules, so that 10 inefficient and 3 efficient rules remain in force unchallenged. Of the 80 relitigated inefficient rules, 72 of the new rules will remain inefficient while 8 will be changed to become efficient. Of the 7 relitigated efficient rules, 6.3 will become inefficient and .7 remain efficient. Again the totals following relitigation favor efficiency: at the subsequent period, 88.3 as opposed to 90 rules are inefficient but 11.7 as opposed to the previous 10 are now efficient.

In this simple model the proportion of efficient rules in force at any period is a function of the stock of efficient and inefficient rules in force at the previous period, the respective rates of relitigation of efficient and inefficient rules, and the proportion of efficient rules announced by judges (the judicial bias toward efficiency). If the rates of relitigation and the judicial bias re-

[13] The difference in the rate of litigation between disputes arising under efficient rules and those arising under inefficient rules will be a function of the extent of the inefficiency.

main constant over time, the share of efficient rules will reach an equilibrium level. The proportion of efficient rules at equilibrium will be greater than the proportion of efficient rules promulgated by judges in any given period, regardless of the relitigation rates or the level of the judicial bias.

Let X_t and Y_t represent respectively the proportion of efficient and inefficient rules in force at period t. Let *a* be the proportion of efficient rules announced by the judiciary, *b* the rate of relitigation of efficient rules, and *c* the rate of relitigation of inefficient rules, each of which is assumed to remain constant through all periods. By definition $X_t + Y_t = 1$, and $c > b$. The proportion of efficient rules in force at any period is represented as follows:

$$X_t = X_{t-1}(1 - b) + a(bX_{t-1} + cY_{t-1}) \qquad (1)$$

Substituting $(1 - X_{t-1})$ for Y_{t-1},

$$X_t = X_{t-1}(1 - b + ab - ac) + ac \qquad (2)$$

It can be shown that in the limit (as t approaches infinity) X will converge to an equilibrium value. To show this, rewrite X_t as

$$X_t = X_0(1 - b + ab - ac)^t + ac\,[(1 - b + ab - ac)^{t-1} + (1 - b + ab - ac)^{t-2} \ldots + (1 - b + ab - ac) + 1] \qquad (3)$$

where X_0 equals the proportion of efficient rules in the base period 0. Letting $Z = (1 - b + ab - ac)$, we know that $Z < 1$, since $o > b$ and $(1 - b) < 1 + a(c - b)$. We can write X_t as

$$X_t = X_0Z^t + ac\,(Z^{t-1} + Z^{t-2} \ldots + Z + 1). \qquad (4)$$

As t goes to infinity, we have

$$X_t = ac/b - ab + ac. \qquad (5)$$

As expected the proportion of efficient rules in equilibrium will increase with increases in the judicial bias toward efficiency and with increases in the relitigation rate of inefficient rules. It will decline with increases in the relitigation rate of efficient rules:

$$\frac{\partial X_t}{\partial a} \geqslant 0 \; \frac{\partial X_t}{\partial c} \geqslant 0 \; \frac{\partial X_t}{\partial b} \leqslant 0 \qquad (6)$$

It is important to appreciate the implications of this model on the exercise of judicial authority. It is true, of course, that greater judicial hostility to efficiency will lead to a lower equilibrium level of efficient rules. But the difference in the rates of relitigation between efficient and inefficient rules places an important restriction on the extent to which judges who prefer inefficiency can implement their preferences. Table 2 shows equilibrium levels of efficient rules, holding the rate of relitigation of efficient rules

TABLE 2
EQUILIBRIUM PROPORTION OF EFFICIENT RULES (%)
RELITIGATION RATE OF EFFICIENT RULES HELD CONSTANT (.02%)

		Relitigation Rate, Inefficient Rules			
		.04	.06	.08	.09
	.7	82.4%	87.5%	90.3%	91.3%
Judicial	.6	75.0	81.8	85.7	87.1
Bias	.5	66.7	75.0	80.0	81.8
(% Efficient)	.4	57.1	66.7	72.7	75.0
	.3	46.2	56.3	63.2	65.9

constant, for plausible values of judicial attitudes toward efficiency (within a range of 40 percent of the mean) and for selected relitigation rates of inefficient rules. Note that "judicial bias" represents the proportion efficient of all rules promulgated by all of the judges within a given jurisdiction over a long period of time. Thus a .3 judicial bias measure could not be achieved if only a small set of judges were hostile to efficiency or if judges were to exercise their hostility in only a selected set of cases. Rather such a measure would require deep and systematic hostility.

Table 2 shows that where judges are relatively indifferent to the allocative effects of their decisions or where the number of decisions hostile to efficiency is roughly equal to the number of decisions sympathetic to efficiency (bias = .5), the equilibrium level of efficient rules will be predominantly efficient. Where judges on the whole prefer efficient outcomes (bias = .6 or .7), the preference is strengthened and the number of efficient rules that survive becomes very large. But efficient rules will comprise a substantial and in most cases a predominating component of legal rules in force even where judicial hostility to efficiency is high (bias = .4 or .3). For example, where judges promulgate efficient rules only 30 percent of the time and the relitigation rate of inefficient rules is .06, efficient rules will dominate at equilibrium, comprising 56 percent of total rules in force.

Table 2 confirms a second limitation on judicial discretion. Regardless of judicial bias, an increase in the relitigation rate of *inefficient* rules will lead to an increase in the equilibrium share of *efficient* rules. The relitigation rate is an indirect measure of the extent of the inefficiency of individual rules. As rules become more inefficient and impose greater costs on the parties subject to them, the stakes of the disputes will increase and the litigation rate will rise. Although it may initially seem paradoxical, as judges promulgate rules imposing greater inefficiencies on society, judicial influence on the proportion of efficient rules in force will decline because each of the rules individually will be less likely to avoid challenge. The proportion of inefficient rules will be maximized where the rules themselves are only negligibly inefficient.

The tendency of legal rules to become efficient over time is independent of judicial bias or the method of judicial decisionmaking. It follows rather from the limitations on the opportunity set of cases available for judicial decision, limitations imposed by independent economic variables that determine the cases that are litigated.[14] Efficient rules "survive" in an evolutionary sense because they are less likely to be relitigated and thus less likely to be changed, regardless of the method of decision. Inefficient rules "perish" because they are more likely to be reviewed and review implies the chance of change whatever the method of judicial decision. In a state of dichotomous rules (assumed for the previous examples), this tendency toward efficiency could be thwarted only if judges could choose an inefficient rule in every case, without exception or error. If judges were to occasionally err then the tendency toward efficiency could not be reversed.[15] If judges were able only to choose rules achieving partial inefficiency, even if they could do so infallibly, the set of legal rules still would tend over time to contain more efficient rules than judges desired, because rules that imposed greater inefficiency would be more likely to be relitigated.[16] It is evident, furthermore, that the tendency of the common law over time to favor efficient rules does not depend on the ability of judges to distinguish efficient from inefficient outcomes. Even where judges are ignorant of the allocative effects of their judgments, they will be led by the litigation decisions of individual parties to promulgate rules that increase the relative proportion of efficient rules.

The tendency toward efficiency is a function of the common law process according to which legal rules are generated from the investment in litigation by individual parties and the parties' investment is systematically determined by the allocative effects of prior legal rules. This suggests, therefore, that efficient outcomes will tend to dominate for all disputes resolved by this process including not only rules derived from the common law itself but also

[14] This analysis is derived from Gary S. Becker, Irrational Behavior and Economic Theory in the Economic Approach to Human Behavior 153 (1976).

[15] The tendency will exist no matter how low the rate of error. But note that these examples assume (unrealistically) that the proportion of inefficient rules promulgated will remain constant over a long period of time, and that the probability of a particular allocative outcome in a dispute regarding any given legal rule will be unrelated to the allocative outcome in any previous dispute regarding that rule (this qualification does not deny precedential influence). If judges, however, are able to selectively reverse rules that are efficient, the proportion of inefficient rules promulgated may rise. Furthermore, where the judicial bias has shifted, there may be a greater tendency in the short run to litigate specific rules that appear inconsistent with the judiciary's new attitude so that the effective judicial bias might appear quite extreme.

Although efficient rules may remain unchallenged where judges clearly have manifested hostility to efficient rules, the settlement of disputes arising under such rules may approximate inefficient outcomes. As with Holmes, the model in this paper construes the law to mean "The prophecies of what the courts will do in fact . . ."

[16] This suggests that where legal rules have been designed to achieve a redistribution of wealth the rules will evolve so that the redistribution will occur efficiently.

rules interpreting legislation and construing provisions of the Constitution. To the extent that a statute or an interpretation of a statute imposes inefficiencies, it will be more likely to be overturned because of the greater likelihood of relitigation. Similarly, within the class of possible constructions of a given constitutional provision, those constructions with relatively more efficient allocative effects will tend over time to survive. It is immaterial to this result that one of the parties to a dispute regarding a statute or a constitutional provision may itself be the government (such as the Justice Department or an administrative agency) whose investment in litigation may be determined by the maximization of something other than dollar returns. Where government suits are brought under legal rules that are inefficient, the stakes will be higher and defendants will be more likely to resist the suits and force litigation.

It is important to appreciate the generality of the hypothesis. Professor Rubin explains that the tendency toward efficiency will be realized only where both parties have a continuing interest in the particular class of disputes so that they will take directly into account more of the costs of the inefficiency of a given rule. This view, however, is not correct. The greater costs imposed by inefficient rules will generate greater litigation whether the particular parties to a dispute bear all of the costs of the rules or not.[17] Professor Rubin argues that where both litigants are indifferent to the future allocative effects of a rule, the judgment with respect to these litigants will have distributive effects only. He infers that each party's decision to litigate, as a result, will be based on the size of the potential judgment alone.[18] But to understand the effects on litigation of the inefficiency or efficiency of rules, it is important to ignore the individual case and to consider the effects on the set of all disputes.[19] It should be apparent that of that set of disputes where neither party possesses a continuing interest in the legal rule, there is likely to be more litigation among those arising under inefficient rules (because the stakes are higher or the number of disputes greater) than among those arising under efficient rules.

With respect to the probability of litigation, a legal rule is like any commodity. A change in relative prices (here, as between efficient and inefficient rules) will change the distribution of consumption choices toward relatively

[17] See Rubin § II B-C and my note 10 *supra*, for a qualifying comment. Professor Rubin must accept this point since he acknowledges that a given rule may impose costs on parties other than the parties to the dispute that generated the rule. See Rubin § II-C.

[18] Rubin's analysis confused the allocative effects of given rules with other determinants of litigation or settlement. Rubin's assumption, for expositional convenience, that the parties possessed identical expectations of the outcome of the case, suggested that all disputes for which neither party had a continuing interest in the dispute would be settled rather than litigated. See Rubin § II-C.

[19] Emphasized in Gary S. Becker, *supra* note 14, at 167-68.

cheaper and away from more expensive commodities.[20] It is unnecessary to assume that consumers possess continuing consumption interests in a particular commodity in order to predict their responses to relative shifts in prices, although such interests may influence to speed of consumer adjustment to such shifts. Similarly, it is unnecessary to assume that individual litigants possess continuing interest in a particular class of disputes in order to predict the response in the litigation rate to an increase in the proportion of inefficient legal rules.

A relative shift from efficient to inefficient legal rules will influence both the number and intensity of disputes regardless of the characteristics of the parties to the disputes. Inefficient rules impose excessive costs, and excessive costs can be predicted to lead to nonoptimal consumption, whether of accident avoidance, contract compliance, or solicitude for another's property. Where the total costs of accidents and accident avoidance under a particular legal rule are higher, there will be nonoptimal investment in avoidance. The accidents that occur may be more severe or may be greater in number or the investment in avoidance may be greater than if the rule were changed. As a result, the litigation rate for inefficient rules will be higher.

Similarly, for the set of disputes in which only one party has a continuing interest in the allocative effects of a given rule, disputes arising under inefficient rules are more likely to be litigated than those arising under efficient rules. Professor Rubin concludes as to such cases that the tendency with respect to efficiency is indeterminate.[21] But again he fails to distinguish the decision to litigate the individual dispute from decisions for the set of all disputes. Professor Rubin notes correctly that where one party alone possesses continuing interest, the stakes of the case to that party relative to his opponent will be greater[22] and the party may be willing to invest more in the

[20] This analysis is well known. See Gary S. Becker, Economic Theory 19-24 (1971). For commodities it is assumed that the price changes are compensated; in the context of litigation, that the wealth effects on the consumption of litigation from a shift between inefficient and efficient rules is negligible, a reasonable assumption. The wealth effects of a particular decision on the rate of litigation within the society are likely to be small since the costs of litigation typically constitute a tiny fraction of an individual's purchases. Where wealth effects, to the contrary, are large, this conclusion does not follow.

[21] Rubin § II-C. Rubin supports his hypothesis by the description of 19th century nuisance law in Joel Franklin Brenner, Nuisance Law and the Industrial Revolution, 3 J. Leg. Studies 403 (1974). According to Brenner, the common law applied different (stricter) standards of proof in suits against factories by inhabitants of industrial towns than in suits by inhabitants of the country. This distinction may be quite consistent with economic efficiency. Brenner did not study whether the wage structure compensated workers coming to industrial cities for the disagreeable conditions. Regardless of inefficiency, both legal standards appear to have been derived from disputes between landowners (and especially wealthy landowners) and factories, both of which, one would imagine, had continuing interests in the dispute. *Id.* at 415-20.

[22] We must assume that there are other parties absent from the dispute whose interests are similar to the party without continuing interest; otherwise it would be efficient for the party with the continuing interest to spend more and dominate more.

litigation. The common law has attempted to deal with this problem of malrepresentation by various means such as equitable bills of peace, exceptions to collateral estoppel, the statutory class action, and more generally by adopting a style of decisionmaking that appears to take the interests of the absent parties into account.[23] The larger investment of one party to a dispute may in fact influence the allocative effect of a rule in a given case, but even if the rule favors the party with the continuing interest, if it is inefficient, it will generate more future disputes (because it generates more accidents or accident avoidance) and consequently it will be more likely to be overturned.

II.

The analysis in this paper can be distinguished from other attempts to explain and predict judicial behavior by its disregard of individual holdings and its focus on systematic changes in the aggregate set of legal rules in force. The set of legal rules can be analogized to the set of consumer decisions in a market. Like consumers, judges are restrained by a budget, derived from the aggregate budget of litigants, which determines the cases that proceed to judgment. As mentioned above, where the opportunity set of commodity choices changes, legal rules in the aggregate, like consumer decisions in the aggregate, can be expected to be shifted toward the relatively cheaper commodities (efficient rules).

Previous efforts of lawyers and political scientists to predict the content of the law have concentrated, to the contrary, on the conscious or unconscious motivations of judges that lead to particular holdings in individual cases. Such efforts, however, are as heroic as predicting the market response to a change in price by analyzing the specific motivations of individual consumers. Just as it is unnecessary for the prediction of market responses to explain the psychological processes that have led individual consumers to choose or to reject particular products,[24] it is unnecessary for the prediction of the course of the law to explain the mental processes that have led individual judges to particular holdings.

This section reviews some of the more prominent theories of judicial behavior to suggest how their predictive power can be enhanced by analysis of the variables that determine the survival of legal rules. The study of the law since Langdell has focused on the published opinions of judges. These

[23] For a discussion of equitable bills of peace see Yuba Consolidated v. Kilkeary, 206 F. 2d 884 (9th Cir. 1953); 1 John Norton Pomeroy, Equity Jurisprudence §269 (5th ed. Spencer W. Symons 1941). For a discussion of rules of estoppel see Richard A. Posner, Economic Analysis of Law § 21.9 (2d ed. forthcoming 1977). For an example of tacit consideration of the interests of individuals not parties to the litigation, see Benjamin N. Cardozo, The Nature of the Judicial Process 21 (1921); Boomer v. Atlantic Cement Co., 26 N.Y. 2d 870 (1970).

[24] Gary S. Becker, *supra* note 14.

opinions constitute, of course, the most recent and authoritative statements of the principles that will control particular disputes, and the tendency to emphasize them is encouraged by the demand for predictions of decisions that will be immediately forthcoming rather than of more substantial long-term changes in the character of legal rules. Excessively narrow attention to current decisions, however, neglects two aspects of the common law that are essential for understanding it. First, such attention ignores the broader corpus of rules and principles which remain effective as controlling precedents but which are infrequently litigated. Second, concentration on judicial opinions creates the hazard of losing sight of the processes that cause certain disputes and not others to be litigated. Every student of the law appreciates, of course, that a judge can decide only cases that come before him, but it has been a universal although implicit assumption of studies of judicial output that the cases that proceed to judgment represent an unbiased sample of the society's disputes.

An early and now notorious explanation of judicial behavior is that of Jerome Frank who, building on his understanding of modern psychology,[25] argued that the factors determining legal rules were the innumerable unconscious personal biases of judges.[26] He concluded that except to the extent that published opinions and announced rules of law were autobiographical, they provided no predictive ability for future decisions. "The law var[ies] . . .", Frank explained, "with the personality of the judge."[27]

Although his view retains currency,[28] Frank was criticized in his own time on grounds that presage in some respects the analysis in this comment. Dean Pound reproached Frank for insisting on the unique, single case which Pound thought may or may not actually be significant, rather than attempting to understand "the uniform course of judicial behavior." According to Pound, Frank and other realists ignored aspects of the common law process

[25] Frank was criticized for giving insufficient attention to the scope of contemporaneous psychological studies. Mortimer J. Adler, Legal Certainty in Law and the Modern Mind: A Symposium, 31 Colum. L. Rev. 91, 92 (1931).

[26] Jerome Frank, Law and the Modern Mind 106, 362 (1931). Frank argued that "the judge's sympathies and antipathies are likely to be active with respect to the persons of the witness, the attorneys and the parties to the suit. His own past may have created plus or minus reactions to women, or blonde women, or men with beards, or Southerners, or Italians, or Englishmen, or plumbers, or ministers, or college graduates, or Democrats. A certain twang or cough or gesture may start up memories painful or pleasant in the main. Those memories of the judge, while he is listening to a witness with such a twang or cough or gesture, may affect the judge's initial hearing of, or subsequent recollection of, what the witness said, or the weight or credibility which the judge will attach to the witness's testimony." *Id.* at 106.

[27] *Id.* at 111-16, 150.

[28] See Sheldon Goldman, Behavioral Approaches to Judicial Decision-Making: Toward a Theory of Judicial Voting Behavior, 11 Jurimetrics J. 142 (1971). For another modern evaluation of Frank see Bruce A. Ackerman, Law and the Modern Mind by Jerome Frank, Daedalus, Winter 1974, at 119.

that render nonrational judicial action unimportant. "[T]he logical and rational element and the traditional technique of application, or art of the common-law lawyer's craft . . . tends to stability and uniformity of judicial action in spite of the disturbing factors."[29] In a similar vein, Mortimer Adler criticized Frank for neglecting the restraints of the common law process on judicial discretion. Although a judge's "psychological prejudices and his hunches . . . are undoubtedly large factors in determining his disposition of the case, . . . [a judge] must nevertheless operate within the range of possible alternatives defined by an exhaustive analysis of the plurality of legal doctrines."[30]

Pound's first criticism is that Frank wrongly emphasized idiosyncratic judicial behavior, and it is true that the evidence that Frank summoned to support his theory consisted of anecdotes and confessions by various judges unable to explain some of their more difficult decisions.[31] Erratic decisions, as Pound indicates, would appear less significant if one were to consider—as a theorist must—a large sample of decisions. The second aspect of Pound's and Adler's criticism, however, is that there are characteristics inherent to the common law process that suppress irrational variations by encouraging their correction. This paper has argued that individual judges may be irrational, just as individual consumers may be irrational, yet the rules in force, like reactions in the market, may in sum exhibit strong rational characteristics. Economic variables, not psychological attributes of judges, will lead to regularities in the cases that come before judges. As a result, Frank's finding that the decision in any individual case was unpredictable was not sufficient to support his conclusion that the law itself was unpredictable.

A sophisticated variant of Frank's approach is that of modern political scientists who attempt to predict the character of the law chiefly from the ideological attitudes of judges.[32] This work has attempted to increase predictive ability by aggregating data of the backgrounds and perceptions of judges, and by selecting and narrowing the range of judicial response by

[29] Roscoe Pound, The Call for a Realist Jurisprudence, 44 Harv. L. Rev. 697, 706-07 (1931). Note that Pound's was not a consistent criticism. Elsewhere Pound criticizes the realists for "faith in masses of figures." *Id.* at 701. Pound suggested as a substitute theory that the course of the law could be explained by what he called the "ideal element," that judges do what they ought to do. See, for example, *id.* at 700.

[30] Mortimer J. Adler, *supra* note 25, at 105. Adler's view is similar to Edward H. Levi's. See text following note 37 *infra*. The constraints of the common law process that Adler perceived were doctrinal limitations as opposed to economic limitations leading to greater survival of efficient rules.

[31] Jerome Frank, *supra* note 26, at 102-17, 137, 143-45.

[32] Glendon A. Schubert, The Judicial Mind Revisited (1974); *id.*, Judicial Policy-Making (rev. ed. 1974); Sheldon Goldman & Thomas P. Jahnige, The Federal Courts as a Political System (2d ed. 1976). For an earlier review of this work see Glendon Schubert, Judicial Process and Behavior, 1963-1971 in 3 Political Science Annual, 73, 94-103 (James A. Robinson ed. 1972).

abstracting certain characteristic legal issues with respect to which it is most plausible that ideology will influence judicial decisions.[33] These studies, however, have weaknesses similar to those of Frank. First, they ignore except in an extremely narrow sense forces that lead certain cases to be brought to judgment.[34] Second, they tend to measure the "law" of a given period or the influence of the judiciary by the content of current decisions.[35] By neglecting those decisions that fail to generate continuing litigation, which are likely to comprise the predominating component of legal rules in force, these studies attribute excessive influence to measurements of the background of the current judiciary.

Various legal scholars have responded to Frank's characterization of judicial decisionmaking by emphasizing the limitations on judicial discretion imposed by the common law process. Their analysis is similar in many respects to the model in this paper.[36] A prominent example is Edward H. Levi's *An Introduction to Legal Reasoning.*[37] Levi explains that the common law process develops legal rules from reasoning by example. For a given decision a judge surveys the set of rules of law announced in earlier similar cases and applies one of the rules to decide the case at hand. The law changes as the similarities perceived between current cases and certain former cases increase. A new legal category or similarity can be proposed by one of the litigants and if the idea is accepted it will displace an earlier legal concept.[38]

[33] See Sheldon Goldman, Voting Behavior on the United States Courts of Appeals Revisited, 69 Am. Pol. Sci. Rev. 491 (1975). Goldman for example classifies cases in categories such as "Criminal Procedures", "Private Economic", "Injured Persons" and identifies judicial outcomes such as "For the injured in federal torts cases" and "For the injured or the fatally injured's estate in automobile accidents."

[34] Goldman and Jahnige mention that subsequent litigation provides "feedback" that influences judicial decision, but their only examples of "feedback" are test cases, too narrow a set. Sheldon Goldman & Thomas P. Jahnige, *supra* note 32, at 238-42. See, as further examples of studies of the judicial process that neglect the determinants of litigation, those debating the influence of the Supreme Court: Robert A. Dahl, Decision-Making in a Democracy: The Supreme Court as a National Policy-Maker, 6 J. Pub. Law 279 (1957); and Jonathan D. Casper, The Supreme Court and National Policy Making, 70 Am. Pol. Sci. Rev. 50 (1976). But see another contribution to this debate, William M. Landes & Richard A. Posner, The Independent Judiciary in an Interest-Group Perspective, 18 J. Law & Econ. 875, 895 & n.41, 896-901 (1975).

[35] Sheldon Goldman, *supra* note 33; Robert A. Dahl, *supra* note 34.

[36] *E.g.*, Henry M. Hart, Jr. and Albert M. Sacks, The Legal Process: Basic Problems in the Making and Application of Law (mimeo. class materials Harv. U., 2 vols. 1958); Edward H. Levi, An Introduction to Legal Reasoning (1948); Herbert Weschler, Toward Neutral Principles of Constitutional Law, 73 Harv. L. Rev. 1 (1959). For further references see the sources cited in Bruce A. Ackerman, *supra* note 28, at 123, 128 n. 26. Ackerman has designated these scholars the "Legal Process" school.

[37] Edward H. Levi, *supra* note 36.

[38] *Id.* at 1-8. For an earlier formulation of a similar model of the common law see Benjamin Cardozo, *supra* note 23, at 41-44, 47-49.

The similarity to the model in this paper lies in Levi's view that judicial discretion is constrained by the set of available socially acceptable legal categories. According to Levi, even though an idea may at one time have been rejected by a court, once it achieves standing in the society it will be suggested again in a subsequent case. The court thus will be offered the opportunity to reinterpret the prior decision and adopt the rejected idea. When adopted, the idea will be extended in later cases and further defined, as it is applied more generally and related to other accepted ideas.[39] The scope of judicial influence, therefore, is restricted by the tendency of decisions that conflict with controlling social concepts to be relitigated and, thus, redefined and reinterpreted.

The chief limitation of Levi's theory is its ability to predict the content of the legal rules that will develop from the common law process. The theory predicts that legal decisions will be controlled by ideas that have won acceptance in the society,[40] but it offers no means of determining which ideas are likely to prevail. Levi, for example, describes in some detail the gradual adoption and extension of different standards of liability for injuries caused by "inherently dangerous" products, but his theory explains this development only as "a reflection of a period in which increasing governmental control and responsibility for the individual were thought to be proper. No one economic or social theory was responsible . . . [A]s changes came about in the manner of living, the social theory moved ahead to explain and persuade."[41]

Levi's model of the judicial process, however, generates empirical propositions similar to those offered in this paper. A social idea or legal category is more likely to be replaced by a different idea, according to Levi, the more often alternative concepts are proposed. Similarly, a new legal category is more likely to be accepted by a court, the more often it is suggested to the court as the appropriate ground for judicial decision. Levi relates the frequency of such proposals, that is of relitigation, to the set of controlling ideas in the society. But, presumably, regardless of the content of the social consciousness, predictable differences in the rate of relitigation of certain legal rules will generate the same result. This is not to suggest that prevailing social concepts have no influence on legal doctrines. But until theories are devised relating social welfare policies or other ideas to litigation rates, one can increase predictive power by concentrating on more narrow characteristics of legal rules that can be shown with greater confidence to affect litigation.

A more recent explanation of judicial behavior is that of Richard A.

[39] Edward H. Levi, *supra* note 36, at 5-8, 33, 61, 73.

[40] *Id.* at 6.

[41] *Id.* at 102. See also pp. 8-27.

Posner in *Economic Analysis of Law*. Earlier in the paper I criticized Posner's explanation of the stimuli that might lead judges to choose efficient outcomes.[42] Posner's hypotheses, however, have generated substantial dispute among legal scholars. It is worthwhile reviewing some of the differences between Posner and his critics because the theory proposed in this paper, I believe, renders many of them moot.

Posner's explanation of judicial behavior attempts to predict various means by which a judge can increase his individual welfare by altering the content of his decisions. Posner initially comments that the common law system appears designed to both suppress and make insignificant the personal pecuniary gains to a judge from a particular decision. Rules of judicial ethics prohibit judges from deciding cases in which they have personal interests. Rules of evidence and procedure tend to conceal the distributive consequences of particular decisions.[43] Posner adds that the wealth effects to a judge from any single decision are likely to be small.[44] This contention has been forcefully contested by Arthur Leff and Morton Horwitz, who argue that the wealth effects of a judicial decision on certain social classes of which the judge may be a member can be quite large—in some cases, according to Horwitz, "enormous."[45] Since it is virtually impossible to measure empirically the wealth effects of a given decision, this dispute is irresolvable. Yet the theory in this paper suggests that even where judges are able in individual cases to directly enhance their own pecuniary welfare, they will remain unable to systematically alter the character of the law. The wealth effects of a particular decision on the rate of litigation are likely to be small,[46] and thus the principal determinants of the allocative effects of legal rules remain beyond judicial control.

Posner's theory of judicial motivation argues that since judges will be typically unable to achieve direct pecuniary gain, they will turn to other decision rules that will enhance their welfare, albeit less directly. Posner initially believed that many judges aspire to higher judicial or political office, so that if efficiency were valued by society, a judge might attempt to improve his chances of advancement by announcing efficient legal rules. In the second edition of *Economic Analysis of Law* Posner suggests that ambition to advance is less important than judges' more general desires to "impose

[42] See text surrounding notes 5-7.

[43] Posner, Economic Analysis 322. Note that the efficient character of these rules supports the hypothesis of this paper. The litigation rate is likely to be higher for procedural disputes than for other disputes since the costs are lower of litigating issues developed by argument rather than by trial. As the litigation rate increases, the tendency toward efficient rules increases.

[44] Posner, Economic Analysis 325-27.

[45] Arthur Allen Leff, Economic Analysis of Law: Some Realism about Nominalism, 60 Va. L. Rev. 451, 471 (1974); Morton J. Horwitz, *supra* note 7, at 100.

[46] See note 20 *supra*.

their preferences, tastes, values, etc. on society."[47] Much of Posner's work has shown that many common law doctrines crystallized in the 19th century, a period, he argues, in which efficiency may have been more highly valued by the society and by common law judges.[48] This description of common law decisionmaking, however, has been assailed by Arthur Leff and by James E. Krier. Leff criticized Posner for failing to explain why the judicial process is systematically less sensitive to distributive consideration than the legislative process, and Krier argued that judges themselves may prefer distributive to allocative consequences.[49]

A reformulation that bases the content of the common law on the preferences and values of judges only pushes the inquiry one step farther back. Since there are no theories for the prediction of judicial tastes, there is no increase in our understanding of the law. This paper has attempted to set forth an alternative theory that does not rely on determination of the preferences or ideology of individual judges. According to this theory, the dispute over judicial preferences becomes less important because although the ideology of individual judges may influence the rate of adoption of common law rules as well as the equilibrium level of efficient values, it cannot affect the process that leads to the survival of efficient or inefficient rules.

III.

It is important to appreciate that this paper has not shown that the rules of the common law are or ever will be completely efficient. It has suggested only that the common law process incorporates a strong tendency toward efficient outcomes. It is an implication of this theory that the rate at which efficient outcomes will be achieved will be a function of the nature of the judicial bias for or against efficiency,[50] the frequency of relitigation of inefficient rules (itself determined by the costs of litigation versus settlement, the precedential effect of the rules, and the extent of their inefficiency), the rate of change of the social conditions that underlie various disputes, and the adaptability of earlier surviving precedents to the efficient resolution of new disputes. It is a further implication that areas of the law within which characteristic disputes have remained relatively consistent over time, such as admiralty, sales, or procedure, are more likely today to be dominated by

[47] Posner, Economic Analysis 325. Richard A. Posner, Economic Analysis of Law § 19.7 (2d ed. forthcoming).

[48] Posner, Economic Analysis 327. Richard A. Posner, A Theory of Negligence, *supra* note 4.

[49] Arthur Allen Leff, *supra* note 45, at 471-73. James E. Krier, Book Review, 122 U. Pa. L. Rev. 1664, 1696 (1974).

[50] The effect of judicial bias on the rate of change toward efficiency and the ultimate equilibrium level suggests that the attention of Richard Posner and his critics to preferences of judges is not irrelevant. It is my own view that efforts to develop theories of judicial preferences will be no more successful than efforts to develop theories of consumer preferences.

efficient rules; and there is evidence supporting this hypothesis.[51] Perhaps a more important suggestion of the paper, however, is that the predictive ability of attempts to explain the character of common law decision making is likely to be enhanced by more careful attention to the forces that systematically affect the amount of litigation.

[51] For a discussion of the evolution of common law rules of admiralty see William M. Landes & Richard A. Posner, Salvors, Finders, Good Samaritans, and Other Rescuers: An Economic Study of Law and Altruism (forthcoming); of rules of sales see K. N. Llewellyn, On Warranty of Quality and Society: II 37 Colum. L. Rev. 341, 392-93 (1937); Grant Gilmore & Charles L. Black, Jr., The Law of Admiralty §§ 3.7-3.8 (2d ed. 1975); of procedure see Posner, Economic Analysis 322.

[11]

WHY IS THE COMMON LAW EFFICIENT?

*PAUL H. RUBIN**

POSNER, in *Economic Analysis of Law*,[1] argues persuasively that the common law can be best understood as an attempt to achieve economic efficiency. He is less persuasive in his explanation of why this is so—his argument is essentially that judges may as well decide in terms of efficiency, since they have no other criteria to use. To an economist accustomed to invisible hand[2] explanations of efficiency in the marketplace, this justification seems weak.

Of related interest is the analysis by Landes,[3] Gould,[4] and Tullock[5] of the decision to litigate a dispute rather than settle. All have concluded that in general, parties will settle out of court. But, for the common law to remain efficient, it must change as conditions change; changes in the common law require that some cases be litigated. Does the rationality of the common law rest on irrational behavior of litigants?

In this paper I show that these issues—the presumed efficiency of the common law and the decision to use the courts to settle a dispute—are related. In particular, this relationship will occur because resorting to court settlement is more likely in cases where the legal rules relevant to the dispute are inefficient, and less likely where the rules are efficient. Thus, efficient rules may evolve from in-court settlement, thereby reducing the incentive for future litigation and increasing the probability that efficient rules will persist. In short, the efficient rule situation noted by Posner is due to an evolutionary mechanism whose direction proceeds from the utility maximizing decisions of disputants rather than from the wisdom of judges.

Section I of this paper contains an analysis of the framework which will be used to discuss pressures for efficiency. Section II contains the actual analy-

* Associate Professor of Economics, University of Georgia. The author would like to thank Gordon Tullock, Carl Jordan, and an anonymous referee for comments on an earlier version of this paper.

[1] Richard A. Posner, Economic Analysis of Law (1972).

[2] For a general discussion of invisible hand explanations, see Robert Nozick, Anarchy, State and Utopia (1974).

[3] William M. Landes, An Economic Analysis of the Courts, 14 J. Law & Econ. 61 (1971).

[4] John P. Gould, The Economics of Legal Conflicts, 2 J. Leg. Studies 279 (1973).

[5] Gordon Tullock, The Logic of the Law (1971).

sis, in which it is shown that efficiency occurs in situations where both parties to a dispute have an ongoing interest in cases, and that efficiency need not occur if one or both parties do not have such an ongoing interest. Section III contains some complications and extensions. The last section is a summary.

I. General Framework

Throughout this paper, I use an example of accident liability to illustrate the arguments. The particular example does not matter, for, as Posner has shown, torts, property, and contract law can all be analyzed within the same framework.[6] Suppose there is a certain type of accident which costs X when it occurs. Parties of type B are the victims and parties of type A the defendants if the accident occurs. Liability may be placed on A or on B. If liability is placed on A, the optimal solution for A is to spend S_A on accident avoidance and allow N_A accidents to occur; conversely, if liability is placed on B, S_B will be spent on avoidance and N_B accidents will occur. Assume also that this is an either/or situation: the technology of avoidance in this case is such that there is no joint action which A and B could take to further reduce accident and prevention costs. For purposes of analysis, assume that it is efficient for liability to be placed on B; that is,

$$T_B = S_B + N_BX < S_A + N_AX = T_A \quad (1)$$

where T_A and T_B represent total present value of accident costs plus prevention costs for parties A and B respectively. Equation (1) indicates that this total cost is less if B is liable than if A is liable.

Efficiency requires that A not be made liable for the accident; the most efficient solution is for B to spend S_B and for there to be N_B accidents. Whether B will spend S_B on avoidance or A will spend S_A depends on the current liability assignment—that is, on the decision which the parties expect the courts to reach if there is an accident and litigation occurs. Courts are somewhat bound by precedent. Thus, if precedents favor B, then S_A will be spent and total accident costs will be T_A; conversely if precedents favor A. (Because we have eliminated the possibility of joint action, one situation or the other will occur.)

Define R as the probability that B will win the suit if an accident occurs and the parties litigate. The value of R is defined by precedent: if $R > .5$, precedents favor B and B is likely to win if the case is litigated. If $R < .5$ precedents favor A. We assume throughout the paper that both parties agree on the value of R. The current liability assignment is then efficient if $R < .5$. It is assumed throughout that judges are likely but not certain to decide on

[6] Richard A. Posner, *supra* note 1, at 98-102.

the basis of precedent. As shown below, it is the possibility of changing current precedents which sometimes makes litigation worthwhile and which will in some circumstances lead to efficiency.

The Coase theorem[7] indicates that placement of liability does not matter: if A were made liable, he would simply pay a bribe to B in order to induce B to avoid accidents; as indicated by (1), this would be the efficient solution. This will in fact occur if the costs of paying the bribe are sufficiently low; however, it is possible that the transactions costs will be greater than (T_A-T_B), the saving from shifting liability to the efficient bearer. In this case, if he is liable, A will accept liability rather than paying B. Even if it is feasible for A to bribe B, there will be some transactions costs involved in paying the bribe. In Section II, it is assumed that paying a bribe is not feasible; in Section III the case of feasible bribery is examined.

II. Analysis

Given the basic situation discussed above, there are some cases in which there will be pressure for the law to evolve towards efficiency. The crucial point is the interest which the parties have in decisions as precedents. Thus, some legal cases involve individuals with a one-time interest in the outcome, while other cases involve corporate bodies of some sort—government agencies, labor unions, firms, insurance companies. Such organizations would have an interest in legal cases as precedents as well as interests as litigants.[8] Insurance companies, for example, would be concerned with future liability cases as well as with a particular case. In analyzing the relation between efficiency and litigation, there are three basic situations which must be considered. In part A, the situation in which both parties have a substantial interest in the case as precedent will be considered. Part B discusses the situation in which only one party is interested in the case as precedent. Part C considers the situation where neither party is interested in the case as precedent.

A. *Both Parties Interested in Precedent*

If both parties to a certain type of legal dispute have a substantial interest in future cases of this sort, then precedents will evolve towards efficiency, the common law situation posited by Posner. If rules are inefficient, there will be an incentive for the party held liable to force litigation; if rules are efficient, there will be no such incentive. Thus, efficient rules will be maintained, and inefficient rules litigated until overturned.

[7] R. H. Coase, The Problem of Social Cost, 3 J. Law & Econ. 1 (1960).

[8] Richard A. Posner, The Behavior of Administrative Agencies, 1 J. Leg. Studies 305 (1972), discusses the interest of agencies in settling cases for use as precedents.

Substantial interest in precedent refers to a situation in which the party is likely to be in many such cases in the future. In effect, such parties are concerned with the entire stream of costs, T_A or T_B, rather than with X, the damages from one particular accident. Start with an inefficient rule—A is held liable if accidents occur, so that A is now spending S_A on accident avoidance and N_AX on damage payments for those accidents which still occur. An accident has just occurred; the parties must decide whether to settle or litigate.

If the case is litigated and B wins, he is paid X; if A wins, he does not pay X in this case, and, in addition, A saves T_A in the future, but B must begin to pay T_B. Court costs for each party are C. The value to A of a court settlement is

$$V_A = R(-X) + (1-R)T_A - C \tag{2}$$

and to B:

$$V_B = R(X) + (1-R)(-T_B) - C \tag{3}$$

The parties can settle out of court if

$$-V_A > V_B \tag{4}$$

which simply says that a settlement can be reached if the expected loss to A of going to court is greater than the expected gain to B. If this is so, there is room for negotiation. Conversely, if (4) is not satisfied, the parties will litigate. In this example, litigation will occur if

$$(1-R)(T_A - T_B) > 2C \tag{5}$$

Here, $T_A - T_B$ is the cost of the inefficient legal rule. As this becomes larger, litigation is more likely. Conversely, as R becomes larger (that is, as the inefficient rule is more entrenched) litigation is less likely. As court costs are higher, litigation is less likely. Finally, if the current rule were efficient (that is, if T_B were greater than T_A), (5) would never be satisfied, so that there would be no litigation.

What will happen? If the parties go to court, B will probably win, since both parties agree that $R > .5$. However, whenever this stituation arises in the future A will again go to court. At some point, some court will find in favor of A; at this point, the law has been changed and is now efficient. From that time on, precedents will favor A in comparable cases. Since there is no deadweight loss to party B when he is forced to bear liability (i.e., no term comparable to $T_A - T_B$), B will not find it worthwhile to go to court when such an accident occurs; instead, B will spend S_B on avoiding such accidents and bear the cost N_BX of those which do occur.

It is now possible to define precisely the meaning of substantial interest.

A's interest in this sort of case is substantial precisely if T_A is large enough so that (5) is satisfied. As this problem has been defined, it is not relevant whether B has a substantial interest or not; however, as we will see in the next section, both parties must have a substantial interest if efficiency is to be guaranteed.

What if both parties are insurance companies with ongoing interests as either defendants or plaintiffs? Then both A and B become interested in $T_A - T_B$, the efficiency savings from future cases. It can easily be shown that, if both parties are equally likely to be on either side of such cases in the future, (5) is unchanged so that the pressure for efficiency will be maintained.

We have thus shown that if rules are inefficient, parties will use the courts until the rules are changed; conversely, if rules are efficient, the courts will not be used and the efficient rule will remain in force. An outside observer coming upon this legal rule would observe that the rule is efficient; but this efficiency occurs because of an evolutionary process, not because of any particular wisdom on the part of judges. If judges decide independently of efficiency, we would still find efficient rules. Intelligent judges may speed up the process of attaining efficiency; they do not drive the process.

B. *Only One Party Interested in Precedent*

If only one party to a dispute is interested in future cases of this sort, there will be pressure for precedents to evolve in favor of that party which does have a stake in future cases, whether or not this is the efficient solution. This is because a party with a stake in future decision will find it worthwhile to litigate as long as liability rests with him; conversely, a party with no stake in future decisions will not find litigation worthwhile.

Let us continue our example: an accident has happened to a certain B. As the law now stands A is likely to win the case—that is, $R < .5$, and both parties agree on the value of R. However, B has a stake in the result of this decision; A has no such stake. That is, this type of case is an ongoing case for B, but a one time case for A. If B goes to court and wins, then in the future he will save S_B per period. T_B is the present value of the stream of accident costs to B as long as he is liable. Thus, if the courts are used and B wins, he receives X from A as a result of this accident; in addition, he saves T_B in the future. On the other hand, if A wins, he does not pay X; A is, by assumption, not interested in future decision. The value to A of a court case is:

$$V_A = R(-X) - C \tag{6}$$

and the value to B is:

$$V_B = R(X) + R(T_B) - C \tag{7}$$

In this case, A will be willing to pay $R(X) + C$ to avoid a court settlement; B will be willing to accept $R(X) + R(T_B) - C$. Therefore, there will be no settlement if

$$R(T_B) > 2C \tag{8}$$

From (8), we see that, unless R is very small (that is, unless precedents are extremely clear and unfavorable to B), or unless court costs are large, B will find litigation worthwhile. Moreover, each time such an accident occurs, B will again go to court rather than settling. As such behavior continues, at some point some court may rule in B's favor. At this point the rule favors B, and B will therefore cease taking precautions to avoid accidents. Rather, party A will begin spending S_A on accident avoidance. When such accidents again occur, the A who is involved will pay X to B, rather than litigate, since A has no future interest in the case.

This same argument could be turned around: if A has an ongoing interest in this type of case and B does not, then A will go to court until a favorable ruling is obtained; from this time on, precedents will favor A, and this rule will persist, since no B will find litigation worthwhile. Thus, when one party has an ongoing interest in a type of case there is a tendency for cases to be litigated until a precedent is established which favors this party. There is no tendency for efficiency in this situation.

This case appears to describe the evolution of nuisance law in the nineteenth century.[9] By the end of this century, those causing nuisances were largely factories, which would have ongoing interests in liability rulings; conversely, those suffering from nuisances were largely individuals with no such interest. (That is, factories were concerned with T_B, but individuals were indifferent to T_A.) The evidence indicates that nuisance law did in fact largely favor factories and firms, rather than individuals.

C. *No Interest in Precedent*

If neither party is interested in precedents, the current rule will persist, whether it is efficient or inefficient. That is, if neither party has an ongoing interest in cases of this sort, then neither will force use of the courts. All such cases will be settled on the basis of the current rule, whatever it might be. Since cases will not go to court, there will be no pressure to change this rule.

Again begin with the situation in which an accident has occurred. A certain party of type B has lost X and is considering suing the party A who is liable. Both parties agree that the probability of B winning is R. If there is no

[9] See Joel Franklin Brenner, Nuisance Law and the Industrial Revolution, 3 J. Leg. Studies 403 (1974), for a discussion which is consistent with this argument.

interest in precedent, then the exact value of R is irrelevant for our purposes. We assume risk neutrality since, as we shall indicate below, risk aversion would complicate the analysis without changing the results.

Clearly, if this is the entire problem, the parties should settle. To A the expected value of a court settlement is

$$V_A = -RX-C \tag{9}$$

and to B it is

$$V_B = RX-C. \tag{10}$$

The parties can settle out of court if (4) is satisfied; this becomes

$$RX + C > RX-C \tag{11}$$

which is obviously met. Thus rather than going to court, A can pay some amount L to B, where

$$RX-C < L < RX+C \tag{12}$$

and this will be better than a court settlement for both parties. This is the essence of the arguments as to why most cases may be expected to be settled out of court. If the parties are risk averse, we replace terms in (9) and (10) with their utility equivalents. For risk averse individuals, the utility of a lottery is less than the utility of the expected value of the lottery; thus, in (4) the left side becomes relatively larger and the right side relatively smaller. Risk aversion makes out of court settlements relatively more likely.

In this situation, the courts will be used only if the parties disagree about the value of R. However, there is no reason to assume that such disagreement is related to the efficiency of current rules. Thus, as long as there is agreement about the probability of decisions, the legal rule will not change; and if there is disagreement and consequent pressure for rule change, there is no presumption that changes would be in the direction of increased efficiency. This situation is presumably that which exists when disputants are individuals with little ongoing interest in solutions. Furthermore, disputes would ordinarily be settled in accordance with current legal rules; it would be unusual for such cases to go to court, and there is no presumption that rules in such cases would be efficient. However, to the extent that the types of legal cases involving individuals are the same types of cases as those involving corporate bodies, this conclusion must be modified for, as we have seen, there is pressure for efficiency in the latter type of case, whereas individual disputants will accept the existing rule, whether it is efficient or not.[10]

[10] See Section III, C.

III. Some Complications

In this section I consider in turn: situations in which bribery is feasible; costs of out-of-court settlements; public good problems; situations in which different types of parties are interested in the same type of case; and some applications to statute law.

A. *Bribery*

Assume again that liability is currently inefficiently assigned—that, A is liable. As mentioned in Section I, it may be possible in this case for A to bribe B to take precautions, rather than taking precautions himself. As before, define T_A and T_B as the present value of the stream of costs if liability is placed, respectively, on A or B; from (1) we know that

$$T_B < T_A. \tag{13}$$

Define T_N as the present value of costs to A of bribing B to take precautions. T_N would include normal aspects of transactions costs—costs of finding the relevant B, of actually making the payments, of monitoring B's behavior, etc. A will find it worthwhile to bribe B if

$$T_N < T_A - T_B \tag{14}$$

that is, if the cost of paying the bribe is less than the saving from taking efficient precautions. Even in this case, however, there is a deadweight loss—an efficiency loss caused by the actual cost of paying the bribe, T_N.

Even with the bribe, there will still be N_A accidents per period. One of these accidents has occurred. A is now liable to pay X to the injured B. As above, A must decide whether to pay or to litigate. If A settles out of court or loses the case in court, he must then spend $T_N + T_B$; he must continue to negotiate with parties B and pay the accident costs of these parties. If B loses, then he must pay T_B—that is, in the future A will not be liable if this type of accident occurs, so that B will spend S_B on avoiding such accidents. In addition, if B loses, he will not be paid X, damages in the accident which has already occurred. Thus, there is a $(1-R)$ chance of B losing T_B. For A, the expected value of going to court becomes

$$V_A = R(-X) + (1-R)(T_B + T_N) - C \tag{15}$$

and for B

$$V_B = R(X) + (1-R)(-T_B) - C. \tag{16}$$

This occurs because, once A has won a case, the law is changed—precedents now favor A, rather than B. This is the essence of judge made common law.

The parties will again settle out of court if (4) is satisfied; but this now becomes

$$(1-R)T_N < 2C. \quad (17)$$

They will go to court if (17) is reveresed:

$$(1-R)T_N > 2C \quad (18)$$

The parties will go to court if the expected present value of the costs to A of negotiating with B in the future to have B take precautions is greater than the total court costs. What has happened is that T_N, the present value of these negotiation costs, is a cost to A but not a gain to B. The stakes in the case are asymmetrical, so that there is less possibility of a settlement between the parties. Notice also that T_N is in this situation the present cost of the inefficient legal rule.

The situation described above is again that in which both parties have an ongoing interst in decisions. It is likely that this will be the only relevant situation for bribes; if B does not have such an interest, then it is likely that B will be unidentifiable in advance. In this case, it is likely that the cost of A of bribing B would be prohibitive, and the analysis used in Section II B would be relevant.

Notice also that there is no relationship between court costs and bribery (transactions) costs. The decision as to whether or not to bribe B is made before the accident occurs; the decision as to whether to go to court is made after an accident has happened. Our argument is that A is likely to go to court to save *future* transactions costs. Of course, as shown in (18), if court costs are high enough relative to the present value of transactions costs, the case will be settled; but this simply says that if court costs are greater than the costs of the inefficiency imbedded in the current rule it is not worth changing the rule.

B. *Settlement Costs*

Throughout, we have ignored the costs of settling the dispute out of court. This action will have some costs, and as these costs increase, the probability of going to court increases. Formally, such costs can be included in our analysis simply by redefining C everywhere as net court costs—the difference between court costs and settlement costs. The level of net court costs is itself an important parameter in our models. As can be seen from (5) and (18) the courts are more likely to be used in overturning inefficient rules as court costs are smaller. Gould[11] has argued that high court costs have the desirable effect of reducing inefficient litigation; but it must be pointed out that such

11. John P. Gould, *supra* note 4, at 296.

costs also have the undesirable effect of reducing efficient litigation—litigation aimed at overturning inefficient rules.

C. *Different Types of Parties, Same Type of Case*

In Section II we saw that when only one party has an ongoing interest in a type of case, precedents could be expected to evolve in favor of that party. Conversely, when both parties have an interest, precedents should evolve toward efficiency. However, it is possible that some cases of a certain type will involve only one party with an ongoing interest, while other cases of the same sort will involve two such parties. In this situation, there could easily arise a conflict—when only one party has an ongoing interest, the inefficient solution may be favored, while when both have such an interest the efficient solution will be favored.

It is possible that cases of this sort would be continually litigated. However, if this were to happen, parties would observe that precedents would not be binding, and this would reduce the incentive for litigation. A more likely solution is for parties to differentiate the cases, so that one sort of precedent would govern cases with one corporate body and a different set of precedents would govern cases with two corporate bodies. The law would then be inconsistent; but no litigant would have an incentive to capitalize on this inconsistency, and therefore it would continue to exist.[12] This explanation for legal inconsistency would seem to be a fruitful area of research for scholars trained in the law.

D. *Public Good Problems*

Once a decision is reached in a case, the decision is a public good.[13] It affects all parties of type A and B. Thus, a party of type A may decide not to litigate a case, even if such litigation would be efficient, in the hope that some other A may do the litigating and save the original A court costs. However, Equations (5) or (18) are not particularly stringent: In many cases, court costs are not prohibitively high. Nonetheless, we might expect some free rider problems. Our model would predict, for example, that large companies would be involved relatively more in litigation than would small companies.

[12] It might appear that the inconsistency would lead some disputants to litigate in the hope of capitalizing on the inconsistency. However, both parties would be aware of this possibility, and thus there would be no asymmetry. Our analysis rests on assuming that litigation occurs only when there is an asymmetry between parties.

[13] See Gordon Tullock, Public Decisions as Public Goods, 99 J. Pol. Econ. 913 (1971).

E. *Application to Statute Law*

Statute law is often inefficient.[14] However, in some cases lobbying for passage of statute law can take the place of deciding to litigate in our model.[15] Thus, if some law were proposed benefitting one well defined small group at the expense of another well defined small group, and if the group which would lose would lose more than the gaining group would gain (*i.e.*, if the law were inefficient), then the potential losers would be able to outspend the potential gainers, so that we would not expect the law to be passed. Thus, we would expect that inefficient statute laws would correspond to our analysis of the situation in which only one party has an interest in precedent; that is, such laws would be passed at the expense of large groups which would not be able to effectively lobby against their passage because of free rider problems.

IV. Summary

We have shown that the efficiency of the common law, to the extent that it exists, can be explained by an evolutionary model—a model in which it is more likely that parties will litigate inefficient rules than efficient rules. If decisions are made randomly, there will be a movement in the direction of efficient laws. The same model provides an explanation for using the courts to settle some disputes, rather than relying on out of court settlements.

The evolutionary pressure comes from behavior of litigants, rather than judges. We therefore found it useful to study behavior of potential litigants, classified according to their interest in cases as precedents. We found that when neither party is interested in precedent, there is no incentive to litigate, and hence, no pressure on the law to change. When only one party is interested in precedent, that party will litigate until a favorable decision is obtained; the law in such cases will favor parties with such an ongoing interest. When both parties have an ongoing interest in a type of case, there will be pressure toward efficiency. When different types of parties have an interest in the same type of case, we would expect inconsistencies to exist in the law.

Finally, we would predict that the evolution toward efficiency, in those cases where there would be such an evolution, would be faster as current rules are more inefficient, as net courts costs (court costs less settlement costs) are lower, and as inefficient rules are less soundly entrenched.

[14] Paul H. Rubin, On the Form of Special Interest Legislation, 21 Public Choice 79 (1975).

[15] This point is due to Gordon Tullock.

ADDENDUM: COMMENT ON "THE COMMON LAW PROCESS AND THE SELECTION OF EFFICIENT RULES"

Professor George L. Priest in his comment[16] has provided a valuable extension of my results. However, this extension is purchased at some cost, and this cost is perhaps greater than Priest himself realizes. It appears that his relatively informal discussion in fact hides some of his assumptions. He is of necessity assuming something more than ". . . that transactions costs in the real world are positive."[17]

I assume throughout my paper that both parties agree on the probabilities of victory for each of them. Priest claims that he avoids this assumption, and that I make the assumption for "expositional convenience."[18] This is not so: the assumption is made for substantive, not expositional, reasons. One must make some assumption about probability estimates of the parties; it is my feeling that the assumption of equal probability assessments is more easily justified than Priest's implicit assumption of differing estimates. Specifically, rational informed individuals (or their attorneys) will have the same estimates about probabilities of any given judicial decision. To assume otherwise is tantamount to assuming ignorance by one or both parties, and as a methodological principle I prefer to avoid assuming any such ignorance wherever possible. Once ignorance is assumed, it is very easy to prove anything, and thus to derive tautological models. Priest's form of the ignorance assumptions—that each party is as likely as the other to misjudge probabilities of victory—is perhaps more innocuous than most such assumptions, but it is nonetheless an assumption I prefer to avoid.

(Priest does not explicitly make any assumption about probability estimates. However, it is a well known result that rational, risk neutral or risk averse individuals with symmetric stakes in a case will not go to law. Thus, cases will be litigated only if one of these assumptions is violated. I assume asymmetric stakes to motivate my litigants. Priest denies this assumption; therefore, he must be assuming different probability estimates. He claims to be concerned only with the number of cases which will be litigated under alternative rules and not with the motives for such litigation. But it is dangerous to make assumptions about aggregate behavior without considering the behavior of the individuals which make up the aggregate.)

In this paper I desired to show how litigation would occur in a world with no ignorance, and how efficiency would be achieved in such a world. Specifically, I desired to show how rational behavior of litigants would lead to

[16] George L. Priest, The Common Law Process and the Selection of Efficient Rules, 6 J. Legal Studies 65 (1977).

[17] *Ibid.*

[18] *Id.* at 73, n. 18.

efficiency of legal decisions. I succeeded in this. Of course, to the extent that parties to disputes do in fact disagree about probabilities, Priest's mechanism would obtain, and his comment is to this extent a valuable extension of the model. However, I feel that the process described in this paper would be empirically more important in driving rules to efficiency than would Priest's process, for litigation will invariably occur if stakes are asymmetrical in my model, while Priest's mechanism is driven by random errors in perception by the parties.

I agree fully with Priest's point about judges. As stated in various places in my paper, the evolutionary model which I develop focuses attention on decisions of potential and actual litigants rather than on judges in driving the model.

[12]

Precedent

Frederick Schauer*

What does it mean for a past event to be *precedent* for a current decision? And how does something we do *today* establish a precedent for the future? Can decisions really be controlled by the past and responsible to the future, or are appeals to precedent just so much window dressing, masking what is in reality a decision made for today only?[1] And even if precedent *can* constrain decisionmakers, why should a procedure for decisionmaking impose such a constraint? Why should the best decision for now be distorted or thwarted by obeisance to a dead past, or by obligation to an uncertain and dimly perceived future? Equally important is the question of weight. When precedent matters, just *how much* should it matter? If we are to be shackled to the past and beholden to the future, just how tight are those bonds, and what should it take to loose them?

An appeal to precedent is a form of argument, and a form of justification,[2] that is often as persuasive as it is pervasive. The bare skeleton of an appeal to precedent is easily stated: The previous treatment of occurrence X in manner Y constitutes, *solely because of its historical pedigree*, a reason for treating X in manner Y if and when X again occurs.[3]

---

* Professor of Law, University of Michigan.

Earlier versions of this article have been presented at faculty workshops at the University of Chicago, the University of Michigan, the University of Texas, the University of Toronto, the University of Virginia, and Yale University. The conventional form of thanks for these opportunities and attendant audience insights is insufficient to express fully my gratitude to the institution of the faculty workshop, which combines ideally the means for exploring one's ideas with others and the informality necessary for truly cooperative intellectual interchange. I would also like to thank Alex Aleinikoff, Larry Alexander, Edward Cooper, Patrick Gudridge, James Krier, William Miller, William Pierce, Thomas Rowe, Terrance Sandalow, Kim Scheppele, Carl Schneider, Peter Westen, and James Boyd White, whose willingness to take time from their own work to comment on mine has made this article better than it otherwise would have been.

1. Recall Justice Roberts' fear that Supreme Court decisions might come to be treated like "a restricted railroad ticket, good for this day and train only." Smith v. Allwright, 321 U.S. 649, 669 (1943) (Roberts, J., dissenting).

2. There is no difference between the logical structure of an *argument* and that of a *justification*, but the different terms suggest separate events within a larger rhetorical setting. Arguments are made prior to a decision, and thus are made *to* a decisionmaker. Justifications, on the other hand, are provided after a decision is made or an action is taken, and are given *by* the decisionmaker.

3. Standard treatments are found in R.W.M. Dias, Jurisprudence 162-217 (4th ed. 1976); G.W. Paton, A Text-Book of Jurisprudence 179-95 (D. Derham 3d ed. 1964); P. Fitzgerald, Salmond on Jurisprudence 141-87 (12th ed. 1966). Traditional approaches with a more modern cast include C.K. Allen, Law in the Making 161-382 (7th ed. 1964); R. Cross, Precedent in English Law (3d ed. 1977).

Appeals to precedent do not reside exclusively in courts of law. Forms of argument that may be concentrated in the legal system are rarely isolated there, and the argument from precedent is a prime example of the nonexclusivity of what used to be called "legal reasoning." Think of the child who insists that he should not have to wear short pants to school because his older brother was allowed to wear long pants when *he* was seven. Or think of the bureaucrat who responds to the supplicant for special consideration by saying that "we've never done it that way before." In countless instances, out of law as well as in, the fact that something was done before provides, by itself, a reason for doing it that way again.

Reliance on precedent is part of life in general. The law's lack of an exclusive claim on precedential reasoning suggests that we should dig beneath the use of precedent in this or even any legal system. I would thus like to look at precedent, at least initially, without the baggage of particular legal doctrines and without the encumbrances of a theory of law or judicial decision. By removing these potentially distorting constraints, we may see things that have previously been blocked from view. And having abstracted the analysis by looking at precedent outside of the law, we may then be able to glimpse a different picture of the use of precedent *in* law, and of what it means to "do law," to operate in a specifically legal form.

I. The Forward-Looking Aspect of Precedent

An argument from precedent seems at first to look backward. The traditional perspective on precedent, both inside and outside of law, has therefore focused on the use of yesterday's precedents in today's decisions.[4] But in an equally if not more important way, an argument from precedent looks forward as well, asking us to view today's decision

4. A noteworthy exception is MacCormick, *Formal Justice and the Form of Legal Arguments*, 6 Etudes de Logique Juridique 103 (1976). Considering the future implications of today's decisions is central to the notion of adjudication according to principle. *See* Golding, *Principled Decision-Making and the Supreme Court*, 63 Colum. L. Rev. 35 (1963); Greenawalt, *The Enduring Significance of Neutral Principles*, 78 Colum. L. Rev. 982 (1978); Wechsler, *Toward Neutral Principles of Constitutional Law*, 73 Harv. L. Rev. 1 (1959). But principles, in and out of law, are expressed in words, and the existing discussion of principles involves the problem of imagining what future cases might later come within the domain now described by a particular set of words. That, as I will discuss presently, is distinct from the question of what later decisions might be taken to follow from the first decision. Implicit in what I say, therefore, is a distinction between what is said and what is done. Much of the discussion of principled decision-making focuses on being constrained tomorrow by what we *say* today. That is important, but it is not the same as being constrained by what we *do* today. Moreover, the focus of the "neutral principles" literature is on the commitments necessarily, or at least ideally, made by a single decisionmaker. That differs from the effect of a particular decision on some *other* decisionmaker possibly not sharing the same views.

More significantly, a careful study of precedent must confront the extent to which sticky and substantially nonnormative social or linguistic characterizations may impede the ability of a formulator of a principle to draw certain intrinsically sound distinctions or to employ certain intrinsically justifiable groupings. This problem, separate from the problem of decision according to principle, is central to understanding the concept of precedent.

as a precedent for tomorrow's decisionmakers. Today is not only yesterday's tomorrow; it is also tomorrow's yesterday. A system of precedent therefore involves the special responsibility accompanying the power to commit the future before we get there.

Thinking about the effect of today's decision upon tomorrow encourages us to separate the precedential effect of a decision from the canonical language, or authoritative characterization, that may accompany that decision. Looking at precedent only as a backward-looking constraint may produce a distorted preoccupation with the canonical statements of previous decisionmakers. The precedents of the past, especially judicial precedents, come neatly packaged, with selected facts and authoritative language. Dealing with the use of past precedents thus requires dealing with the presence of the previous decisionmaker's *words*.[5] These words may themselves have authoritative force, what Ronald Dworkin calls the "enactment force of precedent,"[6] and thus we often find it difficult to disentangle the effect of a past *decision* from the effect caused by its accompanying words. More pervasively, even a previous decisionmaker's noncanonical descriptions channel the way in which the present views those past decisions. So long as the words of the past tell us how to view the deeds of the past, it remains difficult to isolate how much of the effect of a past decision is attributable to what a past court has *done* rather than to what it has *said*.

Nonjudicial precedents of the past also arrive at the present carrying with them their original characterizations. Suppose a child is allowed to stay up past her bedtime in order to watch a television show her parents thought particularly educational. Two weeks later, the child again wants to stay up late to watch a television show. The child will probably argue, "Two weeks ago you said I could stay up late to watch an educational show. Well, this show is educational too, so you have to let me stay up late tonight." That argument moves discussion away from the decision to allow the child to watch a particular show to what the parents *said* in making the decision. And then the argument resembles one over application of a specifically formulated rule such as a statute. If the parents had set out a rule, in advance, that bedtime was 8 p.m. except when an educational show was on later than 8 p.m., the discussion would differ little from that in which a precedent is accompa-

5. This relationship among facts, facts as found by the court, decision of the court, and announced reasoning of the court is at the heart of the English debate about *ratio decidendi*. *See* Goodhart, *Determining the Ratio Decidendi of a Case*, 40 YALE L.J. 161 (1930); Goodhart, *The Ratio Decidendi of a Case*, 22 MOD. L. REV. 117 (1959); Montrose, *Ratio Decidendi and the House of Lords*, 20 MOD. L. REV. 124 (1957); Montrose, *The Ratio Decidendi of a Case*, 20 MOD. L. REV. 587 (1957); Simpson, *The Ratio Decidendi of a Case*, 20 MOD. L. REV. 413 (1957); Simpson, *The* Ratio Decidendi *of a Case*, 21 MOD. L. REV. 155 (1958); Simpson, *The* Ratio Decidendi *of a Case*, 22 MOD. L. REV. 453 (1959); Stone, *The* Ratio *of the* Ratio Decidendi, 22 MOD. L. REV. 597 (1959). In somewhat different language, it is also the centerpiece of E. LEVI, AN INTRODUCTION TO LEGAL REASONING (1948) and K. LLEWELLYN, THE BRAMBLE BUSH 51-66 (1930).

6. R. DWORKIN, TAKING RIGHTS SERIOUSLY 111, 318 (1977); *see also* R. WASSERSTROM, THE JUDICIAL DECISION 35-36 (1961).

nied by simultaneous explanatory language. This is precisely because such language will be treated later like a specifically formulated rule.[7]

The passage of time compounds the difficulty of disentangling a precedent from its specific linguistic account, because the process of characterizing a decision does not end with its first formulation. We necessarily and continuously reinterpret the past as we proceed into the future. People other than the initial decisionmakers use and talk about, and in the process recharacterize, the decisions of yesterday. The story of a decision changes as it passes from generation to generation, just as words whispered from child to child do in a game of "telephone." Past decisions thus come to the present encrusted with society's subsequent characterizations of and commentary on those decisions.[8]

At the moment when we consider the wisdom of some currently contemplated decision, however, the characterization of that decision is comparatively open.[9] There is no authoritative characterization apart from what we choose to create. In making a decision, we must acknowledge its many possible subsequent characterizations, and thus the many directions in which it might be extended. Yet despite this seeming indeterminacy of the future precedential effect of today's decision, awareness of the future effect of today's decision pervades legal and nonlegal argument. Lawyers and others routinely deploy a battery of metaphors—the slippery slope, the parade of horribles, the floodgates, the foot in the door, and the entering wedge are but a few—to urge decisionmakers to consider the future effect of today's decisions. Undergirding each of these metaphors is the belief that even an uncharacterized precedent can influence the future.

Thus, only the precedents of the past, and not forward-looking precedents, stand before us clothed with generations of characterizations and recharacterizations. When we look at today as a precedent for the future, we remove the distraction of the canonical effect of simulta-

7. *See* Schauer, *Opinions as Rules* (Book Review), 53 U. CHI. L. REV. 682 (1986). One of the more important discussions of legal reasoning takes decision according to rule and decision according to precedent as identical forms of reasoning, and groups both under the rubric of "precedent." R. WASSERSTROM, *supra* note 6, at 56. To neglect the difference between decision according to a specifically formulated rule and decision according to an unformulated decision seems a distorting reduction. But even if one is inclined towards reductionism, taking decision according to precedent as a species of decision according to rule, *see* Westen, *On "Confusing Ideas": Reply*, 91 YALE L.J. 1153, 1163-64 (1982), is a more plausible reduction than the reverse. Wasserstrom's terminology does, however, have the advantage of stressing the essential "pastness" of both rules and precedents. On this idea of pastness, see Lehman, *Rules in Law*, 72 GEO. L.J. 1571, 1573 (1984).

8. Think about the way in which cases "mean" something different today than they did when first decided, especially when a case has passed from the legal into the larger culture. Brown v. Board of Education, 347 U.S. 483 (1954), "stands for" something today to the public quite different from what it did to the public in 1954. It would be rather odd if this shift in meaning did not affect the understanding of this case in the legal culture as well.

9. I will presently argue that the available characterizations constitute a more limited set, but a case yet to be decided still presents a menu of possible characterizations larger than that of a precedent of the past.

neous explanatory language, and we can better understand how being constrained by precedent often involves something different from being constrained by specifically formulated normative language.

II. Isolating the Argument from Precedent

We can use the past for many purposes, but not every use of the past involves reliance on precedent. Initially, we must differentiate an argument from precedent from an argument from experience. The first time a child sees a red coil on top of a stove he may touch it, but when he sees the red coil again he knows its dangers and keeps his fingers safely clear. When a physician sees a certain array of symptoms that in the past have indicated typhoid, she will probably diagnose typhoid when those symptoms again appear. And many judges would describe the process of sentencing as based substantially on this type of experiential reasoning.

In each of these cases, a present array of facts similar to some previous array leads a decisionmaker to draw on experience in reaching a conclusion. But despite the superficial similarity of these cases to the use of precedent, the reasoning process here is different. When reasoning from experience, the facts and conclusions of the past have no significance apart from what they teach us about the present. The probability that the present will be like the past both determines and exhausts the value of the previous experience. If we believe that the current case ought to be decided differently, no purely precedential residuum remains in the calculus. Moreover, if we now believe that the previous decision was incorrect, we will completely reject the value of the experience. But if we are truly arguing from precedent, then the fact that something was decided before gives it present value despite our current belief that the previous decision was erroneous.

An argument from experience need not be based on the experience of the present decisionmaker. Unwilling or unable to do as much thinking, looking, or testing as a previous decisionmaker, the current decisionmaker may choose to conserve present decisional resources by relying on the prior decisionmaker's experience: "If Cardozo decided this way, who am I to disagree?" Although people may describe this form of reasoning as "precedent," it is significantly different from a narrower, more central notion of precedent as a norm limiting the decisionmaker's flexibility. When the choice whether to rely on a prior decisionmaker is entirely in the hands of the present decisionmaker, the prior decision does not *constrain* the present decision, and the present decisionmaker violates no norm by disregarding it. I want to view precedent as a *rule* of precedent, and not as a nonrule-governed choice by a decisionmaker in an individual case to rely on the prior decisions of others.[10]

If precedent is seen as a rule directing a decisionmaker to take prior decisions into account, then it follows that a pure argument from precedent, unlike an argument from experience, depends only on the *results* of those decisions, and not on the validity of the reasons supporting those results. That two plus two today equals four is true, but it does not become more true because two plus two equalled four yesterday. When the strength of a current conclusion totally stands or falls on arguments for or against that conclusion, there is no appeal to precedent, even if the same conclusion has been reached in the past. If precedent matters, a prior decision now believed erroneous still affects the current decision simply because it is prior. Only if a rule makes relevant the result of a previous decision regardless of a decisionmaker's current belief about the correctness of that decision do we have the kind of argument from precedent routinely made in law and elsewhere.

In referring to past and present decisionmakers, I presuppose that, as institutions, the past and present decisionmakers are identical or of equal status. If a pure argument from precedent is valid, the earlier decision has a status that must be respected by a later decisionmaker, and that status is imposed by the rule of precedent independent of other status differentials. Lower courts, for example, are expected to respect the decisions of higher courts. But the hierarchical ordering of decisionmakers implicates considerations different from those involved when a decisionmaker is constrained by *its* previous actions as opposed to the orders of its superiors in the hierarchy.[11]

A naked argument from precedent thus urges that a decisionmaker give weight to a particular result regardless of whether that decisionmaker believes it to be correct and regardless of whether that decisionmaker believes it valuable in any way to rely on that previous result. Shorn of any embellishments, the reasons for respecting an argument from precedent may seem far from obvious. But before turning to that issue, we must first deal with the logically prior questions of whether precedent *can* matter, and if so, how.

III. CAN PRECEDENT CONSTRAIN?

A. *Rules of Relevance*

Reasoning from precedent, whether looking back to the past or ahead to the future, presupposes an ability to identify the relevant pre-

10. A decisionmaker might choose to adopt a "rule of thumb" to assist the process of deciding whether to rely on the experiences of others. But as long as the decision whether to adopt and follow the rule of thumb remains solely one for the decisionmaker, then it is not behavior that is rule-governed in the sense that it is guided by some external norm of behavior. *See* Urmson, *The Interpretation of the Moral Philosophy of J.S. Mill*, 3 PHIL. Q. 33, 34 (1953).

11. Note that while contemporary usage has collapsed much of the difference between precedent and *stare decisis*, it should be clear that I am talking about the latter in its strict sense.

cedent. Why does a currently contemplated decision sometimes have a precedent and sometimes not? Such a distinction can exist only if there is some way of identifying a precedent—some way of determining whether a past event is sufficiently similar to the present facts to justify assimilation of the two events. And when we think about the precedential effect in the future of the action we take today, we presuppose that some future events will be descriptively assimilated to today's.

No two events are exactly alike. For a decision to be precedent for another decision does not require that the facts of the earlier and the later cases be absolutely identical. Were that required, nothing would be a precedent for anything else. We must therefore leave the realm of absolute identity. Once we do so, however, it is clear that the relevance of an earlier precedent depends upon how we characterize the facts arising in the earlier case.[12] It is a commonplace that these characterizations are inevitably theory-laden.[13] In order to assess what is a precedent for what, we must engage in some determination of the relevant similarities between the two events. In turn, we must extract this determination from some other organizing standard specifying which similarities are important and which we can safely ignore.

A parent's decision to let a daughter wear high-heeled shoes at the age of thirteen is scarcely precedent when a son then asks to be permitted to wear high-heeled shoes at that age. But a parent's decision to let that daughter stay up until ten o'clock will be relied upon justifiably by the son when he reaches the same age. A judgment finding tort liability based on the ownership of a black dog is precedent for a judgment regarding the owner of a brown dog, but not for a judgment regarding the owner of a black car. This is so only because a principle, or standard, makes dogness relevant in a way that blackness is not. Consider who among Alan Alda, Menachem Begin, and Dave Righetti is most similar to Sandy Koufax. One is the same age, another has the same religion, and a third is employed in the same occupation. The same point about the role of theory in assessing similarity undergirds Holmes' facetious description of the "Vermont justice of the peace before whom a suit was brought by one farmer against another for breaking a churn. The justice took time to consider, and then said that he had looked through the statutes and could find nothing about

12. A characterization may be a simple word or phrase, as when we characterize a 1957 Chevrolet as a *car*, a *vehicle*, or an *antique*. But a more complex description of what this event is an example of is still a characterization.

13. *See, e.g.*, Shiner, *Precedent, Discretion and Fairness*, in LAW, MORALITY AND RIGHTS 93, 97 (M.A. Stewart ed. 1983) (if following precedent is to be logically derived, then the instant case and the precedent case must have ascertainable, legally relevant properties). Indeed, even less skeptical theorists about precedent agree on this. *See, e.g.*, R. CROSS, *supra* note 3, at 182-92 (although in later stages judges are often misled in their reliance on precedent, the first stage in judicial reasoning by analogy is the determination of the relevant likeness between the previous case and the one before the court).

churns, and gave judgment for the defendant."[14]

It should be clear, therefore, that only the intervention of organizing theory, in the form of *rules of relevance*, allows us to distinguish the precedential from the irrelevant. Precedent depends upon such rules. And these rules themselves are contingent upon both time and culture.[15] Holmes used his churn story to show that legal similarity is determined by broad and theory-soaked descriptions like "property" rather than by the nature of the objects involved. Would we draw that conclusion today? The existence of distinct principles for some classes of goods (consumer goods and securities, for example) shows that the rules of relevance in Holmes' time are not necessarily those of today. Consider the difference between 1865 Mississippi and 1985 Michigan in determining whether a decision about the competency of a white physician as a witness was precedent for a case involving a black physician as a witness. The race of the witness, now considered as irrelevant in determining expert competency as height or weight, at another time and place virtually disposed of the issue. Precedent depends on rules, and those rules themselves depend on context.

With rule-dependency and context-dependency in mind, let us return to the forward-looking aspect of precedent. What is it to hope or fear that a decision will establish a precedent for some other decision in the future? Why do some people fear that allowing restrictions on Nazis because they are Nazis will establish a precedent for restrictions on socialists because they are socialists, even though the distinction between a Nazi and a socialist is obvious, accessible, and easily justified?[16] To worry about a precedential effect in the future, or to worry that a specific future event will be analogized to today's case, presupposes some rule of relevance. Rarely does someone at the time of the first decision think that almost the exact same facts will arise again. Rather, the thought is that this decision will establish a precedent for some different array of facts, one that contains some points of identity with the array of facts currently presented. Imagine a faculty meeting considering a request from a student for an excused absence from an examination in order to attend the funeral of his sister. Invariably someone will object that this case will establish a precedent allowing students to be excused from examinations to attend the funerals of grandparents, aunts, uncles, cousins, nieces, nephews, close friends, and pets.[17] Implicit in this objection is a rule of relevance that treats death as a relevant similarity, "caring" as a relevant similarity, and any distinction between siblings and other meaningful relationships as irrelevant. In

14. Holmes, *The Path of the Law*, 10 HARV. L. REV. 457, 474-75 (1897).

15. *See* Gordon, *Critical Legal Histories*, 36 STAN. L. REV. 57, 125 (1984).

16. I am, of course, referring to the discourse surrounding the American Nazi Party's effort to march in Skokie, Illinois. *See generally* A. NEIER, DEFENDING MY ENEMY (1979).

17. *See generally* Schauer, *Slippery Slopes*, 99 HARV. L. REV. 361 (1985).

some form or another, this type of rule of relevance inheres in any assertion of similarity.

A rule of relevance may also be explained as a choice among alternative characterizations. To use the same example, the student's sister is simultaneously a woman, a sibling, a relative, a blood relative, and one with whom the student has a "meaningful relationship." How the relationship is characterized will determine whether later cases will be classed as similar. Thus, one who worries about establishing a precedent, or for that matter one who wants to establish a precedent, has in mind a characterization that the future will give to today's action, some category within which tomorrow's decisionmaker will place today's facts. The issue is one of *assimilation*, how we will group the facts and events of our world. The power of precedent depends upon some assimilation between the event at hand and some other event. This grouping may come from a simple characterization that includes both events, such as the phrase "censorship" to include restrictions on the speech of both Nazis and socialists. Or the assimilation of the two events may come from a more complex rule of relevance, such as the rule that enables people to group government assistance to New York City, Lockheed, Chrysler, and farmers while distinguishing all of these cases from loans to students and veterans. In this case there is still some "heading" under which some but not all instances are likely to be grouped. Regardless of simplicity or complexity, some grouping of the two events under one heading remains necessary for the operation of a system of precedent. The task of a theory of precedent is to explain, in a world in which a single event may fit into many different categories, how and why some assimilations are plausible and others are not.

B. *Categories of Decision and Categories of the World*

Identifying the central place of a rule of relevance is only the first step. We must still locate the source of the rules enabling us to call something similar to something else. Only by looking to the source can we determine if that source constrains, or if a decisionmaker may classify the black dogs as easily with the black cars as with the dogs of other colors.

1. *The articulated characterization.*

In seeking to locate the sources of characterization, we can take a large first step by noting the important distinction between decisions containing and those not containing canonical language. At times a decision will be accompanied by an articulated and authoritative characterization of the decision and its underlying facts. This *articulated characterization*, not unlike an articulated and specifically formulated rule, constrains the use of subsequent and inconsistent characterizations. Suppose the faculty grants the request of the student who wishes to attend the funeral of his sister. Suppose further that the grant of the request is accompanied by a written explanation specifying that the excuse was given so that the student could attend the funeral of a member of his immediate family. This characterization of a sister as a member of an immediate family will in subsequent cases constrain (although by no means absolutely[18]) those who desire to characterize this precedent more broadly, such as by characterizing a sister as a relative, or as a close companion. A similar constraint would operate if the faculty that granted the first excuse attempted to narrow the precedent by denying an excuse in a subsequent case involving a father, mother, or brother.[19]

In classical legal theory, articulated characterizations are often considered mere dicta,[20] but I do not want anything to turn on the questionable distinction between holding and dictum. Whether the characterizing language is treated as holding or dictum, that language cannot absolutely prevent a subsequent interpreter from recharacterizing the first case.[21] But that interpreter must at least confront an argumentative burden not present without an articulated characterization.[22]

---

18. I find it useful to think in terms of argumentative burdens, rather than in terms of absolute prohibitions. Imagine ordering something in a restaurant that is not on the menu. Ordering off the menu is by no means impossible, but it is certainly more difficult than ordering *from* the menu. Throughout this article I assume this presumptive rather than absolute sense of constraint. For a more substantial discussion, see Schauer, *Easy Cases*, 58 S. CAL. L. REV. 399, 423-26 (1985); *see also* Powers, *Structural Aspects of the Impact of Law on Moral Duty Within Utilitarianism and Social Contract Theory*, 26 UCLA L. REV. 1263 (1979) (discussing "translucency"); Powers, *Formalism and Nonformalism in Choice of Law Methodology*, 52 WASH. L. REV. 27 (1976) (discussing "translucency").

19. The two situations are not exactly equivalent, and a sort of "ratchet effect" seems to characterize the way in which constraints operate more in one direction than in another. Expansion seems more defensible than contraction, and it is important to think about why expansion of a given decision seems to flow more easily than contraction. A starting point may be the observation that we do not lead our lives under the *expressio unius* maxim. Except where something special about the context demands it, it is not a rule of discourse that what we say is all we have to say. But it *is* a rule of discourse that one does not willy-nilly go back on what one has already said. In some contexts, however, including most legislation and *perhaps* including case law, it is our understanding that what is said simultaneously says something and marks the outer limits of a domain. Thus the *expressio unius* maxim presupposes the existence of two groups— the group actually specified and the larger group, which could have been specified but was not. The question is one of deciding, given the absence of specification, what this larger group is. And this, in turn, will be largely a function of whether that larger group *could have* been specified. If there is no reason to suppose that it could not have been, then we are likely to take extension to that larger group in a later case as being as inconsistent with the first case as would be outright contradiction.

20. *See* R. CROSS, *supra* note 3, at 79-86. *Compare* Goodhart, *Determining the Ratio Decidendi of a Case*, 40 YALE L.J. 161 (1930) (the principle of law that is the stated basis of a decision is not binding precedent) *with* Montrose, *Ratio Decidendi and the House of Lords*, 20 MOD. L. REV. 124 (1957) (reason given for the decision is binding) *and* Simpson, *The* Ratio Decidendi *of a Case*, 21 MOD. L. REV. 155 (1958).

21. *See* E. LEVI, *supra* note 5, at 9-27. The *locus classicus* is K. LLEWELLYN, THE COMMON LAW TRADITION 85-91 (1960).

22. Even if there *is* a distinction between holding and dictum, the existence of dicta creates an argumentative burden that would not have been present had the first court said nothing at all. We commonly talk of "mere" dicta as a way to justify ignoring some language in a case, but it is worthwhile to consider the effect of having to go through that exercise compared with the situation in which no such troublesome language exists.

Thus the articulated characterization acts like a specifically formulated rule. Rules can be broken, but to justify breaking a rule is more difficult than to take the same course of conduct in pursuit of or in the absence of a rule. Where there is an articulated characterization, therefore, the question whether precedent can constrain may collapse into the question whether rules can constrain. The issue is then the extent to which authoritative language can control, channel, or constrain decisionmakers purporting to interpret that language. This issue has been rehearsed for decades,[23] but it is different from the question whether a decision *qua* decision can also exert meaningful pressure on subsequent decisionmakers.

The special problem of precedent thus appears most clearly when we remove the obscuring smokescreen of an articulated characterization. No decision in the real world is completely devoid of characterizations. Even a mere statement of facts is undoubtedly a characterization. Nevertheless, it is heuristically useful to imagine an event and a decision, without an authoritative statement of what the event is an example of. In this case, it appears possible for a subsequent decisionmaker to adopt any rule of relevance at all—or at least so many alternative rules of relevance that precedent appears to impose no constraint. Precedent's forward-looking aspect reveals this open-ended quality, for the forward-looking use of precedent is somewhat closer to the notion of a collection of facts without an authoritative characterization. Prior to a decision, no single authoritative characterization presents itself in the way that it does with a decision already made. Instead, one concerned about what the future might do with today's decision worries that this decision might be taken by the future to constitute a component of any number of categories extending this decision in different directions. When one fears that restricting Nazis may establish a precedent for content-based restrictions on other speakers, the fear is fueled precisely by the absence, at the time the fear is expressed, of any authoritative characterization separating Nazis from socialists. When faculty members fear the precedential effect of allowing some excuses from examinations, the fears are expressed in ways not present when specifically formulated *rules* are proposed, exactly because the absence of either rules or a canonical statement of the action in this case leaves open a wide choice of possible characterizations for the future to place on this decision. In any situation that lacks an articulated characterization, the central problem of precedent remains: Are there constraints on the assessment of similarity when few events are intrinsically similar to others? When there is no authoritative rule of relevance for a particu-

23. *See generally* J. PAUL, THE LEGAL REALISM OF JEROME N. FRANK (1959); W. RUMBLE, AMERICAN LEGAL REALISM (1968); W. TWINING, KARL LLEWELLYN AND THE REALIST MOVEMENT (1973); Schlegel, *American Legal Realism and Empirical Social Science: The Singular Case of Underhill Moore*, 29 BUFFALO L. REV. 195 (1980).

lar situation, is it not then illusory to think of the precedent as in any way constraining?

2. *The roots of characterization.*

We can now rephrase the problem. For any given decision, are there restraints on the possible categories of assimilation connecting the facts now before us with the facts before a future decisionmaker? Or is the choice of category completely up to the future decisionmaker, who can choose the category that *a posteriori* justifies the decision made on nonprecedential grounds? The problem is to determine what constrains a decisionmaker's control over the categories of assimilation.

In exploring the question of a decisionmaker's control over the categories of assimilation, it may be useful to examine the philosophical controversy about categories, universals, and natural kinds. Under one view, the source of categories of assimilation is scarcely a problem at all. Philosophical theories that we can call "naturalist"[24] argue that much of the world is divided into intrinsic categories, which the language of human beings merely recognizes.[25] Under this view, brown rocks differ from brown shoes because rocks and shoes are different. Period.

The legal analogue of philosophical naturalism lies in one corner of that chamber of juristic horrors called "formalism." Under a rigid formalist[26] conception of precedent, rules of relevance track the natural and largely immutable patterns of the world around us, creating therefore no real choice[27] among rules of relevance on the part of either the

24. Actually the standard label in philosophy for this perspective is "realism." This standard label, however, is best avoided here. The term "realism" is distracting enough in a context in which Legal Realism is being discussed, but that term is doubly confusing in light of the fact that, as shall be shown, philosophical realism is the polar opposite of Legal Realism. This ought to give pause to those who too easily use terms like "formalism" and "realism" in place of case analysis. But it won't.

25. I ought to feel guilty about presenting in one paragraph the entire problem of universals, and doing so in a way that seems to make most of classical and modern metaphysics preposterous. But this is not an essay on metaphysics, and the relationship between categories of decision and categories of the world can best be presented by use of these admittedly crude descriptions of much more highly nuanced positions. Useful introductions to the philosophical views caricatured here include R. AARON, THE THEORY OF UNIVERSALS (2d ed. 1967); H. STANILAND, UNIVERSALS (1972); UNIVERSALS AND PARTICULARS (M. Loux ed. 1970). For a sampling of contemporary discussion of these issues, see STUDIES IN METAPHYSICS (P. French, T. Uehling, Jr. & H. Wettstein eds. 1979).

26. It is unlikely that any person actually held in pure form the caricatured position that today is described as "formalism," although if one is searching for isolated passages the writings of Cesare Beccaria, William Blackstone, and Jeremy Bentham are fruitful terrain. Somewhat more extreme statements are found in E. WAMBAUGH, THE STUDY OF CASES (1894) and Zane, *German Legal Philosophy*, 16 MICH. L. REV. 287 (1918). I confess that I am using "formalist" as a useful construct rather than as a characterization of the views of particular people.

27. In a relatively uninteresting sense, any actor always has a choice of whether to follow even a clear rule. In a more interesting sense, some rules, or some potential applications of rules, present an unavoidable choice. The question whether my bicycle is excluded by the "No vehicles in the park" rule, *see* H.L.A. HART, THE CONCEPT OF LAW 123 (1961); Hart, *Positivism and the Separation of Law and Morals*, 71 HARV. L. REV. 593, 607 (1958), involves a

creator or the follower of a precedent. The only issue is the manner in which the naturally organized events are to be treated. The question of precedent in formalist theory is whether, having treated *X* in manner *Y* at one point in time, it was ever possible to treat *X* in manner *Z* at another. But to the formalist the only question is the comparative desirability of *Y* or *Z*. The question of why or how it is decided that both sets of facts are *X*s never arises.

Opposed to philosophical naturalism is the view commonly referred to as "nominalism." The nominalist views the world not as naturally subdivided, but rather as demarcated by the artificial labels contingently attached by particular people, particular cultures, or particular languages. Brown shoes and brown rocks are distinguished only because we draw the lines of our experience in certain ways rather than others. In a different world brownness rather than rockness might be more important, putting brown shoes in the same category as brown rocks but not in the same category as blue shoes. For the nominalist the world untouched by human beings contains only particulars, and universals, or general categories of any kind, are all impositions fashioned by people and their language.

Nominalism, too, has its analogue in legal theory, and we call it Realism.[28] Taken with the wide range of characterizations available to a judge, many Realists saw the precedents of the past as invariably susceptible to whatever characterization best fit with the result the judge then wanted to reach.[29] Restrictions on Nazism and restrictions on socialism would be grouped together under the general rubric of "censorship" only if the judge's theory of free speech condemned restrictions on both Nazis and socialists, or if the judge wanted both Nazis and socialists to speak. But if the judge liked socialists and not Nazis, then a different characterization—restrictions on racist speakers, for example—would enable the judge to drive a normative wedge between the two cases. These alternative characterizations were always available, according to the Realists, to enable a decisionmaker to mold the precedents of the past to the needs of the present. And if we in the present could so easily mold the past to conform to our current desires, then so too would the present be malleable in the hands of our successors. For some of the Realists, most notably Jerome Frank, the lesson

choice of a different variety than the question whether, faced with the same rule, I may drive my truck in anyway. My reference in the text to a "real" choice is a reference to a case in which a decisionmaker is faced with a decision among more than one plausible but mutually exclusive rule of relevance, and not to a case in which the decisionmaker has to decide whether to disregard the only plausible rule of relevance.

28. My disclaimer, *see* note 26 *supra*, about real formalists applies equally to the views of real Realists. Again, the caricature may serve as a useful heuristic device.

29. *See, e.g.*, J. FRANK, LAW AND THE MODERN MIND (1930); K. LLEWELLYN, *supra* note 5, at 64-70; Douglas, *Stare Decisis*, 49 COLUM. L. REV. 735 (1949); Radin, *Case Law and Stare Decisis: Concerning* Präjudizienrecht in Amerika, 33 COLUM. L. REV. 199 (1933).

was clear: Judges should make their decisions for today alone.[30] What seems best in *this* case, considering all relevant factors with respect to *these* parties, is what should be done, without any sense of obligation to the past or responsibility to the future.

Realism and formalism, like naturalism and nominalism, are caricatures. The world and the problems we confront in dealing with it lie between these polar extremes. But drawing the caricatures helps illustrate the problem—figuring out how categories of decision relate to categories of the world. And this analysis, in large part, will at least relate to, if not exclusively depend on, some broader outlook about where categories of different types come from, how they change, and how much they resist being manipulated by individuals.

Naturalists and nominalists debate the question of whether the categories of the world come to us in relatively immutable form or whether they are largely the product of the minds and languages of particular cultures. The debate in the context of precedent is parallel but at a different level. The question is not whether there are immutable categories of the world. It is whether the categories used in making a decision are totally within the control of a decisionmaker, or of the decisional environment in which individual decisionmakers operate, or whether categories in some way resist molding by the decisionmakers who use them. When we see the issue in these less grand terms, the case for a naturalist/formalist perspective seems more plausible than it might otherwise seem. Even if nominalist/Realist perspectives do map the long-term workings of language and society, naturalist/formalist perspectives may nevertheless better describe the immediate actions of individual decisionmakers within a given social subculture.

Our nonlegal world inevitably involves and incorporates its own categories of assimilation, its own rules of relevance. Think about why power tools are sold in hardware stores rather than in electrical appliance shops. And think about why we most often group red bicycles with bicycles of other colors rather than with red ties and red meat. Without such classifications our existence would be an undifferentiated sensory bombardment, akin to six radio stations broadcasting on the same frequency.

Many of these larger rules of relevance are implicit in the structure of our language. Despite obvious differences, we refer to both amateur chess and professional football as "games."[31] Despite obvious similar-

30. "Present problems should be worked out with reference to present events. We cannot rule the future." J. FRANK, *supra* note 29, at 155.

31. *See* L. WITTGENSTEIN, PHILOSOPHICAL INVESTIGATIONS 67-71 (G. Anscombe trans. 2d ed. 1958). As with the case of the word "games," I do not take the notion of a rule of language or of life as necessarily containing a specifiable list of necessary and sufficient conditions for the application of the rule. But I do take the categorizations of language and life as rules, in the sense that talking or acting in ways inconsistent with the categories ("Bridge, elephants, and *An American Tragedy* are four of my favorite games.") engenders a range of negative reactions that can be summarized under the heading of "breaking a rule." My view

ities, we have a different word for killing deer in the woods in Vermont than we have for killing cows in the stockyards in Omaha.

Although there is a raging philosophical dispute about whether there are natural classes of the world, many of the nonultimate social categories with which we deal daily have clearly been created by human beings, vary with time and place, and are, like glaciers, constantly in flux despite their apparent immobility. People five feet six inches in height are "tall" in some parts of the world and "short" in others. Placing a shoplifter in the stocks is likely to be considered "cruel" in 1986 in a way that it was not in 1791.

The temporal and cultural contingency of the rules of life and language is not controversial. But it does not follow from the temporal and cultural contingency of rules of relevance that they are subject to change by a given decisionmaker, or even by a particular decisionmaking institution. That a society may change its collective views about what counts as a "vehicle," or what is "liberal," "fair notice," or "cruel," does not mean that the power to accomplish any of these changes exists in the short run, or inheres in individual or institutional decisionmakers. Take for example the question of the student asking to be excused from an examination in order to attend the funeral of a sibling. Would this establish a precedent with respect to cousins as well as siblings? The question cannot be avoided by noting that a future decisionmaker will have to make that decision. The question is whether there is some preexisting linguistic or social category that will group siblings and cousins together for some purposes, and, if so, what effect the existence of that category would have on the future decisionmaker's decision. So too with the possibility that some larger and preexisting category of assimilation will group restrictions on Nazis with restrictions on socialists despite the existence of a plausible distinction between the cases. If there is no such larger category of assimilation, there may be no risk that the desired decision of today will be grouped tomorrow with a decision that we today see as both undesirable and distinguishable.[32] But if such a category of assimilation exists in the larger consciousness surrounding the particular decisionmaking individual or institution, then there will be significant resistance to any decision that would disregard that category.

As noted above, decisionmaking within the legal structure is con-

---

that some sort of rule is necessary for the operation of a system of precedent is thus consistent with Moore, *A Natural Law Theory of Precedent*, in PRECEDENT IN LAW (L. Goldstein ed. 1986), although we differ in a fundamental way on what we consider the source of rules significantly involved in the operation of a system of precedent. Contrasting "particularist" views, effectively criticized by Moore, include S. BURTON, AN INTRODUCTION TO LAW AND LEGAL REASONING (1985); Christie, *Objectivity in the Law*, 78 YALE L.J. 1311 (1969); Stone, *Ratiocination not Rationalization*, 74 MIND 161 (1965).

32. I say "may" because there are phenomena other than a shared assimilating category that may cause a decision made today to increase the probability of occurrence of some feared but different decision tomorrow. *See* Schauer, *supra* note 17.

strained by the comparative fixity of those larger societal and linguistic categories that help to constitute the conceptual apparatus of lawyers and judges. Legal decisionmakers, in purportedly relying on precedent, presuppose certain rules of relevance, and these rules of relevance are unquestionably contingent and subject to change. But if these rules of relevance come to legal decisionmakers from the larger linguistic and social environment, we would be mistaken to call them contingent within the legal decisionmaking subculture.[33] My point is that there is a profound difference between absolute contingency and contingency relative to the decisions then available within a particular domain. Legal rules of categorization are like passengers sitting on a train. In an important way the passengers are moving, but in an equally important way the passengers are sitting still.

As an example of the dependency of legal decisions on the language and conceptualization of the larger world in which law operates, consider *Federal Baseball Club v. National League*.[34] Implicit in that case is the question of whether professional baseball will be assimilated with other members of the larger category "local exhibitions" or assimilated with other members of the larger category "businesses in interstate commerce." Even accepting the Court's dubious premise that one event cannot be a member of both classifications, the decision to put professional baseball in the "exhibitions" category deserves closer inspection. Nothing in the law compelled this result. It was instead influenced by the fact that the larger social and linguistic universe within which the Court operated assimilated a baseball game and a Fourth of July parade into the same category, and thus treated the business of selling entertainment and the business of selling oil as distinct. I am not saying the Court was correct, nor am I adopting the "formalist" view that the law must always incorporate the definitions and distinctions then current in ordinary language. But I am saying that the law speaks largely if not exclusively in English, and relies significantly on social and linguistic categories drawn from its larger environment.[35]

---

33. It is also often the case, especially in law-laden countries like the United States, that the reverse also occurs, that the categories and concepts of the law influence thinking in the larger world around the law. *See* A.V. LUNDSTEDT, LEGAL THINKING REVISED 159-70 (1956); Freeman, *Legitimizing Racial Discrimination through Anti-Discrimination Law: A Critical Review of Supreme Court Doctrine*, 62 MINN. L. REV. 1049 (1978).

34. 259 U.S. 200 (1922); *see also* Flood v. Kuhn, 407 U.S. 258 (1972); Toolson v. New York Yankees, Inc., 346 U.S. 356 (1953).

35. The relationship between ordinary English and the English spoken, written, or interpreted in the legal culture is one of the most interesting potential fields of inquiry in legal theory, but one that has received remarkably little attention in the literature. On the one hand, it would be difficult to deny the extent to which legal language, as a technical language, often operates in a context that makes legal terms have meanings different from those they bear when spoken in other contexts. *See* Schauer, *Speech and "Speech"—Obscenity and "Obscenity": An Exercise in the Interpretation of Constitutional Language*, 67 GEO. L.J. 899 (1979). On the other hand, in an important and largely unexplored sense, legal English must remain attached to ordinary English. It seems intuitively correct to note the way in which technical languages are parasitic on ordinary language. *See* Caton, *Introduction* to PHILOSOPHY AND ORDINARY LAN-

However contingent these categories may be in that larger culture, a court at least bears an argumentative burden if it wishes to depart from these categories. And although I have used an example from law, the point applies to any decisionmaking environment operating within a larger social and linguistic culture.

Thus, the central question involves the degree of control any particular subculture has over these larger categories. In the law, for example, how many of the theories that create theory-laden categories are *legal* theories, theories open to the legal culture to change on its own initiative? Some theories and categories of the law are indeed open to such change, and in those cases a theory of precedent within law relies upon a narrower explanation of how purely legal rules are made and changed.[36] But many other rules of relevance come from the larger world, and, to the extent they are relied upon in framing precedent, the law is inevitably constrained in its short-term ability to alter its own starting points. Precedent rests on similarity, and some determinations of similarity are incontestable within particular cultures or subcultures. If we can view these similarities as subculturally fixed, or subculturally incontestable, while at the same time recognizing their larger contingency, we can recognize that the rule-dependency and context-contingency of precedent do not force the conclusion that all characterizations of a past event are always up for grabs. If the available characterizations constitute a closed and often rather limited set, requiring a decisionmaker to follow some earlier result can substantially affect decisions.

Thus, it seems simply mistaken to argue that the rule-dependency of precedent compels the conclusion that reliance on precedent collapses analytically into reliance on substantive normative rules.[37] The notion of precedent largely depends upon the way in which the categories of the world are frequently larger or more powerful in channeling thought than the categories or comparisons that might be crafted to particular normative purposes. The categories of our existence, the categories that group beanbag chairs and metal desks together as "furniture" and motorcycles and trucks together as "vehicles," transcend specific normative ends. These conceptual categories intrude into diverse places and presumptively create assimilative groupings even where that assimilation may frustrate institutional or individual goals. The grouping of trucks and motorcycles as vehicles is a rule of language, not solely

GUAGE at vii-viii (C. Caton ed. 1963). But working this out for law, and taking into account the way in which law must simultaneously function for professionals within the legal system and for citizens outside it, is a task that remains to be completed.

36. *See* E. LEVI, *supra* note 5. Where Levi goes wrong, *e.g.*, *id.* at 4, is in treating the categories used *in* law as necessarily *legal* categories, ones in control of the legal system.

37. Here I am responding to arguments made in, e.g., N. MACCORMICK, LEGAL REASONING AND LEGAL THEORY 163, 186 (1978); Westen, *supra* note 7, at 1163-64. A similar argument couched in terms of desirability rather than inevitability is Moore, *A Natural Law Theory of Interpretation*, 58 S. CAL. L. REV. 277, 358-76 (1985).

within the control of the regulations of the park department. We must distinguish the rule of language from the rule about the kinds of things we want in the park. If we collapse this distinction, we ignore what is most important—the way in which larger categories and rules of language that generate certain groupings significantly constrain the substantive rules in particular regulatory contexts.[38]

IV. The Price of Precedent

I have argued to this point only that precedent *can* matter, that we may coherently talk about one decision as constraining precedent for another. Sometimes an articulated characterization or an articulated rule of relevance may constrain significantly the range of a category of assimilation. And even without an articulated characterization, the characterizations implicit in our organization of the world, although themselves mutable, still channel the determination of relevant similarities within a decisionmaking institution and narrow the range of possible later analogies. That a system of precedent *can* be constraining says nothing, however, about either the desirability or the degree of those constraints.

In order to examine the justifications for a system of precedent, it is useful to begin by spending some time examining the consequences of adopting such a system. The most obvious consequence, of course, is that a decisionmaker constrained by precedent will sometimes feel compelled to make a decision contrary to the one she would have made had there been no precedent to be followed. Although this obvious consequence is no less important for its obviousness, and although I will discuss issues relating to this consequence in the following section, I want to concentrate now on the forward-looking aspect of precedent, and consider how this angle on precedent reveals consequences not quite so obvious.

A rule of precedent tells a current decisionmaker to follow the decision in a previous similar case. Using the language I have been employing here, we can say that a current decisionmaker is told to follow the decision of a previous case involving assimilable, if somewhat different, facts. But of course the current decisionmaker of today is the previous decisionmaker of tomorrow. Although it may seem counterintuitive, this fact causes the current decisionmaker to be constrained by precedent even if there has been no prior decision.

38. It is important to point out that the persuasiveness of my argument is likely to vary with the size of the domain we are contemplating. If we focus only on appellate cases, in which the system presents us exclusively with situations existing at the margins of rule and precedent, we will see many cases in which decisional constraints are inoperative and few in which they are effective. But if we recognize as well that precedent prevents many situations from being contested and makes other situations more difficult to contest, we will appreciate better the constraints that bind us even while they do not appear regularly on the litigator's agenda. *See* Schauer, *supra* note 18.

Even without an existing precedent, the conscientious decisionmaker must recognize that future conscientious decisionmakers will treat her decision as precedent, a realization that will constrain the range of possible decisions about the case at hand. If the future must treat what we do now as presumptively binding, then our current decision must judge not only what is best for now, but also how the current decision will affect the decision of other and future assimilable cases. Thus, the current decisionmaker must also take into account what would be best for some different but assimilable events yet to occur. The decisionmaker must then decide on the basis of what is best for *all* of the cases falling within the appropriate category of assimilation. In making this calculation, the decisionmaker will discount the future for the possibility that the future decisionmaker will disregard or distinguish today's decision. This discount cannot be complete, however, unless there is some reason to believe that future decisionmakers will feel no pull of precedent. But where future decisionmakers *can* be expected to feel the pull of precedent, today's conscientious decisionmakers are obliged to decide not only today's case, but tomorrow's as well. If the best solution to today's case is identical to the best solution for tomorrow's different but assimilable facts, then there is no problem. But if what is best for today's situation might not be best for a different (but likely to be assimilated) situation, then the need to consider the future as well as the present will result in at least some immediately suboptimal decisions.

The constraints imposed by an obligation to the future can be illustrated numerically. Imagine a series of five decisions, each involving a choice between some variety of *A* and some variety of *B*, where *A* and *B* represent categories subsuming assimilable but in some respects different particulars, *A*(1) through *A*(5) and *B*(1) through *B*(5). And suppose that for each decision in a case of *A*(n) versus *B*(n), it is possible to assess the relative social value of different decisions based on either *A* or *B*. We can then sketch a series of five opportunities for descision:

1.	*A*(1)	55	*B*(1)	45
2.	*A*(2)	30	*B*(2)	70
3.	*A*(3)	40	*B*(3)	60
4.	*A*(4)	45	*B*(4)	55
5.	*A*(5)	60	*B*(5)	40

If each decision were independent of every other decision, the optimal decisions for each case would be *A* in the first case (55 is greater than 45), *B* in the second (70 is greater than 30), third (60 is greater than 40), and fourth cases (55 is greater than 45), and *A* in the fifth case (60 is greater than 40), for a net positive value of +100 (+10, +40, +20, +10, +20) over the five decisions. But suppose instead that the decisionmaker in Case 1 knows that her decision will be followed in some array of future cases involving different particulars but within the same categories. Under these conditions the decisionmaker, knowing that her decision in Case 1 will be followed in Cases 2 through 5, must effectively decide not only Case 1, but the other four as well.

Where precedent matters within a system, the possibility of case-by-case optimization is no longer available, and what is left is the choice of deciding either for *A*(1 through 5) or *B*(1 through 5), a choice of −40 or +40. The rational decisionmaker would choose *B*, +40. That choice of *B*, at +40, although rational in light of the available alternatives, is still suboptimal in terms of the best result for each of the five cases (+40 is less than +100), and is also different from the choice that would be made in the first case if the decisionmaker could think about that case in isolation, and not as precedent for the future. So the choice of *B*, plainly the proper choice if precedent is to be taken seriously, is inferior when compared to the best results theoretically obtainable over a range of cases if each case can be looked at in isolation, and is also inferior when compared to the best result that this decisionmaker would reach in the case at hand.[39]

Accepting the constraints of precedent thus entails taking into account an array of instances broader than the one immediately before the decisionmaker. And this in turn means that although in no case can we make a decision that is better than optimal for that case taken in isolation, in some cases we will make decisions that are worse than optimal for that case taken in isolation. It thus becomes plain that adopting a strategy of reliance on precedent is inherently risk averse, in the sense of giving up the possibility of the optimal result in every case in exchange for diminishing the possibility of bad results in some number of cases.

Thus, if the faculty in the case of the student wishing to attend the funeral of a sibling believes that future decisionmakers will assimilate siblings with all other relatives, and if it also believes that in some significant number of nonsibling relative cases it would be wrong to grant the excuse, then the faculty may plausibly deny the request in the present case even though it believes that it would be right to grant the excuse in this case if the case were taken in isolation. When we look at things this way, we see the price of precedent plainly presented. To the extent that a conscientious decisionmaker takes into account the fact that this decision will, within a regime of precedent, substantially control future decisions with respect to similar but assimilable situations, then the conscientious current decisionmaker must partially make those future decisions as well. When this happens, there will be at least some cases in which the best decision within a regime of precedent is nevertheless a suboptimal decision for the case at hand, with each such case

39. The model I use here is of course an extreme simplification, in part because it ignores the effects of precedents other than *this* decision, and in part because it assumes a monolithic decisionmaker. With regard to the latter assumption, see Easterbrook, *Ways of Criticizing the Court*, 95 HARV. L. REV. 802 (1982). I do not believe that either of the simplifying assumptions distorts my basic point.

being a concrete example of the costs of a system in which precedent matters.

V. The Question of Weight

It should be apparent that the extent to which precedent constrains will vary with the size of the assimilating category. In other words, if the conclusions of one case apply to a sweepingly broad set of analogies (and encourage decisionmakers to make such analogies), then the constraints of precedent are likely to be substantial. Not only will a broad set of subsequent decisionmakers feel the impact of the original decision, but the original decisionmaker will feel a greater obligation in making a decision with such broad application. The bigger the group of cases the original decisionmaker is effectively deciding, the more constraining will be the mandate to treat all of those cases alike. Conversely, if the categories of assimilation are comparatively small, the decisionmaker need consider only a few cases beyond the instant case, and the constraints of precedent will be comparatively inconsequential.

Thus, the extent to which precedent constrains will vary not only with a decisionmaking institution's dependence on categories of assimilation external to its environment, but also on the *size* of those categories. To some extent the question of the size of the institution's categories of assimilation will be a function of the size of the particular categories existing in the larger world. But the strength of the constraints of precedent will also depend on just how much variation a particular decisionmaker is encouraged or allowed to acknowledge.

With respect to many decisions, a theoretically justifiable distinction between two events may be drawn if the full richness of individual variation is allowed to be a relevant factor. Distinguishing, for purposes of eligibility for a tax deduction, a failing steel industry from a prospering robotics industry is hardly unjustifiable. So too might we distinguish in the examination excuse example the good student from the marginal one. Of course, such distinctions are not necessarily wise or just. My point is only that distinctions like these cannot be considered arbitrary. The central question, then, is how many nonarbitrary variations between events will a given decisionmaker be allowed to pursue. If every nonarbitrary variation is open for consideration, then precedent poses only an illusory constraint. But if, instead, decisionmakers must look to that truncation of real world richness that comes from thinking about the world in large and rough groupings, then the constraints of precedent will be substantial.

Because the constraint of precedent might not be an all-or-nothing affair, we must consider the way in which the size of the categories of assimilation might largely determine the strength of precedent. This is admittedly an odd way of thinking about weight, because it is more common to think of the question of size and the question of strength as lying along different axes.[40] But when we turn to precedent this distinction between size and strength collapses.

It might occur to us to say that precedent provides *one* reason for a particular decision without providing a *conclusive* reason. We can certainly imagine a system in which the historical treatment of *X* as *Y* provides for that reason alone a conclusive, irrebuttable argument for treating *X* as *Y* now. But it seems also that a relevant precedent can matter even if it has less weight. For precedent to matter in this nonabsolute way, the historical treatment of *X* as *Y* could be said to provide *a* reason for treating *X* as *Y* now. There might be other reasons for treating *X* as *Y*. More importantly, there might also be reasons for treating *X* as not-*Y*, or as *Z*. To say that precedent provides a reason for deciding in a particular way is not to say that following precedent is what we should always do, all things considered.[41]

In thinking about the possibility that precedent might have less than controlling force, it may be helpful to look briefly at lawyers' usage. Lawyers are fond of talking about "binding" precedent, but what constitutes bindingness needs closer analysis.[42] Some decisions, even within a given jurisdictional ambit, *must* be followed while others, hypothetically, might carry with them some lesser force. In this sense, a

40. *See* Schauer, *Can Rights Be Abused?*, 31 PHIL. Q. 225, 228-30 (1981) [hereinafter Schauer, *Rights*]; Schauer, *Categories and the First Amendment: A Play in Three Acts*, 34 VAND. L. REV. 265 (1981); Thomson, *Some Ruminations on Rights*, 19 ARIZ. L. REV. 45 (1977).

41. I intentionally avoid describing this view of precedential weight as "prima facie." That term, especially as used in the literature of rights and obligations, unfortunately suggests that a prima facie right, rule, obligation, or reason is not "real," or that it disappears when confronted with a more compelling reason. Such a view seems misleading, because nonabsolute rights, rules, obligations, or reasons still serve the purpose of requiring justifications for action stronger or different than would otherwise be required. Because rights, rules, obligations, and reasons *always* serve this purpose, some understanding is lost when we describe them as not real or as being, like the Cheshire cat, subject to disappearing instantly. *See* Schauer, *Rights*, *supra* note 40, at 228-30; Searle, *Prima Facie Obligations*, in PRACTICAL REASONING 81, 88-89 (J. Raz ed. 1978) ("[There is] indeed a valid distinction, between what one has an obligation to do and what one ought to do all things considered. But this distinction is marked quite clearly in ordinary language and does not require the introduction of the term *prima facie* to mark it."); *see also* Hintikka, *Deontic Logic and its Philosophical Morals*, in MODELS FOR MODALITIES (1969). Moreover, a reason need not be as strong as, for example, a presumption. If the force of a precedent were to be taken as presumptive, the question in the second case would be whether, having decided the first case as *Y*, it is possible in fairness to decide the second case as *Z*. *See* R. DWORKIN, *supra* note 6, at 113. As so characterized, those who would urge a different result in the second case carry the burden of proof. But precedent might even be said to constitute a reason (and therefore, *ceteris paribus*, a dispositive reason) without even having the force of shifting the burden of proof. For example, the question in the second case still might be simply one of what ought to be done, with the decision in the first case merely being one of the factors considered in this more open-ended inquiry.

42. My usage here varies from the standard sense in which a binding precedent is different from a precedent that might merely be persuasive. Thus, we say that the Supreme Judicial Court of Massachusetts is *bound* by a previous decision of that court in a way that it is not bound by a decision, even if "on point," of the Supreme Court of Idaho. Here the distinction between the binding and the nonbinding is largely one of jurisdictional ambit. And the question of jurisdictional ambit is in turn inextricably intertwined with the question of authority. Thus, decisions are not binding when there is no relationship of authority between one court or one decision and another.

binding precedent is one that must either be followed or distinguished.[43] This type of bindingness is most commonly associated with the effect of superior court decisions on inferior courts, but it may also occur in the subsequent treatment of an earlier decision by the same court.[44] We can also imagine prior decisions that create precedent, but that may have their precedential value outweighed by other factors. Precedent might in this sense be taken to be only *presumptive.* This approach gives a precedent *necessary* weight without making that precedent dispositive. Therefore, we can distinguish the idea of precedent as a constraint or a reason from the idea of precedent as absolutely binding or constraining.

Although the idea of a presumptive but not absolute reason is sound, that idea may not work with respect to precedent, which in an important way is a special case. In other areas, when we say that a factor or consideration or even a right is overridden, we can describe the overriding event in terms different from those we use to identify the circumstances that create, in the first instance, the necessity of a special justification. Think about equal protection, for example, and that using a classification based on race creates a burden of justification on the state to show that it has a "compelling interest" in employing such a classification.[45] Here the obligation of meeting a higher than normal standard of justification is generated by the existence of a classification based on race. But once that obligation is created, it may be possible, as in *Korematsu*, for the state to provide such a special justification, such as the exigencies of war, *based on reasons that themselves cannot be described in terms of a classification based on race.* Think about the example of telling a lie in order to, say, assist the apprehension of an escaped murderer.[46] The existence of a particularly strong justification does not make the lie any less a lie. The presumptive strictures against lying are overridden by factors not necessarily related, except in this instance, to lying. The act of lying and the act of apprehending murderers, just like the act of classifying by race and the act of successfully waging war, are described in different terms, and at this level of discourse they cannot be reduced to a common currency. The ability to distinguish coverage and protection, scope and strength, and therefore the ability to think about reasons as presumptive, is dependent on this feature—that the possible

43. *See* J. RAZ, THE AUTHORITY OF LAW 183-89 (1979); Simpson, *The* Ratio Decidendi *of a Case and the Doctrine of Binding Precedent*, in OXFORD ESSAYS IN JURISPRUDENCE 148 (A. Guest ed. 1961).

44. This was the traditional English rule, which has been somewhat relaxed of late. *See generally* R. CROSS, *supra* note 3, at 103-52.

45. *See, e.g.*, Loving v. Virginia, 388 U.S. 1 (1967); Korematsu v. United States, 323 U.S. 214 (1944).

46. I. KANT, *On a Supposed Right to Tell Lies from Altruistic Motives*, in CRITIQUE OF PRACTICAL REASON AND OTHER WRITINGS IN MORAL PHILOSOPHY (T.K. Abbott trans. 1973), *discussed in* S. BOK, LYING: MORAL CHOICE IN PUBLIC AND PRIVATE LIFE 39-49 (1978); C. FRIED, RIGHT AND WRONG 54-78 (1978).

overriding events are measured along a different plane than are those events creating the need for special justification in the first instance.

Precedent lacks this feature. The constraints of precedent attach in those instances in which some set of events now before us is deemed to be relevantly similar to some set of events of the past. The condition creating the presumption is similarity. But any overriding condition can always be expressed in terms of the absence of similarity. We never decide not to follow a precedent just because we do not feel like following it, but because something about the instant case is different from the precedent case. And if this is so, then the burden-creating conditions and the burden-satisfying conditions are measured along the same plane—similarity and difference. It is as if the special burden of justification present in the case of racial classifications were capable of being overridden by showing that in this case the racial classification was not that bad, or was not really a racial classification. These are permissible arguments, but they are not arguments for overriding. They are arguments showing that the reasons for requiring an especially strong justification simply do not apply here.

In some sense, then, the question of weight is a red herring, for a precedent is always followed or distinguished.[47] We never face a situation where a precedent presumptively ought to be followed, but some special overriding condition in this case leads us not to follow it. Rather, we say that this case is simply different—that there is actually no relevant precedent to follow or disregard.[48] When the present situation presents factors that ought to control the disposition, we can and will translate those factors into a distinction between this case and the precedent case. Thus, the set of cases in which a precedent is applicable but overridden appears to be an empty one.

We must still address the question of how specifically we will describe the precedents of the past and the events of the present. Although it will always be *possible* to distinguish a precedent, this becomes comparatively harder if we describe and use the precedents of the past in general terms. If subsequent decisionmakers describe and carry on the relevant precedent as a case involving a "car," then an attempt to distinguish an instant case because it involves a red car will be unpersuasive, precisely because the breadth of the description in the

---

47. Or it is overruled. But the possibility of overruling is peripheral to the instant discussion. When a precedent is overruled it goes away, and it will not be an argumentative burden in future cases. When the government demonstrates a compelling interest in an equal protection case, for example, or when any right is overridden by particularly exigent circumstances, the right persists even though it may not control the outcome. *See* Gewirth, *Are There Any Absolute Rights?*, 31 PHIL. Q. 1 (1981); Schauer, *Rights*, *supra* note 40; Thomson, *supra* note 40. But when a precedent is overruled its force comes to an end, and thus it is misleading to analogize overruling a precedent to outweighing it or overriding it.

48. Recall Marsh v. Chambers, 463 U.S. 783 (1983), in which the Supreme Court justified its rejection of the 3-part test of previous establishment clause cases by saying that the historical pedigree of legislative chaplains distinguished this case from other establishment clause cases.

first case substantially limits possible distinguishing factors in subsequent cases.

Thus, the question of strength once again dissolves into the question of size. Because we can always characterize any overriding event as a difference, it makes no sense to draw a distinction between whether a precedent is applicable and whether a precedent controls. Both inapplicability and noncontrollingness express themselves in terms of distinctions between an instant case and some putative precedent case. At the level at which we create the practices of precedent, the strength of the norms of precedent will be reflected in the generality of the categories in which decisions are made. A precedential category of "vehicles" will have greater force than smaller categories of "cars," "trucks," and "motorcycles," which in turn will have greater power over the future than categories of "Buicks" or "Toyotas." No precedential rule can begin to capture this question of size. We cannot say that the appropriate categories of decision are just this big, or just this small. Instead, the rules of precedent are likely to resemble rules of language—a series of practices not substantially reducible to specifics. A system in which precedent operates as a comparatively strong constraint will be one in which decisionmakers ignore fine but justifiable differences in the pursuit of large similarities. At first glance, a precedent-governed system described this way, as one in which relevant differences are suppressed, seems no more justifiable than one characterized as treating prior decisions as important merely because they are prior. So why would any society want such a system?

VI. The Virtues of Precedential Constraint

I have looked at how precedent can constrain, at the strength of its constraints, and at the costs of such constraints in imposing a strategy of suboptimization. What remains is what to some might be the biggest question: Why should a decisionmaking mechanism incorporate substantial precedential constraints within it? Why should a decision in Case 1 constrain a decisionmaker in Case 2 and itself be constrained by the knowledge of this secondary impact?

A. *The Argument from Fairness*

Among the most common justifications for treating precedent as relevant is the argument from fairness, sometimes couched as an argument from justice. The argument is most commonly expressed in terms of the simple stricture, "Treat like cases alike."[49] To fail to treat

49. *See, e.g.*, Goodhart, *Precedent in English and Continental Law*, 50 Law Q. Rev. 40, 56-58 (1934); Wade, *The Concept of Legal Certainty: A Preliminary Skirmish*, 4 Mod. L. Rev. 183 (1940-1941). Useful deconstructions of the idea, partly consistent with what I argue here, include Westen, *The Empty Idea of Equality*, 95 Harv. L. Rev. 537 (1982); Winston, *On Treating Like Cases Alike*, 62 Calif. L. Rev. 1 (1974).

similar cases similarly, it is argued, is arbitrary, and consequently unjust or unfair. We achieve fairness by decisionmaking rules designed to achieve consistency across a range of decisions. Where the consistency is among individuals at the same time, we express this decisional rule as "equality." Where the consistency among decisions takes place over time, we call our decisional rule "precedent." Equality and precedent are thus, respectively, the spatial and temporal branches of the same larger normative principle of consistency.

The idea of fairness as consistency forms the bedrock of a great deal of thinking about morality. Whether expressed as Kantian universalizability,[50] as the decisions that people would make if cloaked in a Rawlsian veil of ignorance about their own circumstances,[51] or simply as The Golden Rule, the principle emerges that decisions that are not consistent are, for that reason, unfair, unjust, or simply wrong.

How can we apply this broad principle of fairness more specifically as a potential justification for adopting a decision procedure in which precedent matters? Initially, the principle that like cases should be decided alike would seem to make an unassailable argument for precedent. But the difficulty of denying that like cases should be decided alike is precisely the problem. The statement is so broad as to be almost meaningless. The hard question is what we mean by "alike."

Recall the discussion of the potential *size* of categories of assimilation. From the perspective of the size of the categories involved, the question is not whether like cases should be decided alike, for at that level of abstraction that norm would engender unanimous agreement. Rather, the question is whether the categories of likeness should be large or small. If the categories of likeness, of assimilation, are so small as to enable a decisionmaker to take into account virtually every variation between separate events, then like cases are indeed being decided alike, yet the norm of precedent scarcely constrains. But if relatively large categories act to group many slightly different particular cases under general headings of likeness, then the stricture of deciding like cases alike makes reliance on precedent a substantial constraint.

The issue is thus not the sterile question of treating like cases alike. It is instead the more difficult question of whether we should base our decisionmaking norm on relatively large categories of likeness, or by contrast leave a decisionmaker more or less at liberty to consider any possible way in which this particular array of facts might be unique. The purely formal constraint of treating like cases alike does not speak to this question. Yet the first of these alternatives describes a system of precedent; the second describes a system in which the constraint of precedent is for all practical purposes absent.

Alone, therefore, the argument from fairness, the prescription to

50. *See* R.M. HARE, FREEDOM AND REASON (1963).
51. *See* J. RAWLS, A THEORY OF JUSTICE 136-42 (1973).

treat like cases alike, does not help us choose between a decisional system with a strong precedential constraint and one with virtually no precedential constraint. If we are to find arguments directly addressing the question of precedent, we must look for substantive reasons to choose larger rather than smaller categories of decision.

B. *The Argument from Predictability*

The most commonly offered of the substantive reasons for choosing strong over weak precedential constraint is the principle of predictability.[52] When a decisionmaker must decide this case in the same way as the last, parties will be better able to anticipate the future.[53] The ability to predict what a decisionmaker will do helps us plan our lives, have some degree of repose, and avoid the paralysis of foreseeing only the unknown.

As a value, predictability is neither transcendent nor free from conflict with other values. Yet predictability plainly is, *ceteris paribus*, desirable. We attain predictability, however, only by diminishing our ability to adapt to a changing future.[54] In the language of precedent, following a precedent at a particular time may produce a decision other than the decision deemed optimal on the facts of the particular instance. Where this divergence is absent, the effect of precedent is minimal. But if following precedent will produce a result different from that which would be produced without the constraint of the rule of precedent, then we have identified a case in which precedent matters. And thus we can rephrase the question: To what extent is a decisionmaking environment willing to tolerate suboptimal results in order that people may plan their lives according to decisions previously made?

When we reformulate the question in this way, it becomes clear that the force of the argument from predictability, even if persuasive in the abstract, will vary with numerous factors whose weight cannot be generalized across all decisional environments. For example, how often will the use of large generalizations prevent making decisions on the basis of unique facts that would be dispositive in a particular case? To answer this question requires delving into a panoply of factors relating to the kinds of decisions that are to be made in a given decisionmaking environment. These factors may include the size of the relevant categories, the likelihood of significant factual variation, and many others that vary from environment to environment. I thus merely note, with-

52. *See generally* A. KOCOUREK, AN INTRODUCTION TO THE SCIENCE OF LAW 165-85 (1930); Marsh, *Principle and Discretion in the Judicial Process*, 68 LAW Q. REV. 226 (1952) (background on the claims of uncertainty and nonpredictability).

53. The argument is often couched in terms of *certainty* rather than predictability. *See* R. WASSERSTROM, *supra* note 6, at 60-66. But some outcomes might be more predictable than others yet still be far from certain. Talk of "certainty" establishes an unattainable standard that serves only to distract from the value of the ability to predict with reasonable confidence what the future might bring.

54. *See* H.L.A. HART, *supra* note 27, at 121-32.

out intending to resolve, that one important issue is the expected *frequency* of suboptimal results.

The *consequences* of such a suboptimal decision provide a closely related concern, one touched on earlier. Once we realize that maintaining a serious regime of precedential constraint entails some number of suboptimal decisions, we see that we can express the price we pay for predictability in terms of some number of decisions in which the predicted result, and therefore the actual result if precedent is followed, is not in fact the best result. But the relationship of these costs to the possible benefits of predictability will vary across different kinds of decisions. When Justice Brandeis noted that "in most matters it is more important that the applicable rule of law be settled than that it be settled right,"[55] he was reminding us of one side of this question. The other side, of course, is that sometimes[56] it is more important that things be settled correctly than that they be settled for the sake of settlement. To take an extreme example, making all capital punishment decisions under a strict precedential rule would satisfy desires for predictability but would also entail putting to death some people who would live if their individual cases were scrutinized carefully. And, at the other extreme, many decisions involving the formalities of contracts or real estate transactions are decisions in which sacrificing optimality for predictability would involve negative consequences that are far from catastrophic.

Finally, it is worthwhile adding to the equation some variability in the value of predictability. Much of what we value about predictability is psychological. I feel better knowing that the letter carrier will come at the same time every day, that faculty meetings will not be scheduled on short notice, and that April brings the opening of the baseball season. Predictability thus often has value even when we cannot quantify it.

Thus, the value of predictability is really a question of balancing expected gain against expected loss. We ask how important predictability is for those affected by the decisions, and we then ask whether that amount of predictability is worth the price of the frequency of suboptimal results multiplied by the costs of those suboptimal results. But there is no best answer to this calculation, for the answer will vary with the kinds of decisions that given decisionmakers are expected to make.

55. Burnet v. Coronado Oil & Gas Co., 285 U.S. 393, 406 (1932) (Brandeis, J., dissenting); *see also* Sheddon v. Goodrich, 8 Ves. 481, 497, 32 Eng. Rep. 441, 447 (1803) ("better that the law should be certain than that every judge should speculate upon improvements").

56. As Justice Brandeis argued with respect to constitutional adjudication in *Burnet*, 285 U.S. at 406. *See also* Smith v. Allwright, 321 U.S. 649 (1944).

C. *The Argument from Strengthened Decisionmaking*

1. *Decisionmaking efficiency.*

When a precedent has no decisional significance as a precedent, the conscientious decisionmaker must look at each case in its own fullness. But when a rule external to the decisionmaker compels reliance on the decisions of others, it frees the decisionmaker from these responsibilities. Although a decisionmaker in a precedential system may in every case consider whether to disregard those constraints,[57] this does not deny that a decisionmaker may choose to follow precedent, nor that a decisionmaker who chooses to rely on precedent is in most cases operating within the norms of the system. Thus, a decisionmaker choosing to rely on precedent may justifiably "relax," in the sense of engaging in less scrutiny of the case, where that decisionmaker chooses to rely on a precedent. And where a *rule* of precedent urges a decisionmaker to relax in this sense, the net product will be a substantial reduction in decisionmaking effort.

In this respect, efficiency may justify a rule of precedent.[58] This argument properly relies on the fact that a regime of precedent allows less reconsideration of questions already considered than a system containing no rule of precedent. If we wish to conserve the decisional resources of the decisionmakers, therefore, we have an independent argument for a system of precedent.

There is something curious, however, about the argument from decisional efficiency. Suppose we have a string of three decisionmakers making three assimilable decisions. Under a regime of precedent, the second decisionmaker must defer to the first, but her deference is based on nothing about either the first or second decisionmakers, because it is also the case that the third decisionmaker must defer to the second. If we consider such a system efficient or otherwise desirable, we must either perceive some actual similarity between the decisionmakers or believe that there is some reason to impose a presumed similarity where none in fact exists. When there is actual similarity, a system of precedent enables a decisionmaker to rely on the similar decisionmaker's conclusion about a similar case. Having found the facts in the instant case similar to some decision of the past, the instant decisionmaker need go no further, because the system of precedent assumes that the same result would have been reached even if the instant decisionmaker started all over again.

57. *See* Kennedy, *Legal Formality*, 2 J. LEGAL STUD. 351 (1973).

58. *See* B. CARDOZO, THE NATURE OF THE JUDICIAL PROCESS 149-50 (1921); K. LLEWELLYN, *supra* note 5, at 64-65; R. WASSERSTROM, *supra* note 6, at 72-74; Heiner, *Imperfect Decisions and the Law: On the Evolution of Legal Precedent and Rules*, 15 J. LEGAL STUD. 227 (1986). The considerations that underlie a rule of precedent may also at times generate specific substantive rules. *E.g.*, Epstein, *A Theory of Strict Liability*, 2 J. LEGAL STUD. 151 (1973).

2. *Strengthening the decisionmaking institution.*

But now let us abandon the assumption of similarity among decisionmakers. If we retain the assumption of assimilability of events, more than mere decisional efficiency must be at work. The system of precedent must operate to dampen the variability that would otherwise result from dissimilar decisionmakers. Why should we encourage this process? One possibility is that it might be thought important to create the aura of similarity among decisionmakers even where none may exist. Using a system of precedent to standardize decisions subordinates dissimilarity among decisionmakers, both in appearance and in practice.

Even more substantially, this subordination of decisional and decisionmaker variance is likely in practice to increase the power of the decisionmaking institution. If internal consistency strengthens external credibility, then minimizing internal inconsistency by standardizing decisions within a decisionmaking environment may generally strengthen that decisionmaking environment as an institution.[59]

The considerations surrounding the argument from decisionmaking efficiency rest upon a broad notion about the value of stability in decisionmaking distinct from anything about the actual decisions made. It is also apparent that any attempt to stabilize decisionmaking in an unstable world is likely to produce some suboptimal results. The argument from enhanced decisionmaking, then, suggests that the efficiency advantages may justify putting on blinders to the full richness of human experience. This is by no means an implausible argument, but its strength will depend upon many of the same factors discussed in the context of the argument from predictability. Likewise, whether this strength is sufficient to outweigh its costs will vary with those same factors. Once it becomes clear that no argument from invariable principle supports either the argument from predictability or the argument from enhanced decisionmaking, the evaluation of these alternatives turns into a weighing of costs and benefits that varies with different decisionmaking settings. Further elaboration must be relegated to discussions

59. *See* Shapiro, *Toward a Theory of Stare Decisis*, 1 J. LEGAL STUD. 125 (1972). It is worthwhile to note that this perspective could explain why the Supreme Court should be constrained by precedent, and, more cynically, why the Court purports to be constrained by precedent even when it is not.

On precedent in the particular context of Supreme Court adjudication and judicial review, the leading recent case is Akron v. Akron Center for Reproductive Health, 462 U.S. 416 (1983); *see also* Thornburgh v. American College of Obstetricians & Gynecologists, 106 S. Ct. 2169 (1986); Vasquez v. Hillery, 106 S. Ct. 617 (1986). For discussion of the issue, focusing on why the Supreme Court should or should not be less constrained by precedent than other courts, see Frickey, *A Further Comment on Stare Decisis and the Overruling of* National League of Cities, 2 CONST. COMMENTARIES 341 (1985); Frickey, *Stare Decisis in Constitutional Cases: Reconsidering* National League of Cities, 2 CONST. COMMENTARIES 123 (1985); Kelman, *The Forked Path of Dissent*, 1985 SUP. CT. REV. 227; Maltz, *Some Thoughts on the Death of Stare Decisis in Constitutional Law*, 1980 WIS. L. REV. 467; Monaghan, *Taking Supreme Court Opinions Seriously*, 39 MD. L. REV. 1 (1979); Stevens, *The Life Span of a Judge-Made Rule*, 58 N.Y.U. L. REV. 1 (1983).

of the goals to be served and the characteristics of decisionmaking in various decisionmaking settings.

D. *Precedent and Stability*

Although the various arguments for incorporating a rule of precedent into a particular decisional environment each retains its own irreducible core of justification, in some sense these arguments coalesce. Arguments premised on the values of reliance, predictability, and decisional efficiency all share a focus on stability for stability's sake. The extent to which stability will be promoted is largely a function of the size of the groupings employed within a decisional domain. We must ask whether, at the extremes, large numbers of differences between instances will be suppressed, thus generating comparatively few large categories, or whether all variation will be taken into account, thus generating many smaller categories. Naturally there are gradations between these extremes. But by viewing the issue this way, we see that the various abstract and formal justifications for precedent all rest on conclusions about what ranges of events we wish to treat in like manner.

At times these size-determining factors may be based on substantive value choices. We may broadly draw the category of "person" in many contexts precisely because we believe it substantively evil to distinguish among people on the basis of race, gender, national origin, or even height. At other times the size of the categories will be controlled by the size of the categories at large in the world. Our language and its accompanying conceptual apparatus often inhibit attempts by decisionmakers to draw fine distinctions among the particulars that inhabit the larger categories of our existence. No amount of stress on particularization, for example, could completely prevent categories like "people," "dwellings," or "vehicles" from hindering a decisionmaker's efforts to see differences among people, dwellings, or vehicles. Finally, and perhaps most importantly, the size of the categories of assimilation may be a function of what we expect to accomplish in a decisionmaking setting. This is particularly germane here, for it links the principle of stability, hovering around all of the separate justifications for precedent, to the particular system actually generated.

Some decisionmaking environments emphasize today—the richness and uniqueness of immediate experience. In those environments we seek the freedom to explore every possible argument or fact that might bear on making the best decision for *this* case, for it is precisely the *thisness* of the case that is most vital. At its extreme, such a system might, and arguably should, deny the relevance of precedent entirely. The virtues of stability would bow to the desire "to get it just right," and in such a framework a past decision would have little if any precedential force. More realistically, perhaps, such a system might still acknowledge precedent, but in small units. For if we see precedents as small units, full of rarely duplicated particulars, we are likely to find few cases in which the current small unit is like some small unit of the past.

By contrast, other decisional environments focus on yesterday and tomorrow, emphasizing the recurrent rather than the unique elements of the human condition. Here precedent has its greatest role to play, generating a format for decisionmaking that channels decisions toward consideration of a comparatively limited number of factors likely to be repeated over time. In the context of this essay, this would translate into the use of larger categories of assimilation, gathering many conceivably distinguishable particulars within the embrace of the larger categories.

Without a universal answer to the question of whether stability is a good thing, we cannot decide whether decision according to precedent is a good thing. Stability may be unimpeachable in the abstract, but in reality stability comes only by giving up some of our flexibility to explore fully the deepest corners of the events now before us. Whether this price is worth paying will vary with the purposes to be served within a decisional domain, and we get no closer to knowing those purposes by understanding the relationship between stability and categorial size. Still, focusing on this relationship is valuable, because it enables us to see more clearly just how stability is achieved and just what kind of price we must pay to obtain it.

VII. Conclusion: Precedent and Law

We can locate most of the foregoing within a picture of law, but a picture that differs in some respects from the usual one. Much of contemporary legal theory presupposes that a successful theory of law must situate the structural phenomenon of law within the framework of the political state. A theory of law that does not explain the difference between the laws of Spain and Texas, on the one hand, and the rules of etiquette, baseball, and private clubs, on the other, is treated as incomplete. I do not want to deny that there are important differences between France and the American Contract Bridge League, and that some or all of these differences might be theoretically examined and explained. But it is equally useful to stress the similarities rather than the differences—to try to show the strong link between the rules of a political state and the rules of a private club. And if the consequent theory of ruleness[60]—explaining the place of rules within all of these diverse entities—fails to distinguish among them, the theory has not failed, for drawing that distinction is not the task of a theory of rules. Just as an analysis of bones may not provide the genetic explanation necessary to distinguish *Homo sapiens* from cats, so too might a theory of rules not be

60. I take the term "ruleness" from Kennedy, *Form and Substance in Private Law Adjudication*, 89 Harv. L. Rev. 1685 (1976).

aimed at distinguishing the rules of the political state from the rules of entities with different functions.

Implicit in this agenda, therefore, is a rejection of the view that a theory of law must identify some form of thinking or decisionmaking unique to legal institutions. No one subscribes to this "uniqueness thesis" in exactly this form, but it has certainly occupied a prominent place in contemporary legal theory.[61] Rejecting the "uniqueness thesis," as I do, may produce the conclusion that legal reasoning is present outside the courts, and that nonlegal reasoning is present within the judicial system. This conclusion may have uncomfortably fuzzy edges, but it makes up in accuracy what it lacks in theoretical elegance.

Rejecting a strong version of the uniqueness thesis, however, does not mean that different forms of reasoning cannot be distinguished. That we cannot definitively situate the nature of law within the workings of the political state does not mean that some forms of decisionmaking do not differ from others. By distinguishing thinking that focuses on the present from thinking that mandatorily encompasses a wider temporal scope, I have tried here to begin exploring one way in which some forms of thinking may differ from others, and one way—the use of precedent—in which this difference may find expression in institutional design.

Even the mention of institutional design may beg the important question, because it assumes, prematurely, that we should design institutions to fit one or another decisional model. It may be better to think in terms of decisional domains, recognizing that certain institutions may contain several such decisional domains working in parallel. For example, courts may at times rely on something close to the theoretical ideal of a system of equity,[62] while at other times they rely more on a rule- or precedent-based approach. When Congress considers a private bill, precedent is rarely mentioned, but when Congress impeaches and tries a president or a judge,[63] precedent rightfully comes into play. Similarly, the Department of Justice may rely less on precedent when establishing prosecutorial priorities than when giving advice to the president with respect to constitutional responsibilities.

61. Think, for example, about Ronald Dworkin's attempt to relate judicial decisionmaking to questions about the institutional role to be played by courts in a liberal democratic society, R. Dworkin, *supra* note 6, about Lon Fuller's conception of the internal morality of law, L. Fuller, The Morality of Law (rev. ed. 1969), and even about H.L.A. Hart's search for a "minimum content of natural law" that would attach to positivist theory the social goals of a political organization. H.L.A. Hart, *supra* note 27, at 189-207.

62. I am referring here to equity as a philosophical and historical ideal, and not to the somewhat oxymoronic if more realistic notion of "rules of equity." For a useful discussion of the Aristotelian ideal to which I refer, see R. Wasserstrom, *supra* note 6, at 84-117.

63. Senator Packwood recently stated, in explaining why he did not vote to convict on one of the articles of impeachment against Judge Harry Claiborne, that "I did not want to establish a precedent that, because you're convicted by a jury, that you're automatically impeached, or, if you're acquitted by a jury, you automatically can't be impeached." Det. Free Press, Oct. 10, 1986, at 12, col. 5.

Understanding the notion of precedent becomes easier when we focus on examples like these, because they force us to look at those settings where the constraints of precedent are largely absent. It would seem odd indeed to criticize Ronald Reagan for not following the precedent of Jimmy Carter with respect to relations with the Soviet Union. This is not to say that the policies of either man cannot be criticized. But the criticism must be substantive, and it is no independent ground for condemnation that a president has failed to follow the policy lead of his predecessor. Many aspects of the administrative process share this characteristic, and, like equity, at least one version of the ideal of the administrative process holds that an agency should be free to consider the fullness of certain problems without the constraints of following its or another agency's prior handling of a different array of highly complex facts.[64]

Equity and administrative law are good examples of the fact that the ideals of rule-free and precedent-free decisionmaking, focusing on the richness of this case without taking on the burdens of the last case or the next case, are just that—ideals. But these ideals remind us that there *is* a difference between precedential constraint and total freedom to decide *this* case in the optimal way, even if the two processes rarely appear in pure form. Yet, by seeing that there is a difference, we see that the extent of reliance on precedent is not fixed, but is subject to change in the same ways as are norms governing any decisionmaking institution. This process does not necessarily depend upon written rules, but reflects the entire array of methods by which decisionmakers assimilate what it is proper to do and what is discouraged.

Thus it may be that decisions for the moment, relatively unconstrained by precedent, are not alien to the courts, and that decisions attendant to precedent are not alien either to the political world or to the private worlds in which we live our lives. This in turn is part of a larger perspective that sees law, in this decisionmaking-process sense, in our nonlegal institutions, and that sees nonlaw, in this same decisionmaking-process sense, in our legal institutions. When we see this we may be entirely satisfied. But we may instead want to challenge the extent of this conflation of function. Perhaps we should view legal institutions, including lawyers and law schools, as part of a larger mechanism—call it society—that needs some institutions that are creative, speculative, adaptive, and risk-taking, and other institutions that are cautious, predictable, and risk averse. These latter institutions might act as stabilizers and brakes, rather than as engines and accelerators, and it may be that both forms of institution together constitute, or at least approach, the ideal mix of decisionmaking structures. Within this mix of structures it should be apparent that precedent, as an inherently

64. *See* Koch, *Confining Judicial Authority over Administrative Action*, 49 MO. L. REV. 183, 210-20 (1984).

constraining form of argument, is more suited to some forms of decision than to others. And it should then be apparent why the constraints of precedent have been and perhaps should be reserved not for our institutions of progress, but for our institutions of restraint.

[13]

BOOK REVIEW

Is the Common Law Law?

THE NATURE OF THE COMMON LAW; by Melvin A. Eisenberg.† Cambridge, Massachusetts: Harvard University Press, 1988. Pp. 197, with notes. $22.50 cloth.

Reviewed by Frederick Schauer‡

For all its ubiquity, the common law remains uncommonly puzzling. We are perplexed by the common law in a way that we are not, for example, by statutory interpretation, because the central features of common law method appear inconsistent with some of the primary assumptions of a traditional view of the rule of law. These puzzling features of the common law are easily stated. First, the rules of the common law are nowhere canonically formulated. Indeed, the absence of a single authoritative formulation is what distinguishes common law rules from legislative rules. Second, common law rules are not made by legislatures; they are created by courts simultaneously with the application of those rules to concrete cases. Third, not only are common law rules created in the very process of application, but also they are applied in—and to—the very case that prompted the rulemaking. Thus, common law rules are applied retroactively to facts arising prior to the establishment of the rule. Finally, and most importantly, common law rulemaking does not merely make new law when there is no existing law. Instead, the lawmaking power of common law courts is more than interstitial, and extends to modifying or replacing what had previously been thought to be the governing rule when applying that rule would generate a malignant result in the case at hand.

These features of common law method combine to generate two separate sources of theoretical difficulty. First, it appears as if the common law allows its rules to be remade in the process of application. If this is so, however, the constraint of the rule *qua* rule seems to disappear; that is, the common law, for all its *talk* of rules, does not seem to be a rule-bound method of decisionmaking. Rather, the rules of the common law appear to be but rules of thumb. They are defeasible when direct application of their background rationales would generate a different result, and

† Koret Professor of Law, University of California at Berkeley.
‡ Professor of Law and Professor of Political Science, University of Michigan.

consequently the rules have no normative force of their own. Rules of this sort, capable of modification at the time of application and thus incapable of constraining that application, differ so much from our ordinary conception of rules as guides and constraints that it hardly pays to speak of them as rules at all.

Second, the values that guide a common law court in modifying or discarding what had previously been thought to be a rule of law are moral, economic, social, and political. But if rules of law are defeasible in the service of such a wide domain of values, then the job of the courts seems not to be restricted to any discrete normative domain distinguishable from the entire normative universe. That conclusion not only calls into question the specific theory of law we call "positivism," but also a number of manifestations of a positivist outlook, including law schools, law professors, law students, bar examinations, legally trained judges, and the West Publishing Company.

Although some of my characterizations may seem a bit apocalyptic, the tensions between common law method and many of the traditional assumptions of the "rule of law" are undeniably real.[1] For Bentham, these tensions were sufficient to banish the very idea of the common law from the law at all.[2] Far from heeding his call, however, common law countries, especially this one, have expanded their use of common law methodology. Although the legislative component in contracts, torts, and property may have increased in recent years, the degree of judicial lawmaking surrounding nominally statutory areas of law has increased more than commensurately,[3] and as a result, common law method flourishes as it has never before. The need for serious theoretical exploration of the nature of the common law has therefore rarely been greater, and Melvin Eisenberg's *The Nature of the Common Law* constitutes an important contribution to this increasingly necessary enterprise.

I

Eisenberg's objective is more to explain than to defend the method

1. The tensions I discuss here are admirably explored in Simpson, *The Common Law and Legal Theory*, in LEGAL THEORY AND COMMON LAW 8 (W. Twining ed. 1986).

2. J. BENTHAM, *A Comment on the Commentaries*, in A COMMENT ON THE COMMENTARIES AND A FRAGMENT ON GOVERNMENT (J.H. Burns & H.L.A. Hart eds. 1977); J. BENTHAM, OF LAWS IN GENERAL (H.L.A. Hart ed. 1970). For a particularly incisive analysis of Bentham's views about the common law, see G. POSTEMA, BENTHAM AND THE COMMON LAW TRADITION (1986). *See also* H.L.A. HART, ESSAYS ON BENTHAM: JURISPRUDENCE AND POLITICAL THEORY (1982).

3. This development is both identified and celebrated in G. CALABRESI, A COMMON LAW FOR THE AGE OF STATUTES (1982); *see also* Eskridge, *Dynamic Statutory Interpretation*, 135 U. PA. L. REV. 1479 (1987); Lagenvoort, *Statutory Obsolescence and the Judicial Process: The Revisionist Role of the Courts in Federal Banking Regulation*, 85 MICH. L. REV. 672 (1987); Note, *Intent, Clear Statements, and the Common Law: Statutory Construction in the Supreme Court*, 95 HARV. L. REV. 892 (1982).

of the common law. Nevertheless, he begins the book with a comparatively enthusiastic defense of judicial lawmaking (pp. 4-7). This defense proceeds from a useful distinction (one of many in this book) between what Eisenberg calls the *by-product* and the *enrichment* models of judicial lawmaking (p. 6). Of course no one denies (unless they are seeking confirmation to a judicial appointment) that judges, especially common law judges, frequently make law. Still, judicial lawmaking under the by-product model is largely interstitial, a necessary evil occasioned by the richness and fluidity of human experience. Life is more creative than law, and instances may arise in which courts—having been entrusted with the task of dispute resolution—must make law in order to resolve the disputes that come within their province.[4]

Under the enrichment model, however, judges are proactive participants in the process of creating law; they are partners with other lawmaking institutions in keeping full the reservoir of rules by which we live our lives and plan our transactions. As Eisenberg maintains, the enrichment model is a more faithful rendition than the by-product model of American common law practice. With great frequency, judges make more law than is necessary to decide the case at hand,[5] and then, in subsequent cases, treat this judge-made law as constraining. This and other evidence suggests that American courts hardly treat the creation of common law rules as something about which they should be bashful. Instead, they embrace the task of lawmaking in those areas that have always been the province of the courts, and, with some eagerness, take on those further responsibilities of lawmaking delegated to them by legislatures.[6]

For my part, I wish that Eisenberg's defense of the practice of

4. Although it is accepted that this is the minimum plausible amount of judicial lawmaking, it is worthwhile noting that even this amount of law creation by the judiciary is the product of systemic choice rather than necessity. Although it is true that no code, or other existing array of rules, can completely cover all contingencies, it does not necessarily follow that any case not covered by existing rules should be the occasion for judicial lawmaking. For example, a decisionmaking system might incorporate a default (or closure) rule such that in the absence of a rule allowing a claim by a plaintiff, the court would be without power to grant relief. Such a rule, undeniably incorporating a defendant bias, would impose the risk of open texture on plaintiffs, rather than, as is now the case, imposing it on legislative lawmaking primacy. I do not claim that such an approach would be desirable. I note it, however, to point out that the impossibility of a gapless code does not logically entail the authority of the courts to fill the consequent gaps.

5. Indeed, the making of excess law is built into the very idea of decision according to principle. Insofar as principled decisionmaking involves making decisions according to some principle the decisionmaker would be willing to follow in future cases, the decisionmaker is in effect deciding not only the case at hand, but all of the cases falling within the ambit of the principle. *See* Golding, *Principled Decision-Making and the Supreme Court*, 63 COLUM. L. REV. 35, 42-50 (1963); Greenawalt, *The Enduring Significance of Neutral Principles*, 78 COLUM. L. REV. 982 (1978).

6. As should be apparent from the text, it is only a coincidence that common law *subjects*, such as torts, contracts, and property, should have been developed by common law *method*, which can be applied to any subject.

judicial lawmaking had been less sketchy. He asserts the need for a continuous enrichment of the supply of legal rules, and asserts as well the incapacity of the legislature to meet that demand (pp. 4-5). At some level of abstraction, this proposition is so plainly true that it demands little argumentative or empirical support. But the question is not whether common law methodology should be banished from American law. The common law is an entrenched component of the American political and legal tradition, and common law methodology has also become a prominent feature of legal life even in countries whose legal systems are broadly civilian. Yet it remains the case that *every* act of judicial lawmaking presents the question of its own legitimacy.[7] A judge facing the unprovided-for case on the edge of existing common law practice unavoidably must decide whether or not to extend that practice.[8] A judge who makes law is simultaneously deciding not to defer to some other lawmaking institution. Moreover, even if the power to make law is so well entrenched as to make defense of it superfluous and attack on it futile, a judge making law in any case is still faced with the same choice that Eisenberg describes in by-product/enrichment terms. A judge finding it necessary to make law for *this* case must nevertheless decide how wide a range of future cases to control.

It may be Eisenberg's point that this society, having already chosen the enrichment model, has in effect made these decisions systemically. Consequently, any individual judge confronting a lawmaking opportunity need no longer be concerned with legitimacy, for that question was decided generations ago. Yet such a conclusion seems curious, for it would lead us to say that, in any particular lawmaking situation, a judge should: (a) make whatever law is necessary to reach the best result in the case at hand; and (b) lay down as broad a rule as is socially desirable. Eisenberg of course does not believe this, as his discussion of the constraints on common law judges amply demonstrates. Moreover, his important analysis of the way that nondoctrinal propositions are at work in *every* case could also be used to show that questions of lawmaking legitimacy are likewise at stake in all cases. Yet without a serious and critical examination of whether judges rather than other political actors should be performing the lawmaking role, Eisenberg's discussion of constraints on judges and judicial lawmaking seems strangely untethered.

Let us look at a concrete example. The Securities Exchange Act of 1934 deals with insider trading in two different ways. In Section 16(b) it proceeds by use of a rather precise rule, unquestionably fuzzy at the

7. *See* Fried, *Two Concepts of Interests: Some Reflections on the Supreme Court's Balancing Test*, 76 HARV. L. REV. 755 (1963).

8. The claim here is not about what happens at the limits of existing law, but rather about what happens at the limits of existing lawmaking practice.

edges, as are all rules, but still deciding some number of cases at the rule-making level.[9] In contrast, Section 10(b), even as explicated in SEC Rule 10b-5, is broad and vague,[10] deciding few cases at the rule-making level, and leaving most cases to be decided in common law fashion as they arise. Thus, even though Section 16(b) has its share of surrounding common law elaboration,[11] and Rule 10b-5 has some component of canonical ruleness,[12] the two approaches to what is more or less the same problem differ strikingly, the difference being explainable largely by the degree to which the common law method is at work.

Presumably this choice, call it the 16(b)/10(b) choice, exists with respect to a host of contemplated legislative enactments. When deciding how to regulate a particular area of human conduct, a legislature must decide whether to adopt the 10(b) model and delegate much of the law-making task to the courts proceeding in common law fashion, or instead to adopt the 16(b) model and make the important decisions at the legislative level, leaving the courts to deal only with those cases around the edges that are thrown up by the limitations of language and the open texture of legal life.

The same kinds of choices exist for judges as well as for legislators. A judge deciding a 10b-5 case might consider herself empowered to make as much law as she sees fit, constrained only by the traditions of common law method. A judge deciding a 16(b) case, however, might see her role differently. She might take the comparative precision of Section 16(b) as a strong indication that Congress did not wish her to act in common law fashion, and thus she might consider her role in these cases to be limited to the by-product model, or perhaps even to something narrower.[13]

I do not seek here to resolve whether the 10(b) model is superior to the 16(b) model (or vice versa), or when one would be preferred to the other. I raise these issues only to show that the common law/code decision, and even the by-product/enrichment decision, are not so settled as

9. Section 16(b), 15 U.S.C. § 78p(b) (1982), regulates "short-swing" profits by making such profits recapturable by the corporation if the transaction took place within a "period of less than six months," and if the person making the profit was an officer, director, or "the beneficial owner of more than 10 per centum of any class of any equity security (other than an exempted security) which is registered pursuant to section 78l of this title."

10. Section 10(b), 15 U.S.C. § 78j(b) (1982), empowers the Securities and Exchange Commission to make rules proscribing any "manipulative or deceptive device or contrivance," and Rule 10b-5, 17 CFR § 240.10b-5(a) (1988), prohibits, inter alia, "any device, scheme, or artifice to defraud."

11. *See, e.g.*, Foremost-McKesson, Inc. v. Provident Sec. Co., 423 U.S. 232 (1976); Blau v. Lehman, 368 U.S. 403 (1962).

12. For example, subsection (b) of the Rule makes it unlawful "[t]o make any untrue statement of a material fact or to omit to state a material fact necessary in order to make the statements made, in the light of the circumstances under which they were made, not misleading." 17 C.F.R. § 240.10b-5(b) (1988).

13. On the possibility of an alternative narrower than the by-product model, see *supra* note 4.

to be without current relevance. On the contrary, these choices remain an everyday feature of legal life. As a result, theoretical exploration of the questions of power and role that inform these choices is no less necessary than it has ever been. Eisenberg helps us to consider these choices by his important and incisive description and analysis of what common law method entails. But at the next level, considering whether and when the common law process ought to be fostered or impeded, he leaves much of the work to be done by the reader or others. It is hard to imagine that a book of this explanatory ambition should have such limited justificatory ambition, and it seems that Eisenberg is probably taking as a given what remains in need of justification. No one should undertake that justification without reliance on Eisenberg's explanation of the nature of the common law. It is a pity, however, that Eisenberg did not spend more time on the justificatory task himself.

II

At the explanatory level, Eisenberg's account of the common law is especially insightful and enriching. This account proceeds from what is probably Eisenberg's most illuminating distinction, the distinction between doctrinal propositions and social propositions. Doctrinal propositions include all those "propositions that purport to state legal rules and are found in or easily derived from textual sources that are generally taken to express legal doctrine" (p. 1). Social propositions encompass essentially everything else, including moral propositions like "it is wrong to abandon one's ill parents," policy propositions like "hindering the progress of the automobile industry will decrease the gross national product of the United States," and experiential propositions such as "Williamsburg is prettier than Newark" (pp. 14-42).[14]

The distinction between the doctrinal and the social tracks the positivist distinction between law and nonlaw. However, the doctrinal/social distinction marks the law/nonlaw distinction in a way that transcends many of the misconceptions commonly found in the literature, in particular the view that positivism is about the necessary separation of law and morality.[15] Rather, positivism is about the ability to identify a normative domain that is smaller than and distinguishable from the entire normative universe. Inquiries into whether such a demarcated domain should, can, or does exist are often obscured rather than illuminated by some supposed law/morality distinction that coincides with the law/nonlaw distinction. As Eisenberg quite properly notes, a doctrinal proposition may incorporate a moral component (pp. 14-15), and the social proposi-

14. These examples are mine and not Eisenberg's.

15. *See* J.W. Harris, Legal Philosophies 16 (1980); *see also* the view criticized in P. Soper, A Theory of Law 101 (1984).

tions of policy and experience have no moral component. Under this picture of positivism, the debate about positivism is not a debate about law and morality. Instead it is a debate, at the descriptive level, about whether, in a particular decisional environment, call it the "legal system,"[16] the norms of decision will consist only (or at least largely) of a pedigreeable set of norms not coextensive with the set of norms generally used by decisionmakers in the larger environment of which legal decisionmaking is but a subset.[17]

Positivism in this sense coincides with Unger's conception of formalism. For Unger, formalism is not necessarily a mechanical process requiring no judgment; instead, formalism is "a commitment to, and therefore also a belief in the possibility of, a method of legal justification that contrasts with open-ended disputes about the basic terms of social life, disputes that people call ideological, philosophical, or visionary."[18] There is no need to distinguish Unger's "ideological" from Eisenberg's "social", for both mark the same distinction between some normative domain with constraining boundaries, on the one hand, and the normative domain that lies without those boundaries, on the other. Under either Eisenberg's or Unger's conceptions of the distinction, it would be possible to assert that a norm was valid (that is, accepted) within a given society while still asserting that it was not a valid legal norm.

Eisenberg advances our understanding of the basic issue surrounding positivism and its opponents not only by properly drawing the distinction between the doctrinal and the nondoctrinal, but also by abjuring the use of a Hartian rule of recognition to identify or pedigree the doctrinal propositions.[19] Instead, Eisenberg understands the rule of recognition to be more of a social practice than a formulated or even formulatable rule.[20] Among these social practices are the enrollment of people in three-year institutions called "law schools", who take examinations called "bar examinations", who call themselves "lawyers", who concentrate much of their professional reading and professional justification on a limited range of materials and books, and so on. These social

16. The word "law" has undeniably strong positive emotive connotations, see Fuller *Positivism and Fidelity to Law — A Reply to Professor Hart*, 71 HARV. L. REV. 630 (1958), and thus it may be unwarranted to attach that label to only a small portion of what under any theory takes place within the institution we call "the legal system." In that respect, Eisenberg's doctrinal/social distinction may better capture what is at stake in discussions of positivism without the distractions of debates over when and where to use the word "law."

17. The description of positivism in terms of a "pedigree" comes from R. DWORKIN, TAKING RIGHTS SERIOUSLY 17 (1982).

18. R. UNGER, THE CRITICAL LEGAL STUDIES MOVEMENT 1 (1986).

19. H.L.A. HART, THE CONCEPT OF LAW 92 (1961).

20. On this theme, see also Simpson, *supra* note 1.

practices produce cultural differentiation,[21] such that there are propositions—"Don't put your elbows on the table"—that are socially valid but not part of this practice, and that there are other propositions—The Rule in Shelley's Case, for example—that are legally valid (accepted within legal practice) but largely unknown outside of that limited environment. By not pausing over the formulation of a rule of recognition, Eisenberg helpfully transcends many of the limitations of traditional discussions of positivism; instead, he asks us simply to observe as a fact the enormous difference between the domain of doctrinal propositions and the domain of normative propositions accepted in the larger society.

It might be, of course, that any difference between the domains of the legal and the social is purely stylistic. That is, it might be that any social proposition has its doctrinal analogue, such that the domains of the legal and the social differ in language only and not in substance.[22] Under this recasting of Realism, the distinction between doctrinal propositions and social propositions is not unlike the distinction between English and French. Not all English propositions are perfectly translatable into French, and not all French ones perfectly translatable into English. Still, there are few things that can be said in French that cannot be said in English. Similarly, although the propositions may not be perfectly translatable, there may be few things that can be said in "social" that cannot be said in "doctrinal".

It is unfortunate that, with the exception of his discussion of precedent (pp. 50-61), Eisenberg nowhere takes the challenge of Realism seriously.[23] He assumes rather than examines the view that there are doctrinal propositions that exclude an interesting range of social propositions (p. 43), and that, conversely, there are social propositions that are unlikely at any given time to be replicated in the existing stock of doctrinal propositions. I happen to believe that to be true, and it is plain that Eisenberg believes it to be true; but Eisenberg and I might be wrong. It might be that a common law judge has a sufficient stock of doctrinal

21. N. LUHMANN, A SOCIOLOGICAL THEORY OF LAW 167-74 (1985); N. LUHMANN, THE DIFFERENTIATION OF SOCIETY (1982).

22. The claim, therefore, would be that most extralegal propositions are replicated as legal propositions. *See* Balkin, *The Crystalline Structure of Legal Thought*, 39 RUTGERS L. REV. 1 (1986).

23. His perceptive discussion of precedent recognizes and absorbs the Realist critique that an unformulated result from a previous case may be described in so many different ways as to be nonconstraining. He thus argues, correctly, that the constraint of a precedent will lie not in its holding, but rather in some proposition that is articulated by the precedent court. This analysis of precedent, what he calls the "announcement approach" (pp. 54-56), avoids the Realist attack on precedent, and would be subject only to those attacks that could equally be levelled against formulated rules. Eisenberg also incorporates a version of Realism insofar as he notes that no one of the three approaches to precedent he identifies has achieved pride of place compared to the others. As a result, the use of precedent becomes technique rather than constraint, usable in ways that serve rather than guide the development of law.

propositions to justify in doctrinal language any conclusion reached on social (that is, nondoctrinal) grounds. If this is the case, then any difference between the universes of doctrinal and social propositions ceases to be either important or constraining, and attention would best be trained on the formation and reception of social propositions within society in general; preoccupation with a realm of doctrinal propositions that merely replicate existing social propositions would be largely pointless. Eisenberg rejects this possibility. His rejection, however, is essential to the entire project, and rests on a picture of the array of doctrinal propositions that might be false. Even if it is not false, Eisenberg's explanation of the nature of the common law is incomplete insofar as it fails seriously to explore an empirical assumption upon which the entire edifice of the common law is grounded.[24]

III

The rejection of Realism, therefore, presupposes an extensionally divergent set of doctrinal and social propositions, a presupposition that Eisenberg explicitly states (p. 43). It is the extensional divergence that makes the interplay of doctrinal and social propositions important and interesting, and it is the extensional divergence that makes it crucial to explore the relationship between them. If we were not dealing with the common law, but with an area of law containing canonical texts of immutable authority, the positivist explanation of the relationship would be easy—social propositions are irrelevant except insofar as the canonical texts fail to answer the question presented by a particular dispute. In such cases, and only then, judges should consult social propositions to make new law interstitially. Classical positivist theory refers to this area as "discretion," where "discretion" designates the use of the full range of social propositions unlimited by doctrinal propositions.[25]

24. He does provide several examples of cases in which doctrinal propositions were repudiated or reformulated on the basis of social propositions. Presumably these examples are themselves counterexamples to Realism, for this tack would be unnecessary if the Realist hypothesis of coincidence were correct. Still, the identification of some examples in which doctrine diverges from social norms in a constraining way no more refutes Realism than identification of some mutually exclusive but equally valid doctrinal propositions proves it. Realism is interesting when it makes a probabilistic claim, that the number of instances in which a doctrinal proposition is available to serve a wide range of divergent social propositions is far greater than traditional legal theory supposes. If this claim is correct, then Eisenberg's examples occupy a small area of the common law, and one not appropriately generalizable into claims about the nature of the common law.

25. See J. Bell, Policy Arguments in Judicial Decisions (1983); H.L.A. Hart, *Problems of the Philosophy of Law*, in Essays in Jurisprudence and Philosophy 88, 106-08 (1983); N. MacCormick, H.L.A. Hart 126-30 (1981); Marshall, *Positivism, Adjudication, and Democracy*, in Law, Morality, and Society: Essays in Honour of H.L.A. Hart 132 (P.M.S. Hacker & J. Raz eds. 1977). Some positivists, it should be noted, would demur to the characterization in the text, claiming that legal rules, legal principles, and legal procedures still form and channel the nature of legal decision even when the rule fails to dictate an answer. *See* N.

When we turn from canonically formulated rules to the common law, we see within positivist theory a parallel answer to the question about the relationship between doctrinal and social propositions. Classical positivist theory holds that social propositions are usable in the process of interstitially making new law; that is, of making law where no previously pedigreed common law doctrinal proposition disposes of the existing case. However, once social propositions are used to create new doctrinal propositions—in other words, once law is made—the new doctrinal propositions assume a canonical status, removable not by the court that created them but only by a legislature.[26] Thus, in both statutory and common law, classical positivist theory has social propositions operating, at most, interstitially, and doctrinal propositions conclusively determining any case to which they unequivocally apply.

The foregoing positivist picture of the common law method is faithful to the foundations of positivist theory. Its only difficulty lies in its falsity. The picture painted by a positivist conception of the common law is not a picture of common law adjudication as it exists in any common law country. Instead, common law adjudication is a process that allows judges to remake the existing doctrinal propositions in the process of applying them. What distinguishes the common law from codified law is precisely its incompleteness. No doctrinal proposition of the form "It is the law that *X*" is immune from revision, for even in cases falling within *X*, it remains within the power of the common law court to announce and to apply retroactively that *X* is now (or really always was) X_l.[27] This power, the power to change what was thought to be the rule at the moment of application, and then to apply that changed rule to the case at hand, supplies the bite for Eisenberg's explanatory analysis. Given this power to change the doctrinal propositions even when, by their terms, they apply to the case at hand, the question arises as to the source of the impetus for change. Here the answer is obvious: social propositions. Social propositions provide the purchase for the modification of hitherto applicable doctrinal propositions. The universe of judicially usable social

---

MacCormick, Legal Reasoning and Legal Theory 246-55 (1978); J. Raz, The Authority of Law: Essays on Law and Morality 194-201 (1979). "There are no pure law-creating cases. In every case in which the court makes law it also applies laws restricting and guiding its law-creating activities." *Id.* at 195. It is not my intent to say that the positivist explanation of the interpretation of canonical rules fits especially well with contemporary American practice, which is increasingly similar to common law method. *See* authorities cited at *supra* note 3.

26. This perspective was embodied in the traditional English approach, which until 1966 prohibited any court, including the House of Lords, from overruling its own prior decisions. *See* R. Cross, Precedent in English Law 6 (3d ed. 1977).

27. This phenomenon is commonly described as "defeasibility." *See* M. Martin, The Legal Philosophy of H.L.A. Hart: A Critical Appraisal 115-43 (1987); Baker, *Defeasibility and Meaning*, in Law, Morality, and Society: Essays in Honour of H.L.A. Hart 26 (P.M.S. Hacker & J. Raz eds. 1977).

propositions thus provides the framework for the use of doctrinal propositions. According to Eisenberg, doctrinal propositions are to be applied or extended only if they achieve a certain level of consistency with other doctrinal propositions within the system, and, more importantly, only if they are congruent with the social propositions applicable to the same type of conduct. Thus, a doctrinal proposition may be discarded if it fails the test of social congruence with respect to the relevant social proposition (pp. 64-76, 146-61). More commonly, a doctrinal proposition may be reformulated when, without such reformulation, it would generate a result different from the one that would be generated by the applicable social proposition (pp. 66-68). The determination of social congruence, Eisenberg stresses, occurs not simply when a judge sets aside or reformulates a doctrinal proposition. It also occurs when a doctrinal proposition is followed. If a decision to set aside a doctrinal proposition is founded on the determination that that proposition is incongruent with a social proposition, then a decision *not* to set aside a doctrinal proposition is a decision, sometimes explicit but usually implicit, that the doctrinal proposition *is* congruent with the applicable social propositions. In other words, as long as the judge has the power to set aside a doctrinal proposition for failure of congruence, and has the power to reformulate a doctrinal proposition for failure of congruence in application, then every application of a nonreformulated doctrinal proposition is a determination of the presence of congruence, a determination that cannot, of course, be made without an examination of the social propositions themselves (pp. 2-3, 146-61).

The importance of this point cannot be overestimated. Although first made years ago by Duncan Kennedy,[28] its recent restatement both by Ronald Dworkin[29] and now by Eisenberg is a welcome addition to our understanding of the nature of law, and goes to the foundations of positivism. Any version of positivism presupposes a realm of the legal that is not congruent with the total realm of norms available to a member of the society in which the legal is located. Consequently, positivism, although acknowledging an epiphenomenal area in which discretion might apply, cannot coexist with the proposition that the larger array of norms, available to defeat the doctrinal proposition in any case, is necessarily a part of the decision in every case. By making this clearer than anyone who has preceded him, Eisenberg has greatly advanced our understanding not only of the nature of the common law, but of the nature of law in general.

28. Kennedy, *Legal Formality*, 2 J. LEGAL STUD. 351 (1973).

29. R. DWORKIN, LAW'S EMPIRE 350-54, 449 n.14 (1986).

IV

At this point, however, Eisenberg's explanatory path becomes treacherous. If social propositions constitute, by definition, the universe of nondoctrinal propositions, and if doctrinal propositions are defeasible in the service of social propositions, then the positivist insight appears to be slipping away. The suggestion that social propositions are the masters in every case seems antithetical to a decisionmaking environment in which a more discrete norm set is controlling. Eisenberg seems properly unwilling to relinquish the core positivist perspective. Although there is considerable divergence between his theory and classical positivism, he is hardly ready to scrap the difference between legal and legislative reasoning, and is thus committed to showing that legal decisionmaking somehow differs from the direct application of social propositions.

Eisenberg's first tack is an attempt to pedigree his social propositions. Not all social propositions, it turns out, can push aside doctrinal propositions: only those with a requisite degree of a particular kind of social support.[30] This, for Eisenberg, serves to distinguish the social propositions a judge may legitimately employ from those to which a judge may personally subscribe. Although Eisenberg's requirement of requisite social support distinguishes the range of judicially usable social propositions from the range of social propositions to which a judge may subscribe, it is not clear that this distinction separates judicial from nonjudicial public decisionmaking. Ideally, any public decisionmaker, whether president, legislator, or bureaucrat, has a positional obligation to decide on the basis of the norms adopted by that decisionmaker's constituency, or norms developed in light of the decisionmaker's role, rather than the norms the decisionmaker holds as an individual.[31] And if all public decisionmakers turn out to have obligations that transcend their own personal beliefs, then the normative field available to the wise judge may not differ substantially from the normative field available to any publicly responsive and responsible decisionmaker.[32]

30.
> The question then arises, what criteria should a moral norm satisfy if it is to figure in common law reasoning? The answer is that when moral norms are relevant to establishing, applying, or changing common law rules, the courts should employ social morality, by which I mean moral standards that claim to be rooted in aspirations for the community as a whole, and that, on the basis of an appropriate methodology, can fairly be said to have substantial support in the community, can be derived from norms that have such support, or appear as if they have such support (p. 15).

Eisenberg adds flesh to this skeleton, and then subjects propositions of policy to a similar requirement (p. 29). Experiential propositions also require a requisite degree of support, but here the support is to come largely from authoritative sources rather than from community sentiment (p. 40).

31. On the idea of a positional obligation, see A.J. SIMMONS, MORAL PRINCIPLES AND POLITICAL OBLIGATIONS 16-23 (1979).

32. This view, assimilating the nature of lawmaking when done by the judiciary to lawmaking when done wisely in the legislative process, is forcefully set forth in J. BELL, *supra* note 25.

Eisenberg, at this point, could go in Dworkin's direction and maintain that courts are limited to the province of principle, leaving other social propositions, such as those of policy, to legislators, administrators, and executives. But Eisenberg refuses to take this path, in large part because it appears to attain analytical coherence and possible normative desirability at the expense of descriptive accuracy. Common law courts rely on policy propositions all the time, and Eisenberg, in attempting to give an account of the common law that explains much of existing practice, is thus faced with the task of admitting the relevance of essentially the full universe of social propositions without seeming to endorse either Realism or Unger's open-ended decisionmaking. This is the path that is especially treacherous.

The dilemma here can also be seen through the window of the analysis of rules. Common law rules are a strange breed. They can be modified at the moment of application to the case at hand, and their modification depends upon the background social propositions. If, as Eisenberg's analysis suggests, a doctrinal proposition should be enforced or extended when and only when it is congruent with the relevant social propositions, and a doctrinal proposition should be discarded or reformulated when it lacks such congruence, then the doctrinal proposition seems to be no more than a rule of thumb.[33] Although rules of thumb are useful guides for prediction and useful to consult when time is short, their defining characteristic is their lack of normative weight. The value of a rule of thumb is limited to indicating the result likely to be reached by the rationales or justifications lying behind the rule (in this case social propositions); but they are intrinsically unweighty, providing no reason for decision *qua* rule independent of the reasons generated by the background social propositions.

If common law rules are only rules of thumb, and hence without independent normative weight, then their prominence in adjudication seems odd. Part of this prominence might just be ruse. The citation of rules for decisions that are in fact based largely on social propositions might just be a way of entrenching a legal culture, distancing that culture from its constituency by a language of its own, and creating a cult of expertise where that expertise appears on closer examination to be absent. In this respect it is no surprise that the common law was the favorite target of the Realists, for the rules of the common law seem more mask than reality.

But let us pass on this hypothesis for now. Although it may be true, it may also be that other constraining factors make the common law

33. On rules of thumb in this sense, see R.M. Hare, Moral Thinking: Its Levels, Method and Point 38 (1981); Smart, *Extreme and Restricted Utilitarianism*, 6 Phil. Q. 344 (1956).

something other than merely a method of unmediated application of social propositions. Eisenberg recognizes the dilemma. On the one hand, he argues, correctly, that social propositions are applicable in every case and that doctrinal propositions appear to be largely unweighty servants to these social propositions. But, on the other hand, he is reluctant to embrace the consequence that seemingly flows from that, the conclusion that common law decisionmaking is essentially identical to decisionmaking that uses all the norms then available to any decisionmaker in that society.

Eisenberg's attempt to salvage the distinctiveness of the common law (from open-ended decisionmaking) appears to rest largely on a move that is reminiscent of Llewellyn.[34] More recently similar themes have appeared in the work of Frank Michelman.[35] Llewellyn, Michelman, and now Eisenberg seek to avoid an account of American law that makes it appear more rule bound than it actually is, but all of them also seek to rescue the idea of legal decisionmaking from collapsing indistinguishably into decisionmaking *simpliciter*. In pursuing this goal, each seeks to locate the gap between common law decisionmaking and social decisionmaking in constraining factors coming either from the legal culture or from the particular method of legal decisionmaking. Each sees constraints in the necessity of written justification; each sees constraints emanating out of special training and acculturation; and Eisenberg contributes to this tradition a special concern with intraprofessional discourse (e.g., pp. 9-13, 18, 40-42, 93, 96-99, 118-21, 154-61). As Eisenberg notes, judges are constantly interacting with lawyers on both sides of a case, and their opinions are incessantly evaluated by lawyers, by other judges, in treatises, and on the pages of law reviews. This type of professional discourse does not, as I read him, ameliorate the potential extensional equivalence between doctrinal and social propositions, for nothing in this professional interchange is designed to entrench doctrinal propositions against the weight of social propositions. What the professional discourse does, however, is mediate the reception of social propositions. If the social propositions usable by the judiciary are presented to it by lawyers, judges, and legal literature, then it may be that the social propositions supported by this group, or, more faithfully to Eisenberg's conception, perceived by this group as being supported by the population, will differ with some frequency from the social propositions supported by the population itself. Under this approach, the legal system differs from Unger's open-ended system not because of the effect of its

34. K. LLEWELLYN, THE COMMON LAW TRADITION: DECIDING APPEALS (1960); *see* W. TWINING, KARL LLEWELLYN AND THE REALIST MOVEMENT 203-69 (1973).

35. *See* Michelman, *Justification (and Justifiability) of Law in a Contradictory World*, in JUSTIFICATION (NOMOS XXVIII) 71 (J.R. Pennock & J.W. Chapman eds. 1986).

rules, but because the social propositions used are screened and translated by the perceptions of those acculturated into the legal system.[36]

This conclusion rings true, although its normative desirability is far from obvious. If doctrine is defeasible in the service of morality and policy, itself a normatively defensible goal, and if the morality and policy that dictates the development of law is the morality and policy as perceived and understood by lawyers and judges, then the nature of legal training and judicial selection needs serious rethinking. This is hardly a bad idea, but the radicalism of this conclusion should not be ignored. If, as Eisenberg argues, doctrinal propositions are largely transparent to social propositions, then the use of social propositions would seem to have the laboring oar in both lawyering and judging. And if this is the case, then the importance of doctrinal propositions in training lawyers, in the practice of law, and in judicial justification needs rethinking. Under Eisenberg's approach, doctrinal propositions are useful guides, but if they are no more than that, it is hard to explain why, except as disguise, they figure so prominently in legal practice.

V

There is, however, an alternative explanation with far less radical implications. This alternative explanation, one that I have referred to previously as "presumptive positivism,"[37] is consistent with the general contours of Eisenberg's account, but refuses to acknowledge that the failure of congruence between a doctrinal proposition and a social proposition is a sufficient condition for the defeasibility, whether by replacement or reformulation, of the doctrinal proposition. Instead, a doctrinal proposition yields to an inconsistent social proposition, or is reformulated in the service of a social proposition, when and only when the degree of inconsistency reaches certain magnitudes. If inconsistency exists to a lesser degree, the doctrinal proposition prevails despite the lack of

36. Eisenberg unwittingly provides an example of this phenomenon in his discussion of social morality as a type of social proposition (pp. 19-21). The following two sentences almost speak for themselves. "The first [objection] is that social morality is not a meaningful concept. People who make this objection are apt to point to an analysis of conventional morality by John Ely in his book *Democracy and Distrust*" (p. 19). Now John Ely is a superb scholar and a fine fellow, but only in a very narrow world would John Ely's views about the existence or nonexistence of social morality be thought central. With millennia of philosophical, theological, and social thought on the subject, and at least generations of sociological thought, to center the debate around John Ely demonstrates the way the legal culture is likely to focus on its own—not always perfect—translations of larger ideas. If this example is typical and not aberrational, then we might expect that the set of social propositions as received and used by the legal culture would in many instances diverge from the set of social propositions received and used by society itself.

37. Schauer, *Formalism*, 97 YALE L.J. 509 (1988); Schauer, *The Jurisprudence of Reasons* (Book Review), 85 MICH. L. REV. 847 (1987).

congruence.[38]

Simply stated, my account asserts that a doctrinal proposition is presumptively controlling even when it is inconsistent with some, or all, social propositions. Only when the weight of the inconsistency is overwhelming is the presumption overcome. From this perspective we can see why the legal culture is skewed to the doctrinal, and why there are all around us manifestations of positivism in the preference for a relatively discrete set of materials, sources, and argumentative modes. But we can also understand why it remains legitimate within the legal system for the doctrinal to yield to the social when the necessities of such an outcome are particularly strong. At times this strength may be embodied in a particularly compelling factual situation, such as that in *Riggs v. Palmer*.[39] At times it may be embodied in a particularly compelling policy argument, as in *MacPherson v. Buick Motor Co.*[40] And at times it may be manifested in a particularly outmoded doctrine or in a particularly compelling moral argument, both of which were present in *Brown v. Board of Education*.[41] But regardless of the source of the overriding considerations, "particularly" is the crucial word. It is central to understanding the idea of a presumption that something more than mere inconsistency is required to overcome it.

The idea of a presumption rests on certain psychological assumptions that may not be correct. More specifically, it rests on the ability of people to accept, in some cases, a decision that, given the facts of a particular case, is wrong. The force of a presumption may require appellate courts to affirm decisions they think incorrect, may require jurors to vote to acquit where they think the defendant guilty, and, here, may require judges to apply and perhaps even to extend doctrines they think at odds with the social propositions that ultimately inform the common law. But presumptions appear to work for appellate judges reviewing the decisions of lower courts and administrative agencies, and they appear to work in the criminal law with respect to the presumption of innocence. Thus there is no reason to assume at the outset that presumptions may not be at work in the development of the common law.

Note that presumptive positivism is compatible with Eisenberg's conclusion that social propositions are at work in every case, not only

38. I am unsure whether Eisenberg's account is compatible with mine. At times (e.g., pp. 66-68) he seems to leave no room for the conceptual space that is integral to my account. But at other times, particularly when discussing the necessity of "substantial" failure of congruence (pp. 70-71), his terminology seems consistent with a presumptive approach.

39. 115 N.Y. 506, 22 N.E. 188 (1889).

40. 217 N.Y. 382, 111 N.E. 1050 (1916).

41. 347 U.S. 483 (1954). I sneak in a constitutional example only to remind the reader that American constitutional adjudication in the Supreme Court seems a central case of common law methodology.

those in which they cause a modification of doctrinal propositions. In the picture I am painting here, every case involves a determination by a common law judge that the doctrine she is applying or extending is not drastically incongruent with the applicable social propositions. The relevance of social propositions in *every* case, therefore, is inconsistent with one of the main tenets of positivism, the existence of a discrete realm of the legal. But, as Kelsen has shown us, the theory of positivism need not be a theory of legal exclusivity with respect to any law-applying act.[42] Thus, it is consistent with the broad positivist perspective to note the dominance of a discrete and pedigreeable array of materials in a domain, and in any decision within that domain, but still to acknowledge that every decision within that domain requires reference to materials—that is, social propositions—not within the pedigreed and discrete set.

It is easy to think that positivism is merely the name for one side of a largely arcane dispute carried on by a small number of Anglo-American jurisprudes. But nothing could be further from the truth. The idea of positivism undergirds any distinctly legal enterprise, whether a law school, a law book, a law review, or a law court. But that it undergirds such ideas does not of course make it correct. And thus the dispute about positivism is not a dispute just about whether Hart or Fuller was right, or about whether Hart or Dworkin is right, or about whether positivism or natural law is right. The dispute about positivism is a dispute about the autonomy of law, about the extent to which law is in any useful way distinguishable from social life, and about the extent to which institutions founded on the premise of some degree of legal autonomy have reason to exist.

From this perspective, presumptive positivism appears to gain in accuracy what it loses in drama. Faced with a debate that has, in one form or another, engaged legal theorists for centuries, presumptive positivism suggests the answer may lie in an understanding of the way that the pedigreed materials intersect and interact with the nonpedigreeable ones. By putting the issue in exactly those terms, Eisenberg has greatly assisted the process of understanding not only the common law, but also the law in general. And, by trying to explain that relationship in terms of presumptions, I have tried to further the enterprise that Eisenberg's analysis has so importantly formulated.

42. H. Kelsen, The Pure Theory of Law (1967). On this theme in Kelsen, see Tur, *Positivism, Principles and Rules*, in Perspectives in Jurisprudence 42 (E. Attwooll ed. 1977).

[14]

The Ratio Decidendi of a Case

In his recent article [1] Professor Montrose contrasts two views as to the correct definition of the *ratio decidendi* of a case. One, which may conveniently be called the classical theory, may be summed up by the proposition that the ratio is " the principle of law which the judge considered necessary to the decision." [2] The other, which was advanced by Professor Goodhart some years ago,[3] will be called the Goodhart theory, and is said by Professor Montrose to be accurately summed up by the proposition that " the *ratio decidendi*

[1] [1946] A.C. 493.
[2] [1957] 1 W.L.R. 638.
[3] [1957] 1 W.L.R. 632.

[1] In (1957) 20 M.L.R., at p. 124.
[2] This is substantially Paton's exposition. See *Jurisprudence* (1st ed.), p. 159, cited by Montrose.
[3] In 40 *Yale Law Journal* (1930), and reprinted in *Essays in Jurisprudence and the Common Law*, p. 1.

of a case can be defined as the material facts of the case plus the decision thereon."[4] Both theories agree that the *ratio decidendi*, once determined, is binding or authoritative, and that it may be determined in a single case taken by itself. Now it is hardly possible to contrast the two theories except in relation to a case where the judge does explicitly state a principle[5] of law, and in this note it will be assumed that the discussion is limited to such a case. In such circumstances it is submitted that the Goodhart theory is indistinguishable from the classical theory.

It must be noted first of all that Goodhart insists that the judge's own statement of the material facts of the case must be accepted, if he makes one; even if his statement is demonstrably wrong one ought not to go behind his findings upon this point. In the second place it must be remembered that a rule of law will always be found to contain two parts; the first specifies a number of facts and the second specifies the legal result or conclusion which ought to follow whenever these facts are found to co-exist. This analysis of the form of legal rules is now too well known and established to require elaboration.

When, therefore, a judge states a rule of law, and treats it as applicable to the case before him, the applicability must depend upon his finding that the *material* facts of that case correspond precisely to the facts specified in that rule, and, this being so, that the conclusion or result specified in that rule ought to follow. The rule stated by the judge ought, therefore, upon the basis of Professor Goodhart's arguments, to be treated as the *ratio decidendi*, since it both contains the court's conclusion and the court's findings as to the material facts of the case. The classical theory and the Goodhart theory, if logically followed out, produce the same result.

It is not so obvious that the same is true if the judge states a rule of law, says that it governs his decision, and then proceeds to show that it does not apply to the facts of the case in question. Suppose that a judge says that an action for negligence can only succeed if the damage which the plaintiff alleges is physical damage to his person or property, and then proceeds to show that upon the facts of the case before him the plaintiff has alleged and proved damage of a different kind, so that he feels bound to give judgment for the defendant. Here the rule stated by the judge specifies facts which are not present in the facts of the case before him. In such a case the judge does however by implication treat the "non-physical" nature of the damage (which is a fact present in the case) as material, and it is by stating the rule and holding it to be inapplicable that he makes his opinion upon this point known. He could equally well have said "The rule of law applicable here is

[4] This is Glanville Williams' summary, *Learning the Law* (3rd ed.), p. 67, cited with approval by Montrose.

[5] No distinction is made in this note between a rule of law, a principle of law or a proposition of law. Although there is certainly a distinction made in common usage, it seems to be too vague to be of much significance.

that in an action for negligence where non-physical damage only is proved the plaintiff ought not to recover." Thus, even in this sort of case it is to the rule of law stated by the judge that we ought to turn to discover the *ratio decidendi*, for again the two theories lead to the same result.

It seems therefore that Professor Goodhart, having said that the proposition of law propounded by the judge may be ignored in determining the *ratio decidendi*, and having advanced weighty arguments tending to show that such propositions make unsatisfactory *rationes decidendi*, fails to see that his own arguments make it obligatory that such a proposition should not be ignored. His own theory is just as much open to the same criticism as he and others have directed against the classical theory [6]—criticism to which there has been as yet no satisfactory reply.

A. W. B. SIMPSON.

[15]

THE *RATIO DECIDENDI* OF A CASE

In his most recent article[1] Professor Montrose raises a number of points which I shall attempt to answer as briefly as possible, following the order in which he himself raises them.

He suggests that I have confused two senses in which the term *ratio decidendi* is used; these two usages both exist, and are, therefore, both "correct." Furthermore, they are separable.[2] Thus, one could, according to Professor Montrose, accept one usage and discard the other, and so say, "I think the *ratio decidendi* (meaning the rule of law explicitly stated by the judge as the basis for his decision) of such and such a case is X, but I do not think it is binding" or, more baldly, "I do not think that the *ratio decidendi* of a case is binding." This, indeed, is what Professor Montrose himself is prepared to do.[3] Such a proposition as the last seems somehow odd in the mouth of a lawyer, and although a person making it could not, once he had defined his terms, be accused of obscurity, he might well be accused of a very eccentric use of language. The reason for this is not difficult to pinpoint—it is that the two usages discussed by Professor Montrose are not separable in the way he assumes. Surely those judges and writers (Professor Montrose excepted) who have meant by the term *ratio decidendi* "the rule of law propounded by the judge as the basis of his decision" have adopted this usage because they have thought that such a rule *is* the rule for which the case is of binding authority. Those who have adopted the other usage ("the rule for which the case is of binding authority") have been, to this extent, in agreement with those who adopt the former usage—they have only disagreed in so far as they think that the rule is to be isolated in some other way. The two usages are only separable in a way which is best explained by saying that the first usage (rule of law stated by judge) includes and implies the second (rule of law for which case is authority), but that the second usage gives no clue as to how the rule is to be isolated. This point appears to me to be completely missed in Professor Montrose's writings on the subject.[4] In a short note I did not raise it, and fail to see why I am criticised for not doing so. Had

[1] (1957) 20 M.L.R. 587, where he criticises my note in (1957) 20 M.L.R. at p. 413.

[2] (1957) 20 M.L.R. at pp. 587–588. The two meanings are "... the rule of law propounded by the judge as the basis of his ultimate decision in the case" and "... the rule of law for which a case is of binding authority."

[3] (1957) 20 M.L.R. at p. 588. "The terminology whereby *ratio decidendi* signifies the rule propounded by the judges should not be allowed to be used to beg the question whether such a rule is of binding authority."

[4] See in particular 2 West Aust.L.R. at pp. 329 *et seq.*

I treated of the "ambiguity" of the term *ratio decidendi* I should have advanced the argument I have just sketched to show that Professor Montrose has added to whatever ambiguity previously existed. Since I never raised the point I do not see that I begged any questions by failing to reproduce Professor Montrose's theorisings upon the usage of the term, nor do I see that the ambiguity he himself thinks exists could possibly be said to operate in relation to the occasions when I use the term in my note.

Professor Montrose objects to my usage both of the word "definition" and of the word "correct" in my description of his article as one which "contrasts two views as to the correct definition of the *ratio decidendi* of a case."[5] By "definition" I meant no more than "rule or rules for determining"—in the context this was obvious. I note that Professor Montrose himself uses the same word with the same connotation.[6] He also twice expressly accepts Glanville Williams when the latter says "The *ratio decidendi* may be defined. . . ."[7] As for the word "correct" I find Professor Montrose using it in the paragraph in which he sets out the subject to be discussed in his first article—"The main question is whether . . . the 'classical view' is still correct"[8]—and it was this sentence which suggested my own brief summary of the point at issue in that article.[9] If he finds the word objectionable when used by Simpson he ought to be ready to explain why it is not objectionable when used by Montrose in the same sort of context. In fact we both used the word in that sense in which it is often used by lawyers—a doctrine is "correct" if it is generally accepted by the courts.

Professor Montrose goes on to suggest an ambiguity in the phrase "facts of the case" as I used it, the ambiguity arising because the word "facts" may mean either "particular facts" or "classes of facts." He would like to separate the two, and writes:—

> "Rules of law specify in their antecedents *classes* of facts . . . cases are concerned with specific actualities."[10]

I fail to see what relevance this distinction, even if it is well founded,[11] can have to what I wrote. The totality of the facts established in evidence in a case may be unique; so too will be

5 (1957) 20 M.L.R. p. 588.

6 (1957) 20 M.L.R. p. 589, n. 11, "Corbin, in commenting on the definition of a contract. . . ."

7 (1957) 20 M.L.R. p. 125, n. 7, p. 587, n. 5.

8 (1957) 20 M.L.R. p. 125. The omitted words are "to use Paton's language" —they refer to the expression "classical view."

9 (1957) 20 M.L.R. 124.

10 (1957) 20 M.L.R. 589 *et seq.*

11 The problem of drawing the line between words signifying "particular" facts and "class" facts is not faced by Montrose. For example, consider his illustration of a "particular" fact pair of words—"Bill Sykes"—a class which might, for all one knows, include many such persons. Take the words separately and the point is stronger.

many of those facts considered individually. It is precisely by treating these "particular" facts—or at least some of them—as immaterial that rules of law capable of use in other cases are constructed. The particular facts thus discarded are immaterial in the simple sense that, if they had been otherwise, then (so long as the "class fact" generalisation would still have been permissible) the decision would have been the same. It is in this sense that lawyers frequently think of facts as being material,[12] and it is in this sense that only those facts of a case are material which correspond precisely to the facts specified in the rule of law which the judge, who decides the case, treats as the rule applicable to that case. This I shall call "the first sense." Nothing turns upon whether these facts are what Professor Montrose would call "particular" facts. Now it is quite true that all the facts established in evidence are "material" in quite a different sense in that they make the "class fact" description permissible. This I shall call "the second sense." Thus, if a rule of law propounded by a judge embodies the word "chattels," without qualification, then the fact that he was dealing with a shot-gun was treated by him as immaterial in the first sense—he indicates that his decision would be the same if he were dealing with a motor-car. In the second sense [13] the fact that he was dealing with a shot-gun was material, since, had the subject-matter of the suit been realty, the generalisation chattel would be inappropriate. If the expression "material facts" is used in this second sense no difficulty of an analytical sort arises over their determination, for all facts established in evidence will be "material." Because of this I should have thought

[12] Amongst them Professor Montrose—see his usage of the words in (1957) 20 M.L.R. at p. 594.

[13] It is in another sense still that all the facts established in evidence are "material" because later judges may select one or more of them as a basis for distinguishing the earlier case. To do this is, as Professor Montrose points out in his discussion of *Tulk* v. *Moxhay* ((1957) 20 M.L.R. p. 594), to explain an earlier case by facts which nobody in the earlier case regarded as conditioning the decision. In his discussion of *Donoghue* v. *Stevenson* ((1957) 20 M.L.R. p. 591) Montrose seems to miss the very point he himself makes in relation to *Tulk* v. *Moxhay*, for he does not distinguish the various meanings of "material." Thus, he uses the admitted fact that under the current practice, a later court is entitled to treat the opaqueness of the bottle in *Donoghue* v. *Stevenson* as "material" (*i.e.*, as a condition precedent to the decision) as an argument for saying that the court in *Donoghue* v. *Stevenson* itself treated it as "material" (*i.e.*, as a condition precedent to the decision). This does not at all follow. He backs up this argument by saying that a judgment must be read *secundum subjectam materiam*. The value of quoting this tag lies, surely, in the fact that it draws attention to three points.

(a) All the facts of the case ought to be looked at to clear up ambiguities in judicial expression.

(b) All the facts of the case may be looked at in the search for arguments for distinguishing that case.

(c) All the facts may be examined if the boundaries of a class specified in a rule of law in that case are uncertain. Thus, in the example used in the text the shot-gun fact tells us that "shot-guns are chattels." This proposition may be a rule of sorts, but I do not discuss the status of such rules here.

that the use of the word in my note was confined to the first sense. I agree that there are considerable difficulties in giving an account of the reasons which induce judges to treat some facts as immaterial (in the first sense) but I never purported to deal with these in a short note—nor did Professor Montrose in his short article. We both assumed that the context would make our meaning clear. At no point did I suggest that I thought that there was any *logical* reason why some facts and not others should be selected as material, and so I fail to see why Professor Montrose finds it necessary to set out Stone's arguments upon this point in a reply to my note.[14] This part of Professor Montrose's reply is introduced by his statement that the fallacy in the proposition I advanced " . . . is clear once it is realised that 'application' of a rule to facts is the converse process to that of generalisation from particular fact to 'class' fact."[15] This difficult sentence seems to mean that the fallacy is clear once it is realised that a judge's finding that a rule applies to a particular case does not depend upon (" is the converse process to . . . ") his finding that the material facts of the case correspond precisely to those specified in the rule of law. This amounts to saying that the fallacy in saying that X is the same thing as Y is clear once it is realised that X is not Y. Perhaps I have misunderstood Professor Montrose. I also find it difficult to comprehend this alleged fallacy for another reason. I wrote about a judge who " . . . treats a rule of law as applicable to the case before him. . . ." A judge does this when he orders that consequence to follow which the rule specifies—this one can surely call applying the rule. The converse process to this I take to be " not ordering the consequence specified in the rule." I do not follow how the converse process can be described as " generalisation from particular fact to 'class fact,' " unless Professor Montrose is using the word " apply " in some eccentric way.[16]

Professor Montrose assumes [17] that I was making an independent point when I wrote [18] " . . . it is submitted that the Goodhart theory is indistinguishable from the classical theory." This was

[14] Stone, *Province and Function of Law*, pp. 187 *et seq.*

[15] (1957) 20 M.L.R. 590.

[16] (1957) 20 M.L.R. 593.

[17] On this see Professor Montrose's article, "Judicial Law Making and Law Applying," (1956) *Butterworths South African Law Review*, p. 187. (The references given by Montrose to this article are misleading.) In it he develops a conception of "law applying." Briefly the argument is that the judicial process is more complex than the formula F (facts) × R (rule) = D (decision) would lead us to suppose; the judge, besides formulating the appropriate rule of law and ascertaining the particular facts of a case has to *apply* the rule—this may involve him in difficulties of interpretation, clarification of the terminology in the rule, etc. In *applying* the rule in this sense the judge may have to formulate subsidiary rules (see note 13, above). Even, however, if this special usage of the word "apply" is adopted the obscurity of Professor Montrose's argument remains.

[18] (1957) 20 M.L.R. 414.

not my intention, but I see that the sentence is not happily framed. As he says, however, nothing turns upon this.

Professor Montrose takes me to task for saying that Stone criticised the classical theory.[19] He says that Stone was objecting to "the English theory of precedent." Stone's actual words were [20]:

> "The English theory of precedent, as formulated by text writers, imports that a particular decision is explained by one *ratio decidendi*, or general proposition of which the particular decision is an application, and which is 'required' or necessary to explain that particular decision. Moreover, this general proposition is to be drawn from that particular case itself."

A footnote then adds,

> "It is as to the mode of drawing it [*i.e.*, the general proposition or *ratio decidendi*] that there is controversy. . . ."

Stone does not enter into this controversy except in notes where he criticises Goodhart's method of drawing it. Since he treats Goodhart as one of the controversialists, it seems fair to treat those modes of determining the *ratio decidendi* which Goodhart controverted as aspects of the controversy to which Stone refers. One such mode is that of the classical theory—you draw out the *ratio decidendi* by accepting the rule which the judge thought was necessary for his decision. All suggested methods of determining the *ratio decidendi* by examining a single case—including the classical theory—are equally subject to Stone's criticism, which is directed against two basic assumptions of what he describes generally as the English theory of precedent. He treats the parties to the controversy as to how the *ratio decidendi* is to be determined and their views on this point as only worth mention in a footnote, since, by criticising the two basic assumptions, he criticises all controversialists alike. The two assumptions are:—

(i) the assumption that the question "What single principle does a particular case establish?" can be sensibly answered at all.

(ii) the assumption that any single rule is logically "necessary" to explain a particular decision.

Both assumptions are inherent in the "classical" theory just as they are inherent in the views advanced by Gray, Salmond and Goodhart. On the classical theory one is clearly committed to the first assumption. Equally, one is committed to the second—one is accepting as sensible the judge's belief that some particular rule was "necessary" to decide the case, and upon Stone's view the judge's belief that some particular rule was "necessary" is as logically untenable as anybody else's belief to the same effect. As he points out, logic alone would permit the formulation of any number of possible rules.[21]

19 (1957) 20 M.L.R. 593.

20 Stone, *op. cit.*, p. 187.

21 On p. 593 ((1957) 20 M.L.R.) I see that according to Professor Montrose, Stone (*op. cit.*, p. 187) pointed out that the Goodhart theory is one which says "that

Finally, Professor Montrose returns to his accusation that I misrepresented the nature of his article by saying that it contrasted the classical theory with the Goodhart theory [22]; this time the basis of his criticism is different. It would have been absurd, he suggests, to have done what I said he did, since this would be to contrast a genus not with another genus but with a species of another genus. This accusation of misrepresentation seems to me to be unfounded. In the first paragraph of his article Professor Montrose sets out the problem he proposes to discuss. This is, in his own words, "whether, to use Paton's language, the 'classical view' is still correct." [23] In contradistinction to the "classical view" he mentions the view of most jurists that the "classical view" is incorrect. The only jurists he mentions are Professor Goodhart and Dr. Glanville Williams. The latter is only mentioned as accurately reproducing Professor Goodhart's view of the matter. I thought, when I wrote the note, there, and I still think, that it was fair to describe the article as one which contrasted the classical view with the Goodhart view. The nature of Professor Montrose's arguments to the contrary is illustrated by the fact that they lead him into a misrepresentation of the Goodhart theory—to maintain the genus-species argument he has to say that Professor Goodhart asserted that the rule for which a case is authority is "constructed by later judges," a proposition never in fact maintained by that writer.[24]

In conclusion, Professor Montrose says that ". . . there is a great difference between the classical theory and the theory which permits cases to be explained by principles other than those propounded by the judge." With this statement I would entirely agree, nor am I prepared to admit that I ever, in my note, suggested the contrary. All that I said was that Professor Goodhart's argument as to the determination of the *ratio decidendi* contains an internal contradiction in that, having said that the rule stated by the judge may be ignored, he then goes on to propound a theory of his own whose basic assumption is that the judge's opinion as to what facts are material must be accepted. This basic assumption, in my view, leads to the conclusion, which Professor Goodhart failed to draw, that the rule stated by the judge ought to be accepted as the *ratio decidendi*. It was with this internal contradiction alone that my note was concerned.

A. W. B. SIMPSON.*

the rule of law for which a case is of binding authority *is not one which is pronounced*, *explicitly* or implicitly, *by the judge in the precedent case*, but which is constructed by later judges" (my italics). I find this hard to reconcile with his statement a few lines further up that Stone "nowhere refers" to the classical theory.

[22] (1957) 20 M.L.R. at p. 593.

[23] (1957) 20 M.L.R. at p. 125.

[24] See Goodhart, *Essays in Jurisprudence and the Common Law*, at p. 25, where the author's rules for discovering the binding principle are stated.

* Fellow of Lincoln College, Oxford.

[16]

BLACKSTONE *v.* BENTHAM [1]

BLACKSTONE'S *Commentaries on the Laws of England* is unquestionably the most influential book on English law that has ever been written, but it would be idle to deny that the book is unread by all but a smattering of English lawyers. The smattering mainly consists of students of jurisprudence, and they usually only read those parts of the *Commentaries* which came under the lash of Bentham's formidable pen. I therefore wish to draw attention to three topics commonly discussed by academic lawyers under the rubric "jurisprudence" on which Blackstone is to be preferred to Bentham. They relate to the doctrine of precedent, the interpretation of statutes and criminal responsibility.

But I must first draw attention to the limited nature of my task. I am not suggesting that Blackstone was, in any sense of the words, greater, cleverer or more influential than Bentham. Bentham was "a man with a master mind," and by "a man with a master mind" I mean someone who changed the way in which people think about important subjects. But for Jeremy Bentham our thoughts on many points of morals and politics would not be what they are. Blackstone was only a professor of English law and a judge. I cannot believe that any of us would describe anyone who has as yet held a chair of English law as "a man with a master mind." Some of them have been good expositors, though none as good as Blackstone, but "master minds," definitely no. As to Blackstone's more exalted occupation, I have yet to hear a capacity to change the modes of thought of mankind numbered among the major judicial qualities.

Nor do I wish, in this its bicentennial year, to challenge the merits of the attack launched by Bentham against Blackstone in *A Fragment on Government* but it is important to place that attack in its proper perspective. Incensed by Blackstone's frequent encomia of the common law and perturbed by the possibility that they would constitute an impediment to legislative law reform, Bentham was determined to destroy Blackstone's reputation. With this end in view he set about writing *A Comment on the Commentaries* in 1774. In the words of Mr. C. W. Everett who discovered the manuscript and published it in

1 [The text of a lecture given at Pembroke College, Oxford, on May 29, 1976. Blackstone is usually associated with All Souls College, Oxford, where he was a fellow from 1743 until his marriage in 1761; but his first Oxford association was with Pembroke College where he became a commoner in 1738. Mr. Reginald Graham, himself a Pembroke man, has generously provided for a Blackstone lectureship to be administered by the college. This, the first lecture, was delivered by Sir Rupert Cross, Vinerian Professor of English Law, the present incumbent of the chair which was first held by Blackstone from its foundation in 1758 until he left Oxford in 1766.—Ed.]

1928, Bentham's plan was "... to take the second and third introductory sections of the *Commentaries*, those Blackstone had entitled 'Of the Nature of Laws in General' and 'Of the Laws of England,' and by demolishing them to lay the whole work under suspicion." [2] He seems to have lost his enthusiasm for the project as a whole on the publication in 1776 of *A Fragment on Government*. This was an elaborate criticism of the comparatively short passage in the *Commentaries* in which Blackstone departed from the analysis of his definition of municipal law in order to make some remarks about government in general and the British constitution in particular. The remarks were ill considered and I accept Leslie Stephen's verdict that they "represent little more than a bit of rhetoric embodying fragments of inconsistent theories" [3]; but, to quote Bentham's own description of the *Fragment*, it is no more than "a comment on a digression stuffed into the belly of a definition." [4]

A Fragment on Government made Bentham's reputation. I am not prepared to go quite so far as to suggest that the publication of *A Comment on the Commentaries* in his lifetime would have marred it, but I feel bound to say that the two portions of the work which I am about to mention, section XV entitled "Common Law Judicial Decisions" and section IX entitled "Interpretation of Laws" are so bad that I would like to believe that it was Bentham's consciousness of their deficiencies which led to his decision not to publish the "demolition" of the second and third sections of the introduction to the *Commentaries* in its entirety. I would entertain this belief all the more readily because I cannot resist the conclusion that Bentham deliberately misrepresented parts of what Blackstone wrote. I only hesitate to affirm the belief because of the impression, derived from writers who know more about Bentham than I do, that the non-publication of so many of his manuscripts was the result of a change in the subject of his immediate interest rather than a decisive change of mind.

My doubts about Bentham's bona fides in his discussion of judicial decision have their source in the difference between his attitude to the common law and that of Blackstone. For Blackstone the common law was "that admirable system of maxims and unwritten customs" [5]; for Bentham it was "that fictitious composition which has no known person for its author, no known assemblage of words for its substance." [6] Each of them was inclined to be hyperbolical on the subject.

[2] *A Comment on the Commentaries*, p. 12.
[3] *English Utilitarians*, Vol. I, p. 240.
[4] *A Fragment on Government*, edited by Wilfred Harrison (1960), p. 81.
[5] *Commentaries* IV, p. 375, 1813 edition.
[6] *An Introduction to the Principles of Morals and Legislation* (Burns and Hart edition), p. 8.

Blackstone was prone to assert that the common law solution of a problem could never be unreasonable, Bentham was apt to say that the common law did not exist. Bentham was a firm believer in codification and his sallies against the common law were a proper means of furthering his cause; but he knew perfectly well that the common law did exist and he descended to the contemptible when he affected not to understand Blackstone's pellucid statements on the subject.

THE PROBLEM OF THE MANIFESTLY INCORRECT DECISION

Nowhere is this more apparent than in the case of Bentham's comments on Blackstone's account of the manner in which eighteenth century courts dealt with the problem of the manifestly incorrect decision, the decision which is contrary to the precedents or to some general rule or principle derived from them. In modern English law there are rigid rules dealing with this matter; but in the eighteenth century it was simply recognised that a previous decision which was contrary to established law could be disregarded. Such a decision was variously described. Sometimes it was said to be "absurd," on other occasions it was said to be "unreasonable" or "unjust." Blackstone stated the eighteenth century position in language used by the judges of his time when he said: "The doctrine of the law then is this: precedents and rules must be followed, unless flatly absurd or unjust: for though their reason be not obvious at first view, yet we owe such a deference to former times as not to suppose that they acted wholly without consideration." [7] He took as an illustration the fact that it had been determined time out of mind that a brother of the half blood could not succeed as heir to the estate of his half brother with the result that it might escheat to the King or other superior Lord. Blackstone recognised that the rule was hard to justify and continued:

> "And therefore, though a modern judge on account of a supposed hardship upon the half brother, might wish it had been otherwise settled; yet it is not in his power to alter it. But if any court were now to determine that an elder brother of the half blood might enter upon and seize any lands that were purchased by his younger brother, no subsequent judges would scruple to declare that such prior determination was unjust, was unreasonable, and therefore was not law."

In words avidly pounced upon by Bentham, Blackstone had previously said that the rule that precedents must be followed admits of an exception "where the former determination is most evidently contrary to reason"; but no fair minded reader of the relevant passages

[7] *Commentaries* I, p. 88, 1813 edition.

could have any doubt about their meaning. A previous decision must be followed although the judge in a subsequent case thinks that the rule applied in that decision was a bad one, but not if he thinks that the judge in the previous case was mistaken as to the law. This doctrine was destined to become subject to stringent limitations once our system of courts assumed its present hierarchical form, but it persisted well into the nineteenth century. As late as 1869 we find Stuart V.-C. laconically stating that a decision of Lord Chelmsford's was mistaken and that he declined to follow it, although that decision was reached after a reasoned judgment allowing an appeal from Kindersley V.-C.[8]

After telling us that the most usual translation of the phrase "contrary to reason" is perhaps "contrary to what I like," Bentham says: "This then is the rule which our Author has found to give a Judge to whom a preceding determination is proposed, 'Follow it' says he, 'unless it is most evidently contrary to what you like.'"[9] All this and a lot more in the same vein from someone who had read and was about to cite Blackstone's hypothetical example of the decision in favour of the elder half brother which no subsequent judge would scruple to declare "was unjust, was unreasonable, and therefore not law." Bentham's rhetoric on the subject of this example is none too easy to follow but he certainly uses language which would lay him open to the charge of confusing *res judicata* with *ratio decidendi*, and failing to distinguish between the conclusive effect of a subsisting judicial decision on the parties, and its effect on judges in subsequent cases.

> "It is supposed to be determination of a court competent to determine, that being the case, so long as this determination remains uncancelled by a superior court it must be law, if by law here be meant obligatory. During this period let anyone take upon him to molest the elder brother in entering upon the lands and he will find himself exposed to punishment as much as if it were the best law in the world." [10]

Whatever the true implications of Bentham's remarks may be, it is clear that Blackstone was using the word "law" throughout the entire discussion in the sense of a rule binding on a judge in a case subsequent to that alleged to constitute a precedent.

The later part of section XV of *A Comment on the Commentaries* does little credit to Bentham as a jurist and none whatsoever to him as a fair minded controversialist. Yet, it may be urged, the comment was only on an account of the eighteenth century solution to the problem of the manifestly incorrect decision, a comparatively small

[8] *Collins* v. *Lewis* L.R. 8 Eq. 708.
[9] *A Comment on the Commentaries*, p. 190.
[10] *Ibid.* p. 197.

matter when set against the scope of *A Comment on the Commentaries* as a whole. Let us turn therefore to section IX in which Bentham criticises the account of the major rules of statutory interpretation given by Blackstone at the end of the second section of the introduction to the *Commentaries*. Surely statutory interpretation is a broad enough subject, and yet Bentham seems to me to be guilty of the same faults of wilful misreading and inept comment to which I have already drawn attention.

STATUTORY INTERPRETATION

Blackstone tells us that "The fairest and most rational method to interpret the will of the legislator, is by exploring his intentions at the time when the law was made, by signs the most natural and probable. And these signs are either the words, the context, the subject matter, the effects and consequence, or the spirit and reason of the law.[11] He then says something about each of the five signs of the legislator's intentions, and Bentham is at his most captious at every point. He begins with the groundless suggestion that Blackstone committed the *bêtise* of saying that the meaning of the words is to be explored by reference to the words themselves.[12] Cast into modern terms, all that Blackstone said was that the words of the legislation are the primary indication of the intention of the legislator, an observation that has been made by English judges from pre-Blackstonian times to the present day.

Blackstone said, as others have repeatedly said since, that non-technical words are to be understood in their ordinary meaning: "their usual and most known signification, not so much regarding the proprietary of grammar, as their general and popular use." He gave as an illustration what he described as the "law" mentioned by Puffendorf which forbade a layman to *lay hands* on a priest and was "adjudged to extend to him who had hurt a priest with a weapon." Bentham asks what point there is in a rule which bids us to do what we should do without the bidding. This is indicative of the naïve belief manifested throughout so much of his work that it is possible for the laws of a sophisticated society to be formulated in terms of indisputable comprehensibility. The question also fails to allow for the fact that words and phrases have more than one ordinary meaning. Rules of interpretation are only needed in disputable cases, and Blackstone was simply saying that a judge will interpret non-technical words in what he considers to be their most appropriate ordinary meaning having regard to the context. Bentham at once proceeds to apply this rule by considering the possibility that the prohibition on the laying of hands

[11] *Commentaries* I, p. 78, 1813 edition.
[12] *A Comment on the Commentaries*, p. 106.

upon a priest might have related to attempts to apprehend the clergy, in which case a strictly literal interpretation would have been appropriate. If only he had referred to Puffendorf, a course he expressly disdained, and consulted the 1749 edition of Kennett's translation of *De Iure Naturae et Gentium*, he would have found that the author was probably referring to one of Montaigne's essays commenting on the extent to which people will go in insisting on their observance of the letter of certain requirements in order to preserve their honour:

> "And a certain person of my time, being reproached by the king that he had laid hands on a priest, stiffly and positively denied that he had done any such thing: the meaning of which was, he had cudgelled and kicked him." [13]

Blackstone took a broad view of the context of a statute. For him it included the preamble and other laws made by the same legislator "that have some affinity with the subject, or that expressly relate to the same point." Bentham appears to have considered that nothing more than all the enacting words of a statute could constitute its context. The speeches of Lord Simonds and Lord Somervell in *Att.-Gen.* v. *H.R.H. Prince Ernest Augustus of Hanover* [14] are, of course, a complete vindication of Blackstone.

Bentham next affects not to understand what is meant by the subject-matter of a statute, but it is in relation to the "effects and consequence," the fourth of Blackstone's signs of legislative intent, that he achieves a degree of futility which I can but hope is unique among his copious and admirable writings. To quote Blackstone *in extenso*:

> "As to the effects and consequence the rule is, that where words bear either none, or a very absurd signification, if literally understood, we must a little deviate from the received sense of them. Therefore the Bolognan law, mentioned by Puffendorf, which enacted 'that whosoever drew blood in the streets should be punished with the utmost severity,' was held after long debate not to extend to the surgeon, who opened the vein of a person that fell down in the street with a fit." [15]

Blackstone is simply making the point that, when considering whether to adopt a particular interpretation, a court is entitled to have regard to its consequences. Bentham, reading the passage in the pig-headed way in which he reads so much of Blackstone, asks whether reference is being made to the effects and consequence of the law or of the act

---

[13] *The Essays of Michel de Montaigne*, 2nd edition revised by W. Carew Haslitt, Vol. 1, p. 298. The suggestion that this was the passage to which Puffendorf was referring was made by Kennett at p. 535 of the 1749 edition of his translation.

[14] [1957] A.C. 436, 461, and 473.

[15] *Commentaries* I, p. 80, 1813 edition.

which it prohibits! He proceeds to make very heavy weather of the example:

> "Now if the man's blood that the surgeon drew was drawn in quarrel, or in the design to rob or murder, the surgeon should be punished as well as anybody else: because the punishing him would contribute to the end: the suppression of the mischievous practice of drawing blood with such design. But if he had no such design, but meant on the contrary to give the patient relief from his disorder, then he ought not to be punished: because the punishing of him could contribute nothing to any such end: . . ." [16]

Once again Bentham might have modified his statement if only he had referred to Puffendorf. He would have come across the following:

> "At Bologna it was enacted that whosoever drew blood in the streets should be severely punished. Upon this law a barber was indicted for opening a vein in the street, and it had like to go hard with him, because it was added in the statute, that the words should be taken precisely, without any interpretation." [17]

Blackstone was stating what is now frequently spoken of as the "golden rule" of statutory interpretation: when the literal meaning of the words produces an absurd result, it must yield to common sense. Like all good expositors he chose as an example a very strong case on account of the express prohibition on "interpretation."

I am not suggesting that a perusal of Blackstone on statutory interpretation is essential to a comprehension of the modern law, but I do wish to stress the striking modernity of his brief account of the subject. In spite of Bentham's great and often beneficial preoccupation with language, I am unaware of anything of much value said by him on the subject of statutory interpretation.

THE CRIMINAL LIABILITY OF VOLUNTARY INEBRIATES

My final example of a difference between the views of Blackstone and Bentham on which that of the former is to be preferred concerns the criminal liability of voluntary inebriates. This is a subject of great contemporary interest on account of the decision of the House of Lords in *Majewski*.[18] It is also a subject on which the English law has changed since the time of Blackstone and Bentham. I am not concerned with crimes, such as those connected with the use of motor-vehicles, in relation to which the fact that the accused had taken drink is an essential or possible ingredient of the offence. I am talking

---

16 *A Comment on the Commentaries*, p. 115.
17 Kennett's translation, 1749 edition, p. 540.
18 [1976] 2 W.L.R. 623; [1976] 2 All E.R. 142.

about conduct which was criminal in the eighteenth century and remains criminal today. Blackstone quotes Coke to whom he attributes the Aristotelian view that, so far from constituting an excuse or mitigation, drunkenness aggravated the offence; and it was not until after Bentham's death that it came to be recognised that self-induced intoxication is a defence in the case of crimes in which it is necessary for the prosecution to prove that the accused did a particular act with a "specific intent," *i.e.* for a particular purpose, and not merely that he did the act intentionally. The result is that drunkenness of a sufficient degree is now a defence to a charge of murder or wounding with intent, but not to a charge of involuntary manslaughter, unlawful wounding or assault. But the jurisprudential problem with regard to the criminal liability of voluntary inebriates is the same today as it was in the eighteenth and early nineteenth centuries. Provided the drunkenness was of a sufficient degree, why should it not be a defence in the case of every criminal charge on which *mens rea* must be proved?

When considering this problem it will be convenient to have in mind the very exceptional case in which the accused was, at the material time, in an extreme state of intoxication, so drunk that he did not know what he was doing. This condition is more likely to be brought about by drugs, or a combination of drink and drugs, than by drink alone; but there is no doubt that the law is the same whatever may be the cause of the intoxication. Majewski was under the influence of both drink and drugs, but several members of the House of Lords confessed to having no doubt that he in fact knew what he was doing when his limbs struck his victims, although the House was unanimous in its affirmative response to the question of law raised by the appeal whether a defendant may properly be convicted of assault notwithstanding that, by reason of his self-induced intoxication, he did not intend to do the act alleged to constitute the assault. A lesser degree of intoxication will suffice to negative a specific intent, but it will be convenient to ignore such cases so that we can concentrate on a situation concerning which the law is the same today as it was in the time of Blackstone and Bentham.

Blackstone dealt with the matter with commendable brevity in book IV of the *Commentaries*:

> "But the law of England, considering how easy it is to counterfeit this excuse, and how weak an excuse it is, though real, will not suffer any man thus to privilege one crime by another." [19]

To my mind the statement that the law will not suffer any man "to privilege one crime by another" is, when properly understood,

[19] *Commentaries*, IV, p. 23, 1813 edition.

the sole and sufficient moral justification of the present position; in all probability it also reflects the intuitive reaction of the common man to the excuse of voluntary drunkenness. It could, of course, be summarily dismissed, as it was dismissed by Markby,[20] with the observation that drunkenness *per se* is no crime, but this would be pedantic. Blackstone was referring to the argument in *Reniger* v. *Fogossa* in the course of which it was said, apropos of a hypothetical case in which, while ignorant of what he was doing, a drunken person killed a man: "But inasmuch as that ignorance was occasioned by his own act and folly and he might have avoided it he shall not be privileged thereby." [21] There would, of course, be no objection to rephrasing Blackstone's justification of the criminal liability of voluntary inebriates, even when they are automata, so that it should read: "A person cannot claim to be totally exempt from criminal responsibility on the ground that he did not know what he was doing when that ignorance was the outcome of intoxication due to drink or drugs voluntarily consumed by him." [22]

Bentham deals with the excuse of drunkenness in Chapter 13 of the versions of *An Introduction to the Principles of Morals and Legislation* which were published under his auspices in 1789 and 1823. When considering what he had to say we must remember that we do not know what were his ultimate conclusions concerning the manner in which the excuse or extenuation should be treated in practice because his penal code has never been published,[23] but we are left in no doubt concerning his theoretical views. The case is one in which punishment must be inefficacious because, at the material time, "the will cannot be deterred from any act." The accused's condition would "be neither more nor less than a temporary insanity produced by an assignable cause." [24]

Professor Hart has characterised Bentham's argument as a "spectacular *non-sequitur*" [25] for he set out to prove that the punishment of people in the condition of the drunken automaton for breaking the law must be inefficacious, but all that he proves is the quite different proposition that the *threat* of punishment will be ineffective so far as they are concerned because they will be unaware of its existence at the material time. The infliction of punishment on these

20 *Elements of Law* (6th edition), p. 361.

21 (1551) 1 Plowd. 1, 19.

22 For a complete statement of the law allowance would have to be made for crimes in which a specific intent must be proved and the accused's conduct does not fall within the definition of a lesser crime depending on proof of a "basic intent" or recklessness, see *Majewski* [1976] 2 W.L.R. 623 at 656; [1976] 2 All E.R. at p. 172.

23 See Professor Hart's introduction to Burns and Hart's edition of *An Introduction to the Principles of Morals and Legislation*.

24 *An Introduction to the Principles of Morals and Legislation* (Burns and Hart edition), p. 161.

25 *Punishment and Responsibility*, p. 19.

people might be most effective so far as potential offenders are concerned on the ordinary utilitarian principle of general deterrence for the example of punishment in such cases might be taken as an impressive sign of the severity of the law. When sober, the automata themselves might come to appreciate the need for caution about taking drink or drugs. Arguments based on the need for preserving public respect for the law can easily be overdone, but it is difficult to believe that such respect would not be diminished if, for instance, someone who had gone on an LSD trip with a friend were to escape altogether from criminal liability for serious personal injuries inflicted on him in the course of the trip.[26]

It is, of course, possible for a penal system to be counter-productive owing to its excessive severity, and considerations of this nature lie at the root of some further remarks by Bentham on the defence of drunkenness which are taken from Dumont's *Traités de legislation.*[27] Bentham had no objection to the infliction of punishment on a voluntary inebriate when the drink was taken " in order to embolden the individual in the commission of the crime," or " where he knows by experience that wine renders him dangerous," but, where these considerations do not apply, he rejects Blackstone's justification of the law's refusal to recognise voluntary drunkenness as a defence in the following words: " The English law does not admit intoxication as a ground of excuse; this would be, it is said, to excuse one crime by another. This morality appears hard and unthinking and it is derived from the principle of asceticism." These remarks would meet with the approval of a number of academic lawyers who object to the rejection of the defence of drunkenness of a sufficient degree to negative intention or recklessness in cases in which the existence of those mental elements has to be established by the prosecution. Such rejection, they contend, infringes the sacrosanct principle embodied in the maxim *actus non facit reum nisi mens sit rea.*

In reply to Bentham and the academics I would ask why it is " hard and unthinking " to refuse to allow people to exempt themselves from criminal responsibility for harm done by their bodies by incapacitating their minds from controlling them. Why should the requirement that intention or recklessness must be proved in order to establish liability for an assault not be subject to what appears to be the wholly reasonable retributive principle that it is unjust to those who remain sober to allow those who become drunk to allege that they were unaware of consequences of their bodily movements of which all sober people would have been aware? This is what

26 *Cf. Lipman* [1970] 1 Q.B. 152.
27 Bowring's *Collected Works of Jeremy Bentham*, Vol. I, p. 79.

Blackstone meant when he said that the law would not suffer any man "to privilege one crime by another."

Bentham's statement that the morality underlying Blackstone's doctrine derives from asceticism was presumably based on the idea that to punish people for harm done while they are drunk, especially when they are so drunk as not to know what they are doing, is, in effect, to punish them for getting drunk; but this point can be met on the best utilitarian principles. Punishment is an evil and the less of it the better. But the evil of inflicting punishment is justified if the harm which is thus avoided is greater than that caused by the punishment. It may be asceticism to blame people for simply getting drunk, but it is sound utilitarianism to seek to prevent people from doing certain kinds of harm while they are drunk. In so far as this object can be achieved by punishment, it is achieved most economically by singling out for punishment those who commit the kind of harm which the law seeks to prevent while they are drunk. To quote the late Professor Plamenatz:

> "On most occasions when men get drunk they do little harm, or they do the kind of harm which we do not seek to prevent by official blame and punishment. We can reduce the harm men do when they are drunk more effectively by punishing them for doing it than by punishing them for getting drunk. . . ."[28]

The adoption of this course would be immoral but for the retributive justification provided by Blackstone. Even if a time should come when we permit the acquittal of those charged with crimes involving proof of recklessness on the ground that they were too drunk to appreciate the relevant risk, and create a separate offence of causing certain types of harm while drunk,[29] recourse for a moral justification of such provision will still have to be had to Blackstone's principle that the law will not suffer any man "to privilege one crime by another."

CONCLUSION

If we grant that Bentham scored a goal with *A Fragment on Government*, the score in my imaginary game between Blackstone and Bentham is 3 to 1 in favour of the former, but it would be a mistake to pay much attention to the score on account of the prejudice of the referee. I have no doubt that any competent lawyer or moralist

28 *Philosophy, Politics and Society*, a collection edited by Peter Lazlett and W. G. Runciman (3rd series), Vol. 1 p. 82–3.

29 See the Report of the Butler Committee on mentally abnormal offenders, Chap. 18, s. 4. It is to be hoped that proposals of this nature will receive more thought than has been devoted to them to date before they are adopted. Why should the suggestion be confined to dangerous offences? If there is to be a separate offence of causing bodily harm while drunk, why not have a separate offence of causing bodily harm in a state of automatism caused by "blind rage"?

could avenge Bentham's defeat were he minded to do so. I wish to conclude with the suggestion that Blackstone's three goals reflect a significant difference between the two men. Bentham was *par excellence* a man dominated by one idea and this was the secret of his success as an influential thinker.[30] From the point of view of moral philosophy the dominating idea was, of course, the fundamental axiom of utilitarianism that the greatest happiness of the greatest number is the measure of right and wrong. It seems to me, however, that a tendency to monolithic thought was occasionally Bentham's undoing at a lower level. Examples are provided by the three matters I have been discussing. The confusion between *res judicata* and *ratio decidendi* in his attack upon Blackstone's views concerning the manifestly incorrect decision was due to his rigorous adherence to the idea that the law is the will of the judge,[31] whether it relates to the order in the particular case or the general rule upon which that order was based. According to Bentham the one criterion of statutory interpretation was the purpose of the legislator, hence his rather silly endeavours to ridicule Blackstone's attempts to make allowance for other considerations. Bentham rightly made the point that the will of the voluntary inebriate cannot be deterred from any act at the moment when the alleged crime is committed, but, rather uncharacteristically, he proceeded to ignore all other relevant utilitarian considerations. Perhaps it is not too fanciful to suggest that, although he was intellectually the inferior of the two men, Blackstone avoided mistakes of this nature because he did not know what it was to be dominated by one philosophical idea. It is my belief that this negative characteristic is essential for anyone who is to be the great expositor of the common law which Blackstone was and Bentham was not.

RUPERT CROSS.

[30] Leslie Stephen, *English Utilitarians*, Vol. I, p. 235.
[31] As a subordinate of the sovereign legislator.

[17]

Two Modes of Legal Thought

George P. Fletcher*

We should begin with a confession of ignorance. We have no jurisprudence of legal scholarship. Scholars expatiate at length on the work of other actors in the legal culture—legislators, judges, prosecutors, and even practicing lawyers. Yet we reflect little about what we are doing when we write about the law. We have a journal about the craft of teaching,[1] but none about the craft of scholarship.

In view of our ignorance, we should pay particular heed to our point of departure. I start with the observation that legal scholarship expresses itself in a variety of verbal forms. Descriptive propositions about the law, normative claims about what the law ought to be, and exhortations to decisionmakers to change the law are but examples of the variety of forms that appear in scholarly writing about the law. My initial task in this article is to work out some important distinctions among these verbal forms. Those distinctions generate a framework that I then use to make two more adventurous claims. I claim first that we can usefully distinguish between two modes of legal thought, which I shall call "committed argument" and "detached observation"; and further, that whether we engage exclusively in one form of legal scholarship or another depends on our implicit assumptions about the nature of law. With these bolder theses defended, I then analyze how scholars can and do make persuasive claims in the mode of committed argument.

I. Claims That Scholars Make

To develop a taxonomy of legal claims, I borrow from the conventional distinctions used in classifying propositions in moral discourse. Academic writings about ethics conventionally distinguish between

* Professor of Law, University of California, Los Angeles.

My thanks to the UCLA Tuesday Night Circle for devoting an evening to the discussion of an earlier draft of this paper. Robert Gerstein, Stephen Munzer, Herbert Munzer, Herbert Morris, Ann McConnell, Drew Cornell, and Guyora Binder helped catch some of my mistakes.

1. The Association of American Law Schools publishes the *Journal of Legal Education*.

Two Modes

normative ethics and meta-ethics.[2] The former consists of propositions asserting that particular conduct is right or wrong, good or bad. The latter consists of analytic and structural propositions about normative claims made by others. In the history of ethics, normative (first-order) claims dominated the field. With the writing of Nowell-Smith[3] and Hare,[4] meta-ethics came into vogue in the middle decades of this century. In the last decade, meta-ethical analysis has taken new turns,[5] and philosophical interest has returned to the traditional task of asserting and defending conceptions of the right and the good.[6]

Meta-ethical claims differ from claims about conventional morality. Though both express views on what others say, their modes of support diverge. Meta-ethical claims focus on the concepts and the language used in ethical discourse. A few paradigmatic examples provide all the data necessary for the meta-ethical analysis. By contrast, claims about conventional morality take the form of descriptive hypotheses. They require the mustering of data. Extrapolation from a few examples can hardly prove claims about the content of conventional moral views.

The taxonomy thus distinguishes three types of statement. *First-order* statements are substantive claims about what is right or wrong, good or bad. *Meta-ethical* statements are propositions about the logical nature of moral discourse—for example, the view that moral statements are mere expressions of personal feeling. *Descriptive* statements are generalizations about the moral views of a particular culture.

To bring these distinctions to bear on legal discourse, we should first address the question: what is a first-order legal statement? Consider the following assertions: "The death penalty is constitutional (or unconstitutional)." "Racial discrimination is tortious (or nontortious)." "Your conduct under these facts renders you liable for damages." These statements follow the pattern of first-order moral statements, such as "lying is wrong" and "the death penalty violates

2. For an introduction to these matters, see Nielsen, *Problems of Ethics*, in 3 THE ENCYCLOPEDIA OF PHILOSOPHY 117 (1967), and J. MACKIE, ETHICS 19-20 (1977).

3. P. NOWELL-SMITH, ETHICS (1957).

4. R. HARE, FREEDOM AND REASON (1963); R. HARE, THE LANGUAGE OF MORALS (1952).

5. The significant works in this movement include R. DWORKIN, TAKING RIGHTS SERIOUSLY (1977), C. FRIED, RIGHT AND WRONG (1978), R. NOZICK, ANARCHY, STATE, AND UTOPIA (1974), and J. RAWLS, A THEORY OF JUSTICE (1971). The revival of normative ethics dovetails with the rejection of utilitarianism and the cultivation of the deontological moral theories. For some comments on this shift in philosophical orientation, see Barry, *And Who Is My Neighbor?* (Book Review), 88 YALE L.J. 629 (1979) (review of Fried's *Right and Wrong*).

6. *See* Wiggins, *Truth, Invention and the Meaning of Life*, 62 PROC. BRIT. ACAD. 331 (1976).

human dignity"; they might therefore seem to be first-order legal statements. Yet there is an ambiguity in both the legal and moral statements that we should bring to the surface.

Let us focus on two instances of the statement, "The death penalty is X": in one case, X stands for a moral predicate, such as "wrong," and in the other, X stands for a legal predicate, such as "unconstitutional." Both the moral and legal versions of the statement, "The death penalty is X," lend themselves to two interpretations. Each statement could be a first-order claim, namely, a substantive assertion that the death penalty is wrong or unconstitutional. Alternatively, it could be a description of the way other people regard the death penalty. The latter interpretation of a constitutional statement would be appropriate if we were reporting the official view of those entrusted with expounding the Constitution. That is, if the Supreme Court had so held, a commentator might report the decision by saying, "The death penalty is unconstitutional," and thereby intend merely to describe a holding of the Supreme Court. A descriptive claim of unconstitutionality would be analogous, then, to a descriptive claim that capital punishment is wrong according to the prevailing sentiments of the society. Let us diagram this analogy thus:

Statement	Support
1. The death penalty is wrong.	A survey of what other people think about the death penalty.
2. The death penalty is unconstitutional.	An authoritative holding that the death penalty is unconstitutional.

Consider now what it would mean for the statement, "The death penalty is unconstitutional," to be a first-order legal proposition. If the statement appeared in a Supreme Court opinion holding the death penalty unconstitutional, we would be inclined to identify the statement as a first-order statement about the Constitution. It would not be a descriptive proposition about the language of the Constitution; nor would it plausibly lend itself to characterization as an interpretation of specific language, such as that of the Eighth Amendment. Yet we might have difficulty perceiving the structural analogy between a legal conclusion in a Supreme Court opinion and a moral conclusion reached in everyday discourse.

Two Modes

The factor of authority distinguishes legal from moral discourse. We are all equally situated to make moral claims about the right and the good. Yet the Supreme Court seems to be in a special position to make statements about the Constitution. A statement in a Supreme Court opinion about the constitutionality of the death penalty enjoys a force that the same words in a law review article would not have. Why should this be so?

To answer this question, we must consider the impact of authority on the nature of legal discourse. We could think of the Supreme Court's statement as either a *declaration* of unconstitutionality or an *assertion* of unconstitutionality. The difference is important. Declarations are acts that have force by virtue of the authority of the declarant. They might be politic or impolitic, useful or deleterious, but they are not true or false.[7] Thus, if the Supreme Court declares the meaning of the Constitution, we might question the political wisdom of the decision, but one could hardly say that the Court's statement was true or false. The Court cannot declare what the Constitution means and at the same time make a mistake about the true meaning of the Constitution.

Assertions are different. An assertion or a claim about the meaning of the Constitution presupposes that the claim could be wrong, though in making the assertion, of course, we seek to get the matter right. Thus, if the Court's conclusion of unconstitutionality is not a declaration, but an assertion, the criteria of truth and falsity come into play.

How then do we decide whether the Court's holding is a declaration or an assertion? To answer that question we must examine the bearing of meta-theories on the logical nature of both moral and legal discourse.

II. Meta-Theories of Legal Statements

As noted earlier, the meta-ethical literature seeks to clarify the logical nature of moral statements.[8] Some philosophers hold that moral statements are but the expression of personal preference.[9] Others argue, more convincingly, that moral claims have a truth value (that is, they are either true or false) and thus are distinguishable from

7. This logical point about "declarations" applies with equal force to all performatives. *See* J. Austin, *Performative Utterances*, in Philosophical Papers 233, 237 (3d ed. J. Urmson & G. Warnock 1979).

8. *See* p. 971 *supra*.

9. For an unembarrassed statement of this position, see C. Stevenson, Facts and Values 10-31 (1963).

reports of personal feelings.[10] Let us call those two theories the "emotivist" and the "assertion" theories of moral discourse. Each has an analogue in meta-theories about legal statements made by the courts. An emotivist theory of constitutional argument holds that if a judge says that the Constitution prohibits capital punishment, he or she is merely expressing a personal bias on the issue. Legal realism, as exemplified by the thought of Jerome Frank, adheres to this view, or to something close to it.[11] The legal version of the assertion theory, by contrast, holds that constitutional statements are claims that have a truth value. Judges can be right or wrong in claiming that the Constitution prohibits the death penalty.

These comparisons highlight an important difference between logical meta-theories of moral discourse and of legal discourse. Although we speak of courts and legislatures "declaring the law," we do not regard moral truth as something that can be declared. Declaring implies that the declarant cannot make a mistake. If the referee declares the runner out, the runner is out: it matters not whether the referee has made a bad call. If a court holds or declares a contract void, the contract is void: it matters not whether the judge has made a bad decision. Declarations are acts as well as statements: J.L. Austin dubbed them "performatives."[12] Their impact on the world derives from the authority of the declarant.

There are some matters about which no one has the authority to make declarations. No one has the authority to declare what is historically true, morally right, beautiful, or even efficient. These are matters that admit only of evidence and reasoned debate. They cannot be resolved by declaration.

The law is different. We assume that the law can be declared—that is, enacted or made. This is, at least, an acceptable meta-theory of legal statements. That moral truth cannot be declared in the same way marks an important difference between the meta-theories of legal statements and those of moral statements. In other respects, they run parallel. Both are sometimes characterized as purely emotive, subjective expressions of feeling. Both are sometimes treated as assertions

10. *See, e.g.*, P. Foot, *Moral Beliefs*, in Virtues and Vices and Other Essays in Moral Philosophy 110 (1978); Urmson, *On Grading*, in Logic and Language (Second Series) 159 (A. Flew ed. 1961).

11. *See* J. Frank, Law and the Modern Mind 32-33 (1930) (legal language as rationalization); *id.* at 119 (psychological factors bearing on judging).

12. J. Austin, *supra* note 7, at 233-52.

of that which might be true or false. The following matrix summarizes these possibilities:

	The statement is:		
	purely emotive	an assertion	a declaration
moral statements	yes	yes	no
legal statements	yes	yes	yes

This scheme enables us to state the precise difference between positivist and nonpositivist theories of law. Legal positivism, as developed in the work of Hobbes,[13] Bentham,[14] Austin,[15] Hart,[16] and Raz,[17] is a meta-theory about the statements that qualify as legally effective. The various nonpositivist or transcendent theories of law also lend themselves to characterization as meta-theories about legal discourse. Let us see why this admittedly novel approach to positivism and its alternatives proves to be more illuminating than the conventional approach to the subject.

Two things recur in the Anglo-American literature on legal positivism. Many legal scholars, including Hart,[18] Fuller,[19] and Richards,[20] emphasize the relationship between law and morality in defining the conflict between positivism and its alternatives. These scholars write that what characterizes positivists is their belief that law and morality are distinct; nonpositivists believe that there is some necessary connection between the status of a rule of law and its intrinsic moral value.[21] Other scholars, particularly Dworkin[22] and Raz,[23] emphasize

13. *See* T. HOBBES, LEVIATHAN ch. 26, at 137 (London 1651) (defining "civil law" as the command of the sovereign); pp. 982-83 *infra* (Hobbes on the "common law").

14. J. BENTHAM, AN INTRODUCTION TO THE PRINCIPLES OF MORALS AND LEGISLATION 301-11 (J. Burns & H.L.A. Hart eds. 1970) (1st ed. London 1789).

15. J. AUSTIN, *The Province of Jurisprudence Determined*, in 1 LECTURES ON JURISPRUDENCE 1, 1-25 (London 1861) (1st ed. London 1832).

16. H.L.A. HART, THE CONCEPT OF LAW (1961).

17. J. RAZ, THE CONCEPT OF A LEGAL SYSTEM (2d ed. 1980).

18. Hart, *Positivism and the Separation of Law and Morals*, 71 HARV. L. REV. 593, 601 n.25 (1958) (listing five traits of legal positivism, including separation of law and morals).

19. Fuller, *Positivism and Fidelity to Law—A Reply to Professor Hart*, 71 HARV. L. REV. 630, 631-32 (1958).

20. D. RICHARDS, THE MORAL CRITICISM OF LAW 22-26 (1977) (treating Hart-Fuller exchange as guide to current state of debate about positivism).

21. *See* Fuller, *supra* note 19, at 655-66 (whether statute merits description as "law" and whether it is binding on judges should be one question).

22. *See* R. DWORKIN, *supra* note 5, at 17 (positivist conception of law stresses "pedigree" of rules).

23. *See* J. RAZ, THE AUTHORITY OF LAW 37, 39-45 (1979) (positivism takes law to be "a matter of social fact").

a second aspect of positivism. They stress the problem of determining whether a particular rule is or is not a valid rule of the legal system. From this latter perspective, the positivist agenda requires a test for definitively determining whether a particular rule does or does not have force in the legal system.[24] The contrasting meta-theory of law acknowledges that there may be principles and policies that hover indecisively at the borders of the system, so that it may not always be possible to determine precisely which rules, principles, and policies belong to the system and which do not.[25]

The first perspective on the problem—the separation of law and morals—derives logically from the latter positivist concern that the asserted existence of a rule of law be subject to formal verification.[26] The assumption of positivist thinkers seems to be that if morality and law were interwoven, there would be no way to devise procedures to determine the legal status of morally controversial rules. That is, if morally bad rules were not "law," then we could not readily determine what was law and what was not. Every rule might be subject to moral controversy. Because we could not resolve the moral disputes, we could not determine objectively which rules had legal force. This is precisely the kind of indeterminacy in the concept of law that positivists seek to avoid.[27]

Positivists have devised a variety of tests for verifying whether a given rule is valid in the system. The earlier emphasis on the "command of the sovereign"[28] has given way to the current view that the

24. This methodological assumption comes through clearly in Kelsen's "pure theory of law." *See* H. Kelsen, Die Reine Rechtslehre (2d ed. 1961). The purity of the theory derives from its emulating the methods of logic and of the natural sciences. *See* K. Larenz, Methodenlehre der Rechtswissenschaft 78-79 (4th ed. 1979) (Kelsen's positivist theory of law can only be understood by "taking the positive conception of science as the point of departure"). The positivist conception of science, like the pure theory of law, stands squarely against unverifiable, metaphysical arguments. *See* H. Kelsen, *supra*, at 80 (similarity exists between natural science and pure theory of law). In *The Concept of Law*, H.L.A. Hart minimizes this aspect of Kelsen's positivism. By contrast, Joseph Raz draws our attention to it. *See* J. Raz, *supra* note 23, at 130-32 (discussing Kelsen's methodology).

25. This point is at the heart of Dworkin's strategy for showing that neither Hart's rule of recognition nor any other "master rule" can provide a formal test determining the content of a particular legal system. *See* R. Dworkin, *supra* note 5, at 39-41.

26. The term "formal verification" is designed to elicit the methodological connection between legal and logical positivism. On the logical positivists' "verifiability theory of meaning," see H. Reichenbach, The Rise of Scientific Philosophy 256-57 (1951). Verification in legal positivism is carried out through the use of formal tests for determining legal validity. *See* p. 977 *infra*.

27. *See* H. Kelsen, *supra* note 24, at 68-69 (injection of moral criteria into notion of validity would render rules valid with regard to some moral systems, invalid with regard to others).

28. *See, e.g.*, J. Austin, *supra* note 15, at 169-72; J. Bentham, *supra* note 14, at 301-02; T. Hobbes, *supra* note 13, ch. 26, at 137.

Two Modes

legal system consists of rules, and perhaps of policies and other standards, whose status is determined by purely formal criteria[29]—by their "pedigree," as Dworkin puts it.[30] These formal criteria identify the agencies that can declare that particular rules or other standards are the law.

For present purposes, it is not important whether the rules in a particular legal system authorize only the legislature to enact the law, or whether in light of constitutional practice, the rules also identify courts as law-declaring agencies. The important point for the positivist thesis is that every legal system has a finite set of rules that determines who can make, enact, or declare the law. It follows that we can properly treat positivism as a meta-theory about who can make legally effective, first-order statements.

The positivist meta-theory also holds that these first-order statements are by their nature declarations rather than assertions about what the law is. This second tenet of positivism, like the first, follows from the methodological assumption that the asserted existence of the legal status of any legal rule be subject to verification:[31] a proposition's status as law cannot be indeterminate. If there are irresolvable disputes about what the law is, the positivist program collapses. To avoid this breakdown, the positivist must insist that the authorized agencies do not assert what the law is; they enact or declare the law.

Unlike positivism, transcendent meta-theories of legal discourse require, at least, that judicial statements of the law be treated not as declarations but as assertions of what the law is. Characterizing legal statements as assertions implies that there is some law about which the court might be mistaken. Yet the body of law at issue is not written. It is neither enacted by the legislature nor declared by the courts. It consists of principles and policies that become the objects of assertions and debate. That judicial holdings are assertions of the law constitutes the basic tenet of transcendent theories of law. These theories, expressed in various ways by Coke,[32] Blackstone,[33] Fuller,[34]

29. H.L.A. Hart, *supra* note 16, at 97-107; H. Kelsen, *supra* note 24, at 9-11.
30. *See* R. Dworkin, *supra* note 5, at 17.
31. *See* notes 24 & 26 *supra*.
32. *See* Dr. Bonham's Case, 77 Eng. Rep. 638, 652 (C.P. 1610) (Coke, C.J.) (statute void as violation of "common right and reason"). *See also* pp. 982-83 *infra* (discussion of Hobbes's critique of Coke).
33. 1 W. Blackstone, Commentaries *71 (in rendering a decision, "the judge may *mistake* the law"; further, "decisions of courts of justice are the evidence of what is common law" (emphasis in original)).
34. Fuller, *supra* note 19, at 661-69.

and Dworkin,[35] are properly called transcendent for they all presuppose a body of law that transcends the positive (enacted) legal sources.

Against the background of these distinctions, we can restate Dworkin's important thesis about the relevance of legal principles in a way that does not invite the misreading that his work typically incurs, and perhaps encourages. The distinction between rules and principles is not a matter of relative specificity, rules being precise and principles relatively imprecise. Although some of Dworkin's language infelicitously suggests this interpretation,[36] his better point lies elsewhere. The significant characteristic of principles is that they come to bear on a legal decision only as a result of a judge's asserting that the principle exists and that it has a particular weight in the circumstances of the case.[37] Principles and their weights in particular contexts are not "declared." No authoritative body informs judges how much weight they should accord the principle, say, that we should never punish an innocent person. This principle might call for one measure of weight in defining the scope of insanity—an issue that bears on guilt and innocence.[38] Yet the same aversion to punishing the innocent might call for a different weight in allocating the burden of persuasion on various other issues that bear on a defendant's guilt or innocence.[39] Knowing the language of the principle—"it is unjust to punish an innocent person"—does not tell us how much weight to accord it in particular situations.

Rules are different, Dworkin argues, because they are either "valid" or "invalid."[40] We are compelled either to accept the "answer [a rule] supplies"[41] or to ignore the rule altogether. The force of a rule is not a matter of weight or degree; it is an "all or nothing" matter.[42] Dworkin's point here is not that rules mechanically entail results in particular cases, but rather that the "logical"[43] status of the rule is categorical. Either it binds us or it does not. The rule might be binding, but nonetheless vague. The "answer" it supplies might not in fact resolve the case at hand, but it would nonetheless be an "answer" in this sense.[44]

35. R. DWORKIN, *supra* note 5, at 22-31.
36. *E.g.*, *id.* at 35 ("Only rules dictate results, come what may.")
37. *Id.* at 26-27 (part of "concept of a principle . . . [is] that it makes sense to ask how important or how weighty it is").
38. *See* G. FLETCHER, RETHINKING CRIMINAL LAW 835-46 (1978).
39. *Id.* at 539-41 (insanity); *id.* at 546-48 (lesser evils in German euthanasia case).
40. R. DWORKIN, *supra* note 5, at 24.
41. *Id.*
42. *Id.*
43. *Id.* (distinction between rules and principles is "logical").
44. *But cf. id.* at 35 ("Only rules dictate results, come what may.") Dworkin's argument

Two Modes

The notion of first-order legal statements helps us understand Dworkin's point in distinguishing rules from principles. Rules are valid because they are declared (by the legislature or the courts) to be valid. In stating the rules applicable to the case at hand, a judge need make no assertions about higher bodies of law. She merely states the "valid" or "authoritative" rule; in so doing, she makes a descriptive statement about some other agency's effective first-order declaration of the rule. In contrast, the judge's invocation of principles entails more than a description of determinable and authoritative sources. She must fathom the weight of the principle in the particular case. This process of gauging the force of the principle requires a first-order legal statement in the form of an assertion of what the law is. Thus, Dworkin's jurisprudence should be seen as a meta-theory of judicial discourse. If judges state and apply rules as well as bring to bear principles, then their discourse consists of descriptive statements about the rules as well as first-order assertions about the principles.

First-order statements about principles represent assertions about the law, yet the "law" in this sense transcends both enacted rules and rules accepted as customary law. We lack appropriate words in English to distinguish between law that is enacted or declared (that is, statutes and cases), on the one hand, and the body of law that includes unenacted principles, on the other. We are linguistically embarrassed in writing both about the Constitution and generally about the law. As a result, we operate with at least two senses of the words "Constitution" and "law." In one sense, the Constitution is the set of ordered words written in 1787 and formally amended twenty-six times. In another sense, the "Constitution" is that body of supreme law that includes, for example, principles of substantive due process.[45] Similarly, "law" is used sometimes to refer just to enacted legal sources and in other contexts to include the unwritten principles that judges assess and expound in reaching decisions. Our language does not capture the distinction between these two senses of law. Because the distinction is critical to the overall argument of this paper, however, it is worth examining the more refined treatment that the distinction has received in civilian legal systems.

unfortunately interweaves two issues of "determinability." The first is the problem that concerns positivists seeking to develop formal approaches to the status of legal rules. *See* note 24 *supra*. The other is the problem of determining the outcome of particular cases. Dworkin's position is that principles are not determined in the first sense, R. DWORKIN, *supra* note 5, at 26-27, but that "a set of principles *can* dictate a result," *id.* at 35 (emphasis in original).

45. *See* Perry, *Abortion, the Public Morals, and the Police Power: The Ethical Function of Substantive Due Process*, 23 U.C.L.A. L. REV. 689, 713 (1976) (Constitution in this higher sense is the "organic" constitution).

The Yale Law Journal Vol. 90: 970, 1981

III. Two Concepts of Law

All of the prominent Continental European languages employ two words for law. One refers exclusively to enacted law and other rules that lend themselves to definitive specification: *Gesetz, loi, ley, zakon, törvény*. Another refers to law in the broader sense that includes unenacted principles: *Recht, droit, derecho, prava, jog*. Each of these dimensions of law requires elaboration.

Taking the German terms as exemplary, we should first note the diversity of contexts in which we would translate "law" as *Gesetz*. Both statutory law and scientific laws are *Gesetze* (in the plural). Significantly, Kant used the term *Gesetz* in defining the categorical imperative: the actor must be able to will the maxim of his action to be a universal *Gesetz*.[46] It is not surprising, then, that German theorists also regard customary laws as *Gesetze*.[47] These are all instances of laws that lend themselves to validation or refutation. We can know precisely what the statutes say, which scientific laws are adequately supported by the data, what the form of the universalized maxim would be, and which customs are treated as binding customary law. Positivists have no trouble recognizing law as *Gesetz*. Indeed, this form of law is the positivist paradigm.

The concept of *Recht* is more elusive. We have no counterpart in contemporary English. The term is used in the following ways. First, the entire law of a culture is its *Recht*. Thus one says: *deutsches Recht, le droit français*. Second, particular bodies of law are identified as dimensions of *Recht*: for example, *Strafrecht* (criminal law), *Verfassungsrecht* (constitutional law). The codes that generate these bodies of law are always described as *Gesetze*, but the law generated by the code is a form of *Recht*. Third, the term "law" is translated as *Recht* in jurisprudential phrases such as "sources of law"[48] and "the rule of law."[49] Fourth, philosophical work on the law is always about the concept of *Recht*. For example, Kant worked out his legal theory in

46. I. KANT, GRUNDLEGUNG ZUR METAPHYSIK DER SITTEN 421 (1785); I. KANT, FOUNDATIONS OF THE METAPHYSICS OF MORALS 44 (L. Beck trans. 1969).

47. *See, e.g.*, 4 W. FIKENTSCHER, METHODEN DES RECHTS 328 (1977).

48. *Rechtsquelle* in German. The English term might mislead one to think that the study of these "sources" is a sociological inquiry rather than one about the factors that properly influence judgments of law. *See* H.L.A. HART, *supra* note 16, at 246-47.

49. The closest term in German is *Rechtsstaat*, which suggests not only the governance of rules but a commitment to the substantive values of *Recht*. *See, e.g.*, M. MARX, ZUR DEFINITION DES BEGRIFFS "RECHTSGUT" 14-16 (1972); G. RADBRUCH, RECHTSPHILOSOPHIE 284-90 (6th ed. E. Wolf 1963).

the *Rechtslehre*.[50] Hart's *The Concept of Law* is translated as a work about the concept of *Recht*.[51] In none of these four contexts would we use any word in English but "law."

In virtually all Western languages, the same word *Recht* refers both to law in the broader sense and to individual rights. Thus, German theorists distinguish between objective *Recht* and subjective *Rechte* (in the plural).[52] This suggests that an appropriate translation for *Recht* would be "Right," for at least in the context of personal rights, our idiom corresponds with the continental pattern. The word "Right" will serve us well as the English equivalent of *Recht*. Yet we should not forget that in most situations the term *Recht* is translated literally as "law."

The Right encompasses not only written and customary *Gesetze*, but the unwritten principles and policies that come to the fore only as a result of assessment, judgment, and judicial assertion. The Right includes personal rights, those based on statute and those asserted as a matter of principle. Significantly, however, the Right also includes duties.[53] For example, the German legal duty to rescue a person in distress[54] is imposed as a matter of Right.

The concept of Right intersects the notions of justice and morality, but is distinguishable from both. Radbruch defines the Right as that dimension of law, realized in a particular cultural context, "whose meaning consists in the pursuit of justice."[55] This account by Radbruch helps us understand the peculiar way in which the concept of Right mediates between the particularities of the legal culture and the universal idea of justice. The Right is crystallized in the work of legislatures and courts. Yet, as Radbruch argues, the "sense" of this work consists in the pursuit of justice.

The critical distinction between the two dimensions of law lies in their relative knowability. *Gesetze* are fully knowable. They are finite and, in this sense, fully determinable. They conceal no mysteries. The

50. The *Rechtslehre* appears as the first half (first volume) of I. KANT, DIE METAPHYSIK DER SITTEN (Königsberg 1797). For an approximate translation, see I. KANT, THE METAPHYSICAL ELEMENTS OF JUSTICE (J. Ladd trans. 1965), which infelicitously renders *Recht* as "justice."

51. H.L.A. HART, DER BEGRIFF DES RECHTS (A. von Bayer trans. 1973).

52. 1 ENNECCERUS-NIPPERDEY, ALLGEMEINER TEIL DES BÜRGERLICHEN RECHTS 428-29 (15th ed. 1959).

53. *See* J. FINNIS, NATURAL LAW AND NATURAL RIGHTS 209 (1980) (perceptively elucidating the role of duties in the concept of *jura*, the Roman equivalent to the concept of Right).

54. STRAFGESETZBUCH [STGB] § 13 (W. Ger.).

55. G. RADBRUCH, *supra* note 49, at 127 ("*Recht* [*ist*]/*die Wirklichkeit, die den Sinn hat, der Gerechtigkeit zu dienen*").

Right, on the other hand, is open-ended, transcendent, undetermined. It can never be fully known. We can assert the truth about the Right, and even make a persuasive case for our position. A consensus might emerge for a particular conception of Right. But the consensus can be at most tentative. A better vision of the Right always remains possible.[56]

The distinction between *Gesetz* and *Recht* corresponds to several distinctions we have already discussed. As *Gesetze*, statutes and case holdings are *declared*. The Right cannot be *declared*, but only assayed, pondered, and asserted. In Dworkin's terminology, rules that apply in "all or nothing" fashion[57] are *Gesetze*, whereas principles are a matter of Right. That principles have "weight" and that judges must gauge the force of these principles in every case are characteristics of the Right. No one can declare the principles' existence and determine the precise weight they should carry.

Because we have no clear concept of Right in English, the single word "law" does double duty. Until the time of Blackstone and after, the "common law" clearly had the connotation of law in the sense of Right.[58] At least since the seventeenth century, however, positivist philosophers have sought to equate the word "law" with enacted law (*Gesetze*). The conflict comes to the surface in Thomas Hobbes's masterful *A Dialogue Between a Philosopher and a Student of the Common Laws of England.*[59] The dialogue provided Hobbes with an opportunity to attack the views of the leading legal theorist of the seventeenth century, Sir Edward Coke. The debate centers on the meaning of the word "law."

Hobbes's student of the common law, who appears to be a stand-in for Coke,[60] argues that our understanding of the law is based on an "artificial perfection of Reason gotten by long Study, Observation and Experience."[61] Thus, "the Law of *England* . . . hath been fined and refined by an infinite number of Grave and Learned Men."[62] To this the philosopher, speaking for Hobbes, responds: "It is not Wisdom, but Authority that makes a Law . . . . [N]one can make a

56. That we cannot determine the Right does not imply that there is no "right" answer; that is, no truth in our claims of Right. On the difficulties of denying the reality of the Right, see Dworkin, *No Right Answer?* 53 N.Y.U. L. Rev. 1 (1978).

57. *See* R. Dworkin, *supra* note 5, at 24.

58. *See* notes 32 & 33 *supra*.

59. T. Hobbes, A Dialogue Between a Philosopher and a Student of the Common Laws of England (J. Cropsey ed. 1971) (1st ed. London 1681).

60. *Id.* at 10-11 (introduction by J. Cropsey).

61. *Id.* at 55.

62. *Id.*

Two Modes

Law but he that hath the Legislative Power."[63] The lawyer concludes that it is not the profession of grave and learned lawyers that has the power to legislate, but solely the sovereign, the King in Parliament, in which "not one of twenty was a Learned Lawyer."[64] The lawyer responds by suggesting that the philosopher has missed the point: "You speak of the Statu[t]e Law, and I speak of the Common Law."[65] The philosopher retorts: "I speak generally of Law."[66]

In this brief exchange we find encapsulated the moves that have recurred in the jurisprudential discussions of the last three hundred years. The lawyer expresses the view that the common law should be understood as a species of Right. This was in fact the view that Coke espoused in the *Institutes*[67] and in *Doctor Bonham's Case*.[68] The philosopher countered that the law is no more than statutory law—*Gesetze*. "It is not Wisdom, but Authority that makes a law."[69] Thus the fictional philosopher captures the positivist position as succinctly as anyone who has played his part in the last three centuries.

The debate about the meaning of "law" continues in our time. H.L.A. Hart and other positivists represent the philosopher's view that the applicable law is reducible to enacted statutes[70] and customary law.[71] Fuller's response to Hart holds, in effect, that the word "law" should be understood as the Right.[72] Statutes must meet certain conditions of moral decency before they merit classification as law in this higher sense. Dworkin takes a different tack to strengthen the sense of Right in American jurisprudence. He asserts that contemporary American law includes principles as well as enacted rules.[73] These principles testify to the ongoing influence of the Right in our legal culture.

As long as the debate between positivist and transcendent legal theories turns on how we ought to use the word "law," there seems to

63. *Id.* Lawyers commonly refer to "the law." Note that the philosopher here refers to "a law." That particular laws emanate from the legislature is easier to defend than the claim that all law has its origin in "authority."

64. *Id.*

65. *Id.*

66. *Id.*

67. *See* E. Coke, First Institute § 138, at 97v. (London 1628).

68. *See* Dr. Bonham's Case, 77 Eng. Rep. 638, 652 (C.P. 1610).

69. T. Hobbes, *supra* note 59, at 55.

70. *See* pp. 975-77 *supra*.

71. On the status of customary law, see H.L.A. Hart, *supra* note 16, at 45-46 (rejecting view that custom cannot be source of law until so declared by courts); H. Kelsen, *supra* note 24, at 230-34 (same).

72. *See* Fuller, *supra* note 19, at 655-66. Fuller implicitly adopts Radbruch's conception of the Right. *See* p. 981 *supra*.

73. *See* pp. 978-79 *supra*.

be little hope of resolving the normative controversy.[74] Yet there might be an alternative strategy for refuting the positivist thesis. Dworkin's strategy is to shift our focus from the phenomenon of "law" in general to the argumentative style of lawyers and judges in the common law tradition. That participants in one system rely on principles and policies that transcend the enacted law, Dworkin argues, should count as evidence against the positivist conception of law.[75] The positivist response, it seems, should be to defend a general meta-theory that abstracts from the particularities of a single system.

IV. Two Modes of Legal Thought

To this point, the argument has followed the conventional jurisprudential pattern of analyzing the posture of judges in interpreting and applying the law. We have distinguished between the meta-theory that judicial pronouncements declare the law and the contrasting position that these pronouncements merely assert what the law is. The former position characterizes legal positivism; the latter view marks transcendent theories of law.

We can now trace the impact of these meta-theories on the aspirations of legal scholarship. Let us consider what scholars might do in a legal culture that assumed the existence of the Right as a dimension of the law and accordingly treated judicial and perhaps legislative statements as assertions rather than as declarations of the law. In a legal culture characterized by a vivid sense of the Right, scholars would presumably participate in the assertion, refinement, and teaching of particular conceptions of the Right. If judges asserted rather than declared what the law is, then surely scholars would have equal if not superior standing to participate in the process that Hobbes's lawyer called "fining and refining the law." This mode of legal thought is appropriately called "committed argument." Scholars would commit themselves to the pursuit and the articulation of the principles that constitute the law as the Right. They would engage in first-order substantive legal argument about the law. This argument would unite them in a dialogue with their colleagues, with judges of their time, and with the legal tradition.

Consider now the mode of scholarly thought that would emerge in

74. To summarize the debate: Hart argues that the word "law" should be equivalent to the German *Gesetz;* Fuller, that it should be equivalent to *Recht,* as understood by Radbruch. The debate thus appears to be an irresolvable dispute about the proper use of the word "law."

75. R. Dworkin, *supra* note 5, at 22-45.

a legal culture that took the tenets of positivism as its foundation. In this culture, everyone would assume that the law consisted exclusively of those rules declared to be the law by the authorized agencies—the legislature and perhaps the courts. It is hard to imagine a version of positivism in which scholars could declare or make law merely by writing an article. Scholars would be limited to describing the law as declared by the official agencies.[76]

This posture of description generates a mode of thought appropriately called "detached observation." The scholar is detached from the actual workings of the legal system. His task is to observe and report what he sees. In the mode of "detached observation," scholars can engage in sophisticated analysis as well as the routine reporting of developments in the courts and legislature. The perspectives offered by the social sciences rescue the observing scholar from trivial commentary. In the posture of the scientist studying the law as a social system, the sophisticated observer makes an important contribution to legal scholarship.

The relationship between legal positivism and these two modes of legal thought bears careful articulation. To engage in committed argument, the scholar must believe that the law exists not only as enacted law (*Gesetze*) but as the Right (*Recht*). The law as Right, after all, is the object of the argument. This means that those who engage in committed argument implicitly subscribe to a transcendent theory of law. Those who refuse to acknowledge that the law transcends enacted legal rules cannot—as a conceptual matter—engage in committed argument. Positivists, therefore, are limited to the mode of detached observation.

The converse logical relationship, however, does not hold. Anyone can detach himself from the legal system and observe the behavior of legal officials. Though positivism precludes committed argument about the law, subscribing to a transcendent legal theory does not prevent detached observation.

There might be the following objection to this analysis.[77] It is true that positivist legal scholars cannot, as positivists, argue about

76. In addition to describing the law, scholars in a positivist legal culture could also exhort the officials to change the law, *see* pp. 986-87 *infra*, and predict what the officials might do. The latter represents Holmes's famous "predictive" conception of law. *See* Holmes, *The Path of the Law*, 10 HARV. L. REV. 457, 461 (1897) ("The prophecies of what the courts will do in fact, and nothing more pretentious, are what I mean by the law.")

77. Professor Barbara Underwood raised this point in her comment on the lecture based on this paper, given at the symposium on February 13, 1981.

the law in the higher sense of Right, but they can argue about what the enacted law ought to be. They can commit themselves to reforming the law, through either the courts or the legislatures. Indeed, the facilitation of law reform provides one of the more persuasive arguments for the limited, positivist conception of law. If the law is enacted, then it also can be changed. As a leading positivist, Bentham was also a committed reformer.

All this is true. Yet there is a significant difference between arguing about the content of the law (as Right) and arguing about what the law ought to be. First, judges are bound by the law—both in West Germany and in the United States. Yet, in neither country are they bound by scholarly claims of what the law ought to be. The West German Basic Law (Constitution) makes it clear that the "law" that binds the judges includes not only the enacted law but also principles of Right.[78] Therefore, in asserting conceptions of the Right, German scholars engage in discourse about the criteria that in fact bind the courts. This does not mean that judges follow the opinions of scholars, as they follow legislative directives. Yet being bound by the Right means that if they concede that a particular position is Right, they are obligated to follow it.[79] In contrast, in a legal system founded on positivism, judges would not be bound by the scholars' conception of good law or sound policy. The judges might well concede that the scholars' recommendations are morally right, but nonetheless could maintain that it is up to the legislature to change the law.[80]

In addition, the effort to elaborate the Right generates a literature that differs from the overt advocacy of law reform. The pursuit of immanent principles leads to an emphasis on the internal structure of the law, expressed both in the structure of the codes and in historical evolution. In the last two sections of this article, I shall illustrate the mode of committed argument with instances of scholarly work on matters of structure and principle. The mode of arguing what the law ought to be, as expressed, say, in the work of Bentham, hardly imitates these features of committed argument. The last thing the legislative reformer would do is stress the authority of history.

78. GRUNDGESETZ [GG] art. 20(III) ("*die vollziehende Gewalt und die Rechtsprechung sind an Gesetz und Recht gebunden*"); *cf. id.* art. 97(1) (judges are "independent and subject only to *Gesetz*" ("*nur dem Gesetz unterworfen*")).

79. Dworkin develops a similar argument about the effect of principles on judicial obligation. *See* R. DWORKIN, *supra* note 5, at 35 ("[i]f a judge believes that principles he is bound to recognize point in one direction . . . then he must decide accordingly"). From this premise, Dworkin reasons that principles may "dictate a result." *Id.* at 35.

80. I am indebted to Guyora Binder for helping me formulate this response.

Two Modes

He would seek to counter, rather than to cultivate, the argument that basic principles inhere in the law as it has evolved. In fact, as H.L.A. Hart has stressed, the positivist advocacy of law reform is linked closely to the emergence of utilitarianism as a moral philosophy.[81] With a commitment to promoting future welfare, utilitarians see little point in arguments of principle based on the accrued legal materials.

V. Examples of Committed Argument in Common Law and Civilian Systems

The two modes of thought are stated here as ideal types.[82] They are methodological constructs that enable us to order and to interpret the complicated flux of experience. In a conflicted legal culture, such as our own, it might be difficult to determine whether particular authors are engaged in the mode of committed argument or are merely describing the authoritative materials. As a matter of style, for example, common-law scholars might prefer to camouflage their normative purposes in descriptive syntheses of the cases or in historical claims about legislative intent. Precisely because the data are unamenable to easy classification, these ideal types enable us to make some useful historical and comparative claims about the relative prominence of the two modes of legal thought.

It is safe to assert that at least until the beginning of the nineteenth century, English legal scholarship was devoted almost entirely to committed argument about the basic principles of the common law. Consider the development of the criminal law. Without the sustained efforts of scholars such as Coke,[83] Hale,[84] and Blackstone,[85] the common law of crime would not have taken shape. The scholars did occasionally cite cases, but the significance and meaning of the cited cases depended not on the language of the reported opinions, but on the interpretation the opinions received in the scholarly literature.[86] In our time, we still encounter committed arguments, sometimes explicit and sometimes camouflaged, about substantive

81. Hart, *supra* note 18, at 601.

82. *See* pp. 1001-03 *infra* (describing the methodology of ideal types).

83. E. Coke, Third Institute (London 1644).

84. M. Hale, The History of the Pleas of the Crown (London 1736).

85. 4 W. Blackstone, *supra* note 33.

86. For a discussion of the conflicting interpretations of the important Carrier's Case, Y.B. Pasch. 13 Edw. 4, f. 9, pl. 5 (1473), *reprinted in* 64 Selden Soc'y 30 (1945), see G. Fletcher, *supra* note 38, at 66-70, 97-98, and Fletcher, *Manifest Criminality, Criminal Intent, and the Metamorphosis of Lloyd Weinreb*, 90 Yale L.J. 319, 328-32 (1980). *See also* 4 W. Blackstone, *supra* note 33, at *201 (analysis of burden of persuasion in criminal cases discussing Oneby's Case, 92 Eng. Rep. 465 (K.B. 1727)).

due process,[87] about cruel and unusual punishment,[88] and about the First Amendment.[89] The ongoing debate about tort liability seems to be conducted sometimes in the mode of committed argument,[90] sometimes as an exchange about what the law ought to be.[91] Alongside these examples of committed argument in the current American literature, the last few decades have witnessed an obvious awakening of sophisticated writing in the mode of detached observation. The campaign in our leading law schools to treat the law as a social science reflects the powerful influence of interdisciplinary observation as a model of legal scholarship.

The contrast between these modes of legal thought helps us focus on the special sense of "legal science" in civilian legal cultures. Given our current equation of "science" with "natural science," we might be inclined to believe that civilians think of "legal science" as a form of detached observation, a mode of scientific analysis of legal data. This translation falls wide of the mark. In many languages, the term for "science" has a broader meaning than the current English word. The German term *Wissenschaft* encompasses both natural science and *Geisteswissenschaften,* that is, humanistic disciplines, such as history and social theory. The humanistic sense of *Wissenschaft* finds expression in the term *Rechtswissenschaft,* or "legal science."[92] This translation is awkward because we no longer have an appropriate word in English to describe the kind of knowledge that scholars acquire by searching for structure and meaning in the legal materials. The phrase "humanistic understanding" might be as close as we

87. *E.g.*, Perry, *supra* note 45, at 694 (restrictions on abortion violate the "inherent" limit on state's legislative authority under police power).

88. For efforts to construe the Eighth Amendment as more hostile to the death penalty than the courts have held, see Goldberg & Dershowitz, *Declaring the Death Penalty Unconstitutional*, 83 HARV. L. REV. 1773 (1970), and Radin, *The Jurisprudence of Death: Evolving Standards for the Cruel and Unusual Punishments Clause*, 126 U. PA. L. REV. 989, 1042-52 (1978).

89. T. EMERSON, TOWARD A GENERAL THEORY OF THE FIRST AMENDMENT 16-17 (1963).

90. The best example is the development of the right of privacy, both prior to legislative and judicial recognition, Warren & Brandeis, *The Right to Privacy*, 4 HARV. L. REV. 193, 204-13 (1890) (protection of privacy underlies diverse bodies of law), and today, when the effort is to elicit the principles reflected in the decided cases, W. PROSSER, HANDBOOK OF THE LAW OF TORTS 804-15 (4th ed. 1971) (arguing that privacy cases express four rationalia for recovery).

91. The most influential current critique of existing practice is Epstein's proposal. *See* R. EPSTEIN, A THEORY OF STRICT LIABILITY: TOWARD A REFORMULATION OF TORT LAW (1980).

92. Though I regard this claim as the prevailing view in Germany today, the point is difficult to establish. For a view close to my own, see K. LARENZ, *supra* note 24, at 165-92 (emphasizing heuristic dimension in *Jurisprudenz* as branch of *Rechtswissenschaft*).

Two Modes

can get to the German idea of *Geisteswissenschaft*, or "science-of-the-spirit."[93]

Although sophisticated forms of detached observation might qualify as empirical "science," the mode of committed argument generates an equally sound form of humanistic understanding. The understanding derives from the scholar's personal commitment to the pursuit and from the ensuing dialogue with other committed participants. Admittedly, the notion of humanistic understanding requires a critical exposition that exceeds my own present learning.[94] The most I can hope to do in this article is highlight some features of a legal culture characterized by the mode of committed argument.

The concept of *Lehre* plays a central role in a legal culture dominated by committed argument. Literally, the term *Lehre* means "teaching," but we think only of religious figures as "teachers" in this sense. The best way to grasp what Germans mean by a *Lehre* is to think of the way we use the term "theory" ubiquitously to refer to nonscientific as well as scientific arguments. Epstein's *A Theory of Strict Liability*[95] or Rawls's *A Theory of Justice*[96] would be appropriately translated into German as *Lehren*.[97] These works are assertions about the basic principles of tort law and of justice. They cannot be proved or disproved. They succeed so far as they speak effectively to those concerned about the same issues.[98]

Humanistic legal "theories" (*Lehren*) come and go. For those that gain a following and become dominant, the Germans reserve the special term *herrschende Lehre*, or "ruling theory." Whether a theory becomes dominant in this sense depends on its substantive merit. The reputations and status of those who urge the theory obviously affect the likelihood of the theory's acceptance. Those that become dominant often find their way into legal opinions and statutory reforms

93. This problem of translation is ironic. Apparently, the German term was coined in order to translate the English term "moral science." *See* G. VON WRIGHT, EXPLANATION AND UNDERSTANDING 6 (1971).

94. The texts with which to begin a deeper study would be W. DILTHEY, EINLEITUNG IN DIE GEISTESWISSENSCHAFTEN (1883), and H. RICKERT, DIE GRENZEN DER NATURWISSENSCHAFTLICHEN BEGRIFFSBILDUNG (1913).

95. R. EPSTEIN, *supra* note 91.

96. J. RAWLS, *supra* note 5.

97. Rawls's translator in fact used the term *Theorie*, which looks more like the English term. J. RAWLS, EINE THEORIE DER GERECHTIGKEIT (H. Vetter trans. 1975). The meaning of *Theorie* in German is more restricted. *See* pp. 990-91 *infra*.

98. For a poignant statement of this position, see J. RAWLS, *supra* note 5, at 50 ("So for the purposes of this book, the views of the reader and the author are the only ones that count.")

and thus bear directly on the exercise of judicial and legislative power.[99]

We should note the connection between "legal theories" (*Lehren*) and some of the other terms we have used in this exposition. These theories are assertions of Right. Judges are bound by the Right, and therefore they must pay careful attention to those theories that become dominant in the literature. The Swiss civil code testifies to the impact of legal theories on the legal process. The first section of the code provides that if the code fails to resolve a legal dispute, the judge should act as though he "were a legislator" in fashioning an appropriate rule.[100] The second half of the provision curtails this grant of legislative freedom: the judge is required to follow "customary law" and "those theories that have stood the test of time" (*bewährte Lehren*).[101] Thus the Swiss judge assesses the leading scholarly theories and attempts to gauge their substantive merit.

Humanistic legal "teachings" address a wide range of problems. Some seek to explicate the underlying structure of issues bearing on liability. A good example is the German theory that classifies the issues of substantive criminal law as matters of definition, wrongdoing, and culpability.[102] Others seek to explicate basic concepts used in legal analysis.[103] More specific "teachings," usually called *Theorien* in German, are directed to the solution of particular legal problems, such as impossible attempts[104] and mistaken self-defense.[105]

In the remaining sections of the article I shall offer some suggestions about the criteria that render "theories" and claims of Right persuasive in Western legal cultures. These suggestions are tentative. They derive from reflection about a few instances in which scholars have sought to cull claims of Right from the available legal materials.

99. One good example is the exhaustive discussion of competing "teachings" on mistake of law in the Judgment of Mar. 18, 1952, Bundesgerichtshof, W. Ger., 2 Bundesgerichtshof in Strafsachen [BGHSt] 194. The court sets forth two competing theories, as developed in the literature, and then explains why it chooses the one that it does. *Id.* at 205-11.

100. SCHWEIZERISCHES ZIVILGESETZBUCH [ZGB] § 1(2) (Switz.).

101. *Id.* § 1(3) (French version says that judge *"s'inspire des solutions consacrées par la doctrine et la jurisprudence"*).

102. This development of this structure and its implications is known as the *Verbrechenslehre*. *See* G. FLETCHER, *supra* note 38, at 406-08.

103. Welzel's *Finale Handlungslehre* ("teleological theory of acting") seeks to clarify the nature of the human conduct relevant to the criminal law. *See* G. FLETCHER, *supra* note 38, at 433-48. The theory is treated as important in itself, regardless of whether it affects the outcome of concrete cases.

104. H. JESCHECK, LEHRBUCH DES STRAFRECHTS: ALLGEMEINER TEIL 429-30 (3d ed. 1977) (discussion of "objective theory" and "subjective theory" of liability).

105. *Id.* at 375 (discussion of various theories on the proper classification of the mistaken belief that one is under attack).

Two Modes

VI. Committed Argument: From Statutes to Principles

As a general matter, claims of Right are likely to be persuasive only insofar as they build on legal materials generally recognized as authoritative in the legal culture. A personal and idiosyncratic vision of the Right might be prophetic, but it is not likely to gain support among others who might indulge, as well, in a private view of the Right. The common materials that ground a claim of Right in shared experience are, as one might expect, statutes and cases. Yet there are some important assumptions that we must make about statutes and prior decisions in order to use them effectively to render a claim of Right persuasive.

In order to explicate these assumptions, I shall examine two common techniques of argument in German private law. If a single provision is extended to an analogous situation clearly not covered by the language of the provision, the rationale of the extension is called *Gesetzesanalogie*; that is, analogy based on a statutory provision.[106] If several specific provisions are taken to stand for a single underlying principle, the rationale for the generalized principle is called *Rechtsanalogie*; that is, analogy as a matter of Right.[107] Both of these analogical arguments are efforts to muster the authority of the code as support for a principle of Right.

For a good example of analogical extension from a single provision, consider the 1958 case of the "Horseman,"[108] in which the German Supreme Court extended a statutory provision for damages to the newly recognized tort of invasion of privacy.[109] The defendant had, without the plaintiff's permission, published a picture of the plaintiff riding a horse in an advertisement for a product generally thought to heighten sexual potency. The advertisement, with its not-so-subtle allusion to the plaintiff's "riding" capacities, allegedly held him up to ridicule. There was little doubt that this publication constituted a wrongful violation of the plaintiff's privacy; yet the plaintiff had suffered no material damage, and section 847 of the Civil Code seems to bar the payment of damages for nonmaterial injuries in privacy cases. The section explicitly limits this form of recovery, as well as

106. *See* I(1) ENNECCERUS-NIPPERDEY, *supra* note 52, at 339-40.

107.. *See id.*

108. Judgment of Feb. 14, 1958, Bundesgerichtshof, W. Ger., 26 Bundesgerichtshof in Zivilsachen [BGHZ] 349.

109. The tort was developed by interpretation of the residual clause "or any other right," which defines the scope of protected interests under the general tort provision. BÜRGERLICHES GESETZBUCH [BGB] § 823 (W. Ger.); *see* Judgment of Apr. 2, 1957, Bundesgerichtshof, W. Ger., 24 BGHZ 72.

damages for pain and suffering, to cases of physical injury, wrongful death, and the "deprivation of liberty."[110] Unless privacy proved to be a form of liberty, the plaintiff could not recover under the terms of the code. It is fairly clear that the term "deprivation of liberty" was conceived originally to apply to cases of tortious false imprisonment.[111] Yet the Supreme Court reasoned that by analogical extension, the term should apply to other forms of liberty, and in particular, to the liberty to sell or withhold one's picture from publication. Significantly, the Court did not rely on a fictitious construction of legislative purpose. Its primary argument was that in light of the proper development of the right to privacy since the enactment of the Code, it would represent "unacceptable contempt of this [newly-recognized] right"[112] to limit section 847 to its original purpose and to refuse a remedy in privacy cases. This argument extending section 847 had already gained acceptance as a scholarly theory or "teaching," and the Court relied heavily on scholarly theory in defending its analogical expansion of the law.[113]

Inferring basic principles from several code provisions has had an even more dramatic history in the development of German private law in this century. Shortly after the Civil Code came into force in 1900, Professor Staub noted that the Civil Code lacked, as it still does, a provision to cover simple cases of improper contractual performance leading to consequential harm—for example, delivering a diseased horse and thus infecting the rest of the buyer's stable.[114] The Code had no general provision on contractual breach, but rather two specific forms of "contractual breakdown."[115] Staub argued that these

110. *See* BGB § 847.

111. Section 832(1) of the BGB explicitly protects "liberty" (*Freiheit*) from intentional and negligent deprivations. If in the cases cited above, *see* note 109 *supra*, the courts had thought of the violation of privacy as the "deprivation of liberty," they would not have developed the new tort under the residual clause, "or any other right."

112. Judgment of Feb. 14, 1958, Bundesgerichtshof, W. Ger., 26 BGHZ 349, 356.

113. *See id.* (even before enactment of the new constitution in 1949, many writers had argued in favor of extending BGB § 847; new constitution commits itself to values that support extension). This case and the law it represents eventually generated a constitutional dispute. In its Judgment of Feb. 14, 1973, 34 Bundesverfassungsgericht [BVerfGE] 269, the Federal Constitutional Court held that because judges were bound by "*Gesetz und Recht*," GG art. 20(3), the expansion of BGB § 847 reflected a constitutionally permissible judicial function. *See* 34 BVerfGE at 286-88. Accordingly, the Court concluded, the judicially developed law on the remedies for breach of privacy constituted the type of "*allgemeines Gesetz*" necessary for a restriction on the freedom of the press under GG art. 5(11). 34 BVerfGE at 292.

114. H. STAUB, DIE POSITIVE VERTRAGSVERLETZUNG (1904). According to the foreword to this edition, the argument was originally advanced in a paper presented in September 1902. *Id.* at 2-3. The Civil Code came into force on January 1, 1900.

115. BGB §§ 284-286 ("delay" in performance); *id.* § 280 (impossibility of performance).

Two Modes

specific forms of breakdown reflected a general principle of liability for contractual breach.[116] Eventually adopted by the courts, Staub's theory of "affirmative breach of contract" has become an established institution in the German law of contracts.[117] That the doctrine has never received statutory embodiment has no bearing on its binding force.[118]

For another good example of inferring a general principle from specific statutory provisions, consider the general recognition of injunctions as a remedy for threatened wrongs. The Civil Code refers to the possibility of a preventive injunction in only three provisions. It could be argued that these three references were intended to exhaust the cases of permissible injunctions, but the contrasting claim of Right has prevailed: the three references are taken to be but the surface manifestations of a general principle permitting injunction as a supplementary remedy in all cases of threatened harm.[119]

Several points about analogical argument are worth stressing. First, these claims do not represent interpretations of vague statutory provisions. Nor do the proponents of the arguments seek to camouflage their assertions of Right with fictions[120] or contrived arguments about legislative purpose. Further, both scholars and judges make these claims of Right, which transcend the enacted law. In the German tradition, at least, scholars often initiate new developments by first refining a new theory in the literature.[121] Even though they might expect the courts to follow their teaching, German scholars occasionally have held to their view of the law even though the courts consistently disagreed.[122]

116. *See* H. Staub, *supra* note 114, at 21-23 (referring explicitly to argument by analogy).

117. O. Palandt, Bürgerliches Gesetzbuch 294-98 (39th ed. 1980); W. Fikentscher, Schuldrecht 249 (1969); *see* Judgment of Nov. 13, 1953, Bundesgerichtshof, W. Ger., 11 BGHZ 80, 89 (positive breach of contract is an established rule).

118. BGB § 12 (misuse of another's name); *id.* § 862 (interference with possession); *id.* § 1004 (interference with owner's rights). All three of these provisions use the set formula: "If further disturbances are feared, the affected party can sue for injunctive relief."

119. O. Palandt, *supra* note 117, at 197.

120. Staub's argument provides a striking example. It might have been possible to solve the problem of affirmative breach by reasoning that the temporary breach rendered the proper performance "impossible" in the sense required by BGB § 280. Yet Staub preferred to assert a principle by analogy rather than engage in this kind of manipulation of the Code's language. *See* H. Staub, *supra* note 114, at 10-11.

121. Two striking examples in the criminal law are the development of extra-statutory necessity as a justification, *see* Judgment of Mar. 11, 1927, Reichsgericht, W. Ger., 61 Reichsgericht in Strafsachen [RGSt] 242; G. Fletcher, *supra* note 38, at 777-84, and the development of mistake of law as an excuse, *see* Judgment of Mar. 18, 1952, Bundesgerichtshof, W. Ger., 2 BGHSt 194; G. Fletcher, *supra* note 38, at 742-46.

122. A good example is the literature's holding that impossible attempts were at

When the courts adopt a scholarly view of the law, we could describe the decision as "making law," but that term—as popular as it might be in our own idiom—obscures the tentative nature of claims of Right. The courts do not "enact" anything in subscribing to particular principles. The principles come to prevail, but they are not legislated.

It may seem paradoxical that a codified system of law would permit and even encourage inferences of Right from the code provisions. The popular image of codified law is that the statutory scheme is not only precise, but also comprehensive. In fact, the French and German Civil Codes are exhaustive in neither sense: they are neither precise nor comprehensive. The distinguishing feature of the European codes, and particularly the German codes, is their structure. The provisions are organized so that some apply across whole chapters and books of the code, and others apply solely to specific problems. Cross-references and interrelationships are assumed. The code cannot be used without first studying its structure and learning to interpret the significance of the position enjoyed by each particular provision.[123]

The implication of a structured code is that the whole conveys more meaning than the collected messages of its separate parts. Meaning is encoded, as it were, in the structure of the code.[124] The coherence of the whole and the interrelatedness of the parts enable us to derive principles from the particular provisions.

The assumption of interrelatedness proves to be essential. Suppose that we had three unrelated statutes that referred to the permissibility of injunctions and a hundred others that were silent on the issue. There would be no warrant, as far as I can see, for inferring a general principle of injunctive relief. As we could not develop a grammar from utterances collected from different languages, we cannot infer general principles from haphazard statutory principles. The

least in part exempt from liability, R. FRANK, STRAFGESETZBUCH FÜR DAS DEUTSCHE REICH, § 43, at 83-84 (18th ed. 1931), while the Supreme Court held that these same attempts were punishable, *see* Judgment of June 10, 1880, Reichsgericht, W. Ger., 1 RGSt 451. The difference between the *Lehre* and the case law reflected deeper differences between the objective and subjective theories of liability. *See* G. FLETCHER, *supra* note 38, at 139-84.

123. It is important, for example, that BGB § 254, defining the principle of comparative negligence, appears in the general part of the second book covering all obligations. It follows that the principles of comparative negligence apply in analyzing liability for contractual breach as well as for tortiously causing harm.

124. In defending the recognition of an "affirmative breach of contract" principle as an institution analogical but extrinsic to the German Code provisions, Staub refers to it as "in-dwelling" in the Code, H. STAUB, *supra* note 114, at 6, and notes cryptically: "For analogy is approved and desired by the Code," *id.* at 22.

well-grounded belief that a statute or constitution reveals a coherent order, then, is the precondition for relying on the statute in making persuasive claims of Right.

VII. Committed Argument: From Case Law to Principles

There may have been a time when common-law scholars believed that all the cases in a particular field of law coalesced in a consistent and coherent set of rules. That faith is hard to maintain today. Anyone who has studied the cases in a particular field knows how difficult it is to find principles that will explain the case results from different jurisdictions and from different times within the same jurisdiction. If European codes resemble coherent languages, each with its own grammar, then the Anglo-American case law today speaks two or three languages at once.

Judges function in this cacophony by picking a line of cases that supports their view of the law and stressing those precedents to the exclusion of all others. Judges, alas, must argue for one conception of the Right. Yet scholars are not under the pressure of decision. They need not decide for one side; they need not decide at all. What, then, should their posture be in coping with conflicted bodies of case law?

In broad strokes, we can trace three scholarly responses to the inconsistencies of the cases. First, the legal nominalists, falsely called "realists," convinced many of us that, try as we may, we cannot derive coherent principles from the subterfuge of legal rationalization.[125] For those who believe that cases have little to teach us about the law, the ongoing orthodoxy of the case method of instruction must prove embarrassing. The most we can do in class is speculate about the "process" or perhaps analyze the extra-legal policy values that should have informed the decision.

The nominalist thesis has triggered its antithesis, a rationalist reconstruction of the common law. The reconstruction proceeds by assuming that judges have implicitly followed some standard of rationality in formulating and applying the rules of the common law. The current literature stresses one version of economic efficiency[126]

125. *E.g.*, J. Frank, *supra* note 11, at 32-41. For a succinct survey of "realism" in its historical context, see Ackerman, Book Review, Daedalus, Winter 1974, at 119 (reviewing Jerome Frank's *Law and the Modern Mind*).

126. The Kaldor-Hicks standard of efficiency requires merely that rights be assigned to the party willing, hypothetically, to pay the most for them. *See* R. Posner, Economic Analysis of Law 10-12 (2d ed. 1977); Michelman, *Property, Utility, and Fairness: Comments on the Ethical Foundations of "Just Compensation" Law*, 80 Harv. L. Rev. 1165,

as the standard supposedly underlying the development of the common law.[127] Using this model of rationality as their starting point, the economic observers read the cases in search of supportive evidence. Of course, there are some striking counterexamples that they cannot explain.[128] And they have yet to furnish an account for the supposed judicial commitment to efficiency as a value.[129] Even if an efficient legal system is good for the society as a whole, it does not follow that it is good for judges as a class. Judicial altruism, as distinguished from maximizing one's own utility, hardly fits the economic model of behavior. Yet these counterexamples rarely embarrass the rationalist economists. If the evidence confirms the model, good for the evidence. If not, the data are dismissed as "strange" and "mysterious."[130]

Neither the nominalist study of process nor the rationalist model of efficiency reflects a scholarly commitment to learn from the experience and reasoning of the common-law cases. Nor is there any particular reason why these variations of detached observation should seek wisdom in the case law. The posture of learning from the cases correlates closely with the mode of committed argument. If scholars are engaged in the pursuit of principles of Right, they are likely to see themselves as sharing a common task with the judiciary. In the view of scholars, at least, scholars and judges would both be committed to the goal of refining the basic principles of the system and thus both would have much to learn from argument and criticism.

This third approach, rooted in the mode of committed argument, generates a method for decoding the multiple messages of the case law. The method starts on the assumption that conflicting ways of thinking about the law, conflicting conceptions of Right, might co-

1173-75 (1967). The Pareto standard of efficiency requires that those who gain from the assignment compensate those who lose. *See* K. ARROW, SOCIAL CHOICE AND INDIVIDUAL VALUES 34-45 (2d ed. 1963).

127. R. POSNER, *supra* note 126, at 179-81; Rubin, *Why is the Common Law Efficient?* 6 J. LEGAL STUD. 51 (1977).

128. Posner concedes that comparative negligence is not the correct economic standard, R. POSNER, *supra* note 126, at 124; yet if there is any principle whose time has come, it is that of comparative negligence. *See* V. SCHWARTZ, COMPARATIVE NEGLIGENCE 1 (1974 & Supp. 1978) (in period from 1950 to 1977, number of states adopting comparative negligence increased from 5 to 32). *See also* Priest, *The Theory of Consumer Product Warranty* (forthcoming 90 YALE L.J. (1981)) (warranties implied in law are inefficient).

129. Leff, *Economic Analysis of Law: Some Realism About Nominalism*, 60 VA. L. REV. 451, 471-74 (1975). In a weak reply, Posner suggests that no problem of group conflict exists in the legal system and that, therefore, judges' interests coincide with those of society. *See* R. POSNER, *supra* note 126, at 415-17.

130. Coase, *The Problem of Social Cost*, 3 J.L. & ECON. 1, 15 (1960) ("[t]he reasoning employed by the courts . . . will often seem strange to an economist"); Posner, *The Right of Privacy*, 12 GA. L. REV. 393, 405 (1978) ("The trend toward elevating personal and downgrading organizational privacy is mysterious to the economist.")

exist. This deeper conflict of principles and methods accounts for the surface inconsistency in the case law. We can see the influence of this method in Kennedy's study of the relative influence of altruism and idealism in the history of contract law[131] and in Ackerman's effort to sort out the different ways of thinking about the takings problem.[132]

This third mode of scholarship provides the foundations for my own studies in torts and in criminal law. In the last segment of the article, I shall reflect on the method implicit in these studies. My purpose is to develop a level of methodological understanding that will elicit the possible links between those studies and other efforts to learn from conflicted bodies of case law.

VIII. Ideal Types and Conflicting Conceptions of Right

In a half dozen or so different fields of tort and criminal law, we cannot but confront the internal tension of American law. The cases on the burden of persuasion in criminal cases remain an unresolved jumble.[133] In the field of accident law, the courts cannot come to a stable view about whether negligence or strict liability represents a better approach to allocating losses.[134] On the subject of larceny, some significant decisions simply do not accord with the prevailing criteria of punishable takings.[135] In the law of impossible attempts, the courts simply defy the philosophy of liability incorporated in our reformed statutes.[136] In these and other contexts,[137] however, we

131. Kennedy, *Form and Substance in Private Law Adjudication*, 89 HARV. L. REV. 1685 (1976).

132. B. ACKERMAN, PRIVATE PROPERTY AND THE CONSTITUTION (1977).

133. *See* Fletcher, *Two Kinds of Legal Rules: A Comparative Study of Burden-of-Persuasion Practices in Criminal Cases*, 77 YALE L.J. 880, 882-84 (1968).

134. *See* Fletcher, *Fairness and Utility in Tort Theory*, 85 HARV. L. REV. 537 (1972) (discussing problem as conflict of paradigms that cut across conventional categories of negligence and strict liability).

135. The prevailing view of larceny requires liability for any intentional taking contrary to the will of the owner. *See* Fletcher, *The Metamorphosis of Larceny*, 89 HARV. L. REV. 469, 514-20 (1976). *But see* Topolewski v. State, 130 Wis. 244, 109 N.W. 1037 (1906) (denying liability for completed larceny despite intentional and possibly culpable taking); Regina v. Miller, 49 Crim. App. 241 (1965) (same). *See generally* G. FLETCHER, *supra* note 38, at 70-76, 86-90; Fletcher, *supra*, at 491-98.

136. The revised statutes typically impose liability as if "the attendant circumstances were as [the actor] believes them to be." DEL. CODE ANN. tit. 11, § 531(1) (1979); *see* Mo. ANN. STAT. § 564.011(2) (Vernon 1979) (almost identical language). Yet the case law persistently rejects this "subjective" approach. *E.g.*, United States v. Oviedo, 525 F.2d 881 (5th Cir. 1976) (conviction for attempted sale of heroin, reversed); United States v. Berrigan, 482 F.2d 171 (3d Cir. 1973) (conviction for attempted illegal correspondence by a prisoner, reversed). *See generally* G. FLETCHER, *supra* note 38, at 139-84 (discussing conflicting theories of attempt liability).

137. *See, e.g.*, G. FLETCHER, *supra* note 38, at 836-39 (discussing conflicting conceptions of insanity); *id.* at 856-74 (discussing conflicting "models" of self-defense).

can still seek to learn from judicial efforts to elaborate principles of Right.

My efforts to derive principles from these conflicted bodies of law is guided by the assumption that, at some earlier historical period, the law was consistent and relatively stable. The first stage of such research requires the identification of this classical period and the explication of the operative rules of law as they were then understood.[138] With regard to the burden-of-persuasion cases, the classical period continued until the late nineteenth century.[139] In the field of accident law, the period of relative stability came to an end in the early nineteenth century.[140] In the law of larceny, the classical conception of the crime began to wither in the late eighteenth century.[141] The dating need not be precise provided that the research reveals some core period of relative stability.

If we can state the law consistently as it might have existed, then we can enter the second and most difficult stage of the method: constructing an account or a rationale of the law as it existed in its consistent phase. Providing this account sometimes requires considerable imagination, for we no longer enjoy an easy familiarity with some ways of thinking that prevailed prior to the ascendency of instrumental legal reasoning in the last century.[142] Generating this account of our own requires that we suspend judgment, at least temporarily, about the Right, and seek to adopt another way of thinking. This exercise requires anthropological sensitivity in approaching our own past, a past that differs in its modes of thinking, but that might nonetheless influence legal intuitions today. The method requires that we take judicial language seriously and at the same time search for an account that will locate the language in its context. Of course, there is no conclusive way to validate the accounts we might offer of early legal practices. In the end, the interpretation of the past succeeds if and only if it renders past practices coherent and, in their own way, plausible.

The third and fourth stages of the method consist in constructing a competing but nonetheless coherent conception of the law based on

138. Though the assumption of a classical period has guided my own research, I have no quarrel with Kennedy's methodology, which seems to accept the reality of conflict at all stages of history. *See* Kennedy, *supra* note 131.

139. *See* G. Fletcher, *supra* note 38, at 524-38; Fletcher, *supra* note 133, at 899-910

140. *See* Fletcher, *supra* note 134, at 560-61. For a slightly different dating, see M. Horwitz, The Transformation of American Law 85-89 (1977).

141. *See* G. Fletcher, *supra* note 38, at 90-102; Fletcher, *supra* note 135, at 502-14.

142. On the rise of instrumental reasoning, see M. Horwitz, *supra* note 140, at 1-30; Dworkin, *Morality and the Law*, N.Y. Rev. Books, May 22, 1969, at 29.

those aspects of the present situation that depart from the past. This requires that we filter off the remnants of the past, state the contrasting mode, and then, by analogy to the second step, develop an account of the modern conception of Right. The modern view admits of more ready understanding, for it is indeed our dominant way of thinking. Still, we might have to state the argument more fully and systematically than commentators, concerned about the small picture, have managed to do.

Comparative studies might be useful in explicating either the traditional or the modern approach to a particular legal problem. Legal systems are often out of phase. What might be a matter of conflict in American law could take a different form in a foreign legal system. German law, for example, now consistently applies the rule that a defendant should receive the benefit of the doubt on all issues bearing on culpability.[143] The American case law, in contrast, remains inconsistent on the matter. The German position might be an instance of one of the competing modes of thought that shape the American case law.

The study of ancient legal systems might confirm hypotheses about the classical position of the common law. In Roman, Greek, and Jewish law, one finds a pattern that arguably confirms the hypothesis that common-law larceny required a manifestly criminal act.[144] Whether ancient legal systems in fact provide this confirmation depends on a structuralist theory of law, a theory that permits one to assume that the rules of larceny emerged in related forms in diverse legal cultures. Without this structuralist assumption, the evidence of Roman or Greek law hardly helps us to reconstruct the rules of the medieval common law.[145]

The fifth and final stage of the analysis consists of both a synchronic and a diachronic analysis. Synchronically, we examine the current state of the law with a view toward diagnosing particular rulings as the expression either of the traditional or of the modern mode of thought.[146] Diachronically, we seek to explain the transition

143. *See* Schönke-Schröder, Strafgesetzbuch § 186, at 1277 n.11 (20th ed. 1980) (discussing exception to general rule that defendant has to prove truth in cases of criminal defamation).

144. The sources are Plato, The Laws para. 874, and 3 Gaius, Institutes para. 189, *reprinted in* 1 Gaius, The Institutes of Gaius 215-17 (F. de Zulueta ed. 1946), and Watkins, *Studies in Indo-European Legal Language, Institutions, and Mythology*, in Indo-European and Indo-Europeans 321, 342-45 (G. Cardona et al. eds. 1971).

145. I am indebted to David J. Cohen on this point.

146. These are some examples: the ascendancy of strict liability in tort reflects the return to principles of reciprocity, *see* Fletcher, *supra* note 134, at 570; shifting the

from the older to the newer mode of thought. In seeking these explanations, some people might search for material causes, such as changes in the form of economic organization. The most I have been able to accomplish is to describe the changes by relating the transition in legal thinking to broader currents in intellectual history[147] and sometimes to movements within the law, such as the drive toward codification of the criminal law.[148]

Though the studies I have published have these methodological stages in common, there are important differences among them. In some instances, such as larceny, the modern conception of criminality has virtually displaced the traditional mode of thought;[149] in others, such as impossible attempts, the two ways of thinking collide in the current case law.[150] Moreover, in some cases, I regard the movement toward the modern conception of Right as progressive; in other instances, I regret the loss of values that were implicit in the traditional point of view. For example, the movement in the law of homicide, from a practice of tainting all those who cause death toward a greater emphasis on personal blameworthiness, strikes me as salutary.[151] The related shift toward requiring the prosecution to prove all matters bearing on blameworthiness also seems to be sound.[152] Yet in other fields, such as larceny and impossible attempts, we could learn much from the values implicit in the traditional ways of thinking.[153]

The explication of the two modes of legal thought illustrates, on a meta-level, a methodology used in studying the substantive law. The mode of committed argument prevailed in the evolution of the com-

burden of persuasion to the defendant reflects the influence of the "private law style" in thinking about the criminal law, *see* Fletcher, *supra* note 133, at 919-25; acquittals in cases of "staged larceny" reflect the influence of manifest criminality as a condition of liability, *see* G. FLETCHER, *supra* note 38, at 86-88.

147. For example, I claim that the movement toward requiring the prosecution to bear the risk of residual doubt correlates with the emergence of a normative theory of criminal guilt. *See* G. FLETCHER, *supra* note 38, at 532-37.

148. This influence seems to have been important in the transformation of larceny. *See* Fletcher, *supra* note 135, at 503-04.

149. *See* G. FLETCHER, *supra* note 38, at 103-13; Fletcher, *supra* note 135, at 514-20.

150. *Compare* United States v. Oviedo, 525 F.2d 881 (5th Cir. 1976) (denying liability for intended but impossible sale of heroin) *with* People v. Rojas, 55 Cal. 2d 252, 358 P.2d 921, 10 Cal. Rptr. 465 (1961) (imposing attempt liability for intended but impossible receipt of stolen property).

151. *See* G. FLETCHER, *supra* note 38, at 343-50, 356-58.

152. On the aborted effort to elevate this rule to a principle of due process, see Mullaney v. Wilbur, 421 U.S. 684, 702-04 (1975) (shifting burden on common-law provocation violates due process). *But cf.* Patterson v. New York, 432 U.S. 197, 205-12 (1977) (shifting burden on Model Penal Code version of provocation compatible with due process).

153. On the respect for privacy implicit in the traditional approach to the scope of liability, see Fletcher, *Legality as Privacy*, in LIBERTY AND THE RULE OF LAW 182 (R. Cunningham ed. 1979).

mon law.[154] Detached observation has since gained influence without displacing the original mode of committed argument.[155] Thus, in legal thought itself, we find the kind of conflict that characterizes the substantive law of torts and criminal law.[156]

What is the best way to describe these competing conceptions of legal thought or of the substantive law? We could make do with the uninformative labels "conception," "mode," or "model." The intriguing question is whether we can claim more for the method by linking it to Kuhn's theory of paradigmatic change[157] or Weber's analysis of ideal types.[158] In my analysis of tort law, I used Kuhn's terminology to capture the combination of normative and stylistic elements in the contrasting "paradigms" of reciprocity and of reasonableness.[159] I am inclined now to appreciate the differences between scientific revolutions and transitions in legal thought. Judges and lawyers seldom propound new theories as a way of bringing change to the legal system. Rather, they frequently attempt to reinterpret history and conflicting precedents as a way of suppressing the significance of a change in practice. Scientists take pride in harvesting new ideas; lawyers and judges see their role as nurturing the tradition. Partly because lawyers in the common-law tradition prefer a low level of philosophical consciousness, the changes they wreak rarely take hold across the board. Though a new mode of thought might gain ascendency, the traditional way of thinking remains available to judges and scholars yet to be socialized in the new mode of thought. The tendency for the old and the new to coexist in a legal culture marks a sharp difference from the pattern of revolutionary change in scientific paradigms.

There are at least three reasons why the notion of "ideal types" is better suited to the synchronic analysis of interwoven conceptions of the Right. First, as Weber stressed in his seminal work, the ideal type need not be fully realized in the cultural material that one seeks to understand.[160] Second, the methodology of ideal types recog-

154. *See* pp. 987-88 *supra*.
155. *See* p. 988 *supra*.
156. Other aspects of the legal culture, such as the ethics of advocacy, lend themselves to the same analysis. *See* Simon, *The Ideology of Advocacy: Procedural Justice and Professional Ethics*, 1978 WIS. L. REV. 29.
157. *See* T. KUHN, THE STRUCTURE OF SCIENTIFIC REVOLUTIONS (2d ed. 1970).
158. *See* M. WEBER, THE THEORY OF SOCIAL AND ECONOMIC ORGANIZATION 328-63 (T. Parsons ed. A. Henderson & T. Parsons trans. 1947).
159. Fletcher, *supra* note 134, at 543-51, 556-64.
160. M. WEBER, *"Objectivity" in Social Science and Social Policy*, in THE METHODOLOGY OF THE SOCIAL SCIENCES 50, 101-03 (E. Shils & H. Finch eds. & trans. 1949).

nizes that to gain understanding of what people are doing, we need to enter into ways of thinking that are foreign to our culturally trained instincts.[161] Third, Weber saw the ideal type as a way of explicating the meaning of social action.[162] The effort to understand partly rejected models of legal thought has the same objective. Particular words come into legal discourse with accumulated associations. By explicating the ideal type supporting an argument relying on these terms, we can understand the deeper significance of the advocate's claim.

The explication of judicial language warrants special emphasis. In constructing the ideal types, we reason from the language of the judicial opinions to the underlying premises that, in turn, lead us to a particular interpretation of the judicial language itself. Several examples illustrate this interdependence of data and explanation known as the "hermeneutic circle."[163] The way in which the term "trespass" is used in judicial opinions generates important evidence to support "manifest criminality" as an ideal type of criminal conduct.[164] Yet only when read against the background of the ideal type does the meaning of "trespass" become clear.[165] Similarly, different conceptions of tort liability induce us to think differently about the concept of fault. In one mode of thinking, fault is negated by proof of an excusing condition;[166] in the contrasting mode of thought, fault is negated by proof of a justification.[167] Thus the phrase "liability without fault" takes on different meanings, depending on whether it is read against the background of one or another ideal type of legal thought.

The hermeneutic dimension confirms the methodology of ideal types as the proper way to explicate conflicting conceptions of the

161. M. Weber, *The Meaning of "Ethical Neutrality" in Sociology and Economics*, in The Methodology of the Social Sciences 1, 41 (E. Shils & H. Finch eds. & trans. 1949).

162. M. Weber, *supra* note 160, at 101; *see* Eldridge, *Max Weber: some comments, problems and continuities*, in Max Weber, The Interpretation of Social Reality 9, 28 (J. Eldridge ed. 1980).

163. *See* K. Apel, Die Erklären-Verstehen Kontroverse in Transzendental-Pragmatischer Sicht 16 (1979) (discussing coining of term by Droysen); M. Heidegger, Being and Time § 32, at 194-95 (J. Macquarrie & E. Robinson trans. 1962).

164. "Trespass" fulfills the same doctrinal role as the German requirement of "breaking." It is significant, for example, that in his dissent in The Queen v. Middleton, L.R. 2 Cr. Cas. Res. 38, 56 (1873), Judge Bramwell stresses the requirement both of "trespass" and of a "privy or forcible taking."

165. Given the principles of manifest criminality, one can make sense of the court's denial of liability for an outwardly innocent taking in Topolewski v. State, 130 Wis. 244, 109 N.W. 1037 (1906). *See* G. Fletcher, *supra* note 38, at 86-88.

166. *See* Fletcher, *supra* note 134, at 551-56 (nonfault functions as excuse in paradigm of reciprocity).

167. *See id.* at 556-60 (nonfault functions as justification in paradigm of reasonableness).

Right.[168] Yet, in relying on Weber's example, we need not assume that legal thought must proceed as does social theory. It may be that for purposes of social theory, the scholar should remain neutral between competing ideal types.[169] In explicating the conflict immanent in the case law, the scholar should also strive for neutrality. Normative preconceptions render it more difficult to enter into the opposing mode of thought and to grasp its persuasive power.

Yet understanding the conflicting mode of thought does not preclude the scholar's continuing in the mode of committed argument and siding with one conception of the Right. In the mode of committed argument, we seek both to learn from the conflict in the case law and to exercise responsibility for the ongoing refinement of the legal system. As we cultivate the virtues of neutrality, we are drawn back into the committed pursuit of principles of Right. We have no choice but to mediate between the indifference of neutrality and the distortion of argument.

168. On the influence of the hermeneutic tradition on Weber's conception of sociological understanding, see Z. Bauman, Hermeneutics and Social Science 69-72 (1978).
169. *See id.* at 72 (discussing Weber's famous speech on January 5, 1914, advocating value-free social science).

[18]

REASON IN THE DEVELOPMENT OF THE COMMON LAW

PLUCKNETT's death has made this a sad occasion. I shall not now venture upon a formal tribute: his books are there, and the volumes of the Selden Society for which he did so much. But perhaps I may record my own belief that for him the voices in the year books were real, and that it was not only the lawyers he heard but also their lay clients. His contribution was to bring legal history back to the task so clearly seen by Maitland of placing the law in its social and intellectual setting. The intellectual influences at work in the earliest days of the common law, and the isolation into which so early and so wilfully it plunged itself, were a theme of Plucknett's two latest books, the lectures in Cambridge on legal literature and in Belfast on the criminal law; and the interest was foreshadowed in his inaugural lecture here. But my own favourite is the volume of Oxford lectures on the statutes of Edward I, in which those laborious technicalities become the answers to real problems in a real society.[1]

What Plucknett was after in that book, as his preface explains, was to show how legal history could help general history. And for one chiefly interested in the Middle Ages, this is the aspect of the subject which comes to seem most important. If I may intrude a rueful note of autobiography, one can spend much time on the technicalities of a law-suit before tumbling to it that what one does not understand are the underlying facts, and even more time gingerly talking with social and economic historians only to find that they do not understand them either, and that your law-suit offers the best hope of finding out. And so a technical inquiry into, say, the workings of an action about rights of common turns itself into an effort to imagine a routine of life.

But though this is the aspect of legal history which has come to give me most pleasure, and which, largely because of Plucknett's work, is today most valued, it is only one aspect of the subject; and it is one which a student of the eighteenth century will find less insistent than a student of the thirteenth. Partly, of course, this

* An inaugural lecture given at the London School of Economics on May 20, 1965.

1 Plucknett: *Early English Legal Literature* (C.U.P., 1958); *Edward I and Criminal Law* (C.U.P., 1960); "The Place of the Legal Profession in the History of English Law" (1932) 48 L.Q.R. 328; *Legislation of Edward I* (O.U.P., 1949).

is because the strictly legal sources form a diminishing proportion of the evidence available to the social and economic historian. But it is also because, as the law moves further from its customary beginnings and becomes a wholly professional business, the legal sources become a less sensitive record of everyday circumstances. Indeed, the growth of common forms of pleading, the associated development of fictions, and the use of the jury to give a general verdict for one side or the other without ever saying what happened—all these things rebuff the inquirer who chiefly wants from his report or his plea roll just a simple slice of life.

Nor is this just a matter of the state of the evidence. The legal sources reflect the conditions of life less well because the law itself responds to those conditions less directly. The professional handling which singled out English customs for transmutation into a major system of law necessitated an increasingly artificial relationship between law and society; and the legal historian must become more and more of a lawyer. His intention shifts from relatively static social facts to problems of change. A change made by legislative act will be straightforward for him; there is a direct and visible relationship between social ill and legal remedy. But from the end of the thirteenth century to the beginning of the nineteenth, legislation played a tiny part in the development of private law. Nearly all of it was done in the courts; and judges do not, as does Parliament, make avowed changes in the law in response to argument about social needs. They do not make avowed changes at all; and that is the point.

Legal change under these conditions has the appearance of a conjuring trick: out of the old hat there comes a new rabbit. It is one of the mechanisms of this that I wish to talk about today; and I have chosen it because it illustrates an old-fashioned aspect of legal history which seems to me to need re-emphasis at the present time. The subject is more than a branch of social history. It is also a legal study which has a relevance for lawyers beyond the claims of piety and curiosity. The legal historian has not finished his job when he has identified the pressures which compelled a change; it is obviously not enough to say, for example, that a law of consensual contract came into being because a mercantile community needed it. He must get inside the court-room and hear how the lawyers did it. It was not a vegetable response but required argument, and not social argument but legal argument, legal analysis. And this is what I mean by the title of my lecture. There has been no plan in the development of the common law, even less, as I shall hope to illustrate, than legal historians have sometimes thought. On the contrary, the absence of plan has been a condition of progress. But each step has involved an intellectual problem to be solved by the application of elementary legal ideas. However much it looks like mumbo-jumbo, we have generally not understood a change until we have heard an argument which would have been at least intelligible, perhaps with a little preparation before and a little grumbling after, to Ulpian or Holmes.

That this argument is likely to have important effects, in the real world as well as in legal theory, may seem self-evident; but it has been variously denied. Holmes is here a relevant name. " The life of the law has not been logic: it has been experience." [2] Whole philosophies were built upon his good sense, and what they came to in their most extreme form was that the logic merely clothes the result and is entirely without consequence. Even this was perhaps only to make uncomfortably explicit some comfortable assumptions behind our talk of an inductive empirical system, and our picture of continuous and painless adjustment to social change. Logic is not so obliging. However small a part it plays in deciding the single case—and that is a controversy I would not dare to enter—it plays a large part in legal development. The reasoning adopted yesterday may not have caused yesterday's result; but it governs the terms in which today's dispute is put to a court, or is not put because the lawyers cannot now make a case of it. The " necessities of the time " make demands which cannot always be met; and when they are met, the effectiveness of the response depends upon the logic of the time.

When the demand is, to speak loosely, for regulation in some new area, it can often be reached easily enough from neighbouring premises; though I shall suggest later that the most accessible premises are not always the most appropriate. But the reversal of principles which have been positively established is quite another thing. Logic is directly matched against experience, and shows its strength most obviously in the rarity of such reversals and the difficulty with which they have been brought about. In the nature of the case, there must be resort to fresh premises. The old principles and reasoning are not controverted but abandoned, and the question is approached with a different set of legal ideas. To anticipate my example, the rules of contract yield a result which is no longer acceptable, so ideas from tort are used instead. But though logic is defeated with its own weapon, its strength is shown again in the consequences. What was unacceptable about the old principle was the result; but the approach probably represented the natural

[2] *The Common Law*, p. 1.

analysis of the problem. Using ideas from tort to reconstruct the law of contract is likely to cause both oddities in contract and deficiencies in tort. Fictions and the like are only a symptom of the deep conceptual artificiality into which logic has forced the common law. And this in turn, or so I shall suggest, has affected and may still affect its capacity for natural response even to new demands.

Such change then is indeed more like a trick than the direct magic which the legislator commands: the rabbit is really taken from a different hat. But in one respect the analogy is seriously misleading: the stage cannot have been prepared. Change becomes possible when two lines of reasoning which have developed, as it were, in different compartments, happen to have come sufficiently close for a situation which has traditionally fallen under the one to be represented as within the other. When they reach into the new compartment the lawyers may be acting deliberately and even disingenuously; something like a legislative intention can be imputed to them. But earlier developments in that compartment cannot have been directed. There have been few strategists on the Bench, and none at the Bar: one seeks an argument to win his case, not to pave the way for a change which is probably beyond imagination. Looking back on it, however, the legal historian will see an unbroken line of development; and he can more easily than any other sort of historian be beguiled into supposing that the end was aimed at when early steps were taken. Obvious though the trap is, it is one into which I, at any rate, repeatedly fall; and I shall later try to show it up in connection with the early steps of the process by which our law of contract was won from the ideas of tort.

But first I must justify the proposition that the compartments involved in this method of change have always been conceptual, that events in say the fifteenth century were not different in nature from modern developments by which the law of contract, supposedly about promises, has been altered by resort to the law about statements. The point has been obscured, and a good deal of seeming mumbo-jumbo introduced into legal history, by excessive deference to the formal aspect of the forms of action. Of course, the existence of boundaries between actions made a difference to the problem of change, which presented itself as a matter of rival forms. But it did not necessarily make change more difficult, because the old rule could be left untouched, harmlessly in force. In the action of debt, for example, the debtor by simple contract could make a general denial of indebtedness, and wage his law on it, until 1833. But from the early seventeenth century this was of no consequence in real life, because he would always be sued in a form of action which required jury trial. Again it followed from the availability of wager that his personal representatives could not be sued at all; and again the practical result was reversed, although the old rule was left standing in the disused enclosure formed by the action of debt. The abolition of the forms of action may well have made major change more difficult for the courts, by making it harder to reverse the result without openly reversing the rule. The continued existence of a partially formal barrier between law and equity may be a condition of the continued potency of equity as a means of law reform; its *in personam* operation has always been the most artless means of making a change without actually saying so. But within the common law itself, the abolition of the forms has left us with purely conceptual compartments, and especially with such textbook headings as tort, or the individual torts, and contract. And in this respect, our position is not very different from that in the early days of the common law. No writ, no remedy; no remedy, no right; slogans such as these have made the forms of action appear as though they were primary entities in the law, with the writs playing the part of a law-giver's code. But the writs were attached by red tape to actions which were mostly there first; and the actions themselves, as their names show, mostly represented elementary legal ideas. It is the names, of course, that have caused the trouble. Trespass and covenant became just the names of actions, or at most of very narrow concepts; and so it became possible to read the report of a discussion five hundred years old as being just about the propriety of an action, when it was really about the analysis of the facts. The nearest modern equivalents would be tort and contract; but these would not be exact, and something must be said of the history of the names as such.

" Covenant " presents the fewer problems. Let us start in the middle. From the early fourteenth century, the king's courts applied an invariable rule to actions of covenant brought before them: the plaintiff had to produce a deed sealed by the defendant witnessing the promise. This rule was the outstanding feature of covenant as an action; and it is easy to assume that if the action embodied any concept it was that of a formal contract under seal. But the rule was an adoption and not aboriginal even in the king's courts; and it was not followed in all local courts, for example in London or in Bristol. There is therefore no reason to withhold from the word its dictionary meaning, *conventio*: it is about the enforcement of agreements or promises. A lawyer today might say of a gratuitous oral promise that a claim would sound in contract, even though he added that by the rules of our law of contract it would fail—and that perhaps the matter might be formulated in deceit or estoppel. What the rules of covenant were in local courts, or indeed in the king's courts before a seal came to be necessary and sufficient, we do not yet know. No doubt they varied from place to place, though one would suppose at least that a plaintiff who had performed his side of a bilateral arrangement would be in a strong position.

This introduces one particular in which not merely the rules but the concept of covenant was narrower than our contract. We regard as contractual most claims arising out of most kinds of transaction; covenant was confined to the purer notion of enforcing agreements or promises. The chief difference comes with the kind of obligation which Roman lawyers would describe as contracted *re*. The medieval lender of money for example did not think of himself as relying upon a promise for its return; and this kind of obligation seems to be the original sphere of the word "contract." The complementary nature of the two categories is illustrated in many claims of jurisdiction by franchise-holders, which mention both covenants and contracts. Both are embraced by our modern contract, because in the revolution of the sixteenth and seventeenth centuries both covenant and debt were replaced by *assumpsit*; and it is an odd twist that while we commonly rationalise even the lender's claim in terms of agreement, the informing notion of covenant, it is "contract" that became the generic name. This must be because "covenant" was disabled by its attachment to a form of action, and because in the course of time it acquired the connotations of that attachment, the promise under seal. Consider for example an early eighteenth-century textbook statement: "A Covenant properly is a Specialty, but by Custom *Conventio ore tenus facta* is binding in *Bristol*." [3] It makes sense only in terms of the action; and the writer would no doubt have been incredulous if told that the special custom of Bristol was a survival from the old general law of what we would call contract.[4]

Even more devious is the history of the word "trespass"; and though I have bored legal historians with it before,[5] this gives me a chance to state the results in less indigestible form and, in some particulars, more correctly. At first trespass meant just wrong, *transgressio*, its dictionary sense. It was more vague than covenant,

[3] *The Law of Covenants* (1711), p. 2.

[4] Our usage would probably not have been accepted by the writer: *cf.* p. 15 where, however, he is quoting a case of 1590; 1 Leon. 208. Blackstone uses "contract" as a generic term including covenants under seal; *Commentaries* (5th ed., 1773), Bk. 3, pp. 153, 155; *cf.* Bk. 2, p. 465.

[5] (1958) 74 L.Q.R. at pp. 195, 407, 561.

as tort is more vague than contract; and like tort it could probably have been defined only in terms of what it was not—not contract and so on. Even that negative approach would leave much of what we can separate off as crime, though the public authority inherent in the notion of crime would not always be the king: in a manor court it might be the lord for a breach of agricultural routine, and in London it might be the city for a marketing offence. The procedural separation of crime is a process which I can lament, but cannot trace—at any rate today. But it starts from the same point as our present story: a legal wrong can be seen as offending not merely any individual who may be harmed but also the authority whose law has been broken. In thirteenth-century England there were many such authorities; and the rule was that trespasses, wrongs, whether prosecuted by public authority or the injured party, were matters for the king's court only when the king was, as it were, the appropriate authority. This appropriateness may be all that was at first meant by the phrase " the king's peace " as opposed, for example, to the " sheriff's peace " of the shire court. But the king's peace was most readily broken by a breach of the peace in the modern sense, so that nearly all trespasses coming before the king's courts were wrongs in which force and arms were alleged. One truly complaining of forcible wrong could seemingly choose whether to make these allegations and bring his case before a royal court, or omit them and sue in his shire court. But the victim of a wrong involving no force had ordinarily no choice: he had to sue in his shire court.

In the fourteenth century the position became artificial. On the one hand, even when force was alleged, the king's interest in the breach of his peace became nominal. A fine was still taken from a convicted defendant, and continued to be taken for centuries. But the stringent process by *capias*, originally given to secure this redress for the king, was now treated as being for the plaintiff's benefit and to secure his damages. And on the other hand, some wrongs involving no possible force could be brought within the jurisdiction by careful wording. My favourite case concerns the buyer of a cask of wine, who left it for later collection, and complained that in the meantime his seller, against the king's peace and with force and arms, to wit with swords and bows and arrows, drew off some of the wine and substituted water.[6] I like to picture the honest cask resisting so stoutly. But artificiality might not have provoked a change had it been for the courts to make it. Presumably, however, the decision lay with the Chancery; and in the third

[6] Y.B. 10 Ed. II, Seld.Soc., Vol. 54, p. 140.

quarter of the fourteenth century they began to seal writs returnable in royal courts for the redress of wrongs in which a breach of the king's peace was not even alleged. Perhaps some lost warrant permitted this; an analogous change concerning nuisances was made by statute in 1382.[7] But so far as our evidence goes it just happened.

Trespass could now come before royal courts with no pretence of royal interest. And because there were no standard forms and a special writ had at first to be composed for each case, the writs, and later the actions and even the wrongs, were distinguished by the name of trespass on the case. But trespass on the case was not at first a legal entity any more than trespass *vi et armis* was. They were all just wrongs, and the jurisdictional accident which had divided them might have been without consequence but for a further accident. It has already been mentioned that in trespass *vi et armis*, originally because of the king's interest, process could be by *capias*. But so convenient did this prove that it was extended to purely private law-suits, first to account, and then by a statute of 1352 to most other important personal actions, which were enumerated.[8] But trespass was not mentioned because in 1352 only trespasses *vi et armis*, which had always had such process, could come into the king's courts at all. A generation later, when other trespasses began to come in, there was therefore no warrant for process by *capias*; and the gap was not formally repaired until 1504.[9] By that time the damage had been done. For more than a century it had continued to matter whether or not a trespass writ was formulated with *vi et armis* and *contra pacem*; and since these phrases had become artificial even when jurisdiction hinged on their use, a criterion for their propriety was hard to find.

The search for a common factual feature of trespasses *vi et armis*, by a process which did not end until the eighteenth century, generated a new legal concept, the oddest artefact of the common law: direct forcible injury. And since the search had been for a distinction between trespass *vi et armis* and trespass on the case, commonly shortened to trespass and case, this concept was attributed to the word " trespass." Large consequences followed both

[7] Stat. 6 Ric. II, st. 1, c. 3, made the old viscontiel writs of nuisance returnable in royal courts at the plaintiff's option. In the case of trespass there was a period of confusion when *contra pacem* was capriciously alleged; 74 L.Q.R. at pp. 224, 563, and n. 24 below.

[8] Account: Stat. Marlborough (1267), c. 23; Stat. Westm. II (1285), c. 11. Debt, detinue and replevin (but not covenant, see n. 26, below): Stat. 25 Ed. III, st. 5, c. 17.

[9] Stat. 19 Hy. VII, c. 9. Process in actions on the case was to be as in debt and trespass. The wording shows that case is regarded as an entity distinct from trespass. It is at about this time that *transgressio super casum* begins to appear as a term of art in the plea rolls.

in law and in legal history. In law trespass became a unitary wrong, to be committed with anything from a deliberate punch to a straying cow; and what reason made out of a pair of chronological accidents may have caused widespread injustice. And though in cases of straying shots and straying motor-cars the courts have lately walked through this ghost—eighteenth-century Gothic, perhaps, rather than medieval—it will probably be some time before the clanking of its chains dies away altogether.[10] In legal history, the assumption that " trespass " had always had its modern meaning elicited from the year books a detailed, coherent and anachronistic account: the law could at first comprehend only the simplest physical injuries, and case was a series of developments by analogy, perhaps with statutory aid, to reach more sophisticated wrongs. It is a plausible sequence, but in the dark age of a legal system and not in fourteenth-century England.

In much the same way as " covenant," then, the word " trespass " became disabled from doing its original work; and " tort " was recruited in its place. The noun and its adverb, *atort*, in Latin *injuria* and *injuste*, appear in the claims and defences of every kind of action from the time of our oldest formularies, and were so used as long as these formal phrases were spoken. In the same wide sense the noun turns up in the year books and early reports, and that is the sense it had for Coke.[11] As late as 1677 a treatise alphabetically arranged, the *Doctrina Placitandi*, uses " Tort " for one of its headings; but what is there discussed is the replication *de injuria, de son tort demesne*, the common answer to a plea in justification.[12] This heading has disappeared from a publication of 1771 passed off as including a translation of the *Doctrina Placitandi*, the author of which used the word rather as we would; one of his paragraphs begins: " There is a great difference between torts and contracts." [13] It was precisely in pointing this difference that the modern usage was first foreshadowed. The *Regula Placitandi* of 1691 says that a plea of Not Guilty is not necessarily fatal in *assumpsit*, " and the reason is because *Tort and Deceit* is alledged "; and it also reports an argument in which counsel says: " Here is

10 *Fowler* v. *Lanning* [1959] 1 Q.B. 426; *Letang* v. *Cooper* [1964] 2 Q.B. 53; [1964] 3 W.L.R. 573. Cattle-trespass is an illuminating oddity. In the Middle Ages it might be deliberate, part of a dispute over rights of common; but the same writ was used to bring accidental escapes before a royal court when *contra pacem* had still to be alleged. This being established, a straightforward writ on the case was never invented; and a proposal in 1953 to make the equivalent change, basing liability on negligence, was rejected when it turned out that the strict liability was more convenient for farmers than delving into questions of fault; Cmd. 8746.

11 Co.Litt., f. 158b.

12 *Doctrina Placitandi*, p. 343.

13 *A System of Pleading*, p. 444.

neither Contract nor Privity betwixt the Parties but *Tort* and Wrong." [14] The writer of 1720 who called his book *The Law of Actions on the Case for Torts and Wrongs* must have been using the word in much our sense; but he still felt it necessary to add the " and wrongs " in explanation.[15] Blackstone speaks of " *torts* or wrongs "—italicizing the " torts " in my edition [16]; and according to Winfield the earliest American textbook on the subject, published as late as 1859, was likewise called *Law of Torts or Private Wrongs*.[17] As our term of art, then, the word is late, later than the contraction in the sense of " trespass," itself an indistinct process. Coke says " trespasser " where we should say " tortfeasor," [18] but he expressly equates trespass *simpliciter* with trespass *vi et armis*.[19] There seems to have been a verbal interregnum in the seventeenth century; and if it follows that lawyers were not using the concept itself, the conclusion is not unacceptable or even surprising. Though useful, tort is not an indispensable idea as is contract. It is not one of the elementary particles of the law, but a class, and a residuary class at that. The practical lawyer deals with individual wrongs, and uses the class only when distinguishing other kinds of legal claim. In the seventeenth century most other kinds of legal claim had lately been taken over by the forms of action in what had been called trespass and would later be called tort, and for the time being such distinctions could hardly be drawn. They were the frontiers over which the conceptual war had been fought and lost.

But in the fourteenth and fifteenth centuries such distinctions were being drawn; and what to hindsight look like the earliest battles in that war were probably no more than arguments about the proper analysis of situations which had never before needed to be analysed. Take first the case of the promise ill performed, for example the doctor who undertakes a treatment and does it so badly that his patient is made worse. Today, at least if he is a private doctor, the patient may sue either in tort or in contract; and

[14] *Regula Placitandi*, pp. 191, 201. Italics as printed.

[15] The book is by no means the same as *The Law of Actions* (1710), as stated in Winfield, *The Province of the Law of Tort*, p. 8, n. 1 (a misreading of *Bibliotheca Legum*).

[16] Blackstone, *Commentaries* (5th ed., 1773), Bk. 3, p. 117.

[17] Winfield, *The Province of the Law of Tort*, p. 8.

[18] *Isaack* v. *Clark* (1614) 2 Bulstrode 306 at p. 313: " . . . it should be a hard case, to make him by this to be a Trespasser, and subject unto an Action upon the Case for a Trover and Conversion, onely by his Denyer to deliver them, being demanded, but there ought to be some other act done by him, to make him thereby to be such a Trespasser. . . ." But earlier in this judgment Coke does use the phrase " Trespassor upon the case."

[19] *The Case of the Marshalsea*, 10 Co.Rep. f. 68b at 76a. *Cf.* 2 *Inst.* p. 170, commenting on Stat.Westm. I, c. 6 (amercement " *solonque le quantity del trespasse* ") where he expressly notes the old wide usage. The statute of 1504 extending *capias* to actions on the case uses trespass in the narrow sense; n. 9 above.

normally it does not matter, so we do not worry about the analysis. Nor did it matter in the local courts which at first necessarily heard such cases. There was no seal to ground an action in covenant before the king's courts, and no royal interest to admit it as a trespass. But neither mattered in local courts; and though in London, for example, there seems to have been a remedy at least since the early fourteenth century, nothing would turn on its classification as trespass or covenant.[20] In the king's courts, that was to be crucial. As a trespass it could come in, and did, as soon as the requirement of a royal interest was dropped; but the requirement of a seal in covenant never was dropped. So it is no wonder that the surgeon, the horse-doctor, the ferryman who overloaded his boat and lost its cargo, figure in the earliest trespass actions heard in royal courts with no royal interest, and no wonder that they all argued for the matter being analysed as covenant. Some local courts might have thought them right, though the question would perhaps occur only to the enrolling clerk who had to give the action a name. In 1325, for example, in Littleport, when the owner of grain sued a maltster for malting it badly, the bishop of Ely's clerk called it covenant.[21] And although the king's judges consistently held that such claims were well laid in trespass, there is no reason to suppose either that they were affirming the obvious or that they were conniving in an obvious cheat, still less that they saw themselves as making a first move towards the replacement of one form of action by another. Certainly they saw both the force of the defendant's argument, and the practical inconvenience of accepting it: "... this action of covenant is necessarily maintainable without specialty, because for such little things one cannot always have a clerk to make a specialty." [22] But the discussions are of a genuine problem, of the same nature as those provoked in more recent times by, for example, a statute governing a successful plaintiff's right to costs by reference to the principal sum he recovers, and then

20 An entry of 1300 looks as though an action in covenant had been brought off; *Cal. of Early Mayor's Court Rolls of the City of London, 1298–1307*, p. 81. But an action of 1320 entered on the City's unprinted Sheriff's Court roll must be in trespass: the defendant *usurpando sibi officium surgici* undertook to cure the plaintiff's feet and applied *diversa medicamenta sua . . . contraria* so that she could not walk; and then, perhaps after a refusal to pay, he *vi et armis* entered her house and made off with her goods. For discussions of the early development of this sort of liability, see Kiralfy, *The Action on the Case*, pp. 138–139; and (1958) 74 L.Q.R. at pp. 571–572.

21 *The Court Baron*, Seld Soc., Vol. 4, p. 140. *Cf. Sel.Cas. Concerning the Law Merchant*, Vol. i, Seld.Soc., Vol. 23, pp. 103–104, a St. Ives action in 1317 for building with inferior materials; but substituting inferior materials for those supplied by the plaintiff was called trespass in London in 1300; *Cal. of Early Mayor's Court Rolls of the City of London, 1298–1307*, p. 82.

22 Y.B. Hil. 48 Ed. III, pl. 11, f. 6 at f. 6d, *per* Cavendish.

fixing different sums for contract and for tort. A class-room question suddenly becomes of practical importance.

I wish I thought I understood so clearly what was going on in the cases in which the defendant did not act upon his promise at all. We can hardly be concerned with a frontier incident here. This is the capital city of covenant; and in the end it fell, and trespass actions became generally available. My campaigning metaphor reflects the pervasive assumption that what happened was somehow intended, that there was throughout an aim to circumvent the requirement of a seal. But this is unconsciously to assume a legislator. The minds we want to get inside are the minds of the lawyers who advised plaintiffs to bring trespass actions. They were not out to reform the law, and they are unlikely often to have proffered the desperate chance that a fundamental rule would be reversed for the benefit of one who had foolishly neglected to comply with it. Even if the occasional obstinate client insisted on fighting a hopeless case, his lawyer had to make an argument. Two kinds of argument have been detected in the year books. In three cases between 1400 and 1425 the plaintiff seems to rely on a simple analogy with the cases of ill performance.[23] And, though it comes astonishingly close to success, this evidently fails on the obvious ground that mere failure to perform a promise cannot be anything but a matter of covenant. Success begins to come with a more sophisticated argument that the defendant has deceived the plaintiff. But for a long time this only works when the defendant has actively done something which disables him from performing his undertaking, for example by conveying to a third party land promised to the plaintiff; and this is generally regarded as a handle by which the matter could be dragged into the ambit of ill performance.

Even though they did not in fact succeed, the earlier cases, before there was talk of deceit, provide the greater puzzle. To sue in trespass for the failure to carry out a promise seems just impudent; and if there was no more to it than a smart lawyer trying on an analogy with ill performance, one would expect it to be treated with contempt. But it was not treated with contempt, and chronology suggests that it was not an attempt to push onwards from ill performance seen as an established base. Although the earliest such action reported by the year books was in 1400, it appears from the plea rolls that they were begun a generation earlier, while the base was being established. In Michaelmas term 1370, for example, writs against bad smiths, bad shepherds and a bad tiler are matched by others complaining of a failure to carry

[23] Y.BB. Mich. 2 Hy. IV, pl. 9, f. 3d; Mich. 11 Hy. IV, pl. 60, f. 33; Hil. 3 Hy. VI, pl. 33, f. 36d.

grain and a failure to sow land; and in Easter term 1891 there are six writs for failure to build or repair buildings and one for failure to mow.[24] The rolls of the Common Pleas for these two terms alone occupy the skins of more than a thousand sheep, so that the numbers of such actions are relatively tiny; and it may mean little that I have not found one actually carried to a hearing earlier than the earliest year book example. Even if there were none, it still looks as though there must have been something more in the background than a false analogy to make trespass actions for breach of covenant seem plausible. Something must have obscured the boundary between trespass and covenant, either generally or in a particular class of case.

That it was something in the class of case is possible. All the early plea roll examples mentioned are of the same nature as the earliest year book cases, failure to build or to repair buildings, to carry, or to perform some agricultural operation. Promises for services may have been peculiar in several ways. For one thing, they must have been the chief casualties of the common law requirement of a seal: promises to pay money and to deliver goods would, in suitable circumstances of mutuality, be enforceable without contractual formality in debt and detinue; but an oral promise to serve would not be actionable in covenant in a royal court even though the promisor had been paid. This would at least be a motive for exploiting any confusion caused by opening the jurisdictional barrier. Then again the labour legislation may have introduced confusion of a different kind by treating refusals to serve and departures from service as wrongs. Indeed, the year books themselves suggest that the early cases may possibly be explicable as actions intended to be based on the Statutes of Labourers, but defective for not expressly saying so; if so, it all began with incompetence in plaintiffs' lawyers rather than their effrontery.[25] Or again we may be up against a more deep-seated source of confusion, something to do with status and contract. Outside the common law failures to carry out agricultural operations, at any

24 CP 40/440, mm. 70 (smith); 260 (marshal); 204d (bailee of sheep; *contra pacem* incongruously alleged, as to which see n. 7 above); 309 (shepherd); 520 (tiler, *contra pacem*); 630d (failure to carry by water); 407d (failure to cultivate and sow). CP 40/521 has many misfeasance actions, including several for bad building. Failures to build are: mm. 96d, 201d, 481 (houses); 340 (mill). Failures to repair: mm. 291d, 387d (both mills). Failure to mow: m. 276.

25 Confusion could arise over the need to recite the statute when counting in an action based on it; Y.B. Hil. 5 Hy. V, pl. 26, f. 11. The close relationship between covenant and the statutory action against the departing servant is often made clear: *e.g.*, Y.BB. Mich. 41 Ed. III, pl. 1, f. 17; Mich. 41 Ed. III, pl. 4, f. 20; Mich. 45 Ed. III, pl. 15, f. 15; Hil. 46 Ed. III, pl. 10, f. 4d; Mich. 47 Ed. III, pl. 23, f. 16.

rate, must have been treated as manorial offences far more often than as breaches of covenant; and apart from tenure, the relationship of employer and employee may not always have seemed legally any more than socially the matter of agreement between persons in some sense equal that an apprenticeship was.

A quite different kind of explanation, not restricted to service agreements, would look particularly to the common law. Since trespass was, as tort is, essentially a residuary category, an uncertainty over its boundary with covenant must have its source in covenant. The outstanding fact about covenant in royal courts, indicated by the year books and driven home by the plea rolls, is that after about the first half of the fourteenth century hardly anybody ever used the action except for the purpose of levying a fine. Agreements in general were given force by conditional bonds, in which the performance desired was not itself promised, but made the condition of avoiding a promise to pay money; and litigation was in debt and not covenant. Promises as such, other than promises to pay money, were not being enforced in the king's courts; so that although the name and the action of covenant embodied one of the most basic legal concepts, that concept was not in fact being put through the refinery of professionally conducted litigation. This whole area of the law was lying waste.

This disuse is itself a likely cause of uncertainty about the scope of covenant; but it may be the product of another. Why was the conditional bond universally used instead of the direct deed of promise? If you had to have a deed anyway, one by which your carpenter promised you a large round sum if he had not built the house by Christmas was no doubt more effective (until equity began to disallow penalties) than one by which he simply promised to build it by Christmas. But it takes two to make a contract, and why should the carpenter always agree? It is possible that this mode of contracting, which contemplated redress for failure to perform, was adopted precisely to avoid the writ of covenant which contemplated no such thing. The writ took shape at a time when almost the only kind of agreement important enough for anybody to want to bring to the king's court was an agreement concerning land, and it embodies the most literal notion of enforcing promises: *praecipe quod teneat conventionem*. The words are appropriate for compelling a performance which is still possible, and inappropriate not only for recouping a loss caused by ill performance but also for recouping a loss irremediably caused by failure to perform, for example failure to plough in time for sowing. Whether or not this inappropriateness was a cause of the rise of the conditional bond and the decline of covenant,[26] it may well have combined with it to produce uncertainty about the proper remedy for an irremediable breach, and to make colourable the use of trespass actions. Surely it was in the minds of those, arguing in 1425 for the propriety of a trespass action for failure to build a mill, who put the extreme case of physical damage flowing from a breach of promise, rain spoiling furniture because of a failure to roof, or floods destroying crops because of a failure to ditch.[27] Surely too it played its part in the disablement cases. As early as 1284 the draftsman of the statute of Wales thought it right to deal expressly with the case of one who promises to convey land to the plaintiff and then conveys it to another; the plaintiff cannot have other redress in his writ of covenant, the statute says, than damages.[28] But in 1442 it seemed a reason for allowing a tortious remedy on those facts: to what end, asked a judge, would the plaintiff have a writ of covenant, even if he had a deed, when the defendant cannot keep his covenant? [29]

For these early cases, I have proposed too many answers, probably all wrong. But the question must be right: the plaintiffs' lawyers did not mean to make history, so what were they up to? It is much easier to see what was in their minds when they started talking of deceit in the disablement cases. At first sight this too looks like a dodge, a second and more sophisticated attempt to pass off as a trespass what was really a breach of covenant. But that is to credit the lawyers with too much vision. Deceit in this context was not snatched from the air, or dragged across from fields as remote as the abuse of legal process or even the giving of false warranties on sale. Such illusions are due to the same accident as befell trespass. That you can wrong a man by tricking him into doing something disadvantageous, was as obvious as it is to us; and in local courts proceedings for this kind of trespass were familiar, sometimes at the instance of public authority, as with a seller dubbing his basket of wares, sometimes at the instance of the party aggrieved. But there was no royal interest in such matters, and so deceit did not generally appear in royal courts. The point

26 After this lecture was given, Mr. C. A. F. Meekings kindly suggested to me a quite different kind of explanation for the disuse of covenant, namely that its popularity as the basis of fines had appropriated it to the conveyancer. Once suggested, a connection seems compelling, and it may perhaps have been through the ubiquitous process. That debt did and covenant did not have *capias* would be a motive for using the conditional bond; and the omission of covenant from the statute extending *capias* in 1352 (n. 8 above) may well have been in the interest of the conveyancer.

27 Y.B. Hil. 3 Hy. VI, pl 33, f. 36d, *per* Babington and Cokayne.

28 Stat. Wales, c. 10.

29 Y.B.Trin. 20 Hy. VI, pl. 4, f. 34 at f. 34d, *per* Newton. The "even if" translates *mesque*; it has sometimes been rendered as "unless" which destroys the force of the passage.

appears clearly from an entry of 1280: a woman had been tricked out of her land by a promise of marriage, and justices were ordered to hear her complaint, whether it was to be classified as a plea of land or trespass or deceit.[30] One particular kind of case regularly came in, however, namely where the court itself was deceived; and so the appearance of deceit in purely private affairs after the requirement of a royal interest was dropped, such as the action on a warranty, has been regarded as a development from the process for deceit of the court like the development of case from the mythical trespass.

The result, as with case, has been to represent as legal inventions or the stretching of analogies what were just early appearances in royal courts of claims familiar elsewhere; and the disablement cases turn out to be another example of this. They are generally taken to begin in 1433, when the defendant was a lawyer retained by the plaintiff to arrange a conveyance of certain land to him; and instead he disclosed the plaintiff's plans and arranged a conveyance to a third party.[31] The accident that he was a lawyer has facilitated a derivation from the old process for deceit of a court. In 1442 the defendant was just a landowner who agreed to convey to the plaintiff, and instead she conveyed to another. When sued in deceit, she staked her case on the proposition that the action should be in covenant; and this was argued out in the Exchequer Chamber.[32] To hindsight the plaintiff's action looks like a clever step on the path to a tortious remedy for non-performance of a promise; but the cleverness may just as well have been in the defendant's objection. The claim was not new even in royal courts. As early as 1401 a manorial steward agreed to arrange a customary tenancy for the plaintiff, and then caused the lord to convey the land to a third party; he is sued in deceit, and in the reported argument it is not even suggested that covenant would be appropriate.[33] Nor is there any hint that this was an innovation; nor was it. In 1382 the would-be founder of a lunatic asylum agreed to buy a suitable property and paid for it; and then the vendor sold it to another.[34] The facts

[30] *Sel.Cas. in King's Bench*, Vol. i, Seld.Soc., Vol. 55, p. 65. "*Dominus rex iniunxit Radulpho de Hengham et Waltero de Wymburn' viua voce quod audirent et terminarent querelam Agnetis de Sperkeford versus Willelmum de Pateny, siue esset de placito terre siue transgressionis seu alicuius collusionis vel decepcionis Agnetis de Sperkeford. . . .*" The proper remedy on such facts was evidently a puzzle; *Brevia Placitata*, Seld.Soc., Vol. 66, p. 122; *Casus Placitorum*, Seld.Soc., Vol. 69, p. 30/3. It seems to have become settled as the writ of entry *causa matrimonii praelocuti*; *cf. Novae Narrationes*, Seld.Soc., Vol. 80, p. cxxxii, n. 4.

[31] Y.BB. Hil. 11 Hy. VI, pl. 10, f. 18; Pasch. 11 Hy. VI, pl. 1, f. 24; Trin. 11 Hy. VI, pl. 26, f. 55d.

[32] Y.B. Trin. 20 Hy. VI, pl. 4, f. 34; Kiralfy, *The Action on the Case*, p. 227.

[33] Y.B. Mich. 3 Hy. IV, pl. 12, f. 3.

[34] *Cal. of Select Pleas and Memoranda of the City of London, 1381–1412*, p. 23.

are indistinguishable from those which sixty years later went to the Exchequer Chamber; but they happened in the city of London, whose courts had no requirement of a seal in covenant. Calling the action deceit rather than covenant was therefore not a dodge but the natural analysis. And as with the simple cases of ill performance, though not so promptly, a genuine difficulty arose when actions came into a jurisdiction where the analysis mattered, where covenant was restricted by a formality.

I cannot today go either forwards or backwards from this point. By going backwards, I mean exploring the boundary between covenant and deceit in local jurisdictions. Perhaps there was none, in that a complaint could be double; even if there was, it is unlikely that the promisor's state of mind was decisive, or indeed that there was any single test. In London it looks as though one would not call it deceit unless at least two conditions were satisfied: that the promisee had paid for the promise, and that the promisor had disabled himself from keeping it, as by conveying land to another. If the promise could still be kept, the action would probably be called covenant and judgment would be for specific performance, which remained, where practicable, a normal remedy in the City. Any idea lingering in the common law that the essence of covenant lay in compelling actual performance may therefore have had a more fundamental origin than the mere words of the writ. On the other hand disablement probably did not amount to deceit in London if the promisor had not been paid. In 1366 a plaintiff had agreed to buy land, giving God's pennies but not paying the price, and had bought timber and made arrangements with a carpenter to build; and his action against the defendant, who had sold to another, was apparently in covenant.[85] Obviously the essence of deceit was being tricked out of something. And it may be—to cast a glance forward in the common law—that the general trespassory remedy for failure to keep a promise, at first apparently available only when the promisee had paid or done his part, was just the simple application of this idea suggested by Ames; and hence the doctrine of consideration. Even if so we still need to find out at what point, if ever, it became a mere matter of chicanery. The development of *indebitatus assumpsit*, for example, whereby a trespassory action could be used to recover debts, looks from its beginning like a brazen manoeuvre to avoid using the action of debt with its wager of law. But it may not be coincidence that centuries earlier we find talk of deceit in London actions against

[85] *Cal. of Plea and Memoranda Rolls of the City of London, 1364–1381*, p. 56.

buyers who have induced their sellers to rely on special arrangements for payment.[36]

I have spent time on these early questions because they interest me most, and because like many inaugurals this is really a sermon; and to the extent that it is directed to legal historians its message, right or wrong, is now obvious—so obvious that I would not presume to state it if it did not constitute a confession of past and probably future guilt. Only at the most minute level of detail can our question " How did it happen? " correspond to a contemporary " How can it be brought about? " It is difficult even to see from a distance what to the lawyer of the time was a life-sized problem; and if we are to see it through his eyes, we have to furnish his mind. Our knowledge of later happenings, the false background of one looking backwards, must be taken out; and the implications of this are as hard to reckon with as those of most truisms. Instead there must be put in a background which includes a framework of elementary legal ideas accommodating the practice of local courts as well as the forms of action available in the king's courts. The making of the common law has too often been imagined as consisting of two distinct phases: first it earned its name by absorbing local custom; and then, having collected all the materials it was ever to have and arranged them into the pattern of the forms of action, it sealed itself off, and developed by rearranging the pattern. Lawyers are credited with more than human cunning, and less than ordinary sense.

But the morals which my lecture is chiefly meant to point are for those who practise and those who teach a system of law which has been capable of exploits, however small the stages by which they were brought about, like the reconstruction of contract out of materials taken from tort. It is a method of development which produces great logical strength in detail and great overall disorder; and in particular, barriers which seem fundamental in other systems are insubstantial in ours. A topical example is our propensity to convert an obligation about an object, such as a matrimonial home, into a proprietary right over it.[37] Lack of symmetry in itself is not

[36] *Cal. of Early Mayor's Court Rolls of the City of London, 1298–1307*, pp. 170–171. *Cf.* the fragment of a thriller at p. 247.

[37] *National Provincial Bank* v. *Hastings Car Mart* [1965] 3 W.L.R. 1. The recent history of licences in general is a good example of development by reaching into a seemingly inappropriate compartment of ideas. For some reason such as the Rent Restriction Acts, the appropriate rules, those concerning leases, yield an undesirable answer; so a new starting point is sought in contract. The special dexterity of equity in making rights *in rem* out of rights *in personam*, that is to say in reaching third parties, depends upon its nominal basis: conscience is a matter of undifferentiated wrong, and the cage of privity is replaced by the illusory tether of notice. But if a property right is created, considerations of true wrong are expelled; consider *L.C.C.* v. *Allen*

of course a defect requiring action; but nor is it a virtue, a sign of good sense to be modest about. It is a fact to be reckoned with, and an important one. Abandoning the natural approach to a problem for transient reasons has compelled a capricious use of legal resources, and elementary ideas have been exploited because they were accessible rather than because they were apt. Over the centuries the landscape has been ruthlessly transformed: whole conceptual areas have been laid waste, and others have been made to support activity beyond what they will naturally bear.

This may be illustrated by a more cavalier raid into history, to collect some remoter consequences of the development of which we have examined the earliest stages in such detail. In contract itself there is the odd career of consideration. At any rate so far as the common law is concerned, it began in *assumpsit*; and it may have been, as Ames thought, the promisee's damage when he expresses the matter as a deceit. But it came to seem so much the essence of contract, that some jurisdictions abolished what they took to be the intrusive binding property of the promise under seal. On the face of it they were extirpating the last trace of our original law of contract; and they incidentally set themselves in its most acute form the general problem of the gratuitous promise for which ideas of justice or policy demand enforcement. Now it is the new rules of contract that have to be evaded; and resort is made more or less whole-heartedly to estoppel, an idea again springing from statement rather than promise. And there is another sense in which none of this may be as novel as it looks. We know little enough about the process by which a seal became necessary, and almost nothing about its becoming sufficient. But it did not begin as a contractual formality; and the magic was surely first seen as precluding discussion rather than as directly giving force to a promise.

Less familiar, but not less striking, are some of the consequences in other parts of the law. *Assumpsit* and the action for breach of warranty absorbed the concept of deceit, and carried it off into contract; and the obvious gap left in the law of wrongs was repaired as late as the eighteenth century by what was regarded as the invention of a new tort of deceit. But more fundamental damage had been done. When deceit was diverted into contract, it was

[1914] 3 K.B. 642. In the common law, the strict liability in conversion is similarly the result of expelling fault from a personal remedy to make it serve a proprietary purpose. It should be added that the common law, although not as productive as equity, has manufactured property rights: the passing of property on a sale of goods came about in a mysterious way; but the lease was a simple matter of adding to a contractual right tort remedies against third parties.

also sterilised: if the actions were to enforce promises, their allegations of deceit had to be emptied of meaning. Deceitful conduct as such was left without specific effect in the common law; and the elaboration of fraud as one of the great categories of equitable jurisdiction reflects this. But it is important not to misread the story. That fraud fell to Chancery and Star Chamber can be taken, especially in association with the old misunderstanding about trespass and case, as showing a primitive poverty of ideas in the early common law, which could comprehend a taking or a blow or duress but nothing so subtle as cheating. This is deeply anachronistic. Deceit miscarried in the king's courts because the lawyers were too clever rather than too stupid, and it had flourished in the local jurisdictions from which the common law was drawn. We cannot be sure whether in those jurisdictions it was seen as a distinct entity which could exist outside a contractual context, but the question would not often arise; that is why the common law was able to manage so long without the tort. Deceitful statements, whether about the quality of goods or otherwise, are generally made to induce a contract; and in London, at any rate, it seems that a natural remedy was to undo the transaction.[38] In this matter the Chancellor was no innovator in substance or in treatment.

So far-reaching have been the consequences of this particular development that it may be instructive to cast up a balance sheet. In place of a single idea we have at least three: warranty denatured by absorption into the contract, representation operating outside it, and the resurrected tort. And there are secondary complications about honest misstatement, which may be disposing us to leave deceit once again without specific effect in civil actions. The tendency to use and then supersede the idea like this deserves thought. It is of course convenient to fix liability on a cheat without having to call him so. But the pressure seems never to have been directed to this end, but to generalising the liability; and it is an accidental result that the cheat comes to mingle unmarked among others caught by the general rule. In the end the elementary concept, a moral as well as a legal one, is used as a foundation which disappears under the rules built on it. And it may be that the idea of negligence is playing a similar part in the law today.

As with deceit, though not so profoundly, the history of negligence has been affected by the interaction between contract and tort; though in this case the story begins with ill performance. This was remedied, as we have seen, by actions which the king's

[38] *Cal. of Plea and Memoranda Rolls of the City of London, 1364–1381*, p. 126 (sale of entailed property as fee simple; the defendant was also imprisoned).

courts categorised as trespass. But the writs generally used the magnetic word *assumpsit*, and the idea of negligence was thereby attracted—not to speak too definitely—into the contractual sphere of influence. In this century there was still some ghost of privity to be laid in fixing a manufacturer with liability to the ultimate consumer of his product; and the story is not over yet. So great is the difficulty of proving negligence in such cases that in some jurisdictions attempts are being made to resort to the idea of warranty. The frontiers are to be crossed again. Either privity must be eluded, and the matter smuggled back into contract, or warranty itself must be returned to its first home in tort.[39] Such an attempt to reverse history has of course a more substantial motive than the difficulty of proof. The situation is one in which the language and concepts of specific individual fault may come to seem inappropriate for governing the incidence of loss. It is at first sight curious that the common law, which makes so little use of deceit, should do so much with negligence as a basis of liability; and the historian, at least, is tempted to wonder how far this owes more to its accessibility than to its fitness for all the purposes which we make it serve. To hold that there is a duty of care in a new kind of situation is the modern equivalent of sanctioning a new writ. But since negligence became a tort, instead of the convenient title for a miscellany, it has been possible for us to go on believing in the difficulty of creating new torts without seeing an incongruity in the growth of negligence; and it has been easiest for us to establish new liabilities, new duties, in terms of duties of care. The tort of negligence is the residuary legatee of the action on the case, itself the residue of the residuary category of tort; and we may, like the clerk who files all accessions under Miscellaneous, be overloading the idea.

And this leads me to my conclusion. Questions like the desirability of reaching the manufacturer by means of negligence are asked more easily in the United States, because the conceptual frontiers are less closely guarded. Multiple jurisdictions and discordant precedents keep authority in its place; and on this side of the Atlantic it may be that we must increasingly rely on legislation for major change. Since I have been at pains to show some of the unreasonable things that reason has made case law do, perhaps I should welcome this prospect; but in some areas, at least, I believe that we should be the losers. The common law has traced odd patterns by following its nose; but this is because it has by and large turned, however clumsily, to tasks needing to be done. There

39 See generally, *Prosser on Torts*, 1955 ed., p. 506. I am indebted to Professor Samuel Donnelly of Syracuse Law School, N.Y., for pointing out to me the relevance of these warranty questions during a session last summer at N.Y.U.

will always be enough such tasks for us to want all means of doing them; and I personally would like to see the welcome proposals for improving our legislative machine supplemented by a relaxation in our rules of precedent. But the growing stiffness of the common law in England may not derive so much from authority as from the submissive attitude authority produces. The chief benefit of more obvious choice is to compel more elementary thought, both about results and about reasoning. The lesson has been tardily learnt, and in this School we are particularly trying to apply it, that the lawyer must attend to the results in real life of his reasoning; but the reasoning remains his special business. It is not enough to turn out a student who merely knows the rule, and not much better if he is merely discontented with it. Whatever is to be the balance between legislation and precedent, the vitality of the law depends upon the enterprise of lawyers in exploiting their elementary materials. And if they have never thought about any law but English law, or any period but the present, they may neither guess the range and qualities of those materials, nor even understand that their business is not to find answers but to make them.

S. F. C. MILSOM.

[19]

Legal Principles and the Limits of Law

Joseph Raz*

Most people tend unreflectively to assume that laws belong to legal systems. "Most educated people," writes H. L. A. Hart, "have the idea that the laws in England form some sort of system, and that in France or the United States or Soviet Russia and, indeed, in almost every part of the world which is thought of as a separate 'country' there are legal systems which are broadly similar in structure in spite of important differences."[1] This includes for most people the assumption that laws differ from non-legal rules and principles. There are, for example, moral rules and principles, social customs, constitutions and regulations of voluntary associations, and so on, which are not laws. Many legal philosophers have tried to justify this common assumption. Various criteria have been offered for demarcating the limits of law, for testing whether or not a particular standard belongs to a particular legal system. Various suggestions have been made concerning the importance of the distinction between what is legal and what is not, and the ways in which, by preserving it, we promote our understanding of law and society. For it has often been acknowledged that the distinction is not an easy one to draw in precise terms, and that any reasonable test would admit the presence of borderline cases. Despite these difficulties many theorists have thought that the distinction is worth preserving, partly because it is not difficult to apply in the majority of cases and partly because it seemed to them crucial for a proper understanding of law and society.

On this, as on almost any other fundamental question, opinions differ. There have been theorists who disputed the possibility of drawing the distinction between laws and non-legal norms, or who thought that far from clarifying it actually obscures our understanding of law and society. Recently, in a powerful article, Professor Dworkin has joined those who challenge the orthodox position that what is law may be separated from what is not. But the way in which Professor Dworkin formulates his conclusion is revealing. "I conclude," he writes, "that . . . we must reject the positivists' first tenet, that the law of a community is distinguished from other social standards by some test in the form of a master rule."[2] He clearly believes that there is no test,

* Senior Research Fellow, Nuffield College, Oxford. M. Jur. 1964, Hebrew University, Jerusalem; D. Phil. 1967, Oxford.

1. H.L.A. HART, THE CONCEPT OF LAW 2-3 (1961).
2. Dworkin, *The Model of Rules*, 35 U. CHI. L. REV. 14, 45 (1967), reprinted under the title *Is Law A System of Rules?*, in ESSAYS IN LEGAL PHILOSOPHY 25, 59 (R. Summers ed. 1968) [hereinafter cited as Dworkin, with page references to the original article and, in brackets, to the reprinted paper].

however complex, which distinguishes "the law of a community" from "other social standards," but he explicitly rejects only Hart's way of drawing the distinction by reference to "a master rule," the rule of recognition. As Professor Dworkin makes clear, he chooses to concentrate his attack on Hart, not just because he is concerned with the defects of Hart's theory, but because it is the most sophisticated version of the view he is challenging. In evaluating Professor Dworkin's case it is essential to try to separate those comments which bear merely on Hart's views from those which go to the root of the matter and cast doubt on the advisability of drawing a distinction between laws and other standards or on the very possibility of doing so.

I am not concerned here with refuting Professor Dworkin's criticism of Hart or of "positivism," as defined by him, in general.[3] My main concern is to argue that there is nothing in Professor Dworkin's arguments to show that there is reason to abandon the attempt to draw the limits of law. I will also suggest some, though by no means all, of the reasons which should lead us to persevere in the attempt. Professor Dworkin's arguments turn on the crucial role that principles play in the law, and it is to the examination of legal principles that we must first turn.[4]

3. If pressed to find allies I will certainly find them among those commonly known as legal positivists. I doubt, however, whether on examination we will find any legal philosopher who fulfills Professor Dworkin's definition of a positivist. His positivist is as rare an animal as the mechanical jurisprudent. But that is a different story.

4. Throughout this essay the expressions "norm," "standard," "rule," and "principle" are extensively used. The sense in which these terms are employed will emerge in the discussion. The following diagram summarizes their relations to one another. Occasional deviant usages (*see, e.g.*, pp. 827-28, 835 *infra*) will be distinguished.

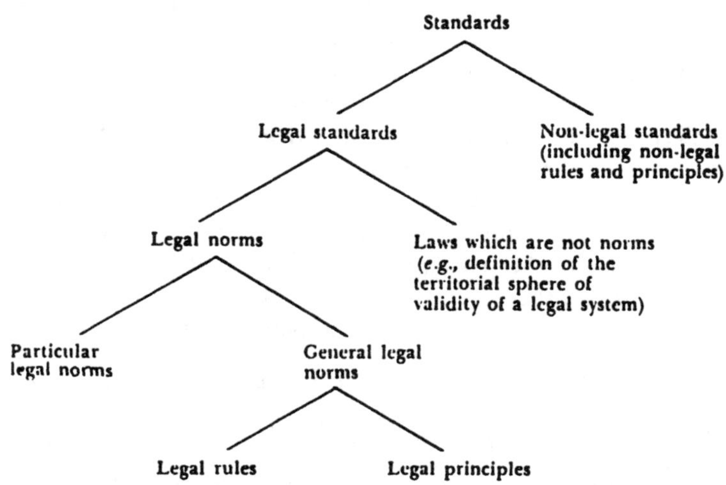

Legal Principles and the Limits of Law

I. Legal Rules and Legal Principles

A. *The Individuation of Laws*

Classifying laws into logically distinct categories has always been one of the major tasks of legal philosophy. Many generations of theorists have shared in repeated attempts to analyze the logical characteristics of laws and to identify and contrast various types of laws in respect of their logical properties. Professor Dworkin's analysis of the nature of legal principles is yet another contribution to this venture. Professor Dworkin calls our attention to a logical distinction between various laws which has been neglected by some, and which he attempts to analyze: the distinction between rules and principles.

The classification of laws presupposes a solution to the more fundamental problem of the individuation of laws, *i.e.,* an answer to the question "What is to count as one complete law?" A brief explanation must be given of both the nature of this problem, and of the reasons an answer to it is presupposed by any classification of laws.[5]

We find our law in statute books and law reports. These are neatly divided into separate judgments, statutes, regulations, by-laws, and so on. It might seem that to find what is one complete law is an easy task. Every section in a statute, every judgment of a court embodies one complete law. But to say this is to misunderstand the question. As Bentham reminded us in 1789:

> What is a law? What the part of a law? The subject of these questions, it is to be observed, is the *logical,* the *ideal,* the *intellectual* whole, not the *physical* one: the *law,* and not the *statute.* An enquiry, directed to the latter sort of object, could neither admit of difficulty nor afford instruction. In this sense . . . [s]o much as was embraced by one and the same act of authentication, so much as received the touch of the sceptre at one stroke, is *one* law: a whole law, and nothing more. A statute of George II made to substitute an *or* instead of an *and* in a former statute is a complete law; a statute containing an entire body of laws, perfect in all its parts, would not be more so. By the word *law* then, as often as it occurs in the succeeding pages is meant that ideal object, of which the part, the whole, or the multiple, or an assemblage of parts, wholes, or multiples mixed together, is exhibited by a statute; not the statute which exhibits them.[6]

5. For a more detailed discussion of these problems, see J. Raz, The Concept of a Legal System chs. 4, 6 (1970).

6. Introduction to the Principles of Morals and Legislation, in J. Bentham, A Fragment on Government with An Introduction to the Principles of Morals and Legislation 429-30 n.1 (W. Harrison ed. 1960).

In a sense Bentham's point is known to every student of law who, when in need to learn the law bearing on a problem, will turn first not to the law reports or statute books but to the legal textbook, whose purpose is to represent the content of the law in an orderly fashion while largely disregarding the fact that any given paragraph may be derived from various statutes and precedents. Authors of textbooks and students of law generally, however, while being largely indifferent[7] to the original divisions of the law by the lawmaker,[8] are equally indifferent to any other attempt to divide the legal material into separate and complete laws. Their interest is in the content of the law; its formal structure does not concern them. Not so the legal philosopher. He is sometimes more interested in the formal structure of laws than in their particular content. To study their formal structure, their logical properties, he must have a doctrine of individuation of laws.

Let me illustrate the point with a few examples. Let us assume that a legal philosopher tells us that all laws are commands. We produce three counter-examples. The first is a section in a constitution saying that "Parliament shall have power to enact laws concerning the rights and duties of property." The second is a section in a statute providing that "every person of age and sound mind shall have power to make a will determining the disposition of his property after death." The third is a statement made by a court in rendering judgment stating that "every person has a right to personal security." None of these, we claim, is a command; therefore, not every law is a command. Have we refuted the theory of our philosopher friend? We have done so only if the three statements we produced are each a statement of one complete law. For our friend may claim, as did Austin and Bentham, for example, that they are merely descriptions of parts of laws or deductions from proper descriptions of laws. He may claim that our constitutional provision does, indeed, establish a law which is a command. It is a command to all to obey any laws made by Parliament regulating the rights and duties of property. This was not the language used by the legislator, but this is the proper description of the constitutional law he made. Statements that Parliament has power to enact such laws made subsequent to the adoption of the constitution

7. Except occasionally for purposes of interpretation.

8. When there is a lawmaker. Much of the law is developed by way of custom and the constantly evolving practices of the courts. Some of the most important laws, as Professor Dworkin reminds us, were not formulated by legal institutions. They underlie institutional activities and are first formulated by commentators.

are true statements of law, but they do not properly describe a law. They are valid deductions from a statement which does properly describe the law and which shows that it is really a command of a special type: a command to obey.

As to our second example, our philosopher friend may claim that, by enacting the section relating to wills which we have quoted, the legislator made not one complete law but a part of many distinct laws, all of which are commands. The laws relating to property, he would claim, are in fact enormously complicated commands prohibiting certain people from interfering with property in certain ways. These commands apply only to people not owning the property or not having certain other rights in it. The commands, therefore, include elaborate specifications of their conditions of application, and the statutory provision we cited is part of these conditions of application. It states in effect that a person should be exempt from the prohibition against interference if, *e.g.*, a deceased owner of the property named him in his will as the future owner, and that other people will be exempt from the prohibition if he subsequently transfers the property or an appropriate right in it to them, etc. Thus, our friend will patiently continue, our mistake was to think that the statutory provision is a complete law, whereas in fact it is merely a part of many laws. Once we understand this, he will triumphantly conclude (expecting us to be able to deal on our own with our third example), we will see that all laws are indeed commands. For, as is by now clear, in his view the court's statement that every person has a right to personal security is not a statement of one law but a summary reference to many. The court in its reasoning alludes to the laws against murder, assault, and false imprisonment, among others, and to the laws commanding violators of these to pay damages.

It would probably be generally accepted that our philosopher friend is mistaken, that not all laws are commands. He is mistaken not because he is employing principles of individuation, but because he has accepted the wrong principles. Every theory about the logical types of laws presupposes a doctrine of the individuation of laws, and for the most part it can be attacked or defended only by attacking or defending its underlying doctrine of individuation. There is no need to tackle here the problem of the individuation of laws in general.[9] It is, however, very important to be constantly aware of it when dis-

9. I have tried to do this elsewhere. J. RAZ, *supra* note 5.

cussing the status of principles. If we do this we will soon realize that not everything which looks like a legal principle is a legal principle, at least not in the sense that Professor Dworkin has in mind.

We often have need to refer summarily to a body of legal rules without specifying their content in detail. Such references are frequently made by courts in the course of justifying their decisions. These references usually take the form of a statement of a principle, but they are not statements of the content of laws of a special type, namely legal principles. They are merely a brief allusion to a number of rules. Someone may say that in his country the principle of freedom of speech is recognized by law. When asked what he means he may say that the only laws setting limits to the liberty to express opinions are concerned with libel and military security; that censorship of films, books and the theatre must be justified by the protection of infants; that there are detailed regulations guaranteeing access to the mass media to people representing all shades of opinions on public matters; and so on. His statement that in his country freedom of speech is recognized by law can thus be seen to be a summary reference to a great number of laws, not a statement of the content of a single law. Another person, by contrast, may say that a certain legal system incorporates the principle of freedom of speech because it contains a law instructing the courts and all public officials to protect freedom of speech in all cases, even those not governed by particular rules. This person's statement *is* a statement of the content of one particular law, and it is a principle in the sense in which Professor Dworkin employs the term. It imposes an obligation and thus guides the action of courts and officials.

Professor Dworkin is only dimly aware of the problem of individuation. He does say that not every statement of a rule is a complete description of it.[10] Many such statements omit many of the exceptions which are part of the rule and which must be included in any complete statement of its content. He is, however, completely oblivious to the importance of the doctrine of individuation to a discussion of principles. In particular, he disregards the fact that some statements by courts which look like statements of legal principles are in fact no more than abbreviated references to a number of legal rules. It seems to me, to take just one of Professor Dworkin's examples of principles, that a court's statement that freedom of contract is not such an im-

10. Dworkin, *supra* note 2, at 25 [37].

mutable doctrine as to admit of no qualification[11] is merely a reference to the fact that there are rules qualifying the freedom of contract and there is a rule granting the courts power to introduce further qualifications. (The exercise of this power is subject to principles guiding the discretion of the courts in general. But these principles are distinct from the power granted to the courts.)

The first lesson to be drawn from applying the doctrine of individuation to the discussion of legal principles is that the apparent multiplicity of principles is deceptive. Some apparent statements of principle are merely abbreviated references to a number of laws, not statements of the content of one complete legal principle.

B. *Conflicts Among Laws*

Bentham, Austin and many others assumed that valid laws do not conflict. They knew, of course, that conflicting statutory provisions and conflicting judicial opinions can easily be found, but they believed that in such cases what is valid are only the laws to the extent to which they do not conflict. In a complete representation of the law of a country all conflicts are resolved by the application of legal rules and principles such as that *lex posterior derogat priori*. The principles of individuation should be so framed to ensure that laws do not conflict. A single law may include many limitative and exceptive provisions, to use Bentham's terminology, qualifying the application of its main provision, and ensuring that it does not conflict with other laws. But one law may not conflict with, and thus qualify, another law.

This is not, however, the way we ordinarily think of the relation between non-legal rules and principles. We know not only that principles like "maximize total happiness" and "strive to increase equality" may conflict when applied to particular cases, but also that rules may sometimes conflict as well. Sometimes one can keep one's promise only by telling a lie. We do not normally think that such conflicts are merely apparent and that each rule in fact includes qualifications such as "keep your promise unless this entails telling a lie." We believe that sometimes we should lie rather than break a promise and sometimes we should break a promise rather than tell a lie, and although what we should do depends on general considerations there is no way of setting all of them down beforehand. We can attend to many problems only when they arise; we are unable to decide what

11. *Id.* at 24 [36].

to do solely on the basis of previously accepted rules. We are on the whole reconciled to the fact that rules may conflict and that they impose obligations which may be overridden in particular cases by contrary considerations.[12]

Professor Dworkin adopts an intermediate position on this issue. Legal rules, he claims, do not conflict whereas legal principles do. Indeed, he turns this into the first distinguishing characteristic between legal rules and principles:

> The difference between legal principles and legal rules is a logical distinction. Both sets of standards point to particular decisions about legal obligation in particular circumstances, but they differ in the character of the direction they give. Rules are applicable in an all-or-nothing fashion. If the facts a rule stipulates are given, then either the rule is valid, in which case the answer it supplies must be accepted, or it is not, in which case it contributes nothing to the decision.[13]

This means, as Professor Dworkin explains, that if a legal rule stipulates that a certain act ought to be done in certain conditions, then, given that in a particular situation the conditions obtain, the act ought to be done. It cannot be argued that it ought not because of a second legal rule which qualifies the first, for on Professor Dworkin's account a legal rule includes all its exceptions and cannot conflict with another rule. "If two rules conflict, one of them cannot be a valid rule."[14] This distinguishes legal rules from legal principles, since the latter may conflict.

This leads Professor Dworkin to the second distinguishing mark of legal principles, which is entailed by the first. Legal principles have certain relative "weights." Some have greater weight than others. This dimension of weight determines what ought to be done in cases to which conflicting principles apply. "When principles intersect . . . one who must resolve the conflict has to take into account the relative weight of each."[15] Since rules do not conflict they do not have this dimension of weight.

I would like to suggest that legal rules may conflict and have weights, and that therefore Professor Dworkin's remarks should not

12. Some philosophers dispute this view, but this is not the place to discuss the general problem in detail. For a convincing argument in favor of the view expressed here, see Singer, *Moral Rules and Principles*, in ESSAYS IN MORAL PHILOSOPHY 160, 167 (A. Melden ed. 1958).

13. Dworkin, *supra* note 2, at 25 [37].

14. *Id.* at 27 [40].

15. *Id.* at 27 [39].

be regarded as defining the characteristics of rules and principles. The issue here turns on which principles of individuation it would be best to adopt. It is possible to devise principles of individuation which guarantee that every rule includes all its qualifications and that no rules ever conflict with each other. But it would be wrong to accept such principles of individuation. The point at issue can best be illustrated by an example. The criminal law includes a rule prohibiting assault. This rule is qualified by various other laws.[16] Assault is permitted in self-defense, in carrying out lawful orders, in cases of necessity. The rule is also qualified by general laws determining the territorial sphere of validity of the bulk of the laws of the legal system concerned. One might wish to claim, as did Bentham, for example, that no statement of the law against assault is a complete description of that law unless it enumerates all these qualifications. One may claim that the qualifying laws are not separate laws but only parts of the law prohibiting assault. To do so would be to accept a very misguided doctrine of the individuation of laws.

Consider the consequences of accepting this view of the individuation of laws. It will mean, of course, that not only the law against assault but also the laws against homicide, rape, and theft, and every other law, will include these and many other qualifying clauses. We will have fewer laws (the doctrine of self-defense, for example, will not be regarded as separate), but those which remain will be enormously complex. They will also be very repetitive, having much of their content in common (the doctrine of self-defense, for example, will be a part of each of the criminal laws).

To accept such a doctrine of individuation is to misunderstand the function of the principles of individuation. Because of the vast amount of legal material which constitutes one legal system, we need to divide it into smaller units called "laws" in order to be able to refer separately to parts of the total legal system. The principles of individuation are the method of carving small and manageable units out of the total legal material in a way which will promote our understanding of the law by classifying laws into various types and by showing how these laws interrelate and interact with one another. The principles of individuation which are necessary to avoid conflicts among laws yield enormously complex laws which are relatively independent; their inter-

16. The definitions of "assault" and some other offenses often include expressions such as "wrongful" and "unlawful." Such words serve to draw attention to the fact that these rules may conflict with other laws which qualify them.

action with other laws is minimized; they are made to be as self-sufficient as possible. This relative independence is acquired at the cost of making each law very bulky; each is derived from a great number of statutes and cases; and they become repetitive. These were also, as we have seen above, the consequences of denying the status of a separate law to the laws conferring powers to legislate or make wills. For these reasons (among others) we must reject any doctrine of individuation which strives to avoid any conflict of rules by making them so much more complex and repetitive.

Instead we should adopt a doctrine of individuation which keeps laws to a manageable size, avoids repetition, minimizes the need to refer to a great variety of statutes and cases as the sources of a single law, and does not deviate unnecessarily from the (admittedly hazy) common sense notion of a law. Such a doctrine of individuation will result in a greater number of laws which interact with one another, modifying and qualifying each other. This approach is closer to the way lawyers ordinarily think about the law, and also illuminates important connections among laws. It focuses attention on the fact that certain groups of laws are affected by certain other laws stipulating doctrines such as self-defense, necessity, etc., while others are not. In short, such a doctrine of individuation better explains the systematic interrelations between various parts of the legal system.

The result is that laws which are not principles may conflict. It is because they conflict or "interact" (to use Professor Dworkin's phrase) that they can modify and qualify one another. Consequently, Professor Dworkin is wrong in holding that principles can be distinguished from other laws because only they can conflict.

This still leaves Professor Dworkin's second point, relating to the "weight" of legal principles, untouched. Legal rules might arguably lack the dimension of weight even though they conflict. But perhaps talking of "weight" here is misleading. Since laws which are not principles conflict, the legal system includes some means of resolving such conflicts. But these means usually determine which one of any two conflicting laws prevails, and the same law always prevails when the two conflict. The law instituting self-defense or mistake of fact as an excuse always overrides the law prohibiting assault. With principles the situation is different. That one principle has more weight, is more important than another, does not entail that whenever they conflict (assuming that no other principle is involved) one ought to follow the more important principle. In determining what is to be done in every case, or type of case, the importance of the principles has to be considered in relation to the amount of good or harm done to the ends they seek to promote. In one case, or type of case, for example, one possible solution may greatly advance the goal of the less important principle, while doing only little harm to the goal of the more important principle. The alternative solutions may cause a great deal of damage to the goal of the less important principle while promoting only slightly the goal of the more important principle. In such cases the less important principle is to be preferred. In other cases the calculation may be different.

By somewhat modifying Professor Dworkin's second point, one might claim that though both rules and principles have relative weights, they behave differently in many instances of conflict. Conflicts between rules are determined solely by their relative importance; conflicts between principles are determined by assessing their relative importance together with the consequences for their goals of various courses of action. It seems to me that this is a correct observation of one important difference between rules and principles (in one sense of "principles") in most legal systems. It would be wrong, however, to regard this as a logical difference between rules and principles, or to take this feature to be a defining characteristic of principles.

First let us observe that there are some types of conflicts in which rules behave like principles. These are cases in which a rule conflicts with a principle. Such conflicts are, of course, possible on Professor Dworkin's account. He thinks that once they are brought before a court they may be resolved by amending the rule to avoid future conflicts. This sometimes happens, but at least before the court's decision and often, as I shall argue below, later, rules do conflict with principles. Such conflicts can be resolved either on the basis of the relative importance of the conflicting laws, disregarding the consequences for each law's goal of the possible solutions (and thus treating the principle as a legal rule is normally treated), or by taking into account both the relative importance of the laws and the consequences for the goals of each of the possible solutions (and treating the legal rule in the way legal principles alone are usually treated). In most cases (though not in all) the second method is followed; but, regardless of which method is used, it is apparent that in these conflicts rules and principles are treated in exactly the same way.[17]

17. Naturally, the assessment of the importance of a rule and of the consequences for its goal of various deviations from it depends largely on the reasons for the rule, which

This observation does not deny that legal rules and principles sometimes behave differently in cases of conflict, and does not preclude one from making this difference the defining characteristic of principles. But it detracts from the attractiveness of such a definition. The reason for rejecting the suggested definition depends on the fact that rules and principles are not exclusively legal concepts. We distinguish between rules and principles in morals and other non-legal spheres. A definition of legal "rules" and "principles" which accounts for the non-legal use of these terms is preferable to any definition which does not fit their non-legal usage. It is quite clear that in many non-legal contexts rules and principles behave in conflict in precisely the same way—the way characteristic of the legal treatment of principles. This is not the place to argue this point at any length. Let us just remind ourselves of the conflict between the rules concerning lying and promising. When such conflicts occur we decide what we ought to do not merely by declaring that one rule is more important than the other and is always to be preferred, but by comparing the good and harm to the values protected by them in every case or type of case, sometimes preferring to follow one rule and break the other, sometimes preferring the opposite. I therefore suggest that the logical difference between rules and principles has nothing to do with the possibility of conflict or the way such conflicts are to be resolved. The different treatment of legal rules and principles in cases of conflict is not entailed by their logical differences but is a result of a legal policy. What that policy is we will be able to see after we establish the logical difference between these types of law.

C. *Rules and Principles Distinguished*

The distinction between rules and principles, as Professor Dworkin rightly observes, is a logical one. Legal rules and legal principles are laws of a different logical type. It would be wrong, however, to suppose that all the laws ordinarily called "rules" are of the same logical type, or that all the laws called "principles" are of the same type.[18]

are sometimes that it promotes the ends of certain legal principles. But in precisely the same way the importance of legal principles and of deviations from them depends on the reasons for the principles—which are sometimes other legal principles. Compare, for example, the relation between the following two principles mentioned by Professor Dworkin: "[T]he courts will not permit themselves to be used as instruments of inequity and injustice." "[T]he courts generally refuse to lend themselves to the enforcement of a 'bargain' in which one party has unjustly taken advantage of the economic necessities of the other." *Id.* at 24 [36].

18. Non-legal rules and principles are also of a variety of logical types, but this need not concern us here.

Legal Principles and the Limits of Law

Compare the rule prohibiting assault or the rule, mentioned by Professor Dworkin, that "[t]he maximum legal speed on the turnpike is sixty miles an hour," with the other rule he mentions, that "[a] will is invalid unless signed by three witnesses."[19] The first two rules erect prohibitions. They are legal norms guiding human behavior by proscribing a certain course of action. The third rule neither prohibits any action nor does it impose an obligation to behave in any way. It is not even a power-conferring rule (this being a type of rule distinct from duty-imposing rules), for it does not confer the power to make wills nor does it confer the power to witness wills. There are other rules conferring these powers on certain classes of persons. The rule itself qualifies the rule conferring power to make wills; it makes the successful exercise of this power depend on three witnesses having signed the will.[20] Such rules, and there are many of them, are not norms, they do not guide behavior directly by providing reasons for action as duty-imposing or power-conferring rules do. Rather they affect one's reasons for action indirectly by qualifying the meaning or application of laws which are norms.[21]

Laws which are not norms are a most important category of laws. They have been neglected by most legal philosophers, who refuse to concede that not all laws guide behavior directly, that instead many guide it indirectly through their logical relations with other laws which are norms. Some of the laws which are not norms are often referred to as "principles." This is particularly true of those laws which govern a vast area of law: that is, those which are logically related to a great number of other laws, qualifying them and modifying their application. Thus the law determining the territorial sphere of validity of most of a country's law (which is clearly not itself a norm) is often referred to as a principle. It is not, however, a principle in the sense in which Professor Dworkin uses this term. (In cases of conflict, for example, it behaves like a rule.) Professor Dworkin is interested in principles which are norms; his principles are principles of obligation, they are standards which "point to particular decisions about legal obligations in particular circumstances."[22]

19. *Id.* at 25 [37].

20. One may argue that it is not a separate law at all but merely part of the rule conferring power to make wills. I will assume that the principles of individuation, for reasons similar to those discussed above, permit one to regard this rule as a separate law. *See* pp. 831-32 *supra*.

21. It should be noted that rules may conflict not only with rules of different logical type but also with rules of the same type. Compare the conflict between the rules concerning lying and promising.

22. Dworkin, *supra* note 2, at 25 [37].

The task of analyzing the various categories of legal and non-legal principles is a considerable one. I am only concerned to point out that not all legal principles are of the type discussed by Professor Dworkin. In the analysis I propose I shall follow him in concentrating attention exclusively on principles of obligation, and in trying to distinguish them, not from all other types of laws, but only from rules of obligation, the type they resemble most closely.

Rules and principles of obligation are similar; for, as Professor Dworkin rightly observes, it is "not always clear from the form of a standard whether it is a rule or a principle."[23] Each states a reason that "argues in one direction."[24] That is to say, each states that a certain class of persons (the "norm-subject") ought to perform a certain act (the "norm-act") in certain circumstances (the "conditions of application").[25] The "ought" in both cases is a prima facie "ought," pointing to a reason for action, not an "ought all things considered." For both rules and principles may be overridden in certain circumstances by other rules and principles or by other reasons. Professor Dworkin creates the impression that the norm-subjects of all legal principles are the courts.[26] But other people and institutions may also be the norm-subjects of principles (though it is true that legal principles, like all other laws, are enforced by the courts). One such example mentioned by Professor Dworkin himself is the American constitutional principle that Congress shall not abridge freedom of speech. Another example is the common law principle of the law of negligence, addressed to all the population and prescribing a duty of reasonable care.[27]

Principles are often stated in ways which leave their subjects unspecified. The statement of the principle, mentioned by Professor Dworkin, that an automobile "manufacturer is under a special obligation in connection with the construction, promotion and sale of his cars,"[28] makes clear that its subjects are automobile manufacturers. It is less clear whether another principle he mentions, that "no one may profit from his own wrong,"[29] is addressed to the public at large or to the

23. *Id.* at 28 [40].
24. *Id.* at 26 [38].
25. This terminology is derived from G.H. VON WRIGHT, NORM AND ACTION ch. 5 (1963).
26. *See, e.g.*, Dworkin, *supra* note 2, at 29-31 [41-44].
27. I shall argue below that Professor Dworkin is wrong in denying (*id.* at 28-29 [40-41]) that this is a principle. *See* pp. 841-42.
28. Dworkin, *supra* note 2, at 26-27 [39].
29. *Id.* at 25-26 [37-38].

courts. A more detailed statement of the principle is needed to determine that. That ordinary statements of principles do not set out in detail all their content should surprise no one, and should not lead to the conclusion that the omitted parts do not exist. In the statement of principles their relative weight is seldom mentioned. Similarly, the conditions of application of principles are sometimes omitted. Some principles are universal in the sense that the norm-act ought to be done whenever there is an opportunity to do so, while others are to be applied only in certain circumstances.

The conditions of application of a principle are not automatically narrowed by the fact that it conflicts with an established rule. The principle that no one may benefit from his wrong always applied to murderers inheriting by the will of the murdered person, despite the fact that their right to inherit was protected until 1889 by a rule. It is because it always applied to such cases that the court in *Riggs v. Palmer*[30] could, as Professor Dworkin reminds us,[31] make an exception to the rule in the case of a murderer. Since principles apply to cases which are regulated by contrary rules, one cannot observe that words like "reasonable" and "unjust" make "the application of the rule which contains [them] depend to some extent upon principles . . . and in this way makes that rule itself more like a principle" and then argue that it is nevertheless only a rule because each of "these terms restricts the *kind* of other principles on which the rule depends."[32] In general, all rules are subject to all principles and may be overridden by any of them in particular circumstances. This is indeed one of the main points which Professor Dworkin is rightly anxious to establish. If a law establishing standards of reasonableness is a rule, then it is liable to be overridden by principles like any other. It is hardly plausible to suggest that the function of words like "reasonable" is to immunize the law against general considerations embodied in certain principles. Their function is to do precisely the opposite. It is true that laws prohibiting unreasonable restraints of trade or damage done by negligence do not in themselves embody or refer to all the considerations embodied in all the principles of law; but no principle does either. They are principles of exactly the same nature as the principle, mentioned by Professor Dworkin, that "the courts must examine purchase agreements [of automobiles] closely to

30. 115 N.Y. 506, 22 N.E. 188 (1889).
31. Dworkin, *supra* note 2, at 29 [41-42].
32. *Id.* at 28-29 [41].

see if consumer and public interests are treated fairly," or the other principle he quotes, that the courts generally refuse to enforce a bargain in which "one party has unjustly taken advantage" of another.[33] They are principles, and like every principle embody one consideration or set of considerations which, though of very great weight in their own sphere, are to compete in particular cases with other more general principles.

The distinction between rules and principles of obligation both in law and outside it turns on the character of the norm-act prescribed. Rules prescribe relatively specific acts; principles prescribe highly unspecific actions. Generic acts, types of acts, are of various degrees of specificity. An act is highly unspecific if it can be performed on different occasions by the performance of a great many heterogeneous generic acts on each occasion. It is more specific to the extent to which there is only a small number of generic acts by the performance of which it is performed. Smoking is a highly specific act which is performed by smoking a pipe, a cigarette or a cigar, but not by many other generic acts. Assault, murder, rape, and speeding are likewise relatively specific acts. Promoting human happiness, respecting human dignity, increasing productivity, and behaving negligently or unjustly or unreasonably are highly unspecific acts. It is because of this that we say rules prescribe or proscribe the first class of acts, whereas principles prescribe the second (to the extent that these types of behavior are governed by norms at all). The distinction between rules and principles is, on this analysis, one of degree, since there is no hard and fast line between acts which are specific and those which are unspecific. Consequently, there will be many borderline cases where it will be impossible to say that we definitely have a rule or definitely a principle.

The suggestion that it is this logical distinction between the type of norm-acts prescribed which underlies much of our ordinary usage of the terms "rules" and "principles" may be greeted with some suspicion. We feel that rules and principles play different roles in practical reasoning whether in the law or outside it and that the suggested distinction does not seem to explain this. In fact, however, the logical distinction does explain some of these differences and it indicates how to explain the rest.

Since highly unspecific acts can be performed by performing on

33. *Id.* at 24 [36].

different occasions a variety of more specific acts, the opportunities for performing them encompass the opportunities for performing the more specific acts and are more general than the latter. Norms prescribing highly unspecific acts, consequently, must be justified by more general considerations bearing on a wider area of human activity. Since we justify considerations which apply to a limited range of situations and actions by more general considerations, principles can be used to justify rules but not vice versa. This is, perhaps, the most important difference in the role of rules and principles in practical reasoning in general, and it can be explained by means of the distinction I have suggested. This does not explain all the differences between rules and principles in the law. These, though dependent on the logical distinction, do not derive from it alone. They depend also on various constraints imposed by general legal policies and goals.

D. *The Role of Principles in the Law*

Let me start with a brief survey of five different purposes for which principles are used in the law. I will then make a general comment on their relation to other laws. The extent to which principles are used for these different purposes varies greatly among different legal systems. Even within one legal system some principles are used for all of them, while others are restricted to a few; and in some branches of the law principles are relied on more extensively than in others I will not try to analyze in detail the role of principles in any particular legal system. My aim is only to isolate some of the different tasks principles may be assigned. These tasks are of a very general nature. Further subdivisions are needed for a complete account of the functions of principles. I will introduce one subdivision in a later section, but otherwise I shall restrict myself to the more general categories. Though the tasks identified can be performed by various types of principles, I shall as before confine the discussion to principles of obligation.

1. *Principles as grounds for interpreting laws.* This is perhaps the most extensive and least inhibited use to which virtually all principles are put. Principles are used for the interpretation of all laws, including other principles of a more restricted application. There is a very strong presumption in most legal systems that other things being equal an interpretation which makes a law conform to a principle is to be preferred to one which does not. Obviously, some interpretations

often conform better to some principles than others, and the courts have to decide which interpretation to prefer. This role of principles is of the utmost importance since it is a crucial device for ensuring coherence of purpose among various laws bearing on the same subject. The importance of this function of principles can be gathered by comparing various legal systems which, despite great similarity in their rules, reach different conclusions in many cases because they apply different principles for their interpretation.

2. *Principles as grounds for changing laws.* The first function of principles merges into the second, since the borderline between an interpretation of a law and its amendment is notoriously a blurred one. Nevertheless the two functions are distinct, and it is not difficult to distinguish between them in the majority of cases. The doctrine of precedent, where accepted, commonly includes the understanding that laws developed through precedent are subject to amendment by the use of principles. This does not mean that judge-made rules are often upset; for, as Professor Dworkin reminds us, principles are often conservative in nature. Subordinate legislation is also subjected to relatively extensive review in light of legal principles. Though subordinate legislation, unlike judge-made law, is often amended on the ground of being in conflict with principles, it is seldom annulled for that reason. Many legal systems, however, stipulate that subordinate legislation must stand some test of reasonableness, thus rendering it void or voidable if it contradicts very fundamental principles. Principles are used much more sparingly when parliamentary legislation is concerned, except in countries which have a formal constitution from which certain principles can be shown to derive.

3. *Principles as grounds for particular exceptions to laws.* Sometimes a law is not applied to a case on which it bears on the ground that to do so in those particular circumstances would sacrifice important principles; but the law is not thereby modified. This may often occur in countries where the doctrine of precedent is not recognized but where principles are allowed to override rules in particular circumstances. In common law countries this use of principles is more restricted, but nonetheless of considerable importance. The principle of laches, for example, is one of a group of principles of equity which is characteristically used in this way. In contrast we may remember that the principle "no one may profit from his own wrong" is characteristically used in the second manner described earlier, *i.e.*, as ground for changing and qualifying rules.

Legal Principles and the Limits of Law

4. *Principles as grounds for making new rules.* When principles but no other laws apply to a certain range of problems, courts act to regulate the area by making new rules. This is a very important way in which the common law develops: new rules are made on the basis of established principles.

5. *Principles as the sole ground for action in particular cases.* There are situations in which what ought legally to be done is determined directly by the application of various principles to the case. This function of principles is radically different from those previously mentioned, for here principles do not operate through the mediation of rules. They are not grounds for the interpretation or modification of rules, nor do they compete with them or serve as grounds for creating them. It is easy to underestimate the extent to which principles are used in this way in most countries. The whole area of sentencing is governed almost exclusively by principles. The activities of public officials and administrative agencies are largely governed by principles in this fashion. The law confers certain powers on the agency and directs it to use them to promote certain policy goals in accordance with general principles. The exercise of discretionary powers is typically guided by principles rather than rules.

It is true, nevertheless, that on the whole there is a marked tendency in the law of many countries not to rely on the direct application of principles but to use them to govern the operation of rules in the ways indicated above. This is particularly true when individuals rather than courts and officials are the norm-subjects of the principles.

Some of the reasons for preferring rules to principles in the direct regulation of behavior have to do with the particular conditions of various countries or of different branches of the law. But at least one general reason for this preference is fairly obvious. Principles, because they prescribe highly unspecific acts, tend to be more vague and less certain than rules. On the other hand, and for the same reason, they are particularly suitable for incorporating into the law very general goals and values, whereas rules are more apt to reflect more concrete considerations which apply to particular situations.

Since the law should strive to balance certainty and reliability against flexibility, it is on the whole wise legal policy to use rules as much as possible for regulating human behavior because they are more certain than principles and lend themselves more easily to uniform and predictable application. It is on the whole advisable to limit the use of principles to govern the creation and application of rules in order to ensure adequate flexibility in changing them and to prevent some of their unforeseen and undesirable effects. Some areas, such as governmental activities, cannot be adequately regulated by rules, and they must be directly governed by principles. But these cases are exceptional. Since in the use of rules the premium should be on certainty, whereas in the use of principles the premium is on flexibility, it is wise to accept relatively simple methods of resolving conflicts between rules which will not detract from the predictability of their application. No similar reasons apply to the methods of resolving conflicts between principles. This explains the difference noted above between the treatment of rules and principles in cases of conflict. The difference stems from reasons of legal policy. It is not a logical difference between the concepts of a rule and a principle.

In fact, all the comments made in this section concerning the relative roles of rules and principles apply only to their use in the law and similar institutions and are not entailed by the concepts of a rule and a principle. In morality, where certainty and uniformity are generally less valued than correctness of judgment, rules have a much more limited role to play than in the law. Principles are to be regarded as governing directly most occasions for action and judgment affected by moral considerations. For the same reason conflicts of rules and conflicts of principles are not, in moral assessments, treated differently.

II. Principles and the Limits of Law

By the thesis of the "limits of law" I mean the position that there is a test which distinguishes what is law from what is not. Professor Dworkin's writings in effect contain three arguments, each of which is partly dependent on his theory of principles, against the thesis of the limits of law.[34] While only two of these arguments are explicitly directed against this thesis, all of them, if valid, undermine it. In the remainder of this article I shall show that each of Professor Dworkin's arguments must fail and that there is good reason to persevere in the

34. "The Model of Rules" is perhaps not altogether clear that all forms of the thesis of the limits of law are to be rejected, though it plainly opposes one version of the thesis by rejecting the tenet "that the law of a community is distinguished from other social standards by some test in the form of a master rule." *Id.* at 45 [59]. Professor Dworkin has, however, confirmed to me in conversation that these arguments are directed against the thesis of the limits of the law generally and has taken such a position in his lectures at Oxford University in 1971.

Legal Principles and the Limits of Law

attempt to construct a test for distinguishing what is law from what is not. I hope in the course of this discussion to throw some light on how such seemingly disparate matters as the thesis of the limits of law, the nature of rules and principles, the role of judicial discretion, and the criterion of the identity of a legal system are related.

A. *Judicial Discretion*

Professor Dworkin's first argument is a result of his theory of judicial discretion.[35] He distinguishes three senses of discretion. In the two weak senses "discretion" means "judgment" and "finality." "Sometimes," explains Professor Dworkin,

> we use "discretion" in a weak sense, simply to say that for some reason the standards an official must apply cannot be applied mechanically but demand the use of judgment. . . .
>
> Sometimes we use the term in a different weak sense, to say only that some official has final authority to make a decision and cannot be reviewed and reversed by any other official. . . .
>
> I call both of these senses weak to distinguish them from a stronger sense. We use "discretion" sometimes . . . to say that on some issue [an official] is simply not bound by standards set by the authority in question.[36]

The thesis that judges have discretion in the strong sense[37] means that there are cases which they are legally entitled to decide and in which no one correct decision is determined by standards of law. The thesis of judicial discretion does not entail that in cases where discretion may be exercised anything goes. Such cases are governed by laws which rule out certain decisions. The only claim is that the laws do not determine any decision as the correct one.

Professor Dworkin argues that (1) the law includes some principles as well as rules. From this he concludes that (2) the courts never have discretion in the strong sense. It follows, though he does not draw the conclusion at this point, that (3) the thesis of the limits of law is wrong. I shall argue that (3) does indeed follow from (2), but that (2) does not follow from (1) and is in any case wrong.

35. *See* Dworkin, *Judicial Discretion*, 60 J. Phil. 624 (1963). Professor Dworkin has reformulated his theory in "The Model of Rules" (*see* Dworkin, *supra* note 2, at 32-40 [44-54]) to meet some of the objections raised by G.C. MacCallum, Jr., in his reply to Dworkin's first paper. *See* MacCallum, *Dworkin on Judicial Discretion*, 60 J. Phil. 638 (1963).

36. Dworkin, *supra* note 2, at 32-33 [45-46].

37. I shall henceforth be concerned only with "discretion" in this sense, and only this sense is involved in what I shall call the "thesis of judicial discretion."

If courts are never entitled to exercise discretion (in the strong sense) it follows that all the reasons, rules and principles which they are entitled to rely on are part of the law. There is one important exception to this conclusion; those standards which are applied because they are the standards of some other legal system or organization, the standards of which the law respects and enforces, are not part of the law. The exception covers those laws of other states which are recognized and enforced according to the rules of private international law. It also extends to contracts and the rules of voluntary associations recognized by law, and to social, moral and religious standards of individuals and communities which are taken into account for some legal purposes (such as mitigation of punishment or exemption from military service) or as creating presumptions of fact as to the behavior or intention of litigants. When referring to such standards in their judgments the courts quite clearly do so not because they are part of the law but because the law makes it its business to recognize and give support, to a certain extent, to standards of other organizations, communities or individuals.[38]

This exception apart (and, however important, it does not affect Professor Dworkin's case against the thesis of the limits of law), it follows from Professor Dworkin's views on judicial discretion that all the reasons which the courts are entitled to use in justifying decisions are part of the law. All the reasons for a decision are legal reasons, for the law uniquely determines which decision is the correct one.[39] Now it seems to me true that on various occasions the courts are entitled to rely on every reason which is endorsed by part of the community for some purpose or other. It follows, therefore, from Professor Dworkin's view on judicial discretion that the thesis of the limits of law is wrong at least to the extent to which it claims that it is possible to distinguish between the law and non-legal social standards.

If, on the other hand, courts do have discretion, then in cases in which they are entitled to exercise discretion they act on standards which are not part of the law. Therefore, though every social standard may figure in a court's decision, it does not follow that all of them are laws. The opportunity is given to those who support the thesis

38. On this problem see Raz, *The Identity of Legal Systems*, 59 CALIF. L. REV. 795 (1971.)

39. The courts may occasionally rely on the wrong reasons. I am concerned here only with the reasons which they are entitled to use.

of the limits of law to draw a distinction between the standards used by courts which are law and those which are not. How is one to decide whether courts do or do not have discretion?

Professor Dworkin is primarily concerned to argue that there are legally binding principles. But this has never been denied by anyone, least of all by the positivists. Indeed, Austin could not have denied that some principles are legally binding while remaining true to his theory of law. The most fundamental tenet of his theory is that the commands of a sovereign are law, and there is nothing to prevent a sovereign from commanding that a principle shall be binding. Professor Dworkin's mistake lies in assuming that when Austin was talking about commands he was referring to what Professor Dworkin calls rules. But this is not the case. Neither does Hart use "rules" in the same sense as Professor Dworkin. By "rules" he means what Professor Dworkin seems to mean by "standards," namely rules, principles or any other type of norm (whether legal or social).[40]

The crux of the argument lies in the inference that since some principles are law judicial discretion does not exist. Professor Dworkin says very little on this. The reason, I suspect, is that he rightly sees that other theorists, not only the positivists, exaggerated the scope of judicial discretion because they failed to attend to the role principles play in the law. They tended to assume that whenever a rule is vague the court has discretion and did not see that sometimes the rule when read in light of some principles is not vague and does not leave room for discretion. "A set of principles," as Professor Dworkin reminds us, "*can* dictate a result."[41] But that it sometimes can does not mean that it always does. And it is this that Professor Dworkin has to establish to make his case against judicial discretion. Unfortunately, he does not even try to establish this point.

I suppose that there might be a legal system which contains a rule that whenever the courts are faced with a case for which the law does not provide a uniquely correct solution they ought to refuse to render judgment. In such a system there would be no judicial discretion. But, whether or not such a system can exist, few if any legal systems in fact contain such a rule. In most legal systems there are at least

40. Of course both Austin and Hart would maintain that *some* principles are not part of the law. But this is no more than to say that they believe in the thesis of the limits of law. It should be noted that I am using "standards" to cover not only norms but also generally accepted reasons for action.

41. Dworkin, *supra* note 2, at 36 [49] (emphasis in original).

three different sources of judicial discretion. Let me survey them briefly.

1. *Vagueness.* Vagueness is inherent in language. It is a problem courts have to face very frequently. As noted above, principles as well as rules of interpretation can sometimes solve problems of vagueness without leaving room for discretion. But principles themselves are vague, and discretion in cases of vagueness cannot be dispensed with so long as courts are entitled to render judgment in such cases.

2. *Weight.* Though principles sometimes limit the scope of the courts' discretion, they tend on the whole to expand it. For reasons noted earlier,[42] the law usually determines with precision the relative weight of rules. Not so with principles. The law characteristically includes only incomplete indications as to their relative weight and leaves much to judicial discretion to be exercised in particular cases. The scope of discretion is in fact doubly extended, since not only must the relative importance of principles be determined, but also the importance relative to each principle of deviating from it or of following it on particular occasions. This matter is usually entrusted to judicial discretion.

That courts have discretion as to weight does not, of course, mean that the law has nothing to contribute to the solution of the case. It contributes some of the elements for a solution, but not all the elements necessary to dictate a uniquely correct solution. In such cases the law dictates what considerations have to be taken into account, but not what weight to assign to each of them or to actions in accordance with or contrary to each of them in particular cases.

3. *Laws of discretion.* Most legal systems contain laws granting courts discretion, not only as to the weight of legally binding considerations, but also to act on considerations which are not legally binding. Such discretion may be, and usually is, guided by principles. These principles, however, do not dictate the considerations to be taken into account, but merely limit the range of the considerations.

One may distinguish between substantive principles, which dictate a goal to be pursued or a value to be protected, and principles of discretion, which guide discretion by stipulating what type of goals and values the judge may take into account in exercising his discretion. Compare the following two sets of hypothetical principles. (a) "Car manufacturers have a duty to protect the public from accidents." "In-

42. *See* pp. 832-42 *supra*.

creased productivity and efficiency should be the prime objective of public corporations." "The validity of standard contracts is contingent on their not taking advantage of the economic necessities of the weaker party." "The law favors security of title." (b) "The courts will not enforce unjust contracts." "Public corporations should act for the general good." "Whatever is *contra bonos mores et decorum* the principles of our law prohibit." The first group of principles set particular considerations to be acted on. They may be vague and they do not specify the weight to be given to each consideration, but the consideration prescribed is clear enough and is not a matter left to the courts' discretion. Principles of the second group, on the other hand, do not stipulate what considerations should be acted on. They merely specify the type of considerations which may be taken into account and leave the rest to the officials or the courts addressed by the principles. Rather than negating discretion, they presuppose its existence and guide it. What is "unjust" or "for the general good" is a matter of opinion and the courts or officials concerned are instructed by law to act on their own views. The law does not impose its own views of justice or the common good. Rather, it leaves the matter to the discretion of the courts or the officials. Many of the principles governing the action of the courts and the executive are principles of discretion.[43] Such principles, far from proving the absence of judicial discretion, are a manifestation of a legal policy to rely on and make use of judicial and administrative discretion in order to increase the flexibility of the law and improve the procedures for its constant review to meet changes in circumstance and opinion.

We must conclude that legal principles do not exclude judicial discretion; they presuppose its existence and direct and guide it. The argument from the absence of judicial discretion against the thesis of the limits of law must therefore be rejected. It should be noted, however, that judicial discretion is not arbitrary judgment. Courts are never allowed to act arbitrarily. Even when discretion is not limited or guided in any specific direction the courts are still legally bound to act as they think is best according to their beliefs and values. If they do not, if they give arbitrary judgment by tossing a coin, for example, they violate a legal duty. A judge must always invoke some general reasons. He has no discretion when the reasons are dictated by law. He has discretion when the law requires him to act on reasons

43. Many of the principles mentioned by Professor Dworkin are of this kind.

which he thinks are correct, instead of imposing its own standards. When discretion is denied the law dictates which standards should be applied by all the judges. When discretion is allowed each judge is entitled to follow different reasons but he must believe that they are the best. Otherwise, discretion can be equated only with arbitrariness, whim, and caprice.

B. *"Sources" of Legal Principles*

Legal principles, like other laws, can be enacted or repealed by legislatures and administrative authorities. They can also become legally binding through establishment by the courts. Many legal systems recognize that both rules and principles can be made into law or lose their status as law through precedent. Rules and principles differ in this respect. A court can establish a new rule in a single judgment which becomes a precedent. Principles are not made into law by a single judgment; they evolve rather like a custom and are binding only if they have considerable authoritative support in a line of judgments. Like customary law, judicially adopted principles need not be formulated very precisely in the judgments which count as authority for their existence. All that has to be shown is that they underlie a series of courts' decisions, that they were in fact a reason operating in a series of cases.

This is recognized by Professor Dworkin. He does, however, add a third "source" of legally binding principles: "judgments of the community at large or some identifiable segment thereof."[44] And he adds in a footnote: "On some occasions, in some kinds of cases, moral principles accepted as standards within the community will figure as good reasons for a legal decision, just as, on other occasions, in other kinds of cases, will standards otherwise established. In this sense, such principles are part of the legal system, if it is helpful to talk about law as a system at all, and the flat statement that law and morals are separate systems is misleading."[45] The morality that Professor Dworkin has in mind consists of those moral views which became social norms in the community. No supporter of the thesis of the limits of law has ever denied that some social norms can be legal norms as well. The legislator can make a social norm into law either by direct enactment or by stipulating that social customs of a certain type should

44. Dworkin, *supra* note 35, at 635 (1963).
45. *Id.* at 635 n.9.

Legal Principles and the Limits of Law

be binding as law. By the doctrine of precedent the courts can do the same. To admit as much does not weaken in the least the thesis of the limits of law.

To challenge the thesis it has to be established that all social norms are automatically (without prior legislative or judicial recognition) binding as law at least to the extent to which they do not conflict with laws created by legislation and precedent. If this were the case in all legal systems the thesis of the limits of law would indeed be badly shaken and would need a far-reaching reformulation. In his subsequent remarks Professor Dworkin implies that this is in fact the case.[46] I think that he is mistaken, and it is worth pausing to examine the source of his mistake.

In most countries one of the most general principles restraining judicial discretion enjoins judges to act only on those values and opinions which have the support of some important segment of the population.[47] There are various grounds on which the principle can be justified, none of which in itself justifies its full scope. It can be justified on democratic grounds; it can be defended by arguing that a judge whose actions affect the fortune of many should not trust his own judgment if it is not supported by learned opinion; it can be argued that laws out of tune with community values are unlikely to achieve their aim or will have some undesirable consequences. Each of these justifications, and others that can be used, interprets the principle somewhat differently. A close study of the matter will no doubt distinguish between various related principles which sometimes reinforce each other and sometimes conflict, or which apply to different situations. All these principles restrain but do not exclude judicial discretion. They do not oblige the courts to enforce any specific social norms. They limit their freedom to act on what they think is right by making it conditional on their ability to show that they are not alone in that opinion. There is, therefore, no reason to regard these principles as converting all social morality into law or as undermining the thesis of the limits of law.

They have, however, a curious, though perhaps not surprising, effect on judicial rhetoric in some countries and especially in the United States. As they should, courts tend to justify judgments based on discretion by arguments designed to show that the decision is a good

46. *Id.* at 635 *et seq.*
47. The main device controlling courts' values and ideology is, of course, not this principle, but the methods of appointing or electing judges.

one,[48] and by other arguments to show that the decision conforms to the views of some segment of the population. Unfortunately, some judges like to claim that the values they endorse are not merely the values of some but embody the national consciousness, represent the national consensus, are universally acknowledged, etc. This is perhaps harmless rhetoric if it is understood as such. Professor Dworkin, however, urges us to give literal interpretation to such pronouncements from the bench. The courts apply what they think are community values. It follows that it is wrong to regard them as acting on their own beliefs as legislators do. They may be wrong in their views of what the values of the community are, but if so they are wrong on a point of law, for since they are bound to apply community values these are part of the law.

This literal interpretation of judicial rhetoric is made possible only if one is prepared to join the courts in endorsing two really harmful myths. One is the myth that there is a considerable body of specific moral values shared by the population of a large and modern country. The myth of the common morality has made much of the oppression of minorities possible. It also allows judges to support a partisan point of view while masquerading as the servant of a general consensus. The second myth is that the most general values provide sufficient ground for practical conclusions. This myth holds that, since we all have a general desire for prosperity, progress, culture, justice, and so on, we all want precisely the same things and support exactly the same ideals; and that all the differences between us result from disagreements of fact about the most efficient policies to secure the common goals. In fact, much disagreement about more specific goals and about less general values is genuine moral disagreement, which cannot be resolved by appeal to the most general value-formulations which we all endorse, for these bear different interpretations for different people.

The courts tend all too often to claim that a specific policy is entailed by belief in some general value, thus avoiding a concrete justification of their decision, maintaining the rhetoric of common goals and community values and endorsing partisan positions without admitting it. Some judges may themselves be captives of the myths they help to perpetuate. But the fact that they are misled should not mis-

48. Though judges are entitled, sometimes, to act as they think best, that they believe the decision is a good one is never a reason for it; they must have reasons for their beliefs.

Legal Principles and the Limits of Law

lead us. Occasional deviations from the canons of good reasoning can be dismissed as mistakes, but when constant use is made of a pattern of argumentation completely devoid of logical validity it is time to distinguish between myth and rhetoric on the one hand and reality on the other. And the law should be understood to encompass reality, not rhetoric.

C. *The Possibility of a Criterion of Identity*

If the thesis of the limits of law is right, there must be a criterion of identity which sets necessary and sufficient conditions, satisfaction of which is a mark that a standard is part of a legal system. Austin's criterion of identity was that all and only the general commands of one sovereign are part of one legal system. Hart has criticized this criterion and suggested another. According to his theory every legal system contains a rule of recognition directed at the courts and imposing on them an obligation to apply those standards which fulfill various criteria set out in the rule.[49] The rule of recognition is a customary rule arising out of the behavior of law-enforcing officials through a period of time. The rest of the laws of the system are valid because they fulfill the conditions set out in the rule of recognition. The general criterion of identity of all legal systems is that each contains a rule of recognition and all those laws satisfying the conditions it stipulates.

Professor Dworkin claims that no adequate criterion of identity can be formulated and that therefore the thesis of the limits of law must be rejected. He directs his attack against Hart's criterion and employs two arguments to show that neither Hart's nor any other criterion of identity can account for the existence of legal principles. I shall argue that one of Professor Dworkin's arguments contains a valid criticism of Hart but does not bear on the possibility of formulating a somewhat different criterion of identity, whereas his second argument fails altogether.

"Hart's sharp distinction between acceptance and validity," the first argument runs, "does not hold. If we are arguing for the principle that a man should not profit from his own wrong, we could cite the acts of courts and legislatures that exemplify it, but this speaks as much to the principle's acceptance as its validity. (It seems odd to

49. For arguments supporting this interpretation of Hart's doctrine, see Raz, *supra* note 38, at 807-08 & nn.23-24.

speak of a principle as being valid at all, perhaps because validity is an all-or-nothing concept, appropriate for rules, but inconsistent with a principle's dimension of weight.)"[50] The concept of validity is said to be inconsistent with the principle's dimension of weight on the ground that one establishes a principle's validity by showing that it has "institutional support"; but the amount of support a principle enjoys determines its weight and is a matter of degree: "[T]he more support we found, the more weight we could claim for the principle."[51] But this is surely mistaken. A principle might have been referred to frequently by the courts as binding, but have little weight. The degree of support may sometimes be evidence for a principle's weight, but it need not be and the two notions are not logically related.

Legal principles may be valid in precisely the same way that rules are. They may, for example, be enacted in the constitution or in a statute, as some of Professor Dworkin's own examples show. It is true, though, that some legal principles are law because they are accepted by the judiciary. But this is true of rules as well as principles. It is, however, an important point which does necessitate a modification of Hart's criterion of identity. But here again Professor Dworkin claims too much. He claims that if the master rule says merely that whatever other rules the community accepts are legally binding then it fails to act as an identifying criterion distinguishing between law and social norms.[52] Had all social customs in all countries been legally binding this would have been a valid criticism. Some countries, however, do not recognize custom as a source of law at all. Those legal systems which do regard customs as legally binding do so only if they pass certain tests. These tests, if they are not set out in a statute or some other law, are laid down by the rule of recognition, which determines under what conditions social customs are binding in law.

The rule of recognition, therefore, does serve to explain the legal status of general community customs. It cannot, however, explain in the same way the legal status of judicial customs. Since it is itself a judicial custom it cannot confer any special status on other judicial customs. Judicial rule-making, as I indicated above, differs in this respect from the evolution of principles by the courts. A rule becomes binding by being laid down in one case as a precedent. It does not

50. Dworkin, *supra* note 2, at 42 [55].
51. *Id.* at 41 [55].
52. *Id.* at 43-44 [57-58].

have to wait until it is accepted in a series of cases to be binding. It is binding because of the doctrine of precedent which is part of our rule of recognition. Principles evolved by the courts become binding by becoming a judicial custom. They are part of the law because they are accepted by the courts, not because they are valid according to the rule of recognition.

Hart's criterion of identity must be modified. A legal system consists not only of one customary rule of the law enforcing agencies and all the laws recognized by it, but of all the customary rules and principles of the law enforcing agencies and all the laws recognized by them.[53] This is an important modification, but it preserves the fundamental point underlying Hart's criterion and shared by many: namely, that law is an institutionalized normative system and that the fact that the enforcement of its standards is a duty of special law-enforcing agencies is one important feature which distinguishes it from many other normative systems. The importance of this feature of law is made manifest by distinguishing between legal and non-legal standards according to whether or not the courts have an obligation to apply them, either because they are themselves judicial custom or because judicial customs make their application obligatory.

Professor Dworkin has a second argument disputing the possibility of formulating an adequate criterion of identity. "True," he says, "if we were challenged to back up our claim that some principle is a principle of law, we would mention any prior cases in which that principle was cited, or figured in the argument . . . . Unless we could find some such institutional support, we would probably fail to make out our case . . . . Yet we could not devise any formula for testing how much and what kind of institutional support is necessary to make a principle a legal principle."[54] In this passage Professor Dworkin is rejecting not merely Hart's version of the thesis of the limits of law but all versions of this thesis. He agrees that if legal and non-legal standards can be distinguished this could only be done by relying on the fact that only legal standards have adequate institutional support in the practice of the courts. He denies, however, the possibility of a general explanation of what counts as adequate institutional support. It follows that it is impossible to provide a general account of the difference between legal and non-legal standards and the thesis of the

53. For a more precise formulation of the criterion and a more detailed examination of the problem, see Raz, *supra* note 38.
54. Dworkin, *supra* note 2, at 41 [55].

limits of law must be abandoned. What is the force of this argument? If a legal system consists, as I have suggested, of those standards which the courts are bound to recognize, we must agree with Professor Dworkin that we need a general explanation of what counts as adequate institutional support. For laws are binding on the courts either because judicial customs make their recognition obligatory or because they are themselves judicial customs. Thus the acceptability of the thesis of the limits of law depends on our ability to explain the concept of a judicial custom. But judicial customs are but a special case of social customs.

What we need is an adequate explanation of the concept of a customary norm. Once we have it we will know what judicial custom is and will have a complete criterion of identity. Hart has provided such an explanation. No doubt it is possible to improve on it, but there is no reason to suppose that the concept of a customary norm defies analysis. It is true that an analysis of the concept does not give us a decision procedure determining for every principle or rule whether or not it has sufficient support to be regarded as a judicial custom.[55] Borderline cases will remain; they must remain, for customary norms evolve gradually. But Dworkin's is a very weak argument, which rejects a distinction because it admits the existence of borderline cases.

55. It is worth reminding ourselves that not every principle is evolved by the courts; many result from legislative action.

Name Index

www.ingramcontent.com/pod-product-compliance
Lightning Source LLC
LaVergne TN
LVHW081342011026
849161LV00013BB/2992
* 9 7 8 0 8 1 4 7 0 6 2 5 1 *